The Power of Comics and Graphic Novels

The Power of Comics and Graphic Novels

Culture, Form, and Context

Randy Duncan, Matthew J. Smith, and Paul Levitz

BLOOMSBURY ACADEMIC
LONDON • NEW YORK • OXFORD • NEW DELHI • SYDNEY

BLOOMSBURY ACADEMIC
Bloomsbury Publishing Plc
50 Bedford Square, London, WC1B 3DP, UK
1385 Broadway, New York, NY 10018, USA
29 Earlsfort Terrace, Dublin 2, Ireland

BLOOMSBURY, BLOOMSBURY ACADEMIC and the Diana logo are trademarks of
Bloomsbury Publishing Plc

First published in Great Britain 2023

Cover design: Rebecca Heselton
Cover illustration by Sonny Liew

A catalogue record for this book is available from the British Library.

Library of Congress Cataloging-in-Publication Data

Names: Duncan, Randy, 1958- author. | Smith, Matthew J., 1971- author. |
Levitz, Paul, author.
Title: The power of comics and graphic novels : culture, form, and context / Randy Duncan,
Matthew J. Smith and Paul Levitz.
Description: London; New York: Bloomsbury Academic, 2023. | Includes bibliographical
references and index.
Identifiers: LCCN 2022059692 (print) | LCCN 2022059693 (ebook) | ISBN 9781350253896 (hardback) |
ISBN 9781350253902 (paperback) | ISBN 9781350253919 (pdf) | ISBN 9781350253926 (epub)
Subjects: LCSH: Comic books, strips, etc.–Technique. | Comic books, strips, etc.–Authorship. |
Comic books, strips, etc.–Social aspects. |
Comic books, strips, etc.–History and criticism. | LCGFT: Comics criticism.
Classification: LCC PN6710 .D863 2023 (print) | LCC PN6710 (ebook) |
DDC 741.5/9–dc23/eng/20230510
LC record available at https://lccn.loc.gov/2022059692
LC ebook record available at https://lccn.loc.gov/2022059693

ISBN: HB: 978-1-3502-5389-6
PB: 978-1-3502-5390-2
ePDF: 978-1-3502-5391-9
eBook: 978-1-3502-5392-6

Typeset by Deanta Global Publishing Services, Chennai, India
Printed and bound in Great Britain

To find out more about our authors and books visit www.bloomsbury.com and
sign up for our newsletters.

Contents

Preface by Karen Green vi
Acknowledgments ix

Introduction 1

Unit I Culture 9

1 Comics in Culture, Comics as Culture 11

2 Making and Reading Comics 26

Unit II Form 55

3 Encapsulation of the Moments 57

4 Composition of the Panels 76

5 Layout of the Pages 103

Unit III Genre 133

6 Genres of Comics 135

7 Memoir Comics 153

8 Superhero Comics 178

9 Beyond Entertainment: Journalism, Documentary, and Advocacy 206

Unit IV Context and Analysis 241

10 The Evolution of American Comics 243

11 Exploring Meanings in Comics 289

12 Writing About Comics 311

Glossary 329
Bibliography 339
Index 362

Preface

By Karen Green

When I began to contemplate the kind invitation to write this preface, extended to me by Matt, Randy, and Paul, my immediate question was: what's my angle? And, after casting about for a few days, I realized that my answer was in the actual title: I wanted to talk about comics and power, or, more precisely, comics and empowerment.

To some degree, there is a story about comics and power inherent in this book's existence. To paraphrase Hemingway, the teaching of comics has been gaining steam gradually, then suddenly, ever since Michael Uslan taught the first accredited comics course at Indiana University, back in 1972. The momentum has truly built over the past decade, with the establishment of undergraduate majors in comics studies, MA programs in comics studies, and even NEH seminars on comics studies. Academic presses are creating monographic series in comics studies, and some, as with the Pennsylvania State University Press' *Graphic Mundi*, even have series devoted to publishing graphic novels.

When I teach my Columbia University course on how to read comics, I see the empowerment my students feel in learning a new language, in understanding how comics work in a manner new to them, and in understanding the visual literacy required to appreciate what comics creators do. I tell them that they are my spores, and at the end of the term they will go out and transmit their infectious passion to others, perhaps even choose comics for a project in another course. It seems to be working. Comics are getting used more and more in teaching here at Columbia, and courses dedicated to the medium are proliferating—such as "Politics, Violence, and the Graphic Novel" in our French Department, and of course "The American Graphic Novel," co-taught by this book's own Paul Levitz. Senior theses, master's essays, and even the occasional Ph.D. here are focusing on comics as a topic.

But that's not the power I wanted to talk about.

Comics can empower the powerless. For groups that have been oppressed, marginalized, ignored, and abandoned, comics provide a voice. And the great thing about making comics is that, as a cartoonist I know once said, they can be made with materials that are easy to steal. Well, of course, that was said in jest, but it's true that with paper, pencil, ink, and brush—and possibly with color markers, inks, and paints—anyone can make a comic. It's nice to have a studio with a drawing desk, an array of brushes and inks, a scanner, and/or a huge monitor with creative software, but it's not necessary. A lot of power resides in the tip of a pencil; after all, editorial cartoonist Thomas Nast famously brought down a corrupt political machine in nineteenth-century New York, using paper and an inkpot. The gateway effort for becoming a cartoonist, the mini-comic, can be made with a pen, a piece of paper, and access to a photocopy machine. That carefully folded mini, which may not even require stapling, can be taken to festivals or offered for sale at a local comic shop. It can be scanned and put up for free on Instagram and/or Twitter—or on a free blog site. Social media provides a very bully pulpit.

What kind of groups do I mean? Refugees and displaced persons. LGBTQIA+ people. The gravely ill and dying. Targets of prejudice or oppression. Those who have transition stories, who've come out under difficult or dangerous circumstances, who've suffered miscarriages or had abortions, who have experiences with mental health issues and/or institutionalization, or who have dealt with aging parents. Not to mention the reporters who tell the stories of any of the earlier groups.

These are genres that have had explosive growth in the past fifteen or so years, but their roots could be seen all the way back in Rodolphe Töpffer's *Histoire de Monsieur Vieux-Bois*, published in the 1830s, then translated into English in 1841 as *The Adventures of Mr. Obadiah Oldbuck*. In that story, a heartbroken man has a series of adventures that lead him to attempt suicide multiple times; he ends up in prison and later is buried alive. It is played for humor and has a happy ending, but it reads pretty dark in places. Wordless woodcut novels in the early twentieth century, from Frans Masereel in Belgium to Lynd Ward in the United States, tell universal stories of social justice. In the 1970s, underground cartoonist Justin Green produced the confessional comic *Binky Brown Meets the Holy Virgin Mary*, which explored his tortured Catholicism and a neurosis that would later be identified as obsessive-compulsive disorder. Green in turn inspired Robert Crumb and Aline Kominsky to produce nakedly honest comics about their own flaws, and Art Spiegelman to explore his parents' Holocaust history. Cleveland comics writer Harvey Pekar, who had been turning mundane stories of life as a VA hospital clerk into comics drawn by a variety of artists, developed cancer and, with his wife Joyce Brabner, produced the graphic novel (and rarely has that ungainly term been less apropos) *Our Cancer Year*.

Are you or someone you love suffering from an illness, or do you just want to learn more? Joyce Farmer's *Special Exits*, Dana Walrath's *Aliceheimer's*, Jennifer Hayden's *The Story of My Tits*, Brian Fies' *Mom's Cancer*, Judd Winick's *Pedro and Me,* to name just a few, offer powerful, sometimes darkly humorous, stories. Do you or someone you love have mental health issues, or have suffered trauma? Comics can engender empathy, can instruct, can make the unknown familiar, in books such as Steve Haines' *Anxiety is Really Strange*; Samuel C. Williams' *At War with Yourself*, which explores military PTSD; Teresa Wong's *Dear Scarlet*, written as a letter to her daughter about post-partum depression; Ellen Forney's *Marbles*, which uses her bipolar disorder to discuss the relationship between mental illness and creativity; Glenn Head's *Chartwell Manor*, relating the physical and sexual abuse he and his classmates suffered at a private school, and the long-term consequences it caused; and the collection *Drawing Power*, edited by Diane Noomin, which gathers moving stories from a wide variety of cartoonists about their experiences with sexual violence and harassment.

Ezra Claytan Daniels' mini-comic—also available for free online—"Are You at Risk for Empathy Myopia?" is truly a comic for our current political moment. This biracial cartoonist sought to explain the value of Black Lives Matter to the white side of his family, and their friends. Eschewing hot-button terms such as "white privilege," Daniels describes the often parochial empathy many people feel and offers a vision of a more all-encompassing version. This is a comic with the power to instruct without offending, offering the possibility of spiritual and emotional growth—without judgment.

Shortly before the Covid-19 pandemic (and, unsurprisingly, comics about the pandemic and its consequences have already begun to appear), and long before the humanitarian crisis caused by Russia's invasion of Ukraine, the head of our Global Studies library division approached me about helping plan an exhibition of comics about refugees, looking at the causes for their flight, their struggle with the decision to leave, the nature of their journeys, and their acclimatization in the countries to which they flee. We pored over the comics in our collection to choose pages to scan and display, in a variety of languages and concerning a variety of countries. Many of these volumes are graphic reportage, allowing an investigative cartoonist to interview people and tell their stories, but some, such as Mana Neyestani's *Petit manuel du parfait réfugié politique*, detail the grueling bureaucratic struggles necessary to live in a new country, often leaving the refugee feeling as if he or she is without a country entirely. Stories such as these humanize refugees, giving them names and faces, depicting the dangers in which they were living, and making a strong case for allowing their entrance to safer harbors.

The books I've mentioned—and so many, many others—allow the suffering to be seen, present their stories in a palatable format, and compel the readers' attention. They give the creators the power of a voice. They offer readers the power of change, of empathy.

As you explore the book you hold in your hand, its authors offer *you* a kind of power, too: the power of understanding, of an expanding mind, of engagement with new forms and new ideas. All education empowers the student; after your time with this book, you may feel empowered to create your own comics, to tell your story. Change a mind. Have your mind changed. So turn the page, start down the path your three authors have provided, and let the power of comics open new doors for you.

Karen Green is the Curator for Comics and Cartoons in the Rare Book & Manuscript Library at Columbia University. She initiated Columbia's graphic novels collection in 2005, expanded to creator archives in 2011, and the curator position was created for her in 2016. She has served as a judge for the Will Eisner Comics Industry Awards, sat on four juries for the Pulitzer Prize in Editorial Cartooning, written a monthly column about comics and the academy for ComiXology, and began teaching the course "Comics: Reading the Medium" in 2014. She has an abiding faith in the power of comics.

Acknowledgments

We acknowledge that this book is a product of so many more people than just its authors, and we owe a debt of thanks to those who lent their expertise and support to its production.

The first edition was enriched thanks to the individual contributions of Allan Asherman, Lara Bachelder, Jerry Bails, David Barker, Robert Beerbohm, Karen Berger, John Mark Boling, Michael Burk, Brian Camp, Tommy Cash, Larry Clowers, Josh Cohick, Peter Coogan, Ashley Corry, Claudia Dattilo, Jamie Daugherty, Jocelin Dean, Jeff Dern, Shel Dorf, Will Eisner, Susan Feuer, Jessica Fisher, Mike Friedrich, Katie Gallof, Sarah Gearhart, Kathleen Glosan, Gary Groth, Claire Heitlinger, Emily Hiscar, Alec Hosterman, Charles Hatfield, Ken Irwin, Denis Kitchen, Travis Langley, Steve Less, Paul Levitz, Benn Linfield, Ryan Masteller, Brian McCoach, Carl Miller, John Jackson Miller, Hiedi Mowrey, Tregg Nardecchia, Max Novick, Robert O'Nale, Gabriella Page-Fort, Laura Pitney, Leonard Rifas, Chuck Rozanski, Carol Sawyer, Randy Scott, Deborah Sessor, Julie Schwartz, Jeff Smith, Susan Sheridan Smith, Bill Spicer, David Stoddard, Jerrod Swanton, Roy Thomas, Maggie Thompson, Hames Ware, John Wheat, Bill Williams, Lauren Wilson, Andrew F. Wood, and the participants on the Comix-Scholars Discussion List. It was also made possible thanks to the support of the original authors' students and colleagues at their home institutions of Henderson State University and Wittenberg University, respectively.

Assistance with the second edition came from David Avital, Steven Brower, Bruce Campbell, James Chapman, James Bucky Carter, Martha Cornog, Jeremy Dauber, Joseph Darowski, Brent Frankenhoff, Karen Green, Milton Griepp, Alec Hosterman, M. Thomas Inge, Ivan Kocmerak, Stephen Lipson, Mark McKinney, Allan Metz, John Jackson Miller, Frank Motler, Jacque Nodell, Kevin Quigley, Mark Richardson, Leonard Rifas, Julia Round, Ben Saunders, Lucia Cedeira Serantes, Marc Singer, Jennifer K. Stuller, Nicolas Theisen, Shaun Treat, and Daniel Yezbick.

Supporting the third edition were Dan Archer, Victor Barjas, Kathleen Berzock, Adam Bessie, Jordan Breedlove, Lucy Brown, Brendan Burford, Eddie Campbell, Neil Cohn, Neil Gaiman, Larry Gonick, Karen Green, Paul Grist, Dean Haspiel, Amanda Kellogg, Peter Kuper, Alec Longstreth, Suzanne Luber, Ibrahim Moustafa, Josh Neufeld, Carolyn Nowak, Linda Perkins, Constantine Petridis, Ted Rall, Leonard Rifas, Joe Sacco, Nick Sousanis, Chris Staros, David Stoddard, James Strum, Seth Tobocman, and Aanchal Vij.

Randy dedicates this third volume to Travis Langley and all the other faculty and administrators who have supported The Center for Comics Studies at Henderson State University.

Matt dedicates this volume to his siblings. To his paternal siblings, Cheryl, Rob, and Cindy, whose love and attention helped raise him, and to his maternal siblings, Tim, Rich, and Dot, who have welcomed him into their hearts later in life.

Paul dedicates this volume to his mother, for *Adventure Comics* #347, and to his father, for *Avengers* #55.

Introduction

Art Spiegelman's graphic novel *Maus* won a special Pulitzer Prize for literature in 1992. The Pulitzer is considered to be one of the highest honors in writing, and for a comic to be recognized alongside the year's best work in literature and journalism was previously unthinkable. But *Maus* is not just any comic. It tells the true story of a Holocaust survivor through an unconventional cast of animals, recounting both the horrors of the Nazi persecution of the Jews in Europe and the enduring pain of survivors and their children. It brilliantly demonstrates the power of comics and graphic novels to communicate ideas through a poignant combination of words and pictures.

While *Maus* was widely praised, the opening line of English professor Lawrence L. Langer's review in *The New York Times Book Review* was fairly typical of how the literary community dealt with the fact that *Maus* was a comic: "Art Spiegelman doesn't draw comics" (1991: 17). Forget that the narrative consisted of hand drawings and word balloons presented in a series of panels; it seems that it could not be a comic because it was good. Unfortunately, this still reflects a common conception of comics.

It is not even that misguided an idea. The majority of comics produced in America have been quickly created, lowest-common-denominator, mass media products targeted at eleven-year-olds. Nowadays, the average person has to go out of their way to even see a comic book, and if they do it will likely be of the costumed superhero variety. But, these books do not accurately represent the variety or potential of the medium. A **medium** is a channel for communicating and includes familiar favorites such as radio, television, or the printed page. When we use the term "medium" in this book, we are addressing the social reality of comics, such as their function as economic commodities. We will also speak of comics as an art form. In choosing this reference, we mean to emphasize the creative aspects of communicating meaning through the comic form. Even the worst of the lot may be talked about as an art form because there is always a set of materials, techniques, and limitations involved in how such work is created.

At their best, comics can accommodate content as profound, moving, and enduring as that found in any of the more celebrated vehicles for human expression. Comics can attract creators who aspire to art and literature, who create works of complexity, passion, and depth. *Maus* received national attention, but many excellent works—such as *The Tale of One Bad Rat*, *It's a Good Life if, You Don't Weaken*, *A Contract with God*, *Ice Haven*, *Monstress, Saga, Epileptic,* and many, many more—are virtually unknown outside the small community of comics readers and are just waiting to be discovered by a wider audience.

What exactly are comics? Why do we consider *Maus* to be comics? We will get to some definitions in short order, but for now let us begin by acknowledging that we are dealing with a particular kind of sequential art, and, with some notable exceptions, art presented in a

Figure 0.1 There are two related stories in *Maus*. The first is that of Art interviewing his father, Vladek, in the present. The second, told through a series of flashbacks, chronicles Vladek's struggle to survive the Holocaust in Nazi Europe. Illustrations from *The Complete Maus: A Survivor's Tale* by Art Spiegelman, *Maus, Volume I* copyright © 1973, 1980, 1981, 1982, 1983, 1984, 1985, 1986 by Art Spiegelman; *Maus, Volume II* copyright © 1986, 1989, 1990, 1991 by Art Spiegelman. Used by permission of Pantheon Books, an imprint of the Knopf Doubleday Publishing Group, a division of Penguin Random House LLC. All rights reserved.

sequence is narrative; it tells a story. As you will see in the next section, there are a number of different manifestations of sequential art, and we find comics and graphic novels to be among the most intriguing of them in terms of their storytelling potential. Thereafter, we will review some of the benefits of studying comics and preview the sections of the book you are about to read (Figure 0.1).

What Are Comics?

The search for a definition must begin with disentangling the term "comics" from the many forms in which it manifests across cultures, including comic strips, comic books, graphic novels, and webcomics. ***Comics*** is a useful general term for designating the phenomenon of juxtaposing images in a sequence. (To **juxtapose** means to place two things side by side.) As comics theorist Scott McCloud (1993) points out, the umbrella term *comics* has also been used to cover cave paintings, Grecian urns, tapestries, stained glass windows, and more. These disparate forms of communication have been treated as a single medium for a number of reasons. Perhaps there is a natural tendency to lump them together because they have some similarities of form. All of the examples given earlier tell a story by presenting carefully selected moments of varying length within panels. A **panel** is simply a discernible area that contains a moment of the story.

Another formal similarity is the potential for use of compositional elements. Perceived distance, angle of view, color, arrangement of elements, simulated lighting effects, and other elements of composition could be used in all of the forms of visual communication mentioned earlier. They all draw upon the same visual vocabulary.

Of course, for the most part, it has been for strategic and political reasons that comics have been defined to include historical artifacts like Grecian urns and the Bayeux Tapestry. This famed tapestry is a horizontal strip of embroidered linen 231 feet long and twenty inches high, created *c.* 1100 CE, that depicts the Norman conquest of England in a sequence of juxtaposed scenes. These and other works of art lend respectability to an otherwise denigrated form of expression. It is a strategic ploy for legitimacy by association.

With this sense of potential in mind, we situate the comics within the array of communication practices that blend/meld text and pictures to varying degrees. As an art form, a **comic book** is a volume in which aspects of the diegesis are represented by pictorial and linguistic images encapsulated in a sequence of juxtaposed panels and pages. Some of the terms within that definition bear some explication. By *volume* we mean a collection of pages connected in sequence. So a comic book might be as brief as only a few sheets of paper or a bound edition as expansive as a several-hundred-page omnibus. It might also be constituted by electronic pages appearing on a tablet or computer. The **diegesis** consists of the characters, places, objects, events, and sensory environment that make up the world of the story. Our definition has a certain utility in helping us to begin talking about comics; however, we acknowledge that it functions best in describing typical or pure cases of the art form. There are some cases lying on the boundaries that may vary from the definition but still meet enough of the criteria to be recognized as comics (Figure 0.2).

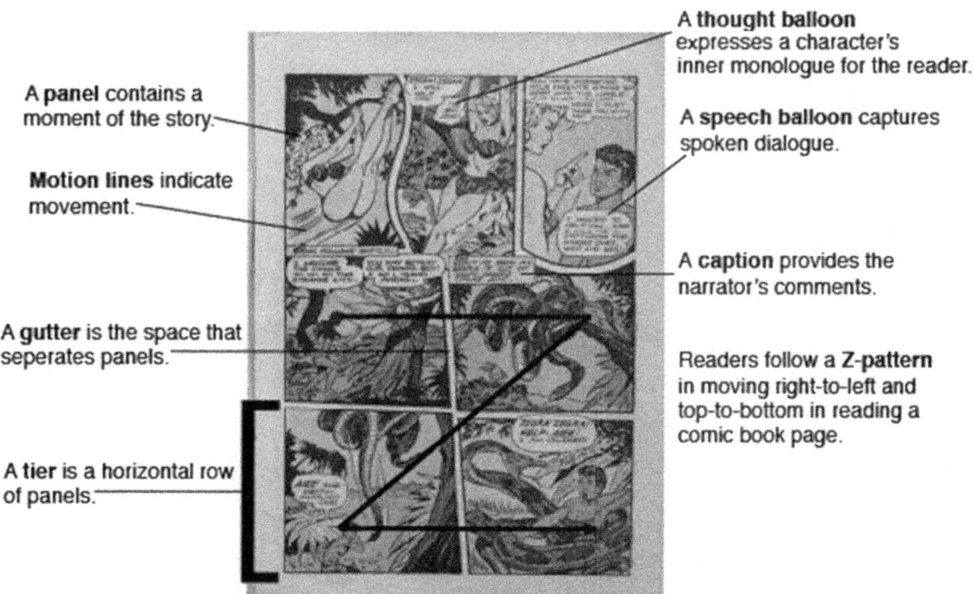

Figure 0.2 This page from *Zegra* #2 (1948) allows us to define many of the basic compositional elements in a comic book page. *Zegra* was published by Fox Feature Syndicate, drawn by Jo Lax, and one of many comics in a genre known as "jungle comics." Graphic by Regina Gasser.

Why call such objects *comic books*, though? The content of *Maus* is certainly not comical, and comic book magazines do not appear to be as handsomely bound or durable as a traditional book. As you will see in greater detail in Chapter 10, most of the early American comic books started out as collections of re-pasted newspaper comic strips. By the time that innovation took hold, the label of "comics" had already been semantically stuck to that art form, even though adventure and science fiction stories not told for laughs had become popular features among them. For nearly a century the label has endured, although it does seem to be a misnomer, given the fact that *comic* books address many more types of stories than just humorous ones, and many comic *books* are produced on rather flimsy materials.

In recent times a number of people have attempted to rehabilitate the image of comic books by using a different term, ***graphic novel***, to describe the more ambitious works in the art form. For creators, labeling their work a graphic novel allows them to distance themselves from the commercial and periodical connotations associated with comic books. For publishers, *graphic novel* is a term that helps elevate the status of their product and has allowed them entrée into bookstores, libraries, and the academy. In practice, graphic novels may be longer than the typical comic book and most often feature self-contained, rather than continuing, stories. While we too use that term in this book, you may well note that the graphic novel meets the definition of the comic book form introduced earlier. While they might be considered manifestations of the same art form, a case could be made that graphic novels exist in a different cultural space and are thus becoming their own medium, distinct from comic books. In the twenty-first century graphic novels are often published by major publishing houses, such as Random House, and bought in traditional or online bookstores by people who do not read comic books. A number of them are even created by cartoonists who are not comic book fans.

Another familiar form of sequential art is the **comic strip**. While strips rely on much of the same vocabulary to communicate ideas as comic books, they tend to use fewer panels in a more rigid layout. The strips come from a tradition of newspaper publishing, where diminishing space allowances have left each strip with a single tier of storytelling possibilities with each daily installment. Comic books came out of the magazine industry and while the number of pages in a typical publication had decreased over the years from sixty-four pages of content down to seventeen at times, the multiple pages allow for greater flexibility in terms of art design and storytelling complexity. Of course, digital comic strips and comic books not only bypass traditional distribution systems but appear in new formats that make the two media virtually indistinguishable (Figure 0.3).

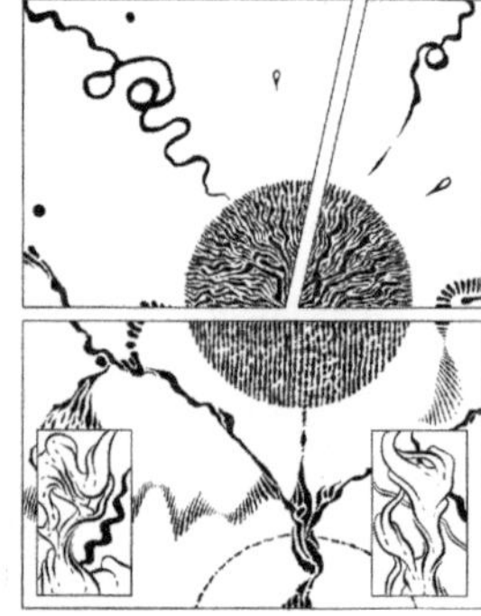

Figure 0.3 In contrast to the representational work of most mainstream comics such as the *Zegra* page in Figure 0.2, this page is more experimental, using shape and design to capture mood. "Page from untitled comic, 2013" is by Andrei Molotiu, author of *Abstract Comics: The Anthology*, and used with permission.

A Comic by Any Other Name . . .

The term "graphic novel" has caused more confusion than it has clarity. It has become increasingly common to hear people refer to almost any form of comics as a graphic novel.

And was it really necessary to have a term for comic books with lots of pages? It seemed to be working just fine to refer to a work as comics, whether it be 1 page, 22 pages, or 800 pages.

The term "graphic novel" might not have seemed necessary, but it has served a variety of needs. Fans wanted a term that would make their beloved art form sound more respectable. Creators such as Byron Preiss and Will Eisner wanted a term that would get their work into traditional bookstores. Once the book stores chains began creating graphic novel sections, mainstream publishers such as Marvel, DC, and Dark Horse were more than willing to have trade collections from their ongoing series marketed as graphic novels if that would get them on the shelves. When librarians wanted to add comics to their holdings they called them graphic novels, hoping a literary-sounding term would garner approval from their supervisors.

Thus, the term "graphic novel" gained popularity as a public relations and marketing device, and quite a successful one. Graphic novel sales have been growing at a lively rate since the late 1990s. By 2006 there were $330 million in graphic novel sales, and in 2020 they topped $835 million (Reed 2022). Of course, some books counted as graphic novels were not what a purest would think of as a graphic novel. Most ongoing print comic book series and many ongoing webcomic series are reprinted in square-bound, sometimes hardcover, trade collections. In recent decades it has become common for story arcs in mainstream comic books to be constructed to fit within a reprint volume (e.g., *Detective Comics* #871–881 collected as *Batman: The Black Mirror*). There are also a number of classic story arcs from the previous century that have been collected in single volumes that might reasonably be considered graphic novels (e.g., *X-Men: Days of Future Past* and *Daredevil: Born Again*).

Not all comics are graphic novels, but all graphic novels are comics. So, don't stress over using the proper label; just enjoy good comics, whatever you want to call them.

What's to Be Gained by Studying Comics?

As noted previously, most people hold a low opinion of comics. To many, comic books and graphic novels are little more than cheap, disposable artifacts of popular culture that are not worth serious reflection or investigation. Given these opinions, what benefits might there be for studying these works? In this section we present three reasons why the medium is worthy of scholarly attention.

First Benefit: Appreciating the Originality of the Art Form

Comic books and graphic novels are unique and powerful form of communication. Perhaps longtime comic book writer Jim Shooter was a bit carried away by his enthusiasm when he claimed, "What we've got is the most portable, limitless, intense, personal, focused, intimate, compelling, wonderful visual medium in creation" (1994: 6). However, it is true that comics tell stories and involve readers in ways that no other art form—not plays, novels, or film—can duplicate. Historian Ron Goulart notes: "What I'd noticed early on was that comics were telling stories in a new way" (2001: v).

Reading often involves more than the mere understanding of words. As journalist Tom Wolfe notes, "reading of words is but a subset of a much more general human activity which includes symbol decoding, information integration and organization" (1977: 427). The very concept of literacy has been revolutionized and broadened. Visual literacy, the ability to understand pictorial information, became one of the basic skills required for communication in the twenty-first century.

The existence of comics has done more than just help undermine the primacy of the printed word. Comics break down, or at least blur, boundaries between word texts and picture texts. Reading comics requires a different type of literacy because on the comics page the drawn word and the drawn picture are both images to be read as a single integrated text. Of course, comics can vary in the degree to which they successfully integrate these two elements, and, as we shall see in later chapters, some theorists propose using the degree of interdependence or interanimation of the linguistic and the pictorial as the primary aesthetic standard for evaluating comics.

Second Benefit: Understanding Historical Significance

There was a time when virtually every kid in America, and quite a few adults, read comic books (Nyberg 1998). Until the television became a fixture in most American homes, the comic book was "the dominant element in the culture of American children" (Lupoff and Thompson 1970/1997: 11). Consider these estimates of comic book readership:

> Between the ages of six and eleven 95 per cent [*sic*] of boys and 91 per cent of girls buy comic books for a steady reading diet. Between twelve and seventeen, the figure falls to 87 per cent of boys and 81 per cent of girls. Between eighteen and thirty, the figure is 41 per cent of men and 28 per cent of women; after thirty, it is down to 16 and 12. But remember, these are steady readers. (Waugh 1947: 334)

It was probably a fairly accurate statement in 1989 when comics historian Mike Benton wrote that "the American comic book has touched the lives of nearly everyone alive today" (11). Although comics have played a less direct role in the lives of most Americans more recently, the appropriation of comic characters

Figure 0.4 Each year US Senator Tom Coburn publishes a report on government spending, and in 2013 the cover appropriated one of the most famous images in comic book history. Compare the image above to the cover of *Action Comics* #1 reproduced in Figure 10.10 on page 255. Art by Josh Trent.

and stories into major film, television, and video game franchises results in a perpetuation of indirect influence into subsequent generations (Figure 0.4).

Third Benefit: Visualizing the Potential of the Medium

In an October 15, 1986, appearance on *Late Night with David Letterman*, Harvey Pekar, writer of the autobiographical comic book *American Splendor*, expressed the potential of the comic book medium in clear, simple terms: "It's words and pictures. You can do anything you want with words and pictures" (qtd. in Witek 1989: 154). Pekar's words proved prophetic, for, as we will see in Chapter 10, 1986 was a watershed year in comic books, and thereafter more and more creators proved that they in fact *could* do anything they wanted with words and pictures.

Notable works since that year have ranged from Alan Moore and Dave Gibbons' deconstruction of the superhero mythos in *Watchmen* (1986) to Martin Rowson's melding of T. S. Eliot and Raymond Chandler in *Wasteland* (1990), to Alison Bechdel's poignant autobiographical novel *Fun Home* (2005) to Emil Ferris' faux-diary *My Favorite Thing Is Monsters* (2017). In 1989, scholar Joseph Witek noted that "a growing number of contemporary American comic books are being written as literature aimed at a general readership of adults" (3). Eric Drooker's nearly wordless fable of the artist in the modern metropolis, *Flood!* (1992); Jason Lutes' *Jar of Fools* (1994), a sparse tale of love, loss, and magic; Howard Cruse's honest portrayal of a gay man's coming of age in the 1960s American south in *Stuck Rubber Baby* (1995); Greg Rucka and Steve Lieber's riveting Antarctica murder mystery *Whiteout* (1998); Dusty Higgins and Ron Wolfe's lyrical Arthurian horror tale *Knights of the Living Dead* (2011); and Gene Luen Yang's twin tales of imperialism and faith in *Boxers and Saints* (2013) are just a few of the literate works that are beginning to fulfill the potential of the medium.

This introduction began with a disparaging quote from Lawrence L. Langer's review of *Maus*. While Langer is loath to acknowledge the work as a comic, he does admit that it is "a serious form of pictorial literature" (1991: 17). And *Maus* is but one of the scores of serious literary works that have shown the medium to be worthy of greater attention and study. However, in the introduction to *Comics: Anatomy of a Mass Medium*, scholars Reinhold Reitberger and Wolfgang Fuchs make one simple point that cannot be overlooked: "Comics are important because we love to read them!" (1971/1972: 7).

What's in This Textbook?

As the subtitle suggests, this book introduces comics in three distinct units: culture, form, and context.

The first unit situates comics as a cultural phenomenon. Chapter 1 (new to this edition) examines how comics as a form of art and communication emerge from and are an influence upon their culture. Chapter 2 considers how the dynamic relationship between the production and consumption of comic works as artists and consumers interact.

The second unit considers formal aspects of comics storytelling. It includes three chapters that explore how comics work to make meaning at three different levels, the encapsulation of moments, the composition of panels, and the layout of pages. Chapter 3 focuses on how the selection of prime moments of action help to depict key elements of storytelling. Chapter 4 examines how the arrangement of visual elements within panels assists with storytelling. Finally, Chapter 5 considers how the layout of the page—or screen—can convey meaning.

The third unit considers comics in terms of their **genres**, or types, of storytelling. Chapter 6 provides an overview of genre theory and reviews a range of the popular genres featured in comics and their characteristics. Chapter 7 casts a spotlight on one of the fastest-growing genres, the memoir, and explores its origins and practices. Chapter 8 takes an in-depth look at the most dominant genre in American comic books, the superhero, in order to better understand its relationship to the form. Chapter 9 (new to this edition) looks at three genres that go beyond entertainment: journalism, advocacy, and documentary.

The fourth unit investigates comics within their wider context. Chapter 10 provides a history of comics as they have grown and matured as a medium for communication. Chapter 11 scrutinizes how we study comics and the cultural practices that are within and surround them. Finally, Chapter 12 (new to this edition) helps to foster thoughtful criticism of comics by introducing readers to the practices of crafting reviews and scholarly analyses.

By the end of this book, careful readers will possess an understanding of how comics are situated in culture, how they communicate meaning through their form, how they manifest themselves in various genres, and how they may be studied and understood.

Turn the page and let's get started!

Discovering: More Online

We invite you to visit us at https://www.bloomsburyonlineresources.com/the-power-of-comics-and-graphic-novels-3 for additional material that didn't make our print edition.

Unit I Culture

1 Comics in Culture, Comics as Culture

In the mid-twentieth century, Donald Duck, his Uncle Scrooge, and his nephews Huey, Dewey, and Louie were among the most popular comic book characters in the United States. Today, comics featuring the Disney ducks sell very few copies in America. Yet in Germany, the comics magazine featuring the ducks sells a quarter of a million copies each week and lavish editions of reprints sell out quickly (Bernofsky 2009).

Why is it that Disney's duck comics have almost no audience in their native land, but are much beloved in another culture? Perhaps the main reason is the work of Erika Fuchs. In 1951 the publisher Ehapa hired Fuchs, a 44-year-old art historian, to provide erudite translations of American comics for their newly launched magazine *Micky Maus*. For more than thirty-five years she was the editor-in-chief of the magazine and translated the comic book adventures of Donald Duck and the other inhabitants of Duckburg into German.

Fuchs did more than merely translate; she adapted the comics to German culture. Fuchs' version of Donald Duck still throws fits and has goofy accidents, but he speaks in complex sentences with alliterate phrases, quotes from German literature, and channels German philosophy. In translating a story set during Halloween, Fuchs changes the holiday to Shrove Monday, a day of parades and costume parties in some parts of Germany. When Huey, Dewey, and Louie (Tick, Trick, and Track in German) want to show their solidarity in resisting bath time they recite an oath from Friedrich Schiller's play *William Tell* (1804).

Generations of Germans, from all walks of life, grew up loving Donald Duck and his family. A "childish" American art form had been made acceptable to German intellectuals. "Even Frankfurt School philosopher Max Horkheimer admitted to enjoying reading Donald Duck comics before bed" (Bernofsky 2009) (Figure 1.1).

Objectives

In this chapter you will learn:

1. how comics function as artifacts reflecting the culture that inspires them, both domestically and internationally;
2. how American studies and media studies provide contexts for studying comics; and
3. how a historical perspective on comics informs understanding of the changing cultural conversation over time.

The core question, "Why engage in the study of comics?", has a simple answer. Like any other media form, the content and processes associated with comics evolve over time and provide a mirror that can help us understand both the culture that forms them and the effect that the

Figure 1.1 "In this house, Dr. Erika Fuchs (1906–2005) lived and translated for more than five decades. Her texts have profoundly crafted the world of Duckburg and enriched the German language." Anecdote about the Disney comics translations by Erika Fuchs. Provided by D.O.N.A.L.D. president Susanne Luber. https://commons.wikimedia.org/wiki/File:Erikafuchsgedenkplakette.jpg

media has on the culture. That seems like circular reasoning, but in fact it's more of a feedback loop: all media are created by individuals who live within, and are deeply influenced by, the culture that surrounds them, and those same creative individuals have a disproportionate ability to affect cultural change. While prior generations of scholars may have rejected the study of comics arguing that the form was too simple to be worthy, it has become clear that the creative content of comics has had profound effects on other media and the broader culture, and with that realization, comics studies have begun to find its place in academia.

Defining our terms before we begin, let us acknowledge that although comics have historical roots in cartoons, our study will focus on comics as a storytelling medium, whether delivered as a "strip" in newspapers, a "book" that is actually a periodical magazine, a "graphic novel" that is a convenient marketing label for a book-format comic, either a collection of previously published periodicals or an original work of book length, or a "webcomic" created and delivered digitally. It's not that cartoons don't share the power of comics to illuminate culture: even the briefest look at, for example, *The New Yorker's* one-panel gag cartoons over the past century provides a powerful exploration of the changing gender roles in that time. But this is already an expansive topic, and focus helps clarity.

A Literary Perspective

One lens to examine comics would certainly be to begin with the body of American literature created in comic forms. Are they literature, and are they ready for study? When asked that type of question about novels a century ago, Oxford don J. R. R. Tolkien demurred, saying they were too new to be considered for the canon of literature. With all due respect to Tolkien's brilliance both as a scholar and as an author, the academic world moved forward with the study of the novel and is now moving forward with the study of comics.

That is not to say that all comics can be considered literature worthy of study for their artistic quality, any more than all prose can be. Much of what is created in any media form is designed simply to be entertainment or to provide information, yet some portion of that body of material proves worthy of further consideration for its artistic quality or insightful commentary on the human condition. It is the power of literature to explore the questions that humankind has pondered for centuries: matters of mortality, morality, spirituality, sexuality, and the unanswered dilemmas of our lives.

But even comics that do not explore such weighty themes can be fertile ground for study as markers of the culture in which they were created and their creators' views of that culture. Consider exploring the comparison between Rudolph Dirks' *The Katzenjammer Kids* and Jerry Craft's *New Kid* (2019). Dirks produced *The Katzenjammer Kids* between 1897 and 1913, and it continues to be distributed in syndication today, making it the longest-running newspaper comic strip. Dirks was influenced by a German children's publication, *Max and Moritz: A Story of Seven Boyish Pranks* by Wilhelm Busch (1865), which tells us something meaningful about the American culture of the period. Unlike the contemporary world, where America is primarily a creator and exporter of cultural content, nineteenth-century America was still largely an importer from the older, more established creative communities of Europe (Figure 1.2).

Figure 1.2 Rudolph Dirks created the mischievous Katzenjammer Kids, who were repeatedly in trouble with their Mama and the Captain. In this August 2, 1903, strip they attempt to shave the Captain's whiskers with a manual lawn mower.

Examining the behaviors of the characters in *The Katzenjammer Kids* also provides insight into the culture of the time. America was in a phase of massive immigration, and the dynamics of child-rearing were far different from those in later generations. The pranks of the kids, and the efforts of the Captain to "civilize" them seem quite anachronistic to our modern eyes. And we shudder at a character like King Bongo, the black monarch of a jungle island. Understanding that these behaviors or stereotypes were representative of this period helps us understand the culture that produced and accepted them.

It's also significant that *The Katzenjammer Kids* reached as large an audience as any cultural content at the dawn of the twentieth century. Before the explosion of mass electronic media, William Randolph Hearst's *The New York Journal* was part of a newspaper empire that would peak with a daily circulation of one in five Americans, and with pass-along readership within families would achieve even deeper reach (based on circulation numbers found in Whyte 2009). Major cartoonists like Dirks were prized contributors and achieved a level of celebrity status almost unimaginable to later generations of comic creators.

By comparison, Jerry Craft's *New Kid* was published in 2019 as an original graphic novel to considerable acclaim, including the prestigious Newbery Medal (the first time awarded to a comic). Craft tells the story of a young man of color admitted to one of New York's most exclusive private schools, and the cultural dissonance he experiences both fitting in with the white, privileged students, and continuing to connect with his original community. Much of Craft's story comments on the effects of economic inequality in our time, on the unintended consequences of affirmative action, and ultimately on the current cultural dialogue surrounding diversity and inclusion—and Craft's ability as a black man to have his story published so widely is in itself a comment on representation. By comparison, the most important cartoonist who was a man of color in Dirks' era, George Herriman of *Krazy Kat* (1913–44), had to pass as white.

On the one hand, *New Kid* is far more widely acknowledged as a work of literature than *The Katzenjammer Kids* was, a mark of how the perception of graphic novels has changed the view of comics. And viewed through the lens of how literature is customarily taught, *New Kid* certainly offers more depth and opportunity for examination. On the other hand, given the shift in how Americans consume media in the last century, it is unlikely that more than perhaps 1 in 100 Americans will actually read *New Kid* as opposed to the near-universal exposure of *The Katzenjammer Kids.* This in itself doesn't make one of the two more worthy of thoughtful examination, but the comparison shows how complex the exploration of comics' place within the culture must be.

An International Perspective

Stepping back from a purely American view of comics as literature requires understanding that the form of storytelling we define as comics has grown in parallel evolution in multiple international traditions, each shaped by its own artistic and cultural forces. Measured by total world circulation, the Japanese form called **manga** (generally translated as "comics") is probably the most significant of the interrelated comics styles. Strongly influenced by the American form in the post–Second World War era, manga is inseparable from traditional Japanese art forms, and deeply intertwined with their animated cartoons, anime. Largely unavailable in the Western world for their first several decades, manga has achieved a large readership in the twenty-first century across most of the globe and has been a powerful influence on comic creators in America and elsewhere.

Can students gain insight into Japanese culture through the comparative study of manga? Since manga forms have been used to tell stories across an even wider range of subject matter than American comics, it seems likely. On one superficial level, it has been observed that in American comics when a protagonist gains extraordinary abilities, their struggle is to choose how to use their uniqueness (see Stan Lee's classic *Spider-Man* line, "With great power there must also come—great responsibility"), while in manga, the challenge is most frequently to fit within the larger society, perhaps reflecting the greater divide between the importance of the individual or the group.

Studying manga can also literally affect how the world is seen. Studies of how humans in different cultures use their vision to "read" emotion in others have shown that in Western cultures people generally look first to others' mouths to judge whether they are smiling or showing signs of aggression (Kuba Krys et al. 2016). By comparison, similar studies have shown that in eastern cultures like Japan's, the first look is to the eyes of other people (Uono and Hietanen 2015). Manga carried this through, exaggerating the expressiveness of eyes in facial expression in comparison to their American counterparts.

The content of manga can also provide useful exploration of comparative literature and views of history. Keiji Nakazawa's *Barefoot Gen (Hadashi No Gen* in the original) tells the story of his experiences as a child during the atomic bombing of Hiroshima and its aftermath. Serialized from 1973 to 1987, it's a lengthy and extraordinarily powerful testimony to a historical moment that is viewed differently in most American literature. The forms of visual exaggeration common in manga combine with the intrinsic horror of the events to provide a very different experience than John Hershey's *Hiroshima* (1946), possibly the most suitable comparable prose work. The details of ordinary Japanese life in the period that Nakazawa captures would have simply been unavailable to an American author unless they resided in Japan for many years. And the specific events that he witnessed were outside any American's direct experience.

Another way to consider comics in the context of world culture is to view them as other national traditions see the form. Comics under the tradition of ***bandes dessinée*** have been regarded more highly in France for many decades, where they are nominally the "ninth art." The Franco-Belgian version of comics has both magazine serialization and book-format (there called "albums") modes and has given the world two of its most enduring series, *The Adventures of Tintin* (1929–76) by Hergé and *Asterix and Obelix* (1959–) by Rene Goscinny and Albert Uderzo. The latter continues with new adventures by the original creators' successors, and each new volume sells over 10 million copies across Europe on publication.

Both of these series are notable for reflecting the creators' (and therefore, the cultures in which they were created) views of the world through the travels of their characters. Tintin had adventures in the Soviet Union, America, and most controversially, the Congo—a volume that has been pulled from circulation in many countries for its depiction of the natives and the Belgian treatment of that territory. Asterix was also a world traveler, though with his stories set in the era of the Roman Empire, the potential for controversy was lessened, and because the volumes were written a generation later, demonstrated fewer issues. Nonetheless, both series give the reader an opportunity to see through the eyes of cultures that are not their own.

Bandes dessinée or manga also gives readers the ability to investigate the taboos of other cultures and compare them to America's. Reading comics from different cultures allows for consideration of why, for instance, American culture is far more tolerant of violence in its media and more intolerant of sexuality than France. Observing how the characters from one culture travel well (or not) also allows scholars to examine specific cultural biases or behaviors. As noted in this chapter's opening anecdote, the Disney comics done by Carl Barks—celebrated as one of America's masters of the form, and still enormously popular in much of Europe six decades after Barks' last work—are unsaleable in the United States to any significant audience of children while Barks' characters like Uncle Scrooge remain popular in other forms. In the reverse direction, *Asterix* has been brought to American audiences by several different publishers, never achieving sales on any meaningful level.

Discovering: Considering Cultural Imperialism

In 1936 cartoonist Lee Falk debuted his long-running syndicated comic strip, *The Phantom*, on the pages of America's newspapers. According to his origin, the Phantom is the latest in a family of crime fighters who have opposed piracy and villainy since the sixteenth century, operating from a base somewhere in the heart of the African jungle. At the start of this heroic legacy, the man who would become the very first Phantom was rescued by a group of African pygmies called the Bander tribe. He, in turn, would help free them from slavery after adopting a costume that invoked the image of their slaver's demon god. The current Phantom continues to provide protection to the Bander tribe. If you read this series from a Western point of view, it may seem like a story that is in keeping with accepted cultural values and norms. Americans in particular are fond of heroic individuals who make a comeback against the odds and manage to not only save themselves but to single-handedly rescue the larger society. However, taken from another perspective, that of the African native, the story is less flattering. Africans are portrayed as either superstitious villains or helpless victims in this story. Either way, it takes a white man to figure out how to free and protect them for centuries; no champion of equal stature to the seemingly immortal Phantom emerges from among their own people.

The idea of a beneficent white hero was a common theme in fiction at the time of the Phantom's debut. White heroes like Tarzan, Sheena, and dozens of other jungle kings and queens were often the stars of novels, newspaper strips, and comic books. Yet the portrayal of these Western-born champions almost always places them in a superior position to the native peoples around them. To readers from these parts of the world, and often those descended from them, such portrayals are insulting. The portrayals devalue both the peoples and the cultures depicted in them. In addition, the portrayals also work to reinforce existing notions of dominance. Thus, to Western readers, such portrayals perpetuate beliefs about the superiority of the white race and Western know-how. In the case of the Phantom, Falk tells us that one white man can do what an entire village of Africans could not: secure the Banders' freedom. Moreover, the continued protection of the Phantom legacy over the tribe for centuries echoes a Western notion that developing nations are childlike and need the supervision of white people.

This, of course, was part of the rationale for European colonialism in the past. While the desire for resources and territory drove colonizers forward, European intellectuals argued that they were doing native peoples of the Americas, India, Africa, Australia, and the Asian Pacific Islands a favor by delivering them from savagery and bringing them the superior European language, religion, and culture. The delivery of such "gifts" was most often made at the end of a gun barrel, as Western militaries first conquered and then "tamed" native people by forcing Western culture upon them (Figure 1.3).

Figure 1.3 Jungle lords were once popular heroes in mass media, but they were problematic figures because of their colonialist and implicit racist messages. Here Ka-Zar, Lord of the Savage Land, asserts his dominance over a group of indigenous peoples. From *X-Men: The Hidden Years* #6 (2000) by John Byrne and Tom Palmer (writer-artists). © 2023 Marvel Entertainment, Inc. and its subsidiaries.

While nearly all nations once under colonial rule have won their political independence, some academics argue that the process of colonialization has only changed tactics, having moved from the use of militaries and missionaries to the tools of mass media. The concern with this new form of colonialism, called **cultural imperialism**, is that dominant cultures can supplant native cultures through the widespread use of broadcast, electronic, and print technology. The dominant invading cultures often produce very attractive media products, which is no surprise given that these are often created using superior technology (e.g., computer-assisted coloring programs) and under the direction of long-term professionals. They also tend to have a head start in learning the business of media when compared to emerging homegrown producers, particularly in terms of establishing and maintaining distribution systems to get the media products into the hands of consumers. Dominant cultures also have typically covered their production costs in their domestic market long before the same product is released abroad. Western publishers can make substantial profits by distributing their products thusly, even if the charges to consumers in a developing country are considerably lower than that for their domestic audience. With much of its overhead covered by sales in its country of origin, a media product can be priced so low in a foreign market that it will even undersell a native product. In the competitive world of media production, the reality is that those who have already made money at it are better positioned to make more money. The unforeseen cost, though, is the erosion of indigenous cultures, as the slicker, cheaper, and more widespread media products provide messages about values, norms, and roles that are different from (if not outright contradictory to) those of native culture. Certainly, America has been charged with cultural imperialism thanks to its highly influential film, television, and, yes, comic book industries. Likewise, we are now seeing Japan exhibiting a similar influence through the widespread distribution of manga.

This brings us back to the *Phantom*, a strip still running today, many years after its creator's passing. The enduring popularity of "The Ghost Who Walks" in newspaper strips eventually led to his appearance in comic books and other media, at home and abroad. In fact, while *Phantom* comic books have been published off and on in America over the years, the Phantom has achieved his greatest popularity abroad. The Phantom is something of a phenomenon in the countries of Scandinavia (Norway, Sweden, Finland), Australia, and, curiously enough, India. In these countries, the comic books have been in continuous publication for more than fifty years, ever since their first introduction, and have been among the bestselling comics in their respective markets. The Phantom can be seen then as an example of imperialism in terms of both the content of its stories and the effect of its distribution. Although the Phantom is not self-consciously propaganda trying to convert readers to adopt its notions of white, Western superiority, it nonetheless propagates that very message through its use of characters and setting. The financial benefits that King Features Syndicate, the owner of the copyright, has garnered through the licensing of Phantom comics around the world are considerable. And while the Phantom may have entertained, if not inspired, audiences in many lands, the lingering question is: at what costs to native identity? Then there is the additional question left in the wake of all characters—including the Phantom, Donald Duck, and Superman—who displace native series: but for the intervention of these commercial endeavors, what alternative heroes might have been imagined around the world?

An American Studies Perspective

Returning focus to America, another way to usefully explore the connections between comics and culture is to use the lens of **American studies**, typically an interdisciplinary approach combining the humanities. Looking at comics this way steps back from the pure "are they literature" question to examining the nexus of historical means of production, distribution, and audiences in conjunction with the content. Longitudinal consideration enables a discussion of how changing technology has affected content and culture long before the digital revolution that current students are living through. Comic strips emerge in part because newspapers achieve the technology to print drawings easily, and gain their initial popularity in part because they are the first part of the paper to be published in color. There is room to investigate the connections between the term "yellow journalism" and its possible roots in Richard F. Outcault's early comic strip *The Yellow Kid* (1895–8), which was the first popular use of color in newspapers.

Ultimately, culture itself is in part shaped by the changing means of communication, as has been evidenced in recent decades by increased **fractionalization** and divisiveness in America that is in part instigated or exaggerated by the fractionalization of our mass media. Looking at the evolution of the (relatively) apolitical media form of comics to demonstrate how these changes both reflect and affect the cultural climate that surrounds us is a useful exercise.

Comics are not always apolitical. As with most creative works, the philosophies of the creators (or occasionally the parties financing the projects) may subtly or unsubtly transmit themselves through the work. An American studies approach would certainly explore instances like the effect of a Quaker-funded biographical comic about Dr. Martin Luther

King Jr. on a very young John Lewis, providing pivotal motivation for Lewis' entry into the civil rights movement. And coming full circle, after becoming a leader in that movement and, ultimately, a long-serving US Congressman, Lewis, would coauthor *March* in 2013 with Andrew Aydin and Nate Powell, launching a graphic novel series intended to inspire current generations of young people to pursue justice through peaceful protest.

Cultural and political shifts also can be accelerated by shifts in technology. Innovations in offset printing that made plate-making and shorter press runs more economical are as much the keys to understanding the underground comix of the 1960s as exploring the drug and protest-fueled subculture of California's Bay Area at the time. Without understanding that the means of production or distribution affect content, and through that the culture, students see an incomplete picture of events.

American studies also encourages students to examine the cultural shifts themselves, examining issues such as why Jackie Ormes' *Torchy Brown in Dixie to Harlem* could only reach a segregated audience in 1937–8, or how the **Bechdel Test** migrated from the narrow audience that first saw it in gay and lesbian-oriented newspapers running Alison Bechdel's *Dykes to Watch out For* in 1985 to the mainstream conversation in the early twenty-first century. (We will take a closer look at the Bechdel test in Chapter 11.) Looking at touchstone moments like this in comics provides a useful measure of the inflection points in the broader society and culture.

A Media Studies Perspective

Alternatively, there is a **media studies** approach to the topic of comics. This would expose students to the unique neurology of how comics are translated into our minds through two separate hemispheres of the brain, unlike most media which travel through a single one. Or follow on the groundbreaking work of Scott McCloud's (1993) *Understanding Comics* and explore why simple drawings can create more immediate identification and association and tracking that through the worldwide acceptance and affection for Charles Schulz's *Peanuts* (1950–2000).

There is a small but important body of evidence developed in studies of the effectiveness of comics as teaching tools that need to be expanded on by media studies scholars so that the power of the form can be properly understood. And as shown in the discussion of the variant forms of comics across the globe, and further considered in the context of the vast array of personal styles used by creators to produce comics, there are undoubtedly subtleties in which styles of comics connect to readers in distinctly different ways.

Taking that question to a high level of complexity, is there some factor intrinsic to the style of manga that enabled it to peak at approximately 60 percent of Japanese publishing content? Or are there intrinsic factors in the Japanese culture that made it more hospitable to manga? And how can the successful transmission of manga to so many other national or regional cultural groups be accounted for if those factors are Japan-specific?

Looked at in all these multiple ways, it is clear that the question of how comics fit within the broader questions of culture is neither simple nor obvious, and provides rewarding territory for scholars to explore. *The Power of Comics & Graphic Novels* is intended as a gateway text on the subject, not a definitive answer, as comics scholarship per se is only a few decades old and still practiced by a comparatively small group of academics. In many ways, comic studies are where film studies were in their nascent form in the 1960s, and seem likely to follow the same exponential growth pattern (Duncan and Smith 2011).

A Historical Perspective

Return then to the central question of comics as culture: where do they fit within the wider question of cultural theory and history, why are they important to study, and how can scholars explore this media form productively? One argument can be developed on a historical basis, notwithstanding this volume's general restriction of its theme to a defined form called comics. The antecedents for the modern form of comics can be traced back to the earliest forms of human communication that survived. If people began communicating through pictures like those that survived in the caves of Lascaux, is it not a fair argument that comics represent simply the most current incarnation of a primal cultural tool?

It is also possible to consider the importance of comics in culture by looking at developmental history. Much of the early artwork by children is presented in simple representational shapes, images that reflect McCloud's (1993) argument on the purity of form. Children translate their vision of the world around them (their culture) to paper as proto-cartoons—and the reflection of that can be seen in some of the most current **diary comics**, memoirs, and webtoons, which often eschew complex artwork for deliberately childlike stick figures and imagery. As scholars go back and study the notable diarists of the past to understand the culture of their times, is it not possible to understand more of our contemporary culture by looking at these immediately published excerpts of our own daily culture? (Figure 1.4).

If culture is considered as the transmission of norms, behaviors, and ideas that shape a society, all the artifacts that are created for those purposes matter. Study of ancient Egyptian culture is not possible without focus on the hieroglyphics laboriously carved that combined illustrations and textual matter to communicate beliefs and information. Knowledge of the Mesoamerican civilizations is enhanced by the study of the "speech scrolls" where they used those dual tools as well. So then can early-twentieth-century Americans be understood

Figure 1.4 Cartoonist Tiffany Babb chronicles her experiences in a series of diary comics called *All about Me*. Used with permission.

without examining the cultural devices that were the single most widely circulated form of entertainment in that culture?

Embedded in the comics of that period—or any later period—are depictions of the gender roles, prejudices, and practices of the time. The content is generally fictional, but to have had value to its audience had to be relevant to the lives they led. Whether decoding the foods eaten from Winsor McCay's *Dream of the Rarebit Fiend* and thereby revealing the popularity of the Welsh Rarebit (an open-faced melted cheese sandwich) *c.* 1904, or tracing the evolving family lives in the shadow of the culturally transforming intrusion of the automobile as represented in Frank King's *Gasoline Alley* (the first American comic strip to age its characters in something parallel to real time from its debut in 1918), comics give scholars biopsies of the culture in which they were created. While these are not times without contemporaneous records that have to be pieced together like archaeologists unearthing ancient cities, it is the nature of contemporaneous records to share the assumptions of the culture in which they were created, and so often to be silent on aspects of them that are presumed "natural." And while some of the same benefits can be achieved by the study of any other fixed cultural artifact, be it in print, film, or digital form, one of the central advantages of studying comics is that they have been less frequently intermediated and less carefully controlled by parties financing their production or distribution.

The Potential for Interpretation

It is true that comics, like all media forms, have been subject to influence by the systems under which they were produced, but the level of that influence has varied widely: from the stultifying effect of the Comics Code enacted after the moral panic and book-burning of comics in the 1950s to the relatively complete artistic freedom of the underground comix movement (see Chapter 10 for full details on these historical moments). And even when there were significant theoretic controls over the production, many comics were created by singular individuals or small teams, operating at high velocity and without detailed supervision, allowing their personal ideologies to permeate the work.

An early example of this is Herriman's *Krazy Kat*, a gender-fluid character at a time when that terminology did not exist nor would acknowledgment of that behavior have been found elsewhere in the widely distributed newspapers of the Hearst publishing empire. But Hearst, the proprietor, was a fan of Herriman's work and so the cartoonist's efforts were not subject to the usual level of supervision or constraint. No contemporaneous research exists to show whether readers noticed, or whether those readers who might have shared that identity felt represented (Figures 1.5a–d).

But whatever Herriman's intent was, and however it was received, it is important to remember that comics, like all forms of cultural communication, exist not only in the creators' imagination but in the minds of those who consume them. A more modern example of this is Stan Lee's and Jack Kirby's *The X-Men* in 1963. On the face of it, it is a heroic fantasy of a handful of characters whose mutations put them outside the norm of the human race, struggling to save humanity from other, more malicious mutants, while having to hide their differences. Lee and Kirby captured the fundamental alienation they were depicting well enough that there is documentation of readers interpreting the story metaphorically to be about their own identity

Figures 1.5a–d George Herriman's *Krazy Kat* turned the traditional cat and mouse dynamic on its ear, as a lovesick Krazy Kat pursues the affections of Ignatz, only to be met with frustration and violent rejection. The gender of either is fluid, though, a point driven home by the final panel in this 1915 strip.

groups, whether racial or sexual. Lee and Kirby, cisgendered heterosexual white men of their time, may have unconsciously thought about the parallels to their own Jewish families' experiences, but the thought that black or LGBTQ readers would identify with the mutants' dilemmas was unlikely to have crossed their minds during the creation.

It is certainly true that from at least the mid-twentieth century onward, out groups like the LGBTQ community have seized upon the form of comics to communicate in increasing numbers and with increasing visibility, reflecting their greater integration into American culture. When Howard Cruse's pioneering *Gay Comix* was published in 1980, it could only be distributed as an underground comix. His story of growing up gay during the civil rights movement of the Sixties, *Stuck Rubber Baby*, was able to be published in 1995 by DC Comics, a unit of one of the largest media corporations. And inspired in part by his work, Alison Bechdel was able not only to publish *Fun Home* in 2006 but to see it turned into a Broadway musical in 2015. (And yet to remain one of the country's most frequently banned books in the next decade.) Examining journeys like this represents part of the opportunity to consider comics' place in the broader culture, and to explore the role they have played in seeding cultural shifts.

Fun Home's translation into a Tony Award-winning musical is only a modest reflection of the great power of comics in translational media, as the audiences for Broadway are perforce restricted to the number of people who can be squeezed into the seats of a theater, performance after performance. The broader impact of comics on popular culture clearly comes in film and television, where the tales crafted for the comics have captured massive audiences. Three of the last decade's top-grossing films of the year have been comics adaptations from Marvel, and the overall percentage of the box office captured by comics-derived films outstrips any other media form as source material. Television is harder to quantify, but the number of programs based on comics is larger today than ever before with successes delivered via traditional broadcast (*Riverdale,* 2017–23), cable (*The Walking Dead,* 2010–22), pay-cable (*Watchmen,* 2019), and streaming (*The Umbrella Academy,* 2019–).

That said, comics have long demonstrated their ability to move beyond the printed page to integrate with the culture. Debuting in 1879, Palmer Cox's *The Brownies* were a late-nineteenth-century proto-comic that became one of the earliest concepts to be translated into a wide range of merchandise, setting the model for the next century's crazes. As early as 1911 McCay took his *Little Nemo in Slumberland* (1905–27) into animation, and newspaper strips like Bud Fisher's *Mutt and Jeff* (1907–83) and *Krazy Kat* followed.

Analyzing: Integrated into Culture

Uniquely in American culture, one fictional property has been central to the creative conversation three times in three different decades. Normally, the pattern for American fads is to burn hot and burn out fast, never to be repeated (how about the mid-1950s television phenomenon *Davy Crockett*, anyone?) or to settle in as a continuing part of the culture at a level that peaks and ebbs with subsequent releases (e.g., *Star Wars,* 1977–). But it is indisputable that *Batman* as created by Bob Kane and Bill Finger in 1939 became the central property in popular culture in 1966 as interpreted in the television series produced by William Dozier and starring Adam West, in 1989 as interpreted in the film directed by Tim Burton and starring Michael Keaton, and again in 2008 as seen in *The Dark Knight* directed by Christopher Nolan and starring Christian Bale.

In studying this cultural phenomenon, scholars must consider the factors that enabled it. One is certainly the oddly protean characteristic of Batman that enables him to have been given such diverse interpretations, from camp to noir, each appearing right for its moment in time. But is another factor that the comics' source material, whose continued publication enables a diverse group of creators to expand upon the original conception and take it in different directions? Or is the corporate ownership and management of the property a factor, guiding it through executions in virtually every available medium American culture has?

Regardless of how a scholar may rank these factors, the result demonstrates powerfully how the creative process that begins in comics has grown to be deeply embedded in the broader culture. Characters and ideas that were given birth in comics have shaped our culture, and other cultures as well. Even the idioms of our language have been permeated by the comics, with phrases like "That's his Kryptonite" being used far from their original meaning. *Superman* creators Jerry Siegel and Joe Shuster wouldn't be surprised, as they envisioned their hero as becoming American folklore, but it is for scholars to take up this subject and discover the full range of linkages between comics and our culture. Whether explored as literature, American studies, media studies, or through any other lens a rich academic journey awaits.

Discussion Questions

1. Are comics "literature" or at least "literary"? What qualities may qualify (or disqualify) them for such categorization in the eyes of learned people?
2. Identify comics you have previously encountered and consider how those comics reflect cultural priorities. In what ways are messages in those comics supporting dominant ideas about cultural norms? In what ways might some of those comic messages challenging dominant ideas?

Activities

1. Select a collection of comics originally produced in the mid-twentieth century and read at least a dozen pages within the collection. Some possible picks might include collections of Frank King's *Gasoline Alley* or Jackie Ormes' *Torchy Brown in Dixie to Harlem*. You can also find a variety of genres represented at https://comicbookplus.com/. Consider what these comics reflect about their cultures? What norms are reflected? What groups are muted or missing? What behaviors are normalized and what behaviors are not? Share your perspective with your instructor and classmates.
2. Consider making a diary comic of your own, chronicling your journey through this comics studies course. For each class session draft a three-panel strip explaining something impactful that you learned or that happened in class that day. Recall that a diary comic does not require a lot of advanced drawing skills and simple stick figures are completely acceptable. At the end of the academic term you and your classmates can compare your journeys by looking back at your collection of comic strips. Here's a template to get you started:

My Diary Comic

Recommended Reading

Comics

Herriman, George. *The George Harriman Library: Krazy & Ignatz.* Seattle: Fantagraphics, 2019–.
Fantagraphics has collected runs of George Harriman's celebrated comic strip, *Krazy Kat*, in a series of reprint editions that bring the surrealist storytelling of one of the most groundbreaking comics to a new generation of readers.

Nakazawa, Keiji. *Barefoot Gen Vols. 1–10.* San Francisco: Last Gasp, 2004–9.
As introduced in the chapter, *Barefoot Gen* is a moving firsthand account of the atomic bombing of Hiroshima. *Gen* is not only a telling example of Japanese manga but a moving tale of surviving the horrors of war.

Scholarly Sources

Serrano, Nhora Lucía, ed. *Immigrants and Comics: Graphic Spaces of Remembrance, Transaction, and Mimesis.* New York: Routledge, 2021.

Serrano and her contributors examine how immigrants and the immigrant experiences have been presented in comics over the last century, from *The Yellow Kid* at the turn of the last century to more recent *X-Men* comics. The selections provide a fascinating examination of how culture is embodied and reflected in experiences where two (or more) cultural traditions come into contact with one another.

Aldama, Frederick Luis, ed. *The Oxford Handbook of Comic Book Studies*. New York: Oxford University Press, 2020.

Aldama has assembled more than three dozen comics experts to examine comics from multiple angles, including selections that focus on "What is a comic?" to what trajectories tell us about the future of comics. Of particular importance to this chapter's consideration is a section of contributions focused on comics as social commentary and as a response to sociopolitical realities.

2 Making and Reading Comics

The architect of the so-called "Silver Age" of superhero comic books, Julius Schwartz, began his career as a fan. Back in 1931—three years before the "official" birth of the comic book—fifteen-year-old Julie Schwartz met fellow teen Mort Weisinger at a gathering of science fiction enthusiasts known as the Scienceers. The next year the two young men gave the fledgling science fiction fan movement momentum when they published *The Time Traveler*, the first nationally distributed fan magazine, or **fanzine**, devoted to science fiction. Two years later, Schwartz and Weisinger turned their avocation into their vocation when they formed Solar Sales Service, the first literary agency for science fiction writers. Their clients included soon-to-be notables such as Ray Bradbury, Otto Binder, H. P. Lovecraft, and Edmond Hamilton.

After Superman was introduced in *Action Comics* in 1938, comic books began attracting both fans and writers of fantastic literature. A number of Solar Sales Service writers, notably Otto Binder and Alfred Bester, made the transition from pulp magazines to comic books. Starting in 1944, Schwartz also ended up working at All-American Comics—later part of DC Comics—editing a wide range of titles over the next forty-five years. As a DC editor, Schwartz not only reshaped the comic book medium but also stimulated the great explosion of comics fandom that occurred in the 1960s.

During the 1940s, while Schwartz was guiding the adventures of Flash, Green Lantern, and the Justice Society of America, some of his fellow science fiction fans were exhibiting the first behaviors of comics fandom: they started saving their old comic books. While the average comic book reader of the time was an eleven- or twelve-year-old, who treated the books as disposable entertainment, the science fiction fans tended to be in their teens or twenties (some even older). For years, they had been filling closets and footlockers with pulp magazines and pocket paperbacks, so it was only natural to do the same with this new form of fantastic literature. And it was only a matter of time before they found one another, thanks in part to Schwartz. In 1961 he began printing the addresses of those who wrote letters to the editor. Rather than relying on chance encounters, now the fans had a way to reach one another and begin to build a community of their own (Figure 2.1).

Julius Schwartz was one of the lucky few fans who managed to make the transition to professional first in science fiction and then in comics, which he hadn't been a fan or reader of before. He not only got to make comics, but he also remembered his roots and helped readers to express their enthusiasm for comic books as fans.

Figure 2.1 Julius "Julie" Schwartz had one of the longest and most illustrious careers in the comic book industry, and to acknowledge the influence he had on the Superman, mythos writers sometimes put Julie into a comic book story. Art from a tribute issue, *Superman* #411 (1985) by Elliot S! Maggin (words) and Curt Swan and Murphy Anderson (art). © DC Comics

Objectives

In this chapter you will learn:

1. how forms and patterns of distribution have shaped the business of comics;
2. how graphic novels have become the most important form of comics;
3. how the industrial and artisan processes shape the nature of the comics created;
4. the characteristics that define comics creators as auteurs; and
5. some of the activities associated with comics fandom.

The month following Comic-Con International in 2009 marked a turning point in the structure of the comics industry: coming off an intense five-day gathering of over 150,000 people that spilled out of the convention center to fill downtown San Diego with activations for entertainment brands, the Walt Disney Company announced the $4 billion acquisition of Marvel Entertainment and Time Warner announced that DC Comics would be reorganized as DC Entertainment and more fully integrated into Warner Bros., moving to Burbank in the foreseeable future. The presence of Hollywood executives, toy and video game company staff, brand licensors, investors, and other business people might have outnumbered the comics publishing people at the convention.

Making Comics in the Twenty-First Century

Comics in America presented a very different picture in the twenty-first century than the field had for most of the previous six decades. Instead of being offered to the public in two distinct forms (the comic book as a periodical pamphlet and the newspaper comic strip) by a handful of specialized publishers and syndicators respectively, and with content highly concentrated in a few genres, the picture had become much more complex. Comics were now being created in a wider range of content than ever before, produced by a diverse group of creative talent operating in many different business arrangements, and delivered through multiple instrumentalities. Three distinct factors triggered this change.

Primary in this transition was the success of comic book properties in translation to film. While these translations had been around for almost a century and had occasionally been highly profitable (*Superman the Movie* in 1978 having been a high watermark), in the twenty-first century they exploded into prominence. In the second decade of the twenty-first century, films derived from comic books had generated in excess of $5 billion of domestic box office receipts (over 5 percent of the total based on boxofficemojo.com data) and had performed well internationally as well. While the causes of this culture shift are difficult to measure as precisely, the evolution of computer graphics permitting more "realistic" and affordable treatment of the dynamic visuals from comics' pages, the arrival of a generation of filmmaking talent who had grown up on the more mature comics material of the 1980s and 1990s, and an increased focus by movie studios on "event" movies (films that were expensive to produce and had an element of branding to drive correspondingly large audiences) all are factors. This directly inspired the acquisition of Marvel by Disney (seeking to enhance their stable of properties with appeal to young males) and the integration of DC into Warner Bros. (seeking greater control over the source material), and because the sale price of Marvel was so large and visible, it indirectly fueled a dramatic increase in investment in other comics companies.

Marvel and DC would continue to dominate the periodical comic book segment, but it was outstripped by growth in other segments in the twenty-first century. With increased focus on their film and television translations, neither company would be the creative engine it had been in its peak years (Marvel in the 1960s and 1970s, DC in the 1980s and 1990s), but would devote most of their line to exploiting their existing properties both in periodicals and as graphic novels.

Many smaller comic companies stepped in to capitalize on the gap in the periodical market, the perceived opportunity to monetize their properties in translation and to take advantage of a wealth of investment capital made available by parties seeking to emulate gains achieved by Marvel's owners. There are now more active comics periodical publishers than at any time since the 1950s. The longest-standing of the so-called independents is Dark Horse, founded in 1986 by Mike Richardson. Successful both in film (*The Mask*, *Hellboy*) and television (*Umbrella Academy*), Dark Horse attracted Chinese investors, and in 2021 was sold to Embracer, a Swedish video game company.

Surpassing Marvel and DC as the largest publisher of comics in America was Scholastic, long a powerful force in traditional children's books. Scholastic had moved into the nascent kids' graphic novel sector in 2005, establishing their Graphix imprint with the acquisition of mass-market rights to *Bone*, previously self-published by its creator Jeff Smith and his wife

Vijaya Ayer over the previous fifteen years. Developing the talent of Raina Telgemeier (*Smile)* and moving cartoonist Dav Pilkey from his previous success as a children's book creator (*Captain Underpants)* to producing graphic novels (*Dog Man*) gave Scholastic the best-selling franchises of the ensuing decades.

In the wake of Scholastic's success, all of the major traditional book publishers in America began to produce graphic novels for children, most setting up separate editorial units ("imprints") to produce them. Like Scholastic, these publishers followed their traditional practices where possible, relying on literary agents to screen and present projects to them (where the traditional periodical comics publishers had rarely encouraged agents), and acquiring only publishing rights, ignoring the opportunity to enter the film and television translation process and leaving those rights to the creators.

Added to its graphic novel production, America's largest book publisher, Penguin Random House, made a complex arrangement with major manga publisher Kodansha to repackage their titles for the American audience. **Manga**, or Japanese comics, has waxed and waned as a part of the graphic novel category in the twenty-first century, usually driven by a specific property or two (*Sailor Moon* initially, *Attack on Titan* most recently). The category is dominated by Viz, a joint venture of Shogakukan and Shueisha, the other two major manga houses. The combination of their own titles and Kodansha's has made Penguin Random House the second-largest graphic novel publisher in the United States.

Further adding to the complexity is a third category of comics publisher: those taking advantage of the digital space. Two large Korean web companies have moved into the American marketplace with fairly similar structures: both Webtoons and Tapas offer platforms that feature enormous lists of user-generated content ("UGC") and a smaller but still substantial collection of content that they finance. Their comics are structured in a vertical scroll, and are available to viewers for free with upcharges for early viewing or downloading. In their native market they have overwhelmed print **manhwa** (the Korean equivalent of manga), and it remains to be seen the size market share they establish in the United States.

Besides these players, Amazon has acquired Comixology, primarily a digital distributor of periodical comics material, and enabled them to begin a line of 'originals' of their own content. There are also literally countless individuals utilizing the open architecture of the web to publish their own webcomics. Some of these monetize their work by selling print-on-demand collections, simple merchandise, or soliciting donations (often via web services like Patreon). The newspaper syndicates of the twentieth century also moved to the web to distribute their comic strips more broadly as the number of papers declined, relying on advertising revenues and the promotional value for their merchandising activities to monetize the effort.

A final category complicating the picture is the existence of Kickstarter as a facilitator. While not a publisher per se, it provides a financing channel for comics projects of all descriptions. From the record-breaking raise of $1.6 million for Boom Studios' BRZKR, a comic collaboration between Keanu Reeves, Matt Kindt, and Ron Garney in 2020, to a horde of smaller projects year after year, Kickstarter provides an alternative method of marketing and funding comics that is as large as a significant publisher.

In 2021, Substack began awarding substantial financial grants (potentially six figures) to creators who will release their comics via Substack's email newsletter platform. In addition to the potential large payments (based on subscriptions), comics creators get access to group health insurance and retain the rights to everything they create. As of this writing, Substack has attracted major comics writers, including James Tynion IV, Nick Spencer, Saladin Ahmed, Chip Zdarsky, Kelly Thompson, Scott Snyder, Jeff Lemire, Brian K Vaughan, and Grant Morrison (Dave 2022).

Overall, comics have entered into an era in which the graphic novel is their most important form. With the expansive definition of graphic novel in the public's mind being the one defined by bookstore merchandising, lumping together reprints of periodical comics, original literary works, nonfiction, and international material like manga, it has become a more welcoming category than the more narrow-focused periodical comics. By the beginning of the twenty-first century, more readers were purchasing comics in graphic novel form than in periodicals, although the intense purchase patterns of the fans still generated disproportionate revenues. In this era, superheroes continue to be the dominant genre sold by traditional comics publishers, and among the most frequently told stories have been periodic reinterpretations of these familiar characters. Doing so has tapped into the mythic qualities of the genre, demonstrating the vitality of heroic mythology for generating stories. It has also meant that mainstream publishing has been fixated on the genre, leaving much of the most progressive and experimental storytelling to independent publishers who have attempted to push the boundaries of the medium well beyond the limitations of just one type of story.

While the industry's superhero mainstream continues to present more and more of the same material, a number of independent publishers have tackled a diversity of genres and even non-genre works. There are dozens of independent publishers, collectively sharing less than 30 percent of the American periodical comics market. Yet, arguably, their contributions do more to advance comics as an art form than anything put out by mainstream publishers throughout this era.

Take for example Image Comics, which got its start competing directly with DC and Marvel in the superhero genre, but in recent years has increasingly gravitated to other genres. In 1998 Image began to publish Eric Shanower's *Age of Bronze*, a retelling of the siege of ancient Troy based on historical sources. Image also achieved critical acclaim with Brian Michael Bendis and Michael Avon Oeming's *Powers* series (2000), which deftly revitalized detective fiction by setting it in the world of superheroes. Likewise, Robert Kirkman's *The Walking Dead* (2003) scored with audiences in telling the ongoing saga of survivors coping in a world of homicidal zombies. The translation of *The Walking Dead* to a popular cable television series then catapulted it to the top of best-seller lists. Despite a foundation firmly rooted in superheroics, Image has grown to be among the industry leaders in marketing other genres for the medium.

Other publishers have been less commercially successful than Image, but have produced works held in high esteem by critics. Fantagraphics has promoted the work of a number of reputable and influential cartoonists, including Chris Ware (*Acme Novelty Library*, 1993), Roberta Gregory (*Naughty Bits*, 1991), Peter Bagge (*Hate*, 1990), Daniel Clowes (*Eightball*, 1989), Carol Lay (*Good Girls*, 1987), and Los Bros Hernandez (*Love and Rockets*, 1982). Many of these cartoonists tell slice-of-life stories far removed from the fantasies offered by mainstream comic book publishers. Another publisher, Top Shelf, has offered everything from memoirs (Craig Thompson's *Blankets*, 2003) to pornography (Alan Moore and Melinda Gebbie's *Lost Girls*, 2006). From established independent publishers like Drawn & Quarterly to recent start-ups like Artists, Writers & Artisans (AWA), independent publishers have set a precedent for the diversity of stories to which the medium can be applied.

In fairness, one must acknowledge that many of the independent publishers have financed their more artistic endeavors by relying on the production of more marketable comic books based on popular licensed properties. Dark Horse has published scores of books based on George Lucas's *Star Wars* film series, Top Cow adapted the *Tomb Raider* video games, Fantagraphics has produced books reprinting Charles Schultz's *Peanuts* strips, and IDW has acquired the rights to the *Star Trek* franchise, a lucrative property that has been published by everyone from Gold Key in the sixties to Malibu in the nineties. At least in this regard, the independent publishers have been in sync with the two major publishers, reproducing familiar narratives in comic book form.

Figure 2.2 Where does your comics dollar go? Industry insiders estimate that 50 percent of the cover price goes to retailers, which they use to pay overhead expenses such as personnel and rent (and still hope to turn a profit). Another 10 percent of the price goes to the distributor, who delivers the comic books from the publisher to the retailer. The remaining 40 percent goes to the publisher, who must divide it among all the creative and administrative talent, as well as the publishing and advertising costs. Original art by Alexander Kostuk for *Thrilling Comics* © 1940 Better Publications, Inc. Graphic by Regina Gasser.

Yet the artistic impact of the independents still resonates, even among the major publishers. In order to attract talent interested in exploring mature themes and retaining ownership of their creative properties, both DC and Marvel have moved toward creating imprints to publish creator-owned content separate from their main lines. Marvel published *Epic Illustrated* from 1980 to 1986, and DC launched Vertigo in 1993 under the editorial guidance of Karen Berger, building on its edgier titles like *Swamp Thing* and *Sandman* before going on to release a number of successful creator-owned series, from Garth Ennis and Steve Dillon's *Preacher* (1995) to Brian K. Vaughan and Pia Guerra's *Y: The Last Man* (2002). After Berger's departure DC shuttered Vertigo in 2019.

Comics Consumption

A number of factors have contributed to the growing popularity of graphic novels. One is the support that graphic novels have been given by professional librarians. Ever since *Maus* won recognition from the Pulitzer committee in 1992, more and more libraries have been adding graphic novels and trade paperbacks to their collections, driven by patron demand that has made comics among the fastest-growing materials that the libraries circulate. This interest came to a flashpoint in 2002, when the American Library Association invited creators Jeff Smith (*Bone*), Neil Gaiman (*Sandman*), Art Spiegleman (*Maus*), and Colleen Doran (*A Distant Soil*) to speak at its annual convention. Since then, libraries have demonstrated even more enthusiasm for graphic storytelling.

Another factor is the surge in popularity of Japanese comics, or manga, in the American market. While the indigenous Japanese comic book industry had operated successfully for decades, it was only in the late eighties, with the translation of manga series like *Akira* (1988), that American audiences began to take note of the comics. Viz Communications began to reprint a range of manga titles for the English-speaking American audience in 1987, but the market for manga grew slowly. Yet by 1997, the market had grown and Viz was joined by competitor Tokyopop.

Technological Influences

As comics continue into the twenty-first century, the wider acceptance comes at a time when the medium's core audience finds itself distracted by more and more competing forms of media engagement. In order to understand the radical changes that are taking place in American comics, it's necessary to step back and look at the changes that are shaking the foundations of the overall publishing industry. The technological shifts of the past decade have significantly undermined the established patterns of book, magazine, and newspaper publishing and are changing how Americans consume all forms of media. While this requires a separate book or course to be fully considered, these macro changes are important background when considering how comics are developing.

First and foremost, technology has shifted to empower individuals with means of creating media that were historically only available to industrial users or individuals making significant investments. The computing power within a basic tablet or smartphone is sufficient to do tasks that were solely the province of publishing companies a generation ago. The work one can do with a basic word processing or desktop publishing program enables the creation of a publication that is a more than adequate substitute for the traditional book, magazine, or newspaper. Layers of cost that were incurred for typesetting, plates, printing, paper, and ink have been stripped away.

Second, to the extent that tasks of creation remain beyond the reach of a single individual, the interconnected nature of the world in the internet age makes it vastly simpler to assemble or finance an enterprise of creation. Writers and artists from across the world can be connected with a few keystrokes and enlisted in the task.

Third, this level of interconnection has made the distribution of content available to all, without the need for complex logistics of shipping or establishing sales networks to reach retailers in many different locations. A homemade video can go on YouTube or a novel that might have languished unread in a drawer can be published digitally.

Finally, these changes have led to an increasing **fractionalization** of all media. Rather than Americans sharing the common experience of a handful of broadcast channels, with popular programs frequently reaching a majority of households, television programming is increasingly delivered without even the use of a television set, and channels reach specific niche audiences. Even the most popular entertainment programs now reach 5 percent of the population.

All of these factors have combined to set the stage for an explosion of self-expression, and an era where a more diverse range of creative voices are speaking out in many media forms, though without the reach that was customarily provided in the more industrial tradition. In short, as Professor Melissa Rosati aptly summarizes, "Publishing is a process, not an industry" (personal communication, 2013). We are in a time where publishing is no longer a term describing a specific industry which is dominated by companies organized to maximize its benefits, but a process that is widely available but increasingly difficult to maximize.

Market Trends

With the disruptions caused by Covid-19 and shifts in distribution patterns data on the most recent years of comics sales are less reliable, but icV2.com (the most solid business site for the field) estimated total comic sales in 2020 at $1.2 billion, relatively level despite the lockdowns shuttering stores for several months. Approximately two-third of these sales were of graphic novel format comics, with most of the other third being periodicals. Available evidence indicates that the graphic novel formats continue to grow, both from increased title variety being available and audience growth, while periodicals remain relatively flat on a month-over-month basis for periods when their retail stores were able to open. Likely to be understated or ignored in the count is the monetization of web comics as well as sales through Kickstarter or other unconventional channels.

Like other media forms, comics experience piracy of their intellectual property on the web. There is no generally accepted tracking of the extent of piracy of comics, but diligent searching would enable a consumer to find virtually any issue they were interested in. Because of the lack of tracking, it is unclear how many potential sales are lost to piracy, but the perceived availability of pirated content contributes to the pressures on publishers for low pricing of digital downloads. Generally, digital formats are offered at the print price initially to protect sales of the physical edition, and then move downward over time to 99¢.

Part of the limitation of statistics for the field is a shifting dynamic of distribution. From 1995 to 2019, virtually all sales to comic shops went through Diamond Comic Distributors, but this has fractionalized. Several large publishers, including Marvel and DC, elected to open other distributors and either withdraw from Diamond or relegate their position to that of a wholesaler or sub-distributor. In addition, comic shops have elected with increasing frequency to purchase graphic novels directly from book publishers or traditional book distributors. This includes graphic novels published by the larger traditional periodical publishers, who have almost all allied with a book publisher for distribution services to bookstores. As a result of these changes, statistics that attempt to identify sales by channel of distribution are probably inaccurate and will remain so until the situation stabilizes and some central data system is established.

Regardless of the limitations on current data, it's clear that the graphic novel has become the dominant form of comics in America and continues to grow.

Periodical comics remain dominated by the superhero genre, or more broadly heroic adventure. A recent hit in the field is *Something Is Killing the Children,* which mixes the tropes of heroics with horror, following the character Erica Slaughter as she chases down and destroys monsters attacking children. Traditional franchises *Batman* and *X-Men* dominate their publishers' lists.

Graphic novels have shown the greatest growth in young children's titles (*Dog Man* titles represent 13 percent of all bookstore-reported sales of graphic novels in 2020), manga titles (up over 50 percent in 2020 led by *My Hero Academia*, and probably capable of more growth as publishers reported difficulty securing print times) and in what are termed middle-grade titles, a much less concentrated category but one benefiting from greatly expanded publishing activity. Titles in the superhero and adventure genres dominated by traditional periodical publishers have shown much less energy in the past years. The powerful advantage of graphic novels over periodicals is not just physical form, but availability: they are generally available where people who are already active readers (a fraction of the American population) are shopping, unlike periodicals which require an intentional shopping activity. It remains to be seen whether the ubiquitous availability of web comics will have the same cannibalization of print in America as it has had in Korea and Japan, where the digital distribution of native and formerly print material has captured the majority of the market.

Distribution, as mentioned earlier, is in flux. Diamond remains the most significant supplier to comic shops, but large retailers have formed their own distribution companies to compete with them, while book stores generally order directly from the various book publishers who also distribute smaller lines than their own (Penguin Random House, the largest, distributes DC, Dark Horse, and other graphic novel lines, as well as Marvel's periodical line while competitor Hachette distributes Marvel's graphic novels).

On a retail level, comic shops remain the principal outlet for periodical comics and a meaningful part of graphic novel sales, while bookstores (brick and mortar as well as Amazon and other web-based outlets) are the largest sellers of graphic novels. Digital distribution of comics content previously published in print remains a modest part of the mix (estimated at under 10 percent of sales), while sales of digital native content are basically unmeasured (icV2.com 2022; Hibbs 2021).

Express Yourself

While new technology has played a powerful role in diversifying comics, a fairly low-tech approach has also captured a cultural trend. People have been creating their own comics and "printing" them on office copiers at least since the early 1970s and the "new wave." The number of these **mini-comics** being created has grown in recent years, as have the comic conventions that are dominated by small presses and mini-comics creators selling their own wares. Events like APE (Amateur Press Expo) or MoCCA (Museum of Cartoons and Comic Art) Fest have yet to grow to the prodigious scale of Japan's Comiket gatherings (where over half a million people come to purchase homemade comics), but they are expanding every year, attracting both more creators and readers.

Mini-comics also represent a methodology for developing a project for future publication. Gene Luen Yang began publishing *American Born Chinese* by selling photo-copied chapters as individual mini-comics in local stores, before connecting with an agent for book-format publication and becoming a National Book Award finalist.

The boundaries of the mini-comics movement are very fluid, as formats represent both personal choices and the limits of inexpensive technology available to specific individuals. Any genre or form that can be imagined has been captured in these publications, few of which reach a wide audience or are archived in an organized form. Unlike the comics that are rigorously listed in *Overstreet's Comic Book Price Guide* or the *Grand Comic Book*

Database, most mini-comics are ephemera, at least so far. They represent a tide of self-expression, unmediated by editors at publishing companies or other influences.

One self-expressive phenomenon that captures both established cartoonists breaking from their major projects and aspiring talents trying to break through is "24 Hour Comics Day." In 1990, theorist Scott McCloud challenged fellow cartoonist Stephen Bissette to do a complete (24 pages) comic in 24 hours. Their private bet inspired others, and a designated 24 Hour Comics Day was organized originally by writer Nat Gertler and has now spread to other countries. Anthologies of some of the best results have been published, and it has even motivated the creation of a similar 24-hour plays project.

The range of potential ways to connect creative effort with an audience through traditional publishing, digital publishing, or do-it-yourself homemade efforts demonstrates the diversity of distribution. Where publishing was formerly an industry, with classic industrial barriers to entry, it is now predominantly a process that an individual can choose to participate in on a variety of paths. For comics, this has opened a medium to diversification of content and audiences, and that diversification is still in progress.

Comics Sales

In media studies, **exhibition** refers to the stage where we find those organizations that engage the consumer in the sale of media products. In times past, the primary exhibitors were newsstand vendors. Today, retailers running comics specialty shops, who sell both new and out-of-print comics, are vital to the industry as points of sale. However, the increasing popularity of more durably bound materials has led to increased shelf space and attention for comics among bookstores and online book vendors. We next explore these competing exhibitors in greater detail.

Specialty Shops

The direct market is the term used to describe comic book specialty shops. Thousands of these shops nationwide sell new comics materials and comics-related merchandise, such as action figures. Many also sell older, collectible comics, and many are involved in other areas of popular culture, including the fantasy role-playing game industry, sports cards, and so forth. Such shops can be found in strip malls, storefronts, and even people's converted basements. They tend to be owned by independent, small business proprietors, and most shops reflect the eclectic tastes of their owners. Comic specialty shop owners are lampooned most notably in popular culture by the character of Comic Book Guy on Fox's long-running television series *The Simpsons*, and the misconceptions that stereotype fosters may be all that many know about such retailers.

In order to draw more positive attention to their stores, owners began sponsoring Free Comic Book Day (FCBD) in 2002. In each of the FCBDs since, thousands of retailers have given away millions of specially printed comic books on one Saturday each May. While the giveaway is a promotion that garners the shops a lot of charitable publicity and increased foot traffic, the real challenge is for them to draw paying customers for the rest of the year. Essential for our consideration is how they do so through the sale of new comics and back issues.

NEW COMICS

Specialty stores sell newly published comics in three distinct formats: periodicals, bound reprint editions, and all-new graphic novels. One distinction among these formats lies in the type of cover binding used to assemble the products and the intended shelf life of the publications. **Periodicals** are what are thought of as traditional comic book magazines. Their covers are typically a glossy paper stock, and they are bound by a series of staples down their spine. Periodicals have an intentionally short shelf life, and most are only expected to be for sale until the next issue is available. New comics are on sale at cover price until the next issue is available, at which point they will likely be moved to the back issue bins. In comics this can be monthly, bi-monthly, quarterly, or even annually for some titles. Issues appear as numbered series and usually contain aspects of serialization, such as recurring characters and continuing plots and subplots from issue to issue. In addition, most periodicals are relatively short on page count, with standard comics today containing thirty-two pages of material (nearly a third of which is advertising). As of this writing, a thirty-two-page comic book sells for $3.99 and up. With some variations in size and printing quality over time, periodicals have always been the backbone of the American comic book industry.

The periodical products of the comics industry present both opportunities and challenges for retailers. On the one hand, the serialized stories in most comic books draw consumers back to the shops month after month. On the other hand, new readers may be discouraged from purchasing an issue in the middle of a series or spending the cumulative money it will take to collect an entire story run in serialized format. The attraction of **bound reprint editions**, then, is in addressing these problems. Bound reprint editions tend to feature stand-alone, finite storylines and may be referred to as graphic novels, although their material is not "novel," as it has already been published. Often these stand-alone stories are a collection of a number of issues that have previously been serialized in periodical publication, much like the way a season's worth of television episodes might be bundled in a DVD collection. Thus, they are substantially larger than a periodical, running from around one hundred pages up to thousands of pages, and their cost might start around $9.99 and run well beyond $75 for a high-quality hardcover edition. Though these prices are considerably higher than the cost of the latest periodical, it is almost always less expensive for the consumer to purchase a collection than a series from the retailer, especially if the original periodicals are long out of print.

The third type of publication is the original **graphic novel** featuring all-new content. Much like other bound editions, such publications typically stand as complete works, but unlike them they tend to debut previously unseen content.

In contrast to a periodical, both bound reprint editions and graphic novels use more durable materials for their binding (at the very least a glossy, cardstock cover) and are intended to have an indeterminate shelf life, so that they may be "on sale" for years to come. In the publishing industry, booksellers classify a book by its binding. Both may be found in a format known as the **trade paperback (TPB)**, characterized by a less rigid, less durable cover (usually cardstock), or **hardcover**, characterized by, well, you guessed it—a firmer, more durable cover. At present, TPBs are the preferred method for reprinting material that has previously been serialized in comic magazines. Both of the leading comics publishers in America, Marvel and DC, regularly collect and republish runs of their monthly titles in TPB form. For instance, Marvel will republish a storyline running across multiple issues of *Amazing*

Spider-Man a few months later in a TPB. With increasing frequency, some publishers are reprinting material in the more expensive hardcover format, too.

Publishing more material in these formats has been an important innovation in the last decades of the twentieth century for the industry, as the more durable, lengthy formats have made comics appearing in this packaging more attractive to bookstores and libraries. These important repositories have made room on their shelves for TPB and hardcover comics.

BACK ISSUES

In addition to the sale of newly published comics, specialty shops will often stock back issues of previously published periodicals. The back issue market can be a lucrative one, as rare and in-demand comic books can draw collectors' dollars well in excess of the prices printed on the covers. Some comics that sold for 10 cents on the newsstands in the 1940s now garner hundreds of thousands of dollars. However, such values are rare and largely dependent on two factors: scarcity and condition. **Scarcity** refers to the availability of a given back issue. Although original runs of some comic books from the 1940s ranked in the millions of copies printed, only a comparative few were preserved. Magazines then, as now, were often trashed or recycled. Because there are fewer copies of such comic books available today, the price demanded for these copies on the market is driven up. For example, in January 1960 DC reportedly circulated over 800,000 copies of its *Superman* (#134) comic book magazine, retailing for 10 cents a copy; a perfect copy of that issue would grow in value to $155 some forty-five years later (Miller et al. 2005: 1318). Conversely, today's fans are much more diligent about retaining and preserving perfect copies, making those comics less valuable. For instance, Marvel Comics released nearly 8 million copies of *X-Men* #1 in October 1991, for $1.50 each. Today, in a market saturated by copies of that comic book, collectors can only expect about $3 on a well-preserved copy.

Of course, comic books are made of materials that deteriorate over time, and so the comparative condition of a comic book also factors into its value. The highest values are assigned to comic books that have the least damage. Borrowing from the terminology of coin collectors, an ideal copy of a given comic book would be in **mint condition**. Coins are made at a mint, which is why a single coin that is in as good condition as the day it was made is said to be in *mint condition*. Comics are not "minted," of course, but the analogy to "as good as it gets" provides a starting point for an elaborate system of grading the condition of comics. Collectors' publications from the *Official Overstreet Comic Book Price Guide* to *The Comics Buyer's Guide* to Comicbookrealm.com report on the values of different grades of popular comics (Figure 2.3).

While grading is a highly subjective process, often resulting in much dickering between seller and buyer, the back issue market embraced a system of third-party grading beginning in 2000 with the establishment of the Comics Guaranty, LLC, or CGC. For a fee, the trained CGC staff grade comics according to a set of objective standards and then apply a numerical value to the condition of the comic ranging from 1.0 to 10.0, where 10.0 is mint condition. The book and an identifying label are then sealed within two sheets of transparent plastic, or **slabbed**, to ensure that the condition is preserved after it has left the evaluator's hands. This system was first practiced by CGC's parent company with collectors of coins and sports cards. However, while both coins and cards can be enjoyed by looking at them through a plastic sheet, comics are meant to be read, and in order to see the interior pages

Do-It-Yourself Grading

While **CGC** keeps its grading standards private, these are the **traditional** condition definitions...

Mint

Abbreviated: **M**
Price is 150% of **NM**

This is a perfect comic book.

The term for this grade is the same one used for **CGC's 10.0 grade.**

Its cover has full luster, with edges sharp and pages like new. There are no signs of wear or aging. It is not imperfectly printed or off-center.

Occasionally referred to as "Gem Mint," a term used by sportscard dealers.

Near Mint

Abbreviated: **NM**
Price is 100% of **NM**

This is a nearly perfect comic book.

The term for this grade is the same one used for **CGC's 9.4 grade.**

Its cover shows barely perceptible signs of wear.

Its spine is tight, and its cover has only minor loss of luster and only minor printing defects. Some discoloration is acceptable in older comics — as are signs of aging.

Very Fine

Abbreviated: **VF**
Price is 66.6% of **NM**

A **Very Fine** copy has beginning signs of wear.

The term for this grade is the same one used for **CGC's 8.0 grade.**

There can be slight creases and wrinkles at the staples, but it is a flat, clean issue with definite signs of being read a few times.

There is some loss of the original gloss, but it is in general an attractive comic book.

Fine

Abbreviated: **F, Fn**
Price is 33.3% of **NM**

A **Fine** comic book is a good-looking copy ... at first glance.

The term for this grade is the same one used for **CGC's 6.0 grade.**

This comic book's cover is worn but flat and clean with no defacement. There is usually no writing on the cover or tape repair.

Stress lines around the staples and more rounded corners are permitted.

Very Good

Abbreviated: **VG**
Price is 20% of **NM**

A **Very Good** comic book is well-read and has some problems.

The term for this grade is the same one used for **CGC's 4.0 grade.**

Most of the original gloss is gone. There are minor markings, discoloration, and/or heavier stress lines around the staples and spine.

The cover may have minor tears and/or corner creases, and spine-rolling is generally permissible.

Good

Abbreviated: **G, Gd**
Price is 12.5% of **NM**

A **Good** copy is a very worn comic book with nothing missing.

The term for this grade is the same one used for **CGC's 2.0 grade.**

Creases, minor tears, rolled spine, and cover flaking are generally permissible in this grade.

Older Golden Age comic books often come in this condition.

Fair

Abbreviated: **FA, Fr.**
Price is 8% of **NM**

A **Fair** copy has multiple problems but is structurally intact.

The term for this grade is the same one used for **CGC's 1.0 grade.**

Copies may have a soiled, slightly damaged cover, a badly rolled spine, cover flaking, corners gone, and tears.

Tape may be present and is always considered a defect.

Poor

Abbreviated: **P, Pr**
Price is 2% of **NM**

A **Poor** copy is damaged and generally unsuitable for collecting.

The term for this grade is the same one used for **CGC's 0.5 grade.**

While the copy may still contain some readable stories, major defects get in the way.

Copies may be in the process of disintegrating and may do so with even light handling.

Figure 2.3 The *Comics Buyer's Guide* provides its readers with an explanation of grading comics in its "Do-It-Yourself Grading" guide. Courtesy of Krause/F+W Media.

of a slabbed comic, one must break the seal of the CGC package and thus invalidate its grading. Still, collectors have not seemed to mind this irony and have reportedly embraced the corporation, with prices of slabbed back issues routinely outselling unslabbed ones in online markets.

Production Processes: Industrial and Artisan

One of the diversifications affecting comics relates to the process. There is now a broader continuum of ways to produce comics than previously was common: According to Mark Rogers (1997), the **industrial process** refers to those places where comics are created as a collaborative product, with the task of developing comics divided among writer, artist, inker, letterer, and colorist, and supervised by an editor. In some less flattering characterizations, this process is labeled an *assembly line*, in which a product is put together in the service of commercial rather than creative priorities. Of course, some of the earliest comics were drafted in this fashion. From the early Eisner-Iger Shop (see Chapter 10) to today's Marvel Bullpen, the production formula of the industrial process still makes most of the profitable comics for sale.

The people who work in the comic book field in America are, generally, either staffers or freelancers. And, of course, some individuals move back and forth between these categories during their careers. A **staffer** is an employee of the publisher with a set salary, regular paychecks, and fringe benefits. Editors, assistant editors, art directors, and production managers comprise the core of the creative staff at most publishers. There are also staff artists who work in postproduction doing minor art corrections, pasting logos and indicia, and whatever else the art director or production manager deems necessary to create a polished product.

Most of the writers and artists who create comic books are **freelancers**, independent contractors who work on assignments for a specified page rate. Most freelancers still do **work-for-hire**. That is, they contract to do work for a specific project with the understanding that the publisher will own the work they produce. Although the publisher may exercise control over this material, most creators have also contracted some form of royalty agreement, which offers them additional compensation based on successful sales performance or reprint editions of their works.

Some writers or artists worked for the same publisher for decades. To fans they might be perceived as a "DC writer" or a "Marvel artist," but, in most cases, they were simply freelancers, working from assignment to assignment. Even when a writer or artist is "assigned" to a monthly title and has some expectation of working on that book long term, the assignment can be changed at the whim of the editor or his supervisors. The only security these creators have is their ability to produce work that the publishers value. And work is not always valued solely for its quality. For editors who have to get books to the printer on schedule each month, speed and reliability can be just as important as talent.

Part of the success that both Marvel and DC have enjoyed has been in their copyright and corporate ownership of the properties they have in their respective catalogs. Most work done in mainstream comics is on a work-for-hire or freelance basis, meaning that the creators are commissioned to design characters and stories for the publishing corporation.

As part of this arrangement, the corporation—not the cartoonist—copyrights the characters featured and the stories told in their publications. On one hand, such an arrangement raises ethical questions about creators' rights. On the other hand, it has ensured the corporations' long-term financial rewards, as the corporate owners can print and reprint successful stories time and again. Even more lucrative is the licensing of comic book characters to other vendors for the marketing of consumer products. Characters like Superman and Spider-Man bring in far more money via their licenses than they make from the sales of their comics.

On the other hand, the **artisan process** describes those comics created by the individual cartoonist who typically does most of the creative work of producing the finished story. Artisan comics often come from smaller, so-called independent publishers. Unlike the industrial process, which often emphasizes the sale of the character featured in a comic rather than the creators behind it, independent publishers are less likely to prioritize regular monthly titles. Unencumbered by the strict production schedules that such periodicals demand, artisan cartoonists can craft a small series of comic books or an entire graphic novel that they can exert full creative control over, rather than relying on an editor to assign portions of the production to other specialists. As Rogers notes, "artisan production has tended to produce comics more varied in scope and more interesting aesthetically. Industrialized production is limiting in and of itself" (1997: 88–9). Just what limits industrialized production imposes on creativity is often a function of the constraints put upon it by owners who tend to be more focused on profitability than creativity.

More recently, as stand-alone graphic novels from artisans have grown in consumer demand and critical respectability, several corporate book publishing houses have become publishers for artisan comics. However, artisan creators are not necessarily beholden to larger publishing houses to get their creations into the hands of readers, as both self-publishing and online publishing outlets present viable alternatives. However, such initiatives may not allow the creator the same reach or level of exposure that traditional publishing houses, well-versed in the techniques of marketing can grant to a work.

Traditional book publishers tend to prefer working with the artisanal process or to rely on creative teams which come preassembled (by collaboration with or without the assistance of an agent). This more closely resembles the process they are familiar with from prose.

The **webcomics** process is a work in progress, but while many webcomics are created using versions of the industrial or artisanal process, the new platforms for webcomics (Webtoons, Tapas) offer tools and systems to assist their creators in producing work that better fits their vertical scroll technology and the tastes of their readers.

An ecosystem has begun to develop to support independent creative work, and parts of it have been utilized by larger entities as marketing tools. Kickstarter is the largest and most obvious of these, as a platform offering crowdfunding for comics projects along with other categories of projects. As originally launched, Kickstarter assumed that the comics creator would also be responsible for arranging printing, shipping, and marketing of their comics, but there are now companies or consultants who offer their services to fill in these gaps and allow the creator to focus entirely on the process of creation. There is also a community of participants on Kickstarter, many of whom are not specifically comics fans or readers, but simply people who like supporting creative efforts. The existence and abundant funding of this ecosystem provides support for many more self-published or small press projects than were possible a decade ago.

Another pathway for supporting creativity is utilizing applications like Patreon, which allow talented people to solicit and collect regular donations from individuals who wish to support their work, like medieval patrons. Many creators offer opportunities to see special work or work in progress as benefits for those contributing via Patreon.

Discovering: Comics Auteurs

Will Eisner believed that because words and pictures should combine as a seamless whole, "the ideal writing process occurs where the writer and artist are the same person" (1996: 111). It is certainly widely held that much of the outstanding work in the comics medium has been produced by a single and personal artistic vision, whether that of a cartoonist or a writer. This same tendency has been recognized in film. The creation of a feature film requires the collaboration of hundreds (sometimes thousands) of individuals. During the 1950s, French film critics like François Truffaut developed the **auteur** theory to explain how out of this very collaborative art a single artistic vision could sometimes emerge. These film critics believed that some directors—though certainly not all—were the artistic driving force, or "author," of the film. The auteur theory identifies certain characteristics of auteurs.

One quality that is often studied about an auteur is one's technical *competence* in using the art form. In the comics medium this means that one must demonstrate an understanding of how to use encapsulation, layout, and composition to effectively tell a story. Frank Miller, creator of *Sin City* and *300*, is known for his ability to depict moments of powerful action using stark contrasts of shadow and light.

A second characteristic that distinguishes the works of the auteur is the recurrence of certain *themes* across works. For decades cartoonist Jim Starlin has been weaving epic tales of cosmic forces, from his early work on Marvel's *Warlock* to his creator-owned *Dreadstar*, to more recent work on DC's *Death of the New Gods*.

A third mark of distinction is the auteur's *stylistic traits*. This may be manifest in a particular writing style, drawing particular layouts, etc. One of Will Eisner's signature effects in *The Spirit* was to make the series title a part of the splash page art so that a city skyline or old newspapers blowing in the wind spelled out "The Spirit" (Figure 2.4).

The fourth consideration is *collaboration*, as auteurs tend to work with the same co-creators time and again. Jeph Loeb and Tim Sale have repeatedly teamed up to produce special projects for DC (*Batman: The Long Halloween*) and Marvel (*Daredevil: Yellow*).

Finally, auteurs often *borrow* ideas and styles from other outstanding creators, evidencing outside influences but reworking them to make them their own. This borrowing may manifest itself in the mimicking of well-known images, phrases, or approaches from other works in the medium, perhaps even their own previous work. For instance, Erik Larsen draws his *Savage Dragon* in a bombastic style reminiscent of the artwork of Jack Kirby.

Figure 2.4 Will Eisner's unique style of varying the logo of his *Spirit* strip is one of the inventive touches that distinguishes him as an auteur of the art form. The Spirit is a Registered Trademark of Will Eisner Studios, Inc. Reprinted with permission. All rights reserved.

Identifying exactly who might be among the auteurs of comics began with the bibliographic work of Jerry Bails and Hames Ware in their multivolume *The Who's Who of American Comic Books*, published in the 1970s. This project took the first crucial step in acknowledging the works of comics creators by giving names and bibliographies to the often uncredited creators of the Golden Age. Since that time, a steady stream of biographies produced by devoted fans has expanded our understanding of the creators and their contributions to the art form. Academics are taking their first steps toward developing a comics **canon**, or definitive collection of auteurs, with cartoonists like Walt Kelly and writers like Alan Moore profiled in book series like the University Press of Mississippi's "Great Comics Artists Series." Creators such as these have mastered the essentials of effective storytelling and managed the limitations of the form.

Comics Fans and Readers

Comic book fans constitute a fascinating and understudied culture. They exert influence over the industry and those who make comic books through their engagement with the industry. In this section we will explore the culture of the comic book fan to better appreciate that influence. We will begin by defining some common terms used to label fans and exploring the roots of the organized fan movement, from its origins in science fiction fandom through to its expression in "Marvel Mania" and beyond. We will examine some of the activities that are manifestations of fan culture, including comic book conventions. But first, we define just what a fan is.

Defining Fans and Fandom

Fans do more than just read and collect comic books. They are more than just casual readers and consumers. Our definition of a **fan** is someone who wants to take part in the dialogue about the medium. Truthfully, many fans want to work in the comic book industry, but for those who don't make it, thinking, talking, and writing about comics is the next best thing. This dialogue takes place in comic book letter columns, in fanzines, on the internet, at comic book conventions, and even at some academic conferences. The content could be anything from an adolescent debate about whether the Hulk could beat up Superman, to a discussion of the psychosexual dynamics in Chris Ware's *Acme Novelty Library*, to a pure and simple appreciation of good storytelling and well-rendered artwork.

Scholar Jeffrey Brown (2001) reports that industry insiders estimate that only 10 to 20 percent of their audience is made up of hardcore fans, with the remaining sales coming from casual readers. And yet, what they lack in numbers, fans more than make up for in fervor. Fans make considerable investments in terms of their finances, time, and emotional involvement because of their love for the medium, its characters, and their creators. So much so, in fact, that to people outside of fandom, their behavior may seem strange. The term "fan" is, in fact, an abbreviated form of *fanatic*, and for many people fandom carries with it the same connotation of mania. Unsurprisingly, then, fans have been characterized in much of the popular press as oddly fixated and thus deservedly marginalized individuals. Media critic Joli Jensen (1992) observes that reports characterizing fans as being obsessed or frenzied in their actions contributes to a social construction of them that separates them from societal norms. Yet the devotion displayed by fans actually is little different than that put forth by other experts in society, such as a literature professor who knows every detail of the works of British poet John Milton, for example. The difference is that society values some cultural products (e.g., Milton), yet does not value the focus of the fans' attention, such as comic books (Figure 2.5).

Figure 2.5 Comic Book Guy has come to embody every unflattering stereotype of the fanboy. Words by Evan Dorkin and art by James Lloyd and Andrew Pepoy. Reprinted from Simpsons Comics Presents Bart Simpson #31. © 2006 Bongo Entertainment, Inc. The Simpsons TM & © 20th Television. All rights reserved.

In recent years, the term **fanboy** has been applied to comic book fans. Initially it was used as a term of derision, meant to demean a person who was "anal retentive, adolescent and emotionally arrested" (Sabin 1993: 68). The most widely recognized manifestation of this insult in popular culture is Comic Book Guy, an overweight, rude know-it-all who runs the comics specialty shop on the television program *The Simpsons*. According to researcher Matthew Pustz (1999), the term "fanboy" first appeared in reference to comics fans on the 1982 cover of *The Official Underground and Newave Comix Price Guide* by cartoonist Bill Griffith, but its use has grown to be contested in recent years. In the fashion of many epithets, the use of *fanboy* has since been co-opted by the fans themselves and is sometimes used as self-deprecating humor. To identify oneself as a fanboy or a fangirl, rather than being labeled as one by others, may be to express one's status as someone who is deeply immersed in comics culture.

Popular conversation has begun to include the term **fandom** as a verb, as in "I'll fandom that." But rather than suggesting the more active role that fan previously meant, it seems to carry the meaning simply of having a deep affection for a property.

Another category of fan group of collectors are **speculators**, people who purchase comics as investments in the hopes that they will increase in value over time. Speculators ran rampant in the early 1990s, when high-profile events like the "Death of Superman" storyline were bringing more people into comics shops, first or anniversary issues were being published with multiple variants (foil, hologram, etc.) covers, and the magazine *Wizard* was assigning ridiculously high values to recent "hot" comic books. Although fans may tout the value of their collections as one defense for their retaining them, most of them collect for the joy that they derive from the medium. To purchase comics as a profit-seeking venture—and to never even read the stories—runs counter to the fans' devotion to the narrative form. And while it is true that many comics have appreciated in value over the years, with copies of *Action Comics* #1 valued at hundreds of thousands of dollars (and one selling for US$3.25 million in 2021), the market is essentially driven by scarcity: The more common a comic book, the less likely it will increase in value. Many speculators who rushed in to buy multiple copies of number one issues in the 1990s have been left with handfuls of comics that have increased very little in value since their publication. Unlike the comic books from the Golden Age, which are now worth tens if not hundreds of thousands of dollars, a lot of these more recent magazines have been carefully protected and stored, leaving them plentiful, not scarce, and leaving speculators rather confounded.

More recently, speculation has intensified in what are termed **key issues**, issues that are more recent first appearances of characters particularly those that are identified as sources of future media translations. These rise rapidly in price, coinciding with the first appearance of a character in a movie or streaming service, and the effect of that is instantly measurable on web platforms like eBay.

As we have thus far discussed, a fan is more than just a strident consumer of comic books. If a fan chooses to engage in the dialogue about comic books, that is almost assuredly being done in concert with others. This interaction initiates one into a community called **fandom**. By no means is fandom a highly centralized community, rather it is a good example of an "imagined" or **virtual community** where people are joined by bonds of mutual interest rather than geographic proximity to one another. Still, there are times when members of the community do convene, most visibly in the event of comic book conventions.

How did this movement begin? How did so many diverse and disparate individuals come to form a virtual community, even before the advent of the internet? At one level, it began spontaneously and chaotically, with thousands of readers across the globe who developed a devotion to the medium. Yet only a handful of these fans took the initiative to reach out and begin the dialogue. We will turn our attention next to those early efforts to reach out to one another and establish connections among those fans.

Fandom Comes of Age

The reality is that most comic book readers never become comic book fans. In the 1940s and 1950s the average comic book reader kicked the habit by mid-teens. Even though the average age at which readers give up comic books has been steadily increasing, there still comes a point at which most comic book readers go cold turkey because comics are considered "uncool" or "childish" within their peer group. But the fans keep reading anyway. Perhaps it was more than just a pun when avid readers of the Entertaining Comics (EC) line of comics in the 1950s called themselves "fan-addicts."

THE EC FAN-ADDICTS

During the 1950s, while Julie Schwartz was overseeing the creation of some exciting space opera titles such as *Mystery in Space* and *Strange Adventures*, comic book readers with a science fiction bent were getting more excited about what was going on over at EC. In 1950, EC began its infamous horror and fantasy line, which included titles like *Weird Fantasy*, *Weird Science*, *The Haunt of Fear*, *Vault of Horror*, and *Tales from the Crypt*. These comics were well-written, exquisitely drawn, and often extremely gory. By 1953, a handful of the older EC "fan-addicts" were producing mimeo-graphed fanzines. By 1955, it was all over. A Senate subcommittee investigated the supposed corrupting influence of comic books, and a besieged industry reacted with a self-regulatory Comics Code that prohibited not only the content but even some of the titles of the innovative EC line (e.g., the word "terror" was forbidden in a title). What might have been the first great movement of comics fandom never got the chance to grow beyond sporadic and isolated outbursts of enthusiasm.

THE SILVER AGE OF COMICS/THE GOLDEN AGE OF FANDOM

Even as the last embers of EC fandom were dying out, another group of fans, who were more excited about superheroes than science fiction or horror, just needed a spark to ignite their movement. It was, of course, Julie Schwartz who provided that spark. *Showcase* #4 (1956), edited by Schwartz, introduced a new version of one of the heroes he had overseen during the Golden Age of comics: Flash. This issue kicked off the great superhero revival and marked the beginning of what became known among fans as the Silver Age of comic books.

The appearance of Flash also galvanized older readers who fondly remembered the original superheroes of the 1940s. What these fans remembered most fondly was *All-Star Comics*, the title that brought the DC heroes together in the Justice Society of America (JSA), the first superhero team. A mathematics graduate student by the name of Jerry Bails began writing to Schwartz, lobbying for the return of the Justice Society. Another fan, Larry Ivie, pitched an idea for a JSA-style team called Justice Legion of the World. Before Schwartz answered these dreams, he whetted appetites a bit more with the introduction of a new Green Lantern in 1959.

But 1960 was the year that comic book fandom really gained momentum. Early that year *The Brave and the Bold* #28 brought the "mightiest heroes of our time . . . together as the Justice League of America" (Jones and Jacobs 1997: 35). Few comic books have been so anticipated, and perhaps no other single comic book did more to create the excitement that fueled the fan movement. In September, Dick and Pat Lupoff published *Xero*, a science fiction fanzine with the first of a series of articles, "All in Color for a Dime," devoted to Golden Age comic books. Also that year, a college student named Roy Thomas wrote to DC asking how he could complete his *All-Star Comics* collection. Gardner Fox, who was scripting the adventures of the new Justice League, told Thomas how to get in touch with Bails. The fans were beginning to find each other.

A similar, though less immediate experience has characterized the comic book letter column. Since the 1950s publishers have printed letters that they have received from readers. Writing a letter to the editor offers fans a way to express their thorough reading of the material. It has also enabled them to connect with others in their imagined community by either producing an ongoing dialogue among them (albeit one printed quite slowly over a period of months) or facilitating a means for them to make one another's acquaintance and pursue a relationship beyond the printed page. (Future *ElfQuest* creators Richard and Wendi Pini famously "met" through an exchange in a letter column and later married.) Though these letter columns offered the fan community an opportunity for interaction in the era before the internet, they had to be viewed with a measure of awareness that they served the publisher's agenda as much as the fans. They were, after all, controlled by the gate-keeping decisions of the editor, who could only run a handful of the volume of letters received each month and probably screened out the most extreme comments. Today, many of the functions of the traditional letter columns have been superseded by the internet, with discussion boards provided by publishers and independent fan-created sites providing fans with even quicker, more voluminous, and unedited commentary. Still, they serve the same social function as the letter column, offering fans an opportunity to express themselves and connect with their peers.

More connections emerged in 1961. Bails, for instance, began contacting his fellow letter writers about Thomas and his ideas for forming an Academy of Comic Art Fans and Collectors. Then Bails and Thomas published *Alter-Ego*, the first comic book fanzine devoted to superheroes. *Comic Art*, the fanzine Don and Maggie Thompson had been working on for nearly a year, came out the following month. Toward the end of the year, two additional Bails-edited fanzines appeared: *The Comicollector* and *On the Drawing Board*, the official newsletter of his newly formed Academy of Comic Art Fans and Collectors. And in December 1961, G. B. Love published *The Rocket's Blast*. The fandom dialogue had begun in earnest.

MARVEL MANIA

Schwartz's decision to revive the superhero genre excited not only fans but competitors as well. The success of the Justice League of America prompted imitation. Martin Goodman's variously named (Timely, Atlas, Marvel) comic book company that had been jumping on bandwagons and following trends since 1939. According to one apocryphal account, after learning about the success of comics featuring the Justice League, Goodman directed Stan Lee (who was his editor-in-chief, his chief writer, and his wife's cousin) to create a superhero team. Lee turned to two trusted and extremely talented collaborators: With Jack Kirby he created the *Fantastic Four*, which became the beginning of the Marvel line; and with Steve Ditko, *Spider-Man*, the most successful of Marvel's characters.

Figure 2.6 Even Marvel comic books parody Stan Lee as a carnival barker. This image from *Generation X* #17 (1996) pokes good-natured fun at the iconic creator with words by Scott Lobdell and Stan Lee and art by Chris Bachalo and Mark Buckingham. © 2023 Marvel Entertainment, Inc. and its subsidiaries.

Stan Lee realized that an involved readership meant a steady market for his product, and he orchestrated a Marvel Mania that rivaled any comics fandom movement before or since. Contemporary caricatures of Lee often depict him as a carnival barker, and, in many ways, this is an apt metaphor. Lee himself has admitted, "as much as I may have contributed to Marvel's success with any stories, editing, creating characters, I think equally as valuable was the advertising, promotion, publicity, and huckstering that I did" (qtd. in Thomas 1998: 11) (Figure 2.6).

The characters and the stories themselves were enough to get fans excited. In contrast to what Lee characterized as the perfect but dull characters of the *D*istinguished *C*ompetition (DC Comics), Marvel heroes had insecurities, they lost their tempers, and when they were not fighting supervillains, they had to deal with all the frustrations of daily living. Fans were also fascinated by the guest appearances, cross-references, and continuing subplots that wove the increasingly complex narrative tapestry. Every issue of a Marvel comic book became a chapter in an ongoing, integrated saga of a fictional realm that became known as the Marvel Universe. Lee, Kirby, and Ditko seemed to be raising the bar for visually dynamic storytelling with each new issue. Yet Lee was not content to let the work speak for itself.

Lee himself spoke directly to the reader in cover blurbs and captions. Because Lee was writing and editing virtually all of the books in those early days, Marvel publications had a consistent tone. The most in-your-face aspect was the tongue-in-cheek hyperbole that permeated the covers, the ads, and even the credits. But the tone was also very direct and personal. Readers felt that they got to know Lee and, through him, the other members of the creative team, which he referred to as the Marvel Bullpen. However, Lee always remained the star of the show. He became the comic book medium's first, and most enduring, celebrity.

Even so, it took Lee a couple of years to find his voice. The development of the Stan Lee/Marvel persona (they became one and the same) can be charted in these early Marvel publications:

Direct and Personal	
March 1962	In *Fantastic Four* #3 Lee institutes a letter column called "The Fantastic 4 Fan Page." Later that year Lee writes, "Look—enough with that 'Dear Editor' jazz," and asks fans to use the salutation "Dear Stan and Jack."
August 1962	In *Amazing Fantasy* #15 Lee breaks the barrier between writer and reader when he writes, "Like costumed heroes? Confidentially, we in the comic mag business refer to them as 'long underwear characters'! And, as you know, they're a dime a dozen! But, we think you may find our Spider-Man just a bit . . . different!"
December 1962	Beginning in *Fantastic Four* #9, Lee expands the credits to include inker and letterer (colorists were not yet credited), growing the notion of the Marvel Bullpen.
January 1963	In *Fantastic Four* #10 Lee and Kirby actually appear in the story and interact with their creations.
February 1963	The splash page to *Fantastic Four* #11 reads, "Special Bonus to our readers! Presenting: The type of story most requested by your letters and post cards . . . A Visit With the Fantastic Four."
March 1964	Nicknames begin to be used in the credits in *Amazing Spider-Man* #10: smiling Stan Lee, Swinging Steve Ditko, and Sparkling Sam Rosen.

By 1963 it did indeed seem that the Marvel Age of Comics had arrived. In that year's Alley Awards—given by the Academy of Comic-Book Arts and Sciences and named for the comic strip character Alley Oop—Marvel won ten of the fifteen professional categories. Lee won in the Best Writer and Best Editor categories, and *Amazing Spider-Man* won for Best Comic Book. Encouraged by the initial fan response, Lee turned up the hype. By 1965 the covers of Marvel Comics bore the label "Marvel Pop Art Productions," and even the credits were mock-dramatic:

> Let Marveldom cheer! Let humanity shout! Stan (the Man) Lee and Jack (King) Kirby have bestowed another masterpiece upon mankind. Exotically embellished by Joe Sinnott. Laconically lettered by Artie Simek. (*Fantastic Four* #73, 1968)

Comics scholar Robert C. Harvey notes that "Lee's was no small accomplishment: his extravagant verbal gyrations gave the books a tongue-in-cheek tone, and this attracted a new readership. Kirby created the visual excitement—the characters and the adventures; Lee created the marching minions of Marvel fandom" (1996: 47).

No comic book company had ever done more to connect with its fans, but Stan Lee continued to seek new channels of communication. In January 1965 Lee instituted the Merry Marvel Marching Society (MMMS)—"an honest-to-gosh far-out fan club in the mixed-up Marvel manner" (Daniels 1991: 106). Historian Les Daniels claims that "Lee never presented the MMMS as anything more than a lot of foolishness, but apparently this very quality made it a big success" (1991: 106). The office was soon flooded with membership applications (Figure 2.7).

Figure 2.7 This image from a Merry Marvel Marching Society advertisement evokes the intertextuality of a 1940s Uncle Sam recruiting poster to solicit club membership in 1965. © 2023 Marvel Entertainment, Inc. and its subsidiaries.

Around the same time, Lee instituted a "Bullpen Bulletins" page in the comic books that provided teasers for forthcoming Marvel comic books and chatty behind-the-scenes news about the writers and artists. The Bulletins page eventually included a little yellow box entitled "Stan's Soapbox." This monthly column is where he most fully developed the Stan Lee persona and most directly connected with his fans: "I tried to write as if the readers were friends of mine and I was talking specifically to them" (qtd. in Daniels 1991: 107). The column was a true soapbox, where Lee often preached his brand of optimism and tolerance, but without ever seeming preachy. Somehow Lee managed to get away with using hip phrases that would have seemed downright silly coming from any other Jewish guy in his mid-forties. His columns were peppered with admonitions for his "True Believers" to "Face Front!" and "Hang Loose!" His pronouncements on the social issues of the day were concluded with "Nuff Said," and he signed off each column with a resounding "Excelsior!"

The printed word was not Lee's only means of communicating with the "minions of Marveldom." His growing celebrity led to personal appearances on the college lecture circuit, television shows, and, of course, comic book conventions.

Comic Book Conventions

Spurred on by the efforts of Schwartz and Lee, comic book fans yearned for a more fully realized fandom, such as many of them had experienced in science fiction fandom, which had been holding conventions since 1939. Because there was a good deal of overlap between science fiction and comic book readers, many members of the comics fan movement were familiar with the convention experience. In fact, science fiction conventions provided a venue for comic book fans to meet and express their enthusiasm. Dick and Pat Lupoff, who included a column about comic books in their science fiction fanzine *Xero*, wore Captain Marvel and Mary Marvel costumes for the masquerade at the 1960 World Science Fiction Convention in Pittsburgh. At the banquet of the same convention, Don Thompson and Maggie Curtis, without being aware of what the Lupoffs were doing with *Xero*, decided to do a fanzine devoted to comics and cartoons.

Four years later, Don and Maggie Thompson (now married) were there when comic book fans assembled for the first event that resembled a convention. In March 1964 Jerry Bails, the chief instigator of comic book fan activity in the 1960s, hosted a proto-con at his home in a suburb of Detroit. A few years earlier, Bails and nineteen other prominent fans had formed the Academy of Comic-Book Arts and Sciences and instituted annual awards, for both pros and fans, which Roy Thomas had suggested they name the Alley Awards.

As executive secretary of the Academy, Bails would be the one to receive the completed ballots. When he received over 250 of them, each with twenty-eight categories, he made an open invitation to any member of the academy to come to spend the weekend at his house and help count the votes. Dubbed the "Alley Tally" by Maggie Thompson, this gathering of about twenty fans had many of the characteristics of later comic book conventions: there was trading and selling of comic books, pages of original comic book art were on display, and there was even a one-man masquerade when Ronn Foss made his dramatic appearance as Rocketman. Of course, the Alley Tally is not considered a true con because it was not openly advertised to all of fandom.

However, a few months later, in nearby Detroit, most of the Alley Talliers and about fifty other fans attended a true convention that was at least partially dedicated to comic books. The Detroit Triple Fan Fair was held at the Hotel Tuller on May 24, 1964. The one-day celebration of fantasy, film, and comics was organized by seventeen-year-old Dave Szurek and fifteen-year-old Bob Brosch. There were no science fiction or comic book professionals in attendance, but fans gave brief talks on film and comics. The highlight for comic book fans was probably Bails' lecture "Comicdom—Past, Present and Future." Shel Dorf, who would take over the organization of the con the following year, recalls that "It was little more than a swap meet. Bob's sister made a big bowl of punch, and there were a lot of card tables with cartons of books" (Schelly 1999: 78).

It took another few months before comicdom had its own convention. According to fandom historian Bill Schelly, "the New York Comicon has traditionally been considered the first real comicon" (1999: 81). Organized by Bernie Bubnis and Ron Fradkin and held in the Workman's Circle Building on Monday, July 27, 1964, the New York Comicon attracted only about fifty fans, but some of the region's leading dealers (Howard Rogofsky and Phil Seuling among them) and even a few comic book professionals were in attendance. Representing Marvel were Spider-

Man artist Steve Ditko and office manager Flo Steinberg. Artist Tom Gill was there representing Gold Key. No one from DC attended, but editors Murray Boltinoff and Julie Schwartz donated some pages of original art for door prizes. This first attempt at a convention was not an unqualified success: it was not well publicized, the room was hard to find and far too hot, and the Monday date was inconvenient for many fans. Bubnis admits that he really had no idea how to organize a convention, but "I just did it because I thought someone should" (Schelly 1999: 81). Among the fans present were future contributors to the field such as Len Wein (*Swamp Thing)* and Marv Wolfman *(The New Teen Titans)*, and future creators in other fields like George R.R. Martin *(Game of Thrones)* and Michael Uslan (executive producer, *Batman* films).

Being held near the heart of comic book production, the New York convention grew quickly. By the second year, there were nearly two hundred fans in attendance. Organizer Dave Kaler, with the help of a network of local fans, made use of industry contacts and arranged for an impressive lineup of professional guests. This time DC was well represented, including editors Mort Weisinger and Gardner Fox, as well as writers Otto Binder and Bill Finger. By the time Phil Seuling, a high school English teacher and prominent comic book dealer, took over running the con in 1968, the attendance was over 700, and it grew steadily thereafter into the thousands. Seuling ran the renamed Comic Art Convention until it faded out of existence in the 1980s, a victim of the increasing cost pressures of New York City as it became more of a tourist destination.

In the late 1960s Shel Dorf moved from Detroit to New York to San Diego and soon fell in with a group of area fans that included future cartoonist Scott Shaw!, Richard Alf, one of the first mail-order comics dealers, and Ken Krueger, a longtime science fiction fan (Shaw 1999: 94–5). It was not long before Dorf was taking groups of fans to visit Jack and Roz Kirby at their home in Thousand Oaks, California. (Like Dorf, the Kirbys had recently moved to California from New York.) This whetted the group's appetite for more pro contact, and in 1969 they began seriously planning a comic book convention. Alf provided the seed money, Krueger provided the know-how from his science fiction fan experiences, Dorf provided the professional contacts, and the rest of the group provided tons of enthusiasm. After a March 1970 one-day con to help raise funds, the first official San Diego Golden State Comic-Con was held August 1–3, 1970, at the U.S. Grant Hotel in downtown San Diego. Over 300 fans showed up to see comic book artists Jack Kirby and Mike Royer, science fiction authors Ray Bradbury and A. E. Van Vogt, editorial cartoonist Bob Stevens, and, probably the biggest name on the ticket, monster maven Forrest J. Ackerman. By 1982 the renamed San Diego Comic-Con had left hotel venues for a new home in the massive San Diego Convention Center and was attracting 5,000 fans. By the end of the decade, the San Diego Comic-Con was the premier comic book convention in the United States and the site of the industry's answer to the Oscars, the Eisner Awards Ceremony. Officially renamed Comic-Con International: San Diego in 1995, the event now attracts over 130,000 attendees a year. Literally dozens of other comic conventions have modeled themselves on the New York and San Diego shows, with smaller but significant and growing attendance.

At the core of the modern convention is the desire of entertainment marketers to connect with the fans who are now recognized as opinion leaders in the era of social marketing. Many larger publishers take advantage of the crowds assembled at conventions to market their latest products and announce forthcoming products in spectacles akin to the unveiling of a new model of a car at an auto show. Film studies send directors and stars to conventions to promote forthcoming theatrical releases and streaming shows. There is also plenty of commerce, with dealers and collectors engaged in the sale and trade of comic books and associated paraphernalia. Artists and independent publishers are also on hand to sell sketches, autographs, and signed copies of their publications. Conventions also present opportunities for aspiring talents to market themselves to editors and try to win the opportunity for a career in the industry.

But more than just a marketplace, conventions are venues for the expression of community. Comic book conventions have a long-standing tradition of making creators accessible to their fans, allowing them to meet face to face. They also permit fans to network with one another, strengthening peer-to-peer relationships. Conventions often feature programming that further enhances the fans' experience or expertise. Panel presentations offered by creators, publishers, academics, and fellow fans allow those attending to engage in close readings of their favorite texts, express their dis/satisfaction with creative directions, and participate in ritualistic ceremonies honoring their favorite creators, among many, many other topics. For many fans the journey to a favorite convention is a pilgrimage to a "sacred" place (Figure 2.8).

Figure 2.8 Comic-Con International draws fans of all ages and apparel and is just one of a number of professionally run conventions that are sponsored around the country and throughout the calendar year. Photo by Karen Stover.

Readers as Well as Fans

Important as comic book fans are to the vitality of the form, comics are sustained by the far larger number of readers whose participation in the field is limited to buying and enjoying the material. Data on the identity of readers was rarely collected by academics or publishers in earlier decades, and what was done as research was often more for marketing purposes than out of unbiased curiosity. With that caveat, it is clear that as comics migrated from sales on the newsstand as a casual purchase by children to being a considered purchase in comic shops or in bookstores, the audience aged and changed.

Today, the industry's conventional wisdom is that the largest number of its American readers are teenagers and adults, with males outnumbering females by a considerable (but diminishing) majority. Proprietary studies have shown that comic book readers tend to be individuals who are heavy readers not only of comics, but of prose, educated more than the average American, and somewhat more frequently found in occupational tracks in the creative and scientific/technology fields. The stereotype of comic book readers is culturally powerful enough to have inspired long-running but affectionate derision on shows like *The Simpsons*, or to provide subtext to let the characters of *The Big Bang Theory* prove their credibility as lovable nerds.

Most readers who shop at comic shops typically remain weekly customers, and are heavy users of the form, with annual buying habits that often go well over a thousand dollars. But an increasing number of readers are people who shop less frequently, either at bookstores, online, or from comic shops, yet focus their purchases almost exclusively on the graphic novel format, buying them for reading pleasure without any particular interest in collecting, speculating, or participating in fandom.

As the diversity of material published in comics is expanding rapidly, the conventional wisdom about its readers is becoming more and more suspect. Clearly, the half-million or more children who purchased *Bone* at schools through Scholastic defy this norm at one extreme, and the sophistication of many graphic novels is expanding it at the other end of the spectrum. It is unclear whether the diversity of material and the diversity of the audience in the United States and Canada will reach the heights of the Japanese manga market (where virtually all subjects are dealt with in manga, and most Japanese who are active readers consume the form), but that is an aspiration of many working in the field.

Analyzing: Comic Book Fandom as Participatory Culture

Comic book fans enact a culture, but many of the raw materials of that culture—the characters, plots, images, and lines pulled from the comics—are almost always the property of other people. Copyright and trademark laws guarantee that the creators of comic book properties own the rights to control and profit from the use of them. (Of course, when a creator makes a comic in a work-for-hire arrangement, it is the publisher who holds the copyright.) Without first securing the permission of the copyright holder, fans who want to produce their own comics featuring popular characters, paint a mural with their favorite character, or even design their own costumes in the likeness of their favorite comic book personality are technically infringing on those rights. The framers of the US Constitution thought that copyright was so important that they enshrined it in that fundamental document with the belief that people who create **intellectual property**—such as books and artwork—should be granted a measure of protection from others profiting from their creativity. The belief is that talented writers, artists, and intellectuals should be able to profit directly from the products of their labor. If someone could simply reprint a novel without its author benefiting from the arrangement, there would be a disincentive for the best and brightest to continue creating new works.

While many people might agree that it is a good idea to have such incentives in place for the creative and intellectual community, few are fully aware of how far copyright protection extends. Fans, in particular, often view the materials put out by the major publishers and independent publishers as contributions to the larger cultural mosaic from which they often sample or poach ideas. "Fans reject the idea of a definitive version produced, authorized, and regulated by some media conglomerate. Instead, fans envision a world where all of us can participate in the creation and circulation of central cultural myths" (Jenkins 2009: 289). Media scholar Henry Jenkins has observed how fans engage in a participatory culture where they borrow characters, plots, images, and other elements from their favorite narratives (e.g., *Star Wars*) to produce their own stories. As you can start to see, though, the rights of copyright holder and the desires of fans can come into conflict with one another.

One infamous case of copyright infringement involving comics took place in the 1970s when the Air Pirates, a studio of underground cartoonists under the direction of Dan O'Neill, parodied the works of Walt Disney. *Air Pirates Funnies* featured a mouse named Mickey and his friends, drawn in the familiar Disney house style but engaged in adult activities like drug consumption and sexual intercourse. Aghast at such an antithetical depiction of their stars, the Disney corporation sued, and the subsequent legal wrangles went all the way to the Supreme Court. While O'Neill's motives for pursuing the case to that level were complex, the situation underscores the seriousness with which copyright holders are willing to defend their ownership.

While the Air Pirates might have been audacious in their parodies, the reality is that people regularly violate copyrighted material. For example, many fans produce their own original **fan fiction** using characters, situations, and images that are under copyright protection. Some of these stories are innocuous amateur attempts at creating additional narratives for familiar mythology. Other fan fiction might delve into areas left unexplored in the copyright holder's canon, such as the notorious **slash fiction**, in which sexual situations might be probed in depth. While such unauthorized uses of their material may upset copyright holders, doing so is a means for fans to embrace the products of mass culture as their own. Fans can thus be both be allies and adversaries in the business of producing comics, with the delicate balance between the copyright holder and audience member's ownership of the material always needing to find a necessary equilibrium.

Discussion Questions

1. What implications does the concentration of ownership have for diverse genres and new ideas to take hold in the mainstream of the industry? What alternatives exist for creators and consumers who want something other than what the mainstream producers are offering?
2. Are comic book fans really any more obsessive about the object of their attention than other fans, like music groupies or television couch potatoes? Are these groups treated with more or less respect than fangirls and fanboys?
3. Imagine you're Stan Lee, and you want to communicate to your "Marvel minions" in the twenty-first century. How would you use social media and the internet to be effective?

Activities

1. Visit both a local bookstore and a comics specialty shop (addresses can be found in your phonebook's yellow pages under "Comic Book Dealers" or at www.comicshoplocator.com). Note the placement of materials published by the Big Two publishers, Marvel and DC, and compare them to those of all other publishers at each outlet. What share of the market do the Big Two publishers seem to command

in terms of shelf space? Is there any noteworthy difference in how the bookstore and specialty shop treat the Big Two and all other publishers? Using these observations as a reference, write an essay in which you reflect on the competition afforded by the exhibition branch of the comic book industry.

2. Conduct an in-depth interview with a comic book fan. The following are a few starter questions, but you will also need to devise additional questions of your own:
   - When did you begin reading comic books?
   - Did you stop reading comic books at any point? If so, why? What prompted you to start again?
   - What do you like about the comic book medium?
   - How have you benefited from reading comic books?
   - Besides reading comic books, do you take part in any other fan activities like attending conventions, collecting related merchandise, posting to a website, etc.? What do you gain from those activities?

Recommended Readings

Comics

Cooke, Jon B., and John Morrow, eds. *Streetwise: Autobiographical Stories by Comic Book Professionals*. Raleigh: TwoMorrows Publishing, 2000.
The men behind mainstream comic books tell of their upbringing, influences, and entrée into the world of graphic storytelling. Sergio Aragonés won an Eisner Award for Best Short Story for his contribution to this anthology, which also features memoirs from two dozen professionals.

Evanier, Mark, and Sergio Aragonés. *Fanboy*. New York: DC Comics, 2001.
Evanier (former assistant to Jack Kirby) and Aragonés (*Mad*; *Groo*) are no strangers to the peculiar behaviors of the fan community. In this humorous take on fandom, they introduce Finster, a fan who takes flights of fantasy to interact with his favorite comic book characters (co-illustrated by some of comicdom's finest artists), even while living out his own misadventures.

Scholarly Sources

Brown, Jeffrey A. *Black Superheroes, Milestone Comics, and Their Fans*. Jackson: University Press of Mississippi, 2001.
Brown investigates how fans interpreted issues of race and masculinity in Milestone Comics, the short-lived DC Comics imprint that featured characters of diverse racial and ethnic backgrounds.

Salkowitz, Rob. *Comic-Con and the Business of Pop Culture*. New York: McGraw-Hill, 2012.
Comic-Con International is a major showcase for the comics, film, television and other entertainment industries, and Salkowitz explores how fans, creators, and marketers intersect to celebrate and promote mass media.

Unit II Form

3 Encapsulation of the Moments

Between a relatively short career as a journalist and a long ongoing career as a popular, multiple award-winning novelist and multimedia writer, Neil Gaiman was a critically acclaimed comic book writer. Gaiman is obviously someone with an affinity and talent for writing, but he had to learn particular techniques for writing comics. During the course of writing the *Sandman* series for DC Comics he mastered the craft, and now he teaches the MasterClass *How to Create a Comic Book*.

For most of his comics work Gaiman wrote full scripts that would be given to an artist to illustrate. Thus, Gaiman made the initial decisions about which aspects of the narrative would be shown on the page and even how they might be encapsulated in individual panels.

The MasterClass staff provide a written overview of the nineteen video lessons in Gaiman's course and some insight into the method he developed for writing comics. After deciding how the narrative would begin and how it would end, Gaiman began determining the beats (major events) in the narrative. By folding sheets of typing paper he created a 24-page mini-comic he used to plan how the beats would be distributed across the pages and how those beats might be turned into panels.

Gaiman was not actually drawing the pictures or even writing the captions and dialogue; his mini-comic (which he never showed to anyone else) was just a notebook in which he was exploring what needed to be drawn and what needed to be written to effectively tell the story he had in mind. He was engaging in encapsulation, the aspect of comic creation that we will examine in this chapter (Figure 3.1).

Objectives

In this chapter you will learn:

1. some of the narrative structures commonly found in comic books;
2. the types and techniques of encapsulation; and
3. the nature of the relationship between the pictorial and linguistic elements of comic books.

Figure 3.1 This "homemade mini-comic" by writer Neil Gaiman is a behind-the-scenes look at how Gaiman communicated to the *Sandman* artists which segments of the narrative should go together on a page © DC Comics.

In 1957 Marshall McLuhan noted that "today we are just beginning to realize the new media are not just mechanical gimmicks for creating worlds of illusion, but new languages with new and unique powers of expression" (119). While McLuhan would have had no problem recognizing the techniques and devices of comic books as a "new language," most comics theorists speak of a comics language merely as a metaphor, because they consider the visual aspects of comic books to have no definite lexicon and no concrete rules of grammar. However, Neil Cohn (*Who Understands Comics* 2021) is doing some fascinating and challenging work applying theories of linguistics and cognitive science to understand how sequences of images in comics literally operate as a language. In this book we do not attempt to explain comic book communication as a type of language, but any serious student of the comic book medium should consider Cohn's work as a supplement and occasionally a counterpoint to the concepts presented in this text.

Creators of comics, whether they be **cartoonists** (who both write and draw the comic) or collaborators (writer, penciler, inker, colorist, letterer), usually consider the **cognitive** (thinking) and **affective** (feeling) responses they hope to elicit from readers of the comic. They attempt to influence these responses through the strategic choices they make about what to show (encapsulation), how to show it (composition), and how to present the relationships of panels on the page or screen (layout). In practice, creators of comics consider a number of these choices simultaneously rather than in a strict sequence, but to examine these concepts at a theoretical level we will deal with each of them in a separate chapter. In this chapter we will explore encapsulation.

Story and Narrative

The comics' form can be used for a wordless visual poem or even a totally abstract series of images, but most comics contain a **narrative** (events and the order in which they are presented) that tells a story. A story has a theme, an idea, or message. Narrative, as we use the term in this chapter, is the means by which a story is told and a theme is communicated.

In **simple narrative** structure there is a conflict or series of conflicts that build in rising action to a climactic moment in which the conflict is resolved. Rather than ending abruptly, the story is often rounded out with a denouement that might show the consequences of the resolution, resonate the theme of the story, or simply re-emphasize the tone or mood of the tale. We expect a story to have a beginning, a middle, and an end; this is what the simple narrative presents. For many years this was the standard story structure for funny animal comics, romance comics, humor comics, and self-contained adventure stories (e.g., *Uncle Scrooge*, the early superhero stories). While simple narratives still exist in the comic book medium, it is now more common for creators of graphic novels, mini-series, and even some serialized comic books to construct **complex narratives** in which the main plot line is expanded by backstory, character development, and ongoing subplots.

The conventional concept of narrativity assumes that events build toward some ultimate resolution of conflict and an ending of the narrative. However, some comics, especially American mainstream comic books, are serialized, continuing stories that have no ultimate resolution and never come to an end as long as there are enough readers willing to purchase the next issue. Even a canceled series is usually left open-ended in anticipation of being revived at some later date.

Literary scholar Marie-Laure Ryan has proposed a number of new modes of narrativity she feels can more accurately describe the various ways in which narrative structures are realized in serialized texts. Two of Ryan's modes seem particularly applicable to comic books.

The first of these is **braided narrativity**. "This type of narrative follows the intertwined destinies of a large [collection] of characters," and rather than an overall plot there are "a number of parallel and successive subplots developing along the destiny line of characters". This mode of narrativity "does not end in an event motivated by the demands of narrative closure, but may be continued ad infinitum by stringing new episodes along destiny lines" (Ryan 1992: 374). Braided narrativity best describes a single title that is creator-owned and tells stories about characters that are not part of a larger fictional universe. *Strangers in Paradise*, *Cerebus*, and *Saga* are good examples.

The popular mainstream superhero comic books, especially those published by DC and Marvel, are part of a sprawling fictional universe, with shaky continuity among the events in all of the titles that comprise the universe. Within these complex fictional structures (where editorial decisions are often driven by commerce), neither characters nor plots are stable concepts. There are often inconsistent, even contradicting narratives across titles and across years. In an effort to appeal to new readers and bring a contemporary feel to characters whose adventures have been published for half a century or more, there are occasional **reboots** that begin a new version of a character or team, often with an alternate telling of events already chronicled in previous issues. For example, Superman's origin has been retold and retooled many times since his first appearance in 1938. In fact, in just

Figures 3.2a–c These three images show increasingly militaristic and ferocious versions of Hawkman, but longtime fans retain a sense of the overall Hawkman mythos despite the character repeatedly being rebooted with different powers, missions, and costumes. *Hawkman* #1 (1964) art by Murphy Anderson; *Hawkworld* #1 (1990) art by Graham Nolan; Savage *Hawkman* #1 (2011) art by Phillip Tan © DC Comics.

a fifteen-year span of the twenty-first century Superman's origin story was rebooted four times: *Superman: Birthright* in 2003; *Superman: Secret Origin* in 2009; *Action Comics* # 1 (New 52) in 2011; *Action Comics* # 977 (Rebirth) in 2017. While longtime readers can be annoyed or even alienated by radical changes to beloved characters, they can also take pleasure in being able to identify how elements from the previous version(s) are modified and integrated into the new "reality" (Figures 3.2a–c).

These continuity-conscious, serialized comic books seem to fit what Ryan calls a **proliferating narrativity**: "In these works, the main plot functions mostly as support for the telling of adventures and anecdotes." It is not the unfolding of an intricate plot or the building of dramatic suspense that holds the reader's interest, but rather "the narrative verve" with which each adventure is related. "The macro structure that holds the micro narratives together is of the most primitive kind; the life of the hero, a family saga, a love affair stretching over a lifetime" (Ryan 1992: 373).

A proliferating narrative is not so much a story as it is a mythos. With the most recognizable and exploitable corporate commodities (e.g., X-Men, Superman, Batman, Spider-Man), the proliferation of the mythos occurs across multiple titles of their own, numerous guest appearances in other titles, novels, television series, motion pictures, video games, merchandise, and even theme parks. Thus, readers/consumers come to know a character through encountering many varied forms of the "character concept." Because a number of these forms are significantly more profitable for the corporation than the publication of comic books, the comic book narrative must sometimes conform to the mythos proliferated in the more popular media.

Speaking in a roundtable discussion with Steve Bissette and Tom Veitch, writer Neil Gaiman has speculated that it is not the superhero character's story that persists in the culture, but rather the character's **state of grace**, a set of powers, appearance, supporting characters, and behaviors that are preserved in a recognizable form for the economic interests of the corporation that owns the character. The colorful costumes, dramatic displays of power, and familiar character traits that constitute this state of grace provide much of the narrative verve that makes reading mainstream superhero comics enjoyable.

A narrative comic is born with the cartoonist or writer imagining, often visualizing, a story. A cartoonist, or writer and artist working together, must determine the segments of narrative that will be used to convey the story. Then they engage in the key activity of **encapsulation**—selecting the key moments of the narrative, each of which will be presented, with picture and (perhaps) words, in a discrete area of the page that comics' theory designates as a panel. A **panel** occupies a finite space on the page and encapsulates a finite, if sometimes indeterminate, span of time. The panel is the basic unit of the comic art form. Panels are the building blocks from which comics are created.

As cartoonist Megan Kelso explains about the comics she loves best, "it's very clear to me that the cartoonist saw the entire world that was represented in the comic, and then carefully chose what to show me" (1999: 229). Comics' pioneer Will Eisner (1985) coined the term "encapsulation" for this process of deciding what to show within a particular panel, but as we will see later there can be broader levels of encapsulation. Eisner stresses that most of the images shown in a comic should be moments of prime action—moments that even though they are just static images on the comics page or screen effectively help the reader to imagine the parts of the action that are not shown. For instance, the images in Figure 3.3 provide enough information for the reader to imagine the action of walking to and getting into a car.

Figure 3.3 ***In the Days of the Mob*** **(1971) by Jack Kirby © DC Comics.**

Levels of Encapsulation

The majority of comic book panels are presented in an orderly progression of framed rectangles, usually separated by a white space known as the **gutter**. However, borders are not necessary or defining elements of the panel. Because innovative artists such as Bernie Krigstein, Art Spiegelman, Joe Quesada, and David Mack are constantly finding new ways to use the very elastic form of the comic book, it is not always easy to recognize or define a panel. Not all comic book panels are enclosed by a border, and not all pictures enclosed by a border function as a panel (see Figure 3.4). On page three of "Fight Night" (see Figure 4.17) a metaphorical fight in a boxing ring is presented in two rectangles separated by a white gutter space. However, the figure of the protagonist extends into both rectangles and a sound effect created by an action in the second rectangle appears in the first rectangle. Are these rectangles really functioning as two panels or are they just portions of one panel? What constitutes a panel is not always clear-cut.

Figure 3.4 Just because a picture or a word is enclosed by a frame does not mean it functions as an independent panel. How many panels are there on this page from Blankets (2003)? Copyright Craig Thompson. Used with permission from Drawn & Quarterly.

While the term "encapsulation" is generally used to refer to the act of creating panels, it is also true that there is encapsulation, a deciding of what to show, at the levels of scene and sequence. The major narrative units within the story are **sequences**. A sequence is comprised of related and usually consecutive **scenes**. Scenes are imprecise units of a narrative that usually, but not necessarily, have unity of time and space and portray a continuous action. Scenes are unified by a central concern, be it a location (e.g., a newspaper office), an incident (e.g., a chase), or a stream of thought (e.g., pondering a decision).

In comic books and graphic novels there is the potential for the page to operate as a distinct unit of meaning within the narrative, and creators must make conscious decisions about which panels will appear together on a page. Many artists use **thumbnail breakdowns** as a way of planning which panels to put on a page, and then visually composing that page. These are quick sketches, often little more than stick figures, used to break a narrative down into visual moments of prime action (the pictures necessary to get the reader to imagine the parts of the narrative that are not depicted on the page). These encapsulation decisions are made in concert with layout decisions, such as the panel size needed to effectively communicate ideas and emotions. Comics creators can choose from a continuum of page breakdowns, ranging from presenting a substantial portion of the narrative on one comics page of many small panels to using a full-page panel for only one instant and one word of the narrative. We will examine layout choices in more depth in Chapter 5.

The primary concern of encapsulation is deciding which moments of the narrative to put on the page. Comics theorist Robert Harvey (1996) writes that "the selection of what is to be pictured is greatly influenced by the quantity of story material (how much exposition is required, how much action, what must be depicted in order to prepare for subsequent events, and so on) and by the available space" (178). There is also a constant dynamic between what *is* shown and what *could* be shown.

One aspect of this dynamic is **syntagmatic choice**, the process of selecting which panels to present from the possible consecutive progression of narrative images that could

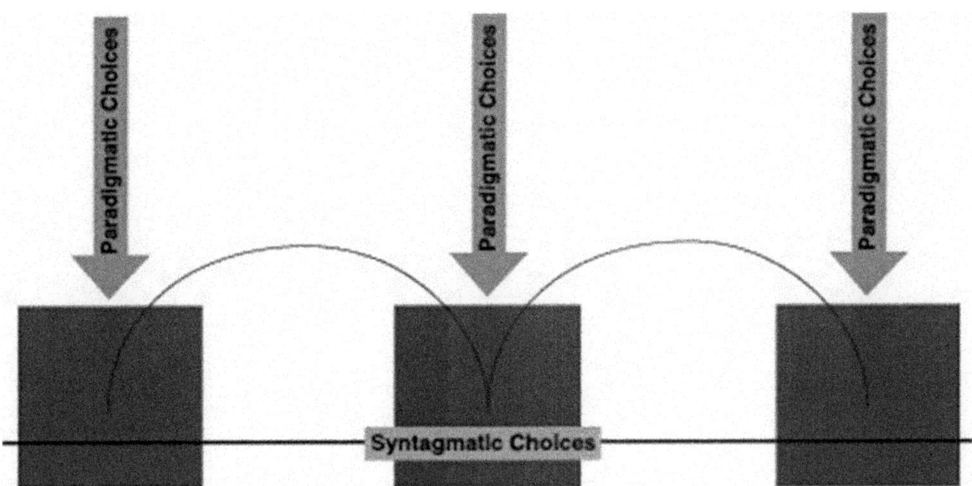

Figure 3.5 This is a visual metaphor for how comics creators make choices about the sequence of moments to encapsulate along a horizontal syntagmatic axis and at each panel make decisions on a vertical *paradigmatic* axis about the particular images to use to convey particular moments.

be placed on the page. This process is vaguely analogous to selecting the word order to create a sentence. The images of syntagmatic choice are arranged along the horizontal axis to form scenes and sequences of the overall narrative. Of course, this "horizontal axis" is merely a metaphor for how panels are strung together in one's mind to form a linear narrative; the layout of panels on a page is not strictly linear. And, as we discuss in more depth later, when the reader actively engages with constructing a narrative flow from the encapsulated moments the shown (prime action) moments can convey intervening moments of the story that are not shown (Groensteen *Comics* 2013: 37) (Figure 3.5).

At each panel and at each image (be it a picture or word) in a panel, the syntagmatic intersects with the vertical axis of the **paradigmatic choice**, the chosen images and all the images that could have made sense or communicated nearly the same meaning at the same point in the panel (see Figure 3.5). According to film scholar James Monaco (1977), a paradigmatic connotation results from comparing, not necessarily consciously, the image shown with "its unrealized companions in the paradigm" (131). Or, as media scholar Jonathan Bignell (1997) explains it, "every sign present has meaning by virtue of the other signs which have been excluded and are not present in the text" (14). For both the syntagmatic and the paradigmatic choices, meaning is created by a combination of the present and the absent.

We see the end result of syntagmatic and paradigmatic choices, but we do not get to see the process. We almost never get to see the images an author/artist considered for a story but did not include. It is not quite the same thing as seeing the rejected images, but perhaps we can get a better grasp of the concept of paradigmatic choice by considering how different artists have chosen to encapsulate the same scene. Batman's origin has been presented in scores of comics over the years, but the basic elements have remained fairly stable—the Wayne family ventures into a bad part of town, they are robbed at gunpoint, and young Bruce Wayne sees his parents shot and killed right in front of him. Figure 3.6a–d shows four depictions of the moment immediately after the fatal shots are fired. The four

Figures 3.6a–d Four examples of the paradigmatic choices made to depict the moment after Bruce Wayne's parents are killed. Clockwise from left: a) *Detective Comics* #33 (1939) words by Bill Finger and art by Bob Kane and Sheldon Moldoff; b) *Batman* #200 (1968) words by Mike Friedrich and art by Chic Stone and Joe Giella; c) *Batman* #232 (1971) words by Danny O'Neil and art by Neal Adams and Dick Giordano; d) *Batman* #404 (1987) words by Frank Miller and art by David Mazzuchelli © DC Comics.

encapsulations of that moment vary in use of dialogue, Bruce's proximity to his fallen parents, the presence of the killer, etc. In one instance the bodies of the Waynes are not even shown.

The Reductive Nature of Encapsulation

Comics are reductive in creation and additive in reading. That is, creators reduce the story to moments on a page by encapsulation, and readers expand the isolated moments into a narrative (which is, of course, never exactly the same as the story the comic's creator(s) had in mind).

The most prevalent reductive device in comics is **synecdoche**, using a part to represent the whole or vice versa. For example, in the majority of panels, only a portion of a character's body is drawn to represent the reality of the entire body (see Figure 3.7). This is true even more often for objects (cars, building, etc.). For instance, in panel one of Figure 4.17 "Fight Night," all we see is a horizontal bar and a hanger, but we understand that to represent a closet. In the static medium of comic books, the frozen moments of prime action stand for the entire action. If this reduction is done with thought and skill, readers understand the whole from the parts presented. For instance, in the third tier of panels of Figure 9.8 *The Disaster Capitalism Curriculum*, the picture shows the teacher handing a practice test to one student, but we imagine a line of students moving past her and each student getting a test packet.

Figure 3.7 Will Eisner demonstrates a type of synecdoche in which a panel showing only a portion of the character actually communicates an impression of the character's entire body. From *Comics and Sequential Art* by Will Eisner. © 1985 by Will Eisner. © 2006 by Will Eisner Studios, Inc. Used by permission of W.W. Norton & Company, Inc.

Metonymy, the use of an associated detail to represent the whole, is another useful reductive device in comics. For instance, on page two of "A Life in Comics" (Figure 5.12) even if Manhattan was not mentioned in a caption, most readers would recognize the top of the Chrysler Building (one of the world's most distinctive buildings) and realize that the city depicted is New York City. The most common metonymy used is the depiction of part of the physical manifestation of an emotion. In his study of the language of film, Director Vsevolod Pudovkin (1975) noted that "there is a law in psychology that says if an emotion gives birth to a certain movement, by imitation of this movement the corresponding emotion can be called forth" (193). In comics as well the gestures, postures, and facial expressions associated with an emotion can be used to represent that emotion. In *Making Comics*, Scott McCloud (2006) provides a lexicon of facial expressions and body language that convey particular emotions. Take a look at Figures 3.14a–c, a page from *Girl Town* (2018), the young woman's changing facial expression and posture lets us know that she is having a strong emotional reaction to the woman's song.

A detail can also represent a whole through a less direct, more indexical relationship based on common usage or conventions. One of the conventions established early on in film and picked up by comic books was that tattered clothes indicate that someone has been in a fight. In the first appearance of Superman there is an extreme example of this. In a series of six panels, Superman deals with a wife-beater. The man, wearing a long-sleeve shirt and tie, is thrown against the wall by Superman and then breaks a knife on Superman's "tough skin." Superman never does anything to rip the man's clothes, but by the fifth panel the man's sleeves are completely torn from his shirt (see Figures 3.8a–b).

Figures 3.8a–b The convention of torn clothing is used to show the ferocity of a fight in *Action Comics* #1 (1938), script by Jerry Siegel and art by Joe Shuster. © DC Comics.

Symbols are another means of economy of expression in comics. Symbols can manifest as a **sequence metaphor**, two juxtaposed images that together create a meaning not present in either image alone. For example, in the first issue of *Aces High* (1955), an image of a medieval knight appears in the sky behind the image of a First World War aviator in his plane. In 1955 this image probably evoked Winston Churchill's famous 1940 speech in which he praised the young airmen of the Royal Air Force as "noble knights," but even today, without that historical context, the co-presence of these two images is the **vehicle** (the image that stimulates a comparison) that creates the **tenor** (underlying meaning) that the aviator is a modern-day knight. Common-lore metaphors are based on a relationship that has become conventionalized by repeated association. Because the moon has repeatedly been depicted as romantic in poetry, song, and film, an image of the moon in a love comic is going to symbolize romance for most readers. Yet visual metaphors are very dependent on context, and a similar drawing of the moon in the *Tomb of Dracula* comic book would symbolize lurking terror.

Since everything in comic books, including characters, is reduced to two-dimensional images, the use of **stereotypes** is prevalent. A stereotype is a recognizable generalization of a type, even though such a culturally perceived type might not exist in reality. Especially when the art style moves away from realism and into caricature, generalizations about characters can be quickly established by exaggerating facial features, physique, hair, posture, clothing, and other artifacts. For example, the way Alec Longstreth draws himself in the second panel of Figure 9.12 plays upon the scruffy "starving artist" stereotype. Comics veteran Will Eisner (1995) often employed what was already a venerable technique in caricature—character renderings based on animals (see Figure 3.9).

What was shown in older (pre-internet) comics needed to be presented with enough context to be immediately comprehensible because doing research to understand what an image represents could be difficult and time consuming. Nowadays, we do not have to own a bookcase full of encyclopedias or travel to a library because, no matter where we are when we read a comic, we are likely to have a powerful computer, with internet access, in our pocket or on a nearby table. Thus, as you read the second page of "A Life in Comics" (Figure 5.12) if you want to more fully understand what Karen Green was experiencing you simply have to ask Siri, Bixby, Alexa, etc. to tell you about The Cloisters. Of course, comics creators should realize that not all readers will make even simple efforts to enhance understanding, and if the encapsulation process reduces the narrative below the threshold at which the meaning of an image is apparent not all readers can be counted on to expand the meaning of the image.

Figure 3.9 Visual stereotyping examples from *Graphic Storytelling and Visual Narrative* by Will Eisner. © 1996 by Will Eisner. © 2008 by Will Eisner Studios, Inc. Used by permission of W.W. Norton & Company, Inc.

Encapsulation of Actions and Motions

Cartoonists have developed a number of techniques to give a sense of movement to the flat, static images on the comics page. The most common technique is simply the posture of the characters. Another frequent technique, used in conjunction with posture, is thin lines (called **speed lines**) or puffs of "smoke" drawn behind a character or object to indicate the direction and rapidity of movement. A third method of communicating movement is drawing, next to a completed figure, a partial outline of the figure in its previous position(s). In the fourth method the artist makes multiple full drawings of the character in action with only slight differences in the character's position each time (see Figures 3.10a–b). With the fifth technique motion is implied to have happened between panels because a figure or object is occupying a different space or assuming a different posture than in the previous panel. A less frequently used variation of this technique, but one that can imply a sudden departure, is the absence of a figure or object from a panel that otherwise has all the elements of the preceding panel (see Figure 3.11). In still another variation, a meta-panel composed of a number of smaller panels can establish a stationary setting that stretches across all the panels, while in each of the smaller panels the same characters or object can be shown at a different place in the setting, thus giving a sense of the figure moving within the frame of the meta-panel.

Figurea 3.10a–b In the top panel, speed lines are drawn in to convey motion. In the middle panel, a path of motion is indicated by a combination of speed lines and repeated figures. In the bottom panel, repeated figures aim for the same effect but without the use of speed lines. *DC Comics Presents* #24 (1980) with words by Len Wein and art by José Luis Garcia-López. © DC Comics.

Figure 3.11 A sudden departure implied by the absence of a figure in the second panel. *Cerebus* #46 (1983) by Dave Sim. © Aardvark-Vanaheim.

Encapsulation of Time

The amount of time encapsulated in a panel can be an instant, a moment, or even a sequence of events. While there are many exceptions, it is often true that the larger the panel, the longer the time span depicted in it. Yet a sequence of events can also be crammed into a small panel, while a splash page can depict a single instant of time. Scott McCloud's (1993) generalization that in comics "time and space are one and the same" dramatically highlights the spatial nature of comic book time and would seem to indicate that the amount of space a panel takes up on the page represents the passage of a certain amount of time, but he is quick to point out "there's no conversion chart" (100). There is no exact formula for how space equals time in the comic art form. And, panel size is not necessarily the result of intention. An artist does not always think about conveying time when she chooses a panel size. Nor does a reader always consider the element of time as he moves through panels of varying sizes. Indeed, Neil Cohn (2013) believes the reading of time in a comic is more conceptual than spatial, and that panel content is more important to this reading than panel size.

The *content* of a panel is almost always relevant to the readers' understanding of the passage of time. When constructing panel content, a creator has to be aware that a reader senses the amount of time elapsed based on their own experience of how long it takes to perform the action depicted. This includes both physical actions and saying or thinking words. While character thoughts or dialogue occupy a span of time within the narrative.

Regardless of how a comics creator intended to encapsulate time, the experience and perception of time in comics rest with the individual reader. Perception of time will vary among readers due to factors such as reading habits and the degree of engagement. For instance, our teaching experience has shown us that English majors who are new to comics tend to focus on words, moving from balloons to captions, and overlooking information provided by the pictures. Depending on life experiences, personal interests, aesthetic sensitivity, and so on, different readers will slow down at different panels to contemplate ideas or to appreciate the artwork.

Although the experience is not the same for every reader, the manner in which time is encapsulated does influence the duration of attention and affects the pacing of the story. In general, the more words in a panel, the slower the reading pace. Thus, effective action scenes usually contain fewer words as the action becomes more intense so that the tempo picks up as the reader moves rapidly from panel to panel.

The narrative pacing in comic books has evolved over time (a concept we will revisit as an aspect of layout in Chapter 5). In older comics both an action and the reactions to that action are often contained in the same panel. Many comic books in the 1940s and 1950s were anthologies, featuring a number of different characters each in their own short stories, ranging from five to fifteen pages in length. And even for those books that contained just one story, that story had to be completed within that issue. Storytelling had to be very compressed. Beginning in the 1960s most serialized comic books became a never-ending mythos (a proliferating narrative) in which subplots are always introducing new conflicts that will develop into the next major conflict for the protagonists. Because there is no pressure to wrap up the story by page twenty-two, the creators of these comics have begun to employ **decompressed storytelling** in which the narrative unfolds more slowly. This approach allows creators to devote more space to an action sequence or to exploring the details of the setting. They can take more time to build suspense. Perhaps most importantly, it makes for more realistic interactions between characters, allowing for more nonverbal reactions and awkward silences; to use an imperfect metaphor, better "acting."

In their examination of the changes in narrative structure in eight decades of superhero comic books Cohn, Taylor, and Pederson (2017) found there has been a shift toward fewer words per panel, more wordless panels, and more close-ups of single characters. Because they are not overcrowding panels with word balloons or captions, comic books with decompressed storytelling also tend to have a better blending of words and pictures.

Discovering: The Creative Goal of the Comics Creator

By Carl Potts

The primary creative goal of the comics creator is to keep the reader immersed in the narrative. In most cases, the narrative will be a story. However, narratives can also be mood pieces, character sketches, educational content, or tales of other types. Unless the project is an instructional piece designed to take the reader through a process taking place in the real world (e.g., assembling a piece of equipment), the creator's goal is to keep the reader immersed in the narrative.

Though the goal is simple, attaining it is often anything but simple and requires a series of sometimes difficult creative decisions and executions. To fulfill the goal, it helps if creators keep several principles in mind.

The primary principle is to *make all creative decisions and executions in the service of the story*. Creators need to provide readers with all the information needed to become absorbed in the narrative while avoiding anything that distracts the audience and breaks their suspension of disbelief.

There are several supporting principles. The first is to *be clear*. Comics creators need to make sure that the reader is visually supplied with all of the information needed to enter and stay immersed in the narrative. The reader's eye path should be as intuitive as possible and, unless there's a specific storytelling need to be less than clear, all visuals should be easily recognizable and understood.

The second supporting principle for comics creators is to *be invisible*. The reader is often unaware of how much information is being visually imparted since some of that information is picked up on a subconscious level. Comics creators sometimes spend many hours, even days, generating and rejecting visuals as they work out a scene that clearly reveals all of the needed information in a well-designed panel that leads the eye intuitively and is juxtaposed properly with the text and the surrounding panels. The reader may look at a panel for only a few seconds, then move on in the story, unaware that the scene took the creator many hours of frustrating labor to work out. This is how it should be. Readers should not be exposed to and distracted by a creator's inefficient struggles to impart the needed narrative elements.

A third supporting principle states that the comics creator should *show, not tell*. Ideally, a comic's visuals will enable the reader can discern most of the tale's major information without having to rely on text. Doing so allows creators to use text in a complimentary relationship when juxtaposed with the visuals and to concentrate on nonvisual information and subtext.

Carl Potts is a writer, consultant, game designer, and former Executive Editor at Marvel Comics. He is the author of The DC Comics Guide to Creating Comics: Inside the Art of Visual Storytelling *(2013).*

Interdependence of Pictorial and Linguistic Elements

Perhaps the most significant element of comic book encapsulation is the unique blend of words and pictures that must occur for the art form to communicate effectively. An important consideration of how language and pictures are encapsulated is the correspondence of the words to the action/scene. Balloons or captions can be **synchronous**, occurring at the same time as the action, or **asynchronous** with the picture. Of course, the relationship between the words and the static image can never be absolutely synchronous, but skillful comics creators make an effort to create panels in which the words correspond to the duration of the action. However, when there are many speech balloons in a panel with a single image, "the picture is appropriate to only some of the conversation—and the remainder of the speeches lose dramatic force because they lack the narrative reinforcement of suitable accompanying visuals" (Harvey 1996: 188) (see Figure 3.12).

Figure 3.12 The bartender in *Scalped* #5 (2007) would have to speak very rapidly to say all the words in his speech balloons before the glass overflowed. Words by Jason Aaron and art by R. M. Guéra. © DC Comics.

Eisner claims that "a protracted exchange of dialogue cannot be realistically supported by unmoving static images," and that, ideally, "the dialogue terminates the endurance of the image" (60). Comics theorist Thierry Groensteen (2007) believes the images of characters engaged in conversation are always desynchronized because each character is "living the moment of their word balloon" (133). Scholars Rheinhold Reitberger and Wolfgang Fuchs (1971, 1972) offer a general rule for the combination of words and images in comic books: "the text must be contained within the picture" (25); in other words, the dialogue must fit with the action shown (see Figure 3.13) The means by which words and pictures work together will be discussed further in the section on composition.

Encapsulation, layout, and composition are not discrete operations that take place in a strict order; they are enmeshed and interdependent. For instance, even as artists are making their thumbnail sketches for the purposes of encapsulation and layout, they cannot help but make some basic decisions about the composition of the images in the panels. In the typical process of comic book creation, the panels are arranged on a page while they exist in only a rudimentary form—as thumbnails sketches. Thus, relationships of panels are established before the details of composition in individual panels are selected and rendered. However, it is in weaving together a sequence of juxtaposed panels into a coherent narrative that readers become most actively engaged in creating the cognitive (meaning) and affective (emotion) end result of reading a comic. Therefore we will save our consideration of layout for Chapter 5, and turn next to the composition of individual panels.

Analyzing: Encapsulation Choices

Let us examine a few of the encapsulation choices made by writer/artist Casey Nowak in an excerpt from their book *Girl Town* (first published under the name Carolyn Nowak, see Figures 3.14a–c). The first panel of page one establishes a location. Not only does the reader know that all the events on the following pages (until a new location is established) take place within the pub, but the panel also conveys some information about the location.

Figure 3.13 In this incident from David Lapham's *Stray Bullets* #8 (1996) the words are spread over a number of panels in order to better fit with the actions pictured. © David Lapham.

It is a small pub in an isolated location, there are not many vehicles in the parking lot, and some patrons might perform karaoke. The second panel is an interior establishing panel, providing a wide view inside the little pub, showing that most tables are empty no one is on stage, and a woman is sitting in a large booth by herself. Having established the setting, Nowak moves to focus on their two protagonists, Jess and Gwen.

It is important to know that Gwen uses the term "friend" sarcastically because neither one of them know the woman in the booth, but earlier in the day Jess had an awkward encounter during which the woman acted strangely. When the proprietor announces the first karaoke participant is Lynette, the strange woman takes the stage in a page-wide panel with no background and the proprietor is colored in a solid grey tone; thus, Lynette becomes the center of attention. Nowak uses the bottom tier of panels to build anticipation. In the first panel Lynette is just standing holding the microphone with a serene smile. The second panel cuts to Jess drinking her beer. Her facial expression is open to interpretation, but based on her brief encounter with the woman Jess might be thinking "This is going to be embarrassing." In the third panel Lynette begins to sing and the wavy ribbon that runs through the three panels of the bottom tier changes color and grows larger to become an unconventional word balloon. As is often true of panels on the bottom right of a page, this panel is a cliffhanger: We wonder what song Lynette will sing. We wonder how good or bad her singing will be.

On the third page, what had been a ribbon swells into a stream of song that weaves through the little pub, and based on Jess' reaction, the song is surprisingly beautiful and heart-wrenchingly sad. The full page is devoted to the progression of Jess' emotional

Figures 3.14a–c ***Girl Town*** **© Carolyn Nowak, courtesy of Top Shelf Productions/IDW Publishing**

response to the song. As we will see in Chapter 5, the page follows a conventional layout pattern, but that is not reality apparent because there are no panel borders. This page demonstrates that panels do not have to be enclosed in lines with white gutters between them in order to exist as moments of encapsulation and to be perceived as such by the reader. Most readers are going to understand that each time a picture of Jess appears on the page it is a different panel, as is the picture that cuts back to Lynette. The final panel of the page shows both Jess and Gwen from a distance. Some readers might sense this distance as stepping back so as not to intrude on Jess' emotional moment, but the encapsulation choice also functions to show the women's different reactions. Gwen's "Wow" punctuates the reader's affective experience of the page.

Casey Nowak's syntagmatic encapsulation choices create a sequential narrative that is easy to comprehend, even if one has not read the previous pages of the story. While there are many other image choices (paradigmatic options) that could have told the same narrative, Nowak's encapsulation choices work so well that it is difficult to imagine moments to show that would have been more effective.

Discussion Questions

1. Figures 3.6a–d shows four different depictions of the same moment from Batman's origin story. Which depiction do you find to be most effective? What is most effective

about it (clarity, emotional impact, etc.)? What are the paradigmatic choices that made this depiction better than the other three?

2. Go to an online site (such as https://comicbookplus.com/) where you can view old comic books for free. Look at some superhero comic books from the 1940s. How does the interdependence of word and picture within the panels of those 1940s comic books compare to the interdependence of word and picture in contemporary superhero comic books? Consider whether or not the words correspond to the duration of the action.

Activities

1. Based on context clues in the first two panels of Figure 9.12 (both words in captions and artwork in both panels), what is your interpretation of the span of time encapsulated in panel 2?
2. In "A Life in Comics" (Figures 5.12 a–g) Nick Sousanis encapsulates quite a few visual allusions to real places, fictional characters, and particular comic strips or comic books. Find a few such images that are not explained in accompanying captions. Do some research and write a brief description of what is being alluded to by these images. Hint: You might have to take a picture of the image and then do a Google image search.

Recommended Reading

Comics

Eisner, Will. *New York: The Big City*. Princeton: Kitchen Sink Press, 1986. [Subsequent editions by DC Comics and W. W. Norton]

In this collection of short, sometimes a single page, vignettes of life in New York City challenges himself to create a substantive narrative within a very limited number of panels.

Russell, P. Craig. *Fairy Tales of Oscar Wilde*. New York: NBM, 1994.

In these adaptations Russell must determine how best to encapsulate Wilde's prose stories. He not only provides drawings that bring Wilde's words to life but adds many wordless panels of visual storytelling that enrich the narrative.

Scholarly Sources

Eisner, Will. *Comics and Sequential Art: Principles and Practices from the Legendary Cartoonist*. New York: W. W. Norton, & Company 2008.

Adapted from his course at New York's School of Visual Arts, Eisner wrote this book to explain the fundamentals of graphic storytelling to aspiring cartoonists. However, as one of the first practitioner-theorists, Eisner also introduced concepts, such as encapsulation, on which comics scholars have built their theories.

Mikkonen, Kai. *The Narratology of Comic Art*. New York: Routledge, 2017.

Mikkonen uses the study of narrative comics as a mean expanding and refining narrative theory. The second section, Graphic Showing and Style, takes a deep dive into the narrative theory to examine how narration as showing operates in comics.

4 Composition of the Panels

When teenager Joe Kubert began drawing comic books in the late 1940s artists usually worked from fairly detailed scripts. Kubert preferred a full script because he liked knowing exactly what words were going to appear in each panel. That information helped him plan his art, both in terms of making sure the art fit with what was happening in the story and physically fitting the drawings into the panel so as to leave room for the necessary caption boxes, speech balloons, and thought balloons. Yet, Kubert still felt his composition choices could "push what the writer has done perhaps one or two steps beyond" what the writer had in mind.

There is a great deal of variation in how writers and artists work together, but the most radical departure from the full script method developed because editor and writer Stan Lee was overworked. During periods when Lee was responsible for writing multiple titles per month he would, with artists he trusted, skip writing a script and just give the artist a brief synopsis of the story he had in mind. Although this approach might have been developed at Fox Publications decades earlier, it became known as the Marvel Method. It evolved to the point that with a gifted storyteller like Jack Kirby, Lee would just verbally communicate a story idea in a couple of sentences. Kirby usually made caption and dialogue suggestions in the margins of each artboard, but Lee, wanting to develop characterization and interject humor, often expanded on those suggestions. That meant that unlike Kubert who composed his panels to allow for the words he knew would be there, Kirby had some of his incredible artwork covered by caption boxes and word balloons.

The full script method gives the writer primary control of encapsulation (the choice of what to show) and, in some cases, a good bit of influence on the composition of images in each panel. Yet, with a few notable exceptions, writers consider their panel descriptions as suggestions and are okay with artists improving on those suggestions. While we will use the term "artist" when we write about composing panels, you should be aware that in some instances, artists are rendering compositional ideas provided by a writer. It all depends on their working relationship.

Artist Fiona Staples has worked with writer Brian K. Vaughn on the *Saga* comic book series for a decade. They discuss each story arc before Vaughn begins to write scripts, and when Staples does receive a script from Vaughn she "likes to read the script and have an emotional experience and then channel that into drawing" (Vaughn qtd. in Holub 2018). Vaughn writes full scripts with brief but clear descriptions of what needs to happen in each panel (the encapsulation), but he leaves most of the decisions about how to show it (composition) to Staples. This chapter is about those "how to show it" decisions, and how those decisions can affect readers.

Objectives

In this chapter you will learn:

1. the elements of composition used in comics panels;
2. the impact art style has on the emotional reactions of the readers;
3. the three functions of images; and
4. the synergistic relationship between words and pictures in comics panels.

Harvey Kurtzman claims that most composition in early comic books "was static, pale, anemic," until Joe Simon and Jack Kirby's work on *Captain America* in the early 1940s created dynamic composition "through opposing lines that clashed and exploded all over the panels" (1991: 20) (see Figure 4.1). The comics of Simon and Kirby, as well as later art by Kirby, certainly had a great deal of influence on the composition in subsequent comic books. However, for some graphic novels or alternative comic books, in which the narrative contains less physical action and more conversation and emotion, the dynamism of Simon and Kirby's style composition can be inappropriate. Keep in mind that in creative hands, the comics form is quite pliable and any generalizations about form, including composition, might hold true for many comics, but certainly not all.

Figure 4.1 An example of the dynamism Joe Simon and Jack Kirby introduced to panel composition. All Winners Comics # 1 (1941) © 2023 Marvel Entertainment, Inc. and its subsidiaries.

Mise-en-scène

As we generalize about composition in comics, we are going to build upon a venerable concept. Film and comics borrowed from theater the concept of **mise-en-scène**, or "putting in the scene." Most of the mise-en-scène elements present on stage or screen can be depicted in a comic book panel: the "actors," background details, color, "lighting," perceived distance, angle, and "movement." Comic books also have some unique elements of composition: visualized sound, the blending of the pictorial and the linguistic, and art style.

Characters/"Actors"

The most important element of mise-en-scène in a panel is usually the character or characters whose actions constitute the narrative. Just as a film actor's performance can enhance a screenplay, the way an artist places and draws the characters in a comic can add nuances and subtext to a writer's script. Artist Sean Phillips says that drawing characters is "all about the acting, how the characters react to what's happening to them" (qtd. in Harper 2014).

Some artists stand up from the drawing board and partially act out what they are going to draw a character doing. Alfredo Alcala believes "the artist shouldn't just be a viewer—he should be involved in the action," and he imagines himself in the situations he is drawing. Alcala also points out that a comics artist is both the actor and the director (qtd. in MacDonald and Yeh 1994: 36). In fact, the comics artist single-handedly fulfills a number of the functions that would be performed by many professionals on a film crew: casting director (giving a character the right look for a part); director (making decisions about blocking, posture, gestures, facial expressions); cinematographer (making decisions distance, angle, and lighting, although the inker often contributes to the latter); production designer (providing the look of everything you see—set design, costume design, props, etc.).

Albert Monteys compares character design to casting a part and his initial drawings of the characters to auditions: "I knew what we wanted to convey in every character and for me it's a very intuitive way, you keep on drawing until you find something that talks to you with the character voice" (qtd. in Snyder 2020).

On stage or in a film a director might instruct an actor to move to a particular mark (location) to deliver a line or perform an action. The planned movement and placement of actors in space is known as **blocking**. We use blocking here somewhat metaphorically because the characters in a comic book do not literally move (although, as we will discuss later, there are a number of techniques for suggesting movement). The artist, sometimes with suggestions from the writer, decides where to place the various "actors" within a panel. If multiple characters are speaking in a panel, then blocking choices are constrained by speaking order—the first character to speak has to be on the left and the last to speak on the right.

Where characters are placed within a panel and how they are placed in relation to objects or other characters can influence the meaning that readers derive from a panel. Characters or objects in the foreground, as opposed to the background, are most likely to command the reader's initial attention. Placement can also influence the perception of power relationships. Generally, characters are perceived as more powerful if placed in the foreground or higher in the panel.

Blocking is only one aspect of acting. Chief among an actor's repertoire are posture, gestures, facial expressions, and vocal quality. On the comics page, the letterer provides the latter, while the artist enacts the other three. For example, on page three of Figure 3.14 the changes in Jess' facial expression and posture convey her reaction to the song. And on page four of "Fight Night" (Figure 4.17d) the contrast between the main character's facial expression and posture in panel six and panel nine conveys that his euphoria is quickly replaced by disappointment.

Let's take a look at how some of these aspects of acting are operationalized in an actual comic (Figure 4.2). The acting in panel one communicates tension. Both Omolola and

Figure 4.2 "Acting" in *Black Panther* # 1 (2022) © 2023 Marvel Entertainment, Inc. and its subsidiaries.

T'Challa sit in a very stiff posture, and they are not looking at each other. T'Challa has his hands in his pockets, a closed posture. In panel two, the body language loosens up a bit. Omolola makes an open hand gesture indicating that she is speaking the truth. T'Challa turns his head to ask a question. In panel three, T'Challa's expression seems to indicate that he is unmoved by Omolola's explanation/apology. In panel four T'Challa and Omolola turn away from each other. Their grief over the death of Jhai has not brought them together but has separated them. T'Challa's facial expression seems to be a mixture of grief, regret, and perhaps shame that his commands led to death and sadness for his subjects. As for vocal quality, notice how the bolded "was" in panels one and four gives emphasis to the statements being made.

Background Detail

In most comic books, figures (visual representations of characters) are the focus of the story and the reader's attention. However, the details depicted behind and around those characters are essential for establishing the setting and mood. Once the setting is established by background details, a vague sense of that setting persists in the reader's imagination, and details tend to become sparse or drop out altogether. In fact, there are times when continued depiction of a detailed setting can be counterproductive to the author's purpose. "When you've got a lot of 'background' detail," warns artist Richard Corben, "it can slow down the pacing of the story and may even detract from what the story is saying." However, Corben goes on to say that "sometimes it may be an important part of the story, such as the setting and the ambiance" (qtd. in Van Hise 1989: 53). In genres such as science fiction and westerns, background details can be as crucial to the narrative as any of the characters. The background details in a panel of original art from *Cowgirl Romances* (Figure 4.3) create a sense of the vastness and ruggedness of the West.

Figure 4.3 ***Cowgirl Romances*** **# 11 (1952). Art by Maurice Whitman. From the collection of Randy Duncan and Douglas Gilpin.**

Color

Most mainstream comic books have traditionally been ablaze with bright primary colors (red, blue, and yellow) Certainly, the colorful costumes are part of the appeal of superheroes. How would the concept of Batman be altered if his costume was a pastel color? Would the Flash seem as fast if he wore gray instead of red? Most mainstream comic book characters, from superheroes to cowboys to ducks, have a recognizable and unvarying color scheme. As European comics scholar Ann Miller points out, color can make the story easier to follow "by allowing characters to be rapidly recognizable from one panel to the next" (2007: 95). Skillful use of color can give a character dramatic impact in a given panel, and in recent decades coloring techniques have become more sophisticated and the color palette has become more varied, "As long as the colorist is aware of providing a contrasting background for [the] sake of clarity," advises colorist Bob Sharen, "the costume colors don't matter that much. Hue and value contrast will make almost any character 'pop' in a given panel." (personal communication, March 21, 1988).

Color can serve a number of affective functions. Color can create or amplify the reader's emotional reaction to the story. "Generally, anger, violence or any impact panel will have a hot color like red, yellow, or orange. Cool colors like blue and purple are used when the mood is sad and depressed" (Glynis Oliver, personal communication, March 15, 1988). Such coloring is used to affect emotions of the readers, but color can also be used to convey emotions of characters (e.g., green to indicate jealousy; gray to represent depression). Over the decades coloring in comics has become less literal and more expressive.

Using black and white instead of color can also affect the meaning of a story. Because many of the most ambitious and critically acclaimed comics works have told their stories without using primary colors, black and white, or at least subtle color (sepia tones, green ink, etc.), has become emblematic of serious comic books. Scott McCloud believes "colors objectify their subjects" and emphasize form rather than meaning, while "in black and white, the ideas behind the art are communicated more directly" (1993: 189, 192).

Figure 4.4 A striking use of chiaroscuro from Daredevil #189 (1982) from writer Frank Miller and artist Klaus Janson. © 2023 Marvel Entertainment, Inc. and its subsidiaries.

Lighting

With skillful use of shading and color, a comic book artist can simulate many of the lighting techniques employed on stage or in film. Will Eisner, drawing on his knowledge of theater lighting, was a pioneer in using lighting effects in comic books. According to Eisner, "an enormous amount of visual storytelling, and enormous amount of environment can be suggested by clever lighting" (qtd. in Viola 1987). Eisner was one of the first artists to bring the mood and the danger of the big city at night to the comic book page by simulating the low-key lighting of the film noir genre.

A comic book artist can use **chiaroscuro**, a stark contrast of light and dark, to funnel attention to a particular point in a panel (Figure 4.4). When the panel is mostly light, dark objects stand out, and when the panel is mostly dark, light objects stand out. According to comics art collector Kenneth K. Kirste, "when evenly balanced, the lighter parts of a work tend to stand out while darker ones recede" (1988: 14).

Distance

The distance from which readers perceive themselves viewing the scenery or action in a panel can influence attention and interpretation. One of the primary functions of the **extreme long view** is to create a context or sense of place. The **long view** can also be used to establish setting at the beginning of the story or scene. Repeated use of long views in a story (especially when not motivated by a scene change) tends to stress setting over character. The **medium view** creates a balance between the character and setting. A specific form of medium view is known in film as the **two shot**. The two shot frames multiple characters interacting so that their reactions to one another can be viewed simultaneously. The **close-up view** emphasizes character over setting because very little of the setting is visible and the character's **affect displays** (emotions indicated by facial expressions) are more in evidence. The **extreme close-up view** is often used to emphasize some detail (e.g., a ring, a scar, a signature) that is important to the plot.

Angle

Linguist Mario Saraceni reminds us that "the point of view from which each individual panel is drawn is a major aspect of the way in which meaning is conveyed in comics" (84). The **extreme high angle**, or bird's-eye view, can be used to present a subjective experience, suggest relationships, or make the reader an omniscient viewer. The **high-angle view** can be used to make something or someone seem small and weak or make the reader feel detached

Figures 4.5a–b A low angle emphasizes Brendan Behan's boisterous, exuberant mood, but then Doran uses a high angle to communicate his sudden swing to a darker mood. *Gone to Amerikay* (2012) © Derek McCulloch and Colleen Doran and DC Comics.

from the action. Panels that present an **eye-level view** tend to create identification with the characters and a sense of involvement in the action. A **low angle** can make the person or object being viewed seem powerful or menacing. The **extreme low angle**, or worm's-eye view, can make whatever is shown seem towering and powerful, but it can also make the reader feel omniscient by taking a vantage point usually unavailable to humans (Figures 4.5a–b).

Movement

While it is true that the images on the printed page are static, there are two types of "movement" that can be implied in comic books: **primary movement** (of people or objects in the frame) and **secondary movement** (of the frame itself). Comics artists have developed certain techniques to convey a sense of movement (see the discussion in Chapter 3), and they have to rely on the reader's imagination to perceive those techniques as actual movement.

Secondary movement, or implied movement of the frame, can be used to direct reader attention, control mood and tempo, suggest relationships, and make the reader feel involved in the action. The changing view in successive panels can mimic the five basic movements of the frame in film: panning (moving sideways), tilting (moving up or down), rolling (tilting to the side or even completely around), tracking or dollying (following a moving subject), and craning (can combine any or all of the other types of movement; a freedom of movement made possible in film by attaching a camera to a crane).

Visualized Sound

In comic books, any sound that is introduced into the story has to be visual, and is, therefore, an element of composition. Voice, sound effects, and music represented in comic books lack the realism found in an auditory medium, but they can be a great deal more expressive than they are in non-illustrated prose.

Figures 4.6a–b The bold and distinctive sound effects lettering created by Howard Chaykin and Ken Bruzenak make sounds a tangible part of the environment in *Time*^{2}: *The Epiphany* (1986) and *American Flagg!* #8 (1984). © Howard Chaykin, Inc.

Comic book dialogue and narration are usually presented in neat, clearly printed lettering. Such lettering is easy to read, but it does little to convey the **paralanguage** (volume, emphasis, rate, vocal quality, etc.) of human speech. Less tidy, but more expressive lettering comes closer to representing qualities of the spoken word. Aspects of paralanguage can be suggested visually by varying the size, thickness, and shape of both the words and the balloons or boxes that contain them.

Because of the "ZAP," "POW," and "ZOWIE" of the sixties *Batman* television series, onomatopoeic sound effects are probably one of the best-known features of the comic book. While such sound effects add the element of "sound" to the action, they also clutter the artwork, and often, probably also due in good measure to the *Batman* television show, seem juvenile. Yet some artists, particularly Walter Simonson, Howard Chaykin, and Ken Bruzenak, have created imaginative sound effects which, rather than impeding the artwork, become part of the page design and could even narrate a sequence of actions that we do not actually see in the panel. For example, in the second image in Figures 4.6a–b, the sound effects communicate that Luther made a heavy belly flop into the snow with a "*splongksh*" sound, grabbed a car bumper that popped off with a "*poinck*," and then the car sped away with a "*vrooom*."

Of the three types of sound, music is the one least effectively represented in comic books. The words of a song, and even the musical score, can be placed in a comic book panel, but for those who are not familiar with the song or do not read music, it is merely text. However, the pictures can give clues as to the type of music and the readers can fill in sounds from their own experiences (Figures 4.7a–b).

Figures 4.7a–b Even though the musical notes in these two panels from Peter Kuper's *The System* (1997) are identical, readers will understand the notes represent different types of music—the type of music to which a stripper might perform and the type of music a young skateboarder might enjoy. © Peter Kuper.

Art Style

Encapsulation, layout, and composition are what comic book creators do; style is how it is done. Contemporary comics artists might "draw" in a number of ways—a pencil, pen, or brush on Bristol board, a stylus on a tablet screen, or even paint on a canvas. Whatever the technology, every mark made on a page or screen has potential consequences for the meanings that will be derived from the panel. According to Eisner, "the reality is that art style tells the story" (1995: 155). The very manner in which an artist draws a line has expressive power. An artist can communicate emotional tone by varying width, direction, curve, or even the number of lines.

Modes of Representation

Most art styles can be categorized into one of two modes of representation. The **cartoon mode**, which grew out of the tradition of caricature, uses both simplification and exaggeration (Witek 2012: 29). Drawings are not detailed, but features (e.g., a bulbous nose or overly large feet) and proportions (e.g., an oversized head) are exaggerated, often for comedic effect. The **naturalistic mode** presents characters and settings as recognizable and conventional representations of either the world we know or presents a world of fantastic science or magic in a "realistic" manner. These modes refer to visual styles and narrative styles that can vary quite a bit in practice, and are not always mutually exclusive.

The realism of the naturalistic mode can create alienation because the reader can see that the character has a very specific appearance that does not look like her, while the simplification of the cartoon mode can create identification because the reader is allowed to see herself in the character. However, too much exaggeration of features in the cartoon mode also creates a specificity, one that marks a character as an **Other**. Exaggeration that is unflattering can further alienation by stressing the imperfections of the Other. Comic scholar and artist John Jennings believes that in comics "the images themselves work better as open ciphers that are filled by the audience" (cited in Batiste, Boelcskevy, and Lewis 2018: 12).

Quality of the Line

The quality of the lines used to create an image can affect how readers react to the image. Drawn lines are always expressive and they can imbue their subject with personality. Straight lines can feel serious or stern. Lines that curve and flow are often perceived to be beautiful or friendly (Bertamini et al. 2016: 154). The quality of a line can be altered (delicate, thick, elegant, or jagged.) to express an impressive "range of moods and emotions" (McCloud 1993: 126). Sean Phillips believes every line makes a difference, especially on faces: "An extra line on the face can age them terribly, or a line that is a millimetre out can make someone ugly" (qtd. in Hogg 2014).

Readers can develop expectations about story content and tone from the style of art before they even read the first panel. A clear line style is usually associated with a lighthearted adventure in which the heroes are sure to triumph over the bad guys (e.g., *Tintin, Tiny Titans*). An ugly (brut) art style is more likely to depict a pessimistic worldview in which triumph is not an option and the best the protagonist can hope for is survival (e.g., Ben Templesmith's cartoon-noir pencils and moody coloring in *Fell*; Keith Giffen's José Munˇoz-inspired style in the "Five Years Later" storyline of *Legion of Super-Heroes* volume 4). These are, of course, generalizations, and plenty of exceptions can be found. For example, in *Jimmy Corrigan: The Smartest Kid on Earth*, Chris Ware tells a bleak story in a clean line style, but the reader soon understands that like the title of the work, the art style is a commentary on the main character's delusions.

Style is difficult to reduce to categories and rules. Harvey (1996) believes that style is too elusive and individualistic to be fully described by the theorist or evaluated by the critic. Perhaps style is impossible to capture in concrete, referential language and must be described with expressive language. For instance, artist Neal Adams described the style of fellow artist Joe Kubert as coming "from a very primitive place," a "gut-level powerful style" full of "gristle," while artist Wally Wood's style has been described as "cool, clean lines and careful balance of light and shade" (Garriock 1978: 90). Jack Kirby's style is distinctive for what critic Thomas Durwood characterizes as "the unprecedented libidinous energy that surges through the main characters as they fight one another in violent scenes of really primal fear and intensity" (1974: 3).

The use of language in a comic book can also have a distinctive style. Certainly writer Stan Lee's captions and dialogue in early Marvel Comics had a distinctive style that was alternately operatic and breezy. Brian Michael Bendis became popular partly due to his ability to write dialogue that mimics the fragments and disfluencies of actual conversation. Brian Azzerello, in his crime comics such as *100 Bullets*, convincingly captures the vernacular of the streets. Eisner believes the best comic books are produced when the artistic style and the linguistic style are unified by a single person creating both the words and the pictures. In fact, Eisner sees comic book "writing" as a creative act done with both words and pictures wherein "the images are employed as a language" (1996: 5)

Discovering: NOT Starting from Scratch

Sometimes the artwork in comics can look very . . . familiar. That is because comics artists might base their art on previously existing images in a number of ways: homage, pastiche, use of reference images, and outright swiping pictures created by other artists.

Homage artwork is very obviously similar to a particular image or a particular artist's style and is often done by an artist who wants to pay tribute to a comic or creator that was personally meaningful to them when they were a young fan. Over the years quite a few comic book cover artists have blatantly, but respectfully, copied the overall design of landmark comics such as *Action Comics* # 1 or *Fantastic Four* # 1.

Pastiche is a form of imitation that can include swiping, but is usually more about mimicking familiar situations and cloning an art style rather than directly copying a drawing. In "A Life in Comics" (Figures 5.12 a–g) Nick Sousanis makes extensive use of pastiche as metaphors for periods of Karen Green's life by activating the associations that readers are likely to have for well-known comics and cartoons (e.g., Little Nemo indicating a dreamer). In Deadpool comics, pastiche contributes to the conventions-breaking humor because Deadpool, who in some iterations knows he is a comic book character, is likely to comment on the particular artist or story segment that is being imitated. Creators of pastiche do not wish to hide what they are doing because the desired effect can only be achieved if readers recognize what is being imitated.

The use of reference images is less obvious, but most comics artist do use them to some extent. In the pre-internet days, artists took photos, tore pages out of magazines, and stored them in file cabinets containing folders with labels such as trains, shorelines, and 1950s cars. Today, artists scan images or collet them online and store them on an app such as Pinterest. Drawing from reference images can give settings greater consistency and a sense of reality.

Some artists take photos of models who are posing following their instructions. Bechdel is one of the artists who use a camera with a timer to photograph herself posing for all the characters in her comics. Steve Lieber points out that "comics storytelling often calls for a sort of exaggerated clarity in the 'acting'" and, thus, artists "rarely find the right pose or expression in other people's photos" (2013). That is why he considers actors or fellow cartoonists to be excellent models.

Of course, there are times when impending deadlines can prompt artists to take shortcuts that involve outright copying, or tracing, someone else's artwork. This is often referred to as swiping. However, swiping is more than just a means of speeding up production of pages. Longtime comics artist Gil Kane admits "most comic artists start off swiping different guys until we have the strength to stand on our own" (qtd. in Van Hise 1989: 101). Stan Drake learned to draw by tracing the art in pulp magazines and later, in preparation for drawing comics with female leads, traced photos in fashion magazines "until I discovered what made them beautiful" (qtd. in Sim 2009). Many artists over the years have swiped poses and entire panels from Jack Kirby's artwork. However, as he was learning to draw comics Kirby himself used many direct swipes from great adventure comic strips, especially those by Alex Raymond and Hal Foster (Figures 4.8a–b).

Sometimes artist swipe, or "recycle," their own earlier artwork. Comics fan blogs are rife with examples of Greg Land repeatedly using the same character poses and

Figures 4.8a–b The same Batman image is used in both Detective Comics # 31 (September 1939) and *Detective Comics* # 33 (November 1939) © DC Comics.

panel compositions. Of course, artists have been doing this since the early days of comic strips and comic books. In the dramatic final panel recounting Batman's origin in *Detective Comics* # 33 the drawing shows the hero is in exactly the same stance (down to the hands) as a drawing in *Detective Comics* # 31. The stance looks almost exactly like a character stance in a panel of the Tarzan comic strip drawn by Hal Foster. Batman co-creator Bob Kane was still doing figure drawings in those days and he was notorious for drawing "inspiration" from pulp magazine and comic strip artwork. And, apparently, if Kane liked an image he had used once he did not mind using it again just a few issues later.

Inferences About Image Functions

In order to understand comic book communication, readers must make inferences about the functions of images, both pictures and words as images on the page (Hatfield 2005: 40–1). Most of these images are used to depict the world of the story, or what is often referred to as the **diegesis**. Readers must distinguish between **sensory diegetic images**, which depict the characters, objects, and sensory environment of the world of the story; **non-sensory diegetic images**, which depict specific memories, emotions, or sensations occurring within characters in the world of the story but undetectable by the senses; and **hermeneutic images**, which are not part of the world of the story, but instead comment on the story and influence how readers interpret it.

Sensory Diegetic Images

We experience the world through our five senses (seeing, hearing, tasting, smelling, and touching). Yet, aside from the tactile sensation of holding and turning the pages of a printed volume, reading a comic book is almost totally a visual experience. And, in fact, the vast majority of pictures in a comic represent visual experience: the people and objects we would see if we lived in the world of the story. Much of what we see in the real world is in motion. A reader can easily imagine similar motion in the world of the story if the artist has successfully employed a combination of the techniques of communicating movement explained in the previous chapter.

Nonvisual sensory experiences have to be suggested by visual imagery, and the readers have to "participate in the acting out of the story" in order to "feel" the sensory experiences suggested by the author's encapsulation and composition choices (Eisner 1996: 57). In the following section we will briefly consider how each of the other four senses can be stimulated and simulated in the readers' imagination by the comic book creators' use of images.

Readers seem to vary in how they experience the sound elements of a comic book. Some are actively engaged in imagining the sound effects and distinct voices of each character, while others understand the content of the dialogue without "hearing" the voices. How a reader responds to the sound images of a comic can be influenced by the skill with which the words are lettered. The expressive lettering of a cartoonist such as Dave Sim or a letterer such as Todd Klein can communicate volume, rate, inflection, and other vocal aspects of human (or Inhuman, gorilla, etc.) speech (Figure 4.9). Some "artists with a strong personality, like Robert Crumb, have a style of lettering—and a matching tone—that is unmistakenly [*sic*] theirs" (Pollman 2001: 17). In other words, we can "hear" an author's distinctive voice telling us a story.

Figure 4.9 Letterer Todd Klein creates a distinctive font and balloon—and thus, a distinct "sound"—for each character in this panel from *Sandman* #47 (1993). © DC Comics.

As comics scholar Gene Kannenberg, Jr. points out in his study of graphic text, even the shape of the balloon in which the text appears can communicate something about the nature of the sound:

> For *thought*, the balloon's edge is scalloped and the tail is replaced by a series of small circles or bubbles. *Whispering* is indicated either by forming the balloon with a dashed

> line or by using smaller-than-normal text. To convey *shouting*, a balloon's edge is spiked, or the text is made relatively larger than that used for normal speech. Similarly, *electronic speech* can be simulated by a jagged-edge or geometrically shaped balloon. *Sarcasm* has even been awarded its own iconic representation, the "dripping" word balloon (2001: 174).

Nearly all comic book lettering is now digitally applied. While computer lettering might lack the spontaneity of hand lettering, it can still be distinctive. Todd Klein has developed over a hundred computer fonts that he sees as "an extension of my personal style."

Dialogue is the type of sound most commonly represented in comic books, but the most dramatically presented sound images are the inventive and often boldly lettered words that represent nonvocal sounds, from the faint impact of a single drop of sweat to the shattering force of a super-powered punch. As evidenced by the Chaykin and Bruzenak sound effects shown earlier, comic creators are constantly developing new means, both subtle and outrageous, to communicate sound.

The sensation of taste is conveyed by both verbal and nonverbal reactions. Words such as "yum" or "yuck" can broadly indicate a positive or negative sensation of taste, but flavors are more precisely communicated by facial expressions. If in one panel a character puts something in his or her mouth and in the next panel is smiling. We take that as an indication of a pleasant taste, whereas we take a contorted face to mean a sour or bitter taste. A smell can be abstractly represented by graphic conventions, often first established in comic strips, such as lines wafting off a freshly baked apple pie. Odor can be implied by showing phenomena commonly associated with strong smells, such as flies buzzing around a garbage can or exaggerated but stereotypical character reactions such as a man holding his nose. In *Fun Home* (2007) Alison Bechdel uses a few scent lines but also takes the unconventional approach of labeling the smells of summer in the city. Bechdel's drawing of a busy New York street is accompanied by seven captions with arrows. One caption pointing down the subway says "urine and electricity," and one pointing at a pedestrian says "Brut" (a cologne popular in the time period depicted).

Subtleties of touch are not easily communicated in the comic form. Generally, only the most extreme tactile sensations, such as punching and blasting, are depicted in comic books. However, when more familiar touch encounters, such as handshakes and embraces, are pictured, they are "felt" in terms of a reader's own experiences of touch. Similarly, a sense of weight or pressure can be conveyed by postures associated with effort and facial expressions associated with strain.

The comic book form cannot truly show the world of the story, but can only suggest it by employing the device of **synecdoche**, using a part of something to represent the whole of the thing. All images on the comic book page stand for more reality than they can depict. First, the images are, by necessity, an abstraction from the real. Comic book drawings are often highly exaggerated or simplified, but even the most detailed drawings or paintings fall far short of reproducing reality. Second, because panels occupy a finite and often small space, the images in them usually show only a portion of objects and beings. Readers use their background knowledge to understand what is not shown. Even if Manhattan was not mentioned in a caption on the second page of "A Life in Comics" (Figure 5.12b), many readers would recognize the distinctive Chrysler Building and understand that it represents New York City.

Figure 4.10 In *Jar of Fools* (1994–7) Jason Lutes uses pictures rather than words in a thought balloon to communicate a hungry man imagining pigeons as a piping-hot meal. From *Jar of Fool*. Copyright Jason Lutes. Used with permission from Drawn & Quarterly.

Non-Sensory Diegetic Images

So far, we have only been dealing with depicting those aspects of the world that can be perceived with the senses. Comics artist must also find ways to represent those aspects of existence—thoughts, emotions, personality traits, and psychological states—that cannot be perceived by the senses. While they cannot actually be seen in the real world, in the comics art form these non-sensory aspects of the diegesis are often represented visually. Sometimes the communication is direct, as with thoughts written out in scalloped thought balloons. Occasionally artists employ pictorial representations of thoughts or feelings (Figure 4.10). For instance, one of the conventions established in comic strips is to use dotted lines and a dagger that seems to be emanating from a character's eyes to indicate the anger behind a look.

Other times, characters' internal states are represented by implication. For instance, in the graphic novel *Blankets* (2003), when Craig awakens the first morning in a strange house and does not remember where he is for a few moments, his confusion is represented by ellipses in the balloon above his head and, in the background, blank panels are interspersed with panels depicting fragments of memory (Figure 4.11).

Hermeneutic Images

Hermeneutic images, whether linguistic or pictorial, are not meant to represent sounds or objects that exist in the world of the story; instead they comment on the story itself. Words that serve a hermeneutic function are not embedded in the story; no one in the world of the story is speaking or thinking these words. Instead, these words are a commentary on the story and are addressed directly to the reader. While these words by necessity exist on the page as images, they are usually bland images, lacking the expressiveness of dialogue or sound effects. They are presented in a straightforward manner so that the focus is on the linguistic content. Readers are not expected to "hear" these words. Of course, there are always exceptions, such as the captions in which Stan Lee, a distinct personality to most Marvel Comics readers of the sixties and seventies, chatted with readers, many of whom imagined his voice.

The most powerful hermeneutic images are pictures that are rich in subtext, implying more than what is literally shown. Three common types of hermeneutic pictures are psychological images, visual metaphors, and intertextual references.

Figure 4.11 Craig Thompson masterfully portrays a confused state of mind in his autobiographical graphic novel *Blankets* (2003). Copyright Craig Thompson. Used with permission from Drawn & Quarterly.

A **psychological image** represents some aspect of a character's personality or state of mind. It operates much like the sort of non-sensory diegetic images illustrated in Figures 4.10 and 4.11). However, diegetic images portraying a state of mind are usually objective, an attempt to portray a "reality" of the world of the story, while hermeneutic images tend to be subjective, reflecting a particular narrative point of view. Consequently, psychological images serving a hermeneutic function are generally more exaggerated than non-sensory diegetic images. For example, the way cartoonist Roberta Gregory draws her parents (Figure 4.12) is not a realistic depiction—the reader is not meant to believe Gregory's mother is so vacuous that her face consists of only a smile and big eyelashes, or that her father has a mouth full of long fangs and squiggly lines emanating from his body. Rather, it is an insight into her attitude toward them, and the constant embarrassment she feels because of how she thinks other people view them.

This is an appropriate instance in which to note that in most cases hermeneutic images are layered over diegetic images. Gregory's drawings comment on her parents (hermeneutic) but also indicate the presence of her parents in the car (diegetic).

Visual metaphors use a picture of one thing to evoke the idea of something else. For example, in *Fun Home* Bechdel uses a visual metaphor to communicate the depth of her father's obsession with the historical restoration of their old home. Bechdel draws her father struggling under the weight of a pillar he carries on his shoulder in a manner sure to evoke Jesus staggering under the weight of the cross, particularly when considered in conjunction with the text in the accompanying captions: "It was his passion. And I mean passion in every sense of the word. Libidinal. Manic. Martyred" (7). In this example, the picture and the text collaborate to carry off the metaphor. What we are terming *visual metaphors* are not always strictly pictorial in nature, because picture images and text images in a panel often work together to create the association.

Figure 4.12 In *Bitchy's College Daze* (1997) Roberta Gregory provides a commentary on the personality of her parents by the manner in which she draws them. Copyright © Roberta Gregory. Courtesy of Fantagraphics Books (www.fantagraphics.com).

It is also usually true that the reader must understand broader contexts than just the information on the page in order to understand the metaphor. The publication of *Maus* brought Art Spiegelman a degree of fame and fortune to which he had not been accustomed. As he worked on *Maus II*, Spiegelman had qualms about his success. On the opening page of the second chapter of *Maus II*, these doubts are not clearly expressed in words but are cleverly suggested by visual metaphors. One of the visual conceits of *Maus* is that all of the Jews, including Spiegelman himself, are drawn as mice. The image of a human head behind the mouse mask seems to indicate that Spiegelman feels he is hiding behind or even defined by his own autobiographical persona from the graphic novel. In the third panel we see Spiegelman's drawing table atop a mound of naked corpses (as indicated by the flies). To read this image as representing Spiegelman's misgivings that he has built his career on the suffering of others, Holocaust victims in general and his own family in particular, the reader must understand the context of Spiegelman's earlier work, the arc of his career, and even aspects of his personality established in his earlier work. It is not uncommon for visual metaphors to derive their meaning from reference to other texts or events—that is, they are intertextual.

Intertextual images remind the reader of something he or she has encountered in other media (movies, books, paintings, TV shows, etc.). Some intertextual pictures refer to real-life events, but of course, most of us only see those events indirectly, as reports in newspapers or on television. A writer or artist might intend for a picture to be an intertextual reference, but whether the picture has the intended meaning for a particular reader depends on that reader's background knowledge. For instance, most Americans over fifty would immediately recognize the panel in Figure 4.13 as a reference to Jack Ruby shooting Lee Harvey Oswald, but the image might have no intertextual meaning for many adolescent and young adult readers.

Even the pencil lines with which a picture is drawn and the brush strokes with which it is inked can have a hermeneutic function. For example, in Figure 4.12 Roberta Gregory's commentary on her parents is communicated primarily by the clean and simple lines for the mother she considers to be simple-minded and a jagged, cluttered style for her always-angry father. Gregory's drawings of her parents, while not pure examples of the styles, tend toward two very different approaches to comics art often referred to as the *clear line style* and *ugly* (or brut) *art.*

Figure 4.13 This drawing of Speedball being shot in *Civil War: Front Line* #7 (2006) is an intertextual picture that will remind many readers of the famous photo or news footage of Jack Ruby shooting Lee Harvey Oswald. © 2023 Marvel Entertainment, Inc. and its subsidiaries.

Three panels from Craig Thompson's memoir graphic novel *Blankets* (2003) illustrate the three functions (sensory diegetic, non-sensory diegetic, and hermeneutic) of comic book images operating on a single page (Figure 4.14). The multiple pictures of the two brothers, Craig and Phil, are clearly sensory diegetic images; they are fairly realistically rendered representations of the brothers as we would see them if we were in the world of the story. The word images in balloons are also part of the sensory diegesis; they represent the spoken words we would hear if we were in the world of the story. The pictures of the landscape in panel one are sensory diegetic images giving us enough details that we can infer a woodland setting. The drawings of the trees are not hyper-realistic, but they clearly provide the idea of trees so we can, through the process of synecdoche, rely on our own experiences of the woods to complete the setting in our imaginations.

Figure 4.14 *From Blankets*. Copyright Craig Thompson. Used with permission from Drawn & Quarterly.

The background details in panel two demonstrate that images can operate in multiple modes. The pictures here do not represent a setting, but two internal faculties not accessible to the senses. They function as non-sensory diegetic images illustrating a blending of Craig's memory and imagination. Yet, due to the subject matter—a winged lizard and angels—and the ornate art style, these background images also serve a hermeneutic function. Thompson uses them to alert the reader that he is an unreliable narrator whose fertile imagination cannot always be trusted. The meaning of these images is only fully understood as a commentary on Craig's fanciful imagination when we consider them in relation to the background in panel three.

It is not unusual for a comic book artist to drop out the background details and focus on characters once a setting has been established. However, in panel three the choice to use no image is clearly hermeneutic when considered in the context of the previous two panels and Phil's dialogue in the panel: the blank background is a visual metaphor for Phil's lack of imagination. This metaphor is reinforced by Phil's matter-of-fact dialogue and the contrast to Craig's vivid imagination represented in the background details of panel two.

In this page from *Blankets*, the pictures and the words work well together to create levels of meaning, but even so, in the first panel Craig is frozen in an awkward stance, in the midst of walking up (or down) a bank, as he speaks a good bit of dialogue. Many comic panels have a less-than-perfect compatibility between words and pictures.

Blending Pictures and Words

Reading comics is an integrated perceptual experience that involves not only the decoding of linguistic and pictorial symbols but an understanding of the **interanimation of meaning** between the words and the pictures. That is, the reader must understand how text and pictures in the same panel each affect the meaning of the other, and how together they create a meaning beyond what is communicated by word or picture alone. Because we cannot simultaneously gaze at pictures and read words, there is not an instantaneous unity of perception, but an integration of two different ways of perceiving information. While never truly blending together, words and pictures do tend to become more like one another as they exist on the comics page. Jessica Abel and Matt Madden's cleverly titled textbook on creating comics, *Drawing Words & Writing Pictures*, reflects the reality that words are rendered as images on the page and pictures become textualized to the extent they can be read to produce meaning.

The blend of pictures and printed words is one of the characteristics that make comics a unique form of communication. However, this blend is not always an exact balance between the two components. Traditionally, the artwork has received the greatest emphasis. Reitberger and Fuchs make the generalization that a comic "is bad—that is it lacks effect—if it is too wordy where a picture would be more striking" (1971/1972: 230). However, a comic book that tackles weighty moral or philosophical issues is likely to rely on words to carry most of the meaning. There are even times when duplication between words and pictures can be effective.

It is the proper emphasis and interaction of pictorial and linguistics that is the basis of effective comics communication. In *Understanding Comics*, McCloud (1993) details categories of word and picture combination. In *word-specific* combinations, the pictures illustrate but do not significantly add to, a largely complete text. In *picture-specific* combinations, words do little more than add a soundtrack to a sequence told with pictures. Words and pictures communicate essentially the same message in the *duo-specific* combination. Cartoonist Art Spiegelman says he used to believe that "repeating what's in a picture in the words is bad comics by definition," but he has come to realize that overlap of the visual and linguistic "can create a strong mood, stronger than when you're given the information only one way or the other" (qtd. in Van Hise 1989: 81). In *additive combinations*, words amplify or elaborate on a picture or vice versa. In rare instances the pictures and the words seem to follow very different, non-intersecting narrative paths in *parallel* combinations. A *montage* combination uses words as integral parts of the picture. The comic book form is at its most powerful when words and pictures go hand-in-hand to convey an idea that neither could convey alone in an *interdependent* combination. Frank L. Cioffi suggests adding another type of word and picture relationship, the *disjunctive*, "where the word and image seem to follow a similar course yet in fact express opposing alternatives" (Cioffi 2001: 98). This type of word and picture combination is most likely to be found in alternative comics that seek to problematize previously held ideologies and deconstruct conventions of comics reading. The use of the disjunctive can create complexity and ambiguity that fits with the postmodern approach to comics.

Images in the Context of Other Images

The comprehension of what each picture image represents and what each text image means can be a virtually instantaneous and barely noticeable operation, but after that first glance, readers immediately begin modifying their understanding of the image by considering it in the context of the other images around it.

Cognitive (comprehension) and **affective** (emotional) reactions to an image are often influenced by reactions to other images in the same panel. For instance, a car shown with speed lines behind it out-distancing another car makes readers think about the speed at which a car can travel. Readers did not necessarily think about the weight of a car until they encountered that cover of *Action Comics* #1, with Superman holding a car over his head (Figure 10.10). The relationship between the images of the car and the man made the weight the most significant characteristic of the car for that particular drawing. In panels depicting a battle, Jack Kirby often drew flying debris that had no clear source, but it effectively conveyed the impact of a blast or a punch.

Figure 4.15 The pictures and dialogue of these two brothers in *Palooka-Ville* #4 (1993) create a contrast from which the readers gain information about each character. From *It's a Good Life, If You Don't Weaken*. Copyright Seth. Used with permission from Drawn & Quarterly.

Quieter and more complex interanimation of meaning can occur in simple conversations (Figure 4.15). In one of his semi-autobiographical comics, Seth depicts a visit with his brother, Stephen. Seth, neat and trim in his coat and tie, is frowning. Stephen, overweight and sloppy in his Bayfield T-shirt, is grinning. Seth holds a pen and Stephen holds a television remote. The assumptions readers make about each character are heightened by the contrast between the images. Understanding the relationship between the images in this panel leads to inferences about the relationship between the brothers. This panel is just one of a series of panels presenting the conversation, and each panel in the series adds more information and potentially alters the reader's assessment of the characters. And, of course, the interpretation of compositional elements in a panel is also likely to be affected by the reality, the individual experience, of each reader. Some readers will understand the interaction between Seth and Stephen through the lens of their own sibling relationships.

Inferences about the relationships between images create a synthesis of those images, an understanding of the panel as a totality. And it is not merely an understanding of the panel as a frozen tableau of related images, but as an event, or most often a segment of an event, spanning a certain period of time. A reader actively engaged with the story incorporates each panel, each segment of time, into the narrative that has been encountered up to that point and into the narrative that has been anticipated based on a scanning or peripheral awareness of yet-to-be-read panels on the page or the adjoining page. The process of incorporation and the flow of the narrative in the reader's imagination is facilitated by the manner in which the panels are arranged on a page, that is, the layout. In comic books and graphic novels the page is a unit of composition and often has a unity of form, operating as a portion of the narrative (a scene) or as an aesthetic piece (beautiful or interesting) that is meant to be experienced as a whole. We will consider layout of the page in more depth in the next chapter.

Analyzing: Art Style and Meaning

Mixing the clear line and brut art styles in the same story can encourage certain responses from readers, particularly when there is a stark contrast in how characters are depicted. In one of a series of "Waiting" vignettes (Figure 4.16) by Linda Perkins and Dean Haspiel, the waitress is drawn in a clear line style that makes her attractive, while customers who ask annoying questions are drawn in an ugly art style that makes them unattractive, if not repulsive. The art encourages a particular perception of the characters—nice waitress and exasperating customers.

Art style always affects readers in subtle ways that they do not consciously process, but when there is a marked change or inconsistency in style, such as drawing the characters in "Waiting" in radically different ways, art style captures a reader's attention and often demands an interpretation.

Of course, reaction to the "Waiting" vignette is not solely dependent on the art style. The drawings

Figure 4.16 "Waiting" in Keyhole # 1 (1996) Copyright Dean Haspiel and Linda Perkins

of the characters have clearer meaning and more emotional impact when considered in relation to the accompanying text, in which the waitress is patiently answering a question already answered in the very menu the customers hold in front of them. Comics readers have to make inferences not only about the function of images but also about the contexts and relationships in which those images appear. Images in a comic do not exist in isolation; they are encapsulated in a panel. And each panel exists within larger units of meaning—the page, the sequence, and the story.

It is not possible for a reader to passively receive meaning from a comic. Even comprehending what each picture represents and what each word means requires some effort, and moving beyond image comprehension to understanding the panel as a whole and how it fits into the overall narrative requires comics readers to make inferences about the functions of images and the relationships between images.

Artist Brent Anderson believes that for a comic to be effective, the reader has to be actively involved in creating meaning. Comics creators facilitate this process with their decisions about what to show and how to show it. If too little information is given then the story is incomprehensible, but if the artist provides too much information then the reading experience is boring. Art Spiegelman warns that if readers focus too much on individual lush illustrations they do not "enter into the panel to panel continuity, which is where comic book magic takes place" (qtd. in Van Hise 1989: 88–90). Says Anderson, "I try to give them just enough communication to be stimulating" (personal communication, August 13, 1999).

Discussion Questions

1. Many carefully selected and crafted details that might give nuance to the meaning of a story can be overlooked as readers are impelled through the story from action to action. This is particularly true for young readers, but even mature readers often do a rapid first reading, to experience the reading rush, and then go back through the book to appreciate elements of craft. Take another, more careful look at a comic book or graphic novel you read recently. Do you find significant diegetic or hermeneutic images you overlooked on your first reading? Does taking these images into account alter your interpretation of the story?
2. Look again at Figure 4.15. What inferences can you make about the personality of each character? What inferences can you make about the relationship between these two characters? Explain how the cartoonist's image choices influenced your inferences.

Activities

1. Design experiments to test one or more of the following hypotheses:
   - H1: language-oriented readers move through a comic book from one grouping of words (balloons, captions, etc.) to another, taking in pictures as secondary information.

- H2: visual-oriented readers move through a comic book from picture to picture, taking in words as secondary information.
- H3: visual-oriented readers are more aware of words as images (lettering technique, color, etc.).
  First, devise a way to measure the language or visual orientation. You might do this with a questionnaire to determine the amount of time each subject spends on reading activities (books, newspapers, etc.) and viewing activities (television, movies, YouTube, etc.). Another approach is to determine each subject's learning style using the free learning styles tests which are available on a number of websites.
- Next, devise a method for determining how each subject goes about reading a comic book. Will you observe them while they read? Will you rely on some form of self-reporting (questionnaire or interview) immediately after the reading? You might want to use a combination of these methods, or devise your own approach.

2. Read "Fight Night" (Figures 4.17a–d) and a) Identify a non-sensory diegetic image and explain what it means; b) Identify two different types of hermeneutic images and explain what meaning they convey.

Recommended Reading

Comics

Liew, Sonny. *The Art of Charlie Chan Hock Chye*. New York: Pantheon Books, 2016.
By mimicking the styles of dozens of comics artists and even particular comics, Sonny Liew uses genre characteristics and composition styles to create interpretive frames for various periods of Singapore's history.

Brubaker, Ed (w), Sean Phillips (A), and Elizabeth Breitweizer (C). *The Fade Out: The Complete Collection*. Portland: Image, 2018.
Sean Phillips' art, based on the meticulous research of archivist Amy Condit, is detailed and evocative of 1940s Hollywood. His use of blocking, posture, and facial expressions creates "acting" that convey a great deal about relationship that is never overtly stated.

Scholarly Sources

Gravett, Paul. *Comics Art*. New Haven: Yale University Press, 2013.
Gravett examines many of the special properties of sequential art, but particularly relevant to panel composition are Chapter 3 Silent Comics and Chapter 7 Style and Individuality.

McCloud, Scott. *Making Comics: Storytelling Secrets of Comics, Manga and Graphic Novels*. New York: Harper, 2006.
In Chapter 1 McCloud illustrates himself improvising a short comic panel by panel, and dealing with composition choices and techniques. The Chapter 2 sections about facial expressions and body language present very specific tools for "acting" in comics.

Figures 4.17a–d "Fight Night" from *Absent Friends* (2004) © Paul Grist

I FIND IT DIFFICULT TO SLEEP DURING THE NIGHT.
THE GUYS IN MY CORNER ARE VERY SUPPORTIVE...
VITAMIN C – THAT'S WHAT YOU NEED...
ORANGES PLENTY OF ORANGES
GUARD YOUR RIGHT
GO FOR IT! GO FOR IT!
SMASH IMINA FACE
OK MUCUS FACE ---
EAT VITAMIN DEATH!!
MUNCH MUNCH
MUNCH MUNCH
BOP
MAYBE IF YOU'D PEELED THEM...
AN APPLE A DAY KEEPS THE DOCTOR AWAY...
GUARD YOUR LEFT
YDOINGREAT! YDOINGREAT!
SMASH IMINA FACE
I FIND IT DIFFICULT TO WAKE DURING THE DAY.

ah...
ah...
ah...
CHOO!
KIND FRIENDS ENQUIRE AFTER MY HEALTH...
SO TELL US... HOW DO YOU FEEL AT THE MOMENT?
BOUNCE
BOUNCE
BOUNCE
I'B FEELIG A BID ROUGG...
LOOK— THIS IS STUPID ...
WE SHOULDN'T BEHAVE LIKE THIS...
I MAKE A PLEA FOR REASON...
OUR LIVES ARE TOO SHORT TO WASTE THEM IN THIS KIND OF SENSELESS VIOLENCE...
Y'GOTTA LIGHT PAL?
certainly -here you are...
YOU SEE? IT JUST GOES TO SHOW THAT WE CAN HELP EACH OTHER - WE CAN BOTH LEARN AND GROW FROM THIS EXPERIENCE ...
IS IT JUST ME OR IS IT GETTING WARM IN HERE?
I AWAKE ONE MORNING...
TO FIND THE BUG ASLEEP AT THE FOOT OF MY BED.
Z

I WATCH IT SLEEPING... SO CALM & RESTFUL, AT PEACE WITH THE WORLD...
Z
OK BUG-
JUST GET OUT OF MY LIFE!
I'LL GET YOU FOR THIS...
YOU'LL BE SORRY...
EXIT
LAYDEEZ AND GENNELMEN ...
AFTER TEN DAZE... THE WINNAH!
KNOCK KNOCK
JOANNA OPENS THE DOOR - BUT I CAN SEE IN HER EYES SHE WON'T BE COMING OUT TONIGHT.
SNIFF
GOTCHA!

5 Layout of the Pages

When she began drawing *Iron Man* (volume 3) in 2000 Alitha E. Martinez was one of only two women doing the lead art on a Marvel Comics title. She is still one of the few AfroLatina comics professionals. Even though she was widely praised for her artwork in *Black Panther: World of Wakanda*, she was recruited for high-profile series such as *Nubia and the Amazons* and has been hired by her alma mater, The School of Visual Arts, to teach cartooning, Martinez still remembers what it was like to have to prove her ability on each new assignment. One way she proves herself is with page layouts that are effective sequential storytelling, but also aesthetically pleasing.

As Martinez reads a script, she envisions it as a movie and watches that "movie" over and over in her mind. Then she begins to draw the "stills" from that movie that represent the moments of prime action. As she is deciding which of those moments need to be together on a page and how they should be arranged she considers which choices will best serve the story. "The hardest part of this," she says "is letting go of my vision of the script to be certain that I'm capturing what the writer and the editor wants" (qtd. in McMillan 2019).

In 2021, Martinez helped create the slightly animated motion comic *Road to Wakanda: Fathers and Sons*, to provide backstory for a forthcoming War for Wakanda expansion for *Marvel's Avengers* video game. To take on this new challenge she adapted her techniques for spatial layouts by adding the element of time. That allowed Martinez to incorporate more of the moments from the "movie" in her mind. Martinez explains: "In comics, too many panels that don't serve the story only slows it down. When a comic is in motion, those shots, that would otherwise be superfluous, actually help the transition from one scene to the next" (qtd. in Stone 2021).

Whether working on print comics or motion comics, Martinez considers herself to be "one part of a collective that is working together to bring the story to life" (qtd. in McMillan 2019). Keep those words in mind as you read this chapter. Even though we will be writing in terms of artists making layout choices, they often do so with input or inspiration from collaborators (Figure 5.1).

Objectives

In this chapter you will learn:

1. the categories of comics page layouts;
2. the tensions between the tabular and liner natures of a comics page; and
3. how readers perform closure to create meanings.

Layout concerns the relationship of a single panel to the succession of panels, to the totality of the page, and to the totality of the story. A cartoonist or writer-artist team constructing a comic book page must consider how the meaning of each panel is affected by the variables of size, sequence, and juxtaposition.

Structure of the Page

In the early years of the comic book medium, the application of both size and sequence was standardized. The first American comic books consisted of newspaper strips cut and re-pasted for a page format. Because most newspaper strips had a standard vertical dimension, it was easy to arrange them in three or four rows across the page. Even after comic books began publishing original material, the three-tier or four-tier format was the standard layout for most comic books of the forties and fifties. Look back at that dynamic *Captain America* page from 1941 (Figure 4.1) and you will see that, despite the slanted, jagged panel border and the action lapping over the border, the page is constructed in **tiers**. In the 1940s, Will Eisner, who was working outside the traditional comic book industry with total editorial control over the weekly newspaper insert he produced, was one of the few artists experimenting with variations of the traditional grid.

In the late sixties and early seventies, more and more artists began to break free of the strict grid layout. For the first few decades, the comics industry standard was for artists to draw on a Bristol board twice the dimensions of a printed comic book. In the late 1960s the standard changed to a smaller, one-and-a-half size, board. The entire board was within the field of vision as artists worked, and they were more aware of the page as a whole and unit of design. This prompted artists such as Carmine Infantino, Gil Kane, Jack Kirby, and Neal Adams to evolve their layout styles. They were soon followed by waves of innovative young artists such as Jim Steranko, Barry Smith, Mike Kaluta, and later Colleen Doran, Jae Lee, David Mack, Karl Kershl, David Aja, J. H. Williams III, etc.

This matrix of bordered panels in tiers, with all the panels and tiers being clearly separated by **gutters** (white spaces between panels), has become known as the waffle-iron grid (or *gaufrier* by the French comics scholars who first applied the metaphor to comics pages). Renaud Chavanne (2010) considers a strip of panels to be the underlying organizing principle of the comic art form. In most comic books and graphic novels tiers of such strips of panels are stacked on a page to form a waffle-grid. If we accept Chevanne's theory, then every comic page layout is a waffle-grid, a variation on the waffle-grid, or a purposeful abandonment of the grid. Perhaps that is true, but let us consider a more precise way to classify the types of comics page layouts.

The classification system that follows was derived from theories of layout advanced by Renaud Chevanne, Benoit Peeters, and Thierry Groensteen. For printed comic books or graphic novels there are three broad categories of page layouts: Conventional, Rhetorical, and Aesthetic.

Conventional Layout

We use the term conventional because a strip of panels of all the same height is still the basic format of comics strips, tiers of such strips were the primary format used in comic

Figure 5.1 Artist Alitha Martinez extends a non-bordered panel across two tiers of the page to create a visually interesting fragmented page layout without disrupting the reading flow. *Nubia and the Amazons* #6 (2022) Stephanie Williams and Vita Ayalya (story), Alitha Martinez and Mark Morales (art) © DC Comics.

books for decades, and, though it might be considered a bit old-fashioned in the 2020s, the waffle-grid (hereafter simply called "the grid") is still employed in many contemporary comic books and graphic novels. Yet even when the convention of the grid is present there are variations in how it is implemented. Grids can be regular, semi-regular, or fragmented.

In a **Conventional Regular Layout** there are generally three or four tiers with two to four panels in each tier. What makes it regular is that all the panels in a tier are the same or close to the same height. While at first glance the lack of panel borders might make the page seem unstructured, the third page of the *Girl Town* excerpt (Figure 3.14) actually conforms to the conventional 3 × 3 waffle-grid, with the slight variation that there are only two panels in the top tier. And because Gwen, sitting on the right in panel one, is exactly aligned with characters in the two tiers below it, the page seems like a 3 × 3 grid. The grid structure is important for understanding this page. The only picture of the singer occupies the center of the page, the middle panel of the middle tier. Being at the center, it is clear she is the source of the emotional impact in the other panels; her song permeates the page.

In a **Conventional Semi-Regular Layout** there is a clear grid structure in which all the panels in a particular tier are the same height, but there is some horizontal variation. A panel unit within the grid might be split to create two smaller panel units. Two or more panel units in the grid structure might be combined to form a larger panel unit. When we use the term "panel unit" we are referring to the underlying structure, not to actual drawn panels.

Look at the four pages of "*Fight Night*" (Figures 4.17 a–d). Each page has at least one tier of four panels. The underlying structure is a 3 (tiers) x 4 (panels) grid. On the second page, in the middle of tiers one and three, you can see instances of two-panel units being combined into one At the top left of page three you can see an instance of one-panel unit being split into two-panel units.

On a page from a Supergirl comic (Figure 5.2) Amanda Conner breaks a panel unit into four small overlapping panel units. The overlapping panels depict distinct moments of time that are very close together to show Supergirl passing out. The fourth, totally black panel, indicates Supergirl is unconscious, and the fact that it overlaps just a bit with the following larger panel indicates that she has been unconscious, at least part of the time, in the spaceship in which she wakes up. It is an unusual use of panels, but easy for readers to understand.

Figure 5.2 Panels from "Supergirl." ***Wednesday Comics*** **(2009) Jimmy Palmiotti (story), Amanda Connor (art) © DC Comics.**

In a **Conventional Fragmented Layout** there is an underlying conventional grid structure, but it can be less noticeable because, in addition to possible horizontal variations, there are vertical variations, panels that extend across two or more tiers. The page from *Nubia and the Amazons* (Figure 5.1) has three panels, each in its own page-wide tier. The

Figure 5.3 *The Unstoppable Wasp* # 5 (2018) Jeremy Whitley (writer), Gurihiru (art) © 2023 Marvel Entertainment, Inc. and its subsidiaries.

second panel has no border and fragments the page because the large drawing of Delphine intrudes into the first panel. It is a fairly mild intrusion and does not disrupt the reading path on the page. Fragmentation in a layout from *The Unstoppable Wasp* (Figure 5.3) might create some confusion about how to move through the panels at the bottom of the page if not for path guidance techniques that we will elaborate on in the Narrative Flow section of this chapter.

Conventional layouts are fairly neutral; they, generally, do not have a great deal of impact on a reader's cognitive or affective responses to a comic. Perhaps that is because the structure is usually somewhat "invisible" to the reader, especially if the reader is absorbed in the narrative. Thierry Groensteen considers page layouts to exist along a continuum ranging from discreet (not calling attention to itself) to ostentatious (meant to be impressive) (2007: 97–9). Conventional layouts tend toward the discrete, but layouts in the next two broad categories are more noticeable, with some of them approaching the ostentatious end of Groensteen's continuum.

Rhetorical Layout

It might seem odd to use **rhetoric**, a term normally associated with spoken language, to describe comic book pages. However, over the centuries communication theorists have expanded the concept of rhetoric and applied it to all modes of human communication, including visual symbols. Yet, our basis for applying the term to the layout of comics pages was there centuries ago in Aristotle's definition of rhetoric: "The art of finding the available means of persuasion in any given situation." The important aspect for our use of the term is that rhetoric adapts to situations. A panel is rhetorical when the size, shape, or placement adapts to the content within the panel or to the deeper meaning that content is meant to convey.

A **Rhetorical Layout** is meant to influence how readers understand and react to the narrative presented in the comic. In fact, the rhetorical layout is a reflection of the artist's own understanding and reaction to the imagined or scripted narrative. While some rhetorical layouts might partially or totally break free from the grid, it is possible to have a layout that fits within one of the conventional categories and also serves a rhetorical function. Rhetorical layouts can be classified into two different, but not always distinct categories: Rhetorical Content and Rhetorical Subtext.

In a **Rhetorical Content Layout** the size, shape, and placement of a panel are determined, to some extent, by the actions or objects contained within the panel (inspired by Peeters 1991, 1998). Take, for example, the first page of Figure 4.17, where a large panel is needed to clearly establish the recurring metaphor of a boxing match. This is a subtle example, but rhetorical layout is admittedly a subjective category. It can be easy to overlook, but if you set out to look for it you might perceive it on almost every page.

The Supergirl page (Figure 5.4) is, for the most part, a semi-regular layout with four tiers of panels and an expanded panel in the third tier. However, "outside" of the grid structure there are six small inset panels that overlap with some of the panels in the grid. In most of the panels, the figure of Supergirl is seen from a long or extreme long distance, which lets the reader know how she is positioned in relation to the spaceship and the aliens. The inset panels, all extreme close-ups of Supergirl's face, let the reader see her emotional reactions

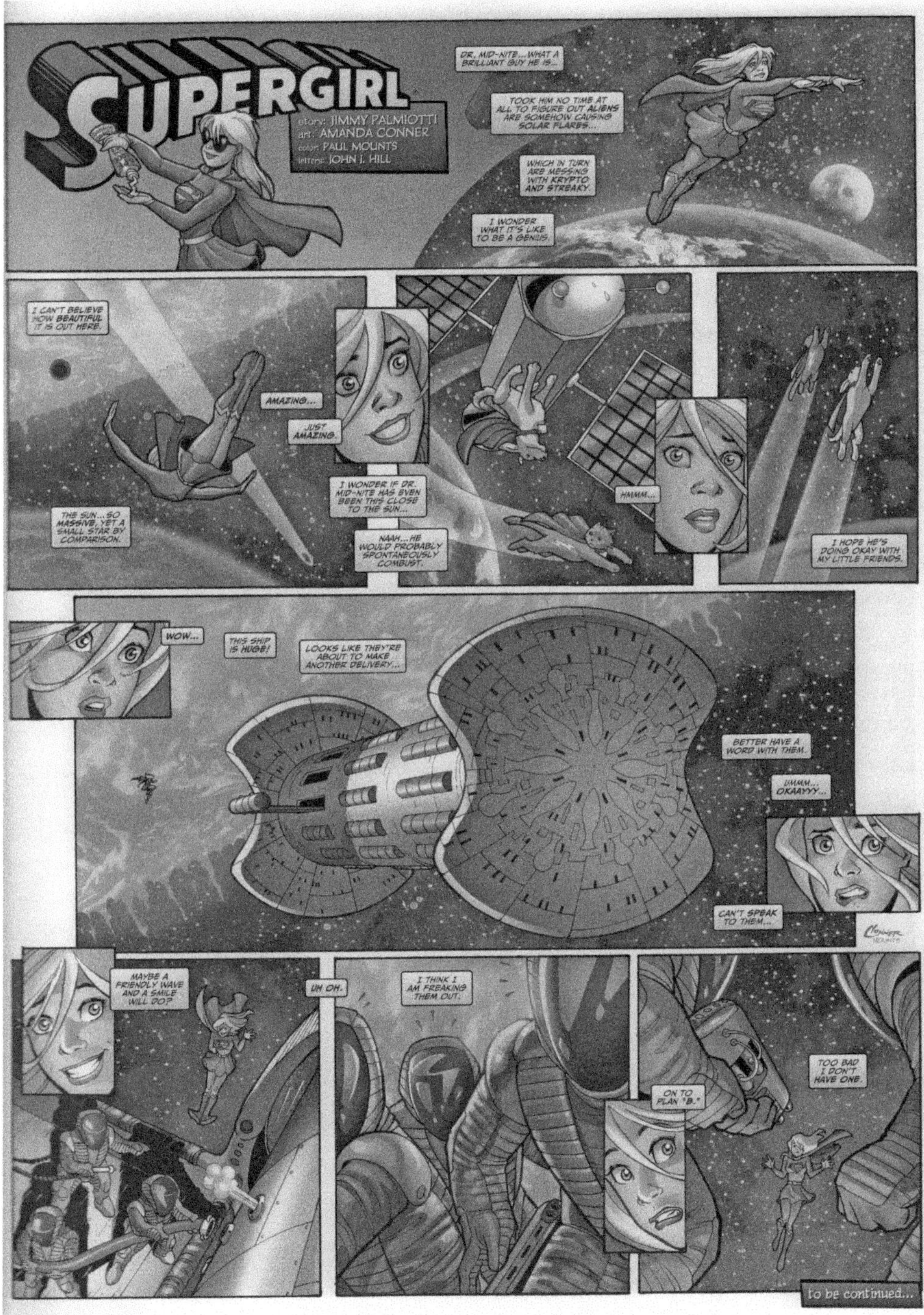

Figure 5.4 "Supergirl." *Wednesday Comics* (2009) Jimmy Palmiotti (story), Amanda Connor (art) © DC Comics.

to the spaceship and the aliens. Supergirl's facial expressions are important actions that require close-up panels in order to be visible to the reader. Perhaps the inset panels are enough to move the page from the Conventional: Semi-Regular category to the Rhetorical Content category. It is a judgment call.

A **Rhetorical Subtext Layout** is meant to enhance the narrative by adding levels of meaning that would not exist in a conventional grid. Certain design elements or perhaps the entire page layout operate as a hermeneutic image that requires interpretation, and that act of interpretation forces the reader to consider a deeper layer of meaning for what is depicted on the page.

In the comic book series *Promethea*, drawn by J. H. Williams III (based on detailed suggestions from writer Alan Moore) virtually every page contains allusions and symbols, and the artwork both reflects and operationalizes mysticism. Many pages have a conventional grid, but sometimes, in a slender panel in the fold, an image or sensation from another "reality" will intrude on the main narrative. On other pages a conventional grid is totally supplanted by a collage of images. On some pages the shapes of panels are evocative of a culture, a genre, a mythic concept, or the sensations (sometimes mystical in nature) that characters are experiencing. *Promeathea*, whose main character is the idea of human imagination, is a story about stories and a treatise on various doctrine of mysticism. There is a narrative, characters are on a quest, but the experience of reading *Promeathea* is more important than following the narrative in the comic book series. Nothing less than complex rhetorical layouts could achieve the effect Alan Moore desired. The pages in *Promeathea* look very different than the average comic book pages, but even layouts that appear to be very conventional can communicate subtext. In the graphic novel *Watchmen*, by Alan Moore and Dave Gibbons, the page layouts are based on the three tier, nine-panel classic waffle-iron grid, but there are width and height variations that are rhetorical in nature. Many of those variations are associated with two larger-than-life characters. Dr. Manhattan appears in tall panels that fracture the grid, not only because he can increase his size, but also to reinforce the idea that he has transcended humanity. Ozymandias considers himself a superior being who has transcended human concepts of good and evil, and his oversized ego is, perhaps, hinted by the large panels he often inhabits.

The third broad category of layout is easier to spot because, by its very nature, it calls attention to itself.

Aesthetic Layout

Most **Aesthetic Layouts** are toward the ostentatious end of Thierry Groensteen's discreet-ostentatious continuum, and Groensteen considers a layout as ostentatious if it is meant to "attract attention to some remarkable quality of itself" (2007: 98). Such remarkable qualities usually consist of a combination of the clever arrangement of the panels on the page and bravura artwork.

Splash pages, two-page spreads, and full-page or two-page panels containing inset panels are the most obvious types of aesthetic layouts. Such pages command the reader's attention and appreciation. They operate as pin-ups that show off the artist's talent. In superhero comics they might also celebrate the prowess or grace of a character (Figure 5.11). On a number of occasions, comics pioneer Will Eisner dismissed aesthetic splash pages as "pretty wallpaper, but poor storytelling" (personal communication, May 4, 1993). Yet, most of Eisner's splash pages for *The Spirit* were carefully, and often cleverly, designed aesthetic layouts. Of course, these aesthetic layouts were the first panel of the comic and set the tone for the story. Readers could spend time appreciating that opening panel, but when they turned the page Eisner wanted them immersed in the narrative.

A page does not have to consist of one large splash page to be considered an aesthetic layout. Some pages that are beautiful to behold contain pictures and words that provide crucial narrative information. You cannot simply admire them and turn the page (Figure 5.5). Some of the best mainstream examples of aesthetic layouts in comic books can be found in the work David Mack and Joe Quesada did on the *Daredevil* series.

Groensteen cautions readers not to be too quick to dismiss a page as merely decorative because ". . . an extremely divided page layout, one that is rowdy or dislocates the frames, will appear as rhetorical (and not as decorative) if it accompanies, highlights, or 'translates' a chaotic situation, a breathless high-speed chase, an alcoholic crisis, or an illustration of the madness of the protagonist" (2007: 99). For example, Jack Kirby drew many magnificent splash pages and two-page spreads suitable for framing but they were not purely aesthetic layouts. They functioned as rhetorical layouts because the size was dictated by the content (vast cosmic panoramas, massive battles with dozens of combatants, the technological jungle beneath Wakanda, etc.) or helped to convey a subtext (the mythic scope of his stories).

You should not think of these categories as mutually exclusive. The rhetorical category in particular can overlap with the conventional and the aesthetic. A page that employs a conventional grid can also serve a rhetorical subtext function, such as in *Watchmen* where the strict use of a nine-panel grid in scenes featuring Rorschach is consistent with his regimented lifestyle and unwavering moral code.

Keep in mind, page layout categories are theoretical constructs, and what creative artists do in practice does not always fit easily with theory. And, the categories themselves have some overlap. What percentage of the height and width variations to a grid have to be motivated by content in order to move the page from a fragmented classification to a rhetorical classification? We do not know or particularly care about the answer to that question. Understanding the concepts of fragmented layout and rhetorical layout are more important than trying to force every comics page into a particular category. This classification system is just a tool for helping you think about the structure of comics pages in a systematic way so that you derive more meaning and satisfaction from reading comics.

Pages on Screens

Most of the theories about how the comics art form communicates are theories about comics on the printed page. By the time this book is published it is likely that many of you will be doing the majority of your comics reading on a screen (as does one of the authors). Whether or not the theories advanced in this and the preceding chapters will be applicable to the screen reading experience depends on the format in which the comic was created and the device on which it is being read. When reading the digital version of a print comic on a tablet pretty much all of the formal theories covered in this book can apply. However,

Figure 5.5 This is an aesthetic layout meant to be appreciated as a work of art, but it also introduces a new character, Maya Lopez, and provides a good bit of information about her. *Daredevil* vol. 2 # 9 (1999) David Mack (story), Joe Quesada (art) © 2023 Marvel Entertainment, Inc. and its subsidiaries.

if you use the guided view that displays one panel at a time you are not experiencing page layout or the same sort of juxtaposition of panels found in print comics.

Older web comics, unless they displayed only one panel per day, used layouts similar to print comics layouts. They used a grid structure, but because they were made for a wide computer screen it was a modified grid, often with only two tiers and more panels per tier. As more people are reading comics on a phone, comics are being formatted as a column of long, narrow images that fit the typical phone screen. Viewing these comics usually involves scrolling and seeing one panel at a time. Because the panels are narrow they tend to show only one character at a time. However, comic creators are finding ways to adapt to these limitations. For example, some have begun to use an occasional split-screen panel, that is two long, very narrow panels side by side (Figure 5.6). These split-screen panels can convey action and reaction, simultaneity, contrast, visual metaphor, a melding of concepts, commentary on character relationships, and possibly much more. Hassan Otsmane-Elhaou (2016) compares the impact of these split-screen panels to the Kuleshov Effect, an early twentieth-century experiment by Soviet filmmaker, theorist, and teacher Lev Kuleshov, that demonstrated the meaning of an image changes as various images are displayed next to it.

Figure 5.6 ***Jaeger*** **(2016) Ibrahim Moustafa (story and art) © Ibrahim Moustafa.**

In moving from page to screen some aspects of the form that current comics scholars consider to be essential might cease to exist. In some instances, we lose the page as a unit of meaning, and without simultaneity and juxtaposition the relationships between panels will be radically different than what is described in this chapter. When we move through a comic panel by panel, never looking at a full page, and when sound and motion are added to a comic it is arguably a different medium. If you experience a comic on an **infinite canvas**, on which the reading path might move in any direction for a (theoretically) infinite digital distance, well, theories about that sort of "layout" are still being developed. Hopefully some of you reading this book will develop new theories of the digital comics form and we will be quoting you in the fourth edition.

Discovery: Thumbnailing It Down

Although every artist has a unique process, many comic professions start their page designs with a process called **thumbnailing**. According to Carl Potts (2013), "Thumbnailing is a form of brainstorming. As with all forms of brainstorming, many of the initial ideas may not prove useful to the story for various reasons (e.g., poor design, wrong angle, too cliched). However, some of the nonuseful thumbnailed may act as springboards, spawning other ideas that could be more helpful." An example of this process is depicted in Figure 3.1, which shows creator Neil Gaiman's thumbnails for a Sandman story.

Thumbnails are not necessarily as detailed as a fully rendered page though they help many artists to conceptualize how they will build the story. "They're like a small model of the final page," says artist Pepe Larraz. "They have to be small because you have to do it very fast, and discard it if it doesn't work. You can't rely too much on it, because they're just tests. On those thumbnails, I design the storytelling, the camera angles, and the panel composition with light and shade" (qtd. in Marnell 2019). Cartoonists Jessica Abel and Matt Madden have observed the variation in approaches among their colleagues, "Thumbnailing can take many forms. Some people draw them small but neat, then blow them up on a photocopier or scanner in order to use the thumbnails as a guide for pencils. Some people's thumbnails are crazy messy."

Whether they be messy or neat, thumbnails may be the way a story itself comes together. Veteran storyteller Walt Simonson reports, "Once the thumbnails are done, I will write the story from the thumbnails. Essentially, what I try to do is to keep everything as loose as possible up to the last moment, to allow for revisions, new ideas, new inspirations, whatever. It keeps the creative process lively along each step of the way and maintains a high flow of energy" (qtd. in Markstein 1994).

The thumbnail: So much power from something so small.

The Tabular and the Linear

Due to the nature of the comic book/graphic novel form, each panel is both an element of encapsulated action (perceived as time) and an element in the design of the page layout (perceived as space). Scott McCloud claims that "wherever your eyes are focused, that's now. But at the same time your eyes take in the surrounding landscape of past and future" (1993: 104). Each page is experienced as both linear (a sequence of events encapsulated in panels) and holistic (a designed, or at least planned, object).

Pierre Fresnault-Derulle (1976) was perhaps the first theorist to stress the relationship and tensions between the tabular (the *planche*) and the linear (succession of panels), and his ideas were expanded on by Benoit Peeters (1998, 2007). It should be noted that when these, and other French comics scholars, use the term *planche* it denotes more than simply page. A *planche* is a designed unit, be it sixteen small panels or a single splash page, that is placed on a page. In this book we are using "page" in much the same way—to mean what is placed on the page, not simply a physical piece of paper or a computer screen.

Andrei Molotiu's concept of **iconostasis**, "the perception of the layout of a comics page as a unified composition" that we "take in at a glance" (2012: 91) provides another perspective on the tabular. Iconostasis emphasizes, and the term itself explains, the tension between the tabular and the linear. If readers deem the page as a whole to be an icon, an image to be admired or at least appreciated, that results in a stasis, a stoppage or at least slowing the reading of the narrative. While iconostasis will always impede, to some degree, the linear impulse to move from panel to panel, Molotiu seems to indicate that the highly designed and highly unconventional page, what we have called aesthetic layout, is most likely to create a strong iconostasis that overpowers the linear impulse.

Comics pages can be not only a unit of design but also a unit of meaning. Pages often encapsulate a full scene or an otherwise meaningful segment of the narrative. We are using the term "unit" to mean a part of a larger, more complex whole, but also to mean something that has a specified function. When a page meets one or both of those definitions it might be said to be a unified composition. A good example of a page with unity of composition can be seen in Figure 5.4. Harkening back to the days when some comic strips occupied a full newspaper page on Sundays, DC Comics published *Wednesday Comics* in a broadsheet format. For twelve weeks *Wednesday Comics* contained one page from each of the fifteen ongoing stories. Because readers were seeing only one page of a story each week, those pages tended to present a narrative segment with its own beginning, middle, and end. Figure 5.4 is one such page from the Supergirl story, written by Jimmy Palmiotti and drawn by Amanda Connor. The first narrative panel (after the title panel) shows Supergirl flying into space, initiating the narrative segment. By the end of the page, in the bottom right-hand panel, Supergirl is in a dire situation, and readers are presented with a cliffhanger that creates anticipation for the installment that will be available next Wednesday. Each tier has its own unity: First tier—departing Earth; second tier—flying through space; third tier—finding the spaceship; fourth tier—encountering the aliens.

We can add to the tabular and the linear a third aspect (and a third tension) of comics layout—Molotiu's concept of sequential dynamism. Molotiu defines **sequential dynamism** as "formal visual energy created by compositional and other elements internal to each panel and by the layout" imparting "a sense of sustained or varied visual rhythms" (2012: 89). Sequential dynamism can, and often does, work in concert with narration, but it is a separate, abstract layer of viewing experience. On some comic pages, the visual energy and rhythm created by panel composition and page layout can lead a reader's eye along an alternate path. Molotiu believes that "by problematizing the reading path, it actually opens the reader's eyes to other formal energies hidden on the page" (2012: 99). While on one level the sequence of narrative comics is based "on the logic of a represented storyline," most comics also provide "a visual aesthetic satisfaction . . . a specifically sequential pleasure, achieved by putting the eye into motion" (Molotiu 2012: 89).

Many, perhaps most, comic book and graphic novel pages have fairly feeble sequential dynamism; low on visual energy and no clear visual rhythm. This is especially true of older comics by creators who often felt underpaid, unappreciated, and were not encouraged to innovate. Figure 5.7 is a page from a *Doc Savage* comic book published in the early 1970s. There is nothing fancy about the panel compositions or page layouts. Artist Ross Andru uses a Conventional Semi-Regular Layout. Yet, this page does have sequential dynamism.

In panel one, the angle of the smoke behind the car, the car itself, and the headlight beams in front of the car all move the reader's eyes from the top left of the panel to the bottom right of the panel. The trail of smoke in panel two at first continues the angle established in panel one. Then the car makes a turn and the street, the trail of smoke, and the sign atop the warehouse all work in parallel to lead the reader's eye to the bottom right corner of the panel. The compositional elements of the first two panels are directing the reader down to panel three.

In panel three there is a reversal of direction. The panel is dominated by the figure of Doc Savage. He is in the foreground, drawn full-figure, and his white pants make him "pop out" from the rest of the panel. The headlight beams from panel one, while not actually crossing into the third panel, point directly down onto the main character, Doc Savage, as if to cast a spotlight on him. The dominant line in this panel is Doc's left leg due to the long stride (creating a sense of energy), the white pants, and the use of foreshortening, a technique that uses distortion to create a sense of depth. That leg is at the same angle as the car in

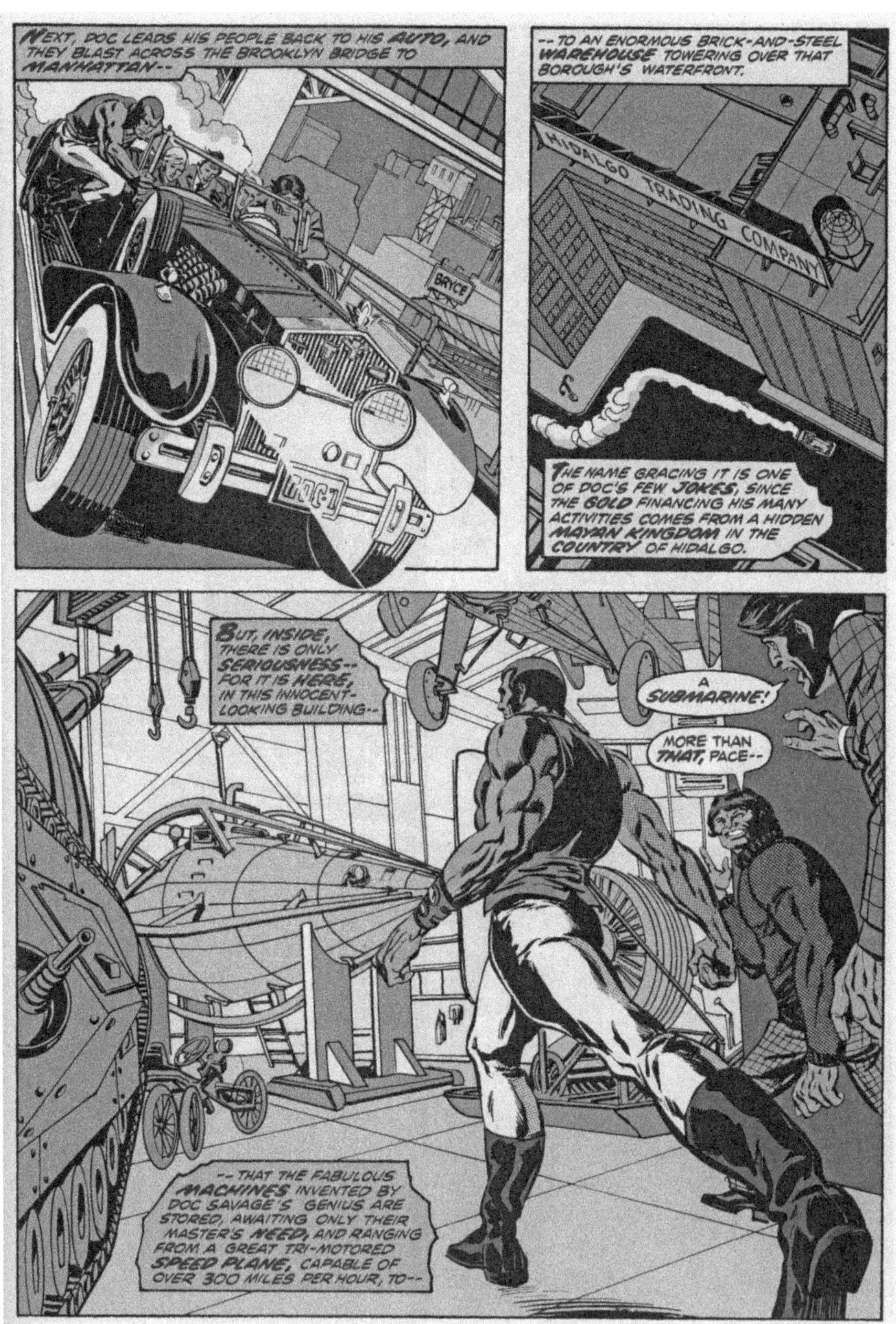

Figure 5.7 *Doc Savage, The Man of Bronze* # 4 (1972) Steve Englehart (script), Ross Andru and Tom Palmer (art) © DC Comics.

panel one, but, because we know he is walking forward, there is a direct clash with the panel one angle. Doc also seems to be walking against the lines that converge at the nose of the submarine and point toward his midsection. Everything about the sequential dynamism of this page leads to the figure of Doc Savage and then puts him in opposition to the initial visual energy. Doc Savage has all these lines pointing against him, but his muscular build and his powerful stride give the sense that he is not going to be held back. After all, that is what adventure heroes do—strive against the forces that oppose them.

Narrative Flow

Narrative flow is a repeated process of developing an understanding of the narrative information within a panel (as it exists within the context of a page layout), adding that understanding to one's understanding of previous narrative information in order to expand the sense of "the story so far," and then moving smoothly to the next panel, where the process continues. In order for there to be a smooth narrative flow there must be a discernable reading path on a page.

Conventional layouts with either a regular or semi-regular application of the grid make it nearly impossible to get off the path. Readers simply follow cultural conventions for reading—the Z reading pattern (left to right, down to the next tier, and then left to right) in the Western world or a reverse-Z for manga. Page structure is unobtrusive, allowing readers to become fully absorbed into the world of the story. Moving from panel to panel becomes an unconscious act.

A conventional layout with a fragmented grid might pose more challenges for a reader. For instance, when a tall panel cuts through all the tiers on the page a reader might ask themselves "Do I read this tall panel now or go down to the next tier?" and therefore experience a moment of blockage. Neil Cohn defines blockage as what occurs when panels are arranged in such a way that readers are uncertain about the reading path to follow (2013). A layout that causes even slight confusion about where to look next on a page can produce "just enough split-second confusion to yank reader out of the world of the story" (McCloud 2006: 33).

In some rhetorical layouts the grid is extremely fragmented or totally absent (at least on the surface). Even when artists have abandoned the grid structure for a complex layout, they usually mean to provide a discernable reading path. However, readers might have to struggle a bit to find that path, and it is unlikely that all readers will interpret an artist's intention in the same way. That can lead to what the comics creators would consider to be a misreading of the comic.

Even if aesthetic layouts do not create a blockage of the narrative flow, they almost always produce a slowing of the flow because they present the tabular as an object that demands attention in and of itself, separate from the narrative. Comics readers, most of whom have an affinity for good artwork, are going to spend some time appreciating the aesthetic qualities of a clever or intricate layout. And, as McCloud warned earlier, even a brief distraction can disrupt the narrative flow and pull the reader out of the world of the story.

While iconostasis, perceiving the page as a designed object, is inherently in conflict, to some degree, with reading comics as a succession of narrative panels, skillfully executed layouts can provide the reader with an aesthetic appreciation of the tabular (the page as a whole) without derailing the linear engagement with the world of the story. When artists know they have created a complex, potentially confusing page layout there are some path guidance techniques they can use to help the reader follow the correct narrative path. For instance, they can draw a word or thought balloon so that it overlaps a panel border, and leads the reader into the next panel, create a string of connected word balloons that cross panel borders, use motion line or character sight lines to indicate the path, or have a figure drawing overlap panel borders.

Look back at Figure 5.3 and you can see how the slight fragmentation at the bottom of the page might cause some reading page path uncertainty if not for the use of a path guidance technique. The natural left-to-right reading order would move a reader's eyes from panel four (the hand slamming down on the desk) to the "I got it. Stay behind me." word balloon in what might seem to be panel five. Instead, reading the word balloon in panel four takes the reader down into the panel below (the actual panel five) because the balloon starts in one panel and extends into the panel below. Then a character's arm that intrudes into panel five leads us over to the character in panel six. Figure 5.8, from an issue of *The Flash*, is a very unusual use of the page (You have to turn the comic book sideways to read it!), and the grid structure is treated as a literal structure on which the characters are climbing. Yet there is a clear reading path. The repeated figures of Dr. Fate and Flash, who are repeatedly overlapping panel borders, form a chain that readers can follow through the two-page spread.

Some comics creators have resorted to numbering panels or using arrows to direct the reader along the correct narrative path. However, as Paul Gravett writes, "It can be argued that it is a weakness of page layout if a comic artist is obliged to indicate the order of panels" (2013: 64).

Closure

The chief task of comics creators is to reduce the imagined story to images encapsulated in panels. The reader must then work at blending those panels into a narrative experience. In order to explain the work the reader performs between and among the panels, Scott McCloud (1993) adapted from Gestalt psychology the concept of **closure**—creating a whole from fragments. As it has been applied to comics, closure refers to the reader applying background knowledge and an understanding of the relationships between encapsulated images to synthesize (or blend) sequences of panels into events, and those sequences of events into an overall story. Building on McCloud's ideas and on theories of perception, cognition, and emotional engagement, philosopher Will Simpson concludes that comics readers "may respond emotionally to either depicted content or to implied content that is available only via the enactment of closure" (2018: para 27).

The comic book reader performs closure within each panel, between panels, and among panels. Earlier in the chapter we examined the inferences a reader makes to create meaning from the fragmentary images within a panel. We now turn our attention to closure between and among panels, the filling in or blending together of panels that transforms the encapsulated moments into a continuous flow of narrative.

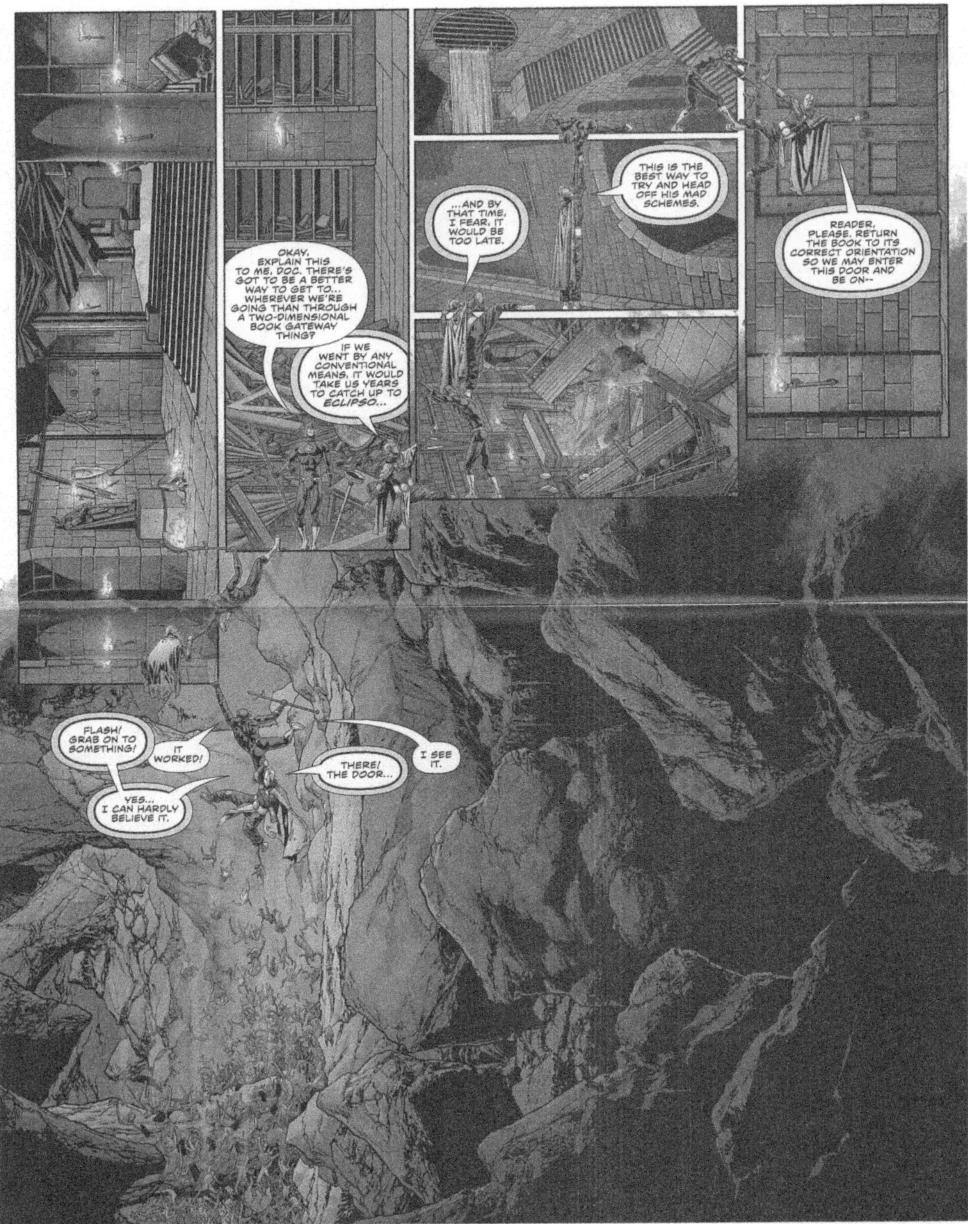

Figure 5.8 ***The Flash*** **#776 (2022) Jeremy Adams (script), Fernando Pasarin and Matt Ryan (art) © DC Comics.**

As a number of comics scholars have noted, panels do not have to be surrounded by a box, and there does not have to be a white space (referred to as a *gutter*) between panels (see Figure 5.9). As Mario Saraceni points out, the gutter is conceptual and does not have to be physically present (2003: 55). Similarly, Jeffery Miller (2000) believes that when McCloud speaks of filling in the gap of the gutter, "we cannot take this to be anything but a metaphor." For Miller, the "sense-making . . . occurs in the interaction between text, reader, and culture."

A number of scholars have proposed alternatives to McCloud's concept of closure. Robert O'Nale (2008) proposes that readers progress through a series of panels not by adding information between panels, but by adding the information in each panel to the background knowledge they already possess, including expectations created by the comic book form itself and that particular book's cover and genre. Neil Cohn (2010) believes that comic readers process chunks of conceptual content (much like we read a sentence) and that those chunks are likely to be related actions (e.g., scenes or sequences) rather than panels. Perhaps when we are reading a comic we are not merely connecting one panel to another, but adding each panel to continually evolving cognitive constructs of scenes, sequences, and ultimately, a narrative.

Figure 5.9 Even though there are no panel borders, this image functions as three panels because the figure of Tim Shea appears three times. *Gone to Amerikay* (2012) Derek McCulloch (story), Colleen Doran (art) © DC Comics.

Closure, or the construction of meaning from fragments, does not occur only between two panels at a time. The reader performs an ongoing construction of meaning by considering each panel in direct relationship to the immediately previous panel and in the context of all previous panels. As Groensteen points out with his concept of **braiding**, the panel relationships can extend even farther because "every panel exists, potentially if not actually, in relation with each of the others" (2007: 146). And these relationships do not simply occur in a linear progression. Each next panel has the potential to provide new information that creates a "retroactive determination" of the meaning of one or more previous panels (Groensteen 2007: 110). On page two of "A Life in Comics" (Figure 5.12b) there is an ornate NY drawn in a style of lettering that might be found in Medieval illuminated manuscripts. That seems odd and unrelated to ten-year-old Karen Green. However, that lettering style retroactively makes sense once we learn on page four that Karen studied medieval history and became a medieval-history librarian. The braiding can be fairly direct or very subtle. A reader's affective and cognitive response to a comic can be influenced by associations or contrasts that are not even consciously processed.

With a Good Comic, Once Is Never Enough

Some of you might be concerned that learning the nuts and bolts of the comics form will ruin the comics reading experience. Not to worry. Unless a comic is poorly constructed or discordant for effect, during an immersive reading (as opposed to an analytical reading) there is a subconscious blending of not only words and pictures, but of all the elements and devices of the comics form (panels, layout, closure, braiding, etc.). As a rule, that subconscious blending does not distract you from the enjoyment of the narrative you are constructing. After years of theorizing, writing, and teaching about the process of constructing meaning from the elements of comics form, your authors can be blissfully unaware of that process when enjoying the latest Marjane Satrapi graphic novel or the most recent issue of *Fantastic Four*.

However, subsequent, more analytical readings can be rewarding. For any comic there is the simple joy of "looking behind the curtain" to see how it's done, but for a more complex comic a second reading will give you a fuller, richer experience of all the work has to offer. In being more mindful of the composition choices, the dynamics of the layout, the use of hermeneutic images, and so on you will discern subtexts and create layers of meaning that did not occur to you as you were propelled through the pages by the flow of the narrative in the immersive reading.

The theories presented here (or elsewhere) cannot completely explain how we read comics. The process is both complex and mysterious. As Hatfield cautions, "comic art is characterized by plurality, instability, and tension, so much so that no single formula for interpreting the page can reliably unlock every comic" (2005: 66). And Cohn believes "the processes guiding sequential image comprehension remain inaccessible to conscious awareness" (2010: 129).

Analyzing: Tabular (page) vs. Linear (sequence)

Both Figures 5.10 (a two-page spread from a Captain America story drawn by Jim Steranko) and 5.11 (a page from the Green Lantern *Wednesday Comics* story drawn by Joe Quinones) have a strong aesthetic quality. And thus, there exists a tension between pausing to admire the page as a whole (the tabular) and engaging with the narrative segments presented on the page (the linear).

Figure 5.10 Captain America # 113 (1969) Jim Steranko (plot and art), Stan Lee (dialogue) © 2023 Marvel Entertainment, Inc. and its subsidiaries.

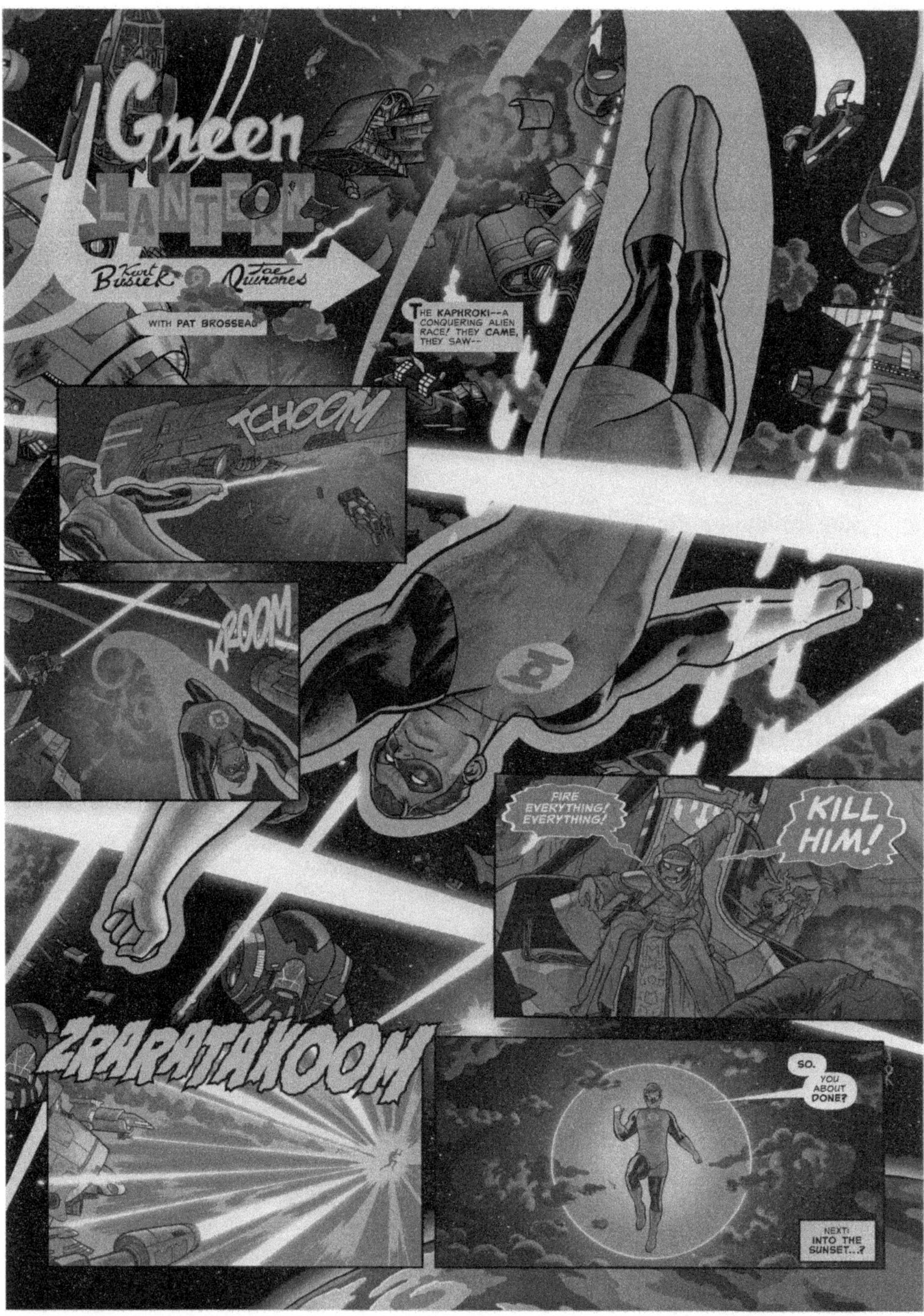

Figure 5.11 "Green Lantern" *Wednesday Comics* (2009) Kurt Busiek (story), Joe Quinones (art) © DC Comics.

Sternako designed the Captain America two-page spread (mega-page) to arrest the reader's attention. The imposing figures in the middle of the spread are shown in dynamic action, mid-leap, and their detailed musculature is on display in the tight, brightly colored costumes. Their arms are stretched out so that they dominate not only the middle but the entire width of the two pages. They are surrounded by a bright yellow background through which lines (of force, energy, excitement?) are radiating. The sequential dynamism is all in the middle of the two-page spread. The rest of the page is very "quiet" by comparison. Their leaping is a moment of dynamic action that seems disconnected from what is going on in the panels on either side of Bucky and Captain America.

The placement of the sequential dynamism and dominant visual appeal in the middle of the mega-page shatters the narrative flow. After looking at the page as a whole, the natural reading path would be to read the two panels of dialogue on the left-hand page. But after reading those panels one cannot move to the next two panels in that tier without crossing over those two giant, muscular, colorful figures and all the lines surrounding them. In the panel stretching across the bottom of the two-page spread the dark clouds, the full moon, and the cemetery are meant to create a certain mood, and the reader should be focusing on Bucky's reaction to Cap's startling announcement. Yet, there are the huge, colorful boots of Bucky and Captain America breaking the mood and intruding on the narrative moment. Readers are invited to glance back up and once again appreciate Steranko's striking artwork. Iconostasis wins out over narrative flow, Yet, stopping and looking at the spread as a whole is not completely satisfying. The aesthetic layout is marred by a conventional tier of bordered panels in which multiple dialogue balloons dominate the small figure drawings. It is a two-page spread that is likely to leave readers impressed, but frustrated.

The Green Lantern page achieves a better resolution of the tensions among the tabular, linear, and sequential dynamism. Our eyes are naturally drawn to the full-page panel of the Green Lantern flying through space. His figure takes up two-thirds of the page, and the fact that he is upside-down (from our Earth-bound orientation) makes the image more striking. We will consider this full page to be panel one. Most readers will want to begin their encounter with the page by engaging in iconostasis, taking time to appreciate the aesthetic pleasure of the page as a whole. There are five bordered panels inset within the full-page panel one. The first two inset panels just provide a closer look at details of the space battle that was established in the full-page panel. Much like with the Captain America page, as readers follow a traditional reading path and move from one bordered panel to the next they have to move across the large, superheroic figure in the middle of the page. Yet, in this instance, the narrative flow is not disrupted because Green Lantern's battle with the Kaphroki spaceships is an ongoing activity, rather than a brief moment of action (the leap). Even as panel four takes our focus inside a Kaphroki ship we know that Green Lantern is still flying around out there, evading energy blasts and blasting back with his power ring, and the large flying figure in the middle of the reinforces that idea.

Discussion Questions

1. For either Figure 5.4 or Figure 5.11, do not look at the words on the page as words, but rather as masses of shapes inside ovals or rectangles. Now, do not look at the

drawings as characters, spaceships, and so on but rather as lines and shapes. The idea is to look beneath the narrative and experience the sequential dynamics of the page. What symmetries, contrasts, trajectories, and rhythms do you see?

2. In this chapter we argued that you cannot be a passive consumer of comics. How would you compare the amount of activity you have to engage in with comics with that of other media? Is comics reading more or less active than engaging with media such as television, books, video games, etc.? Why is this so in each case?

Activities

1. Analyze sequential dynamism and iconostasis on page two of "A Life in Comics" (Figure 5.12b).
2. Make a copy of page two of "A Life in Comics" (Figure 5.12b). Draw panel borders around parts of the page that you think operate as encapsulations of distinct units of the narrative.
3. For "A Life in Comics" (Figures 5.12 a–g), categorize each of the six pages as to what type of layout is being used—conventional, rhetorical, or aesthetic. Provide justification for your choice.

Recommended Reading

Comics

Moore, Alan, and J. H. Williams III. *Promethea*. New York: DC Comics, 1999–2005.
Few comics have had as much variety of page layout as what you will encounter in the *Promethea* series. Many of the layouts are rhetorical, responding to content, intertextual allusions, and even the art style Williams is emulating in a particular issue.

Moustafa, Ibrahim. *Jaeger*. Stela.app, 2016.
For the original version of *Jaeger*, Moustafa developed creative layouts for a narrow phone screen. A few years later *Jaeger* was published as a standard-size graphic novel. Looking at both versions is an opportunity to see how the same story can be told, effectively, in two radically different parameters for layout.

Scholarly Sources

Cohn, Neil. "Navigating Comics: An Empirical and Theoretical Approach to Strategies of Reading Comic Page Layouts." *Frontiers in Psychology* 4, no. 186 (April 2013): n.p. https://www.frontiersin.org/article/10.3389/fpsyg.2013.00186
The article is a good example of the scientific, experimental approaches Neil Cohn and his colleagues have taken to actually test speculative theories about how readers interact with comics.

Peeters, Benoit. "Four Conceptions of the Page: From *Case, Planche, Récit*: Lire la Bande Dessinée." 1998, trans. Jesse Cohn. *ImageText: Interdisciplinary Comics Studies* 3, no. 3 (2007): n.p. https://imagetextjournal.com/four-conceptions-of-the-page/.
This essay explains and expands upon the seminal work of French comics scholars who explored the tensions between the tabular and linear aspects of the comic art form.

Figures 5.12a–g "A Life in Comics: The Graphic Adventures of Karen Green" by Nick Sousanis, which appeared in the Summer 2017 issue of *Columbia Magazine*. Used with permission of Nick Sousanis and courtesy of *Columbia Magazine*.

WHEN GREEN WAS TEN, HER MOM ANNOUNCED:
WE'RE MOVING TO NEW YORK CITY
- A "LAND OF WONDERFUL THINGS."
MAYFIELD DR
HER PARENTS WANTED TO GIVE HER AND HER TWO SIBLINGS EXPOSURE TO CULTURE.
THEY MOVED TO FORT LEE, NEW JERSEY, JUST ACROSS THE RIVER FROM THE CITY.
AS A TEEN, GREEN WAS COMING INTO MANHATTAN REGULARLY. AS SHE RECALLS, THE CITY "WAS DIRTY AND COVERED IN GRAFFITI. IT WAS GREAT. I MISS IT."
IZ THE WIZ!
THE GREENS LIVED NEAR A DRUG STORE THAT HAD SPINNER RACKS OF CLASSIC *MAD* MAGAZINE REPRINTS - WHICH SHE DEVOURED.
MAD
MAD
MAD
MAD
IN HIGH SCHOOL, GREEN FREQUENTLY WALKED ACROSS THE GEORGE WASHINGTON BRIDGE TO EXPLORE THE CLOISTERS MUSEUM.
"I'D NEVER SEEN ANYTHING SO BEAUTIFUL IN MY LIFE."
THE VISUAL STORYTELLING ON DISPLAY IN ARTIFACTS FROM THE MIDDLE AGES RESONATED WITH WHAT SHE SAW IN COMICS.

COMICS SEEMED TO FOLLOW HER EVERYWHERE.

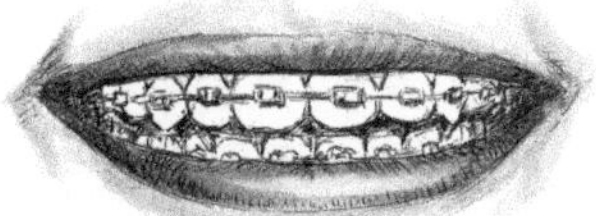

BACK WHEN GREEN WAS 11 SHE GOT BRACES. TO HER DELIGHT, HER ORTHODONTIST HAD STACKS OF *ARCHIE* COMICS.

SHE ENDED UP STAYING FOR HOURS AFTER HER APPOINTMENTS READING...

"I LOVED THOSE COMICS. I THOUGHT THAT'S WHAT HIGH SCHOOL WAS GOING TO BE LIKE. I WAS MISTAKEN."

HIGH SCHOOL PROVED TO BE A DIFFICULT AND TROUBLED TIME FOR GREEN.

IT'S THERE SHE DISCOVERED UNDERGROUND COMICS AND THE COMICS MAGAZINE

HEAVY METAL

- WHICH BLEW HER MIND WITH ITS SLATE OF EUROPEAN CARTOONISTS

after Jim Cherry

- AS WELL AS AMERICAN CHARLES BURNS, WHOSE WORK TOOK HER BREATH AWAY AND SPOKE DIRECTLY TO FEELINGS HIGH SCHOOL EVOKED.

after C. Burns

SHE MADE IT TO COLLEGE IN 1978, BUT DROPPED OUT AFTER ONE SEMESTER AND STARTED BARTENDING, WHICH SHE WOULD DO FOR THE NEXT 15 YEARS.

BARTENDING TAUGHT HER HOW TO WORK WITH AND TALK TO DIFFICULT PEOPLE AND GRIN LIKE A CHESHIRE CAT WHEN SHE WASN'T "FEELING SMILEY."

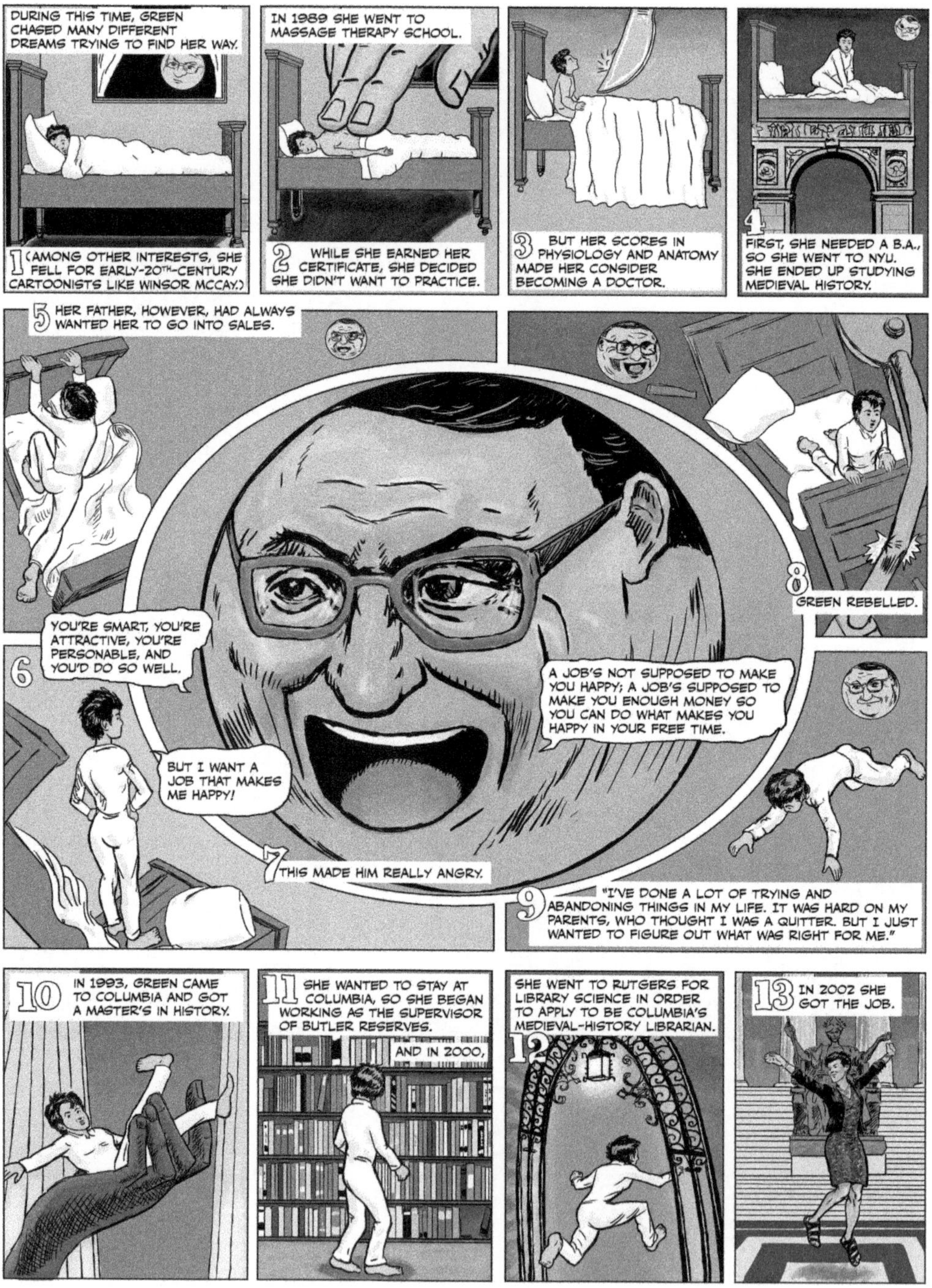

DURING THIS TIME, GREEN CHASED MANY DIFFERENT DREAMS TRYING TO FIND HER WAY.

1 (AMONG OTHER INTERESTS, SHE FELL FOR EARLY-20TH-CENTURY CARTOONISTS LIKE WINSOR MCCAY.)

IN 1989 SHE WENT TO MASSAGE THERAPY SCHOOL.

2 WHILE SHE EARNED HER CERTIFICATE, SHE DECIDED SHE DIDN'T WANT TO PRACTICE.

3 BUT HER SCORES IN PHYSIOLOGY AND ANATOMY MADE HER CONSIDER BECOMING A DOCTOR.

4 FIRST, SHE NEEDED A B.A., SO SHE WENT TO NYU. SHE ENDED UP STUDYING MEDIEVAL HISTORY.

5 HER FATHER, HOWEVER, HAD ALWAYS WANTED HER TO GO INTO SALES.

6 YOU'RE SMART, YOU'RE ATTRACTIVE, YOU'RE PERSONABLE, AND YOU'D DO SO WELL.

BUT I WANT A JOB THAT MAKES ME HAPPY!

A JOB'S NOT SUPPOSED TO MAKE YOU HAPPY; A JOB'S SUPPOSED TO MAKE YOU ENOUGH MONEY SO YOU CAN DO WHAT MAKES YOU HAPPY IN YOUR FREE TIME.

7 THIS MADE HIM REALLY ANGRY.

8 GREEN REBELLED.

9 "I'VE DONE A LOT OF TRYING AND ABANDONING THINGS IN MY LIFE. IT WAS HARD ON MY PARENTS, WHO THOUGHT I WAS A QUITTER. BUT I JUST WANTED TO FIGURE OUT WHAT WAS RIGHT FOR ME."

10 IN 1993, GREEN CAME TO COLUMBIA AND GOT A MASTER'S IN HISTORY.

11 SHE WANTED TO STAY AT COLUMBIA, SO SHE BEGAN WORKING AS THE SUPERVISOR OF BUTLER RESERVES.

AND IN 2000,

SHE WENT TO RUTGERS FOR LIBRARY SCIENCE IN ORDER TO APPLY TO BE COLUMBIA'S MEDIEVAL-HISTORY LIBRARIAN.

12

13 IN 2002 SHE GOT THE JOB.

AS GREEN SETTLED IN AT COLUMBIA, SHE WONDERED WHAT WAS HAPPENING IN COMICS.

SHE BOUGHT A COPY OF PAUL HORNSCHEMEIER'S
MOTHER, COME HOME

- ITS DEPICTION OF FAMILY AND LOSS OPENED GREEN'S EYES TO WHAT COMICS COULD BE AND SPARKED AN IDEA.

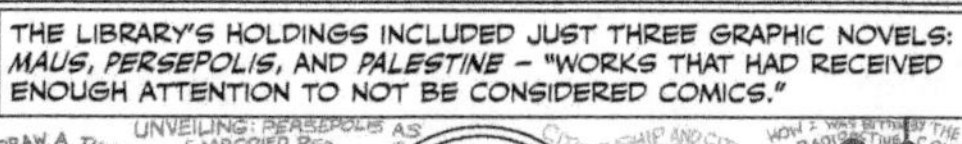
THE LIBRARY'S HOLDINGS INCLUDED JUST THREE GRAPHIC NOVELS: *MAUS*, *PERSEPOLIS*, AND *PALESTINE* – "WORKS THAT HAD RECEIVED ENOUGH ATTENTION TO NOT BE CONSIDERED COMICS."

RECOGNIZING THAT THE STUDY OF COMICS OF ALL SORTS WAS ON THE RISE, IN 2005 GREEN MADE THE CASE THAT THE LIBRARY GET AHEAD OF THE CURVE.
INDISCIPLINE OR, THE CONDITION OF COMICS STUDIES

AND FROM THERE, SHE BEGAN BUILDING A COLLECTION.

IN 2008 GREEN CREATED AN EXHIBITION AT BUTLER, "COMICS IN THE CURRICULUM," DEMONSTRATING WAYS THAT THEMES FROM COMICS COULD BE TAUGHT IN COURSES.

GOTEM
FACULTY IN ENGLISH, NARRATIVE MEDICINE, AND AMERICAN AND EAST ASIAN STUDIES GOT INTERESTED AND NUMEROUS CLASSES HAVE SINCE BEEN OFFERED ACROSS CAMPUS.

Author's note: This is the year I came to Columbia as a doctoral student and first met Karen.

THE COLLECTION STARTED TO TAKE SHAPE.
THEN, IN 2010, OUT OF THE BLUE, LEGENDARY *X-MEN* AUTHOR CHRIS CLAREMONT CONTACTED GREEN TO OFFER UP HIS ARCHIVES.
BAMF
OTHERS FOLLOWED.
THIS BURGEONING CATALOGUE INCLUDES MANUSCRIPTS, SKETCHES, ORIGINAL ART, CORRESPONDENCE, CONTRACTS, AND OTHER MATERIALS,
AND THAT COLLECTION OF THREE? NOW OVER 14,000 VOLUMES!
ZIP
FROM COMICS ICONS LIKE *MAD'S* AL JAFFEE; HOWARD CRUSE, THE FATHER OF GAY COMICS; EARLY BATMAN CONTRIBUTOR JERRY ROBINSON; *ELFQUEST* CREATORS WENDY AND RICHARD PINI; KITCHEN SINK PRESS; AND CARTOONIST MORT GERBERG.

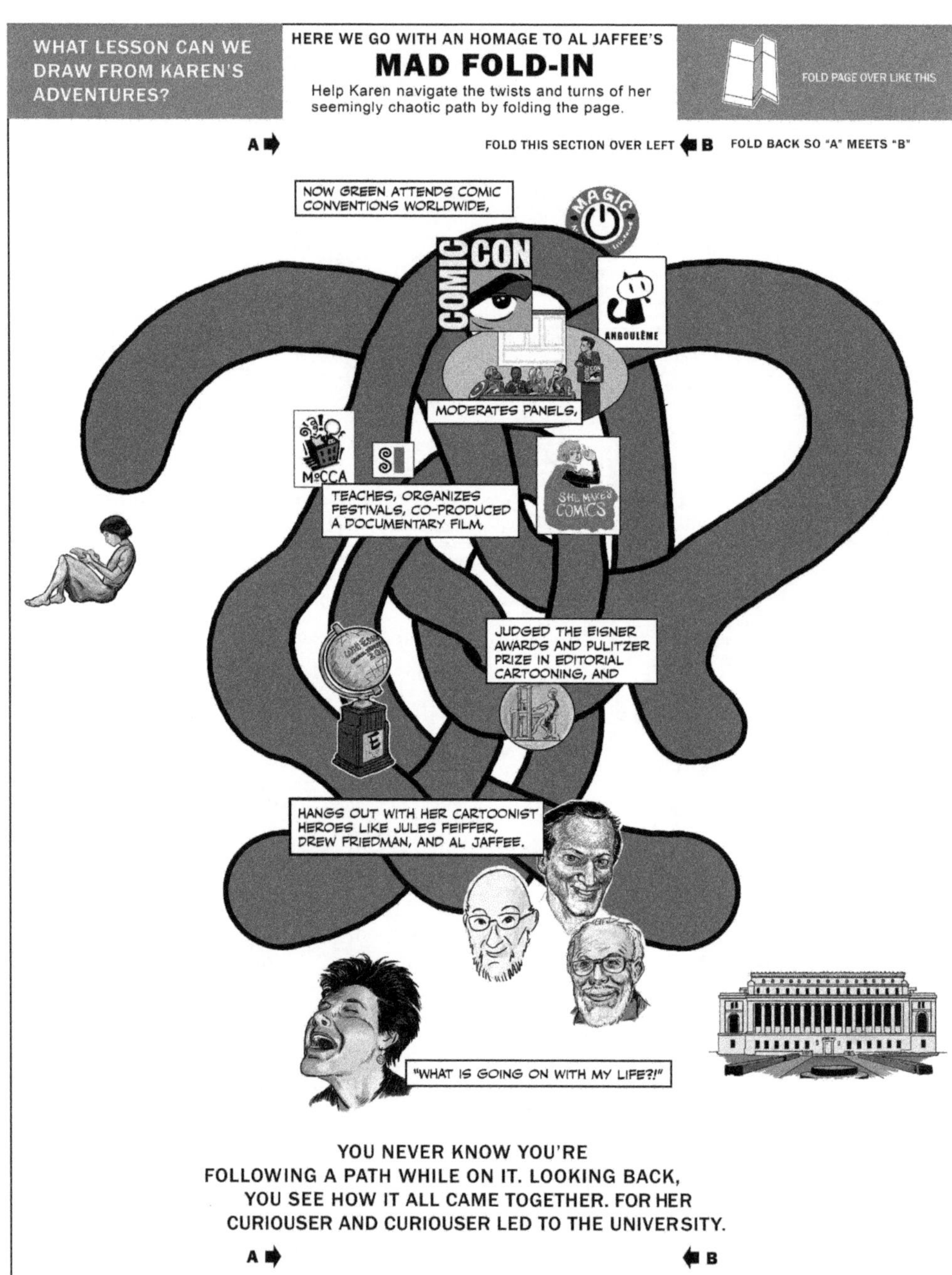

Nick Sousanis '14TC is the author of *Unflattening*, originally his doctoral dissertation written and drawn entirely in comics form, published by Harvard University Press in 2015. He is an assistant professor at San Francisco State U, where he's developing an interdisciplinary program in comics studies. See more at www.spinweaveandcut.com.

Nick Sousanis '14TC is the author of *Unflattening*, published by Harvard University Press in 2015. He is an assistant professor at San Francisco State. See more at www.spinweaveandcut.com.

Unit III Genre

6 Genres of Comics

Absent from the cover of *Startling Comics* #44 (1947) is any wording about its lead feature, Lance Lewis (Figure 6.1). Yet even without a caption or dialogue offering any further explanation, the imagery alone provides regular consumers of popular culture with enough cues that they can quickly discern the type of story in which Lance Lewis stars. Certainly the unusual attire he and his female companion are dressed in offers some guidance. And then there is the man-sized bug attempting to kidnap her, not to mention the rather obvious ray gun Lance is firing at the creature's snout. Either alone or in combination, these cues suggest that this is a story belonging to a particular group of stories called *science fiction*. By 1947, many of the visual conventions associated with science fiction stories had already evolved and become standard, including expectations about the kinds of dress, characters, and technologies one might expect to find in such stories. Science fiction stories had become a staple of American fiction, having found popularity through novels, films, radio broadcasts, comic strips, pulp magazines, and, in time, comic books. Fans of science fiction, like fans of other types of stories, are often motivated to pick up one story after another in that group, giving the producers of media incentive to return to these types of stories time and again. Thus, fans of comic strips like *Buck Rogers in the 25th Century A.D.* and *Flash Gordon* might eagerly purchase this issue of *Startling Comics*, with artwork by comics great Graham Ingels, because its imagery calls to mind those other tales. This is the basis for genre studies, which tries to identify what characteristics make up the kinds of stories that are most often told by our cultural industries and also how the qualities of those media are used to market these types of stories to their audiences.

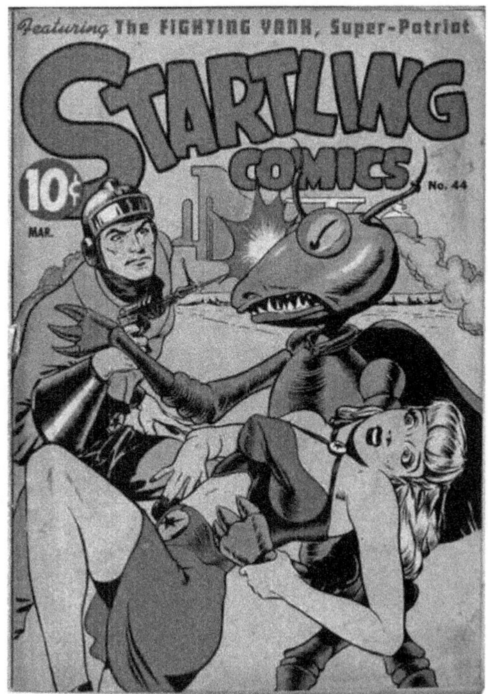

Figure 6.1 ***Startling Comics*' Lance Lewis demonstrates some conventions of a good cover for a science fiction comic. © 1947 Nedor Comics.**

Objectives

In this chapter you will learn:

1. the definition of *genre* and the role it plays in shaping the creation of comics products;
2. the characteristics of genres, including character types, narrative patterns, themes, and other conventions;
3. how westerns, teen humor, romance, funny animals, horror, and other genres developed in comics, and what characterizes each; and
4. how the hybridization of genres helps experimentation and expansion of narrative possibilities.

As a means for studying and better understanding narratives in various media, critics and scholars have identified genres for typing works according to similarities with other works. A **genre** is a way to classify similar types of stories. Genre comes from the same root as *genus*, a term you may recall from biology, which denotes the classification of organisms into groups. Genre studies look for groupings in media such as television, novels, film, and, of course, comics, and provide us with a shorthand for discussing trends and motifs that characterize a given narrative. For instance, film genres include categories for musicals, film noir, and romantic comedy. In comics, genres include teen humor, horror, memoir, and superheroes. The conventions of the memoir and superhero genres in particular have been so richly analyzed that we've set aside treatment of them in their own chapter (Chapters 7 and 8). Not to be overlooked, though, are genres adapted to comics only after popular exposure in other media. For instance, the detective genre has appeared in comics since the medium's inception, but it had already seized the popular imagination through novels, pulp magazines, films, and radio programs before modern comics began to publish stories within the genre in the 1930s. Although comics have often adapted already known and popular genres for their use, they have still placed an imprint on them, influenced by the unique conventions of graphic storytelling.

While genres may enable critics and scholars to talk about the elements that help construct a story, they also help the people who publish comics to find appealing products for particular audiences. From the artistic or creative viewpoint, tapping into a genre allows creators to use known and accepted elements as shorthand for their audience. This frees mental energy and storytelling space to concentrate on the original elements of the narrative that the creators want to introduce. For instance, science fiction fans do not necessarily need to know where Lance Lewis got his ray gun or even what kind of energy it shoots; ray guns seem to be readily accepted by readers of science fiction comics in much the same way that revolvers are accepted as standard issue for detectives. From an economic standpoint, invoking genre is a helpful way to market a story. When the kung-fu craze hit American audiences in the 1970s, it didn't take long for all the major comics publishers to mass-produce kung-fu comics. Among other series, Marvel Comics launched *Master of Kung Fu* (1974–83) and DC Comics responded with *Richard Dragon, Kung Fu Fighter* (1975–7); they each wanted to cash in on the popular trend.

In order to appeal to an audience, though, producers have to walk a fine line between copying what someone else has published and neglecting to fulfill the expectations that an audience brings to the genre. In satisfying these expectations, an entry in a genre must attend to **standardization** to match the conventions of the genre closely enough to be recognized as belonging to the genre. In the sword-and-sorcery comics, which also became popular in the 1970s, this means a story featuring a stalwart sword-wielding hero who roams an exotic land and confronts opposing warriors and monstrous creatures. Balanced against standardization, though, must be **differentiation**, or the innovations brought to the individual narrative or series (Campbell, Martin, and Fabos 2006). In our sword-and-sorcery example, Marvel Comics' popular *Conan the Barbarian* is set in the ancient "Hyperborean Age," a time described as occurring between the fall of mythical Atlantis and the beginning of recorded history. As a matter of distinction, in DC Comics' *Warlord* series, contemporary pilot Travis Morgan crash-lands into Skartaris, a world that exists below the earth's surface and is populated by sorcerers and dinosaurs. These two settings are similar in some regards—both have sorcerers and fantastic beasts roaming about—but different enough to distinguish the two series (among other considerations). As a matter of practice, striking a balance between fulfilling a genre's conventions and introducing innovations allows new series to carve out a niche in a crowded marketplace.

This chapter takes a look at some of the most influential genres adapted to comics. We'll begin by reviewing some of the characteristics common to all genres, and looking at them through the lens of one long-running genre, the western. Next we'll review four other influential genres in comics, namely teen humor, romance, funny animals, and horror, in some depth. We'll also briefly introduce several other genres for your consideration. (You will then have the opportunity to read more in-depth explorations of the memoir and superhero genres in subsequent chapters.) Finally, we'll look at the ways some strips and series break through the artificial boundaries of genre and blend to create hybrid forms. By the end of this chapter, you should have a greater appreciation for the versatility of the comics medium and its ability to create narrative experiences.

Genre Conventions

Genres evolve over time, such that the historic first entry might look markedly different from more contemporary entries. Yet despite such differences, genre studies attempt to identify a set of common characteristics. These characteristics can include the types of characters in such narratives, the way stories are structured, themes the stories revisit time and again, and other conventions (i.e., the way things are often done). Let us look at each of these characteristics, using the western genre to help illustrate them.

Westerns were popular storytelling vehicles for much of the twentieth century. One of the first narrative films, *The Great Train Robbery* (1903), was a western. Many of radio's most successful programs were westerns, including *The Lone Ranger* (1933–55). The longest-running dramatic primetime television series, *Gunsmoke* (1955–75), was a western. And since the turn of the twentieth century, newspaper strips have featured western themes and western characters, many of which were reprinted in the early comic book magazines of the 1930s. Eventually, titles like *Western Picture Stories* and *Star Ranger* (both February 1937) would debut—whole publications devoted exclusively to featuring the genre. Westerns would go on to achieve their greatest popularity in the late 1940s and early 1950s. The biggest sellers of this era were comic books featuring licensed characters, most of them movie and TV cowboys like Gene Autry and Roy Rogers (Horn, *American West*). Publishers who didn't want to pay expensive licensing fees tried their hand with their own original creations, like Marvel's *Two-Gun Kid* (1948) or DC's *Johnny Thunder* (1948). Comics historian Michelle Nolan (1998) estimates that as many as 5,000 western comics were published. Although long a staple in most comics publishers' lines, westerns steadily declined in popularity until the last monthly western comic, DC's *Jonah Hex*, ended in 1985. There are periodic revivals of western comics (Vertigo's *Loveless*), and a number of the original series are offered in reprint editions (such as Marvel's *Rawhide Kid*) to entertain new generations. We now examine what many of them had in common.

Character Types

One of the hallmarks of a genre is the familiar kinds of people who populate it. Certain character types return time and again, creating a recognizable familiarity with the situation for the reader. In the western genre, for instance, we have a number of familiar character types:

- the steely hero, who has an unflinching moral code that may not always reflect perfectly the legal code;
- the grizzled sidekick, whose main function is to provide comic relief;
- the respectable, beautiful woman, whose prim and proper demeanor makes her a socially acceptable love interest for the virtuous hero; and
- the villainous outlaw who disrupts the social order in pursuit of self-serving ends and does so without a moral code or compass.

Figure 6.2 The cover of *Billy the Kid* #63 displays some of the conventions of the western, including the heroic individual and gunplay. Cover art by José Delbo. © 1967 Charlton Comics.

Obviously, some variation on these types (and others) appears from story to story, and series to series, but the recurrence of them in so many instances makes their presence a recognizable part of the genre's formula (Figure 6.2).

Setting

Audiences have come to recognize not only the familiar characters from a particular genre but also the familiar places in which the stories are set. Setting takes into account the location and, if relevant, the time period in which the story occurs. Both place and time help to make westerns readily identifiable. True to their name, westerns are located in the American West, typically in frontier towns complete with wooden buildings, troughs for watering horses, and tumbleweeds blowing down dusty streets. The countryside in the background is often punctuated with buttes and mesas.

Westerns are also recognizable by the time period in which they are set. Most take place in the late nineteenth century when Americans were pushing the frontier west of the Mississippi River. Such expansion into new territory put frontiersmen in conflict with the Native Americans already inhabiting those territories and offered greater opportunities for lawless actions, as the dictates of Eastern civilization—most especially the law—were not fully enforceable at such a distance.

Narrative Patterns

The **narrative pattern** refers to the structure of storytelling. Most stories in the Western tradition follow the Aristotelian model of a beginning, middle, and end, but beyond that overarching structure, genre studies examine what additional patterns are laid upon the framework. For instance, in the western genre, one recurring narrative pattern has the hero encountering a group of townsfolk who are ready to hang an innocent man. The hero must stop the hanging by not only finding the truly guilty party but also bringing him to justice. While in pursuit of the villain, some sort of gunplay ensues, perhaps in the form of a shoot-out. In the end, the hero is almost always proven right, the falsely accused man is freed, and the guilty man is hauled off to jail. Again, within certain variations (the guilty party turns out to be a woman instead of a man in one variation), this pattern is recognized as belonging to the genre because its basic structure has been told so many times. Indeed, many westerns follow a pattern so familiar that it may be called a **monomyth**. A monomyth is the story of the hero's journey, and its basic structure features the hero's separation, initiation, and return, all of which ultimately benefit the community. This structure will be examined again and in greater detail in Chapter 8.

Themes

In addition to character types, setting, and narrative patterns, another major convention involves the repetition of themes. A **theme** is a recurring message either within a narrative or across a series of narratives. A given theme might be included in a narrative either intentionally or unconsciously, but either way it is given special attention by critics, as its repetition is interpreted to mean that the message is significant. A familiar theme in western comics is that of individualism. In the example earlier, where the hero confronts the townsfolk about hanging the wrong man, we see a message about the virtue of individual thought and action over collective thought and action. If the hero is right about the innocence of the falsely accused man and captures the actual criminal, we see that the message of individuality is reinforced as a theme in this particular story. As other stories about individuality come forth from the genre (e.g., the cavalry scout who notifies his comrades about an ambush, the lone marshal who confronts the villain on Main Street for a shoot-out), the strength of the theme, and its relevance to the genre, only increases.

Visual Conventions

Finally, there are recurring storytelling elements that are visual in nature. These conventions include, but are not limited to, the use of certain tools or the clothing styles typically characteristic of the place or time. Such visual cues are signs used to confirm for familiar readers their orientation within the genre, without necessarily having to do much to explain the context to them. Several such conventions are familiar to the producers and readers of western comics. For instance, nearly all western heroes carry a handgun or rifle (although a few prefer bows and arrows). And all are dressed in period clothing—complete with a cowboy hat, of course—and they often appear in the same outfit in issue after issue, almost as if in a superhero costume. Such conventions can make a given genre recognizable almost immediately. In fact, because visual conventions are so often taken for granted, they are often only noticed when they are absent! (The western hero without a hat would be the one who stands out.)

In the next section we'll look at some additional genres and introduce some of the different character types, settings, narrative patterns, themes, and visual conventions that characterize each. As you review them, keep in mind that not every convention has to be present for a story to fit into a genre. But chances are that such conventions have appeared in enough instances that they have become representative of the genre's distinct personality.

Genre Categories

There have been numerous popular genres in the last seven decades of American comics, and to cover even a modest number in depth is beyond the scope of this introductory book. However, reviewing a few of the varied genres should shed some light on the versatility of comics to tell different kinds of stories that appeal to diverse audiences. The following are some of the most influential genres in terms of longevity, popularity, and impact on the medium. We will discuss them in terms of their development and several key elements which characterize each.

Teen Humor

Other than the ubiquitous superhero, teen humor is the only genre to be continuously published since it began in comics' Golden Age. And within the genre, the only character to be in continuous publication is the one who defined it: red-headed, tic-tac-toe-templed Archie Andrews. Archie debuted as a backup feature to superhero lead-in The Shield in *Pep Comics* #22 (1941). Archie and his pals were the brainchildren of MLJ Publishing co-founder John Goldwater, who asked, "Why does every book have to be Superman?" (Robbins 1999: 8). Though the superhero genre was in full bloom at the time, Goldwater charged writer Vic Bloom and artist Bob Montana with the task of producing a feature that used the comics medium to exploit the humorous potential of coming-of-age trials and tribulations. Goldwater already had ample evidence of teenage characters' appeal from other media: Teenagers had begun to emerge as a separate social group in the first half of the twentieth century, and by the time Archie came along in the 1940s the humorous misadventures of teenage protagonists had found an audience among newspaper comic strip readers (beginning with *The Love Life of Harold Teen* as early as 1919), filmgoers (particularly Mickey Rooney portraying Andy Hardy in a series of films began in 1937), and radio listeners (notably the character of Henry Aldrich in *The Aldrich Family*, which began airing in 1939).

Archie's success was immediate, oft-imitated, and enduring. The year following his debut, he was awarded his own title—the first of many—and in due course his pals Jughead, Betty, Veronica, and Reggie all had titles of their own. By 1946 MLJ embraced its star feature by changing its name to Archie Publications. Numerous competitors attempted to imitate Archie's success. Within the company, characters like Bill Woggon's brunette actress Katy Keene achieved popularity, while over at Timely/Atlas/Marvel, another redhead, Patsy Walker, began a decades-long run under the guidance of Stan Lee. Archie Publications, though, ever the leader in the genre, would go on to further success with the introduction of *Sabrina the Teen-Age Witch* and *Josie and the Pussycats* in the 1960s. At the time other publishers were competing with their own teen comics such as *Binky* (DC) and *Tippy Teen* (Tower), but ultimately it has been Archie who has managed to perpetuate the genre he helped spawn. The appeal of Archie, though, was far different from what was later depicted on the CW's television series, *Riverdale.*

Conventions within the comics genre quickly settled around the "Archie style," driven no doubt by Archie Comics' sales success. The series focuses on an ensemble of idealized teenage characters, usually in a high school setting. Although the characters might embody some stereotypes such as the vain prom queen, the clueless schmuck, or the unintelligent jock, most prove to have hearts of gold in the resolution of each story. Stories tend to focus on the most humorous aspects of coming of age, including dating, earning money, and getting access to an automobile. "In a teen comic book all the tensions of dating, of popularity, and of young love are winked at and laughed away" (Benton 1989: 182). The stories are rounded out with a healthy dash of **slapstick**—physical comedy such as a character taking a fall or tearing his pants. The artwork has followed a style which depicts the characters with realistically proportioned bodies but some caricatured facial features (such as Archie's enlarged eyes). At times, female leads like Cheryl Blossom have been criticized as being almost *too* realistic because of their curvaceous figures (Figure 6.3).

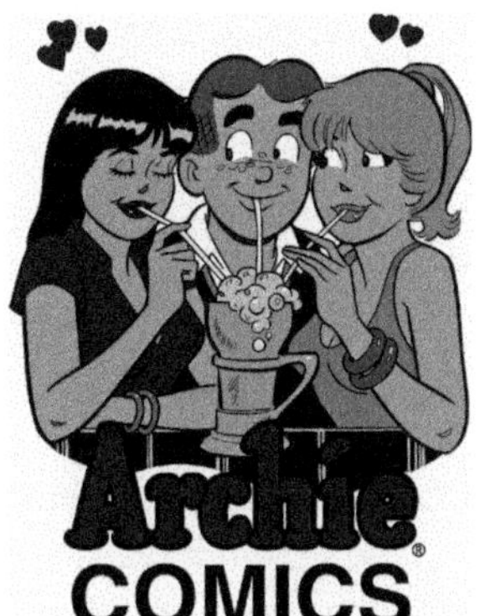

Figure 6.3 America's Typical Teen, Archie Andrews, is forever torn between his attraction to both Veronica and Betty. TM & © 2022 Archie Comic Publications, Inc. Used with permission.

Teen humor comics have traditionally appealed to female rather than male readers, with estimates that as many as 60 percent of Archie's readers are girls, typically ages six to thirteen (Robbins 1999: 12). Part of the appeal seems to be the window that teen humor opens to preteen audiences who think they are finding out about what it is like to be a teenager. As historian Bradford Wright (2001) points out, this is a sanitized perception of the teenage years:

> America's "typical teenager" never uses teen slang, never fights, never smokes or drinks alcohol, always obeys his parents in the end, and betrays only the vaguest hint of his

libido. In other words, he is typical only of the kind of teenager that most adults want to have around. Archie offered young readers a safe glimpse into teen life, while carefully observing the rules of adult society (73).

Not surprisingly, teen humor comics are not made by actual teenagers, but by reasonably mature, established men like Goldwater, Bloom, and Montana, whose works support a light, humorous interpretation of a period of life that can be otherwise fraught with troubling issues.

Romance

Unlike comics in the teen humor tradition that preceded them, romance comics took maturing very seriously, producing a distinct genre that spoke to an overwhelmingly female readership. Typically they were melodramatic in their treatment of young people's struggles with mature romantic relationships. The genre developed right after the Second World War ended when many Americans were settling back into domestic roles. For the next thirty years, romance comics would be a vital part of the comics industry.

The first ongoing title to introduce romance to comics readers was *Young Romance* (1947) from Prize Publications, produced by Joe Simon and Jack Kirby, the same creative team who had created Captain America earlier that decade. The cover of the first issue of *Young Romance* proudly announced that this title was "Designed for the more *adult* readers of *comics*," and that audience, particularly the underserved audience of women readers, responded favorably. *Young Romance* soon had a circulation of over a million copies an issue, and other publishers followed in its wake with titles like *My Own Romance*, *Heart Throbs*, and *First Love*, producing over 120 imitators by 1949.

Romance comics were usually published in anthology format, featuring a collection of three or four stories of a few pages in length, each with a new cast of love-struck characters. Most of the tales were narrated as first-person confessionals, usually with a young woman admitting the burden of some guilt to the reader (e.g., having kissed an older man). Although most of these tales concluded with a happy ending and the destined couple together, a **narrative problematic** frustrated their union for six to eight pages. A narrative problematic is the challenge that must be overcome or resolved before a happy ending can be reached in a story. Oftentimes the path to true happiness was blocked by a female rival for a boy's affection, or an overprotective parent or town gossip could serve as villainous opposition on the pathway to true love (Figure 6.4). Story conflict could also come from within the principal characters, such as a girl who is already involved with a somewhat superficial boyfriend and needs to recognize her true place beside a less articulate but more genuine suitor. Though the titles of the stories could be lurid (e.g., "I Was a Pick-Up" or "You're Not the First"), the

Figure 6.4 Two's company but three's a crowd on the cover of *All for Love* #1 (1958). © Feature Publication, Inc.

books were typically quite tame, especially after the Comics Code came into being in 1954. Although the pairings pointed toward physical relationships, the stories almost never depicted physical intimacy beyond mere kissing. As comics historian Maurice Horn put it, "It was all titillation and no satisfaction" (1985: 73).

The depictions of heroines and heroes in the romance comics were fairly realistic, as readers were meant to identify with the protagonists. However, these depictions could certainly be said to err on the side of idealism, with beautifully coiffed, shapely young women and handsome, well-built young men in the leading roles. Occasionally the portrayals might indulge in a stereotype, like having the blonde lead be the good girl while her brunette rival is the bad girl. More consistently, realities like braces, acne, and excessive weight were rarely depicted among the principal characters. These comics were meant to be fantasy fulfillment, and they depicted their characters accordingly. In due course, "They satisfied a kid's need to know what was ahead, to know that dreams could come true and that life was a simple matter once you found your man" (Scott 1979: 12).

Although romance comics may have given women an entertaining product, they rarely gave them role models who veered far from the societal norms of the mid-twentieth century. Female characters may have narrated the stories, but those characters typically fell into traditional gender roles within the stories themselves. This is not all that surprising when one considers that nearly all romance comics were created by men. Many of these men were talented storytellers, but they were nevertheless portraying their conception of romantic courtship through their own worldview. Even the advice columns featured in many of these magazines were written by men under feminine pen names (e.g., "Julia Roberts") responding to their readers' inquiries.

American society underwent a shift in attitudes toward sexuality and gender roles in the 1960s, and although romance comics attempted to remain in tune with the changes, the creators labored under the restrictions of the Comics Code. Soon romance audiences could find more lurid content in television soap operas and Harlequin paperback novels. Romance comics may have also been undermined by their anthology format, largely lacking a continuing cast of characters with whom readers could establish and pursue **parasocial relationships**. Parasocial relationships develop when people perceive emotional connections to fictional characters or media personalities whom they have never met. These feelings of familiarity may be experienced as intensely as connections to people with whom we have shared relationships. Marvel Comics stopped producing romance comics in 1976 and DC Comics canceled *Young Love*, its last title in the genre, in 1977.

The legacy of romance comics, however, extends well beyond the demise of their leading titles in the late 1970s. Writer John Lustig suggests that the angst-ridden characterization of Marvel Comics' revolutionary superhero characters is indebted to the genre. After all, Stan Lee, Jack Kirby, and many of their fellow collaborators had been working exhaustively on romance comics in the decade prior to the birth of the Marvel Universe. Marvel superheroes often find themselves in challenging relationships, such as the forbidden love between the mutant Scarlet Witch and the android Vision, or the divine Thor's unfulfilled desire to marry his mortal sweetheart Jane Foster. Romance has remained a vital part of the mainstream comics scene.

Of late, the increasing attention directed at a female audience by manga has meant a return to prominence for romance comics within the American comics marketplace. Comics classified as *shôjo* ("little girl") manga are directed at a female audience and feature melodramatic treatments of maturing and relationships. Their central themes often focus on "getting the boy" but also increasingly on "finding oneself" in coming-of-age settings (Thorn 2001: 48). Even mainstream publishers like Marvel and DC have experimented with similarly focused titles like *Spider-Man Loves Mary Jane*, which tell stories from teenager Mary Jane Watson's perspective and are illustrated in the manga style. As they did a generation ago, such romance comics prove that comics are not just for boys.

Funny Animals

The concept of **anthropomorphism**—endowing animals with human qualities—is as old as recorded literature. In the Western tradition Aesop spun fables from ancient Greece (e.g., "The Tortoise and the Hare") and in the Eastern tradition Toba Sōjō depicted animals behaving like humans on *chōjū-jinbutsu-giga* (animal-person caricatures) in twelfth century Japan (these scrolls are considered some of the earliest forms of manga). As a literary device, anthropomorphism acts as a mirror, allowing the storyteller to reflect human characteristics—more often than not, the less flattering ones—back upon the readers in order to enlighten them about the human condition. Encountering animals who speak eloquently, socialize according to human customs, and meet their just desserts when tripped up by their own pride, avarice, or ignorance makes for an entertaining story. Such imagined creatures have fascinated people throughout history and across cultures. It's little wonder then that these "funny animals" would find a home in early comic books (Figure 6.5).

Early comic strips had already embraced animal protagonists by the time comic books came to print. Most notably, George Herriman's strip *Krazy Kat*, launched in 1913, set an aesthetic standard for the genre in the pages of America's newspapers. Yet the fledgling comic book industry did not turn to its newspaper forerunners for funny animal material to fill its pages but to the popular animated film shorts of the day. The first film studio to lend its characters to comic books was Walt Disney, who licensed stars like Mickey Mouse and Donald Duck to Dell Publishing. In 1940 Dell launched the first ongoing funny animal comic book with *Walt Disney's Comics and Stories*. Dell quickly followed up its successful relationship with Disney by establishing contracts with Warner Brothers Studios to use characters like Porky Pig and Bugs Bunny, beginning with *Looney Tunes and Merrie Melodies* (1941), and then enrolled MGM's Walter Lantz creations like Andy Panda and Woody Woodpecker for the first issue of *New Funnies* (1942). Other publishers tried to catch up to Dell's initiative, with first Timely and then St. John Publishing taking on 20th Century Fox's Paul Terry creations like Mighty Mouse in *Terry-Toons* (1942). National Periodicals got into the contest late with Columbia Pictures' the Fox and the Crow in *Real Screen Comics* (1945).

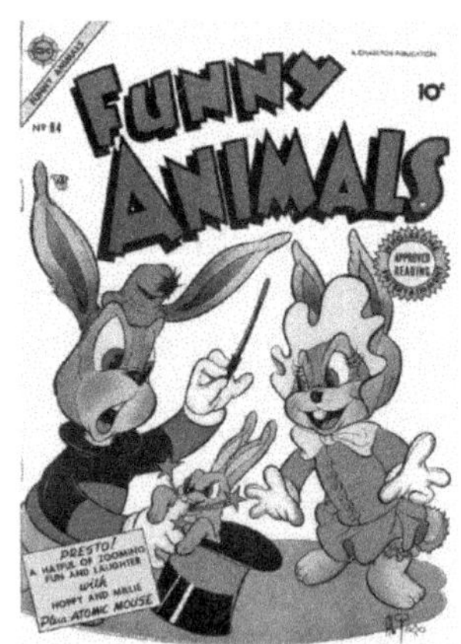

Figure 6.5 This cover by artist Al Fago illustrates a style common among funny animal comics, as anthropomorphic creatures perform human tasks to comical effect. *Funny Animals* #84 (April 1954) © Charlton Comics.

While such adaptations may have been popular with audiences, particularly young children, the translation did not always fare well when moving from one medium to another. For instance, part of the thrill of a Bugs Bunny animated romp is the pacing of the slapstick comedy and masterful vocalizations by voice actor Mel Blanc, but comics cannot convey these qualities. Indeed, the best remembered of the original spate of funny animal comics ultimately proved to be characters that emerged indigenous to the medium. To that end, two creators became synonymous with the genre: Walt Kelly and Carl Barks.

Walt Kelly is highly regarded for the creation of Pogo Possum, an original character who debuted in Dell's *Animal Comics* #1 (1942). Pogo became highly successful in comic books and, beginning in 1949, migrated into a syndicated newspaper strip as well. In fact, while Pogo's comic book career came to end by 1954, his newspaper strip ran nationwide until 1975. Part of the strip's appeal was the genuine satire that Kelly introduced into the Okefenokee Swamp that Pogo inhabited, particularly as he skewered political figures of his day. For instance, Pogo took on Senator Joseph McCarthy during his infamous communist witch-hunts by parodying the senator and his crusade through the character of Simple J. Malarkey. Kelly's savvy satire made Pogo popular enough over the decades that the publishing house of Simon & Shuster issued dozens of collected editions reprinting his adventures. These were among the early forerunners of modern trade paperbacks that regularly collect and reprint comics material today.

Another cartoonist who had an enduring impact on the funny animal genre was Carl Barks, whose work for Dell's Disney line of comics earned him the title of "the good artist" from fans. Disney policy left artists' contributions uncredited—except for Walt himself—in their initial printings. But as fans learned to distinguish the care and style of Barks' work over time, he earned fan recognition despite his anonymity. Between 1942 and 1967 Barks drew hundreds of Donald Duck features and, in December 1947, he introduced fan-favorite character Uncle Scrooge McDuck. To this day, Barks' work is still appearing in reprinted editions of his comics, and he is possibly the most successful American comics creator in Europe.

The earliest funny animal comics, like the fables that preceded them, often focused on some moral lesson: be kind to one's neighbors, always tell the truth, etc. But the appeal for the audience might have been more utilitarian than moralistic. According to historian Les Daniels, "At an age when children had little on their side except the ability to dissemble and a repertoire of alternate fantasy identities, and were surrounded by dumb adults or neighborhood bullies, these images released, quite simply, the power to do infinite things with minimal resources" (1971: 53). Funny animals thus became equipment for the imagination, allowing readers to break free of an otherwise confining life. In regards to their quality of wish fulfillment, then, they may not have been all that different from the superhero comics with which they competed.

The popularity of funny animal comics reached its highest levels during the 1940s and 1950s, though their influence continued throughout the ensuing decades, particularly as subsequent artists began to use the juxtaposition of talking animals interacting with the idiosyncrasies of human society. A new generation of cartoonists tapped into this satirical vein, including Steve Gerber's *Howard the Duck* for Marvel Comics (beginning in 1973) and Dave Sim's epic *Cerebus* (1977–2004), which featured a talking aardvark who held vocations as varied as barbarian warrior and pope. Funny animals continue to allow cartoonists the freedom to explore the human condition, and later examples such as Reed Waller and Kate Worley's sexy soap opera *Omaha the Cat Dancer*, Jim Woodring's anthropomorphic creature Frank, and Jeff Smith's adventurous *Bone* have found a forum among comics' independent publishers.

Horror

Tales of encounters with the supernatural have been fodder for the imagination since people first started storytelling, but the modern fascination with horror fiction can be traced most directly to Mary Shelley's 1818 novel *Frankenstein*. The novel speaks to the awful retribution that comes with disrupting the natural order of things. When scientist Victor Frankenstein builds his Creature using parts of reanimated corpses, he pays for transgressing the natural boundaries between life and death with his own ruination. Horror has been a popular genre in every mass medium, from novels, radio, and films to television, video games, and, of course, comics. Horror stories pick at our collective uneasiness with the unknown, with what lies beyond in the darkness, just out of reach of the revealing light of our primordial campfires. Reading horror stories allows an audience to play out what it fears and in the process allows some catharsis—or emotional release—from those fears.

Given their familiarity in popular culture, it is not surprising that horrific figures like Frankenstein's Creature were featured in anthologies like *Prize Comics* as early as 1940. Eventually whole comic books devoted specificly to the genre emerged, beginning with a one-shot from Avon titled *Eerie*, published in 1946. The first ongoing title came along within the next two years when the American Comics Group started *Adventures into the Unknown* in 1948 and continued to publish it until 1967. But the gold standard in horror comics came from the stable of Entertaining Comics, which published *The Crypt of Terror*—soon changed to the now more familiar title of *Tales from the Crypt*—alongside *The Vault of Horror* and *The Haunt of Fear* beginning in 1950. Under the guidance of publisher Bill Gaines and editor Al Feldstein, EC quickly gained a reputation for clever stories and superior artwork, and even popular fiction author Ray Bradbury allowed some of his works to be adapted by the EC staff. Although the entire run of EC horror comics lasted less than five years, those works have been reprinted again and again. They have even been adapted into film and television directly (e.g., HBO's *Tales from the Crypt*) and had an acknowledged influence on horror fiction in other media, including the works of Stephen King in his short stories and screenplays (*Creepshow*), R. L. Stine in children's books (the "Goosebumps" series), and George Romero and John Carpenter in their films (*Night of the Living Dead* and *The Fog*, respectively).

In the early 1950s EC's success inspired a stampede of imitators, many of whom thought the key to sales rested in increasingly gruesome scenes of violence and gore. The excesses of the horror genre helped fuel a national campaign against the entire comics industry, resulting in the Comics Code, an industry-sponsored censoring program that effectively neutered horror comics and sanitized most future comics exclusively for juvenile audiences (see Chapter 10). Among its prohibitions, the Code forbade the use of the words *horror* or *terror* in any comic book's title and prohibited the use of vampires, werewolves, and zombies in any comic's cast. Despite such restrictions, some of the former horror titles suffered on, but they were much tamer under the auspices of the Code, offering more fantasy and science fiction stories than outright horror. Fear-inducing giant monsters on the order of Godzilla became features in the late fifties and early sixties, offering comics readers some thrills but far fewer chills.

Horror comics eventually found an outlet outside traditional comics magazines, at least until the Comics Code could undergo revision. The re-emergence of horror comics began in earnest in 1964 when Warren Publishing published the first issue of *Creepy*, an anthology attempting to replicate the EC formula for success. *Creepy* skirted the restrictions of the Comics Code by publishing its stories in larger magazine size and in black and white instead of color. The success of *Creepy* led to companion magazines like *Eerie* and *Vampirella*. Wanting to compete with the resurging horror market, comic publishers applied pressure to loosen the Code's restrictions.

When changes to the Code came, they also helped foment changes in the perception of the horrific creatures, as creators began to adopt a view of the monsters as somewhat sympathetic protagonists instead of the misery-inducing antagonists (Mishler 2006). The turn began in 1971 with a revised Code permitting some formerly restricted elements back into full-color comics, repealing the ban on supernatural creatures but still maintaining some taste-related restrictions. Marvel Comics quickly seized the opportunity to release a number of series featuring everything from werewolves to swamp monsters as their leads, the most successful of which was the *Tomb of Dracula* series written by Marv Wolfman and drawn by Gene Colan. During its run through most of the 1970s, *Tomb of Dracula* was an intricately plotted serial, with the world's most famous vampire starring amid a cast of dubious allies and righteous adversaries (including the later-to-be-famous Blade, the Vampire Hunter). Despite his titular role, Dracula was still evil in this series, but a more sympathetic monster would take shape over at DC Comics, where Len Wein and Bernie Wrightson introduced the Swamp Thing character (*House of Secrets* #92, 1971). In 1984 emerging superstar writer Alan Moore took the reins of the Swamp Thing and used the character to move horror comics more from the physical to psychological, emphasizing mood over gory spectacle. A similarly intellectual take on horror came from Neil Gaiman's acclaimed *Sandman* series (1989).

However, not all horror comics subsequent to the Code's revision were more cerebral than visceral. The rise of the direct market meant that comics producers did not have to seek Code approval for newsstand distribution, allowing creators to push the envelope of graphic horror far further than it had been since the Code's introduction in the 1950s. The 1990s saw more blood-soaked series like *Evil Ernie* and *Lady Death* from Chaos! Comics on sale at comics specialty shops alongside the more moody titles of DC's Vertigo line. The emphasis on the horror as the hero, though, would continue to dominate the genre, with successful titles like Mike Mignola's *Hellboy* and Marvel's *Man-Thing* thrusting the supernatural protagonists into the forefront.

As a genre, horror's most obvious characteristic is the insertion of the supernatural into the commonplace. Using fantastic creatures like ghosts or monsters accomplishes this quite readily, especially when their depictions are taken to the extremes of distortion or the grotesque. Of course, what makes these representations really pop is their contrast with ordinary surroundings. So when a werewolf shows up at a movie theater, or a screaming poltergeist haunts a typical suburban home, the shock scares an audience who fears such monstrosities could invade their own commonplace lives. With its emphasis on the visual storytelling elements, comics is an ideal medium for horror stories, as the reader can be reminded of the presence of the supernatural frame after frame, and linger over them as they move through the story at their own pace (Gravett 2005).

A second element common to stories within the horror genre is the element of suspense, the dramatic tension that comes from not knowing the survival of a character or the resolution of a stress-filled situation. Typically, this tension rises throughout the story with additional twists and turns compounding the pressure until the very end of the story. Al Feldstein was particularly revered for his EC comics' twist endings, in which some deviant or evil character would have his comeuppance in the form of poetic justice. For instance, a butcher selling spoiled meat in order to increase his own profits would receive just punishment for his misdeeds, finding himself carved up and displayed in his own meat case by the story's end (*Tales from the Crypt* #32, 1952). Though usually gruesome, horror comics could also aim to be moralistic, relaying a message against greed, jealousy, and other vices. Whether such loftier messages get lost in the spectacle of the accompanying gore is open to debate.

Figure 6.6 Uncle Creepy provided a lighter touch as he narrated spooky stories on the pages of Warren Publication's *Creepy* magazine, a series later resurrected by Dark Horse Comics © 2009.

Because the tension and gore can be so intense, some horror comics have subscribed to a third common feature, softening the delivery of their gruesome tales by having them served up by a host with a sense of humor. Once again EC innovated this trend in horror comics, though Gaines and Feldstein had taken it from early radio programs. In popular radio series like the *Witch's Tale* and *Inner Sanctum*, a creepy narrator introduced and closed each episode. EC did the same with each story, framing their tales with three "GhouLunatics" named the Crypt-Keeper, the Vault-Keeper, and the Old Witch. Each of these characters provided punny segues into and out of the intense stories. For instance, at the end of one tale, the Crypt-Keeper reminds the reader of his own mortality and asks, "Why the *grave* look?" here using *grave* to play on both the deathly theme of the story and to strike an ironic chord about the anticipated seriousness of the reader's reaction. Later horror comics would embrace the GhouLunatics approach, with Warren Publishing giving both its Uncle Creepy and Cousin Eerie similar personalities for its black-and-white magazines (Figure 6.6). DC later cast sparring siblings Cain and Abel as the hosts of its leading horror books, and Charlton Comics featured a whole gang of offbeat hosts, from Dr. Graves to Baron Weirwulf. The hosts also gave those horror comics that featured anthology tales a recurring character to retain audience loyalty from issue to issue. After all, with a number of the featured characters left beheaded, dismembered, or disemboweled by the end of just one story, the host might be the only one in any shape to return with the next issue.

Other Genres, Briefly

In addition to teen humor, romance, funny animals, and horror, other genres popular in the comics have included the following. **Crime comics** depict realistic criminal activities, such as murder, often with a focus on the perpetrator. Contrary to its title, *Crime Does Not Pay* (1942–5) often depicted such criminals as sympathetic anti-heroes—some of them based on real-life convicts—which led to public outcry against their all-too-graphic content. Publishers began to shy away from the genre in response to the objections at the time, though crime comics have found an audience with more mature readers in recent times in works such as Ed Brubaker and Sean Phillips' *Criminal* (2006–).

War comics focus on the life-and-death struggle of combat. Some examples suggest the futility of war while others glamorize the heroics. EC told some of the most poignant war stories in the pages of Harvey Kurtzman's *Two-Fisted Tales* (1950–5) while DC followed the Second World War tour of Sergeant Frank Rock in a series that ran from 1959 to 1988 by Robert Kaningher and Joe Kubert.

The setting for **jungle comics** is captured in its very name. Typically set in the untamed regions of Africa, jungle comics took inspiration from Edgar Rice Burroughs's Tarzan (debuting in 1912), a pulp magazine creation, who became a multimedia phenomenon. Like Tarzan, the protagonists of jungle comics are white heroes and heroines garbed in animal-print swimsuits protecting the environment, its indigenous people, and their white prerogative. Sheena, Queen of the Jungle, is among the most famous jungle queens to have made her mark in comics, debuting in *Jumbo Comics* in 1938 and created by Will Eisner and Jerry Iger.

Kids comics are filled with small characters and big laughs. Kids comics took root in newspaper strips with Rudolph Dirks' *Katzenjammer Kids.* The series debuted in 1897 and ran original material until 2006; reprints are still in syndication, making it the longest-running comic strip in American media history. Marge's *Little Lulu* (debuting in 1935) and Harvey Publishing's *Richie Rich* (debuting in 1957) are other examples of clever children who manage their social world with skill sets well beyond their age.

Just as Hollywood has adapted the intellectual property from comics into films, comics have a long history of adapting features from film and television into comics. **Movie comics** (and/or TV comics) have offered fans interpretations of the filmed adventures or expanded those universes accordingly. Perhaps the most commercially successful film franchise to translate to comics is *Star Wars*, which has produced an extensive expanded universe of material since Marvel first adapted the original film in 1977, adding characters like Gryph and Doctor Aphra to the canon.

Elsewhere in this book, we introduce other genres. Among them, you can read more about underground comix like *Wimmen's Comix* in Chapter 10 and educational comics like *Classics Illustrated* in Chapter 11. There are, of course, even more genres than that, but this brief introduction should give you a sense of the range of possibilities in so much as some of the most commercially viable genres track how the industry has progressed over time.

Analyzing: Hybrid Forms

Although talking about genres requires us to define them in some static ways, the reality of media products is that they are always evolving. In part, this evolution may be attributed to the creative impulses of the cartoonists who are developing new stories to tell. Many of them want to experiment with pushing boundaries by introducing new storytelling elements into their work. The evolution may also be attributed to publishers wanting to find more distinct materials to appeal to their audience in a crowded marketplace. For instance, when the first horror comics appeared, they were nowhere near as gruesome as they would become by the mid-fifties and no one could have foreseen the turn to more moody, psychological horror later in the twentieth century. Put simply, genres evolve.

One of the ways to see the evolution of genre take shape is to note how some comics experiment with hybrid forms. A hybrid might take the familiar character types of one genre and drop them into the narrative pattern of another. For example, in the early 1950s, when both western and romance comics were at the heights of their popularity, a number of publishers experimented with cross-breeding the genres, producing titles like *Western Hearts*, *Western Love*, and *Cowgirl Romances* (Figure 6.7). Similarly, publishers in the 1970s attempted to mix the chills of horror comics with the thrills of love comics, presenting gothic-romance hybrids in titles like *The Dark Mansion of Forbidden Love* and *Haunted Love*. Of course, by far the most experimentation has taken place with the dominant superhero genre, as nearly every conceivable match has been attempted at one time or another:

Figure 6.7 Cowboys discover love on the range in the pages of the short-lived hybridization of western and romance comics (*Cowboy Love* #31, 1955). © 1955 Charlton Comics.

- Superhero + western = the original *Ghost Rider*
- Superhero + teen humor = *Archie as Pureheart the Powerful*
- Superhero + romance = *Young Heroes in Love*
- Superhero + funny animals = *Captain Carrot and His Amazing Zoo Crew*
- Superhero + horror = *Spectre*

And the list goes on and on.

Whether it is for aesthetic exploration or commercial exploitation, the attempts to create and market hybrids have produced some entertaining results. Most of these combinations do not last long, though they can subtly influence a genre. Although a spate of western romances filled the newsstands in the early 1950s, the hybrid was fleeting and the western soon returned to its conventional focus on the male hero, while romance anthologies only occasionally found themselves presenting a love story in a western setting. Other hybrids have been more successful. The combination of horror and superheroes in the pages of *Marvel Zombies* has sold a lot of comics and related merchandise since its debut. Yet whatever their commercial success or longevity, hybrids serve to remind us that comics, as with other popular arts, allow creators to play with their most familiar storytelling techniques.

Discussion Questions

1. How do genres influence your consumption of media? For instance, are you more likely to tune in to a program because it's on SYFY (cable television's

science-fiction-themed channel)? Or would you pick up a paperback because it's a Harlequin Romance? Explain how your own preference(s) for genre(s) influence your selection of media products.

2. Are comics genres products of their times, or do they transcend the times? If you find that they are reflections of their eras, what does a given genre's popularity say about its time (e.g., the rise of sword-and-sorcery or kung-fu comics in the 1970s)? If you perceive that genres transcend their era, what qualities make a given genre popular from generation to generation (e.g., why has Archie's teen humor been able to stay in publication for so long)?
3. Identify two comic genres and then propose a hybridization of them. What features of each would be most relevant to your hybrid narrative? Why do you suppose that the combination would be appealing to an audience?

Activities

1. Conduct a genre analysis of a recent graphic novel. First select one of the genres described in depth in this chapter's readings (e.g., westerns, teen humor, romance, funny animals, horror) and note well the qualities we have discussed that help to define that particular genre. Then select a graphic novel that you perceive as fitting into that genre. (Your instructor may be able to help with some suggestions.) Next, read the graphic novel, noting how it fulfills the characteristic of the genre, such as familiar character types, narrative patterns, genre conventions, and themes (recall that this is all a function of standardization). Also be aware of ways in which it deviates from the genre or other examples within the genre (differentiation). Consider how genre both enables and possibly constrains the storytelling going on in your graphic novel; in other words, what are the advantages and limitations of working within a genre? Your instructor may ask you to submit this analysis as either a written report or an oral presentation explaining how the work fits the genre.
2. It is said that you can't judge a book by its cover, and yet countless impulse purchases at grocery store checkout lanes and bookstore window displays are predicated on the assumption that a good cover *can* sell a publication. Visit your local comic book specialty shop or the graphic novel section of your local library or bookstore in order to locate examples of one of the genres outlined in this chapter. Scan the covers of a number of comics within your selected genre and then pick three covers to analyze in greater depth. Note what you are seeing in terms of genre conventions being displayed on the cover art. How do you know that a selected work actually fits into a given genre? Do the language choices of the title or on any backmatter (e.g., summaries, reviewers' comments, etc.) confirm your inclination that the book fits a specific genre? Do these choices inspire you to want to pick up that particular comic? Come to class prepared to share at least three talking points about how the shorthand of visual communication can be used to successfully (or perhaps even unsuccessfully) suggest a particular genre fit a passing audience.

Recommended Reading

Comics

Smith, Jeff. *Bone*. Columbus: Cartoon Books, 2004.

When Jeff Smith started work on *Bone*, he had a vision of combining anthropomorphic creatures like those that he admired in Walt Kelly's *Pogo* and the grandeur of epic fantasy storytelling that he admired in the works of J. R. R. Tolkien's *Lord of the Rings*. He succeeded in producing a 1,332-page epic (affectionately nicknamed "The Brick" because of its impressive size) that combines the charm and comedic sensibility of short, bone-white creatures with an epic journey to protect the world. Although it is recognizably in the funny animal genre, it is also something more than that and could be considered a hybrid of funny animal and fantasy genres.

Cochran, Russ, ed. *EC Archives*. Milwaukie: Dark Horse Comics, 2013-present.

EC expert Russ Cochran has championed the preservation of EC comics for decades and now partners with Dark Horse to reprint the EC library. Volumes include the genre-defining horror classics from *Tales from the Crypt*, *Vault of Horror*, and *Haunt of Fear*. Also joining them in the series are volumes of EC's *Two-Fisted Tales* and science fiction favorite *Weird Science*.

Scholarly Sources

Labarre, Nicolas. *Understanding Genres in Comics*. London: Palgrave Pivot, 2020.

Labarre argues that genre is an important component of understanding comics publishing and introduces a multifaceted approach for further understanding the impact of genre. A number of case studies examine how the formation and evolution of genres such as horror, funny animals, and science fiction, among others, are influenced by a confluence of publishers' economic motivations, creators' artistic drives, and readers' expectations and responses.

Nolan, Michele. *Love on the Racks: A History of American Romance Comics*. Jefferson: McFarland, 2015.

Nolan traces the development of the romance genre from its roots in teen humor series of the 1940s like *Archie* to the final issue of *Young Love* in the late 1970s. In between are copious details about the evolution and popularization of the genre, including its forays into hybrid genres like western romance.

7 Memoir Comics

At a 1954 Senate Judiciary subcommittee hearing on juvenile delinquency Senator Estes Kefauver held up an issue of *Crime SuspenStories* and questioned whether children should be reading such trash. Nearly sixty years later Senator Patrick Leahy held up a graphic novel at a Senate Judiciary Committee hearing and vowed to make sure all of his grandchildren read it (Wickline 2013). The 2013 hearing was on restoring the protections of the Voting Rights Act and the graphic novel was *March: Book One*, co-written by Representative John Lewis and chronicling his experiences as one of the leaders of the Civil Right Movement in the 1960s (Figures 7.1a–b).

The fact that a Representative would coauthor a graphic novel and a senator would publicly praise a graphic novel seems to indicate attitudes toward comics are much more positive than they were sixty years ago. However, do not expect to see romance, superhero, or teen humor comic books being touted in the Senate. *March* is a memoir and the memoir genre has achieved a respectability not enjoyed by the comics medium as a whole, with the third volume of *March* going on to be the first graphic novel to win the National Book Award for Young People's Literature.

Figure 7.1a In the 1950s James A. Fitzpatrick, chairman of the New York State Joint Legislative Committee to Legislate the Publication of Comics, questioned the suitability of comics for children. Photo by Yale Joel/Time & Life Pictures/Getty Images.

Figure 7.1b In 2013, United States Senator Patrick Leahy promoted the graphic novel, *March* by Congressman John Lewis, Andrew Aydin, and Nate Powell, as worthy of reading, a marked transition in political sentiment about comics from the past. Photo by Win McNamee/Getty Images.

Objectives

In this chapter you will learn:

1. the development of the memoir genre in comics form.
2. the author/narrator/character dynamic that exists in comics memoirs.
3. the typical themes and narrative patterns of comics memoirs.
4. how a comics memoir can intertwine with the identity of its creator.

Defining Memoir

While Gore Vidal, in his own memoir, *Palimpsest*, writes that "a memoir is how one remembers one's own life, while an autobiography is history, requiring research, dates, facts double-checked" (5). In an autobiography there is an emphasis on documenting one's life, providing facts about events, whereas the writer of a memoir is often more concerned with conveying her or his feelings about events. Does this mean a memoir is less true than an autobiography? We will revisit this idea later when we discuss authenticity in memoir.

An autobiography usually spans all of the person's life up to the point of the writing. A **memoir** usually covers a much shorter span of time, and often focuses on particular life-changing incidents and their consequences. Yet, influential life writing scholar Philippe Lejeune defines autobiography as "a retrospective account in prose that a real person makes of his own existence stressing his individual life and especially the history of his personality" (1989: 4). That last part, about the history of a personality, seems to de-emphasize what we usually associate with autobiography, the documented facts of the person's life, and hint at the more emotional, less precise approach of a memoir that explains how a person's most significant experiences molded him or her into the person writing the narrative.

Vidal's definition makes clear distinctions between autobiography and memoir, but in practice many works of life writing are difficult to categorize, and the terms autobiography and memoir are often used interchangeably. Some of the experts we quote in this chapter use the term autobiography but their observations apply to the genre we are calling memoir.

Strict definitions are no longer in vogue because postmodern literary theorists believe memoirists have the right to use any form, including poetry, novels, or comics, they feel works to present their lives (Spengemann 1980: xii). It is not our intent to provide a precise and limiting definition, but rather to describe the conventions of form, content, and style that are characteristic of memoir in comics form.

But first, we provide a very brief consideration of how memoir has developed into one of the most significant genres of comics.

History of Memoir in Comics Form

Memoir took hold in the Western world as stories about the lives of historical figures began to replace the tales of mythic heroes as a way of coming to terms with existence through narrative (Freeman and Brockmeier 2001: 79). The autobiographical impulse began to flourish with the rise of Christianity because the act of confession and the emphasis on having to answer for one's deeds in the afterlife encouraged self-reflection (Freeman and Brockmeier 2001: 80).

Cross-Cultural Roots

The first significant memoir in comics form was the result of a blending of two of the world's major comics traditions, Japanese **manga** and American comic strips. Artist "Henry" Yoshitaka Kiyama used comics to recount the struggles and triumphs he and his friends had as young immigrants to the United States. Kiyama created fifty-two comic-strip episodes he hoped would be serialized in a Japanese language newspaper in San Francisco. No newspaper was interested in this unusual work so, in 1931, Kiyama self-published his collected strips as a book, *Manga Yonin Shosei* (*The Four Students Manga*). At 104 pages long, the work might be considered one of the first graphic novels produced in America. Manga scholar Frederik Schodt discovered the rather obscure book and produced an English translation that was published in 1999 as *The Four Immigrants Manga: A Japanese Experience in San Francisco, 1904—1924*.

The next significant memoir comics were also manga. Shin'ichi Nagashima's *Mangaka Zankoku Monogatari* (*The Harsh Story of a Manga Artist*), published in 1961, presented the first behind-the-scenes stories about the manga industry. Yoshiharu Tsuge's semi-autobiographical story "Chiko," published in *Garo* magazine in 1966, is an early example of what came to be known as *watakushi-manga* (I-comics is Béatrice Maréchal's translation). A few years later *Garo* published the highly influential story "Nejishiki" (1968), the first of Tsuge'a dream comics. Many US comic book fans were first exposed to *watakushi-manga* (and manga in general) in the early 1980s when Educomics published English translations of the work of Keiji Nakazawa. His *Ore wa Mita* (1972) was a brief biography culminating in Hiroshima being devastated by the atomic bomb. In 1973 Nakazawa began expanding the story into the much longer, but more fictionalized *Gen of Hiroshima*. Educomics translated and published the first two installments as *Barefoot Gen* in 1980 and 1981. In 1982 Educomics published *Ore wa Mita* as *I Saw It!* Eventually Last Gasp published the complete *Barefoot Gen* in ten volumes.

Up from the Underground

1972 was the year that a vigorous strain of graphic memoir emerged from the **underground comix** movement in America. The most significant comics memoir of 1972 was *Binky Brown Meets the Holy Virgin Mary* by Justin Green. On the surface the comic might seem sacrilegious and salacious (Green's autobiographical avatar Binky sees penises everywhere), but at its core it is a very revelatory and personal story of a young man tormented by pathological guilt, a form of obsessive-compulsive personality disorder. Green portrayed his internal strife through extensive use of visual metaphor, setting an example that other comics memoirists would follow in depicting their emotional realities. For instance, in the first panel of the book Green is laboriously drawing with a nib pen in his mouth because he is in bondage, enslaved by his compulsive neurosis. On the last page before the epilogue (Figure 7.2) Green's avatar, Binky, is depicted as a fish with a nib pen in his mouth because he "has crawled out of the primeval morass of superstition." *Binky Brown* is considered the genesis of memoir comics in America because "Robert Crumb, Aline Kominsky-Crumb, and Art Spiegelman, credit Green's 1972 comic book with transforming their vision of the potential for telling stories in comics form" (Witek 2011: 227).

Figure 7.2 *Binky Brown Meets the Holy Virgin Mary* (1972) is the seminal comics memoir. © 2009 Justin Green.

Though the titles "The Confessions of R. Crumb" (from *The People's Comics* 1972) and "The Adventures of R. Crumb Himself" (from *Tales of the Leather Nun* 1973) denote memoir, and they are sometimes cited as such, the strips' narratives quickly leave behind any semblance of reality and become sometimes violent fantasies. However, these stories can be taken as highly metaphorical psychosexual self-portraits of Robert Crumb because self-parody and fantasy are part of the lens through which Crumb experiences the world (Witek 1989: 129; Versaci 2007: 40). Aline Kominsky, who would marry Robert Crumb a few years later, began her long career of life writing in comics with "Goldie" in *Wimmen's Comix* # 1 (1972). With the short story "Maus," published in *Funny Aminals* # 1 (1972), Art Spiegelman planted the seed from which he eventually cultivated the graphic novel *Maus*. The original "Maus" was mostly biography, but with "Prisoner on a Hell Planet," published in *Short Order Comix* #1 (1973), Spiegelman crafted a creative memoir, with text that is straightforward autobiography and pictures that are expressionistic and metaphorical.

It was also in 1972 that Harvey Pekar began publishing short stories about his life experience in underground comix such as *The People's Comics* and *Bizarre Sex*. Although he had to continually cajole artists to draw his stories, Pekar was determined to continue documenting his life in comics form and in 1976 he self-published the first issue of *American Splendor*. Jared Gardner believes Pekar's use of "the comics medium to express the daily mundane experiences of a 'working stiff,' to fully explore the complexities of 'ordinary life,' was in many ways as revolutionary as the iconoclasm of Crumb and his colleagues on the West Coast" (15).

Pekar does not always appear in the stories, but Pekar as the narrator is always "present by implication as an observer or listener," making the work a documentation of his direct experience (Witek 1989: 123). *American Splendor* prefigured the reality show focus on quirky, unglamorous subjects engaged in the small incidents of daily life, but unlike reality TV, Pekar refused to introduce contrived conflict between characters. Most of the conflict was of the man against himself variety; Pekar contending with guilt, doubt, and self-loathing. Yet, *American Splendor* stories sometimes had modest triumphs of the human spirit and understated affirmations of life.

Pekar's Disciples

The school of serialized comics memoir that Pekar's work inspired "has tended to stress the abject, the seedy, the anti-heroic, and the just plain nasty" (Hatfield 2005). Three of the most successful representatives of this school are friends who occasionally appear in each other's stories—Chester Brown, Joe Matt, and Seth.

Chester Brown's comics reveal the sorts of things that would normally be a person's secret shame. He began self-publishing *Yummy Fur* as a mini-comic in 1983 and with issue #18 shifted his emphasis to memoir. Personal stories serialized in *Yummy Fur* were published as the graphic novels *The Playboy* (1992) and *I Never Liked You* (1994). The former dealt with Brown's obsession with pornography and the subsequent self-loathing that made it difficult to form relationships with real women, and the latter with his struggles as an introverted adolescent. In the original graphic novel *Paying for It: A Comic-Strip Memoir about Being a John* (2011) Brown used his own story of paying for sex to advocate for his libertarian view that prostitution should be decriminalized.

Joe Matt's comics present a relentlessly unflattering self-portrait. The aptly named *Peepshow* reveals tawdry incidents with exhibitionist zeal and depicts himself as pathetic, whiney, and obnoxious. Matt began *Peepshow* as a single-page strip in 1987 and the collected strips were published as *Peepshow: The Cartoon Diary of Joe Matt* in 1992. He has continued to document his life in an ongoing *Peepshow* comic book that appears sporadically.

The artist known as Seth reinvented himself a number of times. Born Gregory Gallant, he was a naive small-town kid who became a flamboyant punk for a time and eventually transformed into Seth, a mannerly cartoonist who usually wears a vintage suit and hat. In his *Palookaville* comic book, which began publication in 1991, Seth occasionally told stories about his life. A six-issue story arc from *Palookaville* was collected as the graphic novel *It's a Good Life, If You Don't Weaken* (1996), which appeared to be a memoir but was later revealed to be highly fictionalized (more about this book later). Seth's memoir comics, while introspective, self-revelatory, and occasionally unflattering, are far less tawdry than those of his friends Brown and Matt.

Bande Dessinée Memoirs

About the time Pekar's acolytes began gaining attention in Canada and the United States a memoir movement emerged from ***bande dessinée*** (Franco-Belgian comics). Upstart publisher Ego comme X specialized in introspective memoir comics that followed the example of co-founder Fabrice Neaud. In 1994 Neaud began publishing his comics diary in *Ego comme X* magazine and over the years has collected this work in four volumes titled *Journal*.

Edmond Baudoin created one of the earliest *bande dessinée* memoirs, *Passe le temps* (1982), but in the mid-1990s he began taking a "poetic approach to the representation of his own memories and relationships" with work such as *Eloge de la poussiere* (1995), published by L'Association (Beaty 2007: 146). The alternative publisher L'Association issued some of the most innovative and successful *bande dessinée* memoirs. Many of the comics, such as Jean-Christophe Menu's *Livret de phamille* (1995), dealt with the author's life as a cartoonist. Pierre-François Beauchard, who uses the pen name David B., was one of the seven founding members of L'Association and his *l'Ascension du Haut Mal* (published in English as *Epileptic*), serialized in six volumes from 1996 to 2003, is considered one of the masterpieces of *bande dessinée*. The graphic novel details how young David and the rest of his family dealt with his brother's epilepsy, but it also delves into David's interior reality, presenting his philosophies, fantasies, and obsessions. L'Association's other international success was Marjane Satrapi's *Persepolis*, originally published in four volumes, one per year beginning in 2000. Translated into several languages, *Persepolis* found a worldwide readership, spawned a critically acclaimed animated film, was embraced by critics and scholars, and has become one of the most widely taught graphic novels.

Graphic "Novels"

The underground comix were certainly an important stream that feed the current flood of memoir comics, but a number of contemporary cartoonists were inspired by graphic "novels" created by two of the most lauded creators in the history of the comics medium—Will Eisner and Art Spiegelman. The quotation marks around the term novels is an acknowledgment that the term *novel* has traditionally referred to works of fiction, but is being applied to memoir, a form of nonfiction.

In the preface to the 1985 edition of his groundbreaking *A Contract with God*, Eisner tells the readers the stories within "draw on memory culled from my own experiences" and the "narratives are compounded of people and incidents I would have you accept as real" (Eisner 1985: n.p). The final story, most directly drawn from personal experience, features a young man named Willie. Eisner's *To the Heart of the Storm* (1991) is an even more thinly disguised memoir detailing actual events from his young life from 1928 to 1942.

Over the years Art Spiegelman expanded his 1972 short story into the graphic novel *Maus*. The book not only won a special Pulitzer Prize in 1992, but carved out a space for the literate graphic novel in books clubs, school libraries, and college courses. When Marjane Satrapi received *Maus* as a birthday present in 1995 it opened her eyes to the possibilities of the comics medium and inspired her to begin *Persepolis* (Hattenstone 2008). Satrapi was not the only cartoonist to follow in Spiegelman's wake. In the twenty-first century a growing number of ambitious comics memoirs, such as *One Hundred Demons* (2002) by Lynda Barry, *Blankets* (2003) Craig Thompson, *Fun Home* (2006) Alison Bechdel, and *Vietnamerica* (2011) by GB Tran, have been lauded by critics and taught in college classrooms.

Conventions of the Memoir Genre

Rather than attempting to craft a precise definition that restricts what can be categorized as a comics memoir, we seek to understand the defining characteristics of life stories in comics form by examining the conventions of the genre. Following the structure established in the preceding genre chapters, we will consider the characters, themes, patterns, and visual conventions of the memoir genre.

Character Types: The Author/Narrator/Character Dynamic

According to Lejeune's concept of the autobiographical pact, one of the underlying assumptions of memoir discourse is that the author, the narrator, and the protagonist are representations of the same referent, the same being (Herman 2011: 231). Yet Jared Gardner contends "it is a truism of autobiography studies (and of narratology more generally) that the narrator and subject are not one and the same" (Gardner 2008: 10).

These stances are not as contradictory as they might seem at first glance. Even though the protagonist and narrator of a memoir represent the entity that is the author they are not one and the same. None of us are ideologically, spiritually, or even physically the person were many years ago (as a matter of fact, you don't have any of the skin, skeletal, or blood cells you had seven years ago). Human identity is not a static construct. The substance of a memoir is showing how the protagonist, a younger self with a very different worldview than the present self, became, due to the incidents detailed in the memoir, the author.

The layers of self that exist within a memoir are sometimes referred to as the Experiencing I, the Narrating I, and the Authoring I.

The **Experiencing I** is the protagonist of the narrative. In comics the Experiencing I is represented by an **autobiographical avatar**, a performance of earlier self-enacted by dialogue, thoughts, attitude, and, in comics, an image that appears on the page or screen. And in some cases the "voice" in captions is that of the Experiencing I rather than that of a narrator.

Sometimes this avatar is a less literal, more expressionistic, presentation of one's past self. In "Man with Pen in Head" Frank Miller tells about being an extra in the *Daredevil* movie. Most of the text is a straightforward account of his experiences on the set, but Miller draws himself in a style that is a parody of the typical action-packed Frank Miller comic book. Some authors have chosen to give the autobiographical avatar a different name. Justin Green called his younger self Binky Brown (notice the connection created by the color names), Aline Kominsky-Crumb has used the names Goldie (her maiden name is Goldsmith) and Bunch (a truncated version of her nickname Honeybunch) when writing about herself, and for years Eddie Campbell shared incidents and insights from his own life using the "character" Alec MacGarry. An avatar with a different name might be used because the author wants to maintain some emotional distance from the protagonist or wants to emphasize that while the story is representative of their experiences it is not an absolutely factual account.

The **Narrating I** tells the story to the reader. This is most often achieved through "voice-over" narration that appears in captions (However, as noted earlier, captions are not always synonymous with a narrator). Sometimes, the Narrating I addresses the reader through word balloons emanating from an avatar that steps in and out of the **diegesis** (the world of the story), sometimes representing the protagonist of the story and sometimes representing the narrator of the story (Figure 7.3). In other instances the narration in word balloons is spoken by a separate avatar (distinct from the protagonist avatar). This avatar is usually drawn to look like the memoirist looks at the time of the creation of the memoir, but there can certainly be variations (such as the pixie-like winged mini-Chester in Chester Brown's *The Playboy*,

Figure 7.3 The relationship between author, narrator, and subject can be complex. The same avatar slips back and forth between acting within the diegesis and narrating. *It's a Bird* by Steven Seagle and Teddy Kristiansen. © DC Comics.

1992). Occasionally, thought bubbles can function not as the thoughts of the protagonist at a particular moment in the diegesis, but as extra-diegetic commentary by the narrator.

The Narrating I is often the most ill-defined and mutable of the three layers of self in a comics memoir. In some comics the Narrating I is virtually synonymous with the Authoring I (Figure 7.3). In other instances the Narrating I is a character in the narrative, with an on-page avatar and having a persona and a perspective distinct from the Authoring I (Figure 7.4). And the Narrating I is often an unreliable narrator, not always describing events exactly as they happened and not truly representing the viewpoint of either the protagonist or the author.

Figure 7.4 Authoring I Peter Kuper violates conventions as he has his Narrating I persona interact with his Experiencing I persona. *Stop Forgetting to Remember* © 2007 Peter Kuper.

The **Authoring I** is the creator of the work. In some instances, when synonymous with the Narrating I, the Authoring I speaks directly to the reader. In other works, where the story is told by a Narrating I that operates as a character, the Authoring I can recede into the background. Of course, the Authoring I can never fully recede from the reader's awareness in a comic because the reader knows it is the author who created the narrator character and constructed the sentences the narrator "speaks," and, as Benjamin Woo points out, "a drawn image implies that someone drew it" (175).

When the artist draws an image of herself or himself it creates a character-narrator-reader dynamic that does not exist in prose memoirs. In drawing oneself the artist engages in a type of self-definition that does not occur in simply writing about oneself. **Pictorial embodiment** is Elisabeth El Refaie's term for "the different ways in which graphic memoirists' sense of self is linked with the act of visually representing their bodily identities" (8).

El Refaie believes this pictorial embodiment helps the reader form an affiliation (emotional engagement) with the protagonist (9). Modifying the visual style of that self-representation (say from realistic to expressionistic) can influence the nature of the reader's emotional engagement (Figures 7.10 and 7.11). There can also be more substantive changes in self-representation that influence the reader's cognitive reaction. For example, in most of *Maus* Spiegelman draws all the characters, including the Experiencing I Art Spiegelman, as animals in human clothing. However, for seven pages of the "Auschwitz (Time Flies)" chapter he draws all of the characters as humans wearing an animal mask. These drawings of masked characters invite the reader to infer some shift in the meaning of the animal metaphor.

Discovering: How Readers Engage with a Comics Memoir

By Elisabeth El Refaie

What draws readers to memoirs? Scholar Elisabeth El Refaie offers several of their most attractive qualities.

Pictorial embodiment

The term "embodiment" is used in philosophy, sociology, and cultural studies to refer to the key role played by the experience of our own bodies in creating and sustaining our sense of self. In my study of eighty-five graphic memoirs by both North American and European creators (El Refaie 2012), I introduce the notion of "pictorial embodiment" to suggest that for memoirists working in the comics medium, the requirement to produce multiple self-portraits inevitably entails a particularly intense engagement with bodily perceptions and body image. Comics artists also cannot ignore the sociocultural attitudes, norms, and values that make the body and its appearance meaningful, including those related to gender, ethnicity, age, illness, and beauty, for example.

Involvement and *affiliation*

I have identified two main mechanisms used by graphic memoirists to produce an emotional or intellectual response in audiences: "Involvement" describes the sense of connection that individuals may experience with any communicative event, particularly if they are themselves actively engaged in the process of making meaning. Because of the many gaps between individual panels and between words and images in the comics medium, reading comics always requires some degree of active contribution on the part of readers, and many graphic memoirs deliberately exploit and increase this "gappiness." Another way of encouraging reader involvement is through the use of multimodal rhetorical forms such as metaphor, humor, and intertextuality, which are prevalent in the graphic memoir genre and which all leave something to be completed by the audience. "Affiliation," which I use to refer to the reader's emotional engagement with the protagonists, can be encouraged by both verbal and visual means, for instance by giving the reader access to the protagonists' most intimate thoughts, or by showing their facial expressions in a close-up, fully frontal view, so that readers are able to recognize and empathize with the emotions on display. The visual alignment of the reader with the protagonists' point of view may also encourage affiliation.

Performed authenticity

Although most readers now accept that autobiographical truth is always subjective and relative, they are nevertheless likely to expect graphic memoirs to be in some way "authentic." In my view, the creators of autobiographical comics are inevitably engaged in a kind of display or performance of their own fundamental sincerity. This "performed authenticity" typically involves the use of multiple visual signs, such as the physical resemblance between the author and the narrator/protagonist, the choice of a particular style of drawing, and the inclusion of various forms of visual documentation. For example, many graphic memoirists adopt an apparently artless, spontaneous artistic style in order to suggest that they are acting as neutral channels of their own authentic thoughts and feelings, while others draw on the mythical truthfulness that is still associated with photography. Because such visual elements are often perceived by readers to be not directly under the artist's conscious control, I argue, they tend to be perceived as more reliable signals of authenticity than any overt verbal claims or declarations.

Elisabeth El Refaie is the author of *Autobiographical Comics: Life Writing in Pictures and Visual Metaphor and Embodiment in Graphic Illness Narratives.*

Themes

Inherently Rhetorical

Strategic variations of self-representation to manipulate reader reaction are just one indication of how comics memoirs are rhetorical (persuasive). Memoirs are inherently rhetorical because they are "a work of personal selection and justification" (Freeman and Brockmeier 2001: 81). A memoir is a justification for past actions and current values. It is an argument in support of a worldview (Smith and Watson 2010: 7).

A memoir has to be considered a rhetorical construct because it asks to be accepted as authentic even though it can never be a true recreation of the past.

Authenticity Rather Than Truth

A comic is not a recording of what happened, it is a drawing of what the cartoonist remembers doing and feeling. Thus, the imperfections of memory and the demands of storytelling make it impossible to access and present an absolutely true account of the past and a comics memoir must "rely on regimes of authenticity rather than verisimilitude" (Woo 2010: 169).

As young Alison begins to keep a diary in *Fun Home* the Narrating I tells the reader "All I could speak for was my own perceptions, and perhaps not even those" (Bechdel 2007: 141). Memory is often faulty and usually self-serving.

A memoirist's experiences are always mediated through memory and the motives of self-presentation, but in a comics memoir the presentation of those experiences is also shaped by the encapsulation, layout, and composition choices demanded by the comics form. Gardner feels that through "the compressions and gaps" of the comics form foregrounds the "losses and glosses of memory and subjectivity" (6). In his *In The Shadow of No Towers* Spiegelman uses the fragmentation of the comics form to represent his own partial and chaotic memories of being in lower Manhattan on 9/11 (Dony and van Linthout 2010: 183). The act of drawing oneself, often as a caricatured, abstracted avatar, highlights the fact that telling one's life story is always subjective. Aline Kominsky-Crumb (particularly in her Bunch strips) accentuates this by intentionally making the appearance of her avatar inconsistent from panel to panel (Figure 7.5).

The act of molding experience into a coherent narrative requires a selective and distorted presentation of an already imperfectly remembered reality. Even Harvey Pekar, who felt his *American Splendor* stories presented an accurate and honest account of the mundane events of his life, could not show every moment of even a minor incident. He always had to make decisions about which moments of his real-life experience to emphasize (and perhaps enhance) and which moments to totally omit. Peter Kuper says of his memoir work "there is certainly some condensing and just by cherry-picking events I was directing aspects of the reality to make it a more streamlined read" (personal communication, September 23, 2013).

Figure 7.5 Many comics memoirists admit that not everything they present is a fact. From *One! Hundred! Demons!* Copyright Lynda Barry. Used with permission from Drawn & Quarterly.

The memoirist has to shape incidents into a narrative and that often requires creating connections between incidents that did not exist in real life.

Some memoirists use what Benjamin Woo calls "signifiers of truthfulness" to enhance the sense of "this is the way it was" (169). Alison Bechdel makes good use of these "signifiers of truthfulness" in *Fun Home*. The graphic novel is full of documentation—photographs, letters, newspaper headlines, entries from diaries, maps, all drawn in meticulous detail to mimic the original. A realist, representational style of drawing is often used as a bid for authenticity. Other creators gleefully undermine the authenticity of their memoirs by cloaking them in wild content and cartoonish art style. Kim Deitch, for instance, embeds accounts of his own life amid fanciful events and outlandish characters, including a big blue anthropomorphic cat (Jenkins 2012: 7).

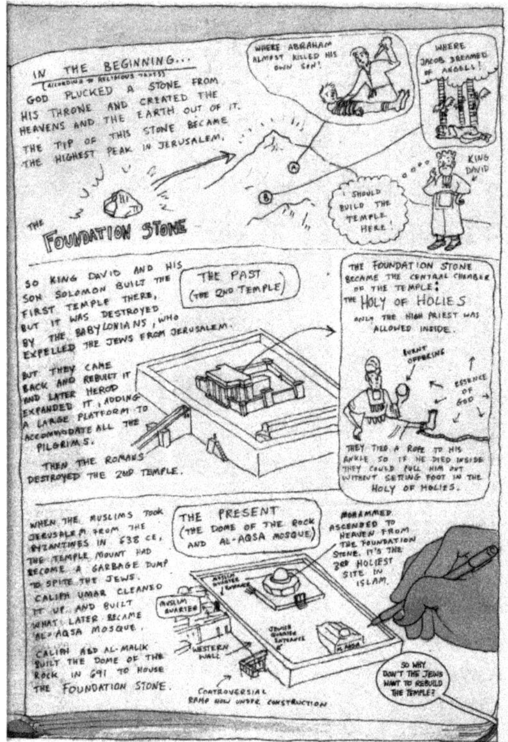

Figure 7.6 Showing the hand taking notes lets the reader know this is not just Sarah's opinion but the information given by the expert tour guide. *How to Understand Israel in 60 Days or Less* by Sarah Glidden © 2010.

The negative light in which some comics memoirists portray themselves, revealing all their foibles, fears, and depraved desires, might be taken as a signifier of truthfulness. George Orwell articulated a common view of life writing: "Autobiography is only to be trusted when it reveals something disgraceful. A man who gives a good account of himself is probably lying" (170). A reader is likely to think "Why would Joe Matt depict himself this way if it was not true?"

Due to the demands of narrative, the fallibility of memory, and the characteristics of the comics form itself, a comics memoir "cannot be read solely as either factual truth or simple fact" (Smith and Watson 2010: 17). Memoirists generally strive to present another kind of truth.

Emotional "Truth" Is More Important than Facts

In the early stages of constructing his memoir Justin Green had "almost a hundred little note cards" on which he had written "factual incidents," but when he finished *Binky Brown* he realized "virtually every incident in the book is allegorical, even though some have a closer foothold in reality" (Green qtd. in Rosenkranz 2011). Most comics memoirists are not obsessed with detailing the verifiable facts of the past, but rather with communicating how they feel about that past. As Phoebe Gloekner says, "factual truth has little significance in the pursuit of emotional truth" (179).

Gloekner, whose work is often categorized as memoir, declares "I am not an autobiographical cartoonist" and says she aspires "to create characters who can be universally understood despite being constructed with details so numerous that they could only refer to a particular situation" (179). When readers make an emotional connection with the work it is often through identification with the protagonist, narrator, or author. This is how the emotional truth of the work is experienced. There are particular shared understandings that are attempted by many comics memoirists and are thus identifiable themes of the memoir genre in comics. Some memoirists assiduously avoid teaching a lesson or providing a moral to the story and simply take the approach of this happened to me, take from it what you will. Yet, one or more of the themes discussed as follows are usually manifest in their work.

Figure 7.7 A visual metaphor can be used to express the emotional truth of an event. *Epileptic—I walked home* © L'Association—David B.

Healing (Therapeutic Confession and Catharsis)

According to Georges Gusdorf, "the task of autobiography is first of all a task of personal salvation" (39). Laurie Sandell, author of *The Imposter's Daughter* (2009), "hoped that by shedding the light of truth on his [her father's] falsehoods, she could overcome her own problems with intimate relationships and Ambien and alcohol abuse" (qtd. in Rosenkranz 2011). In the opening panel of *Binky Brown* the narrator declares that this comic book is not being created solely to entertain readers but "also to purge myself of the compulsive neurosis" (Green 0). David Small says his motivation for creating *Stitches* (2009) "was, first of all, a very selfish one, I wanted—I should say I needed very badly—to remember some things in order to mature" (Small qtd. In Rosenkranz 2011).

A number of comics memoirists have referred to their Catholic backgrounds and compared the act of writing a memoir to the sacrament of confession. The act of telling others about their pain or shame seems to have a therapeutic effect for some memoirists. In 1968 Art Spiegelman's mother committed suicide. Four years later he attempted to channel his anger toward his mother into the four-page memoir comic "Prisoner on the Hell Planet," Later Spiegelman admitted "I don't confuse Art and Therapy (making Art is cheaper), but I *did* think Hell Planet had helped me 'deal' with Anja's suicide" (Spiegelman 2008: 4). David B's way of coping with his brother's illness was to create the graphic memoir *Epilectic* and "by means of it to attain love for his sibling and to realize his own true self in the process" (Tabachnick 2011: 115).

Profile: Sarah Lightman

Born: Sarah Lightman
April 26, 1975
London, United Kingdom

"I am not sure if I could have survived my life without also drawing it. . . . Often I make art about questions and situations in my life before I have even discussed them with friends and family" (qtd. in Gravett 2013).

Career Highlights

2001	Earns her MFA in Painting, Slade School of Art, University College London.
2008	Curates the exhibition "Diary Drawing" at the Centre for Recent Drawing.
2009	Co-founds, with Nicola Streeten, Laydeez do Comics in London, a graphic novel forum, now with branches in Leeds, Bristol, Dublin, San Francisco, and Chicago.
	Chairs the first Women in Comics Conference at the University of Cambridge.
2010	Debuts "Graphic Details: Confessional Comics by Jewish Women" exhibit at the Cartoon Art Museum in San Francisco.
2012	Creates and exhibits first animated films based on her diary drawings: "The Reluctant Bride" and "Family."
2014	Authors, "Life Drawing: Autobiography, Comics, Jewish Women," in *The Routledge Handbook of Contemporary Jewish Cultures*, edited by Laurence Roth and Nadia Valman.
	Edits *Graphic Details: Jewish Women's Confessional Comics* containing, essays and interviews about the touring exhibit. The book won the Eisner Award for Best Scholarly/Academic Work, The Susan Koppelman Prize for Best Edited Book on Feminist Studies, and an Honorable Mention Jordan Schnitzer Book Awards (Jews and the Arts)
2015	Writes *The Book of Sarah*, an autobiographical graphic novel.
2018–21	Honorary Research Fellow, Birkbeck, University of London

Memoir comics are an important part of Sarah Lightman's life. She has maintained a comics diary for many years, she promotes memoir comics as a curator and arts journalist, and she studies them. Lightman's Ph.D. dissertation at the University of Glasgow is forthcoming from Penn State University Press as "Dressing Eve and Other Reparative in Women's Autobiographical Comics." She is interested in how comics that present true stories of trauma can help heal both the artist and the reader.

Figure 7.8 Sarah Lightman. Photo used with permission.

Sarah Lightman is also a comics creator. Creating a visual diary of her life, using drawings, photos, and text, became a source of solace for Lightman when she was an overwhelmed undergraduate at The Slade School for Art. She began to think of this ongoing narrative of her life as The Book of Sarah (after all, her siblings Esther and Daniel already had their books of the *Bible*). Sarah's first graphic novel, was published by Myriad Editions in 2019. Sarah also creates animated films using her drawings. She says "I want to take pain and unhappiness in my life and make something beautiful from them" ("Sarah" 2012).

Lightman feels that while much has been written about how Jewish men created the well-known comic book superheroes, the role of Jewish women in shaping the comics art form has largely gone unexplored. She is particularly interested in revealing the role of Jewish women in the emergence of the memoir genre, whom she considers to be the *superheroines* of everyday life. Lightman co-curated, with journalist Michael Kaminer, the touring exhibit *Graphic Details: Confessional Comics by Jewish Women.* The exhibit features original work by eighteen influential creators and has been touring worldwide since 2010. She is currently co-editing *Jewish Women's Comics: Borders and Bodies.*

Lightman teaches Graphic Narratives at The Royal Drawing School and conducts comics workshops throughout the UK.

How Self-Concept Is Formed

Joe Matt says part of his motivation for creating memoir comics is "to analyze myself, to strive for self-awareness and self-understanding" (Matt qtd. in Rosenkranz). The acts of forming self-concept and performing identity are not only readily apparent in most memoirs, but often at the core of the memoirist wants to express. Your self-concept is the collection of beliefs you hold about yourself. Entire books have been written about the complex process of forming a self-concept and scholars across various disciplines have different theories about how the process occurs, but for the brief space we have here An individual's self-concept is formed from **reflected appraisals**, **social comparisons**, and **self-perception** (Hybels and Weaver 2011: 35–40).

REFLECTED APPRAISALS

Our self-concept is, to a great extent, the result of our interactions with others and our perceptions of what they think of us. (Wallace and Tice 2012: 124). In *Arab in America* (2008), Lebanese-born Toufic El Rassi shows how, as an eighth grader in a mostly white Illinois school, he felt like a weirdo when he started getting facial hair much sooner than his "rosy cheeked peers" and they called him "beardo" (5).

Some of these appraisals are so prescriptive that they function as "scripts" we are expected to follow in acting out our lives (James and Joneward 1971: 68). In the semi-autobiographical *Bitchy's College Daze* (1997) the protagonist, Midge, is occasionally plagued by thoughts bubbles in which a parent is a dispensing advice. In one instance Midge imagines her mother saying "Now, dear . . . don't you think it would be more proper if . . ." (Gregory 1997: 15). The rest of the bubble is obscured by a drawing of her mother's vacuous face (Figure 7.9).

Figure 7.9 The author has his self-concept influenced by a reflected appraisal. "Hero" by Brent Anderson in *Streetwise* (2000). © Brent Anderson and used by permission.

Other people are the "mirror" in which we see ourselves, and the cartoonist creating a memoir is almost literally holding up that mirror as they draw the verbal and nonverbal reactions that express other people's impressions of them.

SOCIAL COMPARISON

Humans form their self-concepts in part by assessing how well they are doing compared to their peers. These comparisons are often based on status symbols such as clothes, cars, homes, electronic gadgets, and the number of social media followers. We also compare ourselves to successful role models, both real and fictional, whom we aspire to emulate. Early on in *Darkroom: A Memoir in Black and White* (2012) Lila Quintero Weaver tells of her family's immigration from Argentina to Alabama in 1961 and her ten-year-old sister Lissy's first day in her new school: "In a room full of Anglo children, Lissy felt dark and conspicuous. A few rows over a girl named Cheryl radiated everything Lissy found enviable. Everything American."

The perceived achievements, abilities, opinions, and possessions of others serve as benchmarks for our self-evaluation (Festinger 1954). Scores of social psychologists have further developed the concept of social comparisons and some of those theorists (Vallacher 1980; Gecas 1982; Schwalbe 1985) identified competence and morality as the two major dimensions of an individual's self-evaluation. When Justin Green's avatar Binky Brown goes from a Catholic school to a mostly Jewish public school he feels like a dunce compared to the other students because "they could think and ask thought-provoking questions" (Green 1972/2009). Conversely, the young Joe Sacco avatar in "Voyage to the End of the Library" feels superior to most of the library's patrons, who he characterizes as "arrested development cases" with "miserable literary expectations" (Sacco 2003: 113, 115).

SELF-PERCEPTION

Perceptions about height, weight, athleticism, intelligence, and talent, especially when those attributes garner you strongly positive or negative attention (reflected appraisals), play a vital role in how you define yourself. In Will Eisner's *The Dreamer* (1986) young Billy has the confidence to start his own studio because he perceives himself as a competent artist due to all the positive reflected appraisals he has received. However, most comics memoirs devote more attention to negative self-perceptions. Eddie Campbell's memoir comics tend to be highly introspective, with the Experiencing I ruminating on his character flaws. In Campbell's four-page "I Have Lost My Sense of Humor" strip for the *Autobiographix* (2003) anthology he depicts himself as pretentious, silly, resentful, spiteful, and self-destructive.

Even when the author does not mention self-perception those perceptions are evident on the comics page because "the requirement to produce multiple drawn versions of one's self necessarily involves an intense engagement with embodied aspects of identity, as well as with the sociocultural models underpinning body image" (El Refaie 2012: 4). Aline Kominsky-Crumb's tendency to draw her Bunch avatar as ugly and much heavier than she is in reality gives some insight into her body image self-perception.

Self-concept is a central theme in many memoirs because the memoirist is writing about a much younger, often adolescent, self that was in the throes of forming a self-concept. In writing about oneself the memoirist has to turn inward and confront self-concept, but the act of drawing oneself "seems to offer a unique way for the artist to recognize and externalize his or her subjectivity" (Hatfield 2005: 115). Creating a memoir comic is always a performance of identity.

How Identity Is Performed

Self-concept is interior, but identity is exterior; a matter of engagement and performance. Elizabeth Bruss considers memoir to be a performative act that "exemplifies the character" of the author (300).

Contrary to Popeye's declaration that "I yam what I yam and tha's all what I yam" (Fleischer 1933), a real human's identity is complex and multifaceted. A person's identity can have social facets (both formal and informal membership in groups), role facets (parent, teacher, member of a culture), and personal traits and characteristics that constitute a sense of self separate from the social or role self (Oyserman, Elmore, and Smith 2012: 74). An important aspect of social intelligence is understanding which facet of identity to perform in a particular situation.

Performing identity, sometimes referred to as impression management, is a matter of "controlling information in order to influence the impressions formed by an audience" (Schlenker 2012: 542). Anyone who regularly uses social media, the self-presentation of creating profiles and the selective disclosure of posting and tweeting, is well practiced in performing identity.

Traditionally autobiographies have been written by "great" men and women, and the goal of the autobiography has often been to reinforce that image of greatness in the public mind. Memoirs are more limited in scope, encompassing a period or incident rather than an entire life, and are more likely to examine human foibles than to lionize them. Although Douglas Wolk does characterize some comics memoirs as trying to prove "the author's pain and sadness are more sad and painful than yours" (Wolk 2007: 203), few comics memoirists seem to be striving for traditional self-glorification. In fact, some memoirists, such as Joe Matt, seem to be using their comics as a means of purging guilt by confession or the self-mortification of revealing the aspect of themselves of which they are most ashamed. Yet, even in the most self-effacing of memoirs the authors are likely to present some justification of their lives and seek a degree of acceptance of who they are (or perceive themselves to be).

Defense of the Author's Identity

We all have certain beliefs, attitudes, and values that are central to our idea of who we are; in social judgment theory these are known as our anchor points (Sherif, Sherif, and Nebergall 1965). These anchor points provide some stability to the sense of self over time, and they determine the thoughts and actions we find acceptable for ourselves and others. Just as the movement of a ship at anchor is limited by the length of the anchor chain, we identify with individuals, groups, causes, and ideologies that seem to be built on beliefs and values close to one of our anchor points and feel alienated from those that stray too far from that anchor point.

A memoir can be a defense of these anchor points, of a worldview. In most of Harvey Pekar's stories he is actively discontented with his life, but his musing (a major source of Pekar's malaise is that he overthinks everything) often justify his outlook—If his life was not a constant struggle he might have anything to write about. Besides, he rationalizes, one should not put too much emphasis on happiness because "Y'might be happy for awhile but then y'get old an' sick an y'die" (Pekar 1986: 2).

However, some people do change, and if we reject an aspect of our self-concept (pull up anchor) and move to a worldview we once found unacceptable we usually feel the need to justify the change. For example, Craig Thompson, who had grown up in a very devout Christian family, devotes a number of pages toward the end of *Blankets* to explaining why he is no longer a Christian.

Narrative Patterns

Within the overall narrative structure of a beginning, middle, and end, there are more specific narrative structures that are commonly used in the memoir genre.

Slice of Life

A **slice of life story** is usually an unvarnished, documentary presentation of a particular incident. It often lacks the structure of a traditional story and might not have an inciting incident, resolution, or even conflict. Such memoirs usually present fairly mundane incidents. One of Harvey Pekar's *American Splendor* stories is about walking to and from the post office on a Saturday morning and another is titled "Standing Behind Old Jewish Ladies in Supermarket Lines."

Occasionally memoirs that follow this pattern can present a more unusual slice of life in which the Experiencing I is dealing with an ongoing problem (e.g., addiction, neurosis) or traveling in an exotic, possibly perilous, locale. Josh Neufeld's *A Few Perfect Hours* (2004) and Craig Thompson's *Carnet de Voyage* (2004) are travelogue diaries that present no grand adventures, just a series of incidents and impressions. What constitutes a slice of life narrative is in the eye of the beholder, but when the events become too adventurous or the presentation too expressionistic most readers are not going to think of the memoir as a slice of life story.

Particularly thin slices of life are depicted in diary comics, usually a few brief panels posted on a quotidian basis on the web. James Kolchalka's *American Elf*, a fourteen-year project begun in 1998 epitomizes the now-popular form, but subsequent practioners have often varied from his illustrative style reducing it to stick figures or simplistic sketches, with the events and observations more important than the cartooning itself. Diary comics have also been used for specific purposes of communication or propaganda, such as Lydia Wysocki's 2019 use of a daily comic in support of a strike by the University and College Union members in the UK.

This Is How I Became Me

Most memoir is more than a statement of "This is who I am." Rather, it serves a self-continuity function—it is an explanation of how the Experiencing I became the Authoring I (Bluck et al. 2005: 109). People reinforce their current self-concept by modifying and organizing memories into a coherent narrative "compatible with their current goals and situation" (Schlenker 2012: 548). In a sense all memoirs do this, but it is a distinct narrative structure when there is a Narrating I who appears on the page as a character in the present day and doles out the narrative in a series of flashbacks. This type of narrative tends to be structured around turning points, particularly critical decisions made by the Experiencing I.

Redemptive Arc (Learning to Cope)

This pattern was established in the fourth century by Augustine and introduced in the early part of this chapter. His *Confessions* details his progression from rowdy youth to hedonistic rhetorician to guilt-ridden Christian convert and finally to a spiritual awakening that allowed him to transcend the temptations and disappointments of the material world and live for a higher purpose. A **redemptive arc** narrative generally has four stages: The Setup, The Problem, The Pain, and The Coping.

The Setup presents the ordinary world before the onset of the problem, or at least a limited awareness of the problem, possibly due to denial. Some memoirs minimize this stage and dive right into the problem.

The Problem stage shows the onset of the conflict or the moment in which the Experiencing I acknowledges there is a conflict. The protagonist is usually embroiled in some relationship conflict, but in most comics memoirs the true problem is an internal conflict stemming from desires, fears, or addictions.

The bulk of the memoir is usually devoted to detailing The Pain caused by the problem. The final stage is the Coping. We chose to call this stage coping rather than redemption or cure because rarely are there happy endings where all problems are solved. Occasionally there might be some degree of transcendence of the problem or the pain (e.g., putting the problem into perspective), but the coping usually takes the form of the protagonist finding the courage to commit to an ongoing struggle.

In David Small's graphic novel *Stitches* the *setup* establishes young David's life in an unhappy, emotionally repressed family. His ordinary world is bad enough but the *problem* phase begins when a disturbing growth is discovered on this neck. The *pain* involves multiple operations, loss of his voice, and the fact that he gets little information and no emotional support from his parents. His *coping* begins when he moves out of his parents' house at sixteen. He achieves a transcendence of sorts through his art (which gives him back "his voice") and an eventual better understanding of his parents.

The arc of the journey is not always limited to the memoirist, nor the tools to the narrow definition of comics within the graphic novel memoir form. Roz Chast's *Can't We Talk About Something More Pleasant?* (2014) balances comics narration with collage and other forms to tell the story of coping with her aging parents, and Nora Krug's *Belonging* (2018) goes even further by incorporating illustrated prose and documents to track the process of investigation and redefining her family history after discovering her uncle had been a Nazi.

It should be noted that the elements of the redemptive arc are not always presented in the order outlined earlier. And the arc may be dispensed with entirely when the format requires. *Drawing Power* (2019), edited by Diane Noomin, collected over sixty short graphic stories of women coping with rape and harassment. These critical moments in the cartoonists' lives were told in brief, capturing the drama and horror of the events, but foregoing the arc as a consequence of the form.

Visual Conventions

As Rocco Versaci points out, "both the hand lettering of the text and the drawn images encourage readers to see the story as the author's personal expression, and these devices represent how a given memoirist 'sees' the world" (39). Memoirists have two general approaches—realism and expressionism—to how to create these representations of their worldview.

Realism

Realism in comics attempts to depict people, objects, and motivations in a manner that reflects most people's real-life experiences. The storytellers usually avoid exotic locales and overly dramatic confrontations and instead focus on average people engaged in everyday activities. The artwork is representational, an unexaggerated likeness of the person or thing it represents. Rather than hyper-realistic art, such that by Neal Adams or Alex Ross, a memoirist taking a realist approach might use line drawings that simplify in order to reveal the essence of a person or situation. Characters are rendered as average, ordinary people (A stark contrast to the attractive faces and perfect physiques of all those superheroes in mainstream comic books). The reader's point of view on characters is most often at eye-level, the way we encounter others in everyday life. The page layouts are usually simple. Groensteen (2011, 2013) claims that a regular, what he calls waffle-iron grid, page layout mimics the rhythm "of existence itself, the clock of life as it ticks by" (Groensteen 2013: 143–4) (Figures 7.10a–b).

Expressionism

Whereas realism is used to present an objective depiction of events, **expressionism** is used by memoirists for presenting a character's subjective point of view or an inner, emotional

Figures 7.10a–b Bryan Talbot's relatively realistic depiction of Mary Talbot (as can be seen by comparison to her photo) fits Mary's very straightforward account of emotional moments. *Dotter of her Father's Eyes* by Mary and Bryan Talbot. © 2012 Dark Horse Books.

reality. As Scott McCloud has pointed out, all drawing carries "an expressive potential" (McCloud 1993: 124), but expressionist art contains blatant distortions and exaggerations to convey emotion. Roberta Gregory draws the face of her semi-autobiographical avatar Midge in a simple but representational manner but she grossly distorts the mouth, often extending it well beyond the boundary of Midge's face, to express a range of emotions from exultation to anger. In a genre for which emotional truth is more important than facts, expressionistic art can be a powerful tool for the memoirist (Figures 7.11a–b).

Figure 7.11a Some of Joe Sacco's drawings of himself are rather self-deprecating compared to how he actually looks, but they dramatically express his emotional state. *Notes from a Defeatist* by Joe Sacco © 2003 Fantagraphics.

Figure 7.11b Photo of Joe Saco. © Don Usner.

Image Functions

A comics memoir need not be all realism or all expressionism. In fact, the comics form makes it easy to shift from a realistic representation of the world to an expressionistic display of an author's subjectivity (Beaty 2007: 164). This shifting of style involves a shifting of the dominance of the three primary image functions described in Chapter 5.

Sensory diegetic images simply depict the world of the story and the actions of the characters. Any story about real events is going to be composed largely of sensory diegetic

Figure 7.12a Sensory diegetic images presenting people, places, and events in the world of the story.

Figure 7.12b Non-sensory diegetic images convey young Spiegelman's emotional reaction upon first encountering *Mad Magazine*.

Figure 7.12c Hermeneutic images give the reader clues about Spiegelman's attitude toward comic book constructions of masculinity, and how to interpret the story that follows. Excerpt(s) from *Breakdowns: Portrait of the Artist as a Young* %@&*! by Art Spiegelman, © 1972, 1973, 1974, 1975, 1976, 1977, 2005, 2006, 2007, and 2008 by Art Spiegelman. Used by permission of Pantheon Books, an imprint of the Knopf Doubleday Publishing Group, a division of Random House LLC. All rights reserved.

images, but this image function is dominant in the realistic approach. For instance, Harvey Pekar's stories seldom contain any images that are not part of a current or remembered real environment (Figure 7.12a–c).

Non-sensory diegetic images represent what a character, usually the Experiencing I, is feeling. This usually involves the introduction of expressionistic elements into the artwork. For instance, when Mary Fleener wants to convey a character's altered state, due to emotional intensity or drug use, the environment around a character's head or sometimes the head itself will fragment into what Fleener calls a cubismo technique (a style of kinetic abstraction drawing inspiration from ancient Egyptian art and Picasso).

Hermeneutic images are usually an indication of what the Authoring I thinks about the actions and feelings of the Experiencing I, and, as such, do not represent anything that is actually happening in the world of the story. Hermeneutic images are used sparingly, if at all, in a realistic memoir, and extensive use of such images makes a narrative expressionistic.

Of course, the function of an image is not always easy to determine because that function can be affected by the interaction with text, interaction with other images in a sequence, interaction with images with many pages removed (**braiding**), or even the layout of panels on a page. On a comics page "words and images can be presented as representational, symbolic, allegorical, associative, and allusive, or they may work in several modes at once" (Witek 2011: 229). Images can also be used in purposely ambiguous ways, resulting in readers having varied perceptions of the functions performed by those images.

Contradictory Images

Occasionally what is drawn on the page is inconsistent with or outright contradicts what is written on the page. Many memoirists, acknowledging that memory can be imprecise and self-serving, realize they cannot always make clear distinctions between facts and memory, between reality and subjective experience. To highlight this ambiguity comics memoirists might purposely present images that contradict the dialogue or narration (Figure 7.13).

Figure 7.13 The pictured action (or inaction) directly contradicts the text description in the caption. Reprinted with permission from "How to Star in a Singaporean Soap Opera" by Josh Neufeld from *A Few Perfect Hours*. Copyright©1998 and 2004 by Josh Neufeld. All rights reserved.

Analyzing: The Lasting Effect of Creating a Memoir Comic

Perhaps when we tell stories about our lives "these stories become our experience of those lives" (Williams 2011: 356). Mentally visualizing the past can be vague. Making that visualization more tangible by drawing it requires greater specificity of detail, making the memory more concrete (even if partially invented). The process of creating a memoir is necessarily reductive because not every incident can be included. Katie Green, author of *Lighter than My Shadow* (2013), says "I've often felt when I make a choice to leave something out, then I'm not only leaving it out of my story but out of my memory" (qtd. in Williams 2011: 363). It seems the act of life writing both changes and solidifies the author's personal history.

Not only can writing a memoir create a new understanding of one's past, but it can also alter one's self-concept and identity in the present. For some authors their identity becomes conflated with the work, particularly with the autobiographical avatar presented in the work. Justin Green felt "branded with Binky Brown" and "craved an identity apart from my best known work" (Green 2009: 60).

And the more popular the memoir, the more it becomes not only an integral part of the author's identity in the world but a part of the author's self-concept. The 2004 "Pop Art" strip (reprinted in the 2008 edition of *Breakdowns*) opens with the Art Spiegelman avatar in a shadow and running from something off-panel. In the second panel he stops and turns to look at a giant figure of a mouse in a suit (the image of how Spiegelman drew his father in *Maus*) rising out of the ground. He says, "No matter how much I run I can't seem to get out of that mouse's shadow" (2008: n.p.). It is a comment on his father's lasting influence in his life, but also an acknowledgment that Spiegelman will forever be introduced as the Pulitzer Prize-winning author of *Maus*. In a number of interviews Spiegelman has compared being forever linked with his acclaimed graphic novel to having a 500-pound mouse breathing down his neck.

In more positive experience, Raina Telgemeier's choice to recount her "years of dental hell" in 2010's *Smile* was not only therapeutic but transformative of her career into dominating the graphic novel best-seller list for much of the following decade with a series of sequels that varied from memoir to fictionalized tales with their roots in her experiences.

Discussion Questions

1. Alison Bechdel acknowledged that her graphic novel *Fun Home* was "in many ways a huge violation of my family" (Chute 2006: 1009). Consider the ethics of memoir. Does the writer of a comics memoir violate norms of self-revelation? Are there revelations that might be hurtful to living persons? Might living persons be embarrassed by their visual representation in a memoir?
2. What sort of evidence would have to be incorporated into a comics memoir in order to persuade you to accept the narrative as true?
3. What are some of the motivations for creating memoirs? If you were to create a narrative about a particular incident or period of time in your life, what purpose would it serve to tell that story?

Activities

1. In most memoirs the younger version of the narrator (the Experiencing I) is transformed (gains new insight, modifies his or her value system, gains a new purpose, etc.). For a particular comics memoir, describe how the transformation was communicated. Is it by means of the Narrating I's commentary, through the Experiencing I's actions, by changes in visual depiction, or by other means?
2. Explore how the development of self-concept is presented in comics memoirs. Write a short paper or give a brief presentation giving two examples of the main character in a comics memoir receiving or responding to reflected appraisals and two examples of the main character in a comics memoir making social comparisons.
3. Consider the opening pages of a number of comics memoirs. If there is a Preface or Introduction to the comics memoir, how does it create a context for experiencing and understanding the memoir that follows? Why did the author chose to begin with a particular incident or narration? Does the opening create a context or expectations for how you will experience and understand the rest of the story?

Recommended Reading

Comics

Guibert, Emmanuel. *Alan's War: The Memories of G.I. Alan Cope.* New York: First Second Books, 2008.

Alan Cope was drafted at eighteen and sent to Europe to fight in World War II. Cartoonist Guibert recorded his friend's recollections of coming of age in those extraordinary circumstances and turned them into a poignant comics memoir.

Tran, G. B. *Vietnamerica*. New York: Villard, 2010.

American-born GB Tran makes remarkable use of the comics form to document his gradual engagement with his family history and realization of the harrowing experiences in war-torn Vietnam that shaped his parents.

Scholarly Sources

Chute, Hillary. *Graphic Women: Life Narrative and Contemporary Comics*. New York: Columbia University Press, 2010.

Chute's examination of the work of five female cartoonists whose use of the multilayered narrative techniques of the comics form to present personal struggles and universal truths reveals the potential of memoir comics.

Kunka, Andrew J. *Autobiographical Comics*. London: Bloomsbury, 2017.

Kunka details the rise of autobiographical comics, explains the cultural contexts in which they occurred, and provides theoretical approaches for analyzing them.

8 Superhero Comics

A week after the opening of *Iron Man 3*, Creed, the seven-year-old son of friends, had a serious talk with one of the authors about the movie. He loves Iron Man (he has the DVDs of the previous movies, scores of toys, the Halloween costume, etc.), and he loved the latest movie, but he was distraught that there might not be any more Iron Man movies. After all, at the end of *Iron Man 3* Tony Stark destroys his suits of armor and implies he is done with being Iron Man. And that did not seem right to this earnest young fan. As Creed said, "Superheroes don't quit."

In that simple statement he might have encapsulated the essence of the superhero as manifest in American popular culture. It speaks not only to the durability of the genre but to the very nature of the heroism these characters display. Countless comic book stories have reiterated that what makes superheroes heroic is not their extraordinary powers but their perseverance in the face of overwhelming odds. And like the characters themselves, the superhero genre has not only persevered but ultimately prevailed in the marketplace.

In this chapter we will examine the nature of superheroes, the conventions of superhero stories, and how the superhero genre has come to dominate not only the mainstream American comic book industry but summer box office at movie theaters around the world (Figures 8.1 and 8.2).

Figure 8.1 **Creed MacNamara prepares to go trick-or-treating as Iron Man. Photo Courtesy of Patrick and Tina MacNamara.**

Figure 8.2 **Invincible Iron Man #81 (#425) (2004) art by Adi Granov. © 2023 Marvel Entertainment, Inc. and its subsidiaries.**

Objectives

In this chapter you will learn:

1. the roots of the superhero concept;
2. the defining characteristics of the superhero;
3. the conventions of the superhero genre;
4. how the superhero genre has evolved; and
5. the appeal of the superhero concept.

Roots of the Superhero Concept

Although Superman was and still is the purest embodiment of the superhero, the concept was not born fully formed that spring day in 1938 when Superman made his debut in *Action Comics* #1. The familiar aspects of the superhero—the powers, the costume, and the dual identity—had all existed before Superman made the scene, albeit not quite in that combination. Even the superhero's penchant for individual initiative and "regeneration through violence" has always been engrained in the American mythos (Nevins 1996: 27; Early 2004: 71), and the extraordinary adventures of the buckskin-clad heroes of early American literature such as Natty Bumppo and larger-than-life pioneers like Daniel Boone prefigure the superhero. Unfortunately, it seems the superhero also has roots in darker aspects of the American experience—costumed vigilantes whose brutality was often fueled by racial hatred.

Comics historian Chris Gavaler (2015) posits that the white-robed and hooded Klansmen of Thomas R. Dixon, Jr's *The Clansman: A Historical Romance of the Ku Klux Klan* (1905) "are the first twentieth-century dual-identity costumed heroes in American literature" (179). While perhaps the most notorious, the Klan is not the only instance of costumed vigilantes in America. Almost seventy years earlier, a popular novel morphed the Boone and Bumppo heroic frontiersman type into a grisly costumed adventurer.

The protagonist of Robert M. Bird's *Nick of the Woods* (1837) is Nathan Slaughter, a mild-mannered Quaker who is driven to seek vengeance on the Shawnee chief who killed his family. Nathan maintains a façade of pacifism, but when the need arises he dons buckskins and a buffalo-like headdress to wage a deadly one-man war against any Native Americans who threaten white settlers. This mysterious avenger, who carves a cross on the torso of the men he kills, is known to the settlers as Nick of the Woods and to his indigenous foes as *Jibbenainosay*, the Spirit-that-Walks [Perhaps an influence on The Phantom, The Ghost Who Walks?].

Following the Civil War, Southern Missouri experienced an influx of saloons, prostitutes, and bandits. In response, a vigilante group that came to be called Bald Knoppers formed in April 1885. They wore matching vests or tunics and frightening masks topped with twisted devil horns. Other vigilante groups in the region adopted the name and a similar look. One Bald Knobbers faction, of relatively well-to-do citizens, banded together to protect their property from outlaws, while in other parts of the state poor farmers donned Bald Knobber costumes and used violence to try to cleanse the wickedness they felt new arrivals had brought to their counties (Hix 2017).

In retrospect, we see these vigilantes as the villains they were, but there is no denying that they display some of the core elements of the superhero genre. They all wore costumes that kept their identities secret and undertook what, in their own twisted minds, they considered to be pro-social, even heroic missions.

However, Peter Coogan (2006) is probably correct that the earliest comic book superheroes were more directly derived from three primary streams of adventure-narrative figures: the science fiction superman, the pulp magazine übermensch, and the dual-identity vigilante. Most of these figures first appeared in novels or pulp magazines. The Shadow, the Lone Ranger, and the Green Hornet were born on the radio. Lesser-known characters like Dr. Occult and the Clock originated in comic books. Some characters, such as the comic strip strongman Popeye and the swashbuckling film heroes played by Douglas Fairbanks, which Joe Siegel and Jerry Shuster acknowledged as influencing their creation of Superman, do not fit easily into any of Coogan's categories. And, while the list in Figure 8.3 contains only the major characters in these three streams, it does provide an overview of the development of the superhero formula that became codified with Superman and, soon after, Batman.

Science Fiction Supermen	Pulp Übermensch	Dual Identity Vigilantes
		Robin Hood 1377
Frankenstein 1818		
		Nick of the Woods 1837
	Nick Carter 1886	
		Scarlet Pimpernel 1905
John Carter 1912	Tarzan 1912	
		The Gray Seal 1914
		Zorro 1919
Hugo Danner 1930		
		The Shadow 1931
		The Lone Ranger 1933
	Doc Savage 1933	The Spider 1933
		The Bat 1934
		Dr. Occult 1935
		Green Hornet 1936
		The Phantom 1936
		The Clock 1936
Superman 1938	The Batman 1939	

Figure 8.3 **Peter Coogan (2006) has traced the development of the superhero as flowing from three streams of adventure-narrative figures.**

Superman is the culmination of all three traditions, but his abilities are perhaps most directly influenced by a character named Hugo Danner, who appeared in Phillip Wylie's 1930 novel *Gladiator*, a book which Jerry Siegel had given a very favorable review in his fanzine. Early in the novel young Danner tells his father, "I can jump higher than a house. I can run faster'n a train. I can pull up big trees an' push 'em over" (Wylie 1930/1976: 44). Later, when Danner goes to war, he finds that his skin is invulnerable to bullets, and only exploding mortar shells can wound him. In his early adventures, Superman's more limited powers were described in a similar way. In *Action Comics* #1 (1938), Clark Kent discovered he could "hurdle a twenty-story building . . . raise tremendous weights . . . run faster than an express train . . . and that nothing less than a bursting shell could penetrate his skin!" Hugo Danner's father cautions him that when people find out about his strength they will fear him, just as Pa Kent warns young Clark, "This great strength of yours—you've got to hide it from people or they'll be scared of you!" (*Superman* #1).

Superman's early displays of power are also similar to the prodigious feats of strength Earthman John Carter (from the 1911 Edgar Rice Burroughs novel *A Princess of Mars*) was capable of on Mars due to the lesser gravity. In fact, the explanation of Superman's powers was modified in *Superman* #1 (1939) with the addition of "The smaller size of our planet, with its slighter gravity pull, assists Superman's tremendous muscles in the performance of miraculous feats of strength!"

Over the years Superman writers and editors have borrowed a number of elements from the pulp magazine hero Doc Savage, including the name Clark, a fortress of solitude in the Arctic, and a code against taking life. The Superman creators also seemed to have been inspired by the Scarlet Pimpernel (from the 1905 novel of the same name), who is perhaps the most direct progenitor of the dual-identity convention. Just as the effete Percy Blakeney is despised by a wife who loves his dashing alter ego, the Scarlet Pimpernel, Lois Lane (in the first forty years of stories) feels disdain for timid Kent, but swoons over Superman.

Discovering: Supermen Before Superman

George Bernard Shaw's 1903 play *Man and Superman, a Comedy and a Philosophy* highlighted concepts of the perfected human being, the superhuman, that had developed in the latter half of the previous century. There was Friedrich Nietzsche's concept of an Übermensch who would transcend petty morality and the need for concepts such as God. Then there was the Eugenics Movement, the desire to improve the human race through selective breeding. There was much inherently unsavory and un-American about the Eugenics Movement and it fell out of favor as the emerging science of genetics called some of its claims into question and especially when it was wholeheartedly embraced by European fascists. However, the quest to perfect humanity continued unabated into the 1930s with another movement—physical culture.

The physical culture movement began in earnest in the late nineteenth century when bodybuilding pioneer Eugen Sandow toured music halls posing and performing feats of strength, marketed training manuals and a correspondence course, launched the first physical fitness magazines, and opened the Institute of Physical Culture in London. Promoted by Florenz Ziegfeld, Sandow headlined the 1894 World's Fair in Chicago.

Soon scores of other bodybuilders were soon attempting to emulate Sandow's success. Following the tradition of showmanship that had been established by carnival strongmen billed as superhuman, these bodybuilders marketed themselves as iron men or supermen. When Siegmund Breitbart appeared in Cleveland in 1923 the local newspaper referred to him as a superman (Ricca 2013: 122). After decades of watching European strongmen tour the United States, homegrown superman Bernarr McFadden built his own physical culture empire.

Figure 8.4 The form-fitting superhero costume was probably inspired by the leotard worn by circus strongmen or a simulation of the near nudity of the "supermen" who appeared in physical culture magazines of the time. *The Superman Magazine* 1.2 (1930) © Strength and Health Magazine.

McFadden's *Physical Culture* (begun in 1899) was one of the magazines Joe Shuster read when he could afford it (Ricca 2013: 121). For years the diminutive Shuster read "scores of physical-culture magazines" (Kobler 1941: 76). Was Shuster familiar with the term superman before he and Jerry Siegel conceived of their comic strip character? If he ever happened upon a particular British magazine it would have been unavoidable. *The Superman: A Monthly Magazine Devoted to Mental and Physical Culture* debuted in 1930 and solidified the connection between physical culture and the term superman (Figure 8.4). It was not just the title; the term permeated the magazine. For example, there was an April 1932 article titled "Supermen I Have Known" and in December 1938 there was a feature about C. G. Pillay, "South Africa's Superman."

It is doubtful we will ever know what role, if any, physical culture supermen played in Siegel and Shuster's creation of Superman, but it is clear that Superman was part of the zeitgeist of the early twentieth century.

Realizing that sales of *Action Comics* were skyrocketing solely due to the presence of Superman, the publisher wanted to duplicate that success. Supposedly editor Vincent Sullivan asked young Bob Kane to create another extraordinary hero. Coogan argues that request marks the true beginning of the superhero genre: "Sullivan created the superhero genre because, instead of asking for another Superman he recognized that Superman represented a kind of hero rather than a singular creation. That recognition and the imitation and repetition it caused gave birth to the superhero genre" (Coogan 2006: 203). Kane and his co-writer Bill Finger created a character very different from Superman but no less extraordinary—Batman.

The creation of Batman looks to have been inspired by a number of pulp magazine adventure heroes. The Spider, the Shadow, and the Bat are all probable inspirations for Batman's modus operandi of striking fear into the hearts of criminals as a creature of the night. The Shadow and the Spider, with their intense eyes burning beneath slouch-brimmed hats, create identities meant to terrorize the criminal underworld, but they do not seem to be as direct an influence as the Bat. Five years before Batman's first appearance, in the pages of *Popular Detective* magazine, Dawson Clade decides that in order to pursue the criminals who had framed him, he "must become a figure of sinister import," a "strange Nemesis" to criminals. Just then a bat flies into the room and he exclaims, "That's it! I'll call myself 'The Bat'!" (qtd. in Nevins 2007). Clade then dons a bat costume to become a vigilante crime fighter. After years of preparation, Bruce Wayne sits in his mansion contemplating how to undertake his war on crime. He reasons that to strike terror into the hearts of criminals he "must be a creature of the night, black, terrible." Just then a huge bat flies into the room and Bruce exclaims, "A Bat! That's it! It's an omen. I shall become a bat!" (*Detective Comics* #33)

Shortly after the appearance of Batman, "the floodgates opened, and a host of long-underwear characters began cavorting across the four-color pages of comic book after comic book" (Harvey 1996: 21). If they hoped to emulate the financial success of Superman and Batman, "a publisher had to make sure of instant product identification. In the years just before the War a superhero needed a bright costume, a dual identity, and a wild talent" (Goulart 1970/1997: 229).

No genre suddenly appears full-blown. In the case of the superhero genre new elements (fantastic powers, costumes, and secret identities) were mixed with existing genres. Detective Comics, Incorporated's popular titles, *Detective Comics*, *Action Comics*, and *Adventure Comics*, indicate some of the genre traditions from which the superhero first emerged. Before Superman, "America's greatest adventure strip character," pushed them all aside more mundane adventurers, such as lawmen and soldiers of fortune, had populated the pages of *Action Comics*. Batman, while certainly more fearsome and physical than the characters who proceeded him, has his roots firmly planted in the genre traditions of those first twenty-six issues of *Detective Comics*. From the beginning he was solving mysteries, soon he acquired adversaries who bedeviled him with riddles, and he was eventually touted as the world's greatest detective. The men who created the distinctly different Marvel superheroes in the 1960s had spent the previous decades churning out stories of huge monsters, alien invasions, and teenage romance. All of those elements are part of the texture of the early Marvel superhero tales, and a number of the characters from the 1950s comics were converted into superheroes or supervillains.

Now that we have examined the pulp roots of the superhero concept we will consider the conventions that make superhero comic books a genre connected to, but distinct from, those roots.

Conventions of the Superhero Genre

As we explain more fully in Chapter 6, any genre which has had the time to develop over the course of decades is bound to have a wide variety of conventions that distinguish it. In the following section, we focus on the character types, themes, narrative patterns, and visual conventions that have come to define the superhero genre in comics.

Character Types

The most essential character type of the superhero genre is, of course, the hero. Coogan examined previous definitions of "superhero" and reduced them to three key elements he believes are emblematic of the superhero: mission, powers, and identity. We are adding a fourth element—violence—which seems to be inherent in superhero stories.

The **pro-social mission** of the comic book superhero was established in the early tales of the genre. Young Clark Kent's mother tells him he has a responsibility to use his powers to benefit humanity. Young Bruce Wayne vows he will wage a war on criminals to avenge his murdered parents. In a psychological profile of the superhero personality Bryan J. Dik notes "a characteristic shared by many superheroes is the strong desire to help others, even when doing so involves great personal risk" (2008: 100). By the time of the Fantastic Four's origin story in 1961, the convention was so well established that in the scene where they realize they have gained superpowers from being bombarded by cosmic rays, the gruff Ben Grimm interrupts the long-winded Reed Richards with, "You don't have to make a speech, big shot. We understand. We've gotta use that power to help mankind, right?" (*Fantastic Four* #1, 1961).

The cosmic rays transform Ben Grimm into the monstrous Thing, whose gruesome appearance gives him an understandably bad attitude. He is a radical departure from the typical superhero, who is a specimen of physical and moral perfection. However, the Thing is part of a long-standing tradition of tragic superheroes with deformed bodies and tortured psyches (a fraternity that includes characters such as the Heap, Hulk, and Swamp Thing). Another variation, the **anti-hero**, began with the easy-to-anger Namor the Sub-Mariner, who, from the time he first appeared in 1939, alternating between ally and enemy of the surface world. An anti-hero typically lacks one or more of the qualities associated with the heroic ideal. In the 1970s the Punisher and Wolverine led the way in popularizing a new breed of violent anti-heroes. Yet even the tragic heroes and the anti-heroes, while bitter, angry, or otherwise tainted, will, in the end, "do the right thing" and serve the cause of justice (Figure 8.5).

Figure 8.5 A lesson about the responsibility to use superpowers for a pro-social mission is passed along to Miles Morales (who will become the second Spider-Man in Marvel's Ultimate Universe). ***Ultimate Spider-Man*** **#4 (2011). © 2014 Marvel Entertainment, Inc. and its subsidiaries.**

The second distinguishing characteristic of superheroes is their powers. This element sets superheroes apart from Tarzan, Zorro, Doc Savage, and all the other admittedly extraordinary adventure heroes who preceded them. Superheroes possess fantastic abilities or skills far superior to those of ordinary humans. Part of the appeal of superheroes is that many of the powers, such as shooting energy beams from their eyes or lightning bolts from their fingertips, make for an exciting visual display on the page. The generations of children who have tied towels around their necks, extended their arms, and pretended to fly are testimony to the fundamental appeal of superpowers.

There are a few recognized superheroes (e.g., the Phantom, the Vigilante, and, most notably, Batman) with no superpowers. Kinesiologist Paul Zehr (2008) estimates it would take a healthy young man or woman at least fifteen years of extreme training to perform Batman's physical feats, and then they could only sustain that level of performance for about three years. However, not only is Batman an incredible athlete, a master of all forms of combat, and able to endure massive amounts of punishment and keep going, but he is also the world's greatest detective. In addition, his vast wealth allows him to employ the latest technology in his war on crime. "Uncommon weapons" are often employed by non-powered superheroes and Batman has a utility belt full of them (Camp, personal communication, May 24, 2013). Then there are those non-powered characters more directly augmented by advanced technology. Tony Stark's Iron Man armor gives him power far beyond that of Batman's utility belt.

Interestingly, the more awesome the superhero's powers, the more necessary it is, for purposes of dramatic narrative, that the hero have a limitation. The most famous Achilles' heel in comic books is Superman's adverse reaction to kryptonite, shards of his shattered home world, Krypton. Most DC superheroes, following the Superman model, are limited by some external force. For example, Martian Manhunter passes out in the presence of an open flame and Green Lantern has to recharge his power ring every twenty-four hours. Few Marvel characters have such artificial, external weaknesses. Their limitations are rooted in their own personalities: pride (Thor), brashness (Quicksilver), addictive personality (Iron Man), and even some instances of multiple personality disorder (Moon Knight).

The third distinguishing quality is identity. As Coogan explains it, superhero identity consists of "the codename and the costume, with the secret identity being a customary counterpart to the code-name" (2006: 32). Generally, the superhero name relates to the hero's powers (Flash), attitude (Daredevil), or role (Captain America). The costume is often an externalization of these aspects of the character. For example, Daredevil's costume is solid red with horns on the cowl, and Captain America is virtually draped in the flag. The costume also marks out the superheroes (and most supervillains) from ordinary people (Figure 8.6).

Figure 8.6 Ms. Marvel conforms to the conventions of the superhero. It is her mission to defend her hometown of Jersey City from extraterrestrial and criminal threats. She has the power of changing her body shape and size. Her costumed identity conceals the fact that she is teenager Kamala Khan. From *Ms. Marvel* #4 (2014) by G. Willow Wilson (writer) and Adrian Alphona (artist). © 2023 Marvel Entertainment, Inc. and its subsidiaries.

The secret or dual identity usually involves a stark contrast. In their non-costumed identities superheroes often feign some weakness of character, such as being a coward or a dissolute playboy. The dual identity is also a way for the ordinary person to identify with extraordinary characters. Perhaps one of the most alluring aspects of the Superman mythos is that Clark Kent is an average guy. Danny Fingeroth (2004) believes "the appeal of the secret identity is as primal as ever" and rooted in that feeling most of us have experienced when we feel the world is not giving us enough respect: "Don't underestimate me. I may not be who you think I am" (60). Or, as Umberto Eco (1972, 2004) explains the appeal, "any accountant in any American city secretly feeds the hope that one day, from the slough of his actual personality, there can spring forth a superman who is capable of redeeming years of mediocre existence" (146).

Of course, not every superhero has a dual identity. Marvel Comics has always been less invested in the secret identity than has DC, but the element of a superhero identity is still present in their characters. Namor has no other identity, but he is given the superhero-sounding moniker the Sub-Mariner. The Fantastic Four are celebrities whose civilian identities are well known. Yet, while everyone knows Johnny Storm is the Human Torch of the Fantastic Four, Johnny does still have the codename and costume that constitute the superhero identity. The secret identity was more important in the early decades of the genre, when superheroes were presented as exceptional beings in a world of ordinary people. Modern stories feature superhero action on a grand scale, with few ordinary humans in evidence.

Another defining characteristic of superheroes is violence. Superheroes do not just oppose evil, they fight it. They are usually reacting to the violence of supervillains who harm innocents and threaten the social order. Superheroes restore social order and impose justice by punching and blasting. In the first three decades of superhero stories the violence was mostly "an odd, antiseptic brand of fisticuffs (no blood, no weapons)" and because they were agents of social control the superheroes' violence was treated as legitimate (Ling 1976: 39). In subsequent decades violence in superhero comics has not only become more graphic and brutal but there has been more criticism of this "mythology of regeneration through violence" (Early 2004: 71).

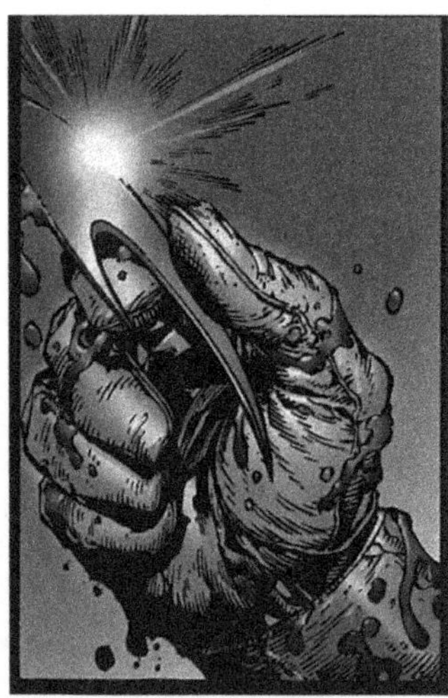

Figure 8.7 Some superheroes engage in a hyper-violent brand of vigilante justice. In his 2006 series Moon Knight began carving his crescent moon symbol into criminals' foreheads after he beat them to a bloody pulp. *Moon Knight* #9 (2007) art by David Finch and Danny Miki. © Marvel Entertainment, Inc. and its subsidiaries.

Theologian Walter Wink (1998) refers to this narrative of "the victory of order over chaos by means of violence," which has been the core of most hero tales throughout recorded history, as the **Myth of Redemptive Violence** (45). Winks finds this myth to be one of the most dominant and destructive forces in Western society. Chris Gavaler is one of a number of scholars that see superhero violence as promoting an ethic of vigilante extremism which seems at odds with their pro-social mission. Russell W. Dalton (2011) also advises that "we should question the entire premise of stories in which our problems are solved by having someone in a costume come in and clobber villains in order to preserve law and order" (ix). Yet Dalton feels compelled to write a book about the benefits of reading superhero comics because he realizes that "at the same time, the average reader can relate to the hero's struggle to do the right thing and to persevere in the midst of adversity" (1). We will revisit some of these thorny issues later in the chapter when we examine the themes of the superhero genre (Figure 8.7).

Sidekicks

The introduction of Robin in 1940 began the rather illogical tradition of adult superheroes taking on teenage sidekicks, often with no powers, in the dangerous fight against the very powerful forces of evil. By many accounts, Robin was introduced to "lighten up" the Batman feature, whose editors were worried that the book might be too intense for some kids. The sidekick was also a convenient device by which writers could have a hero's thoughts expressed in conversation rather than in thought balloons or stilted monologues. Editors and writers hoped the sidekick would provide powerful wish fulfillment for young readers who could project themselves onto the adolescent hero.

Looking beyond the wisecracks and the camaraderie, Stephen R. Bissette (2011) sees in the teen sidekick a disturbing reflection of the real-world exploitation of youth, from child labor to child soldiers. Others have noted sexism in the sidekick convention (Figure 8.8).

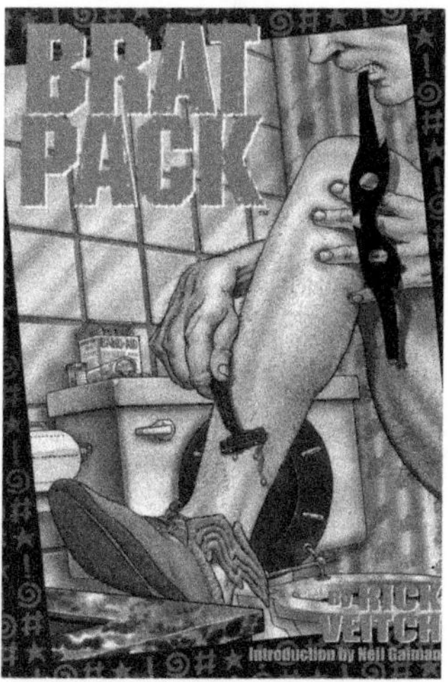

Figure 8.8 ***Brat Pack*** **is a dark, fierce satire that portrays the superhero sidekick concept as silly at best and twisted at its most extreme. Brat Pack ® Rick Veitch.**

During the 1940s and 1950s there were a number of male and female superheroes who fought as a duo, but the female partners tended to be relegated to sidekick status. Not only did the heroine often serve as the damsel in distress for the hero to rescue, but despite the fact they were the same age, the male's superhero name often ended in "-man" while the superheroine's name ended in "-girl" (e.g., Bulletman and Bulletgirl, Hawkman and Hawkgirl).

When writer Stan Lee and the artists at Marvel Comics began creating a new universe of superheroes in the early 1960s, they abandoned the sidekick convention. In fact, teenagers such as Spider-Man, the new Human Torch, and the X-Men were some of the most prominent heroes in the Marvel Universe, although the X-Men did have an adult mentor in Professor Xavier. In 1964 DC let their sidekicks step out of the mentors' shadows and form the Teen Titans. As the sidekicks grew up, they took on new superhero identities (Robin became Nightwing) or assumed the mantle of their mentor (Kid Flash became Flash).

Supervillains

Most of the early antagonists in comics were much less colorful than either the hero or his aide-de-camp. Superman began his career fighting gangsters and corrupt politicians, but it was soon apparent he was not even going to break a sweat that way, and before long he had to contend with villains like Lex Luthor, "the mad scientist who plots to dominate the Earth" (*Superman* #4,

1940). Other extraordinary menaces soon followed. Batman contended with bizarre villains such as Doctor Death, the Monk, and the Scarlet Horde quite early in his adventures. During the 1940s he encountered a colorful, and now familiar, array of Gotham City-based supervillains, among them Penguin, Catwoman, Riddler, and, of course, his arch-nemesis, the Joker. Each of the major superheroes has a similar rogue gallery of villains who return to plague the hero time and time again. Soon, these menaces reached the distinction of being labeled supervillains, making them counterpoints to the superheroes.

Figure 8.9 This image is just one iteration of the perpetual conflict between Dr. Doom and Mr. Fantastic that will be periodically reiterated as long as the *Fantastic Four* comic book is published. Doom will never give up until he proves he is superior to Mr. Fantastic. From *Fantastic Four* #200 (1978), with words by Marv Wolfman and art by Keith Pollard and Joe Sinnott. © 2023 Marvel Entertainment, Inc. and its subsidiaries.

What makes a supervillain different from any other antagonist a hero might encounter? Superpowers and a garish costume certainly contribute to the supervillain persona, but according to scholars Gina Misiroglu and Michael Eury (2006), it is the supervillain's propensity to scheme in operatic proportions that distinguishes him from ordinary criminals. The original Brainiac set out to shrink the city of Metropolis and steal it for his collection, Dr. Doom tries to supplant all other political leaders and establish himself as ruler over the world, and Galactus wants to eat entire planets. The supervillain is a powerfully evil opponent worthy of the incredible power and uncommon virtue of the superhero (Figure 8.9).

The villain is often more integral to the plot than the hero. As scholar Richard Reynolds (1992) points out, superheroes are largely conservative figures, usually content with the status quo. They typically do not seek to redistribute wealth, change sitting governments, or otherwise alter the existing social order. Supervillains, on the other hand, are out to change the world. They may well aim to redistribute wealth (usually to themselves) or unseat elected presidents in order to establish new forms of government (again benefiting themselves, presumably as dictators). Such provocative actions call the comparatively passive heroes into action, moving the story forward in exciting ways. Supervillains are active; superheroes are reactive. In the best of these stories, the hero discovers that defending the status quo challenges him to overcome obstacles he has never cleared before, further refining his qualities as a hero.

Themes

For decades superhero stories have been dismissed as power fantasies for adolescent males. Certainly, for children who might consider themselves powerless in the adult world, a part of the appeal is the freedom and power superheroes display once they cast off their ordinary identities. But there has always been more going on under the surface. There are particular values inherent in the superhero concept, and those values lead to certain themes being explored in superhero genre stories.

The superhero is "a particularly American vision of heroism" (Costello 2009: 14). The exemplar superhero was not only created in America, but the character's very heroism was homegrown: "Superman's powers make the hero capable of saving humanity; Kent's total immersion in the American heartland makes him want to do it" (Engle 1987: 85). Costumed superheroes have become "as iconically American as the Western cowboy" (Darowski 2012: 1) and reflect "what it can mean to be American" (Yockey 2012: 351).

In a series of essays written in the mid-nineteenth century Ralph Waldo Emerson delineates the characteristics of the peculiarly American hero (Gross 1971: 3–17):

Self-reliant (free of the constraints of tradition and society)
Idealistic (hopeful, not cynical)
An unshakeable will
A doer of deeds
A wielder of power

The man of action Emerson envisioned was usually of the more intellectual variety, a philosopher or writer, and his power was in his ideas not his muscles. However, Emerson's concept of applying power to make one's thoughts into reality and become a "finished man" foreshadowed Friedrich Nietzsche's Overman (Übermensch), to which the early superheroes were often compared.

In his 1941 study *The Hero in America*, Dixon Wecter paints a picture of the American hero that is very similar to Emerson's, but Wecter makes some modifications (Americans expect their heroes to be doers of *spectacular* deeds) and emphasizes a few additional characteristics (476–87):

A sense of duty (a responsibility to better community and country)
Confident (as Davy Crockett said "Be always sure you're right, then go ahead!")
Resourceful (The hero could even be a trickster if the deception served a noble cause.)
Has power yet does not abuse it
Humble

It was the early 1940s when Wecter wrote "Vanity or personal arrogance in any form is taboo" (1941: 483). Today, in an era of end-zone dances and self-aggrandizing rappers, we are likely to find cocky Tony Stark (Iron Man) more interesting than the quietly self-assured Steve Rogers (Captain America).

Of course, not all heroes or superheroes are cast in exactly the same mold. As Theodore Gross (2012) points out America is "a pluralistic society in which many kinds of heroes have emerged bearing many different styles" (vi). For example, in the 1960s Spider-Man and Hulk were embraced as counterculture icons because within their fictional universe they were misunderstood and feared, as opposed to the superheroes in the DC Universe who were idolized by the public. (There were not only statues of heroes such as Superman and Flash, but museums devoted to their exploits). Superhero stories are "an American mythology that is forever adjusting to meet society's needs" (Johnson 2012: 2).

Yet, even as superheroes narratives adapt to the nation's changing hopes, fears, and social norms certain aspects of heroism—strength of will, a sense of duty, wielding power and not abusing it—are at the heart of most superhero stories (even if the stories are questioning them).

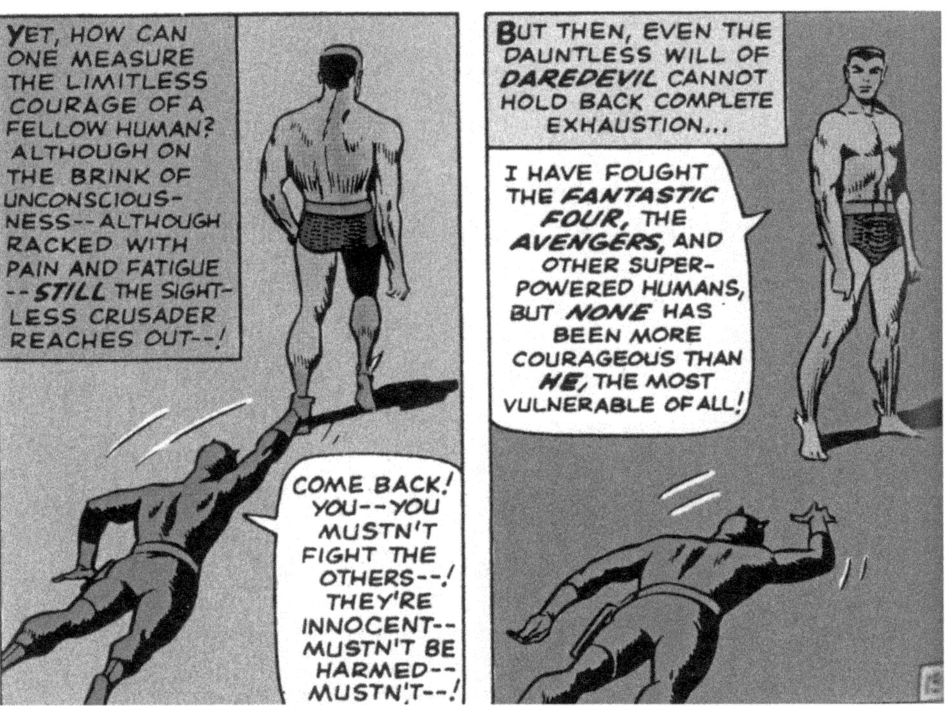

Figure 8.10 Superheroes are heroes not due to their super strength, but due to the strength of their spirit. *Daredevil* #7 (1965). Words by Stan Lee and art by Wally Wood. © 2023 Marvel Entertainment, Inc. and its subsidiaries.

Strength of Will

What makes these protagonists most heroic is not their power, but their persistence. The superhero is often the underdog, facing a more powerful foe or superior numbers, and experiencing temporary defeat. Superheroes are often beaten in the first encounter with a supervillain, or when the odds seem overwhelming they will briefly give in to their doubts, fears, or selfish desires. Yet they always return to the fray, exhibiting a strength of will that reaffirms the strength of the human spirit. "Whether a 'miraculous' return from seeming death, or a return to the right path, the values they embody are too strong to quell or kill" (Fingeroth 2004: 167) (Figure 8.10).

Sense of Duty

Superheroes have always been driven by the ethic of "what one can do, one should do," or as it was stated in the final panel of the first Spider-Man story, "With great power there must also come . . . great responsibility" (*Amazing Fantasy* #15, 1962; see Figure 10.13). Coogan believes that despite the revisionist stories writers might craft or the readings critics might try to impose the core of the superhero concept has remained "aiding the weak against the strong" (Coogan 2006: 238).

Occasionally superheroes question whether or not they are living up to their responsibilities and this provides an opportunity for examining the limits of those responsibilities. At one point in his career Spider-Man resolves to do all that he possibly can to make New York safer. For days he goes without sleep, swinging back and forth across the city fighting villains and rescuing those in danger until his personal life is in a shambles and he is too exhausted to be an effective hero. As Eco points out, from a being of Superman's power, "one could expect the most bewildering political, economic, and technological upheavals in the world," from "the solution of hunger problems" to "the destruction of inhumane systems" (1972/2004: 163). In the 1999 comic book *Superman: Peace on Earth*, Superman dedicates himself to ending hunger in the world, but ultimately fails, finding that more often than not, his efforts create distrust, hatred, or greed. Superman realizes he cannot impose solutions on mankind without compromising his own innate decency and forcing his values on others. Part of the responsibility that comes with great power is the responsibility to not abuse that power. Rather than proactively trying to change the world "the superhero is a figure who serves to return, in narrative form, democracy to its ideals" (Smith 2010).

Examining the Abuse of Power

However, not everyone sees superheroes as such a positive embodiment of American values. Through their actions, superheroes teach the lesson that justice is more important than law. Superheroes are essentially outlaws, masked vigilantes, violating rights and committing assault to bring evildoers to justice. In fact, the superhero genre has sometimes been characterized as being just one aspect of "the metagenre of the vigilante hero" (Hatfield 2012: 123). Robert Jewett and John Shelton Lawrence (2003) believe the superhero genre embodies what they call the Captain America Complex—superheroes use their power to "redeem the world for democracy, but by means that transcend democratic limits on the exercise of power" (35).

Not surprisingly, the superhero genre has been decried as fascist for nearly seventy years. As the genre matured and the stories self-reflective a number of writers have examined the implications of powerful beings taking the law into their own hands. In *Miracleman* (1985) and *Squadron Supreme* (1985), superheroes essentially conquer the world in order to make it better. In *Black Summer* (2007) a superhero decides justice would best be served by violently removing the president of the United States from office.

David A. Pizarro and Roy Baumeister (2013) claim "modern superhero comics (and the films they've inspired) are moral tales on steroids" that satisfy "the natural human inclination toward moralization" (16; 17). However, Pizarro and Baumeister tend to oversimplify the modern superhero tale, treating it as an unambiguous triumph of good over evil (30). Older superhero stories were fairly simplistic and Manichean (absolute good versus absolute evil), but works such as *Watchmen* (1986) and *Brat Pack* (1990) sought to undermine the moral clarity of the superhero genre.

While it is popular for critics to refer to *Watchmen* as a deconstruction of the superhero genre, not all superhero fans read it as such. For many readers the familiar superhero narrative remains intact because the immoral acts Ozymandias commits to serve the greater good clearly make him the supervillain (plus, he's a smug dandy), while Rorshach's badass attitude and unwavering commitment to justice ("Not even in the face of Armageddon.

Never compromise.") mark him as the hero of the story. The moral ambiguity was perhaps more potent for readers of *Identity Crisis* (2004) because they saw familiar DC characters they had long followed and loved immersed in what Grant Morrison (2011) characterizes as "a queasy world of dubious ethics, paranoia, ultraviolence, and sexual assault" (384). *The Civil War* (2006) crossover event had no true villain but instead split Marvel's superheroes into two warring factions that echoed the post-9/11 debate about national security versus personal freedom. One side was led by Iron Man, who imposed draconian and morally questionable measures with the intent of making the world safer. Captain America leads the opposing forces, and even though public sentiment seems to be against him he fights for what he believes to be justice. With admirable characters and reasonable arguments on each side there was no clear victory or tidy resolution at the end of this story.

Narrative Patterns

Origin Story

Because far more people are familiar with superheroes from movies than from comic books, and the first movie tends to explain how the hero came to be, the origin story is probably the most familiar superhero narrative. The origin story is necessary to explain the fantastic nature of the superhero. Comic book historian Ron Goulart (1997) claims, "The most appealing idea to a kid was the short-cut origin, with magic powers thrust upon you. Doing pushups and studying chemistry were too much like school" (Goulart 1970/1997: 230). A fortuitous lightning strike created the powers of Blue Bolt (with a radium chaser), the Human Top, the second Flash (who was simultaneously doused by chemicals), and when Billy Batson says his magic word there is a flash of lightning as he transforms into Captain Marvel. Yet cartoonist Paul Chadwick (1997) believes the origin tales that resonate most strongly with us are the truly transformative experiences that "mine the vein of trauma" because "Nobody travels to the extremes of human character without great suffering. In fact, nobody changes much at all without it" (34).

These superhero origin stories often echo an often-repeated pattern Otto Rank (1959) identified as the myth of the birth of the hero. Following are a few of the key elements from Rank's pattern as they apply to Superman:

child of distinguished parents	son of Krypton's leading scientist
surrendered to the water in a box	sent into space in a small rocket
saved by lowly people and cared for by a humble woman	cared for by a down-to-earth farm couple

(A more detailed explanation of Rank's myth of the birth of the hero is available on the https://www.bloomsburyonlineresources.com/the-power-of-comics-and-graphic-novels-3 site.)

Monomyth

Many of the great hero tales of Western culture follow a mythic pattern similar to the one scholar Joseph Campbell (1968) has described as the classical monomyth. Coogan points out that most superhero origin stories follow the separation-initiation-return structure of the monomyth (2006: 122). The typical monomyth tale ends with the hero returning from his initiation with some wisdom or treasure that will benefit his community. The superhero does emerge from an ordeal, or a happy accident, with power and purpose that can be used to benefit the community, but, due to the serial aesthetic of most comic books, the transformation is only the beginning of the superhero's tale; a tale that will be told in monthly comic book installments and summer blockbuster movies as long as there is a market for the adventures.

The month-to-month comic book adventures of the typical superhero are more likely to follow the pattern of what Robert Jewett and John Shelton Lawrence (2003) call the American monomyth. A Black Marvel story from *All Winners Comics* # 1 (Summer 1941) provides a typical example of the **American monomyth** in superhero comic books.

1. A community is threatened: The Order of the Hood undertakes a "series of robberies and murders never before seen by man."
2. A selfless hero emerges: "Young man-about-town" Dan Lyons slips into an alley and dons his Black Marvel costume.
3. The hero renounces temptation: For stories of this period, the only temptation to renounce was the temptation to give up the struggle when it seemed hopeless. "I'm not afraid to die, but I can't be killed now when the American people need me—I must escape somehow."
4. The hero wins a victory (through superheroism): Black Marvel uses ingenuity and strength to escape from the death-ray chamber and defeat the Order of the Hood.
5. The hero restores harmony to the community: The Black Marvel has "mopped up the Hood gang" and prevented their crime spree.
6. The hero recedes into obscurity: "His work done, the Black Marvel doesn't wait for thanks." Dan Lyons goes back to hanging out with his socialite friends and pretending he is only interested in polo.

The majority of superhero stories in the first few decades of the genre's existence clearly followed this template, but by the mid-sixties new elements were being added to the simple pattern of "discovering the cause of disorder and defeating the transgressor" (Bongco 2000: 102).

SERIAL AESTHETIC: CONTINUITY, MULTIPLICITY, AND REITERATION

Brian Camp (2000) observes that "essentially, superhero stories as we know them are soap operas interrupted by slug-fests," and the "never-ending 'über-soap operas'" are collapsing under the weight of their own accumulated continuity. **Continuity** is the relatedness among characters and events said to inhabit the same fictional universe, and it can pose a problem for creators trying to deal with decades of backstory.

To make matters more complex this continuity has been layered over by a new system of **multiplicity** in which "readers may consume multiple versions of the same franchise, each with different conceptions of the character, different understandings of their relationships with secondary figures, different moral perspectives, exploring different moments in their lives, and so forth" (Jenkins 2009: 20). Rather than confusing readers, continuity and multiplicity

Figures 8.11a–d Fans enjoy multiple versions of Batman that seem very different on the surface but share common elements at their core. *Batman* #700 (2010) art by David Finch and Scott Williams; *Batman: Brave and the Bold* #13 (2010) art by Robert Pope and Scott McRae; *Detective Comics Annual* #7 (1994) art by Enrique Alcatena; *Batman* '66 #1 (2013) art by Michael Allred. © DC Comics.

seem to crystallize some superheroes as archetypes. For instance, not only have multiple creators redefined the Batman character without destroying the character coherence fans value, but "the multiple refractions of the Batman character seem to have made him fuller instead of fragmenting him into obscurity" (Bongco 2000: 146).

In a sense, this represents a move from viewing the superhero as a mythological figure to a folkloric one, where the different versions of the tale share critical commonality that creates recognition that dispels any dissonance. The term **multiverse** was introduced by sf/fantasy author Michael Moorcock in *The Sundered Worlds* (1963) to describe how parallel worlds could have events that would center on a figure who had common characteristics with some differences, what Moorcock described as the Eternal Champion. Neil Stephenson's *Snow Crash* (1992) added the concept of a **metaverse**, a fictional universe existing within a digital reality, but with infinite possibilities. The modern superhero appears to comfortably fit within an overlap of both these concepts, allowing readers (or viewers) to reconcile the Batman of the comics with his analogs in film, television, gaming, and other media, each of whom if examined carefully exhibit dissonant characteristics (Figure 8.11 a–d).

Superheroes, whether they appeared in pulp magazines, comic strips, comic books, or radio, were born into a serial aesthetic that requires both repetition and difference. In ongoing comic book titles some actions are repeated endlessly—using a clever ploy to protect the secret identity, fighting a particular supervillain (most superheroes have fought each of their major nemeses dozens of times). And even though cataclysmic upheavals of society (e.g., a planet of supermen declare war on Earth or everyone on Manhattan turns into a spider) occur with regularity, once the superhero has dealt with the threat both society and the superhero return to the familiar status quo. As Umberto Eco (1972/2004) points out in his analysis of Superman, readers of superhero tales encounter "events happening in an ever-continuing present" (156) in which the hero overcomes obstacles, but does not affect real change in his environment because change would ground the superhero in the temporal and move him one step closer to death (150). As commodities that corporations want to continue to exploit for as long as possible, popular superheroes cannot grow old, die, or fundamentally change; "economics therefore denies any 'definitive' take on a hero" (Taylor 2007: 350).

Marc Singer (1999) believes it is not a story which persists in the minds of superhero comic book readers, but rather a state of being. Expanding on a term he borrowed from comics scribe Neil Gaiman, Singer refers to the alluring aspect of unchanging superheroes as a **state of grace** that consists of the hero's power, appearance, and behavior (Bissette, Gaiman, and Veitch 1989: 195). For example, over the years readers have not so much expected or responded to a particular tale of the Hulk, but rather to "Hulkness"—a scrawny scientist who becomes a huge green (sometimes gray) monster when he gets angry, and who then gets stronger as he gets angrier. If people know only one thing about the Hulk is the often-repeated line from the 1970s TV show: "You wouldn't like me when I'm angry."

Setting

City of Heroes and *Superhero City* are two of the most popular online superhero role-playing games. The titles of these games indicate what everyone knows—superheroes belong in the city. There are some exceptions: Timely Comics heroes roam the globe fighting the Axis, Blue Bolt's adventures take place deep beneath the Earth's crust in the Green Empire, the Silver Age version of Green Lantern is part of a galaxy-wide police force, superhero teams such as the Avengers, and particularly the Fantastic Four, often visit other solar systems or even other

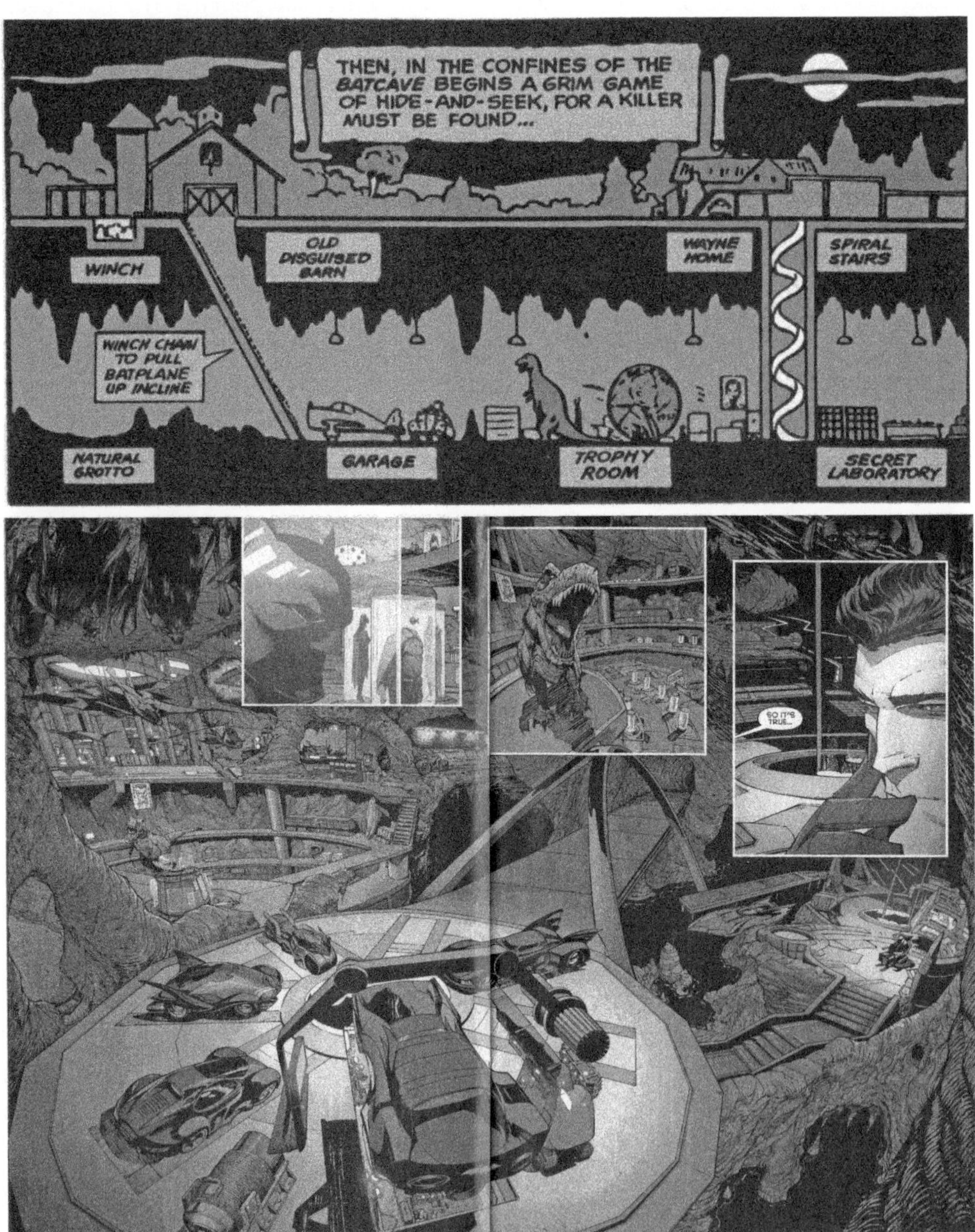

Figures 8.12a–b The look of the Batcave has changed over the years as both technology and comic book art have become more sophisticated. *Batman* #48 (1948) words by Bill Finger and art by Jim Mooney; *Batman* vol. 2, #1 (2011) words by Scott Snyder and art by Greg Capollo. © DC Comics.

dimensions, and Mud Man battles evil in a little seaside town. However, the city is the place where most superheroes are based and where most of their adventures take place.

In Marvel Comics there is very little acknowledgment of a suburban or rural existence. When Marvel characters do travel outside New York it is usually to fantastic realms of myth (Asgard), science fiction settings (The Negative Zone; The Great Refuge), or exotic fictional foreign lands (Wakanda, Latveria). To be in a small town or a rural setting is a trap to be escaped (e.g., the "Terror in a Tiny Town" story in *Fantastic Four* # 236).

Scott Bukatman (2003) notes that "In the mid-1980s, creators began to explore the relation between heroic figure and urban ground, and the city became something more than a generic background for superheroic derring-do" (184). Metropolis, "the City of Tomorrow," has become a symbol of modernity (particularly the vision of technological modernity that was on display at the 1939 World's Fair). Metropolis represents the striving for the Enlightenment ideal of the perfectly rational, perfectly ordered society. Gotham City, on the other hand, manifests a postmodern dystopia. With its twisted architecture and twisted villains, Gotham is anti-rational. Bruce Wayne becomes the world's greatest detective to make sense of the senselessness of Gotham.

A frequently seen specialized setting in superhero comics is the hero or villain headquarters. The most famous of superhero headquarters is undoubtedly the Batcave, with its fleet of vehicles, supercomputers, and bizarre trophies (see Figures 8.12a–b). Many solo superheroes, not requiring a special location for equipment and trophies, simply stash their costumes somewhere in their homes. However, almost all superhero teams have a clearly established base of operations. The Justice League of America started out meeting in a cave but upgraded over the years to a Hall of Justice, a moon-based watchtower, and a satellite with teleportation capability. The Fantastic Four's Baxter Building and the Avengers' Mansion (later Tower) are New York landmarks (proudly emblazoned with their logos) and be so visible and accessible that they are constantly under repair from supervillain attacks. While many supervillains evade the law by living in hideouts or elaborate secret bases, there are some with the financial or political clout to operate from high-profile locations such as Castle Doom or Lexcorp Tower.

Visual Conventions

The visual "vocabulary" and "grammar" of the superhero genre were established primarily by two artists. Burne Hogarth never drew true superheroes, but he took over the Tarzan comic strip from Hal Foster in 1936. The detailed musculature—sometimes referred to as the **flayed look**—and dynamic movement Hogarth used in rendering Tarzan influenced generations of comic book artists. The other artist was Jack Kirby (see profile as follows). While Kirby's figures might seem blockish and stiff compared to the lithe Tarzan of Hogarth, Kirby was even more of a force in creating the visual dynamic of the superhero comic book. Kirby's characters were seldom static; anyone in a costume was either moving or poised to spring into action. "I tore my characters out of the panels," Kirby once said. "I made them jump all over the page" (qtd. in Eisner 2001: 211).

Profile: Jack Kirby

Born: Jacob Kurtzberg
August 28, 1917
New York City

"The secret of my success is the fact that I gave to it. I gave it all I had. There is blood and bone and sinew behind the whole thing."

Figure 8.13 Jack Kirby displayed unparalleled creativity and productivity in his career. Photo by Suzy Skaar and courtesy of the Jack Kirby Museum.

Career Highlights

1941 Simon and Kirby have their first big hit, *Captain America Comics* (for Timely)
1942 The team produces another hit, *Boy Commandos* (DC)
1947 The team launches romance comics with the debut of *Young Romance* (Prize)
1950 The team creates the fondly remembered western *Boys' Ranch* (Harvey)
1954–5 Simon and Kirby publish their own comics under the short-lived Mainline imprint
1957 Kirby experiments with science fiction in "Challengers of the Unknown" (*Showcase*, DC)
1958–61 Kirby does the syndicated SF strip *Sky Masters of the Space Force*
1961 Kirby and Stan Lee revive Marvel and revitalize the superhero with *The Fantastic Four*
1962 Kirby and Lee introduce Marvel's mythical hero, Thor, in *Journey into Mystery*
1963 Kirby and Lee create *The X-Men*
1965–6 *The Fantastic Four* introduces the Inhumans, the Silver Surfer, Galactus, and the Black Panther
1970 Kirby departs Marvel and launches the Fourth World for DC with *Superman's Pal, Jimmy Olsen*
1971 *The New Gods* expands the Fourth World saga
1972 Kirby launches *Kamandi, the Last Boy on Earth*
1975–6 Kirby returns to Marvel and creates *The Eternals*
1978 Kirby goes to work in animation, providing concepts for children's TV series
1981–4 Kirby experiments with creator-owned comics in the direct market with *Captain Victory* and the *Galaxy Rangers* (Pacific)
1994 Kirby dies, age 76
2014 Kirby heirs win multi-million dollar settlement from Disney in their attempt to terminate Kirby's grants to Marvel

Jack Kirby (b. Jacob Kurtzberg, 1917–94) is the artist who designed and first drew much of the Marvel Universe in the 1960s. Marvel characters such as the Fantastic Four, the Hulk, Thor, the X-Men, the Avengers, the Silver Surfer, and the Black Panther were co-created (in some cases solely created) by Kirby and first came to life under his pencil.

He designed these trademark characters by telling stories about them: over the decade he worked up the plots for hundreds of Marvel Comics at his drawing board, sometimes in collaboration with Marvel's reigning editor-writer Stan Lee, and sometimes with only loose guidance from Lee (who wrote or rewrote dialogue and captions over Kirby's pages, giving them a distinctive voice). Marvel's production method, typified by Kirby, bypassed scripts in favor of narrative drawing; plots and characters were conjured up through the art. This technique proved very successful: Marvel had been a small, starving company in 1961 when Kirby and Lee jointly launched *The Fantastic Four*, the first of Marvel's new line of heroes, but by 1970, when Kirby left the company, Marvel was a standard-bearer for the comic book medium and celebrated for its hipness, energy, and edge. More than any other artist, Kirby made that change possible.

Kirby's career, though, goes well beyond the Marvel of the sixties. A lifelong cartoonist, he worked from the mid-1930s, when he was a teen, onward until the 1980s. Though Kirby worked in several media, including newspaper strips and animation, it was comic books that earned his reputation. Indeed his work epitomizes the US-style comic book in all its feistiness, roughhousing energy, and eagerness to please: the comic as pulp pamphlet, populist, typically disposable, yet vital, and is considered a major influence on visuals in film and video games as well as comics. Kirby came of age artistically precisely when the comic book medium did, and he internalized, in fact helped set into formula, its brash, accessible ways. Except for his time (*c.* 1943–5) as an infantryman in the Second World War—a time that haunted and informed his work forever after—Kirby worked almost nonstop on comic books, month in, month out, from the late 1930s to the late 1970s.

Figure 8.14 This page from *New Gods* #7 (1972) illustrates the kinetic energy of Jack Kirby's art as the master storyteller packs explosive action and literal explosions into the sequence panel after panel. © DC Comics.

Kirby belonged to the first generation of cartoonists for whom comic books were new and exciting. Even as the medium struggled to its feet, the young Jacob Kurtzberg got work elsewhere: in the Fleischer animation studio (*c.* 1935–7) and in several newspaper syndicates (1936–9). For the latter he used various pseudonyms, having not yet adopted the name "Jack Kirby." His earliest comic book stories per se came in 1940. From 1941 to the mid-1950s he collaborated with business and creative partner Joe Simon, with whom he ran the prolific Simon & Kirby studio. When Simon became the line editor at Timely—later known as Marvel—in late 1940, he brought Kirby with him, and the two cemented their partnership with the hit *Captain America Comics*, launched early in 1941 (the character would be revived in 1963). Fired from Timely for moonlighting, the two settled in at rival publisher DC, where, in 1942, they created the seminal "kid gang" comics, *The Newsboy Legion* and *The Boy Commandos*. Kirby's work caused a sensation: even by the time he was in his mid-twenties, he inspired scads of imitators with his rousing, dynamic cartooning style, which conveyed movement and conflict with a violent intensity, smashing through panel borders and assaulting the page. Simon and Kirby served, and Kirby regrouped in the postwar period, doing work for publishers Harvey, Hillman, and especially Prize, for which they created the romance comic book genre with *Young Romance* in 1947. That extremely lucrative genre helped keep Simon & Kirby profitable for much of the next decade. The studio employed many other artists and did work in multiple genres. Simon and Kirby's self-publishing operation, Mainline, debuted in 1954, unluckily just in time for an anti-comic book crusade, or moral panic, that put legal and political pressure on comic book publishers and prompted the adoption of the self-censoring Comics Code late that year. The industry's near-collapse, propelled by the panic as well as shifts in magazine distribution and in the larger media landscape (e.g., consider the rise of television), wrecked Mainline and forced Simon and Kirby to find what work they could do separately. Kirby picked up both comic book and newspaper work, notably the syndicated strip *Sky Masters of the Space Force* (1958–61). Legal and workplace frictions cost Kirby that strip as well as freelance work with DC, and so it is that he came to work mostly for Marvel (as we now call it) in the late 1950s—the same place he had been fired from in 1941.

The seminal Marvel period followed, revitalizing comic books with a new and grander approach to superheroes, one based on continuity, deeper, more conflicted characterization, and greater sophistication and irony than before. Editor Stan Lee held up Kirby as an example for other artists to follow, in fact had Kirby lay out a great many comics for other pencilers, and gave Kirby increasingly free rein to develop an expanded canvas, with stories of cosmic scope and pomp. Many now recognize Kirby as Marvel's co-creator as well as chief artist, though the controversy over precisely who created what at Marvel continues to this day. The debate over Kirby's contribution has sparked not only litigation but also calls for boycotts and protests by other creators. Indeed Kirby's career story is a window into the vexed issues of copyright, creator ownership, and work-for-hire practices in the comic book industry; many today see his career, particularly his lack of equity in Marvel and lack of control over his creations, as a tragic and sobering example. The fact that those creations have become far more successful than anyone in the 1960s could have imagined makes his case particularly poignant.

Kirby followed his seminal Marvel period with a string of eccentric superhero and science fiction comics in the seventies, most notably a cluster of comic books for DC collectively known as the Fourth World (1970–4): *The New Gods*, *Mister Miracle*, *The Forever People*, and Kirby's run on the long-lived *Superman's Pal, Jimmy Olsen*. These comics shared a common world, epic scope, and mythic approach to the superhero. Commercially, Kirby's most successful comic of the decade was the post-apocalyptic adventure *Kamandi, the Last Boy on Earth* (1972–8, though by Kirby only to 1976). In the eighties, after bailing out of comics and entering TV animation, he returned to make a key contribution to independent, creator-owned comic books with two SF series for upstart publisher Pacific, *Captain Victory and the Galactic Rangers* and *Silver Star* (1981–4). These projects, published exclusively for the direct market, belonged to Kirby solely and earned him royalties, thus setting an important example for younger talent and validating the option of working with independent publishers. However, this was to be the end of Kirby's serious engagement with the comics field.

Kirby's reputation hovers somewhere between that of the ultimate commercial jobber, one who would adapt to any genre and try his hand at any sort of comic, and that of an untaught but inspired genius who used pulp formula to create very personal stories. In fact he did both, jobbing like mad to support his family, rolling with the punches, and adapting to the comics world as he found it, but also in turn adapting that world to his own talents and making the raw ingredients of the medium, particularly superheroes, into his own quirky mythology. Kirby's quirks, viewed as lovable by some and distracting by others, amount to one of the most distinctive, immediately recognizable styles in the comic book world. Arguably, he rescued the superhero from obsolescence, became the dynamo that powered the genre's revival, and laid the groundwork, visually and conceptually, for the comic book market today.

—*Charles Hatfield*

Charles Hatfield is the author of the Eisner Award-winning *Hand of Fire: The Comics Art of Jack Kirby* (2012).

Another aspect of the look of superhero comics is the eroticism of skintight spandex stretched over impossibly muscled and improbably proportioned bodies. In the early decades of the genre, the emphasis was on the eroticism of tight, and often skimpy, costumes on curvaceous superheroines. While the male superheroes were obviously big, powerful guys, they were often drawn as blockish and without much muscular definition. In the 1960s artists like Neal Adams and Jim Steranko revived Hogarth's flayed look, in which every muscle stands in sharp relief as if the covering skin had been removed. Adams and Steranko were highly influential artists in the genre, and most artists who followed devoted themselves to lovingly rendering bulging muscles, including many that cannot be found on the human body. The distortion of the superhero body accelerated during the eighties and nineties to the point that if there is any eroticism left, it is based on an abstraction of breasts and biceps rather than an emulation of the human form. While there has in recent years been some turning back to more reasonable portrayals of superbodies, one can still find plenty of female superheroes with long stick legs and huge breasts, and plenty of male superheroes with such distorted "colossal anatomies" that they "are moving toward unconscious self-parody" (Taylor 2007: 351). As female readers and creators of superhero comics became more prominent in the twenty-first century, this characteristic became less common and was viewed as less acceptable, though it remained part of many artists' styles (Figure 8.15).

Figure 8.15 Cartoonist Don Simpson pokes fun at the unrealistic anatomy of some superhero depictions in his Megaton Man caricature. Megaton Man TM and © Don Simpson, all rights reserved.

Because comic books are a visual medium, the ritualistic display of a hero's power has become another stylistic convention of the superhero genre. Numerous panels over the years have been devoted to Flash running on water and Thor calling down lightning bolts. Certain poses are often associated with the display of power. The image of Superman with one arm fully extended and one bent, flying up, up, and away, is familiar from both comic books and merchandise. And when Spider-Man swings around New York, he does so in a distinctive, if somewhat awkward-looking manner, with his knees up to his shoulders.

Analyzing: The Enduring Appeal of Superheroes

Superheroes established the comic book as a commercially viable medium in the United States, and it is superheroes who have defined the comic book in popular perception. In twenty-first-century America the superhero is ubiquitous. From Sesame Street's "Hero Guy" and "Super Grover," to Eminem's music videos "Superman" and the Batman and Robin homage "Without Me," to "Orkin Man" commercials, the concept of superheroes pervades our culture (Fingeroth 2004: 169). There are even dozens of real-life costumed crusaders, including promotional characters, people just having fun, and a few serious crime fighters, listed at the World Superhero Registry.

Hundreds of superhero programs, both live-action and animated, have aired on television since *The Adventures of Superman* debuted in 1952. There have even been reality shows such as *Who Wants to Be a Superhero?* and *Stan Lee's Superheroes*. Box Office Mojo lists almost 100 feature films in the superhero category. Seventeen of those films have grossed over $200 million. Four of the top ten highest-grossing films worldwide are superhero movies (Box Office Mojo). *Avengers: Endgame* grossed more than $2 billion in just eleven days (Rubin 2019).

Obviously, to corporations (Disney and Warner at the moment) that own them, superheroes are a commodity to be exploited for profit, but why have they so captured the popular imagination?

In the late 1930s, when the first comic book superheroes began to appear, many individuals were facing the economic devastation of the Great Depression and felt overwhelmed by the mighty machinery and vast structures of the modern world. In Superman and his ilk, they found mythical characters who could rise above the skyscrapers that dwarfed the ordinary human and transcend the forces of modernity that besieged humanity (Regalado 2000: 1). Writer Christopher Knowles (2007) contends, "All superheroes are essentially savior figures," and that is why they "traditionally enjoy greater popularity—with children and adults—in times of national stress" (111). Superhero tales are not so much a fulfillment of a wish for power as they are an optimistic statement about the future and an act of defiance in the face of adversity (Regalado 2000: 12) (Figure 8.16).

Figure 8.16 Scott Bukatman says Superman is "a walking, flying figure of utopian progress" that "prefigures in his mode of perception and spatial negotiation the development of the city of tomorrow" (198). *Superman* #204 (2004) art by Jim Lee and Scott Williams. © DC Comics.

Progress is one of the prime American values (Steele and Redding 1962). Particularly in the early twentieth century, America, reveling in its new status in the world, wanted to break with the traditional, the "old world," and embrace the new and improved. (Think how often that phrase is used in advertising.) It was apropos to have a Superman Day at the 1939–40 World's Fair because the purpose of the Fair was to present the vision of "the world of tomorrow" (televisions, robots, interstate highways) and Superman was soon touted as "the man of tomorrow." That title was not so much a promise that humans could attain his power but as comic book writer Elliot S! Maggin says "Superman is an aspirational figure. He shows us how to be better people ourselves by being the best person he can be" (Roberson 2011). While Superman might have been a metaphor for human moral progress, Batman, more in tune with the physical culture craze of the early twentieth century, provided a more attainable ideal of human physical and mental perfection.

Writer Jeph Loeb and scholar Tom Morris (2005) believe superheroes can serve as "moral examples. Superman can inspire us. Batman can keep us going even when the going is very tough. Spider-Man can help us understand that the voice of conscience is always more important than the cacophony of voices around us, who may be condemning us, belittling us, or just dismissing what we think of as so important" (19).

Superheroes can also be "friends." And that's not really as sad or weird as it sounds. Behm-Morawitz and Pennell (2013) claim that "the appeal of the superhero can partly be explained by the phenomenon of fans getting to know superhero characters in ways that are similar to how they form attachments to friends, neighbors, and loved ones," and forming a parasocial relationship that fulfills attachment needs. A reader who has followed Iron Man's adventures for decades is likely to know more about Tony Stark than he does about his real-life friends. Fans can genuinely care about a character's ups and downs (fictional though they are) and feel a sense of familiarity, often using a nickname (Spidey, Supes, Cap, etc.) to refer to the character. In Dana Anderson's (2013) phenomenological examination of the experience of superhero comic books he explains "Dr. Strange and Captain Marvel would appear in my mind, not as characters from a book or movie, but as reiterations of people I knew and respected and, more than anything else, wanted to be" (67). For Anderson, "the comics themselves weren't books so much as visits with friends" (67).

Of course the appeal of a particular superhero or even the meaning of the entire genre can be a very individual and personal matter. And those meanings can change over time because "the superheroes and their stories have grown with the audiences that consume them, and their formulas, conventions, and narrative worlds must alter to follow suit, injecting new, unpredictable, and more challenging characterizations that keep readers engaged" (Ndalianis 2009: 10).

The superhero is recognized as a particularly American creation and is often seen as an embodiment of American ideology. However, many beyond America's shores mistakenly interpret the superhero as merely a symbol of power. The meaning of superheroes on their native soil can be found in Will Kane, of the movie *High Noon*, who stays to face the gunmen seeking revenge even though no one in town will stand with him or appreciates what he is doing. The meaning can be found in Raymond Chandler's private detective Phillip Marlowe, who risks his life in the service of justice, even though he seldom has a client paying him to do so. The superhero is the same Emersonian hero who strode down the main streets of Western towns and the mean streets of Los Angeles, leading a life of duty, courage, and individual effort.

As discussed earlier, the phenomenal success of comics' translation to film and television in the past decade has generally been viewed as good for the form. The largest portion of this success has been driven by superhero characters, whether treated in ways that mirrored the heroism of their comics (e.g., the Marvel Cinematic Universe), or that focused on titles that explored the darker potential of superheroes (e.g., *The Boys* and *Watchmen*). What is not clear is whether this success in other media has unfortunate collateral effect on the comics, by satisfying the public's desire to consume superhero fiction "better" or more conveniently than the comics themselves. Will their own success be more dangerous to the heroes than any supervillain is yet to be seen.

Discussion Questions

1. If you could have one superpower, what would it be? What do you find appealing about this power? How does what you find exciting about the power relate to the supposed "power fantasy" appeal of superheroes?
2. Apply one or more of the definitions of "superhero" presented in this chapter to a fictional hero who has not normally been labeled as a superhero (e.g., Buffy the Vampire Slayer, Luke Skywalker, or Katniss Everdeen). What does your comparison reveal about the qualities that make a superhero? What does it reveal about the hero you have chosen?
3. In the section on narrative patterns we do not attempt to describe the definitive story structure for the superhero genre but, rather, provide a number of theories (by Coogan, Gertler, Camp, Eco, and Singer) of the superhero genre tale. Which of these theories best describe the superhero stories with which you are familiar?

Activities

1. In 1989 comics historian Mike Benton identified what he called the "Significant Seven" superheroes. Benton claims that "out of the hundreds of superhero characters, seven stand out as the most historically important: Superman, Batman, Wonder Woman, Spider-Man, Captain America, Captain Marvel, and Plastic Man" (*Comic Book* 178). Your task is to revise Benton's list into a "Significant Ten." Justify the addition of each character by explaining how that character has contributed to or changed the superhero genre.
2. Choose a superhero character with whom you are very familiar, and create a program that would be handed out to attendees of a funeral of that character. Assume that the character's secret identity is public knowledge after his or her death. So, just one funeral to memorialize both identities.

Format: Single fold letter-sized piece of paper printed on both sides, or the digital equivalent thereof. The program must include a very brief obituary but might almost include quotes from what you think might be some of the character's favorite poems, books, or songs.

There should be a listing of who is speaking, praying, reading passages of scripture (if that is appropriate for the character), playing an instrument, or singing during the service. This can be a mixture of real-world people and characters from the fictional universe in which your selected character exists.

Programs usually include a picture of the person. You should be able to find plenty of images of the character online, but an original drawing is also acceptable. Usually, there is an image of something associated with the person, or, sometimes, a background image.

To get an idea of the type of content that often appears in funeral programs you can look at:

https://www.funeralprogram-site.com/memorial-bulletin-programs
or
https://www.pinterest.com/funeraltemplate/printable-funeral-program-templates/

Recommended Reading

Comics

Busiek, Kurt, and Brent E. Anderson. *Kurt Busiek's Astro City: Life in the Big City*. La Jolla: Homage Comics, 1995.

Kurt Busiek lovingly crafted the fictional Astro City and its numerous superheroic inhabitants in homage to the superheroes he grew up admiring. Within these city limits, he explores both the heroism and the humanity of beings with powers and abilities far beyond those of mortal men.

Gold, Mike, and Robert Greenberger, eds. *The Greatest Superman Stories Ever Told*. New York: DC Comics, 1987, 2004.

This trade paperback collects a sampling of some of the most entertaining Superman stories published during the character's first fifty years, including selections from creators Jerry Siegel and Joe Shuster, definitive artist Curt Swan, and comic greats Jack Kirby, Alan Moore, and John Byrne.

Scholarly Sources

Hatfield, Charles, Jeet Heer, and Kent Worcester, eds. *The Superhero Reader*. Jackson: University Press of Mississippi, 2013.

The editors provide an excellent analysis of the current state of superhero studies. They have also assembled an impressive sampling of intelligent commentary on the cultural, aesthetic, and historical aspects of the superhero.

Saunders, Ben. *Do the Gods Wear Capes? Spirituality, Fantasy, and Superheroes*. New York: Continuum, 2011.

Saunders demonstrates how the appeal of the superhero is fundamentally metaphysical, and how the superhero genre, by its very nature engages readers in ethical and existential questions.

9 Beyond Entertainment

Journalism, Documentary, and Advocacy

Pioneering comics scholar Sol Davidson journeyed to Mexican jungles, the Australian outback, the Andes Mountains of South America, and the Altamira cave complex in Spain to see firsthand the prehistoric cave paintings that are often touted as the forebears of comics. He was surprised to find that these paintings were "located only in the dim recesses of caves" where they were unlikely to be seen by anyone other than the artist. Davidson concluded that such paintings, for instance a spear pointed at the heart of a mammoth, were not meant to celebrate a kill or glorify a powerful hunter, but rather that "the painting was a wish, a prayer that the bison or mammoth would be the victim of tomorrow's hunt for food and survival. Like the finest in all religions, the prayer was personal, uniquely the artist's vision of what the future should hold" (Davidson 2008).

As organized religion developed there was sometimes reluctance to use art as a means of religious practice. Early Judaism prohibited art that depicted divine beings or humans since they were made in God's image, and associated works of art with idolatry, based on the second commandment: "Thou shalt not make unto thee a graven image, nor any manner of likeness, of any thing that is in heaven above, or that is in the earth beneath, or that is in the water under the earth" (Exodus 20:3). Islam continues to maintain a rather strict prohibition against depictions of Allah, the Prophet Muhammad, and, to a lesser extent, other Muslim holy people.

There have been periods during which some factions of the Christian faith have discouraged or even prohibited depictions of divine figures. However, for the most part, Christianity has embraced art, including juxtaposed, sequential images (comics?) such as narratives on a series of tapestries or stained-glass windows, as a way to give belief a more tangible form than thoughts, or even words. A seventeenth-century Christian manuscript created in Ethiopia, *Teʾamire Maryam* (The Miracles of Mary), while mostly text, contains thirty-two painted scenes of miracles performed by the Virgin Mary. At one point in the book a particular miracle is shown in a series of pictures, within distinct panels, on two

Figure 9.1 ***Te'amire Maryam (The Miracles of Mary)*** **seventeenth Century, Ethiopia.**

facing pages. This is a devotional use of the comics form that goes beyond entertainment (Figure 9.1).

Objectives

In this chapter you will learn:

1. how the emerging genre of comics journalism developed;
2. how comics have been used as instruments of persuasion and propaganda; and
3. how the various documentary modes can be applied in comics.

Unlike private prayers painted deep within caves, most uses of the comics form that go beyond mere entertainment are created with the intent to educate or persuade an audience. In this chapter we will examine how comics have been effectively adapted to serve as an instrument of journalism, education, persuasion, and, perhaps, propaganda.

Comics as Journalism

Wibke Weber and Hans-Martin Rall (2017) define comics journalism as "an emerging field that combines the journalistic approach with comics to produce news stories" (376). Comics journalist Dan Archer believes this combination of comics and journalism should "give the reader a unique reading experience while simultaneously moving, informing and entertaining them in equal share" (JSK 2013).

As printing technology spread through Europe in the fifteenth-century books were printed for the educated upper class, but sensational events of the day were communicated to the illiterate masses with a series of drawings on cheaply produced single sheets of paper known as broadsides or broadsheets. This was the earliest form of mass-distributed drawn journalism. However, by the mid-nineteenth century more of the merchant class were semi-literate and could afford the inexpensive illustrated magazines and newspapers that were beginning to appear. In newspapers and magazines such as [*Glasgow*] *Northern Looking Glass* (1825–6) in Scotland, *Le Charivari* (1832–1937) in France, *Punch* (1841–2002) in England, and *Harper's Magazine* (1850–) in the United States, artists were using caricature to make fun of all aspects of society, including the rich and powerful. Their work laid the foundation for editorial cartoons that became a standard feature of newspapers in the twentieth century and the short journalism comics found online today.

Closer to comics journalism were newspapers, such as the *Illustrated London News* (1842–2003) and *Frank Leslie's Illustrated Newspaper* (1855–1922), supplemented prose new articles with detailed, realistic drawings. In a few instances, the prose was not necessary because multiple panels of drawings (essentially a comic strip) were used to relate events such as the Klondike Gold Rush. Because the primitive cameras of the day required a subject to remain absolutely still, the major illustrated newspapers and magazines of the nineteenth century sent artists on assignment to provide drawn reports of the action on the front lines of the Crimean War and the American Civil War.

Of course, true comics, sequences of panels, were rare in these publications, and once photographic technology improved, drawn journalism was quickly supplanted by photojournalism. The use of comics, or even drawings, to report hard news was virtually non-existent for most of the twentieth century. It was not until the 1990s that comics journalism truly began.

The Father of Modern Comics Journalism: Joe Sacco

When Joe Sacco traveled to the Gaza Strip and the West Bank in the winter of 1991–2 he had already abandoned print journalism as a vocation. One of the reasons he felt compelled to travel to the Occupied Territories was that he felt traditional journalism had failed miserably in conveying any sense of "who the Palestinians were or what their struggle was about" (Sacco 2007: viii). He was earning his living as a cartoonist at the time, and he intended to do a travelogue comic; however, as the days passed his notes became more detailed and some of his conversations were more like interviews. Sacco had a journalism degree from the University of Oregon, and he admits that "when I got there, some of my old journalism training kicked in" (Sacco qtd. in Sabin 2009).

After a two-and-a-half-month stay in the Palestinian territories Sacco returned home and began the work that resulted in, over a two-year period, nine issues of a twenty-four or thirty-two-page comic book titled *Palestine*. Over the course of those nine issues the comic became less about his own experiences and more about documenting the conditions and conflicts he observed. His art style become less "cartoony" and more realistic as he realized "that the drawings had to reflect the weight of the material" he was presenting (Sacco 2007: ix) (Figure 9.2).

Figure 9.2 Joe Sacco's realistic and very detailed art creates a sense of being there. Sacco, center, is taking a photo that probably served as his reference for this scene. *Palestine* # 4 © 1993 Joe Sacco, published by Fantagraphics Books.

A 1996 two-volume collection of the series won the American Book Award, given for outstanding multicultural literature. When the *Palestine* series was collected into one volume in 2001, the work received even more attention, and people began to realize that Sacco was moving toward a new use of the comics form. In

2001, comics scholar Jan Baetens declared that *Safe Are Goražde*, published in 2000, "set a new standard for graphic journalism" (Baetens 2017: 136). And Joe Sacco had a new vocation—comics journalist.

Sacco began melding the habits of traditional journalism with those of a comics artist—making notes that included visual details, taking photographs that would serve as a reference for drawing, and making simple, quick sketches in the field. His published work was less about his impressions and more about relating other people's stories or documenting facts. Sacco appeared in the comics less often, and when he did it was often as a working journalist, with a notepad in hand. He still drew himself as a bit of a caricature, but his subjects, especially when they are relating a story to him, were rendered in a realistic style (see Figure 7.11a for a sample of Sacco's caricature style). All of these aspects are on display in *Footnotes in Gaza* (2009), a mature work of long-form journalism (more about that term later).

The Rise of Comics Journalism

When Amy Nyberg was theorizing about comics journalism in 2006 she noted that there were relatively few practitioners of the craft because it required developing three skill sets: Newsgathering, the ability to communicate effectively in the comics form, and news writing (110). When Nyberg wrote that article Ted Rall was one of the few cartoonists who had emulated Sacco's in-country reporting. In October 2001, cartoonist Rall, his wife, and his agent traveled to Afghanistan to witness firsthand the effects of the US incursion into that country. He was on assignment from the alternative newspaper *Village Voice* and his dispatches, which alternated between prose, editorial cartoons, and multiple-page comics, sought to "separate propaganda from reality" (Rall 2002: 9) (Figure 9.3).

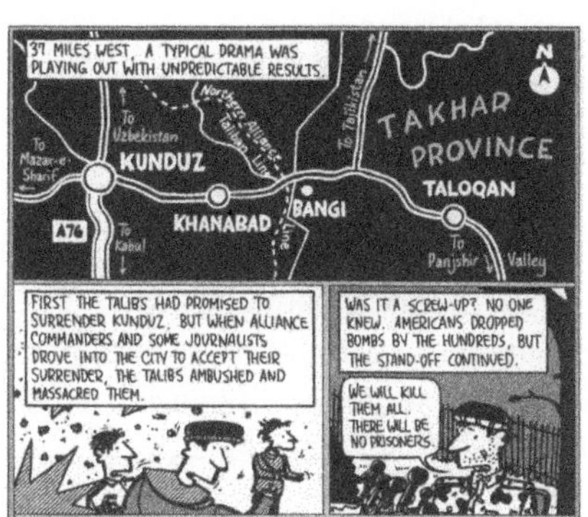

Figure 9.3 Because Ted Rall uses a cartoon style with simplified figures and minimal background detail he was able to file news dispatches in comics form faster than most comics journalists. *To Afghanistan and Back*, updated edition © 2002 Ted Rall, all rights reserved, www.rall.com.

In 2002 Brendan Burford self-published the first issue of *Syncopated*, a collection of short nonfiction comics, some of which contained elements of reportage. *Syncopated* included work by people (e.g., Sarah Glidden, Josh Neufeld, Susie Cagle) who would go on to play major roles in the development of comics journalism. Burford published three volumes over five years, and these were brought together in a single volume, *Syncopated: An Anthology of Nonfiction Picto-Essays*, published by Random House in 2009.

In fact, 2009 was something of a watershed year for comic journalism. Remember, that is the year Joe Sacco's *Footnotes in Gaza* appeared. Also published that year was Josh Neufeld's *A.D.: New Orleans After the Deluge*. Neufeld interviewed a variety of New Orleanians who, primarily due to their financial resources, had very different experiences of

Hurricane Katrina. *A.D.* began as a webcomic serialized in SMITH Magazine during 2007 and 2008. The webcomic got a good bit of mainstream media attention, and when the longer print version appeared, it was nominated for the major comics awards and excerpted in the 2010 edition of *The Best American Comics*.

What follows are a few of the highlights of how the genre of comics journalism developed after 2009.

2010—In 2007 war correspondent David Axe and cartoonist Matt Bors began a webcomic called *War is Boring*. The work was collected into a critically acclaimed print edition in 2010.

2010—The Cartoon Movement site was founded with partial support for the Netherlands government. The content was primarily political cartoons, but over the years the site has developed a network of more than 500 cartoonists from all over the world, a number of whom continue to create comics journalism.

2011—Comics journalist Dan Archer became a Knight Journalism Fellow at Stanford University, where he focused on incorporating interactivity and multimedia into his work.

2011—Josh Kramer self-published *Cartoon Picayune*, an annual magazine of journalism in the form of comics, for eight issues from 2011 to 2016. In 2016, with Em DeMarco, Kramer created The CoJo List email newsletter to promote comics journalism.

2012—Symbolia, an iPad-only magazine devoted to comics journalism, attracted top talent, but only lasted for two years.

2013—Founded by Frank Bourgeron in conjunction with a publishing group and a number of investors, *Le Revue dessinee* (*The Drawn Journal*) has proven to be the most profitable comics journalism venture. The magazine was selling about 20,000 copies per issue in 2018 (Gubitosa 2021: 76).

2013—Editorial cartoonist Matt Bors established *The Nib* to provide an outlet for political satire, journalism, essays, and memoir in comics form. New comics appear online each weekday and a print magazine is published three times a year.

2017—*The New York Time Magazine* devoted an entire issue to retelling some of their most compelling prose stories in comics form.

Due to the time it takes to produce a single comics page, comics are unlikely to play a major role in daily, deadline-driven journalism. Yet, some print media have assigned cartoonists to stories. Sacco has done assignment journalism in comics form for mainstream media such as *Details* (1998), *Time* (2001), *Boston Globe* (2002), *New York Times Magazine* (2003), *Guardian Weekend* (2005), *Harper's* (2007), and *Foreign Policy* (2012). Again, other cartoonists followed the trail Sacco blazed. Andy Warner's comics have appeared on *Slate* and *KQED*. Dan Archer's comics have been published by *The Guardian*, *BBC*, and *Huffington Post*. Susie Cagle's comics have been published by *The Los Angeles Times*, *Chicago Tribune*, *Washington Post*, *Wired*, and *Print* magazine.

Some comics journalists have turned to digital comics as a means of multimedia reporting that incorporates hyperlinked infographics, audio, video, etc. Augusto Paim's *So Close, Faraway!* (2013) is a piece of in-depth, interactive comics journalism about the homeless of Brazil. Bo Soremsky created *Der Kachelmann-Prozess*, a digital interactive comic, as part of his reporting on a high-profile trial in Germany. In 2015, Dan Archer founded Empathetic Media to tell news stories in a new way. The company's *Ferguson Firsthand*, an immersive experience of the Michael Brown shooting through a blend of comics, virtual reality, and augmented reality, was available via Oculus Rift.

We identified Joe Sacco as the most important pioneer of comics journalism, but that does not mean he has been overshadowed by the journalists he inspired. Sacco has been actively producing drawn journalism over the past thirty years. His recent book, *Paying the Land*, an investigation of how mining operations in northern Canada have impacted the way of life of indigenous cultures, was named a best book of 2020 by *The New York Times*, *Publisher's Weekly*, and *The Guardian*. Sacco is still the standard-bearer for journalism in comics form.

How Comics Journalism Is Done

Drawing comics takes time. Comics journalism is slow journalism, not practical for breaking news or even daily reports of any substance. It takes Joe Sacco up to three days to draw one page, and that is after he has sifted through many pages of his notebooks, "whittling them down to a workable narrative" (Marshall 2005: 70). Indeed, "Comics journalism is an incredibly onerous medium—it requires so many specific, labor-intensive, highly technical skills" (Josh Kramer qtd. in Gubitosa 2021: 74).

Some of the most critically acclaimed comics journalism could not be done quickly because the pieces are quite long. Sacco's *Footnotes in Gaza* is 388 pages, not including the four appendices. Neufeld's *A.D.* is 187 pages. Neufeld has commented that "I usually think of even my shorter pieces as a type of long-form journalism" (Josh Neufeld qtd. in Nobel 2020). The approach known as **long-form journalism** was developed in print magazines and newspapers. Long-form journalism can "explore important hard news topics by means of a narrative structure," and focus on real people through "events involving action, dialogue, and a sense of place" (Duncan, Taylor, and Stoddard 2016: 60).

The use of narrative in reportage is associated with literary (or narrative) journalism, a subset of New Journalism. In fact, comics journalism exhibits many of the traits of New Journalism, where the journalist is a participant in events, providing a subjective observation of everyday life that creates emotional immediacy. Factual information is conveyed through dialogue and "literary techniques of prose writing" (Weber and Rall 2017: 382–3).

Josh Neufeld believes "comics journalism stories are most effective when they are told 'in-scene' with people talking, as opposed to using a lot of explanatory captions" (qtd. in Nobel 2020). When the journalist is a participant in those conversations the journalist's point of view is foregrounded. "The sorts of stories that they tell and the ways that they tell them are very human-minded. They're interested in slowly creating relationships with the people that they're interviewing," says Kelp-Stebbins (2022), co-curator of the exhibition *The Art of the News: Comics Journalism*. Kristian Williams (2005) contends that dropping the pretense of objective detachment from the story and emphasizing a personal perspective "adds voice and meaning" to journalism (55) (Figure 9.4).

With such a blatantly subjective approach, the accuracy of comic journalism reporting is likely to be called into question by those who practice traditional journalistic objectivity.

Figure 9.4 A drawing in Joe Sacco's Palestine and the reference photo which informed the drawing. From *Palestine The Special Edition* © 2007 Joe Sacco, published by Fantagraphics Books.

Alissa Quart (2009) acknowledges that works like Neufeld's *A.D.* are not always purely accurate, but claims "they are some of the most emotionally accurate stuff out there." Joe Sacco admits that "The cartoonist draws with the essential truth in mind, not the literal truth" (2012: xii). Notice the differences between a reference photo Sacco took and the panel he drew based on that photo (Figure 9.4). Yet, creators of comics journalism want to have their reporting accepted and that leads them to employ authentication strategies, such as incorporating photographs, images of documents, or even sources cited in footnotes (Weber and Rall 2017: 390).

Let us examine what Josh Neufeld does on one page of his comic *A Tale of Two Pandemics: Historical Insights on Persistent Racial Disparities* to communicate the authenticity of his reporting. The social media posts are drawn exactly as they appeared online so that they operate as verbatim quotations. He displays statistics in a bar graph (a sign of credible evidence) and then provides a citation for the source of the statistics (Figure 9.5).

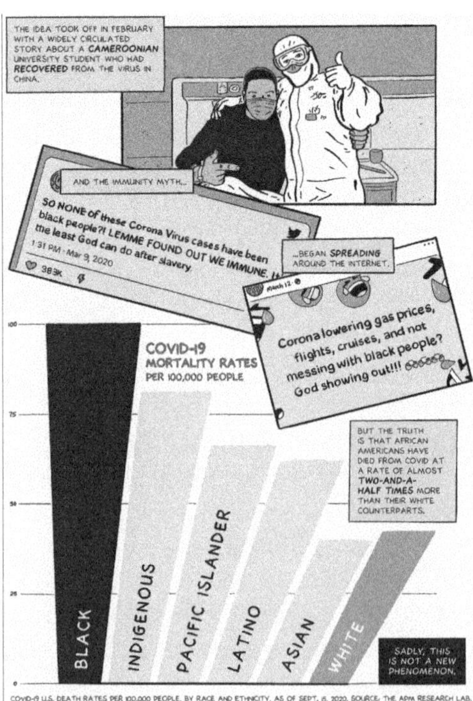

Figure 9.5 Josh Neufeld uses a variety of techniques to authenticate his reporting. *A Tale of Two Pandemics* © 2020 Josh Neufeld.

A "serious" and detailed art style can also be a technique of authentication. As Joe Sacco refined his approach to journalism comics, he moved his avatar to the background, brought his interview subjects and events he was reporting on to the foreground, and adopted a more representational style of art. Comics journalists also tend to avoid speed lines, sound effects, emanata, and other cartooning techniques associated with mainstream humor or superhero comic books. Generally, comics journalists seek to enhance the credibility of their reporting with a realistic rendering style and background details that establish the setting. Of course, there are exceptions. Ted Rall's style (see Figure 9.3) fits the tone of his work, emphasizing the absurdities he finds in even dangerous or tragic situations.

How Readers React and Interact with Comics Journalism

Written journalism is about something that happened in the past, but a visual narrative has a great sense of immediacy; you are encountering it in the here and now. The manner in which a comics journalist encapsulates the prime moments of the reported events in panels "evokes the metaphor of journalism as a 'window on the world'" (Nyberg 2010). The comics journalist is actively showing, not just telling. A reader might get immersed in the facts within sentences and not hear the journalist's voice in prose, but one cannot help but see the journalist's hand in the artwork.

In comics "the journalists aren't a mere voice or talking head but a person with a viewpoint, who is himself/herself participating in the narrative" (Afshana and Din 2018: 531). Comics journalism is often participatory journalism in which the reader gets to see the journalist at work, doing the newsgathering. "Readers are invited to imagine themselves *in place of* the journalist" and participate in the unfolding story (Nyberg 2010).

Comics can humanize subjects, who have a visible presence on the page, more than can prose. Comics can bring us closer to people and places, but, at the same time, can provide more distance from the horrific and tragic than can a photograph. Sacco says "photos of horrible things can be almost unbearable. Drawings have a built in filter" (Weisberg 2012). Sarah Glidden believes comics can make distressing topics more approachable: "A prose piece about Iraqi refugees would be too depressing for my friends to read, but something drawn will make them take a look" (qtd. in Weisberg 2012).

More people are taking a look at comics journalism appearing in print books, newspapers, and magazines, but perhaps most often online at sites such as The Nib, Cartoon Movement, and Drawing the Times. These online sites tend to present a mixture of comics journalism and editorial cartooning. In fact, many of the pieces published on these sites are a blend of reporting and editorializing. Comics journalism developed out of a New Journalism tradition of reporting filtered through a personal perspective and presented in an idiosyncratic style. Comics reporting is (mostly) fact-based, but, in many instances, those facts are presented in a manner that encourages the adoption of a particular belief, attitude, or behavior. As you will see in the next section, many of these characteristics are shared by particular modes of documentary comics.

Comics as Documentary

A **documentary** is a form of nonfiction that shows real people engaged in actual events or interviews real people about actual events. However, that very simple definition would seem to fit the journalism comics discussed earlier. Bill Nichols, in *Introduction to Documentary*, writes that viewing a documentary film is "a way of seeing the historical world directly," but he also acknowledges that "the distinct point of view of the filmmaker shapes" a particular interpretation of that historical world (2010: 14). This still seems a bit like the subjective New Journalism approach used by some comics journalists. A way to further differentiate documentary comics from journalism comics is to consider the six modes of documentary filmmaking identified by Nichols: Expository, Observational, Participatory, Performative, Poetic, and Reflexive (2010: 99–100). The term "mode," as Nichols uses it, refers to both the methods used to create documentary films and the manner in which viewers experience those films.

Comics theorist Pascal LeFèvre (2013) examined the extent to which these modes could be applied to documentaries in comics form. LeFèvre feels the reflexive mode is not a useful category to apply to documentary comics. A reflexive film documentary calls attention to the techniques and process of filmmaking. LeFèvre argues that "all comics by their drawn and thus artificial nature are to a certain degree reflexive" (2013: 53). We agree with LeFèvre's observation about the nature of comics, but we think some nonfiction comics are clearly more reflexive than the average nonfiction comic. Therefore, we will include the reflexive category as we follow the path LeFèvre blazed and explore how Nichols' mode of documentary manifests in documentary comic books and graphic novels.

Participatory Mode

There is as yet no definitive quantitative data about the use of these modes by comics creators, but this might well be the most popular mode of documentary comics. Participatory comics show the creator(s) of the documentary comic interacting with subjects in various ways—interviews, informal conversations, and experiencing events together. In these situations, and even more so when the creators are shown alone, participatory comics emphasize the sensory and emotional experiences of the creators of the comic. Actually, rather than creators it is usually a single cartoonist who both writes and draws participatory documentary comics (Figure 9.6).

Figure 9.6 We see some of the documentarian's decision-making process in "An Encounter with Richard Peterson" from Syncopated: *An Anthology of Nonfiction Picto-Essays* © Brendan Burford, used with special permission.

In "An Encounter with Richard Peterson" the initial focus is solely on Brendan Burford, the creator of the comic, as he walks through the neighborhoods of New York City looking for a story. He becomes interested in the chess players in Washington Square Park, and when he learns that a man named Richie Peterson has been photographing the park for decades, he thinks seeing those photos might give him ideas for an interesting story. The third page of the comic shows Burford's quest to locate Peterson. The first interview with Peterson does not take place until the fourth page of the eleven-page comic. That first interview is followed by informal conversations, and it becomes clear that Burford's documentary is not going to be about chess players in the park, but about Richie Peterson's colorful background. In addition to being a fine chess player, Peterson was a gambling addict, petty thief, and clever con man—an interesting interview subject. Yet, the comic is also about Brandon Burford's search for a story and his strategies for getting Peterson to open up about his life. It documents Burford's participation in creating a documentary comic.

Although, in the previous section, we categorized Joe Sacco as a journalist, some of work clearly fits the definition of participatory documentary. In *Palestine* (1993) Sacco conducts some interviews, but he spends more time simply experiencing events along with his subjects, and, especially in the early chapters, the comic is just as much about Sacco's own sensory and emotional reactions as it is about the lives of the people he is interviewing. The boundary (if there is one) between journalism and documentary is often blurred.

Expository Mode

This is the most common mode for creating a documentary film, but not necessarily the most popular mode of documentary comics. In this mode the creators of comics are unseen. There is a "voice of God" omniscient narrator or a visible expert narrator. A variety of evidence—interviews, documents, photographs, etc.—is used to support a particular perspective or interpretation. While clearly constructing a "rhetorical or argumentative frame" the expository documentary also strives to create an impression of objectivity (Nichols 2010: 105) (Figure 9.7).

Dan Archer and Adam Bessie, authors of *The Disaster Capitalism Curriculum* (2012) announce their intentions in a text introduction to the comic book: "we hope by reporting a well-grounded, thoroughly researched alternative perspective on 'education reform', that readers—and especially our fellow reporters—will see that there is another choice." On the first page of the comic (see Figure 9.7) Archer and Bessie present a portion of an interview with a D.C. public school teacher. The captions contain her words and the pictures function as a reenactment of what the teacher is describing. Notice that the last two panels show her looking at a hypothetical termination notice. This circumstance is continued on the next page (see Figure 9.8), but now the captions contain narration from the documentarians (Archer and Bessie), and the pictures are less literal. The teacher from page 1, after her hypothetical termination, holds a "Failed" sign and the compositional elements of the panel make it seem as if she is a criminal standing in a police lineup.

The middle tier of Figure 9.8 is even more metaphorical. Playing on the acronym GERM (Global Education Reform Movement), the three panels depict a school building getting a

Figure 9.7 ***The Disaster Capitalism Curriculum*** **© Dan Archer (image) (@archcomix) and Adam Bessie (text).**

vaccination. This might seem rather whimsical for an expository documentary. However, the information presented on the page is very evidence-based. The pictures of economist Milton Friedman handing out vouchers to children of color are satirical, but the words in the balloons are in quotation marks and come directly from one of Friedman's books. The 1, 2, and 3 that appear in caption boxes or word balloons indicate that the information comes from sources listed at the bottom of the page. All but one of the pages in the comic book contain such footnotes.

Observational Mode

In this mode creators of comics are unobtrusive both in gathering information for the comic and within the comic itself; they simply convey what they observe about the everyday life of their subjects and do not interact with those subjects. LeFèvre (2013) believes only a pseudo-observational mode is possible in comics because, unlike a camera that simply records what is before it, a drawing is an interpretation of what is observed. A pure use of the observational mode does seem rare in comics; most documentary comics contain some sort of narrator, usually the cartoonist who created the comic. However, a comic can still be constructed in a manner that invites/encourages the reader to adopt an observational stance (Figure 9.9).

Šoba (1998) might not be strictly observational, but creator Joe Sacco recedes into the background much more than in most of his work. Sacco appears on only seventeen pages of the forty-one-page comic. He only has two-word balloons: "How's the leg?";

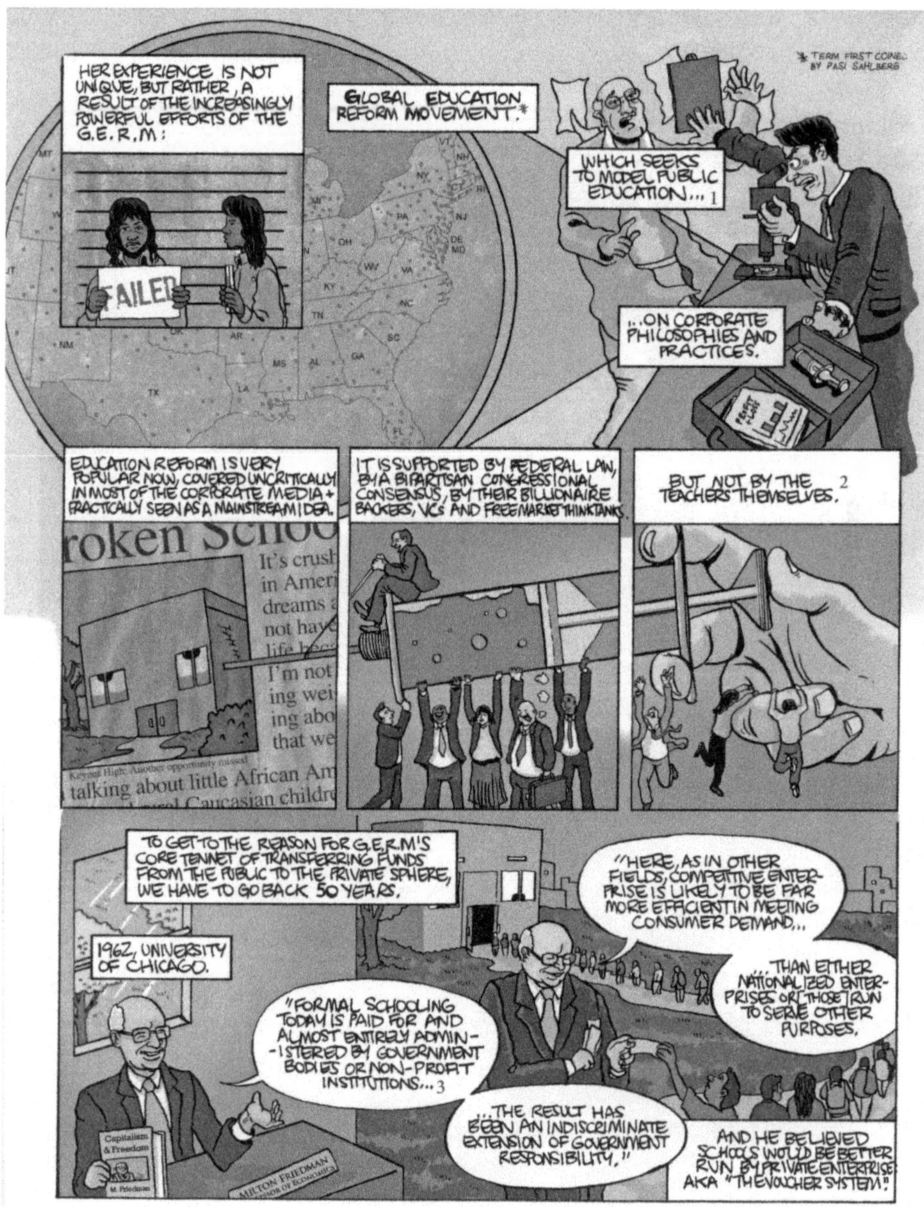

1 Pasi Sahlberg's comments on GERM on his website: **http://www.pasisahlberg.com/blog/?p=68)**
2 More information in Dissent magazine: **http://dissentmagazine.org/article/?article=3781)**.
3 Taken from Milton Friedman's *Capitalism and Freedom*. Check it out online: **http://books.google.ru/books/about/Capitalism_and_Freedom.html?id=iCRk066ybDAC&redir_esc=y**

Figure 9.8 *The Disaster Capitalism Curriculum* © Dan Archer (image) (@archcomix) and Adam Bessie (text).

"She's cute." For most of the book he simply listens and observes. Even though we only see Sacco ask Šoba a single question (and that is in a caption rather than a word balloon) it often seems that Šoba's dialogue must be in response to an interview question. Sometimes when Šoba talks about past events Sacco draws reenactments of those events. Yet, he keeps the comic anchored in the present by frequently cutting back to a drawing of Šoba telling the story. The comic is Šoba's story, a slice of his life that we readers observe along with Sacco.

Figure 9.9 Joe Sacco subtly asks a question in a caption, but mostly he accompanies Šoba and listens to his stories. From *The Fixer and Other Stories*. Copyright Joe Sacco. Used with permission from Drawn & Quarterly.

Performative Mode

This mode does not attempt to present objective facts, but rather presents the documentarian's subjective experience and "embodied knowledge" of particular aspects of society (Nichols 2010: 130). Performative documentaries often contain images that are clearly not meant to convey reality, but represent the documentarian's impressions of a subject or situation. These images require interpretation (they are hermeneutic), and therefore readers of documentary comics using the performative mode are actively engaged in making inferences (Figure 9.10).

Figure 9.10 The nature of money is explored through the perspective of a daydreamer/cartoonist in *The Lovely Horrible Stuff* © Eddie Campbell, courtesy of Top Shelf Productions/IDW Publishing.

The Lovely Horrible Stuff (2012) by Eddie Campbell examines how money and concerns about money permeate most people's lives. Campbell examines the subject with a number of his own experiences, few of which are pleasant—an embezzling travel agent absconds with $5,000 of his money, a sizable loan to his father-in-law leads to animosity on both sides, telling his adult daughter she needs to contribute $50 a month to household expenses leads to an angry confrontation. Campbell uses some traditional documentary techniques. He travels to the Micronesian island of Yap and interviews someone at the Historical Preservation Office to learn how large stone disks became a form of currency in the culture.

He quotes economists Keynes and Friedman. Of course, he also hangs out in a bar and "chats" with William Shakespeare. The review in *The Guardian* claims "Campbell is more concerned with weird facts and flights of fancy than with rigorous analysis," but conveying information in a quirky, idiosyncratic manner is typical of documentaries in the performative mode (Smart 2012).

Poetic Mode

In this approach images of real people, places, or events are the raw material, transformed in artistic ways, used to create patterns, suggest associations, or invoke a mood. Rather than a linear narrative or a logical progression of ideas leading to a conclusion, poetic documentaries are likely to move from aspect to aspect of a place, a life, a profession, a situation, etc. The city symphonies of the 1920s are prime examples of poetic film documentaries. There were no characters and usually no narration; simply an orchestral score accompanied by various images of a large city (Figure 9.11).

Figure 9.11 A "city symphony" in comics form. *The Walking Man* (1992; 2004) © PAPIER/Jiro TANIGUCHI via BCF Tokyo.

The Walking Man (1992, 2004) by Jiro Taniguchi is a graphic novel somewhat in the tradition of the city symphony films. Each chapter shows a man going on a long walk, exploring different parts of a city, and experiencing different conditions. There are chapters titled "Snow," "Rain," and "Starry, Starry Night." The man speaks to his wife at home and occasionally has a brief conversation with someone he encounters on a walk, but the dialogue is sparse. Some chapters are completely silent. The man is often shown from a medium or long distance, surrounded by detailed renderings of the environment. Taniguchi uses a naturalistic style that creates a sense of reality. The presentation is not impressionistic; we are not getting the man's impression of the city. We are experiencing it with him, and each of us is appreciating it (or not) in our own way.

Reflexive Mode

Reflexive documentaries do not explore an outside subject; they reflect back upon the conventions, processes, and techniques by which the documentary itself was created. Perhaps it is a stretch to call *Location, Location, Location* (2016) by Alec Longstreth a documentary comic book. You could consider it to be an advertisement. It is clearly meant to promote The Center for Cartoon Studies. You could consider it to be a memoir. Longstreth describes his life from 2003 to roughly 2013. However, the comic does document, by way of example, the nature of life as a (mostly) freelance artist, and it does so in a matter-of-fact style. It is reflexive because it is a comic about making comics. In the eight-page comic, seventeen of the panels show Longstreth working at his drawing board, computer, or table (Figure 9.12).

Figure 9.12 This mini-comic reflects on the nature of the comics form and the life of a cartoonist. *Location, Location, Location* (2016) by Alec Longstreth, © The Center for Cartoon Studies.

Documentaries bring awareness of little-known aspects of the world (or universe) to a wider audience. Some documentaries are created to make people aware of injustices and/or advocate for a new perspective on an issue. Why is comics form a useful vehicle for educating and persuading? The persuasive power of comics will be explored in the final section of this chapter. For now, let us consider why comics are so good at conveying information.

Why Comics Are Excellent for Informing and Explaining

Research by Piotr Winkielman and colleagues shows that people like "easy-to-use stimuli" (2003: 81), and that "easy-to-process messages are more appealing and persuasive" (86). Comics "significantly simplify and accelerate the process of cognition" (Guruzhalov 2005: 80). Scholars in the Media Education Research Center at Kashmir University agree that one of the chief benefits of comics is "the ability of graphics to help readers digest a vast amount of information in a very short span of time, without actually taking anything from the information but rather making it more engaging" (Afshana and Din 2018: 527). Cheng (2012) contends that comics are very effective for explaining complex processes because they convey the passage of time more clearly than prose can and, unlike a photo which tends to give equal value to every element of the picture, drawn pictures can abstract details and direct attention to the most important aspects of the image.

Juxtaposed images can make it easier to understand relationships, comparisons, or contrasts, which are not only useful for explaining but can provide evidence to support an argument. A sequence of juxtaposed images can provide a clear illustration of processes or cause and effect, but it can also, as you will see in the next section, provide a structure for the logical progression of ideas in an argument.

Comics as Advocacy

Aristotle's writings and teaching in the third century BCE laid the foundation for our modern understanding of persuasion as "the process by which a person's attitudes or behavior are, without duress, influenced by communications from other people" ("Persuasion" 2015). Aristotle believed that whether or not a person was persuaded by an act of communication was determined by a mixture of that person's perception of the credibility of the source (ethos), their emotional response to the message (pathos), and their evaluation of the evidence and logic presented (logos). Centuries after Aristotle conceived these modes of persuasion, a new term, propaganda, became associated with persuasion.

What is the difference between persuasion and propaganda? When the term *propaganda* first appeared in the seventeenth century, it was simply associated with propagating, or spreading, a message. In the early twentieth century the term began to acquire a more sinister connotation. From galvanizing support for the war effort to attempting to dishearten the enemy, communication tactics were "weaponized" during the two World Wars in the first half of the twentieth century.

Terence Qualter (1965) defines **propaganda** as "the deliberate attempt by some individual or group to form, control, or alter the attitudes of other groups by the use of the instruments of communication, with the intention that in any given situation the reaction of those so influenced will be that desired by the propagandist" (27). At first glance, that seems very similar to the definition of persuasion given in the previous paragraph. Yet, that word "control" hints at a greater degree of duress or manipulation.

Propaganda is a subjective label. If we identify with a source and its message, we consider that message to be persuasive. As Kenneth Burke (1950) pointed out, every identification creates an alienation. If a source we are alienated from presents a message that opposes our beliefs, then we consider that message to be propaganda. Because we cannot know what each reader of this book might consider to be propaganda, we will not use that term very often, but, instead, simply use the term persuasion.

Drawing images in an attempt to persuade is an ancient practice. While that cave painting Sol Davidson describes in the introduction to this chapter might have been drawn to implore a higher power to make the next hunt successful, we are going to jump forward, over multiple centuries, to uses of visual persuasion that are more direct precursors to comics.

Caricature, a drawing that exaggerates some aspects of a subject, particularly facial features, was a technique that developed during the Italian Renaissance, and it became a powerful tool for visual persuasion and propaganda. By the eighteenth century, James Gillray was combining caricature with visual metaphor to create deftly satirical and outrageously offensive cartoons and was perhaps the first person to earn his living as a political cartoonist (Robbins and Schulz 1971).

As the number of magazines and newspapers increased in the nineteenth century, so did the frequency of cartooning being used to create persuasive messages. The work of two cartoonists stands out: Charles Philipon and Thomas Nast. In 1830, Philipon began publishing *La Caricature*, a monthly satirical magazine for an upper-class audience, and the less expensive daily broadsheet, *Le Charivari*, for the working class. These publications aggressively attacked the policies and character of citizen-king Louis-Philippe. Philipon's cartoon transforming Louis-Philippe's head into a pear was appropriated by other artists and became a symbol of opposition to Louis-Philippe's rule (Childs 1997). Philipon declared that his magazines used caricature: "to make a mirror for the ridiculous, a whistle for the stupid, a whip for the wicked" (Goldstein 1989: 10). This explains why the magazines were repeatedly seized by authorities and Philipon was prosecuted more than a dozen times and spent most of 1932 in prison (Melby 2009; Cuno 1983).

Thomas Nast was able to take on a powerful political figure without suffering the same harsh retribution. Nast's drawings of suffering and triumph during the American Civil War helped raise the morale of soldiers and citizens on the Union side of the conflict, but Nast became famous and profoundly influenced future visual persuasion with his drawings of William "Boss" Tweed, a corrupt New York politician, getting rich at the city's expense. Perhaps Nast was influenced by Philipon when he transformed Tweed's large head into a money bag. In another cartoon he drew Tweed as a vulture.

Nineteenth-century cartoonists such as Charles Philipon and Thomas Nast developed a new style of cartooning that found a home in magazines and newspapers, and became what we think of today as editorial cartoons. Single-panel cartoons that appear on the editorial page of a newspaper are clearly meant to persuade, and thus, might put some readers on the defensive. Over on the "funny pages"—the comic strip section of the newspaper—the persuasion was likely to be a bit more indirect. *Pogo*, which debuted in 1948, was a funny animal strip that elicited laughs, but sometimes indirectly addressed such topics such as segregation, communism, and rabid anti-communists, as when it lampooned Senator Joseph McCarthy with a caricature named Simple J. Malarkey. By the time the final *Pogo* strip appeared in 1975, a new, more overtly political type of comic strip was on the scene. *Doonesbury*, which debuted in newspapers in 1970, was the herald of this new age and was followed by strips such as *This Modern World* (1988) and *Boondocks* (1996).

There are many other examples of comic strips that attempt to persuade. However, in keeping with the focus of this textbook, most of our discussion in the rest of this section will deal with comic books and graphic novels. Let us take a look at a few of the highlights of comics used as persuasion or propaganda.

1918—The Bureau of Cartoons, funded by the US government's Committee on Public Information (CPI), encouraged cartoonists to use their comic strips to support the war effort. The Bureau sent a weekly bulletin, suggesting specific themes and techniques to more than 750 cartoonists (Rifas 2021). A September 28, 1918 bulletin encouraged cartoonists to "consider yourself a Liberty Bond salesman" and reminded them that "every time you draw a cartoon you have the opportunity of helping to win the war" (Creel 1918: n.p.).

Late 1939—The Shield, the first patriotic-themed superhero, appeared in MLJ's *Pep Comics* # 1 (cover date January 1940). The following year, a new star-spangled superhero, Captain America, was shown punching Hitler on the cover of his debut issue. More patriotic heroes—Fighting Yank, Miss Liberty, The Eagle, Uncle Sam, etc.—soon followed, and apparently the Department of War thought they were effective morale boosters. The US Army was probably the largest customer for the American comic book industry, shipping millions comic books to soldiers overseas (Gabilliet 2010; "Superman's" 1942) (Figure 9.13).

1943–4—In German-occupied France, cartoonist Vincent Krassousky (also known as Vica) created propaganda cartoons for the Nazi newspaper *Le Téméraire* and then produced

Figure 9.13 Comic book characters, especially patriotic-themed superheroes were used to sell war bonds. "Your Life Depends on It!" in Captain America Comics #19 (1942), Stan Lee (script) Al Avison (pencils) © 2023 Marvel Entertainment and its subsidiaries.

the propaganda *bande dessinee* albums *Vica au Paradis de l'U.R.S.S*, *Vica contre le service secret anglais*, and *Vica défie l'Oncle Sam*. The comics combined anti-Semitism and other racist imagery with a cartoon style and slapstick action. In one comic President Roosevelt's "henchman" recruits gangsters from prison to bolster the US Armed Forces. Uncle Sam, leading troops into Africa, parachutes from a plane and lands in a field of cacti planted by Vica.

Cold War Comics

1947—*Is This Tomorrow* makes the argument that if Americans are not vigilant communists will take control of the media, infiltrate the US government, and indoctrinate generations of school children. Other comic books—*How Stalin Hopes We Will Destroy America*, *The Red Iceberg*, *Blood is the Harvest*, etc.—also warned children about the communist threat.

1948—Malcolm Ater's Commercial Comics, Inc. created *The Story of Harry S. Truman* for the Democratic National Committee to use in the presidential campaign. Three million copies were printed and distributed (Rifas 2010: 162). In the following decades Ater created campaign comics for candidates for governorships, the US Senate, and the presidency of the Philippines. The anti-communist messages in these books were fairly mild, but Ater did help elect the politicians who would wage the Cold War.

1949—Governments became major publishers of Cold War comics. When the People's Republic of China was formed in 1949, the government increased the production of propaganda comics "made with the express purpose of educating the readers and teaching them the correct revolutionary way of looking at things" (Strömberg 2010: 70). By the early 1960s, more than 560 million copies of these mini-comics had been circulated (Rifas 2010: 163). Beginning in 1949 with a comic book distributed in South Korea, Thailand, French Indo-China, and Indonesia, the United States Information Agency (USIA) published millions of copies of anti-communist comic books (Rifas 2010), and in 1953 USIA created a weekly anti-communist humor strip, *Little Moe*, that ran in more than 500 newspapers in fifty-eight countries (Rifas 2021: 49).

1957—The pacifist Fellowship of Reconciliation created *Martin Luther King and the Montgomery Story* to advocate for a nonviolent, civil disobedience approach to the struggle for equality. The comic book circulated through civil rights groups and churches, catching the attention of young civil rights activist John Lewis and eventually inspiring him to relate his own experience in comics form, the critically acclaimed *March* trilogy (2013–16).

1961—"This Godless Communism," a ten-chapter story warning children about the threat of world domination by communists, was serialized in *Treasure Chest of Fun and Fact*. *Treasure Chest* was distributed to parochial schools from 1946 to 1972. (Strömberg 2010: 66).

1960–70—Jack Chick self-published a few short, pamphlet-style comics (*Why No Revival?*; *A Demon's Nightmare*) during the 1960s. In 1970 he established Chick Publication and for forty-five years produced hundreds of three-inch by five-inch comic books, or **Chick tracts** as they became known, containing rather vicious screeds against rock music, Catholicism, homosexuality, Islam, Freemasons, and Halloween. According to the archives at Yale University, Chick tracts have been translated into more than 100 languages and more than 800 million copies have been distributed worldwide (Chick Tract Collection).

1971—Marvel Comics editor and scripter Stan Lee received a request from the US Department of Health, Education, and Welfare to use the popular Spider-Man character to encourage young people to avoid drug use. *Amazing Spider-Man* issues 96 through 98 show Peter Parker's friend Harry Osborn in a downward spiral of drug addiction. At DC Comics a drug addiction story was already being created when the Marvel story was published. In DC *Green Lantern/Green Arrow* issue 85 it was revealed that Green Arrow's sidekick Speedy was a heroin addict.

1973—Spire Christian Comics teamed with Archie Comics to publish nineteen comics using the characters and characteristic humor of Archie Comics to promote Christian ideology. They were reprinted many times and sold millions of copies worldwide.

1976—Leonard Rifas founded EduComics which, in conjunction with Kitchen Sink Enterprises, published *All-Atomic Comics*, warning about the dangers of nuclear power plants. Most of the EduComics publications both educated and advocated: the two issues of *Corporate Crime Comics* condemned corporate greed and corruption; *The Big Picture* was created to support protests against the World Trade Organization.

1978—Project Gen began publishing English translations of Keiji's Nakazawa's *Hadashi no Gen*, as *Barefoot Gen,* volume one. The work is a brutally realistic account of the horrible devastation wrought by an atomic bomb and a critique of militarism.

1979—Seth Tobocman and Peter Kuper founded *World War 3 Illustrated*, an anthology of social commentary in comics form. According to the ww3 website, the magazine is "run by a volunteer collective of political activists and artists." As of this writing, the fifty-second issue was published in 2022.

1984—*Grenada: Rescued from Rape and Slavery* was commissioned by the Central Intelligence Agency to convince the inhabitants of the island of Grenada and the American public that the American-led invasion of the island in 1983 was necessary. This comic is perhaps just the tip of the iceberg of the psychological operations (psyop) comics that were created and distributed by government agencies in the waning years of the Cold War and beyond.

1991—During the Gulf War, Joel Andreas created *Addicted to War: Why the U.S. Can't Kick Militarism* to explore who benefits from the long history of US foreign wars. When the US invaded Afghanistan after 9/11 Andreas created an expanded version of the book. The post-9/11 War on Terror inspired a number of cartoonists, such as those in the anthology *The Bush Junta* (2004), to critique the political and corporate leaders who perpetuate and benefit from the military-industrial complex.

Twenty-first century—There has been an explosion of advocacy and propaganda comics created by non-government organizations, government agencies, activists, etc. Hundreds of small print-run, often self-published comic books have been created to support or oppose various causes. Also, many of the online sites mentioned in the journalism section (e.g.—The Nib, Drawing the Times) publish some subjective journalism along with outright editorial or advocacy comics.

2012—Benjamin Worku-Dix founded PositiveNegatives to produce comics about international human rights and social issues. PositiveNegatives produces comics for the groups mentioned earlier.

2016—The election of Donald Trump elicited a visceral response from a number of comics creators. Françoise Mouly and Nadja Spiegelman edited two issues of the radical and politically progressive comics anthology *RESIST!* 58,000 copies of the first issue were given away at women's marches protesting the inauguration of Trump. Other anti-Trump comics followed, including *The Unquotable Donald Trump* (2017) and *Never Show Weakness: Trump in Power* (2020). There were also a few satirical comics, such as *My Hero Magademia* (2018) and *Space Force: Chepo Team* (2020), that cast Trump in a more heroic role, while still poking fun at his appearance, policies, and mannerisms.

How Comics Can Persuade

There has been very little direct analysis of the persuasive techniques used in comics, and virtually no experimental research on the subject. One limited experiment was conducted in 2017 by Zackary Vernon for his master's thesis at Texas State University. Vernon wanted to determine if "a comic book about real queer people" might improve the attitudes of students with a mid to high level of prejudice, as determined by the Attitudes Towards Lesbians and Gays Scale. The results of the experiment "showed reduced levels of prejudice in all but one of the participants, with the levels of difference varying significantly" (Vernon 2017, xii).

The persuasive effect of a particular comic is determined, to a great extent, by the knowledge, beliefs, and attitudes each reader brings to the act of reading. The impact is personal. And, contrary to the results of Vernon's experiment, the impact is usually slight. A single persuasive message seldom creates a substantial change in beliefs or attitudes. However, comics, as a medium and an art form, have some built-in advantages.

Each individual's reading of a comic is influenced, whether they realize it or not, by a network of interwoven attitudes about the comics medium, the comics industry, and even particular titles, characters, creators, etc. Due to those attitudes, and the "invisible" nature of the comic form, the persuasion in a comic is often undetected, and thus, potentially more potent.

PERSUASION DUE TO THE NATURE OF THE MEDIUM

The lowly cultural status of the comic strip and comic book mediums can actually make them more persuasive. Because readers consider comics to be frivolous entertainment and "enjoyable rather than manipulative" they let their guard down; they don't apply critical thinking to what they are reading (Turner 1977: 27).

Editorial cartoons, which comment on current events with gleeful bias and vicious caricature, appear on the editorial page of a newspaper. Due to this placement and content readers know that editorial cartoons are intended to be persuasive messages, and, when that message is counter to their beliefs and values readers go on the defensive and think about counter arguments. Comic strips, which are generally considered to be neither news nor commentary, appear in the entertainment section (with a few exceptions, such as controversial *Doonesbury* strips). Comic books do not even have the respectable surroundings of a newspaper. The majority of the population, even if they love the movies based on them, still consider comic books childish.

Devoted fans of mainstream serialized comic books are not dismissive of the medium but still might overlook the persuasive techniques employed because they are so immersed in the narrative and the characters. Research on the **mere exposure effect** (Zajonc 1968) has shown that the familiar is more likable than the less familiar. Thus, regular readers of serialized comic books are more susceptible to persuasion due to their devotion to the medium.

Even if a comic does impact an attitude or a belief, the reader might not perceive the change to be the result of reading a comic (Murray 2011: 182). Because readers are engaging with a comic book as mere entertainment any "arguments" presented in the book are likely to circumvent critical faculties and be processed on an unconscious, emotional level (Murray 2012: 130). That is, readers will engage in what Petty and Cacioppo (1986) termed **peripheral processing** (as opposed to **central processing** that involves a more conscious and deliberate evaluation of propositions and supporting evidence). Peripheral processing of comic books can occur because the reader is caught up in the narrative, emotionally engaged with the characters, or appreciates the artwork. This characterization is certainly not true of every reader and every comic book reading experience, but peripheral processing is more likely to happen with comic books than with most graphic novels because comic books are, generally, expected to be less serious than graphic novels.

Of course, sometimes those expectations can create a contrast effect that can make a comic more impactful. "Comics come with baggage that's useful for what I'm trying to do," says war correspondent David Axe, who created a webcomic recounting his experiences. "Comics lull you into a false sense of security. You think, this will be funny or at least unserious. Then we hit you with the explosions and the dismemberment. That contrast lends a sharpening effect to the awfulness and violence" (Axe qtd. in Shachtman 2010). However, when *War is Boring*, the webcomic created by Axe and cartoonist, Matt Bors, was collected and published as a hardcover book that was favorably reviewed by the mainstream media, it was considered to be a graphic novel, and there were no expectations that it would be funny or unserious.

While graphic novels and comic books are essentially the same art form, they have become distinct mediums due to differences in production, readership, and marketing. There are traditional book publishers who have a line of graphic novels, but they are unlikely to ever publish issues of comic books. There are some avid readers of graphic novels who have never read a comic book. Perhaps the greatest difference is in how graphic novels and comic books are marketed. We will have more to say about that in the industry section.

The important point for this section is that graphic novels, in comparison to comic books, are seen as a more respectable medium with more serious content. While readers might expect nothing more than light entertainment from a monthly comic book, such as *Captain Carrot and his Amazing Zoo Crew!*, they anticipate that a square-bound graphic novel, such as *March*, might address important topics with some depth and sophistication; it has something to say. Readers are likely to expend more mental effort and engage in central processing, which means applying critical thinking to the content. Therefore, graphic novels do not always have the full advantage of "invisible" persuasion that comes from not being taken seriously.

PERSUASION DUE TO THE NATURE OF THE INDUSTRY

Another context that can affect the reception of the message in a persuasive comic is the reader's attitude about the industry that produces the comics. Over 2,000 years ago, Aristotle observed that ***ethos*** (source credibility) is the most powerful means of persuasion. Thus, a particular comic's ability to influence a particular reader is determined, to some extent, by how that reader feels about the industry as a whole, a particular publisher, or the creative personnel associated with a comic. Because there are distinct national and cultural differences in production and attitudes toward those producers, we will focus on comics as encountered in the United States.

Comic strips, because they appeared in a respectable medium, the newspaper, were openly read by a wide range of ages and across social strata. In 1945, when newspaper delivery drivers went on strike, New York Mayor Fiorello La Guardia ordered municipal station WNYC to read the comics to their audience every day until the strike was over, and he personally read some of the Sunday comic strips to the audience of his weekly *Talk to the People* radio program ("New York").

The comic book industry did not enjoy the same support from authority figures. In the 1940s and 1950s Stan Lee (then Stanley Lieber) was ashamed to tell his neighbors he was a comic book editor and writer (Stan Lee 2002: 57; Joan Lee qtd. in Blake 2002: 61). During that same period there were many warnings about the dangers of reading comic books, with some educators warning comics would stunt children's intellectual development, and psychologists, sociologists, and politicians claiming comics could warp children's sense of morality and lead to a life of crime.

When comic books were "sanitized" by the self-imposed Comics Code in the mid-1950s adults stopped attacking them and stopped reading them. Until the mid-1980s, drugstores, newsstands, and other venues usually displayed comic books on spinner racks with a metal sign on top proclaiming "HEY!! KIDS COMICS." That is still the image—comic books as relatively harmless junk reading for children—that persists, with most people who are not hardcore fans (Figure 9.14).

The immense popularity of superhero movies has made Marvel Comics and, to a lesser extent, DC Comics recognizable brand names, but it has not done much to change the attitudes of the general public toward the source material for those movies. While comic books are unlikely to persuade the average person based on the credibility of the medium and industry, that does, as explained earlier, mean that people are not likely to recognize or critically examine persuasive message within comic books. Of course, longtime, dedicated fans have a different relationship with the medium and the industry.

Figure 9.14 The spinner rack at the local drug store hailed children with a clarion call: "Hey!! Kids Comics" Denis Kitchen Publishing Co., LLC.

Longtime readers of comic books can develop a **parasocial relationship** with a favorite writer, artist, or, more likely, character. A parasocial relationship is a feeling of knowing, liking, and even having an emotional attachment to a fictional character or a real person with whom you have no actual relationship (Cohen 2004). Any recurring character in a regularly appearing comic strip or comic book series might be the object of a parasocial relationship, but research has indicated that "for some readers the primary appeal of superhero comic books is not the fight scenes nor the colorful costumes, but rather a relationship with the 'person' in the costume" (Duncan 2020: 231). Some characters in superhero comic books have a fairly well-developed "life" because they have been appearing in monthly comics for decades, have relationships with many other characters in a large (sort of) unified fictional universe, are featured in a variety of merchandise, and, in recent decades, have almost certainly appeared in other mediums. Dedicated fans have ample opportunity to get to know and become attached to such characters. One of your authors admitted, during a conference keynote address, that he feels closer to Peter Parker than to any of his forty-two first cousins.

A parasocial relationship with a real person works a bit differently because a reader might have some, slight though it be, connection with a comics editor or creator. A fan can actually meet and chat with a favorite writer or artist at a comic book convention. Many comics creators use personal websites and blogs, fan forums, and social media to build their brand and establish connections with fans. Even brief connections are likely to strengthen the parasocial relationship for a fan.

A strong parasocial relationship often means that the reader identifies (shares a sense of interest, attitudes, or values) with the person or character. Kenneth Burke (1950) modified Aristotle's concept of ethos by stressing that considering a source to be credible means we identify with that source. Burke felt that **identification** and persuasion were virtually the same thing. Thus, a comics fan might come to identify with an ideology that a favorite writer has expressed in the stories they tell or statements they make online. Strong identification with a character might even mean that a fan would emulate attitudes or actions of the character. For instance, a "What would Deadpool do?" approach to situations; which, in most instances, is probably not the way to go.

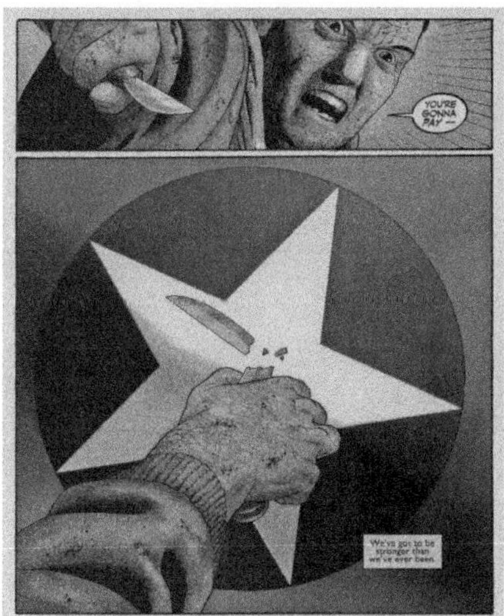

Figures 9.15a–b Captain America vol. 4 # 1 John Ney Rieber and John Cassaday (storytellers) © 2023 Marvel Entertainment and its subsidiaries.

Captain America is a more noble role model. In fact, in both film and comic books, he is the moral center of the Marvel Universe. Thus, when Captain America makes a choice or takes a stand on an issue, his choice operates as a persuasive argument. In a story about the aftermath of the 9/11 attacks, a father, mad with grief over his daughter's death, tries to stab a young Arab-American who just happens to be walking down the street. Captain America intervenes, and his voice-over and dialogue provide a moral compass that was much needed in the months following 9/11 (see Figures 9.15 a–b).

Readers of alternative comics or webcomics might not consider themselves to be as fanatic as readers of superhero comic books. They feel that unlike the heavily marketed superhero comics that mainstream publishers are intent on foisting upon readers, so-called alternative comics are gems they have discovered for themselves. Plus, they consider the content to be more genuine because, free of the constraints of greedy corporate masters, alternative cartoonists have used an artisan (as opposed to industrial) process to express personal visions. Due to these factors they might feel a more personal connection (i.e., identification) with the cartoonist.

The attitudes a reader has about the publisher and or creators of a comic can determine their resistance or susceptibility to the persuasive message within that comic.

PERSUASION DUE TO THE NATURE OF THE ART FORM

In this section we will focus on comic books and graphic novels because their multiple full pages allow for strategies of juxtaposing, sequencing, and braiding not possible in a comic strip. As explained in Chapters 3, 4, and 5, a comic book or graphic novel comes into being through the application of many creative choices about what to show (encapsulation), how to show it (composition), and how to arrange it (layout).

Encapsulation. The concept of encapsulation is usually applied to individual panels, but someone, usually an editor, must decide what to show on the cover. The cover creates a context that can influence a reader's cognitive and affective response to the narrative presented in the comic book or graphic novel. The cover often alerts potential readers to the type of narrative contained within—action, romance, mystery, suspense, and so on, or signals that the comic will be more informative than the narrative. That can help sell a book, but if the cover creates an expectation the comic fails to meet then the reader is likely to be disappointed.

For typical narrative comics, the writers and artists want to show the moments of prime action so that readers can weave those moments into a coherent story. For a comic that intends to persuade, the selection of what to show is guided by the specific purpose of the comic. A specific purpose is how the comic's publisher and creative personnel want readers to be affected by the comic, and that affect can consist of any or all of the following: what they want readers to know; what they want readers to feel; what they want readers to do. Thus, images and words are chosen to inform, evoke emotion, or motivate.

Persuasive messages seldom provide a balanced consideration of all perspectives. They tip the scales in favor of the perspective they promoting by using strategies that intensify what is good about their point of view or policy, and what is bad about opposing points of view or policies and downplay both the negative aspects of their perspective or policy and what is good about opposing perspectives or policies (Rank 1976). Encapsulation in a persuasive comic always involves a degree of card stacking, including only that information that supports the perspective being advanced. When opposing points of view are acknowledged they are often presented through a technique known as **strawman**, a partial representation, or even misrepresentation, makes the perspective seem foolish and easy to refute (Figure 9.16).

Figure 9.16 ***An Army of Principles*** **© 1976, donated to public domain 2022.**

An Army of Principles: *The History and Philosophy of the American Revolution*, was written by an American citizen and published in 1976, the bicentennial of the United States of America. Thus, it is not surprising that the four panels summarizing the ending of the American Revolution (see Figure 9.9) intensify negative aspects of the British perspective. This is done primarily through the use of visual metaphors. The drawing of King George III on a rocking horse brandishing a (toy?) sword might be read as the King being childish and out of touch with reality, especially due to his playing at the battle and his toy horse being put in contrast to the real soldiers and horses depicted in the same panel. The use of a cat (in this instance, a fraidy cat) to represent England and a mouse to represent the American colonies, emphasizes the power disparity between the foes, yet the demeanors of the avatars indicate the mouse is triumphant, or at least confident. Visual metaphor is also used to intensify the positive (from the American perspective) resolution of the conflict, with doves carrying olive branches soaring upward toward the light. This segment of the comic can be considered a strawman argument because it presents a British perspective characterized by poor leadership, debt, fear, and defeat.

According to Kenneth Burke (1966), our vocabulary acts as a terministic screen because the words we apply to describe/understand our sensory experiences construct our individual reality. The encapsulation process in panels is a sort of **terministic/imagistic screen**, creating a particular reality with the words and pictures that are shown. Take a look back at "A Life in Comics" by Nick Sousanis (Figures 5.12 a–g), which presents a brief biography of Karen Green in six pages of words and pictures. While Karen no doubt engages in many mundane activities, what readers perceive as they encounter the terministic/imagistic screen created by Sousanis is a life full of literature and art.

Layout. Layout involves the placement of panels on a page, and that placement creates juxtaposition, panels placed in close proximity to one another, thus inviting (compelling?) readers to make comparisons, contrasts, or other connections between the adjoining panels. Contrasting images can work as an argument because what is presented in one panel might seems more desirable than what is represented in the adjoining panel. *Passional Christi und Antichirsti*, a pamphlet produced under the supervision of Martin Luther in 1521, might be considered a forerunner of propaganda comics. It contains thirteen pairs of woodcut illustrations that support Luther's claim of corruption in the Catholic church by contrasting the holy actions of Jesus with the corrupt actions of Pope Leo X (Wareham 2016). In Figure 9.9, the doves (a symbol of peace) are in stark contrast to the soldiers in the panel to the left and the destruction in the panel above them. Take a look at Figure 9.14 and you will see a number of ways in which the Miles Morales character stands in contrast to the people in the panel behind him. The layout and composition choices prompt the reader to assign meaning to these contrasts.

When it is not apparent that panel contents are different and contrasting, a reader might assume a close association between the panels. This could be particularly true if the panels have some elements of structural sameness (e.g., of equal size and on the same tier of the page). The effect can be positive, our evaluation of image A is enhanced by being next to image B, or negative if our negative evaluation of image A is transferred to the adjoining image B (e.g., guilt by association). These types of associations are a form of the **Kuleshov Effect**, in which the meaning of one image is altered by the image that follows it in sequence. For instance, a single panel of someone handing money to a cap driver wearing a turban is simply the depiction of a common (back when people used cash) functional act. However, when that same panel is preceded by a panel of someone tucking money into a stripper's G-string, and the hands in both panels are at the same angle, most readers are going to make some association between the two panels (see Figure 9.17). Now the cab driver panel might be read as someone, who like the stripper, has to work an undesirable job to survive because his social status limits his opportunities.

Laying out panels on a page also creates a sequence, and sequence can operate as an argument by implying a cause-and-effect relationship. Look at the sequence of four panels across the bottom of page four of Figure 5.12. In the first panel, Karen Green (still being drawn in the style of the Little Nemo comic strip character) is off balance and uncertain as she "falls into" working on a master's degree at Columbia University. In the second panel she is walking hesitantly as she begins to work at the Butler Library. In the third panel she is running as she completes a library science degree and applies for a job at Columbia. In the final panel, the drawing looks like the real Karen Green and she is jumping for joy, with arms raised triumphantly. This sequential "argument" leads us to the conclusion that her association with Columbia University, and particularly the Butler Library, caused Karen to become her true or best self.

Figure 9.17 ***The System*** **© 1997 Peter Kuper, published by DC Comics.**

When we consider visual "arguments" across multiple panels, especially on the same tier, Stephen Toulmin's model of argument might be a useful tool. The basic structure of the Toulmin model progresses from left to right thusly: Grounds (the data we already know)—Warrant (information, that when combined with the grounds, justifies making a claim)—Claim (the main point of the argument). Toulmin's model also accounts for Backing (evidence) for the Grounds and the Warrant, and Conditions of Rebuttal under which the Claim would not be true, but most visual arguments in comics are not going to reach that level of complexity. Kress and van Leeuwen (2006) note that in a left-to-right reading culture panels on the left side of the page are the "given" (the grounds, etc.) and the panels on the right are the "new" information (the warrant). Thus, in a sequence of panels that are arguing for a particular policy or point of view, when the warrant (the new information) is added to the grounds (the given) the sequence might lead to a claim (see Figure 9.18). President Carter's given that the United States should not fight wars to seize oil is followed by a new initiative of transitioning to renewable energy and this grounds and warrant lead us to the claim, in the third panel, that such changes will create a future in which the sun is shining, birds are singing, and children are smiling. Such clear sequential arguments are

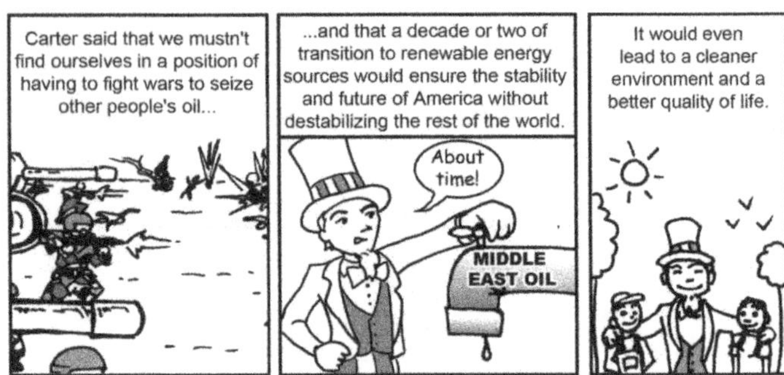

Figure 9.18 ***We the People: A Call to Take Back America*** **by Thom Hartman. Adapted by Gene Latimer and Paul Burke; illustrated by Neil Cohn. © 2004 by Thom Hartman.**

fairly rare. Even in comics meant to be persuasive, arguments are often spread over an entire page or multiple pages, and it might be that many readers do not even recognize them as "arguments."

When encountering, processing, and interpreting visual stimuli the human brain "starts with the simplest type of information and then moves on to increasingly more complex data," and that sequence of cognition "1) shape, 2) color, 3) content" (Lischer n.d.) influences how a reader deals with the information they encounter as they turn to a new page in a comic. A reader might first be aware of the structure of the page layout, the shapes of the panels, and then the dominant color on the page. Only then does their attention turn to the details of how elements in panels are composed (Figure 9.19).

Discovering: Graphic Medicine and the Case of Covid-19

Few things have upended the functions of daily life and endangered public health as much as the SARS-CoV-2, the novel infection known better as Covid-19. A global pandemic disrupted almost every form of human interaction as it swept the globe throughout 2020 and cost thousands of people their very lives. One tool in helping to resist the disease's spread—and deal with its impact—was the use of comics, and more specifically a type of educational comics considered under the banner of **graphic medicine**. "Graphic medicine is an interdisciplinary field within the health humanities that encompasses the creation, use, and study of comics in medicine and health" (Callendar et al. 2020: 1061). While the formal study of graphic medicine predates the pandemic, with regular national and international conferences and a growing body of scholarship exploring the use of comics in health care, the arrival of Covid-19 reiterated the value of using comics to convey information and document experiences related to our well-being.

Comics are valuable in healthcare contexts because they can feature simplified characters, who may be perceived as more widely acceptable to a variety of readers/patients. Comics also allow the reader to play an active role in the creation of meaning, including giving the reader control over the pacing of the processing of information (Callendar et al. 2020). As seen in Figure 9.18 fuzzy bunny that is divorced from gender, race, and other sociocultural markers is more universally accessible and the information it presents may be easier to comprehend given the level of engagement of the reader and the pacing with which a reader may consume it.

According to Ciléin Kearns and Nethmi Kearns (2020), comics also add a powerful persuasive element by framing their information through narratives. Presenting information through story is one of the chief strategies of the anti-vaccine movement—the very antithesis of graphic medicine; the anti-vaccine movement relies on individual anecdotes to universalize claims. The medical community often responds to these unsubstantiated stories by producing straightforward presentations of data—a counter-strategy that may seem cold and detached and lack resonance with readers. Information presented in the framework of a story, as "Baffled Bunny" does, likely has a greater impact as it engages the reader's imagination.

And while many Covid-19-era comics are focused on convincing audiences to take action to protect themselves, others are exercises by practitioners and patients at processing their experiences, showing what they have gone through in treating or recovering from the disease. Such comics are "frequently used as a way to deal with more

Figure 9.19 "Baffled Bunny in OK with That" by Sonny Liew in consultation with Dr. Hsu Li Yang, Professor Alex Cook, and Dr. Hannah Clapham © 2020.

distressing emotions and provide levity in challenging situation" (Callendar et al. 2020: 1062). And so, whether for the good of one's physical health or mental health, comics can be a strategy and a salve for a world facing a health care crisis.

Composition. We have already discussed, in Chapter 4 Composition, how the quality of the line, the use of color, etc. can affect the emotional response to a picture (e.g., curved lines are beautiful or friendly; straight lines are stern; the clean line style tends to make a character likable; the ugly (brut) art style can make a character unlikable), and we will not revisit those concepts in-depth here. However, we do want to acknowledge that for at least the past 100 years there has been a growing recognition of the importance of imagery in persuasion (and thinking in general).

In *Public Opinion*, a landmark study of how people in a modern democratic society come to know what they know, Walter Lippmann (1922) claims "pictures have always been the surest way of conveying an idea" (162). Due to the human tendency to impute "human nature to inanimate or collective things" the events, movements, forces, etc. of the world exist in our minds as person-like allegories (159). These impressions become even more abstracted and simplified because "human qualities are themselves vague and fluctuating" and "are best remembered by a physical sign" (160). Lippmann gives the example of the history, geography, social structure, and populace of England being embodied by the drawings of "John Bull, who is jovial and fat, not too clever, but well able to take care of himself" (160). The pictures in our heads are a vital aspect of how we think, and "We cannot be much interested in, or much moved by, the things we do not see" (161). Pictures are even more powerful and memorable when they have tangible form on the page (or more likely nowadays on the screen) (Figure 9.20).

Figure 9.20 The Uncle Sam of the World Wars, now elderly, befuddled, and seemingly homeless, confronts his would-be replacement—the Uncle Sam of the information age. *Uncle Sam* by Steve Darnall (writer) and Alex Ross (artist) © 1997/1998 DC Comics.

Visual arguments in persuasive comics sometimes function as **ad hominem**, which, rather than dealing with the substance of a person's ideas, seeks to discredit the individual by attacking their character. In comics, this attack might include words (negative adjectives, ethnic slurs, etc.), but will often involve pictures (visual associations and, most potently, the way the individual is drawn). A primary visual tool for ad hominem is caricature, which exaggerates physical characteristics to make the subject seem ridiculous or unattractive, invoking the age-old formula of ugly equals bad. John Bull, as described earlier was an essentially positive caricature, but during the Second World War German propaganda depicted John Bull as even more obese and bedraggled. As the Second World War progressed, the US government's Office of War Information (OWI), by way of the Writers' War Board (WWB), urged comic book publishers to depict German and Japanese soldiers as grotesque and vicious (Hirsch 2021: 46). Many of the caricatures were so loathsome that the ad hominem was quite explicit. However, in some instances visual arguments can be more potent when the pictures merely imply meaning, requiring the reader to be more active in completing the argument (Figure 9.21).

Figure 9.21 This representation of the German military as a primitive, bestial giant echoes popular propaganda posters of the era. Young Allies # 3 (1942) Stan Lee (w) Al Gabriele (a) © 2023 Marvel Entertainment and its subsidiaries.

ENTHYMEMATIC NATURE OF COMICS

By their very nature, comics involve readers in creating the meaning. Each reader creates his

Figure 9.22 "Words Do Matter" in Marvel's Voices: Legacy # 1 John Ridley (writer), Olivier Coipel (artist), Laura Martin (colors) © 2023 Marvel Entertainment and its subsidiaries.

or her own narrative by weaving together the discrete panels with inferences about the implied, but now shown, actions or event that occur between the panels. Comics creator and theorist Scott McCloud (1993) borrowed from Gestalt psychology to describe the additive process of comics reading as closure, emphasizing what readers imagine in the gutter, the white space between panels. Of course, acts of closure, adding personal knowledge and perspectives to the fragmentary information provided on the comics page in order to create a meaningful narrative, can occur among the images in a single panel, between pages, and within the totality of the work. All of these levels of closure require active reader participation, and that is why rhetorical theorist Kathleen Turner (1977) characterizes the act of closure in comics reading as enthymematic. An enthymeme implies, rather than explicitly stating, one or more premises of an argument.

J. Anthony Blair (2005) states that because pictures do not have the communicative specificity of words, "visual arguments are typically enthymemes—arguments with gaps left to be filled in by the participation of the audience" (52). The meaning of visual syntax becomes fluid, indeterminate, and more subject to the viewer's interpretational predispositions. This relative indeterminacy of visual syntax plays a central part in the processes of visual persuasion, and this seeming "deficiency" of visual syntax is arguably one of its principal strengths (Messaris 1997: xiii). Aristotle considered the enthymeme to be a very effective persuasive technique because the audience completes the argument for themselves and might not even perceive they have been persuaded by someone else. Of course, creators of persuasive comics do try to guide the closure that readers will perform, and they hope the completion of an enthymeme will result in acceptance of the argument they intended to make.

Analyzing: "Invisible" Persuasion

In the three-page (Figure 9.22) story titled "Words Do Matter" (see Figure 9.14) there is no dialogue, only caption boxes containing the words of an omniscient narrator. The first caption contains one word—"You." The encapsulation, composition, and layout choices make it perfectly clear the "you" is addressed to Miles Morales, who is also Spider-Man.

Miles appears twice on the page, once in his everyday clothes and once in the Spider-Man costume. However, Miles, not Spider-Man, is the dominant figure on this page. Miles wears a bright red jacket, and all the people behind him are in muted blue and gray clothing. Miles is shown in full figure, but the lower bodies of the people behind him seem to be fading away. Miles overlaps the panel borders. He is not contained within the panel the way the people behind him are; he exists in a suprapositioned panel. The caption in the second panel reads "You are different." Miles is young and Black, and the people behind him in the second panel are older and mostly White.

The "You are different" caption appears again in the bottom panel, which shows Miles as Spider-Man defeating a horrific villain. But in this panel, the word "different" is struck through and replaced with "distinct." This is a change of the terministic screen, the vocabulary through which experiences are filtered in order to create an individual conception of reality. This edit of the caption transforms Miles from the Other (in comparison to those people behind him) into a singular, remarkable human being. By contrast, the people standing behind Miles, due to the muted colors and fading of the image, seem to lack power.

This story featuring Miles appears in the comic book *Marvel's Voices: Legacy*, an anthology of short stories celebrating some of the Black heroes of the Marvel Universe. The title ("Word Do Matter") echoes the phrase Black Lives Matter. And this story, like the rest of the book, is meant to matter; the creators aspire to have an effect beyond entertainment. As Nic Stone, the mother of two Black boys, alludes to in her introduction to the anthology, among the book's persuasive effects is the ability to inspire Black children to see themselves as superheroes.

Discussion Questions

1. The Fellowship of Reconciliation, the publisher of *Martin Luther King and the Montgomery Story*, say they "attempt to practice the things that Jesus taught about overcoming evil with good." Toward the end of the comic book they encourage readers to apply this nonviolent approach to the civil rights movement with what they call "The Montgomery Method." What techniques do the authors of this comic book use to persuade readers to follow this method? The comic can be found online here: https://comicbookplus.com/?dlid=66823 or here: https://www.thehenryford.org/collections-and-research/digital-collections
2. What are the differences between New Journalism and a documentary (particularly the expository and participatory modes)?

Activities

1. Read the Society of Professional Journalist's Code of Ethics. Then read a piece of comics journalism at http://www.susiecagle.com/comics/, www.joshcomix.com/work/stories/, or www.archcomix.com, and determine how it conforms to and deviates from the SPJ Code. Write a short report on your evaluation. The SPJ Code can be found here: https://www.spj.org/ethicscode.asp
2. Read a comic book at the Comics with Problems site (http://www.ep.tc/problems/) or at the University of Nebraska's Government Comics Collection administered by Richard Graham. Is the comic book operating primarily as journalism, persuasion, or documentary? Provide support for your answer.

Recommended Reading

Comics

Sacco, Joe. *Journalism*. New York: Metropolitan Books, 2012.

This book collects Sacco's shorter reportage pieces that were published in various magazines, and newspapers.

Spiegelman, Art. *In the Shadow of No Towers*. New York: Pantheon Books, 2004.

Spiegelman responds to the US War on Terror with a relentlessly creative blend of diatribe, journalism, and documentary, presented in the form of a toddler's board book.

Talbot, Bryan. *Alice in Sunderland*. Milwuakie: Dark Horse Books, 2007.

Talbot's narration of the documentary begins with him standing on a theater stage wearing a rabbit mask. It is a very performative documentary of the history and mythology of Sunderland, England.

Scholarly Sources

Duncan, Randy, Michael Ray Taylor, and David Stoddard. *Creating Comics as Journalism, Memoir & Nonfiction*. New York: Routledge, 2016.

This textbook combines the perspectives of a journalist, an artist, and a comics scholar to explore the history of nonfiction comics and provide practical advice for creating memoir, reportage, or documentary in comics form.

Hirsch, Paul. *Pulp Empire: The Secret History of Comic Book Imperialism*. Chicago: University of Chicago Press, 2021.

Hirsch provides a fresh and detailed looked at how newspaper cartoonists and comic book publishers responded to the US government's pressure to employ comics as propaganda during the Second World War and the subsequent Cold War.

Adams, Jeff. *Documentary Graphic Novels and Social Realism*. Bern: Peter Lang, 2008.

Adams explores how composition and sequencing choices create a visual realism that make comics an effective medium for documenting social crises.

Unit IV Context and Analysis

10 The Evolution of American Comics

This chapter provides a narrative about the development of the comic book and graphic novel. We intentionally note that this is *a* history rather *the* history about the growth of the medium. Every historical narrative privileges certain perspectives in its delivery, and this history is no different. As such, this narrative reflects the perspectives and experiences of its authors, who although raised in different parts of America, still view the development of comics and graphic novels from an American perspective. The story of comics and graphic novels is bigger than any one nation's experience, but to provide a comprehensive account of all of the cultures and peoples who contributed to the comics and graphic novels of today would be a much larger project than one chapter in an introductory textbook could successfully address. So, we are acknowledging up front that the history we are about to tell is *a* narrative but by no means *the* only narrative about how comics came about.

In addition, our approach considers the development of comics and graphic novels from the perspective of them being both a medium and an art form. As noted previously in this textbook, comics are a medium in the sense that they are produced by cultural industries for consumption by large audiences. Comics are also an art form in that they are crafted by skilled artisans and can function as expressions of those artisans' cultural values and responses to the world around them. As we shall see, the evolution of comics is a product of both commerce and art.

Objectives

In this chapter you will learn:

1. the continental roots of comics as an art form;
2. the ways in which comic strips and pulps contributed to the emergence of the American comic book;
3. how publishers turned comic books into a stand-alone medium, building on the success of the superhero genre;
4. how the underground movement developed and spread its influence throughout the industry; and
5. how subsequent cycles of boom and bust have been influenced by the audience and the editorial direction of the major publishers.

Early Roots

Sequential art dates back to the beginning of humanity's artistic expression. Between 10,000 and 25,000 years ago, juxtaposed images in sequence used to convey simple narratives were painted or scratched onto cave walls in France and Spain. Since that time humanity has engaged in a wide array of image sequencing practices, or sequential art, ranging from Egyptian tomb paintings (*c.* 1300 BC), to the Bayeux Tapestry (*c.* 1100 AD), to Mexican codices (*c.* 1500 AD).

However, the sequences of images painted on cave walls, carved into stone, baked onto clay, or woven into elaborate tapestries are far removed from the modern manifestations of sequential art—comic strips, comic books, and graphic novels—in terms of production, distribution, and function. Perhaps comics, in the broadest sense of the term, have existed as an art form for millennia, but sequential art forms employed as popular entertainment media are, as art historian David Kunzle puts it, "children of the printing press" (1970: 133).

As the movable-type printing press technology spread throughout Europe, so did a new form of popular entertainment—the broadside (sometimes referred to as a **broadsheet**), a single large piece of paper with a series of images on it, usually accompanied by text. Although the text was placed above or below the image rather than incorporated into it, the broadsheet manifested the essential form and function of the modern comic strip. Broadsheets were the first type of sequential art to create a degree of interdependence between picture and text. Broadsheets were popular in Germany, France, England, and Holland from about 1450 to 1800, and they were often sold at fairs and festivals. Governments and churches attempted to use this powerful new mass medium to disseminate news and teach moral lessons.

Beyond broadsides there were myriad influences on the evolution of sequential art. Indeed, many of the techniques of sequential art that we associate with comics were developed piecemeal by dozens of medieval book illustrators. Art historian Daniele Alexander-Bidon has demonstrated that in these copiously illustrated, single-copy manuscripts created for the very wealthy, "one finds page layouts, balloons for words or thought, onomatopoeia, movement lines, containment by frames or going outside them, fast movements split into several images, and graphic relations between contiguous images" (qtd. in Groensteen 1998: 108–9). There is not enough space in this chapter to cover all the influences, however, we can proceed with a survey of some of the major eras and influential figures who have helped shape the medium as it now manifests itself in the twenty-first century.

William Hogarth: Sequential Artist

William Hogarth (1697–1764) laid the foundations for popularizing sequential art. Comics historian Maurice Horn claims that Hogarth's "drawings can be acknowledged as the first direct forerunners of the comic strip" ("Hogarth" 321). Early in his career, Hogarth was a painter who promoted himself as an artist and made considerable supplemental income by selling prints of his paintings. Hogarth produced seven sets of sequential narratives on "Modern Moral Subjects." The first three of these sets were originally done in the form of paintings: "A Harlot's Progress" (1731), "The Rake's Progress" (1735), and "Marriage

Figures 10.1a–b William Hogarth first marketed sequential art through prints of his painting series "A Harlot's Progress" (1731). The first plate shows the lead character's arrival in London and the second her role as a kept woman. By the last plate, scavengers are picking over her estate after her death from syphilis.

a la Mode" (1743). While the six paintings (or prints) in "A Harlot's Progress" do have a deliberate sequence and do tell a rudimentary story when they are juxtaposed, as comics historian Mike Kidson points out, the visual sequencing within each image "is confused and inconsistent," and "we understand the series as a narrative because of what it depicts, not because of the way in which it is composed" (1999: 79). However, Hogarth refined his narrative technique. "The Rake's Progress" displays a "much more considered approach toward visual sequencing," and "Marriage a La Mode" has a "much more strip-like and consistent left-to-right construction" (Kidson 1999: 79–80) (Figures 10.1 a–b).

Prints of Hogarth's work were quite popular with London's upper class, but he seemed to want to reach a broader audience, so Hogarth himself authorized copies that could be sold at a fraction of the cost of the originals. By the fourth series, "Industry and Idleness" (1747), Hogarth was reducing his initial investment of time and money by skipping the painting altogether and converting from copperplate engraving to a sort of "enhanced" etching. However, Hogarth's authorized prints were still too expensive for most of London's middle class. But due in part to the availability of cheap pirated prints, Hogarth's work did cross class boundaries. It may well be that Hogarth's importance in the history of comics stems as much from his marketing ability and his marketability as it does from his artistic or storytelling ability.

Rodolphe Töpffer: Father of the Comic Book

The son of a well-known artist, Rodolphe Töpffer (1799–1846) had a lifelong desire to be a painter. Yet art was never to be more than a sideline for Töpffer. He became a teaching director of a boys' preparatory school and engaged his creativity in scholarly writing. It was his scholarship, particularly a translation of the speeches of Demosthenes (1824) and a study of the *Iliad* (1831), that earned him the chair of Rhetoric and Belles-Lettres at the Academy in Geneva. Töpffer went on to write more scholarly treatises and a number of critically acclaimed short stories. However, he is best known for what began as "doodlings" done to give his artistic yearnings an outlet and to delight his students at the prep school.

It was with these *la litterature en estampes* (picture-stories), as he called them, that Töpffer made "a decisive break with older formats and that he initiated a new form of expression" (Groensteen 1998: 107–8). Töpffer created at least seven picture-stories between 1827 and 1844. The first, *Les Amours de M. Vieux-Bois*, was created in 1827, but not printed until 1837. Töpffer's first published album was *Histoire de M. Jabot*, drawn in 1831, printed in 1833, and published in 1835. These picture-stories were usually published as oblong albums, some close to 100 pages long.

One of Töpffer's innovations was that he used the medium of sequential art to tell entertaining fictional stories. Morality tales and propaganda were replaced by slapstick tales of absurdist anti-heroes who struggled against the whims of fate. Yet his greatest innovations were not in content but in form. Historian John Geipel speculates that it was due to his poor eyesight that Töpffer developed "the 'shorthand,' epigrammatic style of drawing that became the stock-in-trade of the later strip cartoonists" (1972: 136). This sketchy (cartoon) style allowed Töpffer's panel compositions and panel sequences to be much more dynamic than any work that had preceded him. "He made broken lines more suggestive than continuous ones, and by abandoning the academic concept of three-dimensional, anatomical drawing, he learned how to render movement. His art is all movement, breathless, relentless; it is the movement for the movement's sake" (Kunzle 1970: 139).

His work might not have been preserved if not for the positive comments of German writer Johann Wolfgang von Goethe. As Goethe wrote about Töpffer in a letter to Eckermann: "If, for the future, he would choose a less frivolous subject and restrict himself a little, he would produce things beyond all conception" (1875: 503). The content of Töpffer's work never became serious, but he began to take the form itself seriously. In his *Essai de physiognomonie* (*Essay on Physiognomy*), written in 1845, Töpffer proclaimed that "the picture-story, which critics disregard and scholars scarcely notice, has greater influence at all times, perhaps even more than written literature" (3). He also recognized that he had created a truly blended art form, where pictures without text would have only vague meaning, and text without pictures would have virtually no meaning. Likewise, each segment (or panel) derives its meaning from what has gone before and what follows. With Töpffer, "the transition from illustration in the Hogarthian sense to composition of an entire story in pictorial terms was complete" (Wiese 1965: xvii).

Töpffer's works were rather quickly translated into a number of different languages, including English. One of the English translations of *Histoire de M. Vieux-Bois*, perhaps a pirated copy of a British edition, made its way to America in the early 1840s as *The Adventures of Obadiah Oldbuck*, a supplement to the *Brother Jonathan* newspaper. The American edition was 8½ × 11 and forty pages in length. It was printed on both sides of the paper, with six to twelve panels per page. In other words, it looked a lot like a modern comic book (Beerbohm 2003). After only a few of his albums had been published, Töpffer began to inspire imitators, including the famed illustrator Gustave Doré (1832–83), whose *The Labours of Hercules* (1847) was a picture-story album that followed the Töpffer model in form, tone, and style but was superior in draftsmanship. Töpffer had created the art form, now it just awaited a medium of transmission, a means of production and distribution (Figure 10.2).

Figure 10.2 Rodolphe Töpffer's *Les Amours de M. Vieux-Bois* (1837) represents one of the earliest experiments with publishing sequential art.

Coming to America: Comics Strips and Pulp Magazines

Figure 10.3 Thomas Nast was the cartoonist who began to define American icons. This is his first Santa Claus from "Christmas Poems" (J. M. Gregory, 1863–4).

American readers had already been exposed to comics with the importation of *The Adventures of Obadiah Oldbuck* and the influence of the Continental comics began to inspire American cartoonists. A number of humor magazines debuted in the 1850s beginning with Thomas W. Strong's *Yankee Notions*, which was followed by *Nick Nacks* and *Comic Monthly*. These magazines featured multi-panel cartoons, some serialized over a period of months, which focused on everyday life (Beringer 2015).

A different strain of influence on comics took its inspiration from the highly successful British humor magazine *Punch* (1841–2002), later mimicked in the United States through satirical magazines such as *Puck* (1871–1918). *Punch* focused on single-panel comics and even coined the term **cartoon** to refer to a humorous drawing (rather than a rough sketch for a painting). But American cartooning began to evolve its own creative ambitions with the work of the German-born Thomas Nast (1840–1902) who was brought to the country at age six. Nast was the first American cartoonist to create lasting cultural icons, drawing defining versions of Uncle Sam, Santa Claus, and the Democratic donkey and adding the Republican elephant and Columbia to the visual lexicon. His most important work was the creation of Tammany Tiger and the cartoon campaign against Boss Tweed and the Democratic machine that controlled much of New York politics. Tweed viewed Nast as dangerous enough to offer bribes that could equal $1 billion in 2013 buying power if Nast would leave the country and abandon his efforts. Nast turned them down, and his cartoons ultimately played a role in bringing down Tweed, as well as influencing American politics on a wide range of issues (Figure 10.3).

The American comic book industry grew out of two roots: newspaper comic strips and pulp magazines. The format and commercial infrastructure grew primarily out of a repackaging of the comic book's closest cousin, the comic strip. Part of the investment capital, the talent, and even some of the heroic archetypes were derived from the pulps.

The first characters to populate the comic book pages did not wear capes or leap tall buildings. They tended to be youngsters with names like Buster Brown, Little Nemo, and The Katzenjammer Kids, and their hijinks entertained semi-literate masses who bought newspapers just to follow their daily misadventures. The first mass media products that began to look like modern comic books—and were called comic books—were actually reprint collections of popular newspaper comic strips. More than a thousand books of comic strip reprints were published between 1897 and 1932 (Beerbohm and Olson 2008). The first and most famous of the comic strip kids to have a collection of his adventures reprinted in book form is the Yellow Kid. The strip that became known as *The Yellow Kid* began as a single-panel cartoon by Richard Felton Outcault (1863–1928). In 1894 Outcault began doing weekly drawings of slum life for the *Sunday World* newspaper. It was not until May 5, 1895, that he titled his cartoon *Hogan's Alley*. Most of the urchins and street toughs he drew wore the conventional clothing of tenement kids. However, one bald, barefooted, jug-eared kid by the name of Mickey Dugan inexplicably wore a nightshirt. As Mickey gained prominence in the strip, he became the chief source of dialogue, and the dialogue appeared not in a word balloon, but written on his nightshirt (Figure 10.4). Legend has it that a printer used Mickey's nightshirt as the test area for new yellow ink, and thereafter he became known to readers as the Yellow Kid. The Yellow Kid was an immensely popular character, and he was widely merchandized. In March 1897, the publication of the *Yellow Kid Magazine* marked "the first published collection of an American comic strip" (Benton 1993: 14). Since *The Yellow Kid* had demonstrated that comics could dramatically increase newspaper circulation, he was soon joined on the comics page by *The Katzenjammer Kids*, *Mutt & Jeff*, *Foxy Grandpa*, and many others. The most popular of the comic strips were collected and reprinted in a variety of formats (Beerbohm and Olson 2008).

Figure 10.4 Hully gee! Richard F. Outcault's comic strips featuring the Yellow Kid helped to sell newspapers and then other merchandise.

While *The Yellow Kid* utilized much of the language of comics, it was still essentially a single-panel cartoon. In 1903, an artist named Clare Briggs experimented with *A. Piker Clerk,* a multi-panel comic in the pages of *The Chicago American*, but the series did not last long. The multi-panel comic that hit it big was Bud Fisher's *A. Mutt*, which debuted in the pages of *The San Francisco Chronicle* in 1907 but would soon be renamed *Mutt and Jeff.* Unlike Briggs' attempt, Fisher's effort was widely imitated and helped to shape the syndicated comic strip boom that followed. Significantly, the multi-panel strip helped to refine the notion of timing in comics, as humor could be derived from events in sequence. With multiple panels to work with, the comic strip artist would move beyond sight gags and one-liners and present humor with a setup and punchline. For example, in one early *Mutt and Jeff* strip, Jeff decides to buy himself a straw hat to replace the top hat he typically wears. When he shows off the hat, Mutt takes note of its flat shape and gives it a toss in Jeff's direction, ultimately poking him in the eye. The humor (such as it is) is dependent on the sequencing of events across the strip. Henceforth, strips (and later whole pages in comic books) would further popularize the storytelling potential of the form.

Just as the comics art form was developing in newspapers, at the dawn of the twentieth century, pulp magazines were beginning to replace dime novels as a form of cheap entertainment for the middle class and educated lower class. Beneath their often lurid covers, pulp magazines contained rough-edged wood-pulp pages filled with crude but powerful storytelling that helped establish most genres of popular fiction and launched the careers of many of America's best-known writers, from Ray Bradbury to Raymond Chandler. Most of the pioneering publishers of the comic book format were in some way associated with the pulp magazines. The promise of revenues from the increasingly popular comic books lured a number of pulp publishers to shift resources to comic book publishing. Many of the pulp writers (and a few of the artists) followed their publishers into the new medium (Bell and Vassallo 2013) (Figure 10.5).

Figure 10.5 **The Spider was the Master of Men—and the pulp magazines—well before Batman and other mystery men debuted in the comic books. © 1940 by Popular Publications, Inc. Copyright renewed © 1968 and assigned to Argosy Communications, Inc. All rights reserved. The Spider is a registered trademark of Argosy Communications, Inc. Used with permission.**

The pulps had introduced heroes such as Tarzan (1912) and Zorro (1919), but sales peaked in the 1930s with the introduction of the "hero pulps." Each hero pulp featured a single recurring hero of remarkable appearance and extraordinary abilities. Both Tarzan and Zorro had appeared in various pulp magazines for years, but in 1931 the Shadow became the first character to appear in a magazine created specifically for his adventures and bearing his name: *The Shadow, A Detective Magazine*. A few years later, *Doc Savage*, *The Spider*, and other eponymous hero pulps appeared on the newsstands. With their costumes, secret identities, and abilities beyond those of ordinary mortals, it is easy to see that this new breed of pulp heroes had a direct influence on the superhero comic books that appeared in the late 1930s and early 1940s. Ironically, the immense popularity of their progeny, such as Superman and Batman, is one of the factors that led to the rather precipitous decline of the pulp magazine industry.

The Modern Comic Book Takes Shape

The American comic book industry was born at Eastern Color Printing Company in New York. In 1929 Eastern Color printed *The Funnies*, the first product from George Delacorte's Dell Publishing Company. *The Funnies* was a sixteen-page tabloid-format collection of comic strips that came out on Saturdays and sold for 10 cents (it was later reduced to 5 cents). *The Funnies* lasted about a year and a half—thirty-six issues. *The Funnies* is significant for a number of reasons. It was the beginning of Dell, a company that was destined to become one of the most prolific and successful comic book publishers. Also, while still consisting of one-page comic strips, it contained original material, not reprints of newspaper comic strips. And perhaps most importantly, it gave a couple of Eastern Color employees ideas.

Eastern Color also printed the color Sunday comics for most of the major newspapers in the northeast. Harry I. Wildenberg, the sales manager at Eastern Color Printing, did not really care for comic strips, but he realized the powerful impact they could have on newspaper circulation. He reasoned that if the comics could sell newspapers, they could be used to sell other products as well. In 1933 Wildenberg sold the Gulf Oil Company on the idea of using comics as a gas station giveaway with a fill-up. In a direct imitation of the format of Dell's *The Funnies*, *Gulf Comic Weekly* was tabloid-sized and contained original, full-page comic strips. For Wildenberg, the motivation was simply to sell printing contracts that kept the Eastern Color presses rolling.

Wildenberg might not have cared for comics, but one of his salesmen, Maxwell Charles Gaines, seemed to have a true affinity for the medium. M. C. Gaines enthusiastically joined his boss in promoting comics in book form. In 1933 Wildenberg and Gaines produced *Funnies on Parade* as an advertising premium to be given away by Proctor & Gamble. This was the first of the comic strip reprint collections to have the look of what came to be called a comic book: 7½ × 10½ with a paper cover. Increasingly, Eastern Color's association with books of comics resulted from the efforts of Gaines. For the rest of 1933 Gaines and Wildenberg continued to promote advertising premium books and print runs began to exceed 100,000 copies. Gaines' most famous efforts, and perhaps the true beginning of the comic book industry, were three books that confusingly bore the same name: *Famous Funnies*.

The first of these publications was issued in 1933 and titled *Famous Funnies: A Carnival of Comics*. This book of comic strip reprints was packaged and printed by Eastern Color for Kinney Shoe Store, Milk-O-Malt, and other clients as a giveaway. Legend has it that Gaines stickered a 10 cent price on the covers of a few dozen of the books and talked some newsstands into participating in his experiment. They sold out over the weekend, and the news vendors wanted more. Gaines is often credited with being the first person to have the idea of selling a book of comics as a product in and of itself, but, of course, books of comic strip reprints from publishers such as Cupples and Leon had been selling briskly for decades (Figure 10.6).

Figure 10.6 Third time's the charm: *Famous Funnies* makes its third debut. © 1934 Eastern Color Printing Company.

The second book, *Famous Funnies, Series One* #1 was issued by Eastern Color in partnership with George Delacorte in early 1934. It consisted of reprints, portions of which were from *Funnies on Parade* and *Famous Funnies: A Carnival of Comics*. To test the market for comic books as a product, approximately 40,000 copies were published to be sold in chain stores for 10 cents.

Finally, in May 1934, the third *Famous Funnies* #1 debuted. With this book, Eastern Color Printing Company went beyond merely packaging and printing books of comics and established itself as the first major comic book publisher. When the second issue of *Famous Funnies* came out, it was the first product that looked like the modern comic book to be sold monthly on the newsstands. Newspaper comic strip reprints were the mainstay of the book, but original filler material began to appear after the first few issues. *Famous Funnies* lasted until 1955, for a total of 218 issues. Thus, Gaines and Wildenberg demonstrated the marketability of the new medium and laid the foundations of the comic book industry.

Figure 10.7 Will Eisner recalls the assembly-line production process practiced in shops in *The Dreamer* (1986). From *The Dreamer* by Will Eisner. © 1986 by Will Eisner. Used by permission of W.W. Norton & Company, Inc.

The Shop System

The shop system, or studio system, was developed in the mid-thirties to meet the sudden and growing demand for original material to fill comic books from new publishers with no editorial resources, or pulp publishers moving into the new medium of comics. Without existing editorial expertise or departments in-house, this form of outsourcing presented a way into the lucrative comic book marketplace. The shops usually packaged entire books for the publishers, largely unsupervised. The usual setup was a large one-room studio with writers and artists working at rows of tables. In some shops an artist was responsible for an entire feature, but in other instances each artist did a particular aspect of a feature and it was passed along in an assembly-line fashion (Figure 10.7).

More than a dozen small shops formed during the 1940s, including Funnies, Inc. (who had assembled the contents for *Marvel Comics* #1), C. C. Beck and Pete Costanza Studio (who did much of the Captain Marvel material for Fawcett Comics), and Harry "A" Chesler's Shop. Chesler's approach was a typical comic book factory that produced material quickly and cheaply with an assembly-line approach. Eight to ten artists worked at rows of drafting tables on the third floor of an old tenement building with creaky, dusty wooden floors and no air conditioning. The writers worked down the hall or worked at home and brought the scripts to Chesler. The shop produced stories for more than a dozen comic book publishers. Particularly notable was Eisner & Iger, founded by Will Eisner and Samuel "Jerry" Iger, as Eisner would have important impacts on the field's development over the next seven decades. Also a product of this system was another pair of young storytellers, Joe Simon and Jack Kirby, who either as partners or independently would go on to have a significant impact on American comics.

Profile: Will Eisner

Born: William Erwin Eisner
March 6, 1917
New York City

"To me, I write about living and the art of living. My villain is Life itself. Human beings are struggling to survive."

Career Highlights

1936 Goes into business with Jerry Iger to operate one of the first comics production shops.
1940 Begins *Weekly Comic Book* (aka The Spirit Section) with *The Spirit* as the lead feature.
1948 Formed the American Visuals Corporation to produce instructional comics for government and corporate clients.
1973 Begins teaching at the School of Visual Arts.
1975 Receives the Lifetime Achievement Award at the International Salon of Comic Books in Angoulême.
1978 Publishes what is regarded as the first prominent graphic novel, *A Contract with God*.
1985 Publishes *Comics and Sequential Art*, a how-to book for cartoonists and the rudimentary formalist theory of the comic book art form.
1988 The Oscars of the comics, the Eisner Awards, are named in Will's honor.
1995 Receives the Milton Caniff Lifetime Achievement award from the National Cartoonists Society.
2005 *The Plot*, Eisner's first nonfiction graphic novel and his last major work undertaken before his death, is published posthumously.

Growing up in the Jewish ghettos in Brooklyn and the Bronx, Will Eisner decided that art would be his means to a better life. While still a teenager, Eisner partnered with established editor Jerry Iger to form the Eisner-Iger Shop, a comic book shop that packaged comics for Fiction House, Fox Comics, and other publishers. A few years later Eisner dissolved his partnership with Iger when he was offered an opportunity unique in the history of comic books: *The Des Moines Register and Tribune Syndicate* wanted Eisner to create a supplement to be inserted into newspapers across the nation. The *Weekly Comic Book* supplement later renamed *The Spirit Section*, contained three features—*Lady Luck*, *Mr. Mystic*, and *The Spirit*.

The syndicate wanted *The Spirit* to be a superhero comic. In early stories the character had a hidden crime lab and even a flying car, but soon Eisner was reshaping the malleable concept into stories of every imaginable genre, and the only remaining concessions to superhero conventions were a simple domino mask and a pair of gloves. Many of the stories began with a dazzling splash page that set the tone. On the pages that followed Eisner experimented with layout and composition. Comics historian Michael Barrier says, "Eisner was in those years the comic-book equivalent of Orson Welles: he was the first complete master of a young and heretofore unformed medium" (1988:

197–8). For many of Eisner's contemporaries and generations of artists who followed him, *The Spirit* was the textbook from which they learned how to create comic books.

Eisner's experiments with *The Spirit* were interrupted in the spring of 1942 when he was drafted into the US Army. While in the Army, Eisner worked in the Ordnance Department, where he produced comics about equipment maintenance. The experience convinced Eisner of the educational and business potential of comics. A few years after he was discharged, Eisner formed American Visuals Corporation to produce the educational and corporate comics that would become the focus of his career for the next twenty-five years. When he shut down American Visuals in the early 1970s, Eisner began teaching at the School of Visual Arts, a college co-founded by newspaper strip cartoonist Burne Hogarth. Among Eisner's students were many future artists, including Joe Quesada, who went on to a long tenure as Marvel's chief creative officer.

In the mid-seventies, inspired by the independence and mature content he saw in underground comix and needing an expressive outlet for the tragic loss of his teenage daughter, Eisner created *A Contract with God and Other Tenement Stories* (1978), a collection of four short stories about the lives of New York tenement dwellers. Although not the first to create a long work in comic book form, nor even the first to use the term *graphic novel*, Eisner might deservedly be considered the champion of the modern graphic novel because he showed the potential of the new format by using it to tell intimate human dramas, and his continued work over the next two decades to promote the form. In his early sixties Will Eisner began blazing a new trail in the comics medium, and he followed *Contract* with more than two dozen graphic novels of heartbreak and perseverance.

Will Eisner influenced generations of cartoonists, entertained and moved thousands of fans, and worked tirelessly to evangelize comics as a valid form of artistic expression and an effective form of educational communication. When he passed away at age eighty-seven, Eisner was still an ambitious creative genius striving to break new ground in his chosen art form (Figure 10.8).

Figure 10.8 Will Eisner in his role as a teacher from unpublished story boards. © 2008 by Will Eisner Studios, Inc.

New Fun

Major Malcolm Wheeler-Nicholson began the publishing company that would become the cornerstone of the new comic book industry. In 1934 he founded National Allied Publications, which later became National Periodical Publications and ultimately DC Comics. As a cavalry officer, Major Wheeler-Nicholson had had his share of adventures in exotic corners of the globe. After retirement from the military, he made a living writing military adventures and historical swashbucklers for pulp magazines such as *Argosy* and *Adventure*. However, Wheeler-Nicholson took note of the new medium of comic books. He decided to try a different approach to publishing comic books by publishing all-new content (he was probably unaware of Delacorte's failed attempt with *The Funnies* in 1929). Perhaps he reasoned that if reprints books could sell so well, a book with original material should do even better, or perhaps he published new material because he thought it would be cheaper than paying the licensing fees for comic strip reprints. Whatever his motivation, in early 1935 he published *New Fun Comics*, a regularly published comic book containing original material.

New Fun was far from an immediate success. Wheeler-Nicholson's Fourth Avenue office began to fill up with unsold copies of the book. Distributors were reluctant to give valuable rack space to an unproven commodity such as the comic book, and they were especially cautious with a book that had totally unknown characters. Despite the lack of sales and a lack of funds, late in 1935 Wheeler-Nicholson added another title, *New Comics*. By this time *New Fun* had been changed to *More Fun*, and the books were being edited by former contributors Vincent Sullivan and Whitney Ellsworth. Perhaps they were paid regularly, but the Major was so unreliable about paying the writers and artists that he had an almost constant turnover of staff. Of course, this meant there were plenty of opportunities for new talent. For instance, two youngsters from Cleveland, Jerry Siegel and Joe Shuster, did a number of features for the Major's comics, including "Dr. Occult," "Slam Bradley," and "Federal Men." However, the Major could not be convinced to publish their favorite feature, "Superman."

Sales of Wheeler-Nicholson's comic books remained shaky, and he was becoming further in debt to a man by the name of Harry Donenfeld. The Major's books were distributed by Independent News, which Harry Donenfeld and his partner Jack Liebowitz had formed in 1932. Independent News had advanced Wheeler-Nicholson funds that he had never paid back. Donenfeld also owned the printing plant that printed the covers for the Major's books, and the Major was behind on paying those printing bills. So when Wheeler-Nicholson wanted to add a third title, *Detective Comics*, to his line of comic books, he was forced to do so in partnership with Donenfeld and Liebowitz. In fact, when *Detective Comics* debuted in 1937, it was the product of a newly formed company—Detective Comics, Inc.—with Wheeler-Nicholson and Liebowitz listed as the owners. Harry Donenfeld was an energetic and aggressive entrepreneur. In addition to being a printer and distributor, he published pulp magazines. Perhaps he saw his association with Wheeler-Nicholson as an easy way to move into the new comic book field. If so, he was correct. By the end of 1937, Donenfeld forced National Allied Publications into bankruptcy to gain control. After the Major's departure, Detective Comics, Inc.—commonly referred to as DC Comics—would go on to become the most enduring publisher of American comic books (Figure 10.9).

Figure 10.9 Pioneering comics writer and publisher Malcolm Wheeler-Nicholson helped launch the American comic book business. © Finn Andreen.

Action Comics

Wheeler-Nicholson returned to writing for the pulps, and almost immediately after his departure the fledgling comic book enterprise he had left behind began to blossom into an empire. Donenfeld and Liebowitz's three titles—*More Fun Comics*, *Adventure Comics*, and

Detective Comics—were selling well enough to keep the presses running, but comic books did not become a big business until the introduction of their next title, *Action Comics*.

Of course, the first issue of *Action Comics* introduced Superman, a character who single-handedly established the identity of the American comic book. Writer Jerry Siegel was always a bundle of nervous energy, always wired. Artist Joe Shuster was very quiet. He was small, but worked out a lot to try to be more muscular. In 1933, while still high school students in Cleveland, the boys produced a mimeographed fanzine, *Science Fiction*. For the third issue, Siegel wrote and Shuster illustrated a story titled "The Reign of the Superman." The title character was a bald villain (who looked a lot like future arch-villain Lex Luthor). Later in the year they toyed with the idea of making their Superman villain into a hero. By 1936 Shuster had sketched various poses of the not-yet-published Superman with a couple of phrases, including "The Greatest Super-Hero of All Times." The Superman costume was no doubt derived from a number of sources, but prominent among them were the outfits worn by strongmen in the circus and the physical culture magazines Shuster loved (Ricca 2013).

Figure 10.10 This cover might have seemed ridiculous to some adults in 1938, but it has become an iconic and often imitated image because *Action Comics* # 1 is arguably the most important comic book in the industry's history. © DC Comics.

Siegel and Shuster's original goal was to do a newspaper strip, but they also tried comic book publishers. They got seventeen rejection letters. One said: "We are in the market only for strips likely to have the most extraordinary appeal, and we do not feel the Superman gets into that category" (Goulart 1986: 85). Despite the lack of encouragement, Siegel and Shuster kept submitting their Superman strip. Ultimately, DC editor Vincent Sullivan decided to purchase the feature for *Action Comics*. The pair was paid ten dollars a page for that first thirteen-page story. So, for $130 to split between them, Siegel and Shuster sold all rights to Superman, who would go on to become one of the most lucrative merchandising properties of all time (Figure 10.10).

When Harry Donenfeld saw the first *Action Comics* cover, with Superman holding a car over his head, he thought it was just too wacky. Superman stories continued to appear, but for the next five issues the covers featured more conventional adventure heroes: aviators, Mounties, and such. By the fourth issue of *Action Comics*, sales figures were impressive. Donenfeld did a newsstand survey and found out that kids were not asking for *Action Comics*, but for "that magazine with Superman on it" (Goulart 1991: 78). Starting with issue twelve, Superman's image or name graced every cover thereafter.

Superman was both the triumph and the tragedy of the comic book medium. Within a few years, *Action Comics* and its spin-off title, *Superman*, were each selling over a million copies a month. Superman assured the financial success of the new industry. Unfortunately, he also assured that the comic book medium would be forever (well, at least so far) associated with adolescent power fantasies of muscular men in tights. The legion of "long underwear" imitators that followed Superman cemented this image in the popular imagination.

Super-Imitators

Superman's first direct competitor had a very short career. Donenfeld's accountant, Victor Fox, probably saw the sales figures on *Action Comics* before anyone else in the company, realized Superman was a goldmine and left DC to stake his own claim. Moving to a different floor in the same building that housed DC, he formed Fox Features Syndicate and commissioned the Eisner-Iger Shop to create a Superman imitation called Wonder Man. *Wonder Comics* #1 was cover-dated May 1939. *Wonder Comics* only lasted two issues, and Wonder Man himself didn't even make it past the first one: DC immediately sued Fox for infringement of copyright. Fox, however, did not go away. Over the next few years his company published plenty of less-Superman-like superheroes, including the Flame and the Blue Beetle, supplied by the Eisner-Iger Shop and others.

Another superhero inspired by the success of Superman had a much longer career, probably because he was sponsored by Superman's publisher. In 1939 DC introduced its second major superhero—and comicdom's second most recognizable icon—the Bat-Man (the hyphen was dropped in short order). When twenty-two-year-old contributor Bob Kane queried about Siegel and Shuster's successful Superman feature, Editor Vince Sullivan suggested Kane work up his own costumed character. The following Tuesday, Kane came back with a Batman story. The first Batman story was published in *Detective Comics* #27.

The story had been co-written, or perhaps totally written, by Kane's collaborator, Bill Finger, drawing heavily on pulp roots and a story in *The Shadow* pulp magazine. Finger wrote most of the early Batman stories, and Kane had other assistants and ghosts from very early on ("Detective" 2014). In fact, by 1948 Kane was doing very little of the actual drawing. The first two stories were credited to "Rob't Kane." Thereafter, every single Batman story was credited to "Bob Kane" until 1968. The early comic book publishers could not conceive that the kids reading the stories actually cared who had created them, so the majority of early comic books gave no writer or artist credits. In a few cases, as with Kane, they followed the model of the comic strips, where a single person, usually the artist, received sole credit. Publishers bought a product and they didn't care who assisted or ghosted for the artist they made the check out to. Everyone, including the assistants and ghosts, accepted the practice.

The arrival of Batman firmly established the superhero as a bankable genre for the emerging industry. In short order other imitators would be cashing in on the genre's popularity and a veritable boom in superheroes followed over the next several years. Debuting in 1940, Fawcett Publications' Captain Marvel—as conceived by Bill Parker and C. C. Beck—shared many of Superman's abilities but his adventures were told with a lighter tone and a more cartoonish art style. The Comics featuring Captain Marvel were soon outselling comics with

Superman or Batman. Timely Comics was already having some success with characters they had introduced in 1939: Angel (who wore a costume but had no powers), The Human Torch (an android who could burst into flame and throw fireballs), and Namor the Sub-Mariner (the hot-tempered king of Atlantis who vacillated between hero and villain). In 1941 Joe Simon and Jack Kirby created Captain America for Timely, the company that would eventually be known as Marvel Comics. Also in 1941, Gaines' All-American Publications delivered a version of the superhero for female readers by introducing Wonder Woman, created by William Moulton Marston and drawn by Harry G. Peter.

By the summer of 1941 comic books were selling at the rate of 10 million copies a month. There were more than twenty-nine comic book publishers, and over 150 different titles were being published (Stevenson 2008). By 1943 the US comic book market "totaled 18,000,000 monthly copies, constituting a third of total magazine sales, to a value of $72,000,000" (Ames and Kunzle 2007: 552). It was an incredible number of comic book pages to be produced each month, and the boom would not last indefinitely.

Post-War Popularity and Backlash

In 1946 only one new superhero character was introduced—Marvel's Blonde Phantom. By the end of 1947 circulation on almost all superhero titles began to falter. Even *Captain Marvel Adventures* was down nearly 2.5 million from its 1944 peak of 14 million copies annually (Benton 1993: 39 & 41). However, the comic book industry as a whole was still robust, and it was beginning to diversify. Over the next few years superheroes were overshadowed by a number of genres: funny animals, teen humor, romance comics, westerns, crime comics, and horror comics.

The most consistently popular of these genres, funny animals, began in 1940 with Dell's *Walt Disney Comics and Stories*. The title "lasted for more than forty years and probably achieved the highest overall circulation of any comic book in history" (Benton 1993: 158). In 1941 Dell also licensed the Warner Brothers cartoon characters. Funny animal titles helped Dell grow into the largest comic book company in the world. The funny animal genre also contained some of the best work ever done in the comic book medium. In 1942 Carl Barks began an uncredited twenty-five-year stint writing and drawing hundreds of adventures of ducks (Donald, his nephews, and his very stingy Uncle Scrooge McDuck). These are probably the most frequently reprinted and translated American-made comic book stories, and Barks was eventually credited for his work due to efforts by fans and scholars. Barks' material achieved particularly large and enduring audiences in Europe, where Disney comics magazines continued to be exceptionally popular well into the twenty-first century laying claim to more than half the worldwide comics market (Arthur 2007).

The longest-lasting of the diversification attempts of the 1940s began in 1941, influenced by the popularity of the *Andy Hardy* teen films of the period. Without any superpowers beyond the ability to stay forever young and foolish, Archie Andrews and his Riverdale friends would hold the record for continuous publication only exceeded in comics by Superman and Batman.

Romance comics got their start in 1947. Significantly, it was the team of Joe Simon and Jack Kirby, who had honed their craft in the studio system before making their name with superhero comics such as Captain America, that produced *Young Romance* #1. It took a few years for romance comics to find an audience, but they reached a peak of popularity in 1950 when they accounted for more than a quarter of the entire comic book market.

A short boom in western comics occurred in 1948. Western comics dated back to the late 1930s when there had been a few short-lived western comic books, but the genre took off in the early 1940s, with books devoted to movie cowboys like Gene Autry and Hopalong Cassidy. By 1948, Fawcett's *Hopalong Cassidy* was selling over 8 million copies annually. Noting this success, other publishers began introducing their own cowboy characters. DC even converted the superhero title *All-Star Comics* into *All-Star Western* to capitalize on the audience's newfound interest.

Yet the real comic book boom of 1948 occurred with crime comics. In 1942, Lev Gleason Publications had changed his flagship title, *Silver Streak Comics*, into the first monthly crime comic book, *Crime Does Not Pay*. Initially, the circulation was barely over 200,000 (a lackluster figure for the time) (Benton 1993: 125, 155). However, circulation climbed steadily until the book was selling over 1.5 million copies a month in 1948. Gleason's book had a slow and steady rise to success, but for the rest of the comic book industry, the crime comic burst onto the scene suddenly and with dramatic results. The ten crime comic book titles of 1947 were joined by twenty-three new crime titles—ten of them beginning with the word *crime* or *criminal*—in 1948 (Stevenson 2008). Even family-friendly Dell attempted to tap into the trend with *Dick Tracy Comics*. Virtually every publisher had at least one crime comic book in 1948.

Crime comic books got a great deal of attention that year. In July, a medical symposium on "The Psychopathology of Comic Books" was presided over by Dr. Fredric Wertham, the senior psychiatrist for the New York Department of Hospitals. Citizens' groups formed to push for regulation or banning of comic books. Some towns even held comic book burnings in order to exorcise the threat of crime comics from their communities.

In response to these concerns, a few publishers, including William Gaines of EC, formed the Association of Comics Magazine Publishers (ACMP) in July 1948. They created a code of standards and an ACMP seal to be put on comic book covers. However, the majority of publishers simply ignored the ACMP, and it soon faded away. Most publishers were not worried about a bit of public outcry. After all, business was booming. A record 425 titles were published in 1948, and that shot up to 592 titles in 1949 and 696 in 1952 (Stevenson 2008). But the media attention did not go away. ABC radio broadcast the program "What's Wrong with Comics?" The Cincinnati Committee on the Evaluation of Comic Books published the findings of their study in the February 1950 *Parents Magazine*. They concluded that 70 percent of comic books contained objectionable material.

EC Comics' "New Trend"

The concerned citizens in Cincinnati and elsewhere must have been appalled by the comic books that appeared later in 1950. William Gaines had inherited the newly renamed Entertaining Comics in 1947 when his father, M. C. Gaines, died in a boating accident. William began reshaping the small line of comics. Soon *Tiny Tot Comics* and *Animal Fables* were replaced by *Crime Patrol* and *Saddle Justice*. The new books seemed to have a bit more market appeal, but Gaines was still not satisfied. So, he decided to shake things up. In

1950, with the help of Editor-writer-artist Al Feldstein, Gaines launched the EC "New Trend" line of comic books: *The Vault of Horror*, *The Haunt of Fear*, *Weird Science*, *Weird Fantasy*, *Crime SuspenStories*, *Two-Fisted Tales*, and *Crypt of Terror* (which was later renamed *Tales from the Crypt*).

The EC line of comics was intelligently written, wonderfully drawn, and as gory as hell. EC historian E. B. Boatner says,

> EC horror opened new vistas of death from sources previously unimagined by the reader. Victims were serial-sectioned by giant machines, eaten by ghouls, devoured by rats—from inside and out—pecked by pigeons, stuffed down disposals, skewered on swords, buried alive, dismembered and used as baseball equipment, hung as living clappers in huge bells, made into sausage and soap, dissolved, southern-fried, hacked by maniacs in Santa Claus suits, and offed in unusually high percentages by their wives or husbands (qtd. in Slade 1999).

The readers, many of them older than the average reader of a few years before, seemed to love it. EC had the strongest fan following the industry had yet seen. Some of these self-styled "EC fan-addicts" started the first fan-produced magazines. EC was helping to fuel the incredible growth of the comic book industry. By 1954, the presses were churning out 150 million books every month. At the beginning of the year there were over 600 different titles being published (Benton 1993: 53). But 1954 was a turning point. The comic book industry had reached its peak and was about to plummet downhill.

Backlash Against Comic Books

It is doubtful the American public had ever confused comic books with literature, but at least for the first decade of its existence, the public did seem to be rather accepting of the new medium. That benign attitude began to erode in the late 1940s as articles about the pernicious effects of comic books began to appear in popular magazines such as *Collier's* (March 1948), *Reader's Digest* (August 1948), and *Ladies' Home Journal* (November 1953). The negative publicity came to a crescendo in 1954 with the publication of Fredric Wertham's book *Seduction of the Innocent: The Influence of Comic Books on Today's Youth*. Although later reviews of his papers established that his research was deeply flawed (Tilley 2012), Wertham's book fueled fears that comic books were one of the causes of juvenile delinquency. Actually, since not that many Americans read books, Wertham's message reached more people by way of an excerpt that appeared in *Ladies' Home Journal*.

In the spring of 1954, a Senate Subcommittee to Investigate Juvenile Delinquency in the United States held hearings on the effects of comic books, and Dr. Wertham was called as the star witness. They also called EC publisher William Gaines. While most of the comics industry professionals who testified admitted that there had been excesses and declared that comic books had to be made more suitable for children, Gaines remained rather defiant. When confronted by Senator Estes Kefauver with a cover that showed a man with a bloody axe in one hand holding the severed head of a woman in the other, Gaines maintained that the cover would only be in bad taste if the man was "holding the head a little higher so that the blood could be seen dripping from it" (Goulart 1991: 216). None of the senators seemed to agree with this aesthetic judgment. The Subcommittee concluded that American kids

Figure 10.11 A crowd cheerfully burns stacks of comic books at a rally in Binghamton, NY, in 1948. St. Patrick's Academy yearbook, Vincent Hawley collection, courtesy of David Hajdu.

were being fed "a concentrated diet of crime, horror, and violence" that had to be eliminated (Kefavuer 1955: 32). While most parents did not read Wertham's pedantic book or watch the boring hearings, they could hardly avoid the basic message that filtered through the mass media: Comic books are bad for children (Figure 10.11).

In response to the rising criticism, comic book publishers established the self-regulatory Code of the Comics Magazine Association of America on October 25, 1954. This time most of the publishers joined the association. According to the Code, "all scenes of horror, excessive bloodshed, gory or gruesome crimes, depravity, lust, sadism, [and] masochism shall not be permitted." The Code even prohibited using the words *horror* or *terror* in a title. The public outcry provided an opportunity for publishers like Dell, DC, and Archie, who were putting out relatively unobjectionable material, to eliminate some of their competitors who were specializing in crime and horror comics (Figure 10.12).

Figure 10.12 The Seal of the Comics Code let parents know that a comic book had passed the censors, but its adoption meant that the entire industry began pandering to juvenile content.

The comic book industry fell on hard times in the latter half of the 1950s for a number of different reasons, some of them unrelated to the anti-comic book crusade. For one thing, it was during the fifties that television became the dominant mass medium. At the beginning of the decade, television sets were in barely 10 percent of the homes in

America, but by the end of it, 90 percent of American homes had at least one television. Reading in general declined as people's fascination with television grew. And certainly kids had less incentive to spend 10 cents of their allowance on a comic book when they could follow the televised adventures of Robin Hood and Zorro for free.

The thinning of the ranks of comic book publishers was due in part to a natural boom-and-bust cycle. The profits of the so-called "Golden Age" of comics had attracted more publishers than the market could support. Even though enthusiasm for superheroes had waned in the post-war years, publishers found other genres—romance and westerns, then crime and horror—to fill the void. The industry as a whole remained strong in 1954, with 625 comic book titles and an annual revenue of $90 million (Stevenson 2008; Benton 1993: 53). New titles were still flooding the market, but sales of individual titles were down significantly from the previous decade, and new publishers came and went quickly. A number of publishers did fold after the imposition of the Code, but most of those were recent start-ups that had tried to capitalize on the very trends that the Code banned. The only major publisher that left the comic book business specifically due to the Code was EC. And although EC had to cancel all of its crime and horror titles, they managed to stay in business for a couple more years by switching to the so-called "New Direction" comics, such as *Aces High* and *Psychoanalysis*. However, comic circulation went down pretty much across the board. By 1957 there were 150 fewer titles on the stands than in 1954 (Stevenson 2008). The comic book industry was definitely slowing down.

Throughout the 1950s, comic book publishers would focus their resources on briefly popular genres, only to abandon them as sales faltered and shift their resources to the next "hot" genre. After having to leave behind crime, horror, television comics, and other genres, the major publishers found a familiar last line of defense. By the early 1960s, most of the industry was making a gradual return to the concept that had spawned the Golden Age of comic books—the superhero.

The Superhero Reborn

The return to superheroes was tentative. Atlas had tried it first in 1954 with revivals of Sub-Mariner, the Human Torch, and Captain America. The Human Torch and Captain America comics only lasted for three issues each. These characters were popular during the Second World War, but without the threat of the Axis powers, the characters needed a new raison d'être. And publisher Martin Goodman had never been timid about having his characters enter the fray of current events. On the cover of his own book, Cap was billed as "Captain America . . . Commie Smasher." This attempt to revive superheroes and profit from the "red scare" was derailed by the "comic book scare" that was reaching a crescendo in 1954 with the Senate Subcommittee hearings.

It was, however, the industry's establishment of self-censorship that once more made superheroes an attractive genre for publishers. The sanitized violence and moral purity of superhero comic books might not have been as titillating as the sexy and gory books of the early fifties, but they were a good fit with the standards of the new Comics Code. In late 1955 DC introduced their first new superhero in years, the Martian Manhunter, as a backup feature in *Detective Comics*. While this visitor from Mars had plenty of superpowers, he operated more as a detective than a superhero in his early stories. It would take a new twist on an old hero to get the superhero revival going.

Schwartz and the Fans

The true flashpoint of the superhero revival was *Showcase* #4 in 1956, when DC attempted a revival of a character that had bowed out five years prior: the Flash. Unlike Atlas' earlier approach to reviving the same character, DC, under the editorial guidance of Julius "Julie" Schwartz, experimented with reviving the *concept* of the Flash. This Flash had similar powers to his predecessor, but a different identity and costume. By 1959, sales of the Flash's trial runs in *Showcase* warranted his continued adventures, and an emboldened Schwartz attempted a second revival, this time with a makeover of Green Lantern. Both characters benefited by a pervasive sense of modernity in their new incarnations: Flash's secret identity was now a forensic police scientist (predating their presence on television by two decades) and Green Lantern a test pilot (modeled on Chuck Yeager, a then-current celebrity). Spurred on by a second success, Schwartz pursued reviving the concept of the superhero team, first piloted by DC in the 1940s with the Justice Society of America in the pages of *All-Star Comics*. Schwartz opted to update both the team's name—changing "society" to "league" with the same instinct for currency—and its roster. Along with his two new stars, the Flash and Green Lantern, Schwartz added the Martian Manhunter and stalwart characters Aquaman and Wonder Woman. Superman and Batman were also members, but they were largely consigned to cameo roles in the group's earliest adventures. In 1960 the Justice League of America debuted in the pages of *The Brave and the Bold* #28, and in 1961 *Justice League of America* became the best-selling new title of the year. There was no denying that the superhero revival was in full bloom.

In addition to his wizardry for revitalizing stale properties, Schwartz was also a supporter of the emerging comics fandom. **Fans** are audience members who communicate their devotion, and Schwartz understood them, as he himself had been an early organizer among science fiction fans. He took the time to respond to fan letters, to help fans connect with one another, and ultimately to support their gatherings at conventions. Doing so helped these fans feel a connection to each other and to the men who created the comic books they loved.

The Marvels

In the comic book industry, what works well for one publisher is usually soon copied by other publishers, and if there was ever a publisher who could follow a trend, it was Atlas Comics' Goodman. According to legend, Goodman was on a golf outing with DC's publisher, Jack Liebowitz, and Liebowitz happened to mention the sales success of *Justice League*, which got Goodman going. (Whether that legendary exchange happened or not, Goodman would hardly need such a tip, as most of the publishers kept an eye on what was working for the competition.) Goodman directed his lone editor, Stan Lee, to come up with a team of superheroes. For years, Lee had been putting out stories about huge monsters with names like Moomba and Fin Fang Foom, and after twenty years in the business he had grown tired of the routine. According to Lee's account, because he was ready to quit anyway, his wife Joan encouraged Lee to write the kind of comic he *wanted* to write. And that's what inspired Lee, in collaboration with artist Jack Kirby, to try something different with the Fantastic Four.

Fantastic Four #1 debuted in 1961 and featured a take on superheroes that was very different from anything DC was putting out. Superficially, these superheroes had no secret identities, they (initially) wore no costumes, and one of their members was the grotesquely misshapen Thing. Upon closer inspection, readers would discover characters who bickered among themselves, struggled with self-esteem issues, and had financial woes. Lee explains, "The characters would be the kind of characters I could personally relate to: They'd be flesh and blood, they'd have their faults and foibles, they'd be fallible and feisty, and—most important of all—inside their colorful, costumed booties they'd have feet of clay" (1974: 17). This was a marked departure from DC's heroes. DC tended to focus on plot development at the expense of characterization, and as a result, the DC heroes all had "essentially the same personality" and spoke in "the same carefully measured sentences" (Wright 2001: 185). The appeal of Marvel was this more human approach to its heroes.

Lee and Kirby began to turn out flawed heroes one after another. In 1962 they unleashed scientist Bruce Banner's dark side in *The Incredible Hulk*. Then a frail doctor was transformed into the Mighty Thor in the pages of *Journey into Mystery*. But the quintessential Marvel hero came from Lee in collaboration with another artist, Steve Ditko. Lee proposed making a teenager the lead instead of merely the sidekick, but publisher Goodman was lukewarm to the idea and it got relegated to the last issue of a series that was about to be canceled. *Amazing Fantasy* #15 introduced the world to Peter Parker, a teen bookworm who gains the powers of a spider while at a science demonstration. Instead of using his powers to jump immediately into crime fighting, Peter launches into a career in showbiz as the Amazing Spider-Man. His initial pride in his newfound station is squelched, though, when an irresponsible act on his part leads to the death of his Uncle Ben. He then vows to use his abilities for good, and, despite his best intentions, begins a life complicated by an aunt in fragile health, difficulty in making ends meet, and the jealous wrath of a newspaper publisher out to defame him. The problems Peter Parker faced out of costume spoke to his audience, and, perhaps better than any superhero before him, they could identify with Spider-Man. (**Identification** occurs when audiences can see themselves in a character.) The "web-slinger" had problems with family, romance, and money, which seemed like the same problems many of his adolescent readers were facing. As one fan noted, "I *especially* liked Peter Parker being an average guy who is rejected by the in-crowd at school because he had brains. Now here was a comic book character with whom I could identify! If this was Marvel, I wanted more" (Schelly 2001: 42) (Figure 10.13).

And so did a lot of other fans. As Marvel's superheroes grew increasingly popular, Lee and his stable of artists—including Kirby, Ditko, Don Heck, Larry Lieber, and Bill Everett—soon introduced Iron Man, the Avengers, and a revived Captain America. Then came the X-Men, Doctor Strange, and Daredevil. Marvel Comics was gaining fans in part because of the connection readers were making with the characters inside the comics, and in part because they had a favorable conception of the people making those comics. "One reason for the success of the new Marvels, besides the generally high quality of the art and writing, was that Stan Lee created a personality cult around himself. Where DC Comics were edited by a generally faceless lot of men whose names were unknown to the general public, Lee *was* Marvel" (Thompson 1970: 29). Lee addressed the reader in his captions, he developed a "Bullpen Bulletins" page to highlight the goings-on in the Marvel offices, and he hit the college lecture circuit. "For the first ten to fifteen years of Marvel's existence, Lee and his company were selling more than just comic books. They were selling a participatory world for readers, a way of life for its true believers" (Pustz 1999: 56).

Marvel did not actually achieve dominance in the market until the early seventies. In the meantime, prompted perhaps by the phenomenon of the *Batman* television series (1966–8),

Figure 10.13 Stan Lee's prose and Steve Ditko's pose capture the angst of a teenage superhero from *Amazing Spider-Man* #4 (1963). © 2023 Marvel Entertainment, Inc. and its subsidiaries.

plenty of other competitors attempted to jump on the superhero bandwagon, but none of them quite captured either DC's inventiveness or Marvel's humanity. Archie attempted to revive some of its wartime characters like the Shield; Charlton unleashed its "Action Heroes" line, including *Captain Atom*; and Tower Comics introduced Wally Wood's *T.H.U.N.D.E.R. Agents*, which attempted to cross the spy craze in film and television with the superhero craze in comics. Dell, American Comics Group, and even Harvey Comics all jumped on the bandwagon as well, but to short-lived success. By the end of the decade, most of the competitors had moved on to other genres, leaving DC and Marvel the dominant publishers in superhero fare.

The Underground Rises

The rise of other companies attempting to compete with DC and Marvel in the superhero market was not the only significant development for comic books in the 1960s. As we might expect for this fabled decade, something more radical began to happen to comic books as both a medium and an art form.

Spontaneously across America, creative and unconventional young people who had grown up reading the genre fantasies mass-produced by the traditional comic book publishers began to make their own comics. A number of these comics first appeared in college humor magazines and counterculture newspapers. Even when they were published in the familiar pamphlet format, they did not compete with traditional comic books on the newsstands but developed a distribution system of alternative bookstores, record stores, and head shops. The content and even the style of the artwork were a conscious rebellion against the Comics Code restrictions, editorial policies, and genre formulas of traditional comic books. These convention-defying, politically charged, and independently produced comics became known as **underground comix**. As individuals and small presses began to produce alternatives to their products, the traditional, mostly New York-based, publishers became known as the **mainstream**.

The underground comix movement has its roots in the crude little sex comics known as eight-pagers or **Tijuana Bibles**, although there is no proof any were actually produced in Tijuana. The creators of these wallet-sized sex romps had to be much more underground than the comix artist of the 1960s because the eight-pagers were illegal due to both obscenity violations and copyright infringement. The Tijuana Bibles depicted—in graphic detail—celebrities, political figures, or fictional characters using obscene language and enjoying a wide variety of sex acts, some of which were illegal at the time. By far the favorite subjects were characters from the newspaper comic strips (e.g., Popeye finds himself in a threesome with Olive Oyl and Wimpy). If any of the creators of these eight-pagers had been found, surely they would have been both sued and jailed. Cartoonist Art Spiegelman believes that while the eight-pagers did not directly inspire his fellow underground comix artists in the 1960s, "the comics that galvanized my generation—the early *Mad*, the horror and science fiction comics of the fifties—were mostly done by guys who had been in their turn warped by those little books" (1997: 5).

While the underground comix were uninhibited and willfully shocking in the tradition of the sex comics that had existed on the fringes of society, at least a part of their financial success was due to a mainstream comics publisher, Marvel Comics. Underground comix found their most avid fans among college-age readers. Reading comics had been primarily an adolescent or pre-adolescent pastime for decades, but Marvel began to cultivate an older audience just a few years before the undergrounds made the scene. By the mid-sixties, the adventures of Spider-Man, the Hulk, and Doctor Strange were becoming popular on college campuses.

It is likely that the twenty-something comic book reader of the late sixties did not make a clear distinction between mainstream and underground comics. A college-age fan's stack of reading material might have included Marvel's *Doctor Strange* and DC's *Strange Adventures* (featuring Neal Adams' Deadman), along with *Snatch Comics* and *Radical America Komiks*. If Marvel had not already made reading comics hip, there might not have been as many young people ready to go along for the ride when the undergrounds made reading comix rebellious.

The taproot of the undergrounds goes back to another New York-based, but somewhat less than traditional, mainstream publisher. Those science fiction and horror comics Spiegelman claimed galvanized his generation were mostly from William Gaines' infamous EC line that included *Vault of Horror*, *Crime SuspenStories*, and *Mad*. The gore, violence, sensuality, and occasional political commentary strained against and often violated the boundaries of what was considered good taste until EC became the primary target of the newly created Comics Code Authority (CCA). When most of Gaines' titles were denied Code approval and distributors refused to carry them, EC stayed afloat on the back of one title begun in 1952: *Mad*.

By the time the Comics Code had forced the horror and crime titles off the newsstands, *Mad* had been converted from comic book to magazine format. Magazines were not subject to CCA approval and were treated differently by distributors. Sales steadily increased, and by the early 1970s, *Mad* magazine was selling 2.5 million copies an issue (Sabin 1993: 167). However, it was *Mad* the comic book, in particular those early issues edited by Harvey Kurtzman, that planted the seeds from which the underground comix sprouted like wild cannabis. Underground comix historian Mark Estren says Kurtzman is the "person most often cited by the underground cartoonists as a major influence on their consciousness and their style" (1993: 294), and the underground's leading light, Robert Crumb, has referred to Kurtzman as his hero (1988: 5). Kurtzman's satire in those first twenty-eight issues of *Mad* skewered pop culture icons from Tarzan to James Dean, and revealed the fundamental fallacies of our national myths. "Kurtzman is the man who decisively determined the style of humour and satire in the USA after 1950" (Reitberger and Fuchs 1971/1972: 218).

The Underground Digs In

Humor magazines had been a tradition at larger universities for decades, but when the teenagers who had grown up reading *Mad* arrived at college in the late1950s and early 1960s, they reinvigorated campus humor with biting satire and radical views that often led to clashes with university administrators. With a circulation of over 12,000, the *Texas Ranger,* published at the University of Texas in Austin, was among the most successful college humor magazines. It was also central to the genesis of the underground comix.

Gilbert Shelton graduated from the University of Texas in 1961, but when he received his pre-induction notice he decided he had better return to UT as a graduate student to get a draft deferment. With the September 1962 issue (vol. 77, no.1), Shelton took over as editor of the *Texas Ranger*. The comix revolution was underway. Multi-page comics featuring the adventures of Shelton's superhero parody, Wonder Wart-Hog, appeared in all but one of the *Texas Ranger* issues Shelton edited. Wonder Wart-Hog became the first underground comix "hit." Just weeks before his series debuted in the *Texas Ranger*, the "Hog of Steel" was presented to a national audience in the pages of *Help!* and a profile in *Mademoiselle* magazine.

Figure 10.14 Gilbert Shelton's *Fabulous Furry Freak Brothers* would eventually become the best known and most widely marketed characters from the underground comix. © 1971, Gilbert Shelton.

After his one-year stint as editor, Shelton stayed with the *Texas Ranger* for another year as art director. Shelton and his friends must have felt a bit stifled under the new editor, who quickly phased out the Wart-Hog comics. In January 1964 Shelton, Jack Jackson, and Tony Bell published the first issue of *THE Austin Iconoclastic Newsletter* (known simply as *THE*). *THE* ran for five issues as a newsletter, then, starting in the summer of 1964, was a magazine for two issues. At only four pages, the first newsletter was sparse on content, but historically important for the inclusion of the one-page comic "The Adventures of J" by Frank Stack. Though never called by name, J is obviously Jesus; the characters are dressed in Biblical attire and J is popular at a wedding feast because he turns the water into wine. Shelton collected about a dozen of the Jesus strips, convinced another student to run off fifty sets on the Law School Library photo copier, and began passing out the stapled fourteen-page "comic book," *The Adventures of Jesus*. Stack, as editor of the *Texas Ranger* for the 1958–9 academic year, had published a few of sophomore Gilbert Shelton's cartoons, and now Shelton was returning the favor by making Stack's creation into what many consider the first underground comic book.

1964 was also a landmark year for another former *Texas Ranger* staffer. In the fifth issue of *THE*, the following ad appeared: "Have you got your copy of *God Nose Adult Comix* yet? Available exclusively at The Id Coffee House—407 W. 24." *God Nose* was by Jack Jackson, with assistance from Pat Massey and Lieuen Adkins. In his job at the State Comptroller's office, Jackson often had coffee in the capitol cafeteria with some of the guys who ran the state government print shop down in the basement. Jackson supplied the paper, including purple construction paper for the cover, and between jobs and after hours his print shop buddies ran off a thousand copies of the forty-two-page *God Nose* comic book (Wheat 2006: 272). Because Jackson did not want to lose his government job, he signed the *God Nose* book Jaxon, the nickname Shelton had coined for the notes he left his friend around the *Ranger* office. The main character of the comic was a short, large-nosed supreme being who had misadventures in the world of the foolish humans he had created.

God Nose and *The Adventures of Jesus* are the two leading candidates for the "first" underground comic book, among other contenders. And if you consider work in formats other than a stand-alone booklet, the origins of the undergrounds are extremely murky. Underground comix in the standard comic book format, or at least resembling it, did not appear until near the end of the decade, but scores of edgy, obscene, and antiauthoritarian comics were published in college humor magazines and underground newspapers throughout the 1960s. A number of these papers formed the Underground Press Syndicate and shared features, giving aspiring cartoonists wider exposure.

One such cartoonist, Robert Crumb, had been making comic books and fanzines since the age of eight and saw the underground newspapers as a promising venue for his work. In 1967 he began taking LSD and filling sketchbooks in a feverish outpouring of bizarre ideas. Virtually all of the characters for which he became famous—Mr. Natural, the Vulture Demoness, Eggs Ackley, and Angelfood McSpade—were conceived during this period. Even most of the underground press didn't know what to make of Crumb's bizarre visions, but the Philadelphia-based underground newspaper *Yarrowstalks* published a couple of his strips in its first two issues during the summer of 1967. *Yarrowstalks* editor Brian Zahn made the third issue an all-Crumb issue, and at about the same time, New York's *East Village Other* newspaper began to regularly publish Crumb's strips. Energized by the growing acceptance of his work (and quite a few drugs), Crumb produced another book's worth of strips, including "Whiteman" and a page of uncharacteristically lighthearted "Keep on Truckin'" images that were destined to make their way into mainstream culture. He just needed to find someone willing to publish the book.

Crumb's work was already beginning to garner him fans, and two of those fans, underground newspaper publisher Don Donahue and printer Charles Plymell, were anxious to publish Crumb's new work, which they did as *Zap Comix* #1 (1968). While Crumb and his wife Dana made their way through the streets of San Francisco selling copies of *Zap* out of a baby carriage, Donahue sold the majority of the print run to Third World Distribution. "From there they went all over the country," explained Donahue. "The hippie vendors from all over the Bay Area went there to pick up their stuff" (qtd. in Rosenkranz 2011: 71). Within a couple of months, Donahue had to do a second printing, and soon copies of *Zap* were showing up in head shops and record stores across the nation. By the fall of 1968 Robert Crumb was a minor celebrity, and the acclaim from *Zap* led to opportunities that made him a major celebrity. He turned down an offer to do a Rolling Stones album cover, but when Janis Joplin herself asked, he did a front and back cover for Big Brother and the Holding Company's *Cheap Thrills* album. Crumb was only paid $600 for the work, but it became one of the most collectible album covers of all time. Toward the end of the year, Viking Press published a slightly censored sampling of his work from 1965 to 1968 in *R. Crumb's Head Comix*. Crumb's growing fame fueled the growth of underground comix in general (Figure 10.15).

Figure 10.15 Robert Crumb became the star of the underground movement. A panel from Robert Crumb's: "Can the mind know it?" © 2014 R. Crumb. Courtesy of Fantagraphics Books.

Much like the mainstream comic book industry had flourished following the success of Superman, within a few years of the appearance of *Zap*, undergrounds had developed into a strong alternate comics industry, complete with a Berkeley Comix Convention in 1973. At the peak of the underground phenomenon in 1973, there were over 300 comix titles in print, with nearly as many people referring to themselves as underground cartoonists (Rosenkranz 2011: 4), and the average book sold 40,000 copies (Raeburn 2004: 35).

Comix not only defied the sources of authority in conventional society by breaking their taboos, but they also went on a direct attack. Authority figures are presented as inept or brutish and always corrupt. The structures of society, institutions, and bureaucracies, are portrayed as soulless and oppressive. As German media critics Rheinhold Reitberger and Wolfgang Fuchs correctly observed from their outside perspective, "the underground cartoonists and their creations attack all that middle America holds dear" (1971/1972: 219) (Figure 10.16).

Reinventing the Market

Marvel and DC entered the seventies with faltering superhero sales and a slight but growing competition from underground comix and the magazine-format horror comics that were unfettered by Code restrictions. This sent the Big Two scrambling to find the next big thing, and they often attempted to adapt to whatever current trend in popular culture was selling. For example, when interest in martial arts hit Hollywood, the comic book industry began to produce kung-fu features like Marvel's *Master of Kung Fu* (debuting in 1973). As sword-and-sorcery books boomed, the comics industry experimented with adapting that genre, the most successful of which was unquestionably Roy Thomas and Barry Smith's interpretation of Robert E. Howard's *Conan the Barbarian* (1970). Following the lead of magazine publishers Warren and Skywald, who were publishing popular black-and-white magazines, the industry returned to publishing horror comics, revising the Comics Code in 1971 to allow for the inclusion of vampires, ghouls, and werewolves as long as they were "handled in the classic tradition" of "high calibre literary works." Marvel's entries included *The Tomb of Dracula* (1972) and *Werewolf by Night* (1972), but perhaps the most important new horror character developed at this time was DC Comics' Swamp Thing. Debuting in a short story by Len Wein and Bernie Wrightson in the horror anthology *House of Secrets* in 1972, Swamp Thing would return in his own ongoing series later in the seventies and again in the eighties. Under the guidance of British author Alan Moore, *The Saga of the Swamp Thing* was one of the most influential titles of the 1980s, showcasing Moore's sophisticated approach to storytelling.

Figure 10.16 While men like Shelton and Crumb may have achieved recognition beyond the underground community, men were not the only pioneers in the movement. At a time when few females worked in mainstream comics, *Wimmen's Comix* debuted in 1972 and became a significant outlet for the creative expression of female cartoonists in the decades to follow. Cover of issue #14 by Trina Robbins and used with permission.

Despite a downturn in their popularity, superheroes still made up the bulk of comic book titles at this time, and several high points demonstrated that they were still a viable mode for storytelling. Jack Kirby had left Marvel Comics in 1970 for the chance to exercise greater editorial control over his stories at DC. His first project there was a magnum opus, a series of four interrelated ongoing comic book series: *New Gods*, *Forever People*, *Mister Miracle*, and *Superman's Pal*, *Jimmy Olsen*. The story focused on the clash of opposing gods of light and darkness whose ages-old conflict opens a new chapter on Earth. Kirby's "Fourth World" titles would be canceled or reassigned before he could finish the story the way he originally intended, but the New Gods would be integral players in the DC Universe in decades to come. More important than the effect of Kirby's characters on the fictional world, was the effect of the scale of his creative vision on his successors. The Fourth World was the first attempt by a comics creator to construct a complex mythos designed to feature multiple titles, cosmic-scale calamities, and largely unprecedented storytelling techniques. The aspirations Kirby introduced would become frequently used tools of the trade over the ensuing decades.

A more immediate, but no less enduring, success would debut in 1975, when Len Wein and Dave Cockrum re-launched Marvel's *X-Men* series, which had faltered and been canceled in 1970. This time around, though, the creative team didn't simply resurrect the same five Anglo-American teenagers in the lead roles but instead recruited a cast of international characters, including an African woman, a Japanese man, and a Russian teen. Wein ended up stepping aside for another author, Chris Claremont, and Cockrum left thereafter to be replaced by artist John Byrne. Claremont and Byrne became one of the most highly regarded collaborations in the field, and by the decade's end *X-Men* was at the top of the sales charts, a position it rarely relinquished for more than three decades thereafter. The secret to the *X-Men* was both in its popular creative team and in the way it wove the flawed characters and soap opera elements that had been introduced by Marvel in the early sixties together with the attempts to address real-world concerns of the late sixties and early seventies. The *X-Men*'s roster changed (with one member killed in the team's second adventure), the members were often in conflict with one another, and all the while they fought for a world "that feared and hated them" because of their genetic differences. Claremont also became particularly noted for the strength, both physical and emotional, of his female characters, and the diversity of the backgrounds he gave to his cast. Going beyond the inherent metaphor of mutants as an outcast race (which readers frequently saw through the lens of their own experiences as part of a minority, either racially or in terms of their sexual orientation), he brought the history of racism into the work directly. His origin of Magneto, the principal antagonist for the team, connected back to the character's Holocaust experiences as a victim, and made him a textured and tortured person struggling to ensure that "never again" would begin with the survival of the mutants (Figure 10.18).

Figure 10.17 Part of mainstream comic books' innocence died along with Gwen Stacy in the pages of *The Amazing Spider-Man* #121 (1973), in a story penned by Gerry Conway with art by Gil Kane. © 2023 Marvel Entertainment, Inc. and its subsidiaries.

Independents and Alternatives

By the mid-seventies there were only six mainstream comic book publishers—Marvel, DC, Archie, Charlton, Gold Key, and Harvey (and Warren, publishing in a black-and-white magazine format)—and to the majority of comic book fans only Marvel and DC mattered. The term **independent** came to refer to any new publisher that attempted to compete with the established publishers by offering genre fiction comic books intended for a mainstream audience.

The independents came into being through a confluence of creative and industrial factors; creators were attracted by creative freedoms and ownership of their material modeled on the undergrounds, distribution was easily available through the direct market to a small but growing number of comic shops (and based on non-returnable orders, reducing the risks publishers had to take), and printers had available press time caused by the contraction of the mainstream, which for the first time they were willing to sell for shorter runs.

Figure 10.18 This cover of *Giant-Size X-Men* #1 (1975) is etched in the memories of comics fans of a certain age because it was a flashpoint in the history of the American comic book industry. The issue introduced an "all-new, all-different" team of mutant superheroes who would go on to dominate the sales charts for the next several decades. Art by Gil Kane and Dave Cockrum. © 2023 Marvel Entertainment, Inc. and its subsidiaries.

A key example of independent publishing was Eclipse Enterprises. Founded in 1977 by brothers Jan and Dean Mullaney, Eclipse lasted for seventeen years and published 125 different titles, covering virtually every genre. The Mullaney brothers and editor cat yronwode were innovators, taking chances on new formats and daring material, some of which had a lasting impact on American comic books. In 1978 their initial publication was the first graphic novel intended for the emerging comics specialty store market: *Sabre: Slow Fade of an Endangered Species* by Don McGregor and Paul Gulacy. In partnership with Viz Communications, Eclipse brought English translations of Japanese manga to American readers in 1987. That same year, the company pioneered documentary-style comics with "graphic journalism," such as *Real War Stories*, created for the use of the Central Committee for Conscientious Objectors, and *Brought to Light*, an exposé of illegal CIA activities

There were scores of other small publishers with comic books on the market, at least briefly, during the 1980s, like Pacific Comics, Comico, and First Comics, just to name a few. While the overcrowding of the comic book market led to some problems we will examine in a moment, there were also some benefits. The competition from the independent publishers had a positive impact on both the financial and creative practices at the Big Two. Most of these independent publishers paid royalties and allowed creators to retain ownership of their intellectual properties (Figure 10.19). It was not long before DC and Marvel had to offer royalties and at least negotiate ownership rights with the most influential creators. Eventually Marvel and DC created new imprints to publish the type of intelligent, mature material readers had been attracted to in independent offerings. Yet Marvel and DC also treated the independents like farm teams where new talents could prove themselves before trying to break into the majors, and most of the independent publishers and the newcomers who worked for them aspired to join the established mainstream. At the time, there were other cartoonists who were charting a course that took them far from the mainstream, and their efforts did more to revolutionize the art form.

Figure 10.19 Kevin Eastman and Peter Laird conceived of the Teenage Mutant Ninja Turtles as a parody of several popular comic book themes of the day (teenage superheroes, mutants, and ninjas), and doing business as Mirage Studios, they self-published the first comic in May 1984. The Turtles' popularity has transcended comic books as the characters have become a fixture in feature films, animated television programs, video games, toys, and countless licensed products. © 2013 Viacom International Inc. All rights reserved. Nickelodeon, all related titles, characters, and logos are trademarks owned by Viacom Media Networks, a division of Viacom International Inc.

Alternative comic books are usually created by a single cartoonist and present a very personal vision. Many are autobiographical in nature and put more emphasis on the author than on characters. These are self-published or small press works that resist or even satirize the clichés of mainstream genre fiction and valorize their roots in the comix tradition. *Arcade: the Comics Revue* (1975) was conceived by editors Art Spiegelman and Bill Griffith as a means to get comix material on the magazine racks alongside the black-and-white horror magazines (Rosenkranz 2011). The magazine never got distribution beyond the usual underground outlets, and those were dwindling in number by the mid-seventies. After only seven issues, *Arcade* folded, and comics journalist Gary Groth sees *Arcade*'s end as signaling "the last whimper of the underground movement" (Groth 2000: 21). *Arcade* can also be seen not only as "a bridge between the underground and the more experimental approach of *Raw*," but also a transitional publication between underground comix and alternative comics (Sabin and Triggs 2000: 10).

After the hard work and frustration of the *Arcade* experience, Spiegelman swore he would never get involved with producing another magazine, but when he met future wife Françoise Mouly and she suggested they start a comics anthology magazine, he found himself immediately acquiescing. When Spiegelman and Mouly published the first issue of *Raw* in 1981, they thought it might be a one-time venture. It had a print run of only 4,500 but sold out quickly, and both readers and artists who wanted to contribute began asking when the next issue would be published (Rosenkranz 2011: 253). Subsequent issues of *Raw* contained work by such underground stalwarts as S. Clay Wilson and Bill Griffith, as well as emerging alternative cartoonists like Gary Panter and Charles Burns, but the most historically significant aspect of *Raw* was Spiegelman's own contribution. For years Spiegelman had been working on a long-term and very personal project that began as a three-page story in *Funny Aminals* [*sic*] back in 1972. In *Raw* #2 Spiegelman began serializing *Maus* as a mini-comic insert. *Raw*'s bold experimentation with design was an indication that Spiegelman and Mouly aspired to bridge the considerable gap between comics and high art.

In addition to these emerging narratives from domestic talent, there was also increasing awareness of the European tradition among American storytellers. *Heavy Metal* began stateside publication in 1977 and featured translations from *Métal Hurlant*, a French comics magazine that featured science fiction and fantasy stories with explicit adult content. More importantly, it introduced American audiences to the styles of such European talents as Jean Giraud (a.k.a. Mobeius), Jean-Claude Forest, and Milo Manara. Whether domestic or imported, these new varieties of comic books were able to find a substantially different audience than the one that had supported the underground comix, due to a radical change in comic book distribution and marketing that allowed independents, alternatives, and even a few of the residual undergrounds to be sold side-by-side with mainstream comics in a new type of store.

Direct Market

For decades mainstream comic book publishers had taken it for granted that aside from meager subscription sales, the newsstand distribution system was the only way to sell their product. It had always been an inefficient system, and by the 1970s newsstand sales had declined dramatically (Sabin 1993). Bundles of mixed titles were distributed to newsstands, drugstores, and supermarkets, where they were displayed in a haphazard fashion, and each month a large number of unsold issues were returned to distributor warehouses where they were ground into pulp. The system also discouraged many readers from becoming fans because it was difficult to follow a character or storyline when one could not rely on particular titles to be available at the corner store from month to month. Phil Seuling, a Brooklyn high school teacher and comic book fan, had a better idea.

In 1973 Seuling approached all the major publishers with the same deal: If they would give him a 50 percent discount (over time this grew to 60 percent), he would keep the unsold issues rather than returning them for credit (Dean 2006: 51). Seuling had been selling comic books through mail order and at the New York Comic Art Convention, which he had been instrumental in building into the model comic book convention. Unlike the distributors, who cared little and knew less about the comics in their trucks, Seuling knew that during the 1960s, comic book narrative had evolved from stand-alone stories to ongoing soap operas sustained through multiple subplots and crossovers between titles, and he realized most fans were frustrated about not being able to reliably follow the trials and tribulations of their favorite characters. That's why he felt confident he could make money with his scheme. He knew which new titles the fans he dealt with wanted to buy, and any issues not immediately sold would become back-issue stock for the mail order business, which he could eventually sell to fans unable to find those issues at their hometown newsstands.

Seuling was not the only entrepreneurial comics fan in the early seventies. A growing number of teenagers and young adults were using their personal comics collections to set up comic book shops in cheap storefronts or storage sheds in their backyards. Chuck Rozanski, who opened his first store at nineteen and became a Seuling sub-distributor four years later, estimates that in 1974 "there were no more than 30 comics specialty shops throughout the United States and Canada, with another 100 stores that featured comics along with other wares such as books or records" (qtd. in Dean 2006: 51). Seuling, through his newly established Sea Gate Distribution company, offered these retailers a 40 percent discount on new comics—10 to 20 percent better than the newsstand distributors were giving them—and shipped them the precise mix and quantity of titles they needed. As the number of comics shops increased, Seuling set up sub-distributors throughout the country and established what became known as the **Direct Market** system. By the beginning of the 1980s, a number of fans turned retailers turned distributors had challenged Seuling's monopoly and energized the direct market. From fewer than 200 stores in 1974, the comics specialty retail network grew to approximately 3000 stores by the mid-eighties (Dean 2006: 51–4).

Publishers embraced the system. They could take advance orders from retailers and print quantities that more precisely matched demand, and they didn't have to take returns from comic shops; issues that didn't sell within a month or two of their release went into the store's back-issue bins. Marvel created a book, *Dazzler*, to try out a direct-market-only offering. *Dazzler* #1 (1981) sold in excess of 400,000 copies (Sabin 1993: 66). DC followed with limited series, such as *Camelot 3000* (1982), which were aimed at the fan market and began to use better printing, color, and to work outside the limitations of the Comic Code. Limited newsstand distribution and subscription sales continued, but Marvel and DC gradually shifted their marketing efforts to the direct market.

The Direct Market system encouraged other fans to try their hand at publishing, like Pacific Comics, which entered comic book publishing near the end of 1981 and released their first book exclusively for the comics specialty stores. New comic book publishers were not likely to get much rack space if they attempted to compete with the Big Two on the newsstands; those outlets were only interested in carrying proven titles. However, they stood a good chance of getting their product in the comics specialty stores. The fans who ran the comic shops got excited about new characters and concepts, and probably stocked more titles from the upstart publishers than was financially prudent.

It was also an environment that nurtured fans. Stores ordered books based on the tastes of their particular clientele, and fans were almost guaranteed not to miss an issue of their favorite books because retailers used pull lists to put aside each of their regulars' requests as the books arrived each week. On the other hand, the direct market isolated comic books and their readers from mainstream culture, and also isolated comic books from potential new readers. While at first the system seemed perfect for both publishers and fans, there quickly developed what retailer Chuck Rozanski has called "an economic micro-world" and others have referred to as "a superhero ghetto" (qtd. in Dean 2006: 59). The economic health of all segments of the industry—mainstream, independent, and even alternative—became dependent on the Direct Market system, and when the system faltered in the 1990s, the effects would be devastating. In the meantime, comic books would not only explore new markets, but also new genres and formats.

The Rise of the Graphic Novel

In a 1960 lecture to the Bristol Literary Society, novelist John Updike speculated on new forms the novel might take and told the audience, "I see no intrinsic reason why a doubly talented artist might not arise and create a comic-strip novel masterpiece" (Gravett 2006: 8). Updike was not the only person considering the possibility of a more prestigious future for graphic storytelling. Richard Kyle, a prominent and outspoken member of the growing comic book fan community, was aware of the more mature work being produced in European comics and he expressed a desire for similar comics work in America. As early as 1964, Kyle advocated using the terms "graphic story" and "graphic novel" to distinguish serious works from run-of-the-mill newsstand comic books (Schelly 1999: 130). *Graphic novel* was the term that caught on.

Book-format reprints of comics material dated back before the comic books and had been successfully applied to comic book creations beginning with mass-market paperbacks of *Mad* (1954). Original comics material in the format, though, with a level of literary aspiration that could deserve the term novel had been rare, and uniformly commercially unsuccessful, beginning with *Harvey Kurtzman's Jungle Book* (1959).

In 1978 Will Eisner's *A Contract with God*, distributed in both bookstore chains and direct market comic book shops in traditional hardcover and trade paperback formats, garnered wide attention and firmly established *graphic novel* as the term for a longer comics work with literary intent.

Over the past forty years the number of graphic novels in comic books shops and major bookstore chains has steadily increased, due in part to a new generation of alternative cartoonists who, inspired by the work of their underground and independent predecessors, are creating ambitious long-form comics. However, the *graphic novel* section at Barnes & Noble would not be so extensive if not for more Japanese manga reprints being marketed in the United States, and a rather indiscriminate use of the term *graphic novel*. Any work longer than the standard comic book, from Howard Cruse's 210-page hardcover *Stuck Rubber Baby* to a trade paperback collecting seven issues of *Amazing Spider-Man*, might be labeled a "graphic novel" by eager marketers. And nonfiction, such as Joe Sacco's journalism in comics form, finds a home on those shelves as well.

Some comics theorists and critics see the graphic novel label as a burden to the comic book art form. Cartoonist Scott McCloud claims that "in moving from periodical to book, an implicit claim of permanent worth was being made—a claim that had to be justified" (2000: 29). Scholar Charles Hatfield worries that the term "may encourage expectations, positive or negative, that are not borne out by the material itself" (2005: 5). As the 1980s progressed, the comic book industry truly aspired to produce more than mere ephemera, objects that are here today and gone tomorrow. Lending credibility to this aspiration were works that advanced the art of comic books and won attention in the popular press. The three works that engendered the most hope for the future of comics all graced the shelves in what might be the medium's greatest year: 1986.

The Greatest Year

The publication of Art Spiegelman's *Maus: A Survivor's Tale* brought mainstream attention to the potential of comic books to tell stories other than those about superheroes. *Maus* is a memoir about Art trying to relate to his father, Vladek, a survivor of the Holocaust, whose experiences leading up to his internment in a concentration camp are told in flashbacks. The characters, however, are depicted as animals, with the predatory Nazis cast as cats and the persecuted Jews as mice. Spiegelman had actually begun to publish sections of his narrative in underground comix anthology *Funny Aminals* [*sic*] in 1972 and returned to the work in 1977, publishing installments serially in *Raw*. In 1986 he published the collected chapters to much acclaim. While numerous accounts of the Holocaust had been published in the decades since the Second World War, there had never been one quite like *Maus*, and critics took notice. Spiegelman would go on to produce a second volume of the memoir and publish it in 1992. That volume would win a Pulitzer Prize Special Award, the first and only comic book to earn one of publishing's most prestigious prizes.

Given that Spiegelman's work was emerging in the less restrictive confines of the underground movement, it might be expected that his accomplished works would be more artistically than commercially driven. Yet the two other major works of comic's greatest year were issued by a mainstream publisher, DC Comics. In 1986 they had two of the industry's most talented storytellers, Frank Miller and Alan Moore, on projects that took apart the very concept of the superhero.

Frank Miller had already earned a reputation for spinning gritty narratives with his run on Marvel's *Daredevil* series (1979–83) and a mini-series he had done for DC called *Ronin* (1983) when he had the opportunity to create *Batman: The Dark Knight Returns* (1986). The four-part limited series is set several years in the future, where a middle-aged Bruce Wayne finds himself drawn back to his former life as a masked vigilante. His return to crime fighting puts him in conflict with former foes like the Joker and friends like Superman, all in stunning visuals delivered by Miller's pencils, with inks provided by Klaus Janson and a color palette from Lynn Varley. DC even debuted a new square-bound binding for the limited series, calling it "Prestige Format." Miller's take on the Dark Knight drew more attention than the character had received since the campy TV show of the 1960s. Miller brought Batman back to his violent roots and provided a grittier, less sanitized vision of vigilantism. As one critic noted, "the repercussions of this Miller story continue to affect even far less ambitious super-hero tales a decade after its publication" (Nevins 1996: 29). Miller would go on to write a number of special projects for Batman, but his first take on the hero would be his most influential, bearing considerable influence on the darker tone and direction of the film franchise that would debut with Tim Burton's *Batman* (1989).

Like Frank Miller, Alan Moore explores the real-world implications of people dressing up in colorful costumes and taking to the streets to dispense vigilante justice. In late 1986, DC Comics began to publish *Watchmen*, a twelve-issue limited series by Moore in collaboration with artist Dave Gibbons. *Watchmen* is regarded as quite possibly "the most complex and ambitious superhero series ever published" (Wright 2001: 272) due to its layered narrative of plots and subplots all weaving together and leading to an unanticipated climax. Unlike most previous superhero narratives where the protagonists defend the status quo, *Watchmen* features characters—including the Machiavellian Ozymandias and the anti-hero Rorschach—who take steps toward real social change, imposing their vision of what is right upon society, even though doing so comes through amoral means.

Moore had previously explored the horrific side of superheroes running amuck in his *Marvelman* series for the British comics anthology *Warrior* beginning in 1982. Numerous superhero series would explore the trope further, from Mark Gruenwald's *Squadron Supreme* (1985) to Garth Ennis and Darick Robertson's *The Boys* (2006–12). After completing its initial run as a serial, *Watchmen* was reprinted as a trade paperback and marketed as a graphic novel to much critical acclaim and academic analysis. In 2005, *Time* magazine named it one of "the 100 best novels from 1923 to present" alongside such literary luminaries as Harper Lee's *To Kill a Mockingbird* and William Faulker's *The Sound and the Fury* (Figure 10.20).

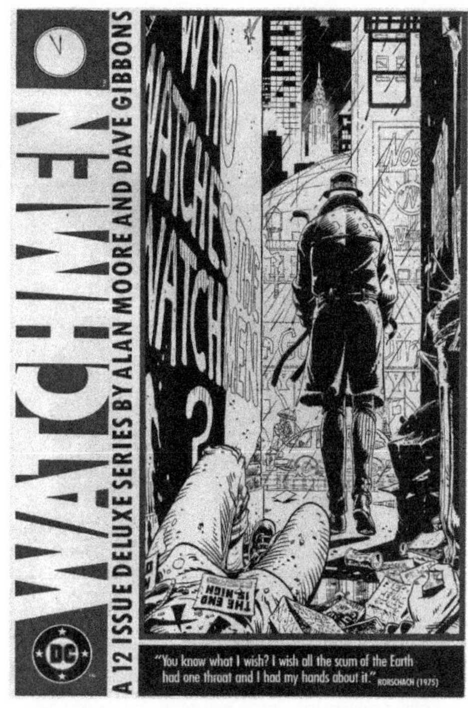

Figure 10.20 DC's house ad for Alan Moore and Dave Gibbons' masterpiece asks, "Who watches the watchmen?" in the aftermath of a violent attack from trench-coated anti-hero Rorschach. Art by Dave Gibbons © DC Comics.

IMPACT OF THE GREATEST YEAR

The three titles that made 1986 comics' greatest year, *Maus*, *Batman: The Dark Knight Returns*, and *Watchmen* each debuted in serial formats but have remained in print since each was published in collected editions. While European comics had a long tradition of publishing so-called albums of comics, such as the Belgian creator Hergé's *Tintin*, collected editions were a rarity in American comics at this time. However, the unparalleled critical and commercial success of the three titles led to their republication in multiple editions, such that none of them have gone out of print since. The enduring demand for these works by the public and by the bookstores and libraries that would stock them and other trades would form a cornerstone in the expanding comics marketplace beyond the newsstand or comic book specialty store. In addition, the darker heroes of *Batman: The Dark Knight Returns* and *Watchmen* were at the forefront of a wave of anti-heroes who grew steadily more popular in the mainstream as the eighties ended and the nineties began. Writer Chris Claremont and a number of collaborators (beginning with none other than Frank Miller) unleashed the feral mutant Wolverine from the X-Men ensemble and turned him into a comics superstar, well known for cutting and impaling his foes with his razor-sharp claws. And the Punisher, who had been created by Gerry Conway as an antagonist for Spider-Man, resurfaced as the lead in his own popular series. In fact, by the early 1990s the gun-toting, death-dealing vigilante starred in three monthly magazines of his own, making him almost as visible a property in the comics as Spider-Man, Superman, and Batman.

Moore also proved to be just one successful import from the UK. Earlier Barry Windsor-Smith cracked the international divide when he was hired to produce the art for Marvel's *Conan the Barbarian* in 1970. By the 1980s, a whole crop of British talent found themselves recruited, especially when DC Comics began to hire talents like artists Brian Bolland (*Camelot 3000*) and Dave Gibbons (*Green Lantern*). Since the critical and commercial success of *Watchmen*, imported talents from the British Isles have had considerable impact on the American comics mainstream. These talents include writers like Neil Gaiman (*Sandman*), Warren Ellis (*The Authority*), Mark Millar (*Civil War*), and Grant Morrison (*JLA*). DC launched its Vertigo imprint in 1993 under the editorial guidance of Karen Berger, building on its edgier titles like *Swamp Thing* and *Sandman* before going on to release a number of successful creator-owned series, from Garth Ennis and Steve Dillon's *Preacher* (1995) to Brian K. Vaughan and Pia Guerra's *Y: The Last Man* (2002).

Celebrity status was being given to more and more creators at this time, such that they could parlay that fame into actual wealth. In 1992 Image Comics emerged when a group of artists sought to win for themselves a larger share of the profit that their talents were generating for America's largest comic book publisher. No company profited more from the expansion of the comics market in the early 1990s than Marvel, and while Marvel long held that it was its stable of attractive characters that drew its audience, it certainly owed a portion of its market share to the talents of the creators who breathed life into those characters. Marvel recognized these creators' influence and capitalized on their appeal. In 1990, they gave artist Todd McFarlane his own *Spider-Man* #1, which sold almost 3 million copies. Another artist, Rob Liefeld, helped sell 5 million copies of *X-Force* #1 in 1991. A few months after that, the Jim Lee-drawn *X-Men* #1 set new industry records by selling 8 million copies. Such massive sales, coupled with lucrative licensing of the original artwork, generated a lot of profit for Marvel, but only a modest percentage of it came back to the artists. Frustrated by Marvel's compensation, the lack of creator ownership over what they were producing, and various creative differences, McFarlane, Liefeld, and Lee joined with four other rising stars, Erik Larsen, Marc Silvestri, Jim Valentino, and Whilce Portacio, to establish their own publishing house (Figure 10.21).

The seven Image founders discovered an eager audience for their initial offerings. Nearly a million copies of Liefeld's *Youngblood* #1 were pre-ordered by retailers. McFarlane's *Spawn* #1 would sell 1.7 million copies. The sales were unprecedented for independent

Figure 10.21 The Image Comics founders reunited in 2008. In the front row, left to right, are Jim Valentino, Jim Lee, and Whilce Portacio; back row, Marc Silvestri, Erik Larsen, Rob Liefeld, and Todd McFarlane. Photo courtesy of *Wizard: The Comics Magazine* / wizarduniverse.com.

publishing, and so were the profits for the creators, who reaped financial rewards many times greater than they had drawing for Marvel on work-for-hire contracts. The seven were hailed as super-stars by the fans, who made Image products so hot that even the venerable DC Comics, the number-two seller in the marketplace, felt the heat. But Image was not without its critics. Given that artists ran the company, its comic books emphasized visual spectacle over story structure or dialogue. Moreover, many of the titles came to rely on stereotypes of hyper-masculine heroes and impossibly proportioned heroines. Finally, as time went by, more and more Image comic books were delivered later and later, frustrating retailers and fans alike. Internal disputes would eventually fracture the alliance among the Image founders, and Image would settle into a distant third, well behind Marvel and DC, in the marketplace. However, Image had proven that creator-owned publishing was not only practical but could be profitable. Other publishers scrambled to create imprints friendly to creator-owned properties, but their development was ill-timed. The boom that the industry had enjoyed for several years was about to go bust.

Fortunes Turn

The success from this concentration on the existing properties was driven by publishers and comic shops catering to speculators, who were creating a "bubble" in comics' value as collectibles. The newsstand market for comics had largely shrunk into secondary importance by the late 1980s, and in particular the Tim Burton-directed *Batman* (1989) film had the effect of massively expanding the sales in comic shops. Most of those sales were to new readers, but there was also a dangerous new perception of comics as an investment product. For several years, all three sectors of the comic book industry had profited from the increased attention that had been directed to the fact that older, collectible comic books had been increasing in value, with some of the most desirable having grown to be worth hundreds of thousands of dollars. This spurred a speculative response from some investors who bought up multiple copies of new comics, hoping that their freshly minted comic books would in short order increase in value. Publishers responded to the growing collectors' market by offering numerous gimmicks to entice these buyers' attention, from covers with special effects like hologram enhancements to copies sealed in polybags. Collectively, they also produced more comic book titles than ever before. Marvel Comics alone was putting out about one hundred titles a month at the height of the boom. Yet the flood of comics would contribute to the expansion's undoing.

The decline in the comic buyers' market came, in part, from the realization among speculators that scarcity is what inflates the price of collectibles. An issue of *Wolverine* published in 1990, whose press run was nearing a million issues, could increase only modestly in value over time. The reason that 1940's *Batman* #1 was worth hundreds of thousands of dollars was because there were so few copies still in existence. Rozanski cites the 1992 "Death of Superman" storyline as the moment of epiphany for many speculators. DC had hyped the story—in which the Man of Steel dies while stopping an Image-inspired muscle-bound monster named Doomsday—in the popular press, resulting in the sale of millions of copies of the story's climax in *Superman* #75. Yet those who bought the issue as an investment would be disappointed in short order: "When these new comics consumers/ investors tried to sell their copies of *Superman* #75 for a profit a few months later, however, and discovered that they could only recover their purchase price if they had a first printing, their bitter disillusionment did much to cause the comics investing bubble to begin bursting" (Rozanski n.d.) (Figure 10.22).

Figure 10.22 The death of Superman garnered national media attention but may have contributed to the end of the speculators' market. The cover of *Superman* #75 by Dan Jurgens and Brett Breeding became an iconic fixture in the world of American comics as the story became one of the best-selling comics of all time. © DC Comics.

As speculators began to walk away from the industry, they left retailers with tons of unwanted backstock, forcing many to close up shop. By 1996, the number of comics retailers shrank from an estimated 10,000 shops to just 4,000 nationwide (Jones and Jacobs 1997: 363). Other woes beset the publishers. With fewer buyers and increased competition for those who remained, many of the publishers went out of business. Distributors also began to feel the bite of a shrinking industry. When Marvel Comics made a bid at vertical integration by setting up an exclusive distribution deal using its own recently acquired distributor, Heroes World, the move spurred other publishers to seek out exclusive deals of their own with competing distributors. Marvel soon abandoned its scheme, and in the aftermath most distributors were driven out of business, except for Diamond Comic Distributors, who emerged from the fracas with a virtual monopoly over comic book distribution in 1994. The mismanagement at Marvel continued until 1996 when the company was forced to declare bankruptcy and reorganize its business. Marvel successfully emerged from the proceedings and even regained its sales dominance over the industry, but by the time it did, it was clear that the sale of periodical comic books was going to be a smaller industry than ever before. Yet a change in format and some clever marketing would allow comics to reach new audiences.

The Proliferation of the Graphic Novel

Arguably, in the course of the last three decades, comic books appear to have entered into an era in which the graphic novel is becoming the most important form of comics. With the expansive definition of graphic novel in the public's mind being the one defined by bookstore merchandising, lumping together reprints of periodical comics, original literary works, nonfiction, and international material like manga, it has become a more welcoming category than the more narrow-focused comics. By the beginning of the twenty-first century, it was likely that more readers were purchasing comics in graphic novel form than in periodicals, although the intense purchase patterns of the fans still generated disproportionate revenues. In this era, superheroes continue to be the dominant genre sold by mainstream publishers, and among the most frequently told stories have been periodic reinterpretations of these familiar characters. Doing so has tapped into the mythic qualities of the genre, demonstrating the vitality of heroic mythology for generating stories. It has also meant that mainstream publishing has been fixated on the genre, leaving much of the most progressive and experimental storytelling to independent publishers who have attempted to push the boundaries of the medium well beyond the limitations of just one type of story.

Independent Comics Achieve Recognition

While the industry's superhero mainstream continues to present more and more of the same material, a number of independent publishers have tackled a diversity of genres and even non-genre works. There are dozens of independent publishers, collectively sharing about 40 percent of the American comics market. Yet, arguably, their contributions do more to advance comics as an art form than anything put out by mainstream publishers throughout this era.

While the industry's third-largest publisher, Image Comics, got its start competing directly with DC and Marvel in the superhero genre, it has in recent years increasingly gravitated to other genres. In 1998 Image began to publish Eric Shanower's *Age of Bronze*, a retelling of the siege of ancient Troy based on historical sources. Image also achieved critical acclaim with Brian Michael Bendis and Michael Avon Oeming's *Powers* series (2000), which deftly revitalized detective fiction by setting it in the world of superheroics. Likewise, Robert Kirkman's *The Walking Dead* (2003) scored with audiences in telling the ongoing saga of survivors coping in a world of homicidal zombies. The translation of *The Walking Dead* to a popular cable television series then catapulted it to the top of best-seller lists. More recent series have continued Image's diversification, including Brain K. Vaughan and Fiona Staples' space opera *Saga* (2012), Kieron Gillen and Jamie McKelvie's fantasy *The Wicked + The Divine* (2014), and Majorie Liu and Sana Takeda's epic *Monstress* (2015). Despite a foundation firmly rooted in superheroics, Image has grown to be among the industry leaders in marketing other genres for the medium.

Another independent publisher, Dark Horse Comics, has also enjoyed commercial success in offering comic books from other genres. Its most high-profile projects have been works by Frank Miller, including the gritty *Sin City* crime comics, which began in 1991, and the historical drama *300* in 1998. Both properties went on to be highly profitable film adaptations. Another recognizable creation, Mike Mignola's *Hellboy*, which first appeared in 1993, has also gone on to enjoy Hollywood film adaptations.

Other publishers have been less commercially successful than Image or Dark Horse, but have produced works held in high esteem by critics. Fantagraphics has promoted the work of a number of reputable and influential cartoonists, including Chris Ware (*Acme Novelty Library*, 1993), Peter Bagge (*Hate*, 1990), Daniel Clowes (*Eightball*, 1989), and Los Bros Hernandez (*Love and Rockets*, 1982). Many of these cartoonists tell slice-of-life stories far removed from the fantasies offered by mainstream comic book publishers. Another publisher, Top Shelf, has offered everything from memoirs (Craig Thompson's *Blankets*, 2003) to pornography (Alan Moore and Melinda Gebbie's *Lost Girls*, 2006). Along with many others, such independent publishers have set a precedent for the diversity of stories to which the medium can be applied.

In fairness, one must acknowledge that many of the independent publishers have financed their more artistic endeavors by relying on the production of more marketable comic books based on popular licensed properties. Top Cow adapted the *Tomb Raider* video games, Fantagraphics has produced books reprinting Charles Schulz's *Peanuts* strips, and IDW has acquired the rights to the *Star Trek* franchise, a lucrative property that has been published by everyone from Gold Key in the sixties to Malibu in the nineties. At least in this regard, the independent publishers have been in sync with the two major publishers, reproducing familiar narratives in comic book form.

Yet the artistic impact of the independents still resonates, even among the major publishers. In order to attract talent interested in exploring mature themes and retaining ownership of their creative properties, both DC and Marvel have moved toward creating imprints to publish creator-owned content separate from their main lines.

One less-visible effect of the growth of the independent market upon the mainstream publishers is the abandonment of censoring review by the Comics Magazine Association of America (CMAA). Since 1954 most mainstream publishers had submitted their comic books for review by the CMAA, particularly if they hoped to sell their magazines on newsstands. However, as the market for comic books shifted from newsstands to specialty shops and new publishers bypassed the association entirely, its seal of approval became less and less significant. In 2001 Marvel abandoned the review process entirely, electing to begin its own self-assessed rating system on its covers, and by 2009 the review program ended. Marvel's Editor-in-chief Joe Quesada notes, "In retrospect, thinking about the Code and the CMAA, let me just put this bluntly, I just think the CMAA did a very poor job with respect to letting people in the general public know that there were comics other than the ones for kids, thus I think in a lot of ways perpetuating the CMAA, and Marvel was a very big part of that." (qtd. in Alls 2001).

Figure 10.23 With the rising popularity of Japanese manga among American audiences, publishers like Marvel began to experiment with the distinctive manga style such as in this cover from *Marvel Mangaverse* by Ben Dunn (artist). © 2023 Marvel Entertainment, Inc. and its subsidiaries.

Another factor is the surge in popularity for Japanese comics, or manga, in the American market. While the indigenous Japanese comic book industry had operated successfully for decades, it was only in the late eighties, with the translation of manga series like *Akira* (1988), that American audiences began to take note of the comics. Viz Communications began to reprint a range of manga titles for the English-speaking American audience in 1987, but the market for manga grew slowly. Yet by 1997 the market had grown, and Viz was joined by competitor Tokyopop. In the first decade of the new century, manga has been the fastest-growing segment of comic book publishing, with dozens of publishers offering translated manga or American-made comics imitating its distinctive style. For several years, the largest retailer for manga was actually the Borders chain of bookstores, not the comics specialty stores' direct market, which further suggests that their appeal stretches beyond traditional comics readers (Figure 10.23).

In Japan, manga storytelling is applied to subject matter that ranges from young children's stories to serious historical works, or even cookbooks. In America, by a low point in the 1990s, comics' subject matter was limited to a very narrow range. The graphic novel format has been the transformative factor in opening that range up.

While a lengthier exploration of genre in comics is the subject of Chapter 6, it is important to consider the dimensions of this process in the diversification of the medium. This is an ongoing process, which will undoubtedly explore new creative territory between the time this book is published and when it is read, but it has already allowed comics storytelling to address many new subjects.

Cartoonists' memoirs have a long tradition, as explored in Chapter 8, but the ability to use comics to tell stories of their lives has proved particularly important to young people. Graphic novels of personal experience, whether fictionalized or not, have been very important to the growth of the medium. Alison Bechdel's *Fun Home* received massive critical acclaim on its publication in 2006, and it's possible to follow the life of cartoonists such as Gabrielle Bell through volume after volume. Memoirs like these seem to have been particularly effective in introducing high school and college-age women to comics, an audience that had been underrepresented for many years.

Figure 10.24 Jeff Smith's self-published *Bone* charmed a new generation of children into reading comics. BONE® is ©2022 Jeff Smith.

Particularly important to creators working in the field was a renewal of what had once been America's primary audience for comics, children. *Bone*, an acclaimed periodical title launched in 1991 by cartoonist Jeff Smith through his own Cartoon Books imprint, became the first major hit comic for children when Smith made a deal with Scholastic Books to publish graphic novel editions and give them a wider distribution than Cartoon Books' own reach had permitted. Scholastic's in-school book sales have long given them a unique reach to children in America, and sales of *Bone* climbed to over a half million copies of the new editions (Figure 10.24).

Creators who prefer the power of comics have also used them to explore historical subjects, like Gene Luen Yang's *Boxers and Saints*, a 2013 National Book Award nominee for its evocation of a critical moment in Chinese history. This project is emblematic of a greater comfort with the use of comics in classrooms, which has also seen textbooks on subjects including economics and science being created in comics form, in the hope that a generation of students who enjoy visual learning will immerse themselves in the subjects more this way.

The potential for comics reaching adult audiences also inspires truly new forms, like Joe Sacco's works that combine traditional journalism with memoir and the graphic novel to document his travels through some of the world's most troubled areas, like *Palestine* (1993). Taking photographs as he travels, Sacco uses them as the basis for comics that tell deeply personal stories of what life is like in the middle of war zones.

There are no large-scale longitudinal studies of comics readers allowing measurement of how each of these projects and formats expands the total audience reading comics in America. Given the minimal overlap with the demographics of the narrow audience that comics periodicals had at their low point in circulation in the 1980s, however, it's clear that the array of new forms and genres have helped comics grow out of the limitations of the direct market.

Beyond the Graphic Novel via the Web

While the graphic novel has been a powerful factor in creating opportunities for diversification of content in comics, it is not the only one, or perhaps the most powerful. The graphic novel format is still limited by the requirement that the creative talent assemble a significant body of work before publication, whether they create it speculatively or financed by others through a traditional publishing contract or crowdfunding through a website like Kickstarter.

Possibly the most important factor in diversification for comics has been the evolution of the internet, and the open access it has provided creative people to make their self-expression available to the public. Because the generation of comic book readers who dominated the field in the 1980s were demographically heavily male, in their late teens and early twenties, and identifiably **early adopters** in marketing terms, it was not surprising that they migrated to the internet very early on. Prior to the introduction of programming languages like html and browsers that made graphic interfaces fairly simple, comics and comic characters were early subjects for computer-aided communication. Discussions that had previously been circulated via fanzines moved over to the web.

Early experiments with comics on the internet appear to date to the mid-1980s, when they appeared on bulletin boards and services like CompuServe, which were accessible by the then-slow modems. In 1991, cartoonist Hans Bjordahl produced *Where The Buffalo Roam*, which billed itself as the internet's first comic strip and was the first to be regularly updated for circulation on an FTP site and via Usenet. As the technology improved to allow easy transmission of graphics, the form evolved into **webcomics**, a term that is broad enough to include both the publication of cartoons essentially identical to traditional newspaper strip comics and interactive forms using software like flash animation. The term **digital comics** is also used, with the distinction in how the comics are distributed.

The turn of the century was a pivotal moment for webcomics, with the launch of two of the most successful in 1998: *Penny Arcade* by Jerry Holkins and Mike Krahulik, and *PvP* by Scott Kurtz. Although the webcomics appeared free on the internet, the cartoonists devised strategies to monetize their work through the sale of print editions, merchandise, and events. Many of these early webcomics worked in the format of newspaper strips and centered on characters who were involved in the world of video gaming, either as players or professionals. In 2000, comics theorist Scott McCloud published *Reinventing Comics*, devoting significant space to evangelizing the potential of webcomics, and the following year web cartoonists gave their own award within their community, while the print-oriented Eisner Awards added a digital comics category in 2005.

The power and challenge of webcomics is their ease of distribution and the difficulty of sustaining them while an audience (and economic basis) builds. A significant number of webcomics are published briefly and abandoned, and efforts to make this easier through collectives and other group mechanisms have repeatedly been developed. There are literally thousands of webcomics available to explore on the web in this fractionalized environment, either as stand-alone websites or on websites that incorporate them. The material that eventually became Jeff Kinney's *Diary of a Wimpy Kid* (2004), an extraordinarily successful children's book series and three films (to date), debuted on an educational website named *Funbrain*, for example. Webcomics can be created in any genre or form, and although many of the successes mimic the newspaper strips, particularly in the rhythm of humor they utilize, other models continue to be explored.

Talent from the traditional print forms of comics has become involved in webcomics as well, and even talent from other creative industries. Joss Whedon was a well-established television and film writer and director by 2008 when he won an Eisner award for best digital comic doing *Sugarshock!* with artist Fåbio Moon. In 2012, *V For Vendetta* artist David Lloyd launched a "magazine" format entitled *Aces Weekly*, with continuing comics in dramatic genres by both established and newer talent. *Aces Weekly* is offered via subscription, with revenues being shared by the contributing writers and artists. As the ability to do different kinds of storytelling in digital comics expands, it is likely that more talent will crossover and explore these possibilities (Figures 10.25 a–b).

Figures 10.25a–b In the digital version of *The Damnation of Charlie Wormwood* by Christina Blanch and Chee, the second panel appears superimposed over the first when clicked. Charlie's dialogue fades as his partner's conversation appears. Panels courtesy of *Thrillbent.com*.

Major publishers produce comics specifically for digital release as well. Most have had their writers and artists do stories of successful properties like *X-Men* in digital formats, and in many cases have followed this with print releases later when enough episodes had been created. Some of these projects have been specifically designed to appeal to people who were not avid comics readers, but who were interested in the properties from their other media forms, and appear to have been successful at attracting fresh audiences to the comics this way. For example in 2013, DC tied into *Injustice: Gods Among Us* with a series of digital comics based on the fighting game, then made them available to their print audience in periodical and graphic novel formats.

Comics publishers have turned to the web as a form of additional distribution for their traditionally created publications as well. Both Marvel Comics and DC Comics developed an "all you can eat" subscription model allowing access to hundreds of its back issues, and most publishers offer digital downloads of their comics both through their own websites and that of a digital distributor like Comixology. Digital distribution now takes place simultaneously with the release of most comics, and the catalog of titles available is enormous and growing, with Comixology, now owned by Amazon, alone advertising over 100,000 comics. Significant percentages of these sales go to customers who are unable to shop conveniently at comic shops, including those in international markets where the English language edition of a comic may be available, but the local language edition may not be for several months, if at all.

There is also an argument for traditional print comics collectors to shift over to digital forms as a way of managing their collections. Many longtime comics readers amass collections of thousands of issues, most often stored in specially designed cardboard containers known as longboxes. These can be overwhelming for an average apartment or home, and can require renting storage units for larger collections. Converting a collection to digital form makes it easily accessible and stored on a single hard drive.

Like other media forms, comics experience piracy of their intellectual property on the web. There is no generally accepted tracking of the extent of piracy of comics, but diligent searching would enable a consumer to find virtually any issue they were interested in. Because of the lack of tracking, it is unclear how many potential sales are lost to piracy, but the perceived availability of pirated content contributes to the pressures on publishers for low pricing of digital downloads. Generally, digital formats are offered at the print price initially to protect sales of the physical edition, and then move downward over time to 99¢.

Analyzing: An Historical Perspective on Acceptance

As we draw this history to a conclusion, we note that as of this writing comics are enjoying greater respectability than at any time in their history. Since 2015 three graphic novels have been awarded the prestigious Newbery Medal. Five graphic novels have been nominated for The National Book Award, and *March: Book Three* actually won in 2016. Comics creators Art Spiegelman, Alison Bechdel, Gene Luen Yang, and Lynda Barry have been recipients of $625,000 "Genius Grants" from the MacArthur Fellows Program, underscoring the value placed on the artistry as practiced by some of the medium's most influential voices.

Comics are also an undeniable portion of the book market, with sales of graphic novels now accounting for a larger portion of book sales than either stalwarts such as science fiction/fantasy novels or mystery novels. The purchase of Marvel by the Walt Disney Company in 2009 has proven to be a very wise investment, as many of the best-loved and most profitable motion picture and television programs are adapted from comic books.

There is a growing public perception that comics have cultural value beyond serving as the source material for popular multimedia entertainment. When one small school district in Tennessee removed the graphic novel *Maus* from the eighth-grade curriculum, outrage swept through both legacy media and social media. This reaction is quite a contrast to 70 years ago when both scholarly journals and dozens of popular magazines condemned the content of comics, there were public burnings of comic books, and politicians were advocating for censorship of comics in order to protect children.

Discussion Questions

1. What is it about the superhero genre that has made it so consistently linked to the comics medium? Or, taken from another perspective, what is it about the comics medium that makes it so favorable to the superhero genre?
2. Aside from those reviewed in this chapter, are there other factors that have contributed to the gradual decline of the comic book market? Why else do you think fewer people, especially young people, read comic books now than they did before?
3. Can you forecast the future of comic books based on recent trends in the industry? What do you think will be the defining characteristics of the next era of comic book history?

Activities

1. There are many important contributors to comic book history whom we barely had space to mention in this chapter, each of them interesting characters in their own right. Research one of these other figures on your own and provide a biography highlighting that person's contributions to the medium. Some suggestions of people to investigate are Tarpé Mills, Matt Baker, Lev Gleason, and Jim Steranko, among many, many others.
2. New trends in the comics industry will come along well beyond the publication date of this book. Visit one of the news websites that follows the business of comics and graphic novels, such as ICv2 or Publisher's Weekly, and examine a recent span of reports on the business of comics publishing. Report back to your instructor and peers what trends extend concepts raised in this chapter and what new trends have been introduced.

Recommended Reading

Comics

Eisner, Will. *The Best of the Spirit.* New York: DC Comics, 2005.
While we might have recommended any number of classic comics to you, Will Eisner's early efforts to innovate within the medium are best captured in his work on *The Spirit*, a series he produced before and after the Second World War. The series captures both the frenetic energy of the Golden Age of comics and Eisner's own creativity in devising new ways to work within it.

Van Lente, Fred, and Ryan Dunlavey. *The Comic Book History of Comics*. San Diego: IDW, 2012.
Van Lente and Dunlavey, also known for their engaging *Action Philosophers!* series, use a canny mix of mostly historically accurate details and irreverent humor to chronicle the history of the American comic book industry.

Scholarly Sources

Dauber, Jeremy. *American Comics: A History.* New York: W.W. Norton and Company, 2022.
Dauber surveys the history of American comics in detail, capturing the way that American culture is reflected in and by its comics. Examples of the groundbreaking and meritorious help to guide readers through decades of growth and development.

Hatfield, Charles. *Alternative Comics: An Emerging Literature*. Jackson: University Press of Mississippi, 2005.
Hatfield traces the development of alternative comics from its roots in the underground comics movement of the late sixties through to its most gifted practitioners of recent years. Along the way, he provides analysis of the trends and tropes in the literary comics published outside of the industry's mainstream.

11 Exploring Meanings in Comics

Many pundits figured that the outcome of the 1948 presidential election was a foregone conclusion. Poll after poll indicated that Republican nominee Thomas E. Dewey would unseat incumbent President Harry S. Truman in the November contest. Despite these dour predictions, the Democratic National Committee (DNC) campaigned on, and among its promotional materials released the first ever comic book biography of a presidential candidate, the sixteen-page *The Story of Harry S. Truman*. The DNC commissioned more than 3 million copies of the comic book and released them in October, just before the election, hoping to bring around undecided voters. In releasing the comic books, the DNC targeted those groups of people most likely to turn to Truman: farmers, African Americans, labor unions, and veterans. Veterans, in particular, were fans of comic books, and the novelty of the unusual venue surely piqued the interest of many other potential voters. The four-color account of Truman's life highlighted many of his most heroic actions—including his own military service, his watchdog activities on behalf of taxpayers in the US Senate, and his leading America to the conclusion of the Second World War—with none of his faults.

Figure 11.1 ***The Story of Harry S. Truman*** **may have influenced some undecided voters to cast their ballot in favor of the incumbent president in a race that was so close that the *Chicago Tribune* famously printed an erroneous edition declaring "Dewey Defeats Truman." Reprinted with permission from the Democratic National Committee.**

While it is impossible to say if the comic book was ultimately responsible for winning over the hearts and minds of undecided voters, Truman won the election by a margin of 1,188,054 votes, which was well within the parameters of the 3 million copies of the comic book that the DNC had distributed. The pollster who had predicted Dewey's win did so too quickly. Many Americans did not make their choice for chief executive until the crucial last weeks of the campaign—weeks when *The Story of Harry S. Truman* had the chance to circulate among many of these voters (Szasz 2000) (Figure 11.1).

Objectives

In this chapter you will learn:

1. how descriptive methods employed by literacy experts have examined comics' potential to help with reading skills;
2. about interpretive methods and deriving meanings through the lens of mythic analysis;
3. how critical methods uncover and seek to change our acceptance of gender stereotypes.

Did *The Story of Harry S. Truman* win the election for president? Can a comic have that much influence on voter decision-making? For that matter, can comics—or any mass medium—produce such direct effects on its audience? Initially, critics attacked comics as inferior, even dangerous, products of culture, stirring fears that they affect their readers in negative ways. Alternatively, proponents of comics have hailed them as effective pedagogical tools for enhancing literacy and second language learning. More recently, critics and scholars have presented a less impassioned response to comics as artifacts of culture, commenting on their symbolic meanings. Though the approaches—and conclusions—have varied since the 1940s, researchers have tried to better understand the comics and their audiences through scholarly inquiry.

What do we mean when we say something is "scholarly?" Scholarship is publicly shared understanding that comes from systematic ways of knowing. Scholarship is subject to review from others, most especially those who have a background in the same area or on the same topic, and is commonly shared in public ways, such as through presentations and publications. Scholarship is more than merely reporting that a phenomenon exists or offering editorial opinion on it. Scholarship seeks to probe and know a phenomenon using methods that go beyond superficial acknowledgment of the subject or simple responses to its existence. Thus, scholarship is a more rigorous way of perceiving subjects and is typically, though not exclusively, the work of experts within a field.

This chapter explores how scholars have studied comics to come to clearer understanding of what they mean to their audiences. Scholars use multiple methods to come to an understanding of comics texts, their creators, and their audiences, far more than we could profile in just one chapter. However, we can group these methods into three broad approaches: descriptive, interpretive, and critical. This chapter provides an overview of each of these three approaches with some specific applications of each in turn. By this chapter's end, you should have a broader picture of the investigations that have gone on and those that are proceeding in the interdisciplinary field of Comics Studies.

Discovering: Milestones in the Development of Comics Studies

The following chronology recognizes only a few of the many pioneering American comics scholars and the accomplishments that have contributed to our understanding of comic books. A larger survey would take into account many more scholars, expanding to include international scholars and those whose work in comic strips and political cartoons also enriched the larger study of comics as an art form.

1947 Cartoonist Frederick Coulton Waugh authors *The Comics*, one of the first histories of comics to include an examination of comic books.

1954 Dr. Fredric Wertham publishes *The Seduction of the Innocent*, the most influential—and devastating—book about comic books ever published.

1959 Sol Davidson graduates from New York University after completing one of the first Ph.D. dissertations focused on comics.

1965 Cartoonist Jules Feiffer produces one of the first critical essays about comics accessible to a wider public audience, published by Dial Press as *The Great Comic Book Heroes*.

1967 The inaugural issue of the *Journal of Popular Culture*, a peer-reviewed academic periodical, is launched under the guidance of founding editor and Bowling Green State University Professor Ray B. Browne. *JPC* and the Popular Culture Association, founded thereafter, help to promote the scholarly study of all popular culture, comics included.

1970 An increasing number of histories of the medium begin to appear, including Jim Steranko's *History of Comics* and Dick Lupoff and Don Thompson's *All in Color for a Dime*. Les Daniels' *Comix: A History of Comic Books in America* joins them in 1971.

1972 Professor Donald Ault offers one of the first university-level courses focused on the study of comics: "Literature and Popular Culture," at the University of California, Berkeley.

1972 An essay translated as "The Myth of Superman" by respected Italian philosopher Umberto Eco first appears in English and becomes an often-reprinted piece of comics criticism (originally published in Italy in 1962).

1973 The first volume of David Kunzle's historical analysis, *The Early Comic Strip*, explores some of the forms of narrative comics that were the precursors to modern comic books.

1973 Scholars assemble at the University of California for the First Berkeley Comic Art Convention, one of the earliest conventions attended by academics.

1976 Editors Gary Groth and Mike Catron begin to transform *The Nostalgia Journal* into *The Comics Journal*, which becomes one of the most prominent and, at times, controversial continuing efforts at comics journalism and criticism.

1979 Cartoonist Robert C. Harvey begins to develop a vocabulary for comics criticism when he publishes "The Aesthetics of the Comic Strip" in the pages of the *Journal of Popular Culture*.

1983 Under the editorial direction of Thomas Andrae and Geoffrey Blum, the first of the thirty-volume *Carl Barks Library* appears, launching one of the earliest collections of comics and criticism in English.

1985 Cartoonist Will Eisner publishes his first textbook on how to create comics, *Comics & Sequential Art*, which while a primer for cartoonists also introduced an academic audience to concepts and terminology for thinking about comics form.

1985 Trina Robbins and catherine yronwode publish *Women and the Comics*, a book-length examination of the contributions of women creators to the medium.

1990 The University Press of Mississippi begins to publish a series of books devoted to comics studies, beginning with Joseph Witek's *Comic Books as History* and M. Thomas Inge's *Comics as Culture*

1992 Peter Coogan and Randy Duncan found the Comic Arts Conference, the first annual American academic conference devoted exclusively to the study of comics which, since 1998, has been held in conjunction with San Diego's Comic-Con International.

1993 Cartoonist Scott McCloud publishes *Understanding Comics: The Invisible Art*, a book of comics theory told in comics form that garners critical acclaim and widespread interest.

1994 Under the editorial direction of Lucy Shelton Caswell, curator of the Cartoon Research Library at Ohio State University, *INKS: Cartoon and Comic Art Studies* becomes the first American academic journal focused exclusively on the comics medium.

1995 The International Comic Arts Festival convenes, bringing together comics scholars from around the world in its first annual meeting (later under the banner of the International Comics Arts Forum).

1999 Professor John A. Lent launches the *International Journal of Comic Art*, a scholarly journal devoted to the study of comics across cultures.

2004 The University of Florida posts the first online refereed academic journal about comics, *ImageTexT: Interdisciplinary Comics Studies*.

2010 High-profile academic presses begin publishing academic serials, such as Routledge's *The Journal of Graphic Novels and Comics* and Intellect's *Studies in Comics*.

2014 The Comics Studies Society is founded as a learned society to promote the field.

Descriptive Methods of Analysis

From popular music to video games, each mass medium seems to come under attack shortly after it becomes popular, and comics were no exception. The first widely published critique came in 1940, when Sterling North, the literary editor for the *Chicago Daily News*, publicly condemned them in an oft-quoted editorial:

> Badly drawn, badly written and badly printed—a strain on young eyes and young nervous systems—the effect of these pulp-paper nightmares is that of a violent stimulant. Their crude blacks and reds spoil the child's natural sense of color; their hypodermic injection of sex and murder make the child impatient with better, though quieter stories. Unless we want a coming generation even more ferocious than the present one, parents and teachers throughout America must band together to break the "comic" magazine. (56)

North outlined a litany of charges against the nascent comic book industry: comic books were aesthetically an inferior publication, they caused eye strain, and they corrupted America's youth by exposing them to violence and sex. Critics who followed his lead would argue that such exposure prompted children to commit wanton antisocial acts. While North was certainly entitled to his opinion about the artistic merits of comic books, any claims about their effects on the physical and mental well-being of America's youth lacked objective study and confirmation at the time. Indeed, much of the initial condemnation of comics stemmed from superficial perceptions of comics' shortcomings rather than a more thorough investigation of their contents or their effects on their audiences. The research conclusions that followed would challenge the claims that comic books caused impressionable minds to pursue violent, even criminal activities. A consensus of media scholars has since agreed that violent media do heighten violent reactions (Rifas 1992), though the conditions under which audiences react to such stimulation are still subject to continued investigation and further understanding.

Descriptive research, such as that conducted by media scholars, seeks to explain the social world: Why do people behave in certain ways or react to certain stimuli the way that they do? Descriptive research seeks to provide explanations to such questions. Typically, answers are discovered through formal processes of observing the behavior of groups of people directly or by collecting reports of their attitudes and experiences through carefully administered surveys.

The initial focus and furor over comics' role in violent behavior were shortly thereafter eclipsed by the rise of a medium that came to dominate the national consciousness even more: television. Consequently, social scientific research into comics' possible deleterious effects subsided for some time. However, interest in comics as an influence on our negative emotions does return periodically. For example, one study found that consumption of violent content in mass media, including comic books, desensitized children to the effects of crime and violence (Lovibond 1967). Still later, Stephen Kirsh and Paul Olczak (2003) investigated how the consumption of violent media content influences people with a disposition toward hostility. They conducted an experiment with two groups of college students, who were first measured for their attitudes toward seeking vengeance. One group read comics with graphic violence, like *Curse of Spawn* and *Evil Ernie*, while the other group read less violent material like the innocuous *Archie* and *Dexter's Laboratory*. The researchers then presented the participants with different scenarios (e.g., being cheated on by one's significant other) and asked them to rate the likelihood of seeking vengeance in each of these situations. When the results were tallied and compared to the initial measures, Kirsh and Olczak (2003) found that after having read the violent comics, people who were high in trait hostility were more likely to consider vengeful responses.

Such conclusions are in sync with other research findings indicating that mass media that offer antisocial messages can—but not necessarily will—encourage those dispositions, and comics seem as likely to promote such responses as any other mass medium. Around the same time that researchers were making inquiries into the effects of comics on their audience's social behavior, interest in comics' effect on audience's reading abilities was also underway.

Literacy

While a climate of fear seemingly motivated the initial research into comics' possible negative impact, it appears that an attitude of hope sustains social scientific research into the medium's educational applications. In particular, a number of scholars have investigated the idea that comics can be used as tools to aid in educating, especially in terms of improving literacy. Research over the past seven decades has demonstrated that comics have the capability to motivate readers, to enhance reading skills, and to aid those engaged in learning a second language.

One of the chief virtues of comics seems to be their ability to motivate readers by turning them on to reading in the first place (Haugaard 1973). Bonny Norton (2003) argues that it is ownership of one's reading material that encourages people, especially young people, to read more. If one is allowed to read what gives one pleasure, then one tends to read more. In the case of children, a problem arises when parents and teachers fail to acknowledge what children enjoy reading. Consequently, other researchers have found that "Those who reported more comic book reading also reported more pleasure reading in general, greater reading enjoyment, and tended to do more book reading." (Ujiie and Krashen 1996: 51). Noted literacy expert Stephen Krashen (1993) claims comics have the benefit of functioning as a bridge to other kinds of reading, as they help young readers develop linguistic competence and an interest in books.

Second, contrary to the criticisms of those who feared that reading comics handicaps a child's ability to read text-only materials, research has confirmed that comics actually do more to promote than retard reading ability. In fact, one of the earliest studies into comics readership found that children who read a lot of comics and those who read few comics actually read about the same amount and types of materials, leading researcher Paul Witty (1941) to conclude that comics were not harmful so long as they remained a part of a well-balanced reading program. Likewise, teacher Florence Heisler (1948) found that reading comics is not indicative of a lack of intelligence; one study by reading specialist Emma Halstead Swain (1978) even found that in comparing groups of students with poor grades to those with good grades, comics were more often read by students earning good grades! Reading experts like Gary Wright (1979) and Robert Thorndike (1941) have found that mainstream superhero comics tend to be written somewhere around the sixth-grade level—about the same level as the average American newspaper—making reading comics something of a challenge for any child less developed than that.

Comics may not be a panacea, though, for struggling readers. Marshall Arlin and Garry Roth (1978) caution that poor students may spend more time consuming the pictures than attending to the words, requiring educators to do more than merely distribute comics if they are to promote textual literacy. We should note here that reading images is still cognitive work and there are potential benefits in developing children's visual literacy, as well as their textual.

More recent research has further suggested that comics may enhance readers' understanding of material and abilities to work with language. Ġorġ Mallia (2007) reported on students involved in an experiment where different groups were asked to read a historical text. One group got a text-only version, a second group got the text with illustrations, and a third group got a comics version of the material. After each group read the material, they were tested for their recollection, comprehension, and knowledge of the history lesson. Statistical analysis of the results showed that students recalled the content of the comic as well as the text with illustrations; those who read the text-only treatment fared the poorest in the comparison. Mallia concludes that comics are at least as effective as the other two options as teaching tools. Similarly encouraging results were found in an experiment run by Michael Bitz (2004) with more than 700 students involved in an after-school program that encouraged them to write and draw their own eight-page comic book as a means for improving their expressiveness. A survey of the students found that 86 percent of them believed that the experience helped their writing ability. Even more impressively, 90 percent of the instructors reported that they thought the students' writing had improved after participating in the project.

Third, comics seem to help facilitate the acquisition of a second language. Researcher Neil Williams (1995) found that the depiction of nonverbal activities provided by comics helps second language learners to understand the text within context. Comics are also attractive as they are culturally current, using the common vernacular rather than artificially perfected grammar and vocabulary, giving the students a less formal entrée into the other culture. Bonny Norton and Karen Vanderheyden (2004) found that Archie Comics were particularly helpful to their second language learners, perhaps because their readers could easily relate to the high school social situations depicted in those comics. They found that the pleasure and enjoyment the readers got from the comics engaged their interest more than some other texts. Moreover, when they could discuss these comics with others in their class, the connection further encouraged their engagement with the language.

Given that comics seem to help with reading motivation, reading development, and second language acquisition, why are they not a more familiar feature in language arts curricula? One argument is that the campaign against comics in the 1950s did such a thorough job of discrediting comics in the public eye that for decades thereafter most respectable researchers steered clear of advocating for the comics. Presumably, most instructors are reluctant to face the scorn of introducing materials that are perceived to be morally and developmentally questionable. However, James Bucky Carter (2007) cautions that we do not know exactly why the vast majority of instructors are hesitant to introduce comics in the classroom and that is an attitude education researchers should investigate.

Another possible explanation lies in the different sets of interpretive skills that today's teachers and today's students possess. Many current teachers were trained to privilege text-based narratives as the only legitimate cultural material worth studying. Thus, educators have not only advocated for traditional, text-based literacy, they have taught it to the exclusion of other forms of literacy. Today's students, however, are immersed in a **multimodal** culture, learning about their world from more than just prose sources. They also communicate through multiple interpretive systems: just consider how a given website uses textual, visual, and aural stimuli simultaneously to communicate its message. Educators like Adam Schwartz and Elaine Rubinstein-Avila (2006) have taken note of this difference and begun to advocate for the teaching of forms of literacy that go beyond just text-based literacy, such as visual literacy and the more far-reaching critical literacy. In order to help educators begin to address these different literacies, a number of academics have begun to publish books that provide guidance to education specialists (see James Bucky Carter

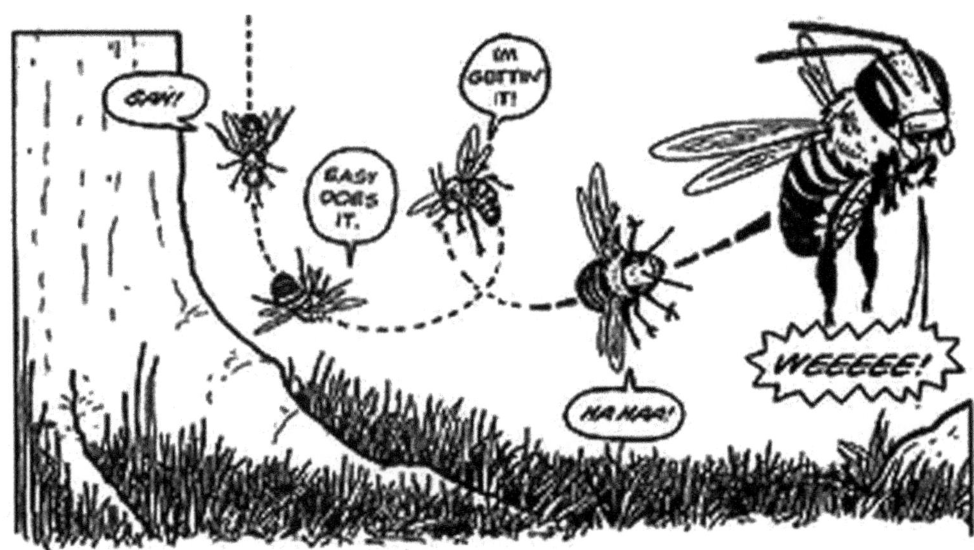

Figure 11.2 Dr. Jay Hosler teaches his readers about the life cycle of the bee while weaving a narrative around one bee in the hive, Nyuki. From *The Way of the Hive: A Honey Bee Story* © Jay Hosler.

2007), language instructors (see Stephen Cary 2004), and librarians (see Michele Gorman 2003) to help them facilitate the integration of comics into their instruction.

There is certainly increasing interest in many areas of education about the power of comics to engage readers. For example, the state of Maryland engaged in the Maryland Comic Book Initiative, employing graphic storytelling in curricula ranging from elementary schools to correctional education. Developed in partnership with Diamond Comic Distributors, once the largest distributor of comics in America, the initiative adds credence to the growing body of research indicating that comics motivate readership and encourage creativity. Likewise, a diverse body of instructional materials is coming forth for the educational market. For instance, Dr. Jay Hosler is a college biology professor and cartoonist who has illustrated books on topics as diverse as the life cycle of the bee and the theories of Charles Darwin (Figure 11.2). Such examples are only the tip of the iceberg in terms of the range and possible applications of comics in educational settings. In fact, graphic novels are even listed under the Common Core State Standards Initiative for education as a text form that students should encounter.

Discovering: Educational Comics

By William B. Jones, Jr.,

The colorful adventures of Superman and Captain Marvel may have propelled early comic books toward popular success, but many parents and educators disapproved, regarding the new medium as a waste of reading time. Some critics, however, decided to fight with fire, and educational comics began to compete with other genres. One of the first, *True Comics*, came from the publishers of *Parents Magazine* in March 1941. The idea was to provide alternatives to superheroes such as real-life heroes like Winston

Churchill or Dwight D. Eisenhower. The market responded with similar publications, such as comics innovator Max Gaines' Educational Comics, which presented *Picture Stories from the Bible* and *Picture Stories from American History.*

But the most enduring of the educational comics was the Gilberton Company's *Classic Comics*, debuting in October 1941 and continuing under the yellow *Classics Illustrated* banner from March 1947 until April 1971. The brainchild of publisher Albert L. Kanter, the series adapted epics, novels, and biographies into comics form, "Featuring Stories by the World's Greatest Authors"—including Homer (*The Iliad*), William Shakespeare (*Macbeth*), Victor Hugo (*Les Misérables*), Charles Dickens (*Great Expectations*), and Herman Melville (*Moby Dick*).

Kanter continually sought to distance *Classics Illustrated* from other comics, which were coming under increasing cultural and legislative scrutiny and attack in the late 1940s and early 1950s. The series distinguished itself, winning awards and improving the quality of its artwork and adaptations under the exacting editorship of Roberta Strauss Feuerlicht.

Classics Illustrated is significant as the first comics series to present complete, self-contained literary stories—a forerunner of the graphic novel. Unlike the standard thirty-two-page, one-shot-release comics model, most forty-eight-page *CI* editions were reprinted, some more than twenty times. Copies could be ordered from the numbered list of titles included in each issue.

By the time the series ceased publication in 1971, the catalog featured 169 titles. Attempts to revive *Classics Illustrated* were mounted by First Publishing in 1990–1 and Acclaim Books in 1997–8. In 2003, Jack Lake Productions, under license from First Classics, Inc., began the ongoing restoration of the original series, using the original plates, proofs, and cover art. Since 2008, a British publisher, CCS Books, has been producing hardcover and softcover remastered *CI* editions for worldwide distribution.

Although *Classics Illustrated* has endured as an icon, it was not without its critics. Educators such as Elinor Saltus complained that while educational comics might have the right intent, the format diminished the quality of the content of the original works. Poet Delmore Schwartz disparaged the dilution or distortion of what he deemed the proper response to authors such as Dostoevsky and Swift. Fredric Wertham blasted *CI*, asserting that "they emasculate the classics, . . . and, as I have often found, do not reveal to children the world of good literature . . . They conceal it" (1954: 36).

Yet from the late 1940s onward, thousands of schools worldwide adopted *Ivanhoe* and other *Classics*, while future writers such as Anne Rice and George R. R. Martin discovered in them pathways to inspiration. As *CI* historian William B. Jones, Jr., noted: "[T]he series was never intended to replace the original works"; instead, what *Classics Illustrated* did was "to make the realms of the literary and historical imagination accessible and immediate" to generations of readers (Jones 2011: 6).

Using comics to educate even while they engage their readership persists to this day, not only with the rebirth of *CI* but also with creators such as Leonard Rifas, Jim Ottaviani, Fred Van Lente, and Ryan Dunlavey independently producing educational comics. Rifas' EduComics has created such topical titles as *All-Atomic Comics* and *Food Comics*. Ottaviani's G.T. Labs has produced comics such as *Two-Fisted Science* and biographies of famous scientists. Van Lente and Dunlavey won acclaim by documenting the lives and ideas of great thinkers in *Action Philosophers!* While these comics will never sell as prodigiously as superhero comics, they posit a loftier purpose for the medium beyond merely making money for publishers (Figures 11.3 a–b).

William B. Jones, Jr., is the author of Classics Illustrated: A Cultural History, 2nd Ed. (2011, rev. 2017) (Figures 11.3 a–b).

Interpretive Methods of Analysis

While descriptive methods help us to understand many things about the culture of comic books, they are not the only tools for examining them. In fact, another set of investigative tools called **interpretive methods** affords an alternate means for study and is particularly useful for looking at the messages within the characters, stories, and artwork itself. Accordingly, scholars who employ interpretive methods pay close attention to the content of comics and attempt to explain what the messages in comic books mean by making specific arguments about the significance of certain messages and using evidence from the texts themselves to support their claims.

Once again, there are numerous methods for conducting such explorations, far more than we could ever hope to catalog in one chapter, but we offer a sample of them here to demonstrate the diversity of possible approaches for analyzing comics. We begin with the method of content analysis and then turn to mythic analysis. For each method, we also present an example of published research using that approach.

Content Analysis

Researchers who use content analysis are interested in the patterns of meaning as they appear across mediated messages. To them, there are insights to be found in counting the number of times a particular portrayal is offered or a certain act is performed in the media. Thus, content analysis involves examining the frequency of selected variables presented in media messages. For example, a researcher might review how often acts of physical violence are portrayed in a genre of graphic novels or consider what roles minorities fill in a comic book series. Content analysis is a **quantitative** methodology, meaning that concepts are counted, tabulated, and discussed in terms of statistics. By quantifying their discoveries, researchers can compare and contrast phenomena in pronounced ways.

Like other studies, content analysis begins with the researcher posing a question. A research question should always guide the selection of a method to study a phenomenon, and content analysis works particularly well for answering questions dealing with patterns and trends across the media. If indeed the question lends itself to content analysis, the researcher proceeds with determining what kind of sample to work within (e.g., what kind of comics should be examined and how many should be reviewed?). The researcher must also define the units for analysis. The key to producing effective content analysis is to work with carefully defined categories (e.g., what qualifies as an act of violence?). From here the researcher uses a coding sheet to begin collecting data by reading the actual media messages and recording the findings. Once all of the examples in the sample have been

Figures 11.3a–b On the top is Alex Bum's painted cover for *Classics Illustrated* #99, Hamlet (September 1952), and on the bottom is George Wilson's painted cover for *Classics Illustrated* #133, The Time Machine (July 1956). Both Hamlet and The Time Machine are immediately recognizable and about as iconic as *Classics Illustrated* covers get; both were used at different times as representative back-cover reorder list icons. *Classics Illustrated* and *Classics Illustrated Junior* trademarks and associated copyrights are the property of First Classics, Inc. All rights reserved.

reviewed, the results are tabulated, interpreted, and reported.

Figure 11.4 Veronica Lodge not only serves as a romantic interest for Archie Andrews but is a symbol of wealth in comics. Cover from *Veronica* #21 (1992) with art by Dan Parent and Henry Scarpelli. TM & © 2022 Archie Comic Publications, Inc. Used with permission.

An example of a content analysis of comic books comes from Russell W. Belk (1987), who reported the findings of his research in the *Journal of Consumer Research*. A professor of business administration, Belk began his project with an interest in how comics might influence young people's expectations and reflect America's preoccupation with material possessions. He asked questions like, "Are the wealthy portrayed positively, or are they treated ambiguously or even negatively?" and "Do [the portrayals] change over time or remain constant?" (26). In order to answer these questions, he conducted a content analysis of four comic book characters associated with wealth: the miserly Uncle Scrooge McDuck from *Donald Duck*, heiress Veronica Lodge from *Archie*, funny animal adversaries *Fox and Crow*, and the world's richest boy, *Richie Rich*. In order to come up with a manageable sample of the hundreds of stories published about these popular characters, many of whom had been in publication since the 1940s, Belk selected a sample of at least twenty published stories from each decade of the characters' publishing history. After an initial review of many of the stories, he then crafted a coding sheet with categories covering seventy themes, values, and character traits that he wanted to count. Assistants, called coders, helped him to review more than 230 samples for quantitative analysis, looking to determine the frequency of activities such as "trying to earn money at a job" and qualities such as "who is portrayed as selfish?" (39) (Figure 11.4).

Belk found a number of interesting portrayals among the individual characters from this analysis and was able to conclude that the comic books taught lessons consistent with accepted values about wealth, namely that wealth should be earned honestly and used responsibly, and that those who did not follow this model suffered misfortune accordingly. For example, while Uncle Scrooge might not be frequently generous, he is shown to have earned all his money through hard work. In contrast, his adversaries, the burglaring Beagle Boys, have their schemes to swindle their way to fortune foiled each time. Because of the extent of his sample, which covered several decades and characters from many different publishers, Belk's thoroughness sustains the strength of the claims he makes about comic book portrayals of wealth. A systematic content analysis allows researchers to lay some claim to a better understanding of the trends presented within the content of the medium's messages.

Mythic Criticism

The previous sections considered methods of examining comics audiences and the comics themselves using quantitative methods of investigation. As an alternative, **qualitative** methods emphasize understanding without necessarily counting. Instead, the researcher's focus is placed on interpreting meaning. Some qualitative methods are designed to look at meanings as interpreted by the audiences, and others explore the meanings constructed by symbols within the text itself. We now turn to just one example of the many qualitative methods aimed at identifying meanings represented within the text itself.

Mythic criticism is a type of rhetorical criticism that examines a given text for its culturally symbolic meanings. The symbols used in the course of a narrative often stand in for other figures or values in a given cultural tradition. All rhetorical criticism is concerned with meaning, and in mythic criticism the researchers carefully review the text to identify how key symbols presented in the text are addressing additional cultural concerns. **Myths** are the stories that a culture tells itself to remind its people of key values and traditions. The ancient Greeks, for instance, clearly valued humility, as they had numerous myths that told of misfortune that followed pride. For instance, there is the story of Arachne, whose pride in her weaving led her to brag that she was better than Athena, the goddess who turned Arachne into the first spider as punishment for her boast. Cultures all over the world still have myths that they espouse today, and the researcher's goal in mythic criticism is to help others see just how such contemporary myths underscore deeper messages. Critics seek to uncover what such stories say that people value. Their work helps the rest of us reflect on the significance of these portrayals of values.

In mythic criticism, the researcher begins by selecting a text, usually one that has already made an impression upon the researcher or one that has garnered a lot of critical or popular attention. The investigator reads this text carefully, often multiple times, noting familiar themes that come through upon each review. This scholar also brings to bear her own familiarity with the larger culture in which the narrative is told, drawing connections between the symbols in the story and the meanings that they connect to the larger culture itself. The researcher then writes an argument, or a case, for the presence and significance of the meanings that she believes are present in the text. This argument is then shared with others through an oral presentation or by publication.

One publication that illustrates mythic analysis comes from Tim Blackmore (2004) and was published in the *International Journal of Comic Art*. Therein, Blackmore argues that Frank Miller's graphic novel, *300*, is mythic in nature, speaking to America's value of selfless heroism. *300* retells the story of the 300 soldiers led by King Leonidas of Sparta who defended the narrow mountain pass at Thermopylae from invasion by a significantly larger Persian army in 480 BC. According to Blackmore, the information that served as Miller's source material, the writings of the Greek historian Herodotus, was itself already highly mythologized, with recent historians casting doubt on several of Herodotus' details, such as his inflation of the Persian army from about 100,000 actual troops to 5 million in the account. Miller himself added to the symbolic, rather than realistic, portrayal in his retelling of the tale by adding details such as making the traitorous Ephialtes monstrously deformed. Whether it is the overwhelming opposition or a horrific appearance, such symbols are included to provide contrast to the bravery and attractiveness of the Spartan heroes. In myths, the story isn't concerned with historical accuracy but with making its point as clearly as possible (Figure 11.5).

The point Blackmore sees in Miller's tale is that Americans should do the heroic thing regardless of personal cost. Interestingly, Miller wrote *300* while America was at peace, not at war. "America's hero, argues Miller, should be heroism," writes Blackmore; *300* "is

Figure 11.5 A mythic analysis of Frank Miller's *300* argues for the connection between the heroism portrayed in the graphic novel and the value of heroism in American culture. *300* © 1998 Frank Miller, Inc. *300* and the *300* logo are trademarks of Frank Miller, Inc. Published by Dark Horse Comics, Inc.

a story of manners, a didactic text about the unimaginable courage it takes to act in a truly civil way" (347). The graphic novel depicting the heroic sacrifice of the Spartans is thus a myth for modern audiences, meant to stir within the members of a free society the desire to stand and defend their way of life. Mythic critiques like Blackmore's help us to appreciate and understand the complexity and sophistication of comic narratives within their cultural context. (We should note here that *300* has a range of potential readings, and other academics have faulted it for potentially ethnocentric and racist depictions.)

Critical Methods of Analysis

Whereas interpretive methods lay bare deeper meanings in comic book texts, **critical methods** pay particular attention to exposing imbalances in social power and advocating for change. The principal subject of analysis in such methods has to do with ideology. **Ideology** refers to a set of sense-making ideas about how the world works. Ideologies aren't hidden—unless they may be considered to be hiding in plain sight—as they are composed of taken-for-granted assumptions about the way the social world is supposed to work. For instance, most of us hold some ideas about people's gender roles, sexual preferences, class distinctions, racial characteristics, ethnic qualities, and national origin, among other markers, that inform how we perceive and interact with them. Ideologies emerge as groups of people develop ways of thinking about relationships between themselves and others in the world. A given set of ideas—an ideology—then helps them manage the world and thus becomes equipment for living. The longer that these ideologies have a hold, the less likely anyone is to question their premises. Thus, an ideology takes on the appearance of common sense among those within a culture that embraces it. However, critical reflection or feedback from those outside an ideology's influence can expose an ideology's biases.

Why is identifying ideology an important intellectual undertaking? Because issues of ideology are entwined with issues of power. Those who benefit from a dominant idea often wield power in society. Consider the idea, still dominant in numerous societies around the world, that men should enjoy more rights and privileges than women. In these societies, this idea is used to benefit the dominant group, in this case, males, and subordinate group, in this case, females. Such an ideology is perpetuated through a number of institutions within a society: the customs of the family unit, the laws imposed by the state, the practices of the religion, and the messages coming from mass media outlets. All of these institutions may be critiqued for perpetuating a given ideology, but our focus is on how the mass medium of comic books shapes and shares such ideas.

Like other artifacts of mass media, comics are produced by individuals or groups of individuals who bring to their works their own preexisting ideas. Whether intentionally or unintentionally, creators' work in comics embodies elements of their ideologies. Some ideological messages find a welcoming audience who accept the creators' stated assumptions as true. This interpretation is called the **preferred reading** and occurs when the creators' intent matches the readers' understanding of the message. Those with a different, if not outright contradictory, set of ideas to those presented by the creators might interpret the messages quite unlike the way they were intended. These are **oppositional readings**, and they lay bare the assumptions presented in the narrative. A word of caution here: readings are not all or nothing, and a **negotiated reading**, where some assumptions are accepted and others rejected, is also possible. The essential point is that ideological assumptions are not always accepted at face value.

In 1999 comics writer Gail Simone posted a list on the internet outlining a number of female leads and supporting characters who had been maimed or killed in mainstream superhero comics. She titled the list "Women in Refrigerators," naming it after a scene in a *Green Lantern* comic book where the protagonist returns home to find his girlfriend's dead body stuffed into a refrigerator. The list also included characters like the former Batgirl, Barbara Gordon, whose spine was shattered when she was shot by the Joker in Alan Moore and Brian Bolland's graphic novel *Batman: The Killing Joke* (1988), and a host of other female characters who had similarly had their identities and powers taken away or otherwise been left for dead. Simone wanted to start a conversation about the treatment of strong female leads in a genre dominated by male characters and presumably catering to a male audience. Were these just derivative plot devices used to stir the male heroes into action, with a Green Lantern or a Batman meting out righteous justice to the perpetrators of these violent attacks? Or were male creators oblivious to their female audience and their needs for identification with strong characters? Simone's posting of the Women in Refrigerators list became a flashpoint in issues of gender and comics, refocusing consideration of women in comics, both from the perspective of characters on the comics page and producers behind the scenes.

One of the ways that ideology works to serve the interests of the dominant group is to define them in contrast to other, less powerful groups in a society. For example, in American society the dominant group has been white males, leaving women and people of color in a subordinate position. Of course, there are additional social groupings that have defined the privileged group, including characteristics defined by social class, ethnicity, sexual preference, nationality, and so on, but we will focus on biological sex and race, as they are among the most often studied discriminators. Such subordinate groups are often portrayed in popular culture as **Other**, a designation that makes them seem strange, unusual, and distant. This designation helps the dominant group define itself through negation (i.e., we know what we are by labeling what we are not), and as these definitions are repeated over time, they become increasingly difficult to dismiss. Those who seek to resist such definitions are therefore very concerned when portrayals that affirm the dominant group's definitions appear in the mass media, as these depictions seemingly verify the depiction's legitimacy. Left unchallenged, these images may be accepted as legitimate, and thus the issue of **representation** becomes central to the practice of ideological critique of the media.

Figure 11.6 People accept this over-simplified depiction as representative of women in the context of a public restroom, but over-simplification is less welcome in more complex symbolic exchanges, like narratives.

Because depictions in comics are abstracted from reality to one degree or another, the selection of traits that a character embodies—both in terms of personality and physical appearance—runs the risk of relying on stereotypical qualities. Most of us are trained within our culture to recognize the shorthand symbols that seek to capture differences in biological sex. Consider, for instance, the restroom signs that use a simple stick figure with protrusions reminiscent of a skirt to indicate the ladies' room. As familiar a figure as this image has become, emerging back in a time when it was considered a norm for women to wear skirts, today's reality is that women do not wear skirts quite as often, and many favor slacks and jeans (Figure 11.6).

Instead, the symbol is shorthand, a convenience for communicating quickly. While most might not object to such inaccurate abbreviations on the doors of public restrooms, when simplistic and unflattering stereotypes appear in more developed messages, like comics, the reliance on stereotypical representations sparks objections.

Images of Women in Comics

The aforementioned trope of women being typecast as victims is, of course, only one of the stereotypes to note. Another objectionable stereotype in mainstream comics is to be found in the physical appearance of the women illustrated. The misrepresentation of women, especially in the last few decades, as extremely thin with disproportionately large breasts has outraged many critics. Going all the way back to comics' Golden Age, artists have a tradition of drawing "good girls"—so-called for how well they were drawn, not how virtuous they were—featuring women with protruding breasts and provocative poses. Some comic book covers of the 1940s were scandalous because they depicted women in form-fitting outfits, accentuating their breasts (a.k.a. "headlights") in particular. By the 1990s, Catwoman was put into an improbable

Figure 11.7 The "Hawkeye Initiative" is a blog where artists mock the conventions of cheesecake shots of female heroes by replacing them with the masculine hero, Hawkeye. The resulting images point out the ridiculousness of unrealistic bodies and hypersexualized poses into which women can be contorted in comics art.

costume that looked as if it was somehow shrink-wrapped to her top-heavy body. At the same time, buxom, scantily clad women became a house style for Image Comics, Marvel released a series of swimsuit specials that cast their heroines in bikinis, and the independent producers of comics like Lady Death took **cheesecake**—the depiction of females in suggestive clothing and poses—to the level of anatomical impossibility (Figure 11.7).

Even comics that do not cast women into the role of sex objects are still apt to define a woman's role as secondary. In a classic study of the ideological implications of the popular British comic *Jackie*, researcher Angela McRobbie (2000) found that young women were consistently being subjected to an agenda that stressed traditional sex roles. Stories dealt with preparation for a domestic role in marriage, notions of idealized romance, and devotion to fashion and beauty. The problem with this, as McRobbie explains, is that "girls are being invited to join a closed sorority of shared feminine values which actively excludes other possible values" (70). In other words, the comics magazine's message foreclosed rather than opened possibilities, rather clearly suggesting that happiness followed becoming a homemaker, and not even mentioning the option of becoming a physician. Consequently, the closure focused young women on adopting values that served the interests of the dominant group: men. American comics fared little better in this regard, though they opened limited possibilities in terms of careers. Some of the most prominent and enduring female icons in comics represent such limited career choices as actress (Archie's Katy Keene) and model (Marvel's Millie the Model). Even those women who have serious careers (DC's Lois Lane) are often featured in stories that emphasize romance.

Of course, inaccurate representations are one problem but lack of representation is another entirely. Quite often women in mass media have a token presence and appear only to serve to enhance the male character(s) in starring roles. Cartoonist Alison Bechdel offered commentary on this type of misrepresentation when she promoted what has become known as the **Bechdel Test** in the pages of her comic strip, *Dykes to Watch out For*, though the test would not permeate the popular consciousness until years after she first introduced it. The test has three basic requirements: that a narrative has at least two female characters; that those characters talk to one another; and that they talk about something other than men. Failing the test suggests the story is biased, and quite a lot of popular stories do not measure up. Just consider how the Invisible Woman is the only female member of the Fantastic Four or how Betty and Veronica's conversation often turns to focus on their romantic rival, Archie.

Part of the problem with the presentation of women in the comics may be attributed to the historic lack of inclusion of women in the industry. Until very recently, the medium has been disproportionately populated by male creators working for male owners, although not always dominated by male readers. In the heyday of comic books in the 1940s, reader surveys suggested nearly an even split among male and female readers (Witty 1941). Still, even comics' most enduring female icon, Wonder Woman, was created by a male—William Moulton Marston—and her stories were principally written by male storytellers for the first nearly fifty years of her publishing history. There have been professional women cartoonists, of course, such as *Miss Fury* creator Tarpé Mills in the 1940s, EC colorist Marie Severin in the 1950s, and *Metamorpho* co-creator Ramona Fradon in the 1960s. Strides for an expanded role for women cartoonists came through the comix underground (edited by Trina Robbins, *It Ain't Me, Babe*, 1970) and the alternative press (Wendy Pini, *Elfquest*, 1978). The industry arguably achieved a milestone when Jeanette Kahn was appointed the high-profile role of publisher of DC Comics in 1976. Since that time, numerous women writers (e.g., Gail Simone), artists (e.g., Raina Telgemier), and editors (e.g., Karen Berger) have contributed their talents to the industry, though women's surest ally has been the growth of the graphic novel market that has allowed them to work in genres other than superheroes, with particular success in terms of creating autobiographical comics (e.g., Marjane Satrapi's *Persepolis*, 2002, Alison Bechdel's *Fun Home*, 2006, and Emil Ferris' *My Favorite Thing is Monsters*, 2017). Complementing these efforts is an increasingly vocal fan community, such as the Sequential Tart and Women Write about Comics, who strive to bring recognition to female creators, characters, and readership. Still, given the prevalence of male creators, male characters, and male themes in contemporary comics, it would be erroneous to assume that the dominant ideology has relinquished its hold on its audience's thinking entirely.

Profile: Trina Robbins

Born: Trina Perlson
August 17, 1938
Brooklyn, New York

"I'm very proud of having rediscovered and brought to the attention of comics fans and scholars so many talented women comics creators who had fallen into obscurity, and I intend to keep at it."

Career Highlights

Figure 11.8 Herstorian Trina Robbins has contributed comics and commentary over the course of her prolific career. Photo courtesy of Ann Sanfedele.

1970 Produced the first comic book entirely by women, the underground one-shot *It Ain't Me Babe*

1972 Collaborates on the first issue of the ongoing series *Wimmen's Comix* and contributes "Sandy Comes Out," the first comics story featuring an openly lesbian character

1983 Publishes her first scholarly book, *Women and the Comics,* with coauthor catherine yronwode

1985-6 Tackles mainstream comic books with *Meet Misty* for Marvel Comics and *Legend of Wonder Woman* for DC

1994 Co-founds the Friends of Lulu, an association that promotes roles for women in the comics industry

2000 With artist Anne Timmons creates *GoGirl!* for Image Comics, a series about a female superhero aimed at young female readers

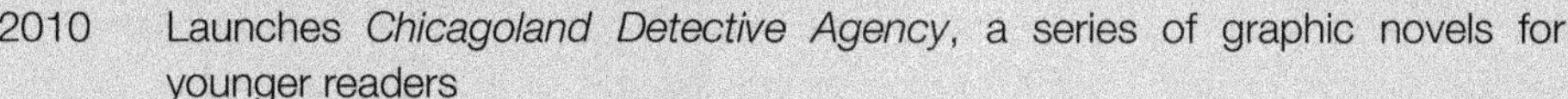

2010 Launches *Chicagoland Detective Agency*, a series of graphic novels for younger readers

2013 Releases her definitive history on women in comics: *Pretty in Ink: American Women Cartoonists 1896–2013* from Fantagraphics Books

Trina Robbins is a pioneer in two realms of comics culture. She was among a cohort of independent female cartoonists who challenged the male-dominated comics publishing industry. Her contributions in magazines such as *It Ain't Me Babe* and *Wimmen's Comix* helped establish her as a role model to talented young women who followed.

But Robbins was also the vanguard in a movement to identify and document the careers and contributions of female cartoonists. As she explains, "I was a cartoonist who moved into scholarly work because none of the comics historians (who were all male) were writing about the women who had created comics, or were at the most giving them a token page or two. As (duh) a woman comics creator, it was a pretty clear what needed to be done, so I did it."

Adopting the role of herstorian, as she dubbed herself, Robbins sought to keep the contributions of her predecessors and peers in view of the scholarly and fan communities in works such as *A Century of Women Cartoonists* (Kitchen Sink, 1993) and *The Brinkley Girls: The Best of Nell Brinkley's Cartoons from 1913-1940* (Fantagraphics, 2009). "My big epiphany in researching my books has been the realization that if you're not written about, you're forgotten." To her credit, other historians have followed in her footsteps and continue promoting the contributions of women cartoonists.

"So many brilliant comics creators have fallen into obscurity, male and female," says Robbins, who also notes, "There is so much more out there besides Batman and Spider-Man" worthy of attention.

In the meantime, she continues to work in comics, adding to series such as *The Chicagoland Detective Agency.* This series is particularly dear to her heart as it is aimed at younger readers: "I love writing for young readers, and until the recent onset of graphic novels there used to be nothing for kids except superhero comics, which were mostly too violent and which girls didn't read." And so Robbins continues to push the boundaries of where graphic storytelling and scholarship are focused, and isn't that just what pioneers are prone to do?

Analyzing: Comics Criticism Comes of Age

Work from all three scholarly perspectives, descriptive, interpretive, and critical, continues to be produced with ever-increasing frequency and sophistication. Yet perhaps the most exciting development in comics scholarship involves work in building a language for critiquing the art form on its own terms. Other media already benefit from the long-standing tradition of developing and using concepts to talk about storytelling devices in their art forms. For example, the field of film studies has over the past century developed a vocabulary for talking about framing, editing, lighting, and setting within a motion picture. Terms like *mise-en-scène* and *noir* are familiar examples of this vocabulary for those who may have already taken a film appreciation course. In similar fashion, scholars in comics studies are now developing a vocabulary to talk about their medium.

According to comics scholar Joseph Witek (1999), this is a relatively recent development in the field and the third in series of phases in the development of a distinct comics criticism. The first phase was characterized by comics appreciation and exemplified in such early works of sustained study as Martin Sheridan's 1942 book, *Comics and Their Creators*, which cataloged the comic strip's creators and their creations. The second step toward a distinct comics criticism came when comics began to be used as evidence for arguments about larger social trends. The method of content analysis, discussed earlier, would fall within the parameters of this phase, and works such as Arthur Asa Berger's 1973 *The Comic-Stripped American* would exemplify it. The third and most mature phase in this process came when thinkers began to approach comics as a narrative medium on its own terms. Witek credits legendary cartoonist Will Eisner with producing the first full-length treatment of this approach in his 1985 *Comics and Sequential Art.*

The groundbreaking work of cartoonists like Eisner, along with others like Robert C. Harvey (1996) and Scott McCloud (1993), have certainly laid much of the foundation for this current work. We have considered concepts like Eisner's encapsulation, Harvey's blending, and McCloud's closure in previous chapters, where we discussed the encoding and decoding of comics and advanced some of our own theories about the art form. Additional language for interpreting comics is also coming from academics. Among those scholars and works offering language for consideration are David Carrier's *Aesthetics of Comics* (2000), Neil Cohn's The *Visual Language of Comics* (2013), Thierry Groenstein's *System of Comics* (2007) and *Comics and Narration* (2013), and *Key Terms in Comics Studies* (2022) edited by Erin La Cour, Simon Grennan, and Rik Spanjers. Through these and other works, we are witnessing the beginning of a more formal approach to comics criticism, one that promises to enrich our understanding and appreciation for the comics art form on its own terms.

Discussion Questions

1. What qualities of the comics form do you find appealing as a reader? How could these qualities help motivate others to want to read comics?
2. Issues of representation in comics often focus on the misrepresentation of groups of people. While women have received unflattering portrayals, other disempowered groups have appeared rarely, if at all. Can you identify some groups that have been absent from comics? Which treatment would be more preferred: to be misrepresented or not be represented at all?
3. What questions are still unanswered about comics' content or their effects on audiences? How could researchers go about finding answers to the questions you have posed?

Activities

1. Using your university's databases and online search engines develop an annotated bibliography for one of the figures introduced in this chapter's sidebar, "Discovering: Milestones in the Development of Comics Studies." An annotated bibliography provides both a citation for a scholarly publication and a brief summary/commentary on the contents of each entry. Be prepared to discuss the major contributions of your figure to the field of comics studies.
2. Conduct a content analysis that closely examines a set of comics for the patterns of messages they send about an ethnic group, profession, institution, etc. The following is an example of the elements that must be defined and the steps that one follows in conducting a content analysis.

Step One: Formulate Your Research Question
Example: "How are journalists portrayed in Marvel superhero comic books?"

Step Two: Identify Your Genre
Example: "Marvel superhero comic books"

Step Three: Outline Your Sample
Example: "Six months worth of Marvel's ten best-selling superhero titles"

Step Four: Designate Your Unit of Analysis
Example: "Depictions of journalists"

Step Five: Create a Coding Sheet of the Categories to be Analyzed
Example:

Title: __________ Issue # ________ Date: ________ Creators: __________
Type of journalist: _______editor _______reporter _______ photojournalist _______other
Look: _______well-dressed _______scruffy _______ casual _______ other

Personality: _______ethical _______unethical _______ brave _______ cowardly

_______angry _______dispassionate _______ other

Bad Habits: _______cigarettes _______ coffee _______ alcohol
_______ disorganized desk ____ sloppy dresser ____ other

Step Six: Review Each Comic in Your Sample and Record a Count of Each Appearance of Your Categories

Step Seven: Write a Paragraph or Two Explaining the Answer to Your Research Question Based on the Patterns Seen in Your Results

Note: **This is just an example!** You need to formulate your own question, select your own universe and sample, construct your own coding sheet, and draw your own conclusions.

Recommended Reading

Comics

Hosler, Jay. *The Way of the Hive: A Honey Bee Story*. New York: HarperCollins, 2021.
The Way of the Hive tells the story of Nyuki the bee in a clever mix of comic adventure and biological fact. Hosler's efforts go to show that comics can be both entertaining and educating.

Classics Illustrated. (1947–71). Available on Comixology at https://www.comixology.com/Classics-Illustrated/comics-series/12470.
From *Hamlet* to *War of the Worlds*, *Classics Illustrated* adapts some of the most regarded works of prose literature to comics form and serves as a touchstone for generations of readers. Much of the catalog is now available for download in digital reproductions.

Scholarly Sources

Kirtley, Susan E., Antero Garcia, and Peter E. Carlson, eds. *With Great Power Comes Great Pedagogy: Teaching, Learning, and Comics.* Jackson: University Press of Mississippi, 2020.
Contributors to this volume help readers to understand a number of ways to teach using comics in their classroom. In addition to the expertise of professional educators, the volume also includes interviews with professional comics creators turned instructors such as Lynda Barry and Brian Michael Bendis.

Giddens, Thomas, ed. *Critical Directions in Comics Studies*. Jackson: University Press of Mississippi, 2020.
Giddens and the contributors to this volume seek to re-examine assumptions about the way that the field of comics studies frames the study of comics. Contributors bring perspectives on a range of topics from health humanities to critical legal studies to question works as diverse as British comics to Marvel's *Deadpool*.

12 Writing About Comics

Each week Victor Dandridge, Jr. and Ryan Seymore take to the internet to post their reviews of the week's latest comic books, graphic novels, and fan-related merchandise. Their vlog, "Black White & Read All Over" is recorded from Seymore's store, Comic Town, in Columbus, Ohio, but has a potential worldwide reach thanks to a YouTube channel. Dandridge is a creator and educator, and the two fans play off of one another as they highlight the latest comics and graphic novels each recommends to the reading public. Their love of the medium is evident through their banter, and their enthusiasm for comics is likely to drive readers to Seymour's store—and others like it around the country (Figure 12.1).

As we have argued throughout this textbook, comics and graphic novels are acts of communication, and as such invite a response from their audiences. Sometimes these fan reactions take place in the conversations that fans have with one another in their local comic shop, an exchange that is echoed in the format of Dandridge and Seymour's conversations; however, it can also take on a more formal response when readers commit to communicating their response in video or written responses.

This chapter covers two kinds of writing about comics: reviews and analyses. Although both forms of writing are critical responses to comics, there are some key differences.

Figure 12.1 Victor Dandridge, Jr. and Ryan Seymore deliver reviews of the latest comic books on their vlog, "Black White & Read All Over." Reproduced with the permission of Victor Dandridge, Jr.

Foremost, we suggest that reviews are about assessing the value of the reading experience while analyses are about interpreting meanings within comics. Another key distinction involves the audience for each. A review can be for anyone interested in reading a comic or graphic novel; an analysis tends to be targeted for an academic audience of one's fellow scholars and students of the medium. And yet both forms of writing help deepen our appreciation for and response to comics and graphic novels. We will explain the process of writing each type of critical response and provide an outline for the potential structure for each. These explanations are intended to help guide you toward generating your own critical responses and engaging in the ongoing conversation about the value of reading comics.

Comics scholar Craig Fischer (2010) has previously identified not two but three types of writing about comics. Fischer proposed a set of categories including *fan appreciation*, *essayistic criticism*, and *academic criticism. Fan appreciation* is a first-person response to reading comics that celebrates the medium, a character, or a creator who inspired someone's love of comics. These tend to focus on the fans' "origin story" of coming to the comics medium and typically lack much critical content for the reader. For example, fan-turned-pro Robert Crumb has written about the influence of cartoonist Harvey Kurtzman on his career. *Essayistic criticism* consists of interviews and reviews that may contain some autobiographical content but are far more rigorous in their evaluation of the comics material. Fischer notes that *The Comics Journal*, which began publication in 1977, is a for this kind of comics writing, and it has a history of interrogating creators and their works for their artistic vision—or lack thereof. Finally, *academic criticism* is employed by scholars who use theoretical concepts—often from fields of study outside of comics studies—to investigate meanings within comics texts. These are often jargon-filled essays and address the interests of other scholars rather than the wider public. *The Journal of Graphic Novels and Comics* from Routledge is an example of a publication that provides scholars with a forum for the exchange of ideas.

Fischer certainly provides a useful set of categories to describe the landscape of comics writing, and we believe that our approach to writing about comics in this chapter expands upon the second of these categories and introduces forms of essayistic criticism. Our review and analysis assignments encourage you to move beyond mere tributes but may not quite take you to the level of mature academic criticism, given the number of years it takes to develop the necessary knowledge base to engage with that writing. Instead, we believe that our presentation of reviews and analyses emerge from essayistic tradition, focusing your response on a more critical discussion of the content of the comics and the experience of reading them.

Objectives

1. To write reviews helpful for other readers about the perceived value of a reading experience; and
2. To write analyses for other critical thinkers about the meanings in comics and graphic novels.

Writing a Review

A **review** is a thoughtful response to a creative work that seeks to guide audience members as to whether or not they should read the work themselves. In effect, a review renders a service to the audience. The author seeks to provide just enough persuasive information for the audience members to make informed decisions. Thus, your primary concern in writing a review is to help your audience determine whether or not the comic or graphic novel is worth their efforts to acquire it and invest their time in reading it.

Reviews tend to be more subjective than objective in nature; however, that does not mean they are simply statements of opinion. Instead, reviews are informed by the reviewer's expertise with the subject matter and explained by claims about the quality or effectiveness of the work supported by evidence from the work itself.

The Review Writing Process

Step one in writing a review is to select a comic or graphic novel. What makes a comic or graphic novel worthy of review? Typically, we think of reviewers tackling recently published works, as this presents a good deal of utility to an audience who regularly consumes the latest publications; Would-be readers want to know whether or not a new publication is worth their attention. However, the practice of reviewing may be applied to any existing work, as the catalog of comics across time and cultures means that readers cannot have possibly read everything and so reviews help them sift through the seemingly endless choices. That said, the likely preferred choice for what you pick up to review is something about which you have some curiosity. For instance, if there is a work in your favorite genre or one by a creator you've previously enjoyed, then it is also a strong candidate for a review.

Step two is to read through the work in its entirety. In all fairness to the creators, you as a reviewer really should read through the whole comic book or graphic novel, even if you find yourself turned off somewhat early in your reading experience. Problems within the early pages of the work may be resolved as it progresses and initial impressions of problems may be clarified as you gather more information. As you read, it is wise to take notes about sections that stand out to you. As your reading goes on, you may want to start to identify themes in the work. Be sure to cite the pages (if numbered) that you are pulling your observations from, as you may wish to refer back to them as you author your review.

Step three is to reflect on your reading experience. What pleased you? What disappointed you? Can you begin to apply concepts from Chapters 3, 4, and 5 of this textbook regarding the creation and interpretation of comics communication to your reading experience? For example, did the writer develop relatable characters? Did the artist lack the ability to coordinate the verbal-visual blending? Is the layout of the pages clear or confusing? Careful reflection can help you to identify the major elements that led you to have a favorable or unfavorable reception of the comic.

Step four is to compose your review. You can begin this process with some pre-writing activities such as brainstorming or outlining. Initially you don't have to worry about expressing your ideas in complete, grammatically correct sentences. At first just try to get your ideas about what is effective or ineffective in the work written down and then structure how to express them as you move along.

As you look over your thoughts, you'll eventually want to weigh out whether you judge the work to be worthy or unworthy of other reader's time. At this point you'll want to capture that judgment by stating it in a thesis. A **thesis** expresses your argument, the central point or conviction put forward in your essay. A thesis basically captures in a single statement whether you are recommending a work or not and the key reason(s) for doing so. For example, you might be recommending the latest memoir comic and capture that by saying, "*My Life in Pictures* is a worthwhile reading experience because it vividly portrays the struggles of coming of age in a small town."

As you continue to compose, you'll want to support your thesis by offering claims. A **claim** is a statement asserting some relevant attribute of the comic. To say that the creators used layout to create an effective reading experience represents a claim. As you can tell, this can be rather subjective in nature. However, reviewers can substantiate their claims by providing evidence.

Thus, step five is to back each claim with evidence. **Evidence** is material pulled from the comic itself to attempt to validate the reviewer's claim. So, if my claim is that the creators used layout effectively, I would supply evidence from the reading. For example, let's say that in a discussion between two characters about the circular nature of life, the creators design the page like a wheel with panels encircling a central hub. That inventive conception with the thematic similarities between topic and rendering might strike you as particularly artistic and support your claim about their effectiveness in employing layout to help carry forward the story.

Step six is to revise. Writing is a process of committing ideas to words and revising them. It's okay to rework, reorder, and even reject ideas, statements, and words along the way. One of the best writing tips we have considered in our own writing is to allow time to step away from a writing assignment and come back to it after some time away, be that an hour, a day, or even weeks later. The fresh perspective afforded by time away from a piece of writing can help you to realize ways to make it clearer in subsequent revisions. If you are fortunate enough to have an editorial partner such as a classmate or writing center tutor, seek out their feedback and revise accordingly. Having an actual reader examine your draft and responding to their suggestions can lead to an even more effective finished essay.

Step seven is to publish. If your review is part of an assignment in a Comics Studies course, this may mean submitting the completed review to your professor by uploading it to the learning management system. If you are engaging a wider audience of fellow comics readers, this may lead to posting it in an online forum or including it in some other venue. Once a review is out there, it becomes an act of communication itself, not only responding to the original comic but inviting feedback from its readers. Who knows? If published online, your review may even be discovered by the original creators themselves!

DISCOVERING: STEPS IN A REVIEW

1) Select a comic book or graphic novel
2) Read the work entirely, making notes as you go
3) Reflect on your reading experience
4) Compose your thesis and related claims
5) Provide supporting evidence for those claims

6) Revise your drafts

7) Publish your complete review

Structuring a Review

Now that you have a sense of how to go about the process of writing a review, we would like to suggest what structure you may find in the finished product. We want to emphasize that the structure presented as follows is not necessarily the order in which a review is written. The order that follows is the final organizational structure that is presented in the published version. Many successful writers start their process by working within the body of their review first and add on the elements that constitute the beginning and ending at a later time, as their process moves toward publication.

We also want to point out that reviews tend to be brief. The role of the reviewer is not to recreate the reading experience for their audience but to provide enough information to either help encourage the audience to go read the work for themselves or save them the time of reading something that's not worth the investment.

Whether as a separate heading or soon within the essay itself, be sure to identify the name of the work, its principal creators, the publisher, and likely the date of publication. This information will prove useful if you give a positive review and readers want to track the work down to check it out for themselves.

The structure of a review should begin with a hook of some kind to arrest the audience's attention. This could be an unfamiliar fact, an anecdote about the work or its creators, or any other device that grabs the reader. For example, in starting a review about your favorite creator's first attempt within a new genre, you might inform the reader of that fact: "Dakota Lee is known for creating memoir comics, but in their latest work they are experimenting with horror fiction for the very first time."

Early on a reader should have some sense of the **valence** of your review, that is, whether it is generally more positive and supportive of the work or more negative and critical of the work. This is likely embodied in your thesis. Continuing with the example begun in the previous paragraph, our thesis might read, "Dakota Lee's *The Big Thrill* provides big chills, as depictions of the horror of being trapped in a haunted house make for a truly spine-tingling reading experience." As this wording suggests, the review indicates a positive reaction by noting that the author achieved "big chills," which is to be taken as a compliment within the horror genre. A review should not be a "who dunnit?" where the big reveal comes at the very end; rather, a reader should be able to perceive how you are judging the work early on in the review.

While readers consult reviews to determine whether or not to pick up a comic or graphic novel, you may not always be in a position to render a "thumbs up" or "thumbs down" verdict on a given work. It is possible that you may have a mixed review, where you find some elements of the comic praiseworthy and others less favorable. Even if they love a work, many reviewers still find some flaw in it, and even the worst work may have some redeemable aspects. The key is to be honest with your audience and let them know the good and the bad in anything you are reviewing for them.

Most reviews also include some summary of the plot and major features of the work early on. We urge you to be rather brief with this summary, as it need not be so detailed as to void the joy of reading the work itself. In fact, reviews should always be aware of how many potential spoilers they may be giving. A **spoiler** is a plot detail that if known beforehand ruins the pleasure of the surprise for the reader. For example, revealing the final fate of the characters following the climax of the work is a major spoiler. It is considered bad form to reveal spoilers unless you forewarn your reader that spoilers are coming (i.e., "spoiler alert"). Instead, there should be just enough details about the characters, setting, and the initial action of the narrative to provide the reader with context for the claims to follow.

The body of a review should consist mostly of claims about the work and evidence from the work to support the claims. In some cases, reviewers might reproduce a panel, sequence, or page from the reading to serve as evidence itself. A review likely consists of more than one singular claim about a work but because reviews tend to be concise in their overall length, they rarely delve into more than a handful of claims. Do note that reviewers will usually introduce their strongest claims first and follow up with less convincing claims thereafter (Figure 12.2).

Figure 12.2 Although we do not know who the storytellers are for this pre-Code story of teenage rebellion, we can recognize that the protagonist, Linda, is standoffish with both her parents and her steady boyfriend, Jimmy. Note how there is literal distance between Linda and her folks, who have fairly mundane expectations for her, and notice how she has her back turned to Jimmy. A reviewer could make the claim that the storytellers were effective in using blocking and body language to communicate what her thoughts were and the narration confirms her feelings of dissatisfaction with her life. St. John Publications produced *Teen-Age Temptations* in 1952.

Reviews typically end with some intentional conclusion, rather than merely trail off after the last claim is offered. A conclusion might be a final statement reaffirming the reviewer's stance, with words somewhere along a continuum ranging from wholeheartedly endorsing the reader to read the work to warning them to stay clear of it. Sometimes reviews offer an overall rating for a work (e.g., "five stars") or alternative advice for the reader, such as suggestions for more favorable works by the same creators or similar works by other creators. In whatever way the review concludes, the key is to end intentionally.

While reviews clearly have a utility function in that they seek to inform and persuade an audience about their reading choices, they can be well-constructed, even entertaining reads themselves. Injecting your reviews with personality and authenticity will encourage readers to connect with you and, ideally, value your judgments.

CHECKLIST: THE STRUCTURE OF A REVIEW

- Hook
- Publication details
- Thesis
- Brief summary
- Claim and evidence (repeat as space allows)
- Conclusion

DISCOVERING: SAMPLE STUDENT REVIEW

The following essay was authored by Victor Barajas, a senior student at Henderson State University majoring in nursing and reviews "A Life in Comics" by Nick Sousanis, as seen on pages 125–131.

Review of "A Life in Comics"

The short story comic "A Life in Comics," written and illustrated by Nick Sousanis, presents the biographical history of Karen Green's interest in comics from a young age that would eventually develop into a flourishing career as a librarian. As noted in the comic, Sousanis first met Green when he attended Columbia as a doctoral student. She no doubt left a lasting impression on Sousanis considering his efforts in this comic to immortalize her life's choices in comic form. The two also clearly make a fantastic team by comics standards since "A Life in Comics" earned Sousanis the Eisner Award for Best Short Story in 2018 (Sousanis). After reading the brief comic, it is easy to see why. By blending the verbal and visual to tell the story of Green's tumultuous journey to become the first curator for comics and cartoons in Columbia's Rare Books & Manuscripts Library, Sousanis presents a captivating look into the value of chasing your interests despite opposition or meandering pathways.

With comics, we typically make snap judgments early based on the illustrator's art style about whether or not we want to invest our time in it. Sousanis's style incorporates an element of realism, which the reader might expect of a biographical work. However, he also makes visual allusions to other works like the *New Yorker's* iconic cartoon style, Medieval manuscript art, *Archie*, Batman, Spider-Man, and more. Sousanis incorporates each of these unique styles to further illustrate the breadth and value of Green's appreciation of cartoons and comics. The inclusion of the different styles is effective because of this choice in instructing the reader about the varied kinds of comics that Green has helped curate and validate in academia.

In unison with the realistic art style, Sousanis also adopts a realistic approach to the prose narrative, which uses dialogue sparingly in favor of expository writing. This rhetorical choice also fits with the biography genre, and it provides the information with an additional layer of credibility. However, even among the more serious narration, there are still elements of humor that maintain the reader's interest and flesh out Green's character as more three-dimensional. At the bottom of page 3, for example, Sousanis explores Green's experience as a bartender and her use of a Cheshire grin to cover up the times she did not want to smile.

Tying to the short story nature of this biographical work, the pacing of the panels is important to keep the reader interested without losing valuable details. Thankfully, Sousanis expertly moves the story along without neglecting elements of Green's experience. By the end of the short comic, the reader can feel that they have truly learned the value of Green's journey as well as the importance of following our interests without giving in to the pressure of capitalism. Part of what keeps the pace moving so well is Sousanis's use of varying panel sizes, positions, and of creative elements like on the final page where the reader is invited to interact with the comic physically by folding the page to conceptualize how outsiders might have seen Green's journey in comparison with how her life's decisions developed.

Whether or not you already see the study of comics as a legitimate academic pursuit, learning about one librarian's importance to that world is made even more interesting by Sousanis's narrative craft. The art style, creative narration, and quick pace reveal a valuable message for any twenty-first-century citizen: our lives may feel directionless or confusing when we are in the middle of our journeys, but when we follow our passions, we can achieve new and wonderful things. Karen Green, Columbia's Curator for Comics and Cartoons, is a fantastic example of the power of letting your interests guide you, so give her and Sousanis a chance. I think you will be pleasantly surprised at the depth of the message they deliver in so few pages.

Works Cited

Sousanis, Nick. "About." *Spin, Weave, and Cut*. Accessed 15 October 2021. https://spinweaveandcut.com/about/.

Writing an Analysis

An **analysis** is an intellectual response to a creative work that seeks to explore deeper meanings found within it. Unlike a review, which is written with a general audience of readers in mind, an analysis tends to be written for a scholarly audience, who tend to have some prior experience in critiquing and sense-making when it comes to creative works. Such an audience certainly includes people like your instructor but frankly also includes your classmates, who may have limited but some experience in critiquing comics up to this point. The author of an analysis seeks to make a strong case to its audience about an interpretation based on a careful reading of the text and reflection on its meanings.

Analyses are also subjective in nature; however, their subjectivity is supported by the detailed evidence and reasoning in the essay. Although analyses seek to make a convincing case, most writers of analyses can recognize that not everyone will share their interpretation of the work and its meanings. What matters is putting forward the strongest case possible to win over the thoughtful consideration of readers.

The Analysis Writing Process

The process of writing an analysis follows a pattern very similar to writing a review, but the pattern bears reiterating just to highlight some of the ways in which an analysis differs from a review. Step one is to select a comic or graphic novel. Although any comic past or present could be subject to analysis, typically works that have found favor with audiences and either been honored with awards like the Will Eisner Comics Industry Awards, "The Eisners," or ones that have made it on to "must reads" lists make for frequent focuses. However, we want to underscore that it is possible to critique any work in this fashion, including those that are poorly executed and those that have undesirable social and political messages. In fact, it is often easier for students to perform an analysis on a work that is not well regarded in order to more readily explore the faults within it or attempt to redeem it through its virtues.

Step two is to read the work entirely and most likely multiple times. The reason for multiple readings is to help you identify those deeper meanings within the work, especially those that may slip by you in a quick, initial scan of the comic. Multiple readings not only help you to bring broader meanings into focus but also identify those details that support the formation of your arguments. Because this process is focused on uncovering such details, it is often referred to as **close reading**. Taking careful notes throughout your reading process will serve you well as you compose the essay. You may want to note the elements of effective storytelling such as plot, character, and dialogue, but because this is comics, you'll also want to consider rendering, framing, and layout. Pay attention to themes, that is any recurring ideas or actions in the story or images in the depiction. For example, you might notice how often characters say something or are shown doing something repeatedly.

Step three is to reflect on the reading experience and begin to consider what deeper meanings may be presented in the work itself. For example, you might ask yourself questions like how were characters from minoritized groups represented in the comic or are there deeper meanings to the color scheme employed by the color artist? Those are specific questions that may not be applicable to all comics. As part of your reflections you may wish to consider how the specific comic succeeded in eliciting a response from you: What did it do well? Where did it fail to perform?

Step four is to compose your analysis. Pre-writing activities like brainstorming and outlining can help you capture key ideas without having to write them all out at first. Subsequent revisions of your initial thoughts can begin to elaborate key ideas in complete sentences.

Here again, a thesis will be key to capturing your argument. With an analysis, the thesis puts forward your central interpretation of the work. It expresses in one statement the argument you are attempting to make with the essay. For instance, in a science fiction comic about first contact between two alien races, your thesis might read, "The graphic novel *First Encounter* is too far removed from the reader's experience to get its audience to feel empathy for the alien species standing in as an allegory for humans on different sides of a political disagreement."

Once you have a thesis, additional claims can be offered to support it. In the case of the earlier thesis, a supporting claim might be to say, "Each alien species is too strangely drawn for readers to see themselves in the aliens' asymmetrical and distorted forms and thus fails to develop empathy for the creatures."

Step five is to back up each claim with evidence from the work itself. In the earlier example, you might support the claim by offering up a description of the aliens, whose asymmetrical bodies and pale skin tones make it difficult for readers to see themselves in their alien forms. When analyzing a comic, images can be used as evidence, although these are usually accompanied by some explanatory text to anchor the meaning of the image (or at least the meaning you want to give it) (Figure 12.3).

Step six is to revise your work. Again, taking time away from your draft to look at it through fresh eyes or relying on an actual pair of fresh eyes from another reader can help you to improve the communication coming through your essay.

Step seven is to publish your essay. This may mean turning in your analysis to your instructor for course credit and/or taking it into another scholarly venue, such as a research conference presentation or submitting it for review in a local, regional, national, or even international journal that specializes in publishing comics studies and popular culture.

Structuring an Analysis

Having discussed the steps in writing your analysis, we turn our attention to the structure of the completed essay. Again, typically the order of elements as they appear in the published essay is not the order in which they are generated. Writers arrive at a final order in subsequent drafts of the essay.

An analysis tends to be more in-depth than a review. Typically, it takes more words to explore the interpretation offered by the thesis and provide sufficient claims and supporting evidence to make a convincing case for the readers.

In order to capture your readers' attention, you want to begin an essay with a hook that can grab their attention. There are a number of strategies you could use in establishing a hook (some of which are covered in the review earlier), but one additional one that you might use for a fuller essay could be to pull in a relevant quote from the dialogue or a panel from a sequence and discuss it in context of the larger meaning of the work.

Readers should also discover your thesis relatively early on in the essay. A thesis is not something you build up to at the very end of your essay; rather, it should be clearly stated relatively early on.

Most analyses also provide some manner of summary of the plot and major features of the work. A summary really should not be the major portion of your essay; give enough details to establish the nature of the work and move into your claims and evidence efficiently. Unlike a review, dropping spoilers seems to be less of an issue for an analysis. That is because audiences are not necessarily relying on an analysis to inform their reading decisions; many are reading an analysis to see what you thought of the work, perhaps having already read it themselves. Thus, if there is something you want to analyze that gives away a major plot point (such as the death of a major character), it may be necessary to discuss that development in order for your analysis to make sense.

The body of your analysis should offer claims and detailed evidence to support your thesis. While you may have the liberty to offer a number of claims in support of your thesis, it is probably better to offer your strongest claims and to back those up with clear, convincing evidence. Going a bit more into detail on your evidence will likely make for a stronger overall interpretation than lots and lots of claims. Here again, evidence might include reproductions of panels, sequences, or pages from the actual comic art itself. Recall that we covered approaches to research in the previous chapter, and noted how the particular methodology you employ is going to govern the nature of your claims and the types of evidence you will use to support those claims.

An analysis should definitely draw itself to a conclusion. The conclusion might briefly review the case presented throughout the essay and reiterate the thesis. You might also reflect on larger lessons the work or your analysis of it has taught you about comics, the topics covered within the work, or even social dynamics surrounding the work or its focus. Some analyses also point to future directions for research.

Figure 12.3 Artist Pete Costanza seeks to make an alien visitor strange but also non-threatening. Note how the oversized ears and bulging eyes are atypical for most humans, making the alien appear to be strange. And yet the soft features leave the aliens unmenacing and in the course of the story the outnumbered alien pose no real threat against humanity. The inferences we make in its features play out in the story where the alien visitors only seek to avoid conflict with humans. From *Forbidden Worlds* #50 (1957) from the American Comics Group.

Because analyses are typically scholarly works, they should include a bibliography of sources you have consulted in the construction of your essay. At an absolute minimum this should include publication information for the comic or graphic novel itself. It may also include sources you consulted in researching the creators, previous scholarship on the same work, or any other source that helped you to talk about the work in context. Although comics and graphic novels are not always clearly flagged in citation systems like that provided by the American Psychological Association (APA), you can consult your instructor or librarian for guidance. For instance, in this textbook we have followed the Chicago Style and thus cite our published comics as follows:

> Author's Last name, First name. Title of Comic Book Issue. City of publication: Name of Publisher, Year published.

You should consult with your instructor as to preferred formatting.

Table 12.1 Key Differences Between a Review and Analysis

A review . . .	An analysis . . .
Is written for a general audience to give advice.	Is written for a scholarly audience to share an interpretation.
Tends to be brief.	Tends to go into some detail, especially with its presentation of evidence.
Carefully avoids spoilers that reveal crucial plot details.	May need to discuss crucial plot points in order to carry forward its argument.
Offers a limited number of claims to support its central argument with limited but compelling evidence.	Offers a number of claims to support is central argument but each with substantive evidence to back it up.
Concludes briefly but intentionally.	Concludes with reiteration and perspective.

The function of an analysis is to explore meanings within a comic's text. The writer is sharing an interpretation of the text and attempting to sway the audience to see the work from that perspective, too. An effective analysis opens up a new perspective for the reader, providing them with a view of the comics art they might not have otherwise been aware of.

CHECKLIST: THE STRUCTURE OF AN ANALYSIS

- Hook
- Thesis
- Summary
- Claims and detailed evidence (repeat as the argument merits)
- Conclusion
- Bibliography

DISCOVERING: SAMPLE STUDENT ANALYSIS

The following essay was authored by Eloise Sumner, a junior exchange student while at Radford University majoring in English Literature and analyzes *Chilling Adventures of Sabrina* by Roberto Aguirre-Sacasa and Robert Hack.

Witchcraft Is Not Used as a Tool of Empowerment in *Chilling Adventures of Sabrina*

"I know you're scared, Sabrina. Because all women are taught to fear power. Own your power." ("Chapter 10: The Witching Hour" 39:18-39:32). In modern literary works, witchcraft is no longer a tool for the marginalization of women; the female power to yield magic over others relinquishes the patriarchal hold on the female body. Yet, the original, male-written narrative of *Chilling Adventures of Sabrina* is arguably not the inspiring, female tale of emancipation that the Netflix show strives to create; while the women are to an extent empowered by their craft, this power is subverted through traditional female presentations. The graphic novel tells the complex narrative of Sabrina Spellman who must choose between witchcraft and the mortal world on the eve of her sixteenth birthday; while witchcraft promises wonders, Sabrina longs for her mortal boyfriend Harvey. As Sabrina comes to make her choice, Madam Satan, her father's jealous lover who recently arose from the dead, orchestrates Harvey's death, leading Sabrina on a dark path of witchery as she attempts to bring him back. In this analysis of Roberto Aguirre-Sacasa and Robert Hack's *Chilling Adventures of Sabrina*, I will argue that witchcraft is not used as a tool for empowerment, but as a means of enforcing archaic and stereotypical representations of women.

The novel implements traditional depictions of witches as inhuman others. When chasing Harvey, the witches are dehumanized to creatures who walk on all fours in this sensory diegetic image (Aguirre-Sacasa and Hack 2018: 85) that would visually depict the witches as wild animals. Aguirre-Sacasa captions the scene, "pray for Harvey Kinkle," wherein the double entendre upon "pray" highlights that Harvey has become the literal "prey," casting the witches as inhuman predators. Indeed, after Harvey's death, the once kind and familial Hilda and Zelda depicted flying over Sabrina's shoulder as Guardian Angels (Aguirre-Sacasa and Hack 2018: 13), cannot hide their inner corrupted form. Hack draws skeletal, decaying bodies (Aguirre-Sacasa and Hack 2018: 99) of monsters that standardize the horror genre: the witches become "the prototype of all evil" (Evans-Prichard as cited in Spence 2017: 6) as was traditionally believed in the Middle Ages. Their callous dismissal of Harvey's death aligns their hideous outward form with their inner immorality and cold-hearted predatory nature. Indeed, Zelda tells Sabrina, "You'll have to do a lot of acting over the next few days," suggesting their previous kindly perception to be a mere performance to hide the vulgarity beneath. Female sexuality is equally implemented as a tool to villainize the witches; the female body was used to persecute witches in the medieval period given their supposed sexual relations with the devil (Schimmelpfennig 2013: 7). In the text, Madam Satan is seen emerging from the lake through braided panels, naked and cloaked in shadow in a visual depiction of dark, wanton sexuality. This chiaroscuro casts her as dangerous and mysterious, given "female sexuality . . . has been the foundation of the construct of female monstrosity" (Santos 2017: 129) and she becomes a threat to corrupting the purity of her victims. Thereby, by aligning witches with both their sexuality and monstrous identity, the witches are visually confirmed to the traditional perceptions of witches as inhuman others.

Furthermore, the sense of empowerment that witchcraft affords the central protagonist Sabrina is flawed. Her identity is entirely constructed around her relationship with her boyfriend, Harvey. It is through this relationship that Aguirre-Sacasa demonstrates her strength as she takes on the traditionally masculine role while Harvey becomes the helpless victim who Sabrina must protect; when Harvey interrupts the witches' dark baptism, Sabrina cries, "Harvey, they'll kill you . . . RUN." (Aguirre-Sacasa and Hack 2018: 85). Indeed, the moment he decides to perform the role of the male hero, he is immediately killed (Aguirre-Sacasa and Hack 2018: 96); the witch holds Harvey in her arms as if he were nothing more than a ragdoll, drenched in blood, demonstrating his incapability of living up to the traditional masculine hero model within the diegesis. Despite this more masculine role, Sabrina is limited by the all-consuming nature of the relationship. She has no other female friends her age and thereby becomes the "isolated heroine" (Jowett 2017) typical of the horror genre; instead of using a coven of witches to draw upon collaborative female strength, Aguirre-Sacasa isolates his heroine so that her constructed personality is predominantly defined by her relationship with a male secondary character. It is the relationship that would draw her into the mortal world, which is arguably a representation of the confining domestic sphere: the encapsulated scene within the panel in which Sabrina dreams of a mortal life is old-fashioned, discolored, and demonstrates Sabrina fulfilling the role of the stereotypical housewife (Aguirre-Sacasa and Hack 2018: 95). While the mortal world promises domesticity, the path of night would condemn her to subservience; women become mere "hand-maiden[s]" (Aguirre-Sacasa and Hack 2018: 82) to Satan, their male ruler: "He is your Master" (Aguirre-Sacasa and Hack 2018: 82), wherein the term "Master" recalls a power hierarchy that would mark the witches inferior, while the brut art style reinforces the pessimistic potential of her future. In this panel, a medium view demonstrates Satan as a towering figure leering over two female witches, highlighting his dominion over them; despite the potential power associated with witchcraft, these witches are limited to servants under a male ruling. This servility thereby associates the witches with the traditional ideology that "because women's bodies were weaker, the devil could reach women's souls more easily" (Reis 1995: 15) and they become puppets under his rule: "you danced for me, girl . . . " (Aguirre-Sacasa and Hack 2018: 82), wherein dancing for a man recalls more sexualized ideals surrounding the female body as an object to pleasure the male gaze. Indeed, Satan's insinuation that she is merely a "girl" depowers Sabrina further, stripping her to the status of a child and inferior. Sabrina is thus entrapped within a male dominating sphere as an isolated heroine, wherein her future outcomes limit her to domesticity or subservience.

Finally, the female antagonist, Madam Satan transforms into the harmful stereotype of the "Crazy Ex-Girlfriend" (McDermott 2018) which seeks to dismiss female emotions. She appears all consumed by her relationship with Sabrina's father, Edward to the extent that after his rejection of her, she commits suicide by jumping into a tiger's cage (Aguirre-Sacasa and Hack 2018: 41). While the action itself is bold, violent, and traditionally un-feminine, she demonstrates her life to be worthless without the companionship of a man. Upon her resurrection, instead of redeeming her previous action, her jealousy leads her to fixate on punishing Edward's family. She isolates herself in acts of petty violence and turns against other women; "Diana. That was the harlot's name." (Aguirre-Sacasa and Hack 2018: 35). Wherein the affect display is one of hate, her hands seen reaching toward the reader, her eyes drawn as skulls to demonstrate deadly intent. She thus falls into the horror trope that would pitch women against women (Jowett 2017), in acts that cast her as dramatic and reduce the true emotion beneath. As a female character, she fails the Bechdel test (Bechdel 1986: 22), conspiring predominantly with a male crow while she replaces her face with that of a more beautiful girl (Aguirre-Sacasa and Hack 2018: 53), which only reinforces the emphasis upon the female sexual body within society. The use of metonymy within the text, wherein Madam Satan is represented by a close-up panel on voluptuous lips (Aguirre-Sacasa and Hack 2018: 53), highlights not only the danger of her sexuality but also the corrupting nature of her words. It is these very words that she uses to corrupt and fool Sabrina in an ultimate act of spite against her ex-lover; "I hope I've earned your trust now, Sabrina." (Aguirre-Sacasa and Hack 2018: 123). Indeed, Madam Satan is a unique character given her resurrected state which allows her to "operate outside of the system" (Aguirre-Sacasa and Hack 2018: 123) that would label her subservient to Satan; she is depicted physically flying, a tenor which highlights her rising above the submissive state Satan desires. Yet, despite Satan's lack of control over her, Madam Satan's life remains male led, controlled by her ex-lover who is predominantly absent in the text, the hurt of his rejection suggesting her need for male validation to be all-consuming.

In conclusion, the *Chilling Adventures of Sabrina* does not use witchcraft to empower women, casting them into archaic roles. They conform to the traditional presentations of witches as inhuman; others, wherein sexuality and their monstrous depictions, suggest their threatening presence. Furthermore, the protagonist's identity and sense of female strength is constructed around her relationship with a boy; the ultimate plot-line devises two futures that ultimately lead her subservient, either to the domestic lifestyle or to a malevolent male ruler. Madam Satan's jealous motivations against her ex-lover weaken her as an antagonist; her liberated state outside of Satan's dominion is thereby undermined as her life continues to revolve around a male figure. Despite the potential witchcraft has to create a sense of power among female characters, Aguirre-Sacasa and Hack create women who are limited by their female identity, conforming to archaic and stereotypical roles.

Bibliography

Aguirre-Sacasa, Roberto, and Robert Hack. *Chilling Adventures of Sabrina.* New York, Archie Comic Publications, Inc, 2018.

Bechdel, Alison. *Dykes to Watch Out For*. New York: Firebrand Books, 1986.

"Chapter 10: The Witching Hour." Chilling Adventures of Sabrina, Season 1, Episode 10, Warner Bros. Television Production, October 26, 2018, *Netflix*, https://www.netflix.com/browse?jbv=80223989.

Jowett, L. "The Final Girl? Isolated Heroines and the Absence of Female Friendship in Teen Horror." *Investigating Identities in Young Adult (YA) Narratives, The University of Northampton, 13 December 2017*, Northampton.

McDermott, Roe. "How the trope of the 'Crazy Ex-Girlfriend' Protects Abusive Men." *Image.ie*, August 7, 2018. https://www.image.ie/editorial/trope-crazy-ex-girlfriend-protects-abusive-men-125052. Accessed November 19, 2021.

Reis, Elizabeth. "The Devil, the Body, and the Feminine Soul in Puritan New England." *The Journal of American History* 82, no. 1 (1995): 15–36. https://doi.org/10.2307/2081913.

Santos, Cristinia. *Unbecoming Female Monsters: Witches, Vampires, and Virgins*. Lanham: Lexington Books, 2017.

Schimmelpfennig, Annette. "Chaos Reigns - Women as Witches in Contemporary Film and the Fairy Tales of the Brothers Grimm." *Gender Forum*, no. 44 (2013): 1–12.

Selisker, Scott. "The Bechdel Test and the Social Form of Character Networks." *New Literary History* 46, no. 3 (2015): 505–23. doi:10.1353/nlh.2015.0024.

Spence, Samantha. *Witchcraft Accusations and Persecutions as a Mechanism for the Marginalisation of Women.* Newcastle Upon Tyne: Cambridge Scholars Publishing, 2017.

Wolff, Cynthia G. "A Mirror for Men: Stereotypes of Women in Literature." *The Massachusetts Review* 13, no. 1/2 (1972): 205–18.

Analyzing: Venues for Publishing

While the audience for your initial review and analysis assignments in this Comics Studies course may be limited to your instructor, our hope is that you will be inspired to take revised versions of those writing exercises—and subsequent ones—a step further. The conversation about comics deserves to have another generation of contributors weigh in with their insights and there are plenty of venues to carry them on to.

Many comics-related websites like *Comic Book Resources* and *Bleeding Cool* publish reviews from a rotating crew of regular contributors. New sites seeking fresh and distinct voices on comics, such as the Eisner-winning *Women Write about Comics*, are venues for rising talent. Breaking into such a gig may take repeated efforts or effective networking relationships, but in the meantime, there is nothing stopping you from publishing your writing on your own website, blog, or vlog, much like Victor and Ryan in our opening vignette.

Your analysis may also find a larger audience as a paper presented as a part of an academic conference. Numerous academic conferences welcome scholarship into comics and there are even stand-alone conferences dedicated to the study of comics, such as the conferences sponsored by the Comics Studies Society and the Graphic Medicine International Collective. There are also several conferences held in conjunction with comic book conventions, including the long-running Comics Arts Conference during San Diego's Comic-Con International and Comics and Popular Arts Conference at DragonCon in Atlanta, among others.

While many academics present their papers at a conference first, they often submit them for wider dissemination in academic publications thereafter. Many academic journals are open to publishing quality scholarship about comics, but there are several periodicals that regularly publish scholarship, including the *International Journal of Comic Art*, *Journal of Graphic Novels and Comics*, and *INKS.* Additionally, there are several online journals that popularize scholarly work, including *ImageText* and *The Comics Grid.*

Given the growth of interest in Comics Studies over the past two decades, by the time you are reading this textbook there are likely to be even more venues for reviews and scholarship available to you. We encourage you to engage with these outlets. If you have enjoyed reading and learning about comics art as much as we have, then the opportunity to talk about them—and talk with others about them—should be your next outlet for exploring the power of comics.

Discussion Questions

1. What makes a reviewer trustworthy to you? By what criteria do you hold their reviews as helpful advice in your own selection of media, be that reviews for films, television, video games, novels, podcasts, or other media? What could reviewers do to better secure your confidence in their reviews?
2. Several frames for conducting analyses exist across the intellectual spectrum, including those that scrutinize texts through the lens of gendered, racial, and socio-economic standings. Pick a comic and then discuss how your demographics might influence your reading of that comic. Are any comics "neutral" when it comes to reading them or does a person's background or situation almost always factor into interpretations?

Activities

1. Agree on a graphic novel among a group of friends or classmates and write independent reviews of the work. Then gather to exchange or read aloud your reviews to one another. Discuss as a group what claims you might have had in common and what claims stood out as different among the members. Use these reviews as a springboard for a more substantive "book club" discussion of the graphic novel.
2. Take an original analysis of a comic or graphic novel and turn it into a conference-style poster presentation. Posters typically consist of several sheets of paper arranged on a corkboard or a tri-fold board (like those used in a middle school science fair). Each piece of paper should contain one abbreviated section of your analysis paper. (Think of no more information than you might find on a presentation slide and recall the impact of visuals—particularly panels from a comic—in communicating ideas.) Gather with your colleagues to create a poster session of your projects to share with students, faculty, and administration in a public forum. Many universities already have internal undergraduate research showcases. Many faculty members have experience creating posters for presentations at academic conference and can provide you with guidance and support.

Recommended Reading

Comics

Barry, Lynda. *Syllabus: Notes from an Accidental Professor.* Montreal: Drawn & Quarterly, 2014.
Syllabus demonstrates Barry's innovative approach to teaching writing through the use of comics illustration. This work encourages readers to find their voices through the creation of comics.

Cham, Jorge. *PhD Comics.* http://phdcomics.com/.
"Piled Higher and Deeper" takes an irreverent look at the trials and tribulations of graduate study and all the strife associated with persevering in higher education.

Scholarly Sources

Brown, Matthew J., Randy Duncan, and Matthew J. Smith, eds. *More Critical Approaches to Comics: Theories and Methods.* New York: Routledge, 2020.
More than twenty experts explain and then model methods for analyzing comics and the culture surrounding them. The methods include tools for unpacking meaning based on viewpoints, expression, and relationships.

Helvie, Forrest C., ed. *How to Analyze and Review Comics: A Handbook on Comics Criticism.* Edwardsville: Sequart Organization, 2021.
Helvie and his contributors cover a range of issues associated with comics criticism, from how to analyze coloring and lettering to strategies for evaluating web comics.

Glossary

aesthetic layout page designs that command the reader's attention and appreciation, often showing off the artist's talent

affect displays emotions indicated by facial expressions

affective reaction emotional responses (e.g., excitement, pity, fear) that arise without conscious effort

album a collection of previously serialized comics in a bound edition

alternative non-mainstream comic books usually created by a single cartoonist and presenting a very personal vision

American monomyth a narrative pattern featuring the hero's journey as one emerges to defend the community before returning to anonymity

American Studies an interdisciplinary field combining the humanities to study cultural phenomena in the United States

analysis an intellectual essay that explores deeper meanings found within a comic

anime Japanese animated films

anthropomorphism literary device where non-human creatures are given human qualities, and usually human failings

anti-hero a protagonist who lacks some of the qualities of an idealized hero

apa an amateur press alliance, whose members publish collections of their works and distribute them to each other

art form a type of creative expression governed by its own materials, techniques, and limitations

artisan process production method that involves principally individual execution of the writing and drawing (and perhaps other roles) in the creation of comics

asynchronous the depiction of sound (dialogue, sound effects, or music) in a panel that is not occurring at the same moment as the events pictured in the panel

auteur the primary "author" of a work who provides a unifying artistic vision, even within a collaborative production process

Authoring I the creator of a work

autobiographical avatar a performance of an earlier self that is enacted by dialogue, thoughts, attitude, and, in comics, an image that appears on the page or screen

autofiction a memoir that blends elements of fiction with truth, as the memoirist remembers it

back issues stocks of comic book magazines older than the most current issue offered for sale by comics specialty shops

bande dessinée "drawn strips" or comics from the Franco-Belgian tradition

Bechdel test a means for critiquing media narratives such as film and comics for gender bias by asking if a story has at least two female character who talk to one another about something other than a male character

blocking the planned movement and placement of actors in space

bound reprint edition a collection of previously printed comics material sold as a stand-alone publication

braiding the concept that panels occurring pages apart can have a relationship that affects their meaning, particularly a retroactive determination of the meaning of the panels occurring earlier in the work

broadsheet an early form of mass communication consisting of a single page of printed material usually with both words and images

Canadian whites comics with black and white interior pages published during World War II

canon a definitive list of the most worthwhile works or most talented creators

cartoon a humorous drawing

cartoon mode a mode of representation characterized by simplification and exaggeration

cartoonist creator who both writes and draws comics

central processing assigning meaning to stimuli based on conscious and deliberate evaluation of propositions and supporting evidence

character types familiar kinds of people who populate a genre

cheesecake depictions of females in suggestive clothing and poses

chiaroscuro a stark contrast of light and dark

Chick tracts small (3-inch by 5-inch) comics viciously attacking any beliefs and practices that did not conform to publisher Jack Chick's worldview

claim a statement asserting some relevant attribute of the comic

close reading the act of carefully —and perhaps repeatedly —examining a comic for identification of its meanings

close-up view a panel that places the reader in a position to view the character over setting because very little of the setting is visible

closure applying background knowledge and an understanding of the relationships between encapsulated images to synthesize (or blend) sequences of panels into events or concepts.

cognitive reaction the process of perceiving, organizing, and interpreting the symbols on the page in order to construct meaning

comic book a volume in which aspects of the diegesis are represented by pictorial and linguistic images encapsulated in a sequence of juxtaposed panels and pages

comic strip a short sequence of juxtaposed panels in which aspects of the diegesis are represented by pictorial and linguistic images

comics juxtaposed images in a sequence

Comics Code Authority an industry-sponsored board tasked with reviewing the contents of comic books before approving them for distribution

Comics Guaranty, LLC (CGC) limited liability corporation that offers the services of a third-party evaluation of a comic book's grading

comics journalism verified accounts of actual events presented in comics form

complex narrative a story structure in which the main plot line is expanded by backstory, character development, and ongoing subplots

composition the selection and placement of visual elements on a comics page and within a panel

conglomerate a large organization made up by many smaller businesses in diverse fields (e.g., the Walt Disney Company owns Marvel Entertainment, ABC Television, and ESPN)

content analysis research method in which the frequency and patterns of selected variables are investigated across media messages

continuity the consistent relationship among different comics stories

conventional layout a strip of panels of all the same height

conventional fragmented layout a page arranged with an underlying conventional grid structure but with horizontal variations and/or vertical variations, including panels that extend across two or more tiers

conventional semi-regular layout a page arranged with a clear grid structure in which all the panels in a particular tier are the same height, but there is some horizontal variation

conventional regular layout a page arranged with three or four tiers with two to four panels in each tier

copyright the legal control that the owner has over intellectual property

crime comics genre depicting criminal activities, such as murder, often with a focus on the perpetrator

critical methods methods of inquiry that seek to expose imbalances in social power and advocate for change

crowdfunding raising money for a project by asking many people to make small contributions

cultural imperialism the erosion of native cultures, including their value systems, language, and traditions, due to the influence of more dominant cultures through the distribution of mass media

decompressed storytelling a technique in which the narrative unfolds more slowly

descriptive research methods of inquiry that seek to explain human behavior, often investigated through observations or surveys

diary comics frequently posted or published brief accounts, in comics form, of incidents or thoughts from a cartoonist's day-to-day life

diegesis the world of the story

diegetic images pictures and words that depict characters, objects, and sensory environment of the world of the story

differentiation the process of distinguishing a narrative from others within its genre

digital comics comics created or distributed via a computer

direct effects theory of mass media consumption that says audiences imitate what they see portrayed in media messages; also known as the "magic bullet theory" of media effects

Direct Market the system of comic book distribution to specialty shops

disjointed panel the words and images that constitute the panel are not contiguous

distribution stage in the mass media industry where entities deliver media products from the producer to the exhibitor

documentary a form of nonfiction that shows real people engaged in actual events or interviews real people about actual events

early adopters people who use new technologies as soon as they are available

eight-pagers crude sex comic books; also Tijuana Bibles

encapsulation selecting images that represent the key moments of the narrative and putting them in a panel

environmental autobiography a memoir that emphasizes the importance of a place (house, town, region, etc.) in shaping an individual's identity

ethos source credibility

evidence material pulled from a comic to support a claim

exhibition stage in the mass media industry where entities sell media products to the consumers

Experiencing I the protagonist in a memoir narrative

expressionism a storytelling style that distorts or exaggerates in order to convey a character's inner, emotional reality

extreme close-up view a panel that places the reader in a position to view some detail (e.g., a ring, a scar, a signature) that is important to the plot

extreme high angle (bird's eye view) a panel perspective that places the reader far above the character or action so as to give the reader a subjective experience, suggest relationships, or make the reader an omniscient viewer

extreme long view a panel that places the reader at a considerable distance from the action so as to ascertain context and setting

extreme low angle (worm's-eye view) a panel perspective that places the reader far below the character or action so as to make whatever is shown seem towering or powerful, or to make the reader feel omniscient through a perspective usually unavailable to humans

eye-level view a panel perspective that places the reader at the same height as the character or action and thus in a position to identify with the characters or feel involved in the action

fan an audience member engaged in the dialogue about comic books

fan fiction original stories using characters, situations, and images that are under someone else's copyright protection

fanboy a term for fans that may be either insulting or used for self-deprecation

fandom the community of fans produced by organized activity; also a verb expressing deep affection for a property

fanzine a fan-produced magazine

flayed look artistic style that emphasizes detailed musculature

fotonovela a comic whose panels consist of a mixture of still photography and text; also known as *fumetti* in Europe

fractionalization to break into parts, especially with audiences

freelancer an independent contractor who accepts work on particular assignments

funny animals genre with anthropomorphic characters in humorous situations

gatekeeper anyone who has the authority to select or modify messages communicated through the media

genre a class or type of an art form as determined by the appearance of similarities with other works

Golden Age reference to the comic book era of earliest mass popularity, roughly dated 1938–1945

Good Girl Art style of comic art in which shapely, stereotypically attractive women are provocatively posed for the pleasure of the male viewer

graphic novel a label applied by creators and publishers to distinguish a comic book, which in practice is longer and perhaps self-contained, in contrast to most periodical comic books

grid a symmetrical page layout of panels and tiers

ground level non-mainstream comic books that allowed creators to tap into the under-ground sensibility and work in genres other than superheroes

gutter the space between panels

hardcover a book published with a comparatively durable cover

hegemony the perpetuation of power disparities in a culture through the capitulation of those disadvantaged by the system

hermeneutic images depictions of what the creator thinks about the actions and feelings of the characters and, as such, do not represent anything that is actually happening in the world of the story

high-angle view a panel perspective that place the reader above the character or action in order to make something or someone seem small and weak, or to make the reader feel detached from the action

historietas "little stories" or comics from the Mexican tradition

horror suspense-filled genre that inserts the supernatural into commonplace settings

hybrid a narrative that combines qualities from two or more genres

iconostasis a perception of the layout of a comics page as a unified composition taken in at a glance

ideology a set of ideas that function as sense-making tools for groups of people

identification the process whereby audiences can see themselves in a character

independent smaller publisher that attempts to compete with the established publishers by offering genre fiction comic books intended for a mainstream audience

industrial process production method that involves collaborators performing specialized tasks in the creation of comics

infinite canvas the idea that for digital comics the progression of panels can go in any direction for a theoretically infinite distance

intellectual property an original work of words, images, or ideas that is legally recognized as being owned by its creator

interanimation of meaning images (picture or text) appearing in proximity (in a panel or on a page) can each affect the meaning of the other, and together create a meaning beyond what is communicated by each separate image

interpretive methods methods of inquiry that examine the content of comics to explain what the messages in comic books mean

intertextual image a picture that reminds the reader of something he or she has encountered in other media (movies, books, paintings, TV shows, etc.)

jungle comics adventure-filled genre set in untamed, natural settings

juvenile delinquency a social condition in which youth engage in illegal activities such as vandalism, theft, and murder

juxtapose to place items side-by-side

key issues issues that are more recent first appearances of characters particularly those that are identified as sources of future media translations

kids comics genre featuring child protagonists in humorous situations

Kuleshov Effect an association in which the meaning of one image is altered by the image that follows it in sequence

layout the relationship of a single panel to the succession of panels, to the totality of the page, and to the totality of the story; involves choices of size, sequence, and juxtaposition

layout dynamics the variations and contrasts of panel size, sequence, and juxtaposition that affects a reader's cognitive and affective response to a page or two-page spread

licensing the assigning of rights by a trademark holder to a licensee to use a character for a marketing application

ligne claire style of drawing that assigns equal value to all the lines within the frame and de-emphasizes shading

literacy the ability to understand and interpret a symbol system, traditionally associated with reading text but now regarded as including visual and other cultural symbols as well

limited series a comic book series launched with definite conclusion planned

long-form journalism long articles or a series of articles that often contain elements of narrative journalism

long view a panel that places the reader at a distance from the action so to establish the setting of a story or scene

low angle a panel perspective that places the reader below the character or action so as to make the person or object being viewed seem powerful or menacing

mainstream comic books produced by the most established and profitable publishers

manga Japanese comics; translated as "irresponsible pictures"

mangaka professional cartoonists working in Japanese manga

manhwa Korean comics

Marvel method a collaborative production which vests most control over the storytelling dynamics upon the artist rather than the writer

Media Studies an academic discipline that examines the content, history, and effects of communication technologies, industries, and practices

medium a channel for communication

medium view a panel that places the reader in a position to view a balance between character and setting

mere exposure effect an interpretation in which the familiar is more likable than the less familiar

memoir a story from someone's life, often focused on particular life-changing incidents and their consequences

metafictional a type of story where the author calls attention to the fact that it is a created work of fiction

metanarration a type of narration where the narrator appears as an avatar on the page

metaverse a fictional universe existing within a digital reality

metonymy the use of an associated detail to represent the whole

mini-comics (or mini-comix) originally designated a 3½ x 4" eight-page comic, but the term has come to refer to any small, homemade comic book.

mint condition a state lacking any detectable flaws

mise-en-scène "putting in the scene;" elements depicted in a comic book panel such as background details, color, lighting effects, distance, angle, simulated movement, visualized sound, the blending of the pictorial and the linguistic, and art style

monomyth the archetypical story of the hero's journey repeated across multiple versions

monopoly a marketplace characterized by only one provider and no competition

movie comics genre featuring adaptations of film and television properties

multimodal a text which communicates through more than one symbol system such as comics (visual and textual) or television (visual and aural)

multiplicity multiple versions of the same character

multiverse a collection of parallel universes

Myth of Redemptive Violence Theologian Walter Wink's term for the ancient and pervasive idea, and frequently used narrative pattern, that the forces of good must use violence to defeat the forces of evil

mythic criticism a research method wherein texts are reviewed for their culturally significant meanings

naturalistic mode a mode of representation in which characters and settings are recognizable and conventional

Narrating I the authorial voice that tells the story to the reader, most often achieved in comics through "voice-over" narration that appears in captions

narrative events and the order in which they are presented

narrative flow a repeated process of developing an understanding of the narrative information within a panel (as it exists within the context of a page layout), adding that understanding to one's understanding of previous narrative information in order to expand the sense of "the story so far," and then moving smoothly to the next panel, where the process continues

narrative pattern the often-repeated structure of storytelling across stories within a genre

narrative problematic the challenge that must be overcome or resolved before a happy ending can be reached in a story (e.g., a rival's diversion)

negotiated reading an interpretation of a message that accepts some of the intent of the creators while rejecting other elements

newwave (also new wave) half or quarter page mini-comics produced by cartoonists independent of any publisher

ninth art title assigned to the comics art form by scholar Claude Beylie, who argued comics and television deserved standing with seven other arts: architecture, music, painting, sculpture, poetry, dance, and cinema

non-sensory diegetic images depictions representing what a character is feeling

oligopoly a marketplace characterized by relatively few competitors

onomatopoeia invented words that mimic sounds

oppositional reading an interpretation of a message that is counter to the creators' intent

origin story narrative that explains the fantastic nature of the superhero and involves a transformation; also referred to commonly as the "secret origin"

otaku originally an obsessive fan in Japan but later embraced as a label for various fan communities as a means to label and distinguish themselves

Other social group that is defined in contrast to the qualities of a preferred group in a society

panel a discernible area that contains a moment of the story

paradigmatic choice the chosen images and all the images that could have made sense or communicated nearly the same meaning at the same point in the panel

paralanguage the qualities of volume, emphasis, rate, and vocal quality that characterize human speech

parasocial relationship the perception of a relationship with figures in the media that develops over time and may have an emotional intensity similar to that of actual shared relationships

peripheral processing assigning meaning to stimuli based on an unconscious, emotional level

pictorial embodiment the different ways in which graphic memoirists' sense of self is linked with the act of visually representing their bodily identities

planchet a designed unit that is placed on a page

preferred reading an interpretation of a message that matches the intent of the creators

primary movement the implied movement of people or objects in the frame

production stage in mass media industry where entities create media products

proliferating narrativity the focus of interest does not reside in the building and resolving of dramatic suspense spanning the entire text (story), but in the narrative verve displayed in relating adventures from the life of the hero (mythos)

propaganda a series of related communication acts that spread a particular interpretation of an event

pro-social mission a hero's attitude to use one's powers for the benefit of humanity

prozine a fanzine with higher production values and produced by a staff with more of a professional than amateur standing

psychological image an image that represents some aspect of a character's personality or state of mind

pulps magazine made of cheap paper and featuring sensational fictional stories (e.g., detective, science fiction, adventure)

qualitative analysis of phenomena using interpretative data

quantitative analysis of phenomena using numerical data

realism a storytelling style that attempts to depict people, objects, and motivations in a manner consistent with most people's real-life experience

redemptive arc a narrative pattern that progresses from the setup that establishes a character's ordinary world to the advent of a problem to the pain caused by the problem, and, finally, to finding a way to cope with, or transcend, the problem and the pain

reboot starting a series over with revisions to the mythos established in the previous incarnation(s) of the series

reflected appraisals our perception of what other think of us

representation the depiction (or lack thereof) and definition of a social group in mass media messages

review a short essay that provides reading advice about a comic to its audience

rhetoric the art of finding the available means of persuasion in any given situation

rhetorical content layout a page arrangement where the size, shape, and placement of a panel is determined, to some extent, by the actions or objects contained within the panel

rhetorical layout a page arrangement that is meant to influence how readers understand and react to the narrative presented in the comic

rhetorical subtext layout a page arrangement that is meant to enhance the narrative by adding levels of meaning that would not exist in a conventional grid

rogues gallery a superhero's collection of foes

romance comics genre featuring melodramatic presentations of romantic relationships

scarcity the relatively limited availability of an object, which helps drive up its value

scene a unit of the story that usually, but not necessarily, has unity of time and space to portray a continuous action.

science fiction comics genre that focuses on the impact of imagined science or technology on society or individuals

secondary movement the implied movement of the frame itself

self-perception the ways an individual thinks about one's appearance, traits, and abilities

sensacionales Mexican comics emphasizing sexuality, crime, and melodrama

sensory diegetic images depictions of the world of the story and the actions of the characters

sequence the compilation of related and usually consecutive scenes

sequence metaphor two juxtaposed images that together create a meaning not present in either image alone

sequential art any artwork with elements arranged in a sequence to tell a story

sequential dynamism formal visual energy created by compositional and other elements internal to each panel and by a layout that imparts a sense of sustained or varied visual rhythm

setting environments in which genre stories are placed

shôjo manga "little girl" comics focused on maturing and relationships

shop system an arrangement where independent contractors produced content for the major publishers, often in an assembly line where different production steps were divided among artists

sidekick a superhero's younger partner, useful as a conversation partner for the hero and a target of wish fulfillment for young readers

Silver Age reference to the comic book era coinciding with the second surge in popularity in superhero comics, roughly dated 1956–1969

simple narrative a story structure in which there is conflict or a series of conflicts that build in rising action to a climactic moment in which the conflict is resolved

slabbed referring to the state of a comic book that has been evaluated and then sheathed between two sheets of plastic by the Comics Guaranty, LLC

slapstick physical comedy

slash fiction stories authored by fans that place same-sex fictional characters into sexual situations

slice of life story a narrative presenting mundane events of everyday life

social comparison our perception of how we compare to peers and roles models in terms of status symbols (possessions, accomplishments, looks, etc.)

specialty shops stores offering comics and comics-related paraphernalia

speculators collectors who purchase comic books as investments

speed lines thin lines or puffs of "smoke" drawn behind a character or object to indicate the direction and rapidity of movement

spoiler plot detail that could ruin the pleasure of the reading experience if revealed prematurely

splash page full-page panel, usually at or near the beginning of a comics narrative, used to establish context or mood

staffer an employee of the publisher (e.g., editor, art director, production manager) with a set salary, regular paychecks, and fringe benefits

standardization the process of including enough recognizable elements so that a narrative clearly fits within a genre

state of grace a set of powers, appearance, supporting characters, and behaviors that are preserved in a recognizable form for the economic interests of the corporation that owns the character

stereotype a recognizable generalization of a type

strawman an argument characterized by partial representation or misrepresentation that makes the perspective seem foolish and easy to refute

superhero a protagonist with a pro-social mission, powers and abilities beyond normal people, a distinguishing identity, and often engaged in violent interactions

supervillain an antagonist who schemes on a grand scale

sword and sorcery fantasy genre characterized by protagonists with antiquated weapons and magical beings

symbols images that represent something else

synchronous the depiction of sound (dialogue, sound effects, or music) in a panel that emanates from and is occurring at the same moment as the events pictured in the panel

synecdoche a part of something that stands for the whole or vice versa

synergy the coordinated release of products tied into a media property to maximize exposure and increase profitability

syntagmatic choice the process of selecting which panels to present from the possible progression of story images that could occur

teen humor genre focused on comedic tales of coming of age

tenor the underlying meaning behind an image

terministic/imagistic screen a filter on our perceptions

themes a recurring message either within a narrative or across a series of narratives

thesis a statement that expresses the central argument of a review or analysis

thumbnail breakdowns quick sketches used to break a narrative down into visual moments of prime action

tiers a row of comics panels

Tijuana Bible crude sex comic books; also eight-pagers

trade paperback (TPB) a comic book usually with more pages than most monthly issues and bound by a cover that is of higher durability than a paper cover but not quite as durable as hardcover

transmedia storytelling communicating different portions of a whole story through different media

two shot a panel that places the reader in a position to view multiple characters interacting so that their reaction to one another can be viewed simultaneously

underground comix independently produced comic books, often socially rebellious

valence the quality of whether a review is generally more positive or negative

vehicle an image that stimulates a comparison

visual conventions recurring images across a genre

virtual community a group of people in relationship to one another who rely on mediated communication because of a lack of geographic proximity to one another

virtuous cycle the more diverse material created, the greater the possibility some of it might interest a purchaser, and the more purchasers that return to sample the experiments, the more diverse material likely to be created

visual metaphor a picture of one thing to evoke the idea of something else

war comics genre focused on the life-and-death struggle of combat

webcomics online publication of cartoons essentially identical to traditional newspaper strip comics as well as interactive forms using software like flash animation

Western genre set in the historic American West and focused on exploring or taming the frontier

work-for-hire an arrangement with a cartoonist in which the publisher retains copyright over characters and story

Yellow Kid Thesis a disputed assertion that the comics medium began with the work of Richard Felton Outcault's *Hogan's Alley*, featuring the character of the Yellow Kid

Z reading pattern the Western practice of starting to read a page in the upper left-hand corner, moving to the right, and then at the end of that tier continuing back to the left-hand side of the next tier, and so on

Bibliography

Abel, Jessica, and Matt Madden. 2008. *Drawing Words & Writing Pictures*. New York: First Second.

Adelman, Bob. 1997/2004. *Tijuana Bibles: Art and Wit in America's Forbidden Funnies, 1930s–1950s*. New York: Simon & Schuster.

Afshana, Syeda, and Heeba Din. 2018. "Innovating the Narrative: A Study into the Emerging Genre of Graphic Journalism." *International Journal of Research in Social Sciences* 8, no. 11 (November): 527–45.

Allen, Todd. 2007. "Online Comics vs. Printed Comics: A Study in E-Commerce and the Comparative Economics of Content." Accessed July 10, 2007. www.businessofcontent.com/dojo/215/v.jsp?p=/comics-ecommerce/index.

Alls, Rob. 2001. "Marvel Press Conference Transcript." *Comics Continuum*. Last modified on May 17, 2001. www.comicscontinuum.com/stories/0105/17/marvelindex.htm.

Ames, Winslow, and David M. Kunzle. 2007. "Caricature, Cartoon and Comic Strip." In *The New Encyclopedia Britannica*, vol. 15, Macropedia 15th ed., 539–52. Chicago: Encyclopedia Britannica, Inc.

"Are Comics Fascist?" *Time*, October 22, 1945, 67–8.

Anderson, Dana. 2013. "The Experience of the Superhero: A Phenomenological Definition." In *What Is a Superhero?* edited by Robin S. Rosenberg and Peter Coogan, 65–70. Oxford: Oxford University Press.

Arlin, Marshall, and Garry Roth. 1978. "Pupils' Use of Time while Reading Comics and Books." *American Educational Research Journal* 15: 201–16.

Arlington, Gary. 1982. "A Recollection." In *The Official Underground and Newave Comix Price Guide*, edited by Jay Kennedy, 35. Cambridge: Boatner Norton Press.

Arthur. 2007. "The Popularity of Disney Comics and Magazines around the World." *Disney Comics Worldwide*. Last modified April 6, 2007. https://www.wolfstad.com/dcw/blog/2007/04/disney-comics-around-the-world/.

Baetens, Jan. 2017. "Other Non-fiction." In *The Cambridge Companion to the Graphic Novel*, edited by Stephen E. Tabachnick, 130–43. Cambridge: Cambridge University Press.

Bails, Jerry, Hames Ware, Michael Barrier, and Jim Vadeboncoeur, eds. 1973–1976. *The Who's Who of American Comic Books*. 4 vols. St. Clair Shores: J. Bails.

Bakwin, Ruth Morris. 1953. "Psychological Aspects of Pediatrics: The Comics." *The Journal of Pediatrics* 42: 633–5.

Barrier, Michael. 1988. "Comic Master: The Art of Will Eisner." *Print* 42: 197–8.

Batiste, Stephanie L., Mary Anne Boelcskevy, and Shireen K. Lewis. 2018. "Interview with John Jennings, Featuring Alternate and Draft Panels from Kindred: The Graphic Novel Adaptation." *Journal of Black Studies and Research* 48, no. 4: 8–18.

Beard, David. 2007. "Deceptive Data: How Diamond Best-Seller Lists Distort the Comics Industry." *The Comics Journal* 283 (May): 19–24.

Beaty, Bart. 2007. *Unpopular Culture: Transforming the European Comic Book in the 1990s*. Toronto: University of Toronto Press.

Beaty, Bart. 2012. *Comics versus Art*. Toronto: University of Toronto Press.

Bechdel, Alison. 2007. *Fun Home: A Family Tragicomic*. Boston: Mariner Books.

Beerbohm, Robert Lee. 1997. E-mail to Comics Scholars' Discussion List, December 4.

Beerbohm, Robert Lee. 1999. "Secret Origins of the Direct Market: Part One: 'Affidavit Returns'—The Scourge of Distribution." *Comic Book Artist* 6 (Fall): 80–91.

Beerbohm, Robert Lee. 2003. "The Originator of Comics." In *The Adventures of Obadiah Oldbuck*, edited by Alfredo Castelli, 50. Napoli: Comicon.

Beerbohm, Robert Lee, and Richard D. Olson. 2008. "The Platinum Age: The American Comic Book: 1883–1938: Further Concise History & Price Index of the Field as of 2008." In *The Official Overstreet Comic Book Price Guide*, 38th ed., edited by Robert M. Overstreet, 367–75. New York: House of Collectible.

Behm-Morawitz, Elizabeth, and Hillary Pennell. 2013. "The Effects of Superhero Sagas on Our Gendered Selves." *In Our Superheroes, Ourselves*, edited by Robin S. Rosenburg, 70–90. Oxford: Oxford University Press.

Belk, Russell W. 1987. "Material Values in the Comics: A Content Analysis of Comic Books Featuring Themes of Wealth." *The Journal of Consumer Research* 14: 26–42.

Bell, Blake. 2002. *I Have to Live with This Guy!* Raleigh: TwoMorrows Publishing.

Bell, Blake. 2008. "Ditko and Stanton." *Ditko Looked Up*. Accessed June 11, 2008. www.ditko.comics.org/ditko/crea/crerstan.html.

Bell, Blake, and Michael J. Vassallo. 2013. *The Secret History of Marvel Comics*. Seattle: Fantagraphics.

Bender, Lauretta, and Reginald S. Lourie. 1941. "The Effect of Comic Books on the Ideology of Children." *American Journal of Orthopsychiatry* 11: 540–50.

Benson, John. 1981. "Is War Hell? The Evolution of an Artist's Viewpoint." *Panels* 2: 18–20.

Benton, Mike. 1989. *The Comic Book in America: An Illustrated History*. Dallas: Taylor Publishing Company.

Benton, Mike. 1991. *Horror Comics: The Illustrated History*. Dallas: Taylor Publishing Company.

Benton, Mike. 1993. *The Comics Book in America: An Illustrated History*. Dallas: Taylor Publishing Company.

Benton, Mike. 1994. *Masters of Imagination: The Comic Book Artists Hall of Fame*. Dallas: Taylor Publishing Company.

Beringer, Alex. 2015. "Transatlantic Picture Stories: Experiments in the Antebellum American Comic Strip." *American Literature* 87, no. 3 (September): 455–88.

Bernofsky, Susan. 2009. "Why Donald Duck Is the Jerry Lewis of Germany." *The Wall Street Journal*. Last modified May 23, 2009. https://www.wsj.com/articles/SB10001424052970203771904574181722075062290.

Berger, Arthur Asa. 1973. *The Comic-Stripped American: What Dick Tracy, Blondie, Daddy Warbucks and Charlie Brown Tell Us about Ourselves*. New York: Walker & Co.

Berona, David. 1995. "Picture Stories: Eric Drooker and the Tradition of Woodcut Novels." *Inks* 2, no. 1: 2–11.

Bertamini, Marco, Letizia Palumbo, Tamara Nicoleta Gheorghes, and Mai Galatsidas. 2016. "Do Observers Like Curvature or Do They Dislike Angularity?" *British Journal of Psychology* 107, no. 1: 154–78.

Bignell, Jonathan. 1997. *Media Semiotics: An Introduction*. Manchester: Manchester University Press.

Biography. 2017. *William Randolph Hearst*. https://www.biography.com/media-figure/william-randolph-hearst.

Bird, Robert M. 1937. *Nick of the Woods, or Adventures of Prairie Life*. Accessed April 2, 2022. https://www.gutenberg.org/cache/epub/13970/pg13970.html.

Bissette, Stephen R. 2011. *Teen Angels & New Mutants: Rick Veitch's Bratpack and the Art, Karma, and Commerce of Killing Sidekicks*. Encino: Black Coat Press.

Bissette, Stephen, Neil Gaiman, and Tom Veitch. 1989. "Change or Die! The Revisionist Roundtable Discussion." In *The One*, edited by Rick Veitch, 188–209. Windham Hill: King Hell Press.

Bitz, Michael. 2004. "The Comic Book Project: Forging Alternative Pathways to Literacy." *Journal of Adolescent & Adult Literacy* 47: 574–86.

Blackmore, Tim. 2004. "*300* and Two: Frank Miller and Daniel Ford Interpret Herodotus's Thermopylae Myth." *International Journal of Comic Art* 6, no. 2: 325–49.

Blair, J. Anthony. 2005. "The Rhetoric of Visual Arguments." In *Defining Visual Rhetorics*, edited by Charles A. Hill and Marguerite Helmers, 41–61. Mahwah: Lawrence Earlbaum Associates.

Bloomberg News. 2007. "Spider Cents Boost Marvel Profits." *Ottawa Citizen*, May 9, 2007, D8.

Bluck, Susan, Nicole Alea, Tilmann Habermas, and David C. Rubin. 2005. "A Tale of Three Functions: The Self-Reported Uses of Autobiographical Memory." *Social Cognition* 23, no. 1: 91–117.

Blumberg, Arnold T. 2005. "Promotional Comics: The Marketing of a Medium." In *The Official Overstreet Comic Book Price Guide*, 35th ed., edited by Robert M. Overstreet, 285–88. New York: Gemstone Publishing.

Blumberg, Arnold T. 2006. "'The Night Gwen Stacy Died': The End of Innocence and the 'Last Gasp of the Silver Age.'" *International Journal of Comic Art* 8, no. 1: 197–211.

Boichel, Bill. 1991. "Batman: Commodity as Myth." In *The Many Lives of the Batman: Critical Approaches to a Superhero and His Media*, edited by Roberta E. Pearson and William Uricchio, 4–17. New York: Routledge.

Bolhafner, Stephen. 1991. "Art for Art's Sake: Spiegelman Speaks on *Raw*'s Past, Present and Future." *The Comics Journal* 145: 96–9.

Bongco, Mila. 2000. *Reading Comics: Language, Culture, and the Concept of the Superhero in Comic Books*. New York: Garland Publishing.

Boxer, Sarah. 2005. "Comics Escape a Paper Box, and Electronic Questions Pop Out." *New York Times*, April 17, 2005, E1.

Branch, Jeffrey C. 1997. "Everything's . . . Archie: The Inside Story of Archie Comics." *Comic Book Marketplace*, October, 32–6, no. 53: 45–51.

Brooks, Tim, and Earle Marsh. 1992. *The Complete Directory to Prime Time Network TV Shows, 1946–Present*. 5th ed. New York: Ballantine.

Brown, Jeffrey A. 1999. "Comic Book Masculinity and the New Black Superhero." *African-American Review* 33: 25–42.

Brown, Jeffrey A. 2001. *Black Superheroes, Milestone Comics, and Their Fans*. Jackson: University Press of Mississippi.

Bruner, Jerome. 2001. "Self-Making and World-Making." In *Narrative and Identity: Studies in Autobiography, Self and Culture*, edited by Jens Brockmeier and Donal Carbaugh, 26–37. Amsterdam: John Benjamins Publishing.

Bruss, Elizabeth. 1980. "Eye for I: Autobiography in Film." In *Autobiography: Essays Theoretical and Critical*, edited by James Olney, 296–320. Princeton: Princeton University Press.

Bukatman, Scott. 2003. *Matters of Gravity*. Durham: Duke University Press.

Burke, Kenneth. 1950. *A Rhetoric of Motives*. New York: Prentice Hall.

Burke, Kenneth. 1966. *Language as Symbolic Action*. Berkeley: University of California Press.

Byrne, John. 1986. "Superman: A Personal View." *The Man of Steel* 1: inside back cover.

Callendar, Brian, Shirlene Obuobi, M. K. Czerwiec, and Ian Williams. 2020. “The Art of Medicine: COVID-19, Comics, and the Visual Culture of Contagion.” *The Lancet* 396 (October): 1061–3.

Camp, Brian. 2000. “What is the Superhero Genre Tale?” Paper presented at the Comic Arts Conference, San Diego, CA, July 21, 2000.

Campbell, Joseph. 1968. *The Hero with a Thousand Faces*. Princeton: Princeton University Press.

Campbell, Richard, Christopher R. Martin, and Betina Fabos. 2006. *Media and Culture: An Introduction to Mass Communication*. 5th ed. Boston: Bedford/St. Martin's.

Carlson, Johanna Draper. 2005. “Online Comic Fandom in 1995.” *Comics Worth Reading*. Last modified December 15, 2005. http://comicsworthreading.com/2005/12/15/online-comic-fandom-in-1995.

Carrier, David. 2001. *Aesthetics of Comics*. University Park: Penn State University Press.

Carter, James Bucky. 2007. “Introduction—Carving a Niche: Graphic Novels in the English Language Arts Classroom.” In *Building Literacy Connections with Graphic Novels: Page by Page, Panel by Panel*, edited by James Bucky Carter, 1–25. Urbana: National Council of Teachers of English.

Carter, Lynda. 2000. “Introduction.” In *Wonder Woman: The Complete History*, by Les Daniels, 9. San Francisco: Chronicle Books.

Cary, Stephen. 2004. *Going Graphic: Comics at Work in the Multilingual Classroom*. Portsmouth: Heinemann.

Cates, Isaac. 2011. “The Diary Comic.” In *Graphic Subjects: Critical Essays on Autobiography and Graphic Novels*, edited by Michael A. Chaney, 209–26. Madison: University of Wisconsin Press.

Chadwick, Paul. 1997. “Not That Old Chestnut!” *Comics Buyer's Guide*, December 12, 1997, 34–5.

Chambliss, Julian C., and William Svitavsky. 2008. “From Pulp Hero to Superhero: Culture, Race, and Identity in American Popular Culture, 1990–1940.” *Studies in American Culture* 30, no. 1: 1–34.

Chavanne, Renaud. 2010. *Composition de la Bande Dessinée* [The Composition of Comics]. Mountrouge: PLG.

Cheng, Kevin. 2012. *See What I Mean: How to Use Comics to Communicate Ideas*. New York: Rosenfeld Media.

Chiarello, Mark, and Todd Klein. 2004. *The DC Comics Guide to Coloring and Lettering Comics*. New York: Watson-Guptill Publications.

Chick Tract Collection (RG 270), Special Collections, Yale Divinity School Library. Accessed April 24, 2022. https://archives.yale.edu/repositories/4/resources/5561.

Childs, Elizabeth C. 1997. “The Body Impolitic: Censorship and the Caricature of Honoré Daumier.” In *Suspended License: Censorship and the Visual Arts*, edited by Elizabeth C. Childs, 148–79 Seattle: University of Washington Press.

Chute, Hillary L. 2006. “An Interview with Alison Bechdel.” *Modern Fiction Studies* 52, no. 4: 1004–13.

Chute, Hillary L. 2010. *Graphic Women: Life Narrative and Contemporary Comics*. New York: Columbia University Press.

Cioffi, F. L. 2001. “Disturbing Comics: The Disjunction of Word and Image in the Comics of Andrzej Mlecyko, Ben Katchor, R. Crumb, and Art Spiegelman.” In *The Language of Comics: Word and Image*, edited by Robin Varnum and Christina T. Gibbons, 97–122. Jackson: University Press of Mississippi.

Clancy, Shaun. 2004. “Hex . . . and Other Blessings: Tony DeZuñiga, the CBA Interview.” *Comic Book Artist* 4: 40–5.

Coale, Mark. 1998. *Breaking the Panels: Over 75 Short Interviews from around the Comics Industry*. Colora: O-Goshi Studios.

Cohen, Jonathan. 2004. "Parasocial Break-Up from Favorite Television Characters: The Role of Attachment Styles and Relationship Intensity." *Journal of Social and Personal Relationships* 21, no. 2: 187–202.

Cohn, Neil. 2003. *Early Writings on Visual Language*. Carlsbad: Emaki Productions.

Cohn, Neil. 2010. "The Limits of Time and Transitions: Challenges to Theories of Sequential Image Comprehension." *Studies in Comics* 1, no. 1 (April): 127–47.

Cohn, Neil. 2013. "Navigating Comics: An Empirical and Theoretical Approach to Strategies of Reading Comic Page Layouts." *Frontiers in Psychology* 4. https://www.frontiersin.org/article/10.3389/fpsyg.2013.00186.

Cohn, Neil. 2013. *The Visual Language of Comics*. New York: Bloomsbury.

Cohn, Neil. 2021. *Who Understands Comics: Questioning the Universality of Visual Language Comprehension*. New York: Bloomsbury.

Cohn, Neil, Ryan Taylor, and Kaitlin Pederson. 2017. "A Picture Is Worth More Words over Time: Multimodality and Narrative Structure across Eight Decades of American Superhero Comics." *Multimodal Communication* 6, no. 1: 19–37.

Comixology. 2013. "About Comixology." Accessed November 29, 2013. http://blog.comixology.com/about_comixology/.

Contino, Jennifer M. 2001. "A Touch of Vertigo: Karen Berger." *Sequential Tart* 4, no. 1. www.sequentialtart.com/archive/feb01/berger.shtml.

Coogan, Peter. 2006. *The Superhero: The Secret Origin of a Genre*. Austin: MonkeyBrain Books.

Cooke, Andrew D., dir. 2007. *Will Eisner: Portrait of a Sequential Artist*. Montilla Pictures. DVD.

Cooke, Jon B. 2001. "Vengeance, Incorporated: A History of the Short-lived Comics Publisher, Atlas/Seaboard." *Comic Book Artist* 16 (December): 14–9.

Costello, Matthew J. 2009. *Secret Identity Crisis: Comic Books and the Unmasking of Cold War America*. New York: Continuum.

Creel, George. 1918. "Bulletin for Cartoonists No. 16." *Bureau of Cartoons*. Committee on Public Information, September 28, 1918. Accessed December 22, 2021. http://historymatters.gmu.edu/d/5052/.

Cremins, Brian. 2003. "'I Asked for Water (She Gave Me Gasoline)': Tim Truman's *Scout* and Social Satire in the Independent Comics of the 1980s." *International Journal of Comic Art* 5, no. 2: 339–50.

Crist, Judith. 1948. "Horror in the Nursery." *Collier's*, March 29, 1948, 22–3.

Crumb, Robert. 1988. "Twenty Years Later." In *R. Crumb's Head Comix*, 1–5. New York: Simon & Schuster.

Crumb, Robert, and Peter Poplaski. 2005. *The R. Crumb Handbook*. London: MQ Publications.

Cruse, Howard. 1980. "Digging the Underground." Lecture to the Cartoonists Guild, Inc., New York.

Cuno, James 1983, "Charles Philipon, La Maison Aubert, and the Business of Caricature in Paris, 1829–41." *Art Journal* 43, no. 4: 347–54.

"D.C. Comics." *Harper's Magazine Online*. Last modified June 2005. http://harpers.org/archive/2005/06/0080579.

Dalton, Russell W. 2011. *Marvelous Myths: Marvel Superheroes and Everyday Faith*. Atlanta: Chalice Press.

Daniels, Les. 1971. *Comix: A History of Comic Books in America*. New York: Bonanza Books.

Daniels, Les. 1991. *Marvel: Five Fabulous Decades of the World's Greatest Comics*. New York: Harry N. Abrams, Inc.

Darowski, Joseph J. 2012. *The Ages of Superman: Essays on the Man of Steel in Changing Times*. Jefferson: McFarland & Company.

Dave. 2022. "The Guide to Comics on Substack." *Comic Book Herald*, February 5, 2022. https://www.comicbookherald.com/guide-to-comics-creators-on-substack/.

Davidson, Sol. 2008. "Educational Comics: A Family Tree." *ImageTexT: Interdisciplinary Comics Studies* 4, no. 2. http://imagetext.english.ufl.edu/archives/v4_2/davidson/.

Dean, Michael. 2006. "Fine Young Cannibals: How Phil Seuling and a Generation of Teenage Entrepreneurs Created the Direct Market and Changed the Face of Comics." *The Comics Journal*, July, 49–59.

Deppy, Dirk. 2006. "Suicide Club: How Greed and Stupidity Disemboweled the American Comic-Book Industry in the 1990s." *The Comics Journal*, July, 68–75.

"Detective Comics, DC, 1937 series." *Grand Comics Database*. Accessed February 17, 2014. https://www.comics.org/series/87/.

Dik, Bryan J. 2008. "When I Grow up I want to be a Superhero." In *The Psychology of Superheroes: An Unauthorized Exploration*, edited by Robin S. Rosenberg, 91–104. Dallas: BenBella Books.

Dony, Christophe, and Caroline van Linthout. 2010. "Comics, Trauma and Cultural Memory(ies) of 9/11." In *The Rise and Reason of Comics and Graphic Literature: Critical Essays on the Form*, edited by Joyce Goggin and Dan Hassler-Forest, 178–87. Jefferson: McFarland & Company.

Dooley, Dennis, and Gary Engle, eds. 1987. *Superman at Fifty: The Persistence of a Legend*. Cleveland: Octavia.

Doubrosky, Serge. 1977. *Fils*. Paris: Galilee.

Drew, Sybil, dir. 2008. *Your Friendly Neighborhood Hero*. Kojanpan Films, 88 min.

Duin, Steve, and Mike Richardson. 1998. *Comics between the Panels*. Milwaukie: Dark Horse Comics, Inc.

Duncan, Randy. 1999–2000. "Toward a Theory of Comic Book Communication." *Academic Forum* 17. Accessed May 19, 2008. www.hsu.edu/default.aspx?id=3508.

Duncan, Randy. 2020. "Parasocial Relationship Analysis: 'Like Losing a Friend': Fans' Emotional Distress after the Loss of a Parasocial Relationship." In *More Critical Approaches to Comics: Theories and Methods*, edited by Matthew J. Brown, Randy Duncan, and Matthew J. Smith, 221–32. New York: Routledge.

Duncan, Randy, and Matthew J. Smith. 2011. "Learning from Film Studies: Analogies and Challenges." *Comics Forum*. Last modified July 15, 2011. http://comicsforum.org/2011/07/15/learning-from-film-studies-analogies-and-challenges-by-randy-duncan-and-matthew-j-smith/.

Duncan, Randy, Michael Ray Taylor, and David Stoddard. 2016. *Creating Comics as Journalism, Memoir & Nonfiction*. New York: Routledge.

Durwood, Thomas A. 1974. "Jack Kirby, Fritz Lang and Balance." *The Harvard Journal of Pictorial Fiction* 1, no. 1: 1–3.

Dziedric, Nancy, and Scot Peacock, eds. 1997. *Twentieth Century Literary Criticism*, vol. 66. Detroit: Gale.

Early, Gerald. 2004. "The 1960s, African Americans, and the American Comic Book." In *Strips, Toons, and Blusies: Essays in Comics and Culture*, edited by D. B. Dowd and Todd Hignite, 60–75. New York: Princeton Architectural Press.

Ecke, Jochen. 2011. "'Solve and Coagula': Alan Moore and the Classical Comic Book's Spatial and Temporal Systems." *Studies in Comics* 2, no. 1: 105–19.

Eco, Umberto. 1972/2004. "The Myth of Superman." In *Arguing Comics: Literary Masters on a Popular Medium*, edited by Jeet Heer and Kent Worcester, 146–64. Jackson: University Press of Mississippi.

Eisner, Will. 1985. "Preface." In *A Contract with God and Other Tenement Stories*. n.p: Kitchen Sink Press.

Eisner, Will. 1995. *Comics & Sequential Art*. Tamarac: Poorhouse Press.

Eisner, Will. 1996. *Graphic Storytelling*. Tamarac: Poorhouse Press.
Eisner, Will. 2001. "Shop Talk with Jack Kirby." In *Will Eisner's Shop Talk*, edited by Diana Schutz and Denis Kitchen, 193–223. Milwaukie: Dark Horse Comics.
El Refaie, Elisabeth. 2012. *Autobiographical Comics: Life Writing in Pictures*. Jackson: University Press of Mississippi.
Endres, Clifford. 1974. "Jaxon Returns: The Long Road Back to Austin." *Austin Sun*, November 7, 1974, 13, 20, 23.
Engle, Gary. 1987. "What Makes Superman So Darned American?" In *Superman at Fifty: The Persistence of a Legend*, edited by Dennis Dooley and Gary Engle, 79–87. Cleveland: Octavia.
Estren, Mark James. 1993. *A History of Underground Comix*. 4th ed. Berkeley: Ronin Publishing.
Evanier, Mark. 2008. *Kirby: King of Comics*. New York: Abrams.
Festinger, Leon. 1954. "A Theory of Social Comparison Processes." *Human Relations* 7: 117–40.
Fingeroth, Danny. 2004. *Superman on the Couch*. New York: Continuum.
Fingeroth, Danny. 2007. *Disguised as Clark Kent: Jews, Comics, and the Creation of the Super-Hero*. New York: Continuum.
Fischer, Craig. 2010. "Worlds without Worlds: Audiences, Jargon, and North American Comics Discourse." *Transatlantica* 10. https://journals.openedition.org/transatlantica/4919.
Fiske, John. 1991. "The Discourses of TV Quiz Shows, or School + Luck = Success + Sex." In *Television Criticism: Approaches and Applications*, edited by Leah Vande Berg and Lawrence Wenner, 445–62. White Plains: Longman.
Fleischer, Dave, dir. 1933. "I Yan What I Yam." Fleischer Studios, September 29.
Freccero, J. 1986. "Autobiography and Narrative." In *Reconstructing Individualism*, edited by Thomas C. Heller, Morton Sousa, and David E. Wellberg, 16–29. Stanford: Stanford University Press.
Freeman, Mark, and Jens Brockmeier. 2001. "Narrative Integrity: Autobiographical Identity and the Meaning of the 'Good Life.'" In *Narrative and Identity: Studies in Autobiography, Self ad Culture*, edited by Jens Brockmeier and Donal Carbaugh, 75–99. Amsterdam: John Benjamins Publishing.
Fresnault-Derulle, Pierre. 1976. "Du Linéaire au Tablulaire." *Communications* 24: 7–23.
Fulce, John. 1990. *Seduction of the Innocent Revisited*. Lafayette: Huntington House.
Gabilliet, Jean-Paul. 2010. *Of Comics and Men: A Cultural History of American Comic Books*. Translated by Bart Beaty and Nick Nguyen. Jackson: University of Mississippi Press.
Gardner, Jared. 2008. "Autography's Biography, 1972–2007." *Biography* 31, no. 1: 1–26.
Garriock, P. R. 1978. *Masters of Comic Book Art*. New York: Images Graphiques.
Garrity, Shaenon. 2007. "The Gail Simone Interview." *Comics Journal* 286: 68–91.
Gavaler, Chris. 2015. *On the Origins of Superheroes: From the Big Bang to Action Comics No. 1*. Iowa City: University of Iowa Press.
Gecas, Viktor. 1982. "The Self-Concept." *Annual Review of Sociology* 8: 1–33.
Geerdes, Clay. 1990. "Comix Wavola." *Comix F/X*, May, n.p.
Geerdes, Clay. 1990. "The Evolution of the Minicomix in the Bay Area, Part 4." *Comix F/X*, May, 6–7.
Geipel, John. 1972. *The Cartoon: A Short History of Graphic Comedy and Satire*. South Brunswick: A. S. Barnes and Company.
George, Milo, ed. 2002. *The Comics Journal Library, Volume One: Jack Kirby*. Seattle: Fantagraphics Books.
Gerber, Ernst. 1989–1990. *The Photo-Journal Guide to Comic Books*. 2 vols. Minden: Gerber Publishing Co.
Gertler, Nat. 2000. "What Is the Superhero Genre Tale?" Paper presented at the Comic Arts Conference, San Diego, CA, July 21, 2000.

Giordano, Dick. 1988. "Introduction: Growing up with the Greatest." In *The Greatest Batman Stories Ever Told*, edited by Mike Gold, 6–11. New York: DC Comics.
Gloeckner, Phoebe. 2011. "Autobiography: The Process Negates the Term." In *Graphic Subjects: Critical Essays on Autobiography and Graphic Novels*, edited by Michael A. Chaney, 178–9. Madison: University of Wisconsin Press.
Goethe, Johann Wolfgang von. 1875. *Conversations of Goethe with Eckermann and Soret*. Translated by John Oxenford. London: George Bell.
Goldstein, Jay. 1999. "Mixx's Sailor Moon Manga Is the Number 1 Graphic Novel or Trade Paperback in America!" *Mixx Entertainment*. Last modified June 18, 1999. http://web.archive .org/web/20001029221527/http://www.mixxonline.com/mixxonline/company/press_releases/ pr_990618_sailor_tops.html.
Goldstein, Robert Justin. 1989. "The Debate over Censorship of Caricature in Nineteenth-Century France." *Art Journal* 48, no. 1: 9–15.
Gordon, Ian. 1998. *Comic Strips and Consumer Culture 1890–1945*. Washington: Smithsonian Institution Press.
Gorman, Michele. 2003. *Getting Graphic! Using Graphic Novels to Promote Literacy with Preteens and Teens*. Worthington: Linworth Publishing, Inc.
Goulart, Ron. 1986. *Ron Goulart's Great History of Comic Books*. Chicago: Contemporary Books.
Goulart, Ron. 1991. *Over Fifty Years of American Comic Books*. Lincolnwood: Publications International, Ltd.
Goulart, Ron. 1970/1997. "The Second Banana Superheroes." In *All in Color for a Dime*, edited by Dick Lupoff and Don Thompson, 229–39. Iola: Krause Publications.
Goulart, Ron. 2000. *Comic Book Culture: An Illustrated History*. Portland: Collectors Press.
Goulart, Ron. 2001. *Great American Comic Books*. Lincolnwood: Publications International, Ltd.
Gramsci, Antonio. 1971. *In Selections from the Prison Notebooks of Antonio Gramsci*, edited by Quintin Hoare and Geoffrey Nowell Smith. New York: International Publishers.
Grand Comic Book Database. 1994–2008. Accessed August 3, 2008. www.comics.org.
"Graphic Novels Hit $375 Million." 2008. *ICv2*, April 18, 2008. Accessed May 18, 2008. www.icv2 .com/articles/news/12416.html.
Gravett, Paul. 2004. *Manga: Sixty Years of Japanese Comics*. New York: HarperCollins.
Gravett, Paul. 2005. *Graphic Novels: Everything You Need to Know*. New York: Harper- Collins.
Gravett, Paul. 2006. *Great British Comics: Celebrating a Century of Ripping Yarns and Wizard Wheezes*. London: Aurum Press Limited.
Gravett, Paul. 2013. *Comics Art*. New Haven: Yale University Press.
Gravett, Paul. 2013. "Sarah Lightman: The Book of Sarah." *Paulgravett.com*. Last modified September 28, 2013. http://www.paulgravett.com/index.php/articles/article/ sarah_lightman_ the_book_of_sarah.
Green, Justin. 2009. "Afterword." In *Binky Brown Meets the Holy Virgin Mary*, 51–63. San Francisco: McSweeney's Books.
Green, Justin. 1972/2009. *Binky Brown Meets the Holy Virgin Mary*. San Francisco: McSweeney's Books.
Gregory, Roberta. 1997. *Bitchy's College Daze*. Seattle: Fantagraphics Books.
Groensteen, Thierry. 1998. "Töpffer, the Originator of the Modern Comic Strip." In *Forging a New Medium: The Comic Strip in the Nineteenth Century*, edited by Pascal Lefèvre and Charles Dierick, 105–14. Brussells: VUB University Press.
Groensteen, Thierry. 2007. *System of Comics*. Translated by Bart Beaty and Nick Nguyen. Jackson: University Press of Mississippi.
Groensteen, Thierry. 2013. *Comics and Narration*. Translated by Ann Miller. Jackson: University Press of Mississippi.

Gross, Theodore L. 1971. *The Heroic Ideal in American Literature*. New York: The Free Press.
Grossman, Lev, and Richard Lacayo. 2005. "*Time*'s Critics Pick the 100 Best Novels 1923 to Present." *Time*. Accessed May 29, 2008. www.time.com/time/2005/100books.
Groth, Gary. 2000. "Independent Spirits: A Comics Perspective." In *Below Critical Radar: Fanzines and Alternative Comics from 1976 to the Present Day*, edited by Roger Sabin and Teal Triggs, 17–27. Hove: Slab-O-Concrete.
Groth, Gary. 2006. "Black and White and Dead All Over." *The Comics Journal*, July, 60–7.
Gubitosa, Carlo. 2021. "The Rise and Fall of Comics Journalism Magazines and Their Legacy: Experience of Graphic Storytelling in the USA, Italy, and France." *Paradoxa* 32: 61–86.
Guruzhalov, Victor. 2005. "Comics in Education: Are They Useful? A Roundtable prepared by Svetlana Malimova." Translated by Seth Graham. *International Journal of Comic Art* 7, no. 1 (Spring): 75–94.
Gusdorf, Georges. 1980. "Conditions and Limits of Autobiography." In *Autobiography: Essays Theoretical and Critical*, edited by James Olney, 27–48. Princeton: Princeton University Press.
Gustines, George Gene. 2005. "Where Superheroes Go for Industry News." *New York Times*, August 2, 2005. Accessed April 21, 2008. www.nytimes.com/2005/08/02/books/02sham.html?_r=2&oref=slogin&oref=slogin.
Hague, Ian. 2014. *Comics and the Senses: A Multisensory Approach to Comics and Graphic Novels*. London: Routledge.
Harper, David. 2014. "Artist Alley: Sean Phillips and the Dark Side of Hollywood in 'The Fade Out'." *Multiversity Comics*, August 20. http://www.multiversitycomics.com/news-columns/artist-alley-sean-phillips-and-the-dark-side-of-hollywood-in-the-fade-out-interview/.
Harrison, Randall. 1981. *The Cartoon: Communication to the Quick*. Beverly Hills: Sage.
Harvey, Robert C. 1996. *The Art of the Comic Book: An Aesthetic History*. Jackson: University Press of Mississippi.
Hatfield, Charles. 2005. *Alternative Comics: An Emerging Literature*. Jackson: University Press of Mississippi.
Hatfield, Charles. 2012. *Hand of Fire: The Comics Art of Jack Kirby*. Jackson: University Press of Mississippi.
Hattenstone, Simon. 2008. "Confessions of Miss Mischief." *Guardian UK*, March 28, 2008, n.p. Accessed October 17, 2013. http://www.guardian.co.uk/film/2008/mar/29/biography.
Haugaard, Kay. 1973. "Comic Books: Conduits to Culture?" *The Reading Teacher* 27: 54–5.
Haynes, Amanda. 2007. "Mass Media Re-Presentations of the Social World: Ethnicity and 'Race.'" In *Media Studies: Key Issues and Debates*, edited by Eoin Devereux, 162–90. Los Angeles: Sage.
Heisler, Florence. 1948. "Comparison of Comic Book and Non-Comic Book Readers of the Elementary School." *Journal of Educational Research* 41: 541–6.
Herman, David. 2011. "Narrative Worldmaking in Graphic Life Writing." In *Graphic Subjects: Critical Essays on Autobiography and Graphic Novels*, edited by Michael A. Chaney, 231–43. Madison: University of Wisconsin Press.
Hibbs, Brian. 2021. "Tilting at Windmills #286: The Era Changes – Part One." *Comicsbeat.com*. Last modified September 20, 2021. https://www.comicsbeat.com/tilting-at-windmills-286-the-era-changes-part-one/.
Hight, Craig. 2007. "*American Splendor*: Translating Comic Autobiography into Drama-Documentary." In *Film and Comic Books*, edited by Ian Gordon, Mark Jankovich, and Matthew P. McAllister, 180–98. Jackson: University Press of Mississippi.
Hinds, Harold E., and Charles M. Tatum. 1977. "Hogarth, William." In *The World Encyclopedia of Comics*, edited by Maurice Horn, 320–1. New York: Avon.

Hinds, Harold E., and Charles M. Tatum. 1992. *Not Just for Children: The Mexican Comic Book in the Late 1960s and 1970s*. Westport: Greenwood Press.
Hirsch, Paul. 2021. *Pulp Empire: The Secret History of Comic Book Imperialism*. Chicago: The University of Chicago Press.
Hix, Lisa. 2017. "Self-Righteous Devils: What Ozark Vigilantes of the 1880s Reveal About Modern America." *Collectors Weekly*, February 24, 2017. Accessed January 29, 2022. https://www.collectorsweekly.com/articles/what-ozark-vigilantes-of-the-1880s-reveal-about-modern-america/.
"Hogarth, William." 1976. In *The World Encyclopedia of Comics*, edited by Maurice Horn, 320–1. New York: Avon.
Hogg, Trevor. 2014. "Criminal Minds: Sean Phillips talks about Ed Brubaker." *Flickering Myth*, November 15. https://www.flickeringmyth.com/2014/11/criminal-minds-sean-phillips-talks-ed-brubaker/.
Holub, Christian. 2018. "Brian K. Vaughan and Fiona Staples Explain Why Saga Is Taking a Hiatus after that Stunning Cliffhanger." *EW*, August 28. https://ew.com/books/2018/08/28/brian-k-vaughan-fiona-staples-saga-hiatus/.
Horn, Maurice. 1977. *Comics of the American West*. New York: Winchester Press.
Horn, Maurice. 1985. *Sex in the Comics*. New York: Chelsea House Publishers.
Hoult, Thomas F. 1949. "Comic Books and Juvenile Delinquency." *Sociology and Social Research* 33: 279–84.
Houston, Frank. 1999. "Stan Lee." *Salon.com*. Last modified on August 17, 1999. www.salon.com/people/bc/1999/08/17/lee.
Hybels, Saundra, and Richard L. Weaver II. 2011. *Communicating Effectively*. 10th ed. Boston: McGraw-Hill.
icV2.com. 2022. Accessed April 8, 2022. https://icv2.com/.
Infantino, Carmine, and J. David Spurlock. 2001. *The Amazing World of Carmine Infantino: An Autobiography*. Lebanon: Vanguard Productions.
Inge, M. Thomas. 1985. "Preface." In *The American Comic Book: An Exhibition at the Ohio State University*. Columbus: Ohio State University Libraries.
Inge, M. Thomas. 1990. *Comics as Culture*. Jackson: University Press of Mississippi.
Jackson, Jack. 1972. "A Phenomenon." *Infinity Four*, n.p.
Jacobson, Nels. 1991. "The Maverick Tradition: Postering in Austin, Texas." *OFFtheWALL* 1, no. 2: n.p.
James, Muriel, and Dorothy Joneward. 1971. *Born to Win: Transactional Analysis with Gestalt Experiments*. Reading: Addison-Wesley.
Jenkins, Henry. 2003. "Quentin Tarantino's *Star Wars*? Digital Cinema, Media Convergence, and Participatory Culture." In *Rethinking Media Change: The Aesthetics of Transition*, edited by David Thorburn and Henry Jenkins, 281–312. Cambridge, MA: The MIT Press.
Jenkins, Henry. 2009. "'Just Men in Tights': Rewriting Silver Age Comics in an Era of Multiplicity." In *The Contemporary Comic Book Superhero*, edited by Angela Ndalianis, 281–312. London: Routledge.
Jenkins, Henry. 2012. "Introduction: Should We Discipline the Reading of Comics?" In *Critical Approaches to Comics: Theories and Methods*, edited by Matthew J. Smith and Randy Duncan, 1–14. New York: Routledge.
Jennings, John, with Damian Duffy. 2007. "Finding Other Heroes." In *Other Heroes: African American Comic Book Creators, Characters and Archetypes*, edited by John Jennings and Damian Duffy, 162–6. [S. l.]: lulu.com.
Jensen, Joli. 1992. "Fandom as Pathology: The Consequences of Characterization." In *The Adoring Audience: Fan Culture and Popular Media*, edited by Lisa A. Lewis, 9–29. New York: Routledge.

Jewett, Robert, and John Shelton Lawrence. 1977. *The American Monomyth*. Garden City: Anchor Press.

Jewett, Robert, and John Shelton Lawrence. 2003. *Captain America and the Crusade against Evil: The Dilemma of Zealous Nationalism*. Grand Rapids: William B. Eerdmans Publishing.

Johnson, Jeffery K. 2012. *Super-History: Comic Book Superheroes and American Society*. Jefferson: McFarland & Company.

Jones, Gerard, and Will Jacobs. 1997. *The Comic Book Heroes*. 2nd ed. Rocklin: Prima Publishing.

Jones, William B., Jr. 2002. *Classics Illustrated: A Cultural History, with Illustrations*. Jefferson: McFarland & Company, Inc.

Jones, William B., Jr. 2011. *Classics Illustrated: A Cultural History*. 2nd ed. Jefferson: McFarland & Company, Inc.

JSK. 2013. "Q&A with Dan Archer: Comics Journalism and the Power of Collaboration." *Idea Lab*. Last modified December 16, 2013. http://www.pbs.org/idealab/2013/12/qa-with-dan-archer-comics-journalism-and-the-power-of-collaboration-2/.

Juno, Andrea. 1997. *Dangerous Drawings: Interviews with Graphix and Comix Artists*. New York: Juno Books.

Kane, Bob, and Gardner F. Fox. 1939. "The Batman Meets Dr. Death." *Detective Comics* #29 (July): 1–10.

Kannenberg, Gene, Jr. 2007. "The Ad that Made an Icon out of Mac." *Hogan's Alley: The Online Magazine of the Cartoon Arts*. Accessed July 7, 2007. www.cagle.com/hogan/features/atlas.asp.

Kannenberg, Gene, Jr. 2001. "Graphic Text, Graphic Context: Interpreting Custom Fonts and Hands in Con- temporary Comics." In *Illuminating Letter: Typography and Literary Interpretation*, edited by Paul C. Gutjahr and Megan L. Benton, 165–92. Amherst: University of Massachusetts Press.

Kasson, John F. 2001. *Houdini, Tarzan, and the Perfect Man: The White Male Body and the Challenge of Modernity in America*. New York: Hill and Wang.

Kearns, Ciléin, and Nethmi Kearns. 2020. "The Role of Comics in Public Health Communication during the COVID-19 Pandemic." *Journal of Visual Communication in Medicine* 43, no. 3: 139–49. https://doi.org/10.1080/17453054.2020.1761248.

Kefauver, Estes. 1955. "Comic Books and Juvenile Delinquency: Interim Report of the Committee on the Judiciary; A Part of the Investigation of Juvenile Delinquency in the United States." Eighty-Third Congress, First Session Pursuant to S. Res. 89, and Eighty-third Congress, second session pursuant to S. Res. 190, March 14 (Legislative Day, March 10).

Kelp-Stebbins, Sarah. 2022. "OHC Cosponsors 'Art of the News: Comics Journalism'." *Oregon Humanities Center*. Accessed March 27, 2022. https://ohc.uoregon.edu/multimedia/news/ohc-cosponsors-art-of-the-news-comics-journalism/.

Kelso, Megan. 1999. "New Voices in Comics 1998: A Roundtable." *International Journal of Comic Art* 1, no. 2: 216–37.

Kendall, David, ed. 2007. *The Mammoth Book of Best War Comics*. New York: Running Press.

Kennedy, Jay. 1982. *The Official Underground and Newave Price Guide*. Cambridge: Boatner Norton Press.

Kidson, Mike. 1999. "William Hogarth: Printing Techniques and Comics." *International Journal of Comic Art* 1, no. 1: 76–89.

Kirsh, Steven J., and Paul V. Olczak. 2003. "Comic Book Violence and Vengeance." In *Perspectives on Violence*, edited by Frederick K. Blucher, 81–92. Hauppage: Nova Science Publishers.

Kirste, Kenneth K. 1988. *Drawn to Excellence: Masters of Cartoon Art*. San Francisco: Cartoon Art Museum.

Knowles, Christopher. 2007. *Our Gods Wear Spandex: The Secret History of Comic Book Heroes*. San Francisco: Weiser Books.

Kobler, John. 1941. "Up, Up and Awa-a-y!: The Rise of Superman Incorporated." *Saturday Evening Post*, June 21, 1941, 14–5, 70–8.

Krashen, Stephen. 1993. *The Power of Reading: Insights from the Research*. Englewood: Libraries Unlimited.

Kress, Gunther, and Theo van Leeuwen. 2006. *Reading Images: The Grammar of Visual Design*. New York: Routledge.

Kuba Krys, C. et al. 2016. "Be Careful Where You Smile: Culture Shapes Judgments of Intelligence and Honesty of Smiling Individuals." *Journal of Nonverbal Behavior* 40: 101–16.

Kunzle, David. 1970. "The Comic Strip." In *Art News Annual XXXVI: Narrative Art*, edited by Thomas B. Hess and John Ashbery, 133–45. New York: The Macmillan Company.

Kunzle, David. 1998. "Caricature, Cartoon, and Comic Strip." In *The New Encyclopedia Britannica*, vol. 15. Macropaedia, 15th ed., 52. Chicago: Encyclopedia Britannica, Inc.

Kuper, Peter. 2005. "Launching World War 3." In *The Education of a Comics Artist: Visual Narrative in Cartoons, Graphic Novels, and Beyond*, edited by Michael Dooley and Steven Heller, 28–31. New York: Allworth Press.

Kurtzman, Harvey. 1991. *From Aargh! to Zap! Harvey Kurtzman's Visual History of the Comics*. New York: Prentice Hall Press.

La Cour, Erin, Simon Grennan, and Rik Spanjers, eds. 2022. *Key Terms in Comics Studies*. New York: Palgrave Macmillan.

Lang, Jeffrey, and Patrick Trimble. 1988. "Whatever Happened to the Man of Tomorrow? An Examination of the American Monomyth and the Comic Book Superhero." *Journal of Popular Culture* 22, no. 3: 157–73.

Langer, Lawrence L. 1991. "A Fable of the Holocaust." *The New York Times Book Review*, November 3, 1991, 17.

Lannon, Keegan. 2013. "Visualizing Words: The Functions of Words in Comics." *International Journal of Comic* 15, no. 1: 287–305, Art. 15.

Lavin, Michael R. 1999. "A Librarian's Guide to Archie Comics." *Serials Review* 25, no. 1: 75–82.

Lee, Joan. 2002. *I Have to Live with This Guy!* edited by Blake Bell, 61. Raleigh: TwoMorrows Publishing.

Lee, Stan. 1974. *Origins of Marvel Comics*. New York: Simon and Schuster.

Lee, Stan, and George Mair. 2002. *Excelsior! The Amazing Life of Stan Lee*. New York: Simon & Schuster.

Lefèvre, Pascal. 2013. "The Modes of Documentary Comics." In *Der dokumentarische Comic Reportage und Biographie*, edited by Dietrich Grünewald, 50–60. Berlin: Christian A. Bachmann Verlag.

Lejeune, Philippe. 1989. "Le Pact Autobiographique" [The Autobiographical Pact]. Translated by Katherine Leary. In *On Autobiography*, edited by Paul John Eaken, 3–30. Minneapolis: University of Minnesota Press.

Leonard, Devin. 2007. "Marvel Goes Hollywood: Calling All Superheroes." *Fortune*, May 28, 2007. Accessed June 3, 2007. http://money.cnn.com/magazines/fortune/fortune_archive/2007/05/28/10003446/index.html.

Levitz, Paul. 2013. "Why Supervillains?" In *What is a Superhero?* edited by Robin S. Rosenberg and Peter Coogan, 79–81. Oxford: Oxford University Press.

Lewin, Herbert S. 1953. "Fact and Figures about the Comics." *Nation's Schools* 52: 46–8.

Lieber, Steve. 2013. "Dilettante 004: Using Photo Reference." *Toucan: The Official Comic-Con & Wondercon Blog*, April 5. https://www.comic-con.org/toucan/dilettante-004-using-photo-reference.

Ling, Paul K. 1976. "A Thematic Analysis of Underground Comics." *Crimmer's: The Journal of the Narrative Arts*, 39–43.

Lippman, Walter. *Public Opinion*. New York: Harcourt, Brace and Company, 1922.

Lischer, Brian. n.d. "The Sequence of Cognition: How to Leverage the Subconscious Language of Design." *Ignyte*. Accessed May 1, 2022. https://www.ignytebrands.com/sequence-of-cognition/#1.

Loeb, Jeph, and Tom Morris. 2005. "Heroes and Superheroes." In *Superheroes and Philosophy*, edited by Tom Morris and Matt Morris, 11–20. Chicago: Open Court.

Lofficier, Jean-Marc, and Randy Lofficier. 2004. *Shadowmen 2: Heroes and Villains of French Comics*. Encino: Black Coat Press.

Lovibond, S. H. 1967. "The Effect of Media Stressing Crime and Violence upon Children's Attitudes." *Social Problems* 15: 91–100.

Lowery, Shearon L., and Melvin L. DeFleur. 1983. *Milestones in Mass Communication Research*. 2nd ed. New York: Longman.

Luckiesh, Matthew, and Frak K. Moss. 1942. "Legibility in Comic Books." *Sight-Saving Review* 12: 19–24.

Lupoff, Dick, and Don Thompson. 1970. "Introduction." In *All in Color for a Dime*, edited by Dick Lupoff and Don Thompson, 7–14. New York: Ace Books.

Lustig, John. 2005. "The Terrible, Tragic (*Sob!*) Death of Romance (Comics!!)." *Back Issue*, December, 16–23.

MacDonald, Heidi, and Phillip Dana Yeh. 1994. *Secret Teachings of a Comic Book Master: The Art of Alfredo Alcala*. Lompoc: International Humor Advisory Council.

Malan, Dan. 1847/1992. "Introduction." *The Labours of Hercules*. Translated by Eric Bosch. St. Louis: Malan Classical Enterprises.

Mallia, Ġorġ. 2007. "Learning from the Sequence: The Use of Comics in Instruction." *Image-Text* 3. Accessed November 9, 2007. www.english.ufl.edu/imagetext/archives/v3_3/mallia/.

Malloy, Alex. 1992. *Comics Values Annual*. Radnor: Wallace Homestead.

Maréchal, Béatrice. 2005. "On Top of the Mountain: The Influential Manga of Yoshiharu Tsuge." In *The Comics Journal, Special Edition Volume Five: Manga Masters*, edited by Gary Groth, 22–8. Seattle: Fantagraphics.

Marion, Philippe. 1993. *Traces en Cases [Traces in Frames]*. Louvain-la-Neuve: Académia.

Markstein, Don, ed. 1994. *Hot Tips from Top Comics Creators*. New York: Fictioneer Books.

Marnell, Blair. 2019. "House of X Artist Pepe Larraz on His Process and Persistence." Last modified August 2, 2019. https://www.marvel.com/articles/comics/house-of-x-artist-pepe-larraz-on-his-process-and-persistence-i-mean-it-a-real-pain.

Marshall, Monica. 2005. *Joe Sacco*. New York: Rosen Publishing Group.

Matton, Annette. 2001. "From Realism to Superheroes in Marvel's *The 'Nam*." In *Comics & Ideology*, edited by Matthew P. McAllister, Edward H. Sewell, Jr., and Ian Gordon, 151–76. New York: Peter Lang.

McAllister, Matthew P. 1990. "Cultural Argument and Organizational Constraint in the Comic Book Industry." *Journal of Communication* 40: 55–71.

McAllister, Matthew P. 2001. "Ownership Concentration in the U.S. Comic Book Industry." In *Comics & Ideology*, edited by Matthew P. McAllister, Edward H. Sewell, Jr., and Ian Gordon, 15–38. New York: Peter Lang.

McAllister, Matthew P., Edward H. Sewell, Jr., and Ian Gordon. 2001. "Introducing Comics and Ideology." In *Comics & Ideology*, edited by Matthew P. McAllister, Edward H. Sewell, Jr., and Ian Gordon, 1–13. New York: Peter Lang.

McCloud, Scott. 1993. *Understanding Comics: The Invisible Art*. Northhampton: Tundra Publishing.

McCloud, Scott. 2000. *Reinventing Comics: How Imagination and Technology Are Revolutionizing an Art Form*. New York: HarperCollins.

McCloud, Scott. 2006. *Making Comics: Storytelling Secrets of Comics, Manga and Graphic Novels*. New York: Harper.

McLuhan, Marshall. 1967. "Essay 11 [unnamed]." In *McLuhan: Hot and Cool*, edited by Gerald Emanuel Stern, 119–23. New York: Signet.

McMillan, Graeme. 2019. "Omni Lets Artist Alitha E. Martinez Create the Future of Comics." *The Hollywood Reporter*, August 12, 2019. https://www.hollywoodreporter.com/news/general-news/omni-lets-artist-alitha-e-martinez-create-future-comics-1230630/.

McRobbie, Angela. 2000. *Feminism and Youth Culture*. 2nd ed. New York: Routledge.

Meehan, Eileen R. 1991. "'Holy Commodity Fetish, Batman!': The Political Economy of a Commercial Intertext." In *The Many Lives of the Batman: Critical Approaches to a Superhero and His Media*, edited by Roberta E. Pearson and William Uricchio, 47–65. New York: Routledge.

Melby, Julie L. 2009, "Charles Philipon's La Caricature." *Graphic Arts*. Last modified February 4, 2009. http://blogs.princeton.edu/graphicarts/2009/02/charles_philipons_la_caricatur.html.

Mercier, Jean-Pierre. 2004. "'Remember Folks, It's Only Line on Paper': Robert Crumb and the Art of Comics." In *54th Carnegie International*, edited by Laura Hoptman. Pittsburgh: Carnegie Museum of Art.

Messaris, Paul. 1997. *Visual Persuasion: The Role of Images in Advertising*. Thousand Oaks: Sage Publications, 1997.

Miller, Ann. 2007. *Reading Bande Dessinée: Critical Approaches to French-Language Comic Strip*. Bristol: Intellect.

Miller Frank. 2003. "Man with Pen in Head." In *AutobioGraphix*, edited by Diana Schutz, 5–10. Milwaukie: Dark Horse Books.

Miller, Jeffery. 2000. Posting to Comics Scholars Discussion List, March 17, 2000.

Miller, John Jackson. 2008. *Comics Chronicles*. Last modified April 24, 2008. www.comichron.com.

Miller, John Jackson. 2013. "2012 Comic Book Sales Figures." *Comichron: The Comics Chronicles*. Accessed July 28, 2013. http://www.comichron.com/monthlycomicssales/2012.html.

Miller, John Jackson, Maggie Thompson, Peter Bickford, and Brent Frankenhoff. 2005. *Comics Buyer's Guide Standard Catalog of Comic Books*. 4th ed. Iola: kp books.

Miller, Rachel. 2018. "Keep out, or Else: Girls' Diaries in Comics." *Public Books*. Last modified May 4, 2018. https://www.publicbooks.org/keep-out-or-else-girls-diaries-in-comics/.

Mishler, James. 2006. "Horror Comics: Tricks & Treats through the Ages." *Comic Buyer's Guide*, January, 24–6, 28–30, 32, 34.

Misiroglu, Gina, and Michael Eury, eds. 2006. *The Supervillain Book: The Evil Side of Comics and Hollywood*. Canton: Visible Ink Press.

Molotiu, Andrei. 2012. "Abstract Form: Sequential Dynamism and Iconostasis in Abstract Comics and Steve Ditko's Amazing Spider-Man." In *Critical Approaches to Comics: Theories and Methods*, edited by Matthew J. Smith and Randy Duncan, 84–100. New York Routledge.

Monaco, James. 1977. *How to Read a Film*. New York: Oxford University Press, 1977.

Moore, Matt. 2013. "Rep. John Lewis' Graphic Novel Tells His Civil Rights Story." *Online Athens Banner-Herald*. Last modified August 13, 2013. http://onlineathens.com/local-news/2013-08-13/rep-john-lewis-graphic-novel-tells-his-civil-rights-story.

Morrison, Grant. 2011. *Supergods: What Masked Vigilantes, Miraculous Mutants and the Sun God from Smallville Can Teach Us about Being Human*. New York: Spiegel & Grau.

Mullaney, Dean. 1987. "Publisher's Introduction." *In Real War Stories no. 1*. Forestville: Eclipse Comics.

Murphy, T. E. 1954. "For the Kiddies to Read." *Reader's Digest*, June, 5–8.

Murray, Chris. 2000. "Propaganda: Superhero Comics and Propaganda in World War Two." In *Comics & Culture: Analytical and Theoretical Approaches to Comics*, edited by Anne Magnussen and Hans-Christian Christiansen, 141–56. Copenhagen: Museum Tusculanum Press.

Murray, Chris. 2011. *Champions of the Oppressed? Superhero Comics, Popular Culture, and Propaganda in America During World War II*. Cresskill: Hampton Press.

Murray, Chris. 2012. "Propaganda: The Pleasures of Persuasion in Captain America." In *Critical Approaches to Comics: Theories and Methods*, edited by Matthew J. Smith and Randy Duncan, 129–41. New York: Routledge.

Nakazawa, Jun. 2005. "Development of Manga (Comic Book) Literacy in Children." In *Applied Developmental Psychology: Theory, Practice, and Research from Japan* edited by David W. Shwalb, Jun Nakazawa, and Barbara Shwalb, 23–42. Greenwich: Information Age Publishing.

Ndalianis, Angela. 2009. *The Contemporary Comic Book Superhero*. New York: Routledge.

Nelson, Gayle, and Ron Truner. 1999. "The Last Gasp Story." *Last Gasp*. Last modified January 1999. www.lastgasp.com/alg.

Nevins, Jess. 2007. "The Bat." *Pulp and Adventure Heroes of the Pre-War Years*. Accessed November 29, 2007. http://geocities.com/jjnevins/pulpsb.html.

Nevins, Mark David. 1996. "Mythology and Superheroes." *Inks* 3, no. 3: 24–30.

"New York Newspaper and Mail Deliverers Union Strike." 2017. The Chester Gould Dick Tracy Museum. Accessed January 23, 2022. https://www.dicktracymuseum.com/newspaper-strike#:~:text=New%20York%20City%20Mayor%20Fiorello,adventures%20for%20July%208%2C%201945.

Nichols, Bill. 2010. *Introduction to Documentary*. 2nd ed. Bloomington: Indiana University Press.

Nobel, Carmen. 2020. "Documenting Serious Issues with Comics Journalism: An Interview with Josh Neufeld." *The Journalist's Resource*. Last modified November 16, 2020. https://journalistsresource.org/media/documenting-pandemic-comics-journalism/.

Nolan, Michelle. 1997. "Patriotic Heroes . . . the Red, White & Blue of WWII." *Comic Book Marketplace*, June, 13–8.

Nolan, Michelle. 1998. "Collecting the Western Genre!" *Comic Book Marketplace*, July, 23–6.

Norrington, Stephen, dir. 1998. *Blade*. New York: New Line Cinema. DVD, 120 mins.

North, Sterling. 1940. "A National Disgrace." *Chicago Daily News*, May 8, 1940, reprinted in *Childhood Education* 17: 56.

Norton, Bonny. 2003. "The Motivating Power of Comic Books: Insights from Archie Comic Readers." *Reaching Teacher* 57: 140–7.

Norton, Bonny, and Karen Vanderheyden. 2004. "Comic Book Culture and Second Language Learners." In *Critical Pedagogies and Language Learning*, edited by Bonny Norton and Kelleen Toohey, 201–21. New York: Cambridge University Press.

Nyberg, Amy Kiste. 1998. *Seal of Approval: The History of the Comics Code*. Jackson: University of Mississippi Press.

Nyberg, Amy Kiste. 2006. "Theorizing Comics Journalism." *International Journal of Comic Art* 8, no. 2: 98–112.

Nyberg, Amy Kiste. 2010. "*Culture Pulp*: The Art of Journalism." Presented at the Popular Culture Association Annual Conference, St. Louis, Missouri, April 2, 2010.

O'Nale, Robert. 2008. "The Gestalt Function of Comics." Paper presented at the 16th annual Comics Arts Conference, San Diego, California, July 24–27.

O'Neil, Dennis. 1992. "Green Thoughts." Introduction to *Green Lantern, Green Arrow: The Collection*, by Dennis O'Neil. New York: DC Comics.

Orwell, George. 1946. "Benefit of Clergy: Some Notes on Salvador Dali." In *Dickens, Dali and Others: Studies in Popular Culture*, edited by George Orwell, 17–184. New York: The Cornwell Press.
O'Sullivan, Judith. 1990. *The Great American Comic Strip*. Boston: Bulfinch Press.
Otsmane-Elhaou, Hassan. 2016. "Laying out Digital Comics: Jaeger." *Strip Panel Naked*. Accessed December 10, 2016. https://www.youtube.com/watch?v=zlMj8W9X2gc.
"Over 3,300 Graphic Novels Released in '07." 2008. *ICv2*. Last modified March 6, 2008. www.icv2.com/articles/news/12186.html.
Overstreet, Robert M. 1970. "Introduction." In *Comic Book Price Guide*. Cleveland: Robert M. Overstreet.
Overstreet, Robert M. 2005. *Official Overstreet Comic Book Price Guide*. 35th ed. New York: Gemstone Publishing.
Oyserman, Daphna, Kristen Elmore, and George Smith. 2012. "Self, Self-Concept, and Identity." In *Handbook of Self and Identity*, 2nd ed., edited by Mark R. Leary and June Price, 69–104. Tangney: Guilford Press.
Paine, Albert B. 1980. *Thomas Nast: His Period and Picture*. New York: Chelsea House.
Peeters, Benoit. 1983. "Les Adventures de la Page." *Consequences* 1: 32–44.
Peeters, Benoit. 1991. *Case, planche, récit: comment lire une bande dessinée*. Tournai: Casterman.
Peeters, Benoit. 1998/2007. "Four Conceptions of the Page: From *Case, Planche, Récit*: Lire la Bande Dessinée." Translated by Jesse Cohn. *ImageText: Interdisciplinary Comics Studies* 3, no. 3: n.p. https://imagetextjournal.com/four-conceptions-of-the-page/.
Pekar, Harvey. 1985. "Stories about Honesty, Money, and Misogyny." Interview by Gary Groth. *Comics Journal* 97: 44–64.
Pekar, Harvey. 1986. "Short Weekend." In *American Splendor: The Life and Times of Harvey Pekar*. Garden City: Doubleday & Company.
Pekar, Harvey. 1988. "The Potential of Comics." *The Comics Journal* 123 (July): 81–8.
"Persuasion." 2015. *Encyclopedia Britannica*. Last modified October 7, 2015. https://www.britannica.com/science/persuasion-psychology.
Petty, Richard, and John Cacioppo. 1986. *Communication and Persuasion: Central and Peripheral Routes to Attitude Change*. New York: Springer-Verlag.
Phillips, Charles. 1991. *Archie: His First 50 Years*. New York: Abbeville Press.
Pilcher, Tim, and Brad Brooks. 2005. *The Essential Guide to World Comics*. London: Collins & Brown.
Pizarro, David A., and Roy Baumeister. 2013. "Superhero Comics as Moral Pornography." In *Our Superheroes, Ourselves*, edited by Robin Rosenberg, 19–36. Oxford: Oxford University Press.
Pollman, Joost. 2001. "Shaping Sounds in Comics." *International Journal of Comic Art* 3, no. 1: 9–21.
Potts, Carl. 2013. *The DC Guide to Crating Comics: Inside the Art of Visual Storytelling*. New York: DC Comics.
Pudovkin, Vsevolod I. 1975. "Film Technique." In *Film: An Anthology*, edited by Daniel Talbot, 189–200. Berkeley: University of California Press.
Pustz, Matthew. 1999. *Comic Book Culture: Fanboys and True Believers*. Jackson: University Press of Mississippi.
Qualter, Terence H. 1965. *Propaganda and Psychological Warfare*. New York: Random House.
Quart, Alissa. 2009. "The Rise of True Fiction." *Columbia Journalism Review*, November/December. https://archives.cjr.org/feature/the_rise_of_true_fiction.php.
Raeburn, Daniel. 2004. "Two Centuries of Underground Comic Books." In *Strips, Toons, and Bluesies: Essays in Comics and Culture*, edited by D. B. Dowd and Todd Hignite, 34–45. New York: Princeton Architectural Press.

Rall, Ted. 2002. *To Afghanistan and Back*. New York: NBM.

Rank, Hugh. 1976. "Teaching about Public Persuasion: Rationale and a Schema." In *Teaching and Doublespeak*, edited by Daniel J. Dieterich, 3–19. Urbana: National Council of Teachers of English.

Rank, Otto. 1959. *The Myth of the Birth of the Hero and other Writings*. New York: Vintage Book.

Rasula, Jed. 1990. "Nietzsche in the Nursery: Naïve Classics and Surrogate Parents in Post-War American Cultural Debates." *Representations* 29: 50–77.

Raviv, Dan. 2002. *Comic Wars: How Two Tycoons Battled over the Marvel Comics Empire—And Both Lost*. New York: Broadway Books.

Reed, Calvin. 2022. "How Comics Got to Now." *Publishers Weekly*. Accessed April 19, 2022. https://www.publishersweekly.com/pw/by-topic/industry-news/comics/article/89013-how-comics-got-to-now.html.

Reed, Robbie. 2008. "Secret Origins of the DC Implosion." *Dial B for Blog*. Accessed June 11, 2008. www.dialbforblog.com/archives/252.

Regalado, Aldo. 2000. "The Superhero Genre: Revisited and Reinterpreted." *Partial Proceedings of the 8th Annual Comic Arts Conference*, San Diego, California, July 20–22, 2000.

Reid, Calvin. 2008. "Graphic Novel Market Hits $330 Million." *PW Daily*, February 23, 2007. www.publishersweekly.com/article/CA6419034.html?q=Graphic+novel+market+hits+%24330.

Reitberger, Reinhold, and Wolfgang Fuchs. 1971/1972. *Comics: Anatomy of a Mass Medium*. Translated by Nadia Fowler. Boston: Little, Brown and Company.

Reynolds, Richard. 1992. *Super Heroes: A Modern Mythology*. London: B.T. Batsford Ltd.

Ricca, Brad. 2013. *Super Boys: The Amazing Adventures of Jerry Siegel and Joe Shuster – The Creators of Superman*. New York: St. Martin's Press.

Ridley, John. 2007. "Three Writers are Drawn by the Allure of Comics." *NPR*, October 17, 2007. www.npr.org/templates/story/story.php?storyId=87867518.

Rifas, Leonard. 1982 "Introduction." In *I SAW IT*, by Keiji Nakazawa, 1. San Francisco: EduComics.

Rifas, Leonard. 1992. "Fredric Wertham, Scientist." Paper presented at the Comic Arts Conference, San Diego, California, 1992.

Rifas, Leonard. 2000. "Cold War Comics." *International Journal of Comic Art* 2, no. 1: 3–32.

Rifas, Leonard. 2010. "Educational Comics." In *Encyclopedia of Comic Books and Graphic Novels*, edited by M. Keith Booker, 160–9. Santa Barbara: Greenwood.

Rifas, Leonard. 2021. *Korean War Comic Books*. Jefferson: McFarland.

Roberson, Chris (w), J. Michael Straczynski (w), Jamal Igle (a), Diogenes Neves (a), and Eddy Barrows (a). 2011. *Superman* #713. New York: DC Comics.

Robbins, Daniel, and Juergen Schulz. 1971. *Caricature and its Role in Graphic Satire*. Providence: Museum of Art, Rhode Island School of Design.

Robbins, Trina. 1996. *The Great Women Super Heroes*. Northampton: Kitchen Sink Press.

Robbins, Trina. 1999. *From Girls to Grrrlz: A History of Comics from Teens to Zines*. San Francisco: Chronicle Books.

Rogers, Mark C. 1997. "Beyond Bang! Pow! Genre and the Evolution of the American Comic Book Industry." Ph.D. diss., University of Michigan.

Rogers, Mark C. 2006. "Understanding Production: The Stylistic Impact of Artisan and Industrial Methods." *International Journal of Comic Art* 8, no. 1: 509–17.

Rosenkranz, Patrick. 2002. *Rebel Visions: The Underground Comix Revolution, 1963–1975*. Seattle: Fantagraphics Books.

Rosenkranz, Patrick. 2011. "The ABCs of Autobio Comix." *The Comics Journal*. Last modified March 6, 2011. www.tcj.com/the-abcs-of-auto-bio-comix-2.

Rovin, Jeff. 1985. *The Encyclopedia of Superheroes*. New York: Facts on File.

Rozanski, Chuck. "Death of Superman" promotion of 1992. *Tales from the Database*. Accessed April 3, 2022. www.milehighcomics.com/tales/cbg127.html.

Rubenstein, Anne. 1998. *Bad Language, Naked Ladies, and Other Threats to the Nation: A Political History of Comic Books in Mexico*. Durham: Duke University Press.

Rubin, Rebecca. 2019. "*Avengers: Endgame* Crushes $2 Billion Milestone in Record Time." *Variety*, May 5, 2019. https://variety.com/2019/film/news/avengers-endgame-2-billion-record-time-1203205293/.

Ryan, Marie-Laure. 1992. "The Modes of Narrativity and Their Visual Metaphors." *Style* 26, no. 3: 368–87.

Sabin, Roger. 1993. *Adult Comics: An Introduction*. London: Routledge.

Sabin, Roger. 1996. *Comics, Comix, & Graphic Novels: A History of Comic Art*. New York: Phaidon Press Inc.

Sabin, Roger. 2009. "Notes on Sacco's Footnotes in Gaza." *Eye* 29. Last modified November 29, 2009. http://www.eyemagazine.com/blog/post/notes-on-saccos-footnotes-in-gaza.

Sabin, Roger, and Teal Triggs. 2000. *Below Critical Radar: Fanzines and Alternative Comics from 1976 to the Present Day*. Hove: Slab-O-Concrete.

Sacco, Joe. 2003. *Notes from a Defeatist*. Seattle: Fantagraphics Books.

Sacco, Joe. 2007. "Some Reflections on Palestine." In *Palestine, The Special Edition*, viii–xxii. Seattle: Fantagraphics Books.

Sacco, Joe. 2012. *Journalism*. New York: Metropolitan Books.

Said, Edward. 2001/2007. "Homage to Joe Sacco." In *Palestine: The Special Edition*, edited by Kim Thompson, v–vii. Seattle: Fantagraphics Books.

Saltus, Elinor C. 1952. "The Comics Aren't Good Enough." *Wilson Library Bulletin* 26: 382–3.

Sam, Salgood. 2015. "Flow, & the Eyelines!" *Making Comics with Salgood Sam!* Last modified June 6, 2015. https://makingcomics.spiltink.org/flow-the-eyelines/.

Saraceni, Mario. 2003. *The Language of Comics*. London: Routledge.

"Sarah Lightman: Laydeez do Comics," *Jerwood Visual Arts Blog*. Last modified November, 1 2012. http://blog.jerwoodvisualarts.org/?p=1318.

Sassienie, Paul. 1994. *The Comic Book*. Edison: Chartwell Books.

Saunders, Ben. 2011. *Do The Gods Wears Capes? Spirituality, Fantasy, and Superheroes*. New York: Continuum.

Savage, William W., Jr. 1990. *Commies, Cowboys, and Jungle Queens: Comic Books and America, 1945–1954*. Hanover: Wesleyan University Press.

Shachtman, Noah. 2010. "War is Boring? Not in This Comic Book." *Wired*, August 17, 2010. https://www.wired.com/2010/08/war-is-boring-not-in-this-comic-book/.

Schelly, Bill. 1999. *The Golden Age of Comic Fandom*. Seattle: Hamster Press.

Schelly, Bill. 2001. *Sense of Wonder: A Life in Comic Fandom*. Raleigh: TwoMorrows Publishing.

Schlenker, Barry R. 2012. "Self-Presentation." In *Handbook of Self and Identity*, 2nd ed., edited by Mark R. Leary and June Price Tangney, 542–70. New York: Guilford Press.

Schmitt, Ronald. 1992. "Deconstructive Comics." *Journal of Popular Culture* 25: 153–61.

Schreiner, Dave. 1994. *Kitchen Sink Press: The First 25 Years*. Northampton: Kitchen Sink Press.

Schwalbe, Michael L. 1985. "Autonomy in Work and Self-Esteem." *The Sociological Quarterly* 26: 519–35.

Schwartz, Adam, and Eliane Rubinstein-Avila. 2006. "Understanding the Manga Hype: Uncovering the Multimodality of Comic-Book Literacies." *Journal of Adolescent and Adult Literacy* 50: 40–9.

Scott, Naomi, ed. 1979. *Heart Throbs: The Best of DC Romance Comics*. New York: Simon & Shuster.

Screech, Matthew. 2005. *Masters of the Ninth Art: Bandes Dessinées and the Franco-Belgian Identity*. Liverpool: Liverpool University Press.

Selby, Chip, dir. 2004. *Tales from the Crypt: From Comic Books to Television! 2004*. Monsters. DVD video, 56 mins.

Shannon, Claude, and Warren Weaver. 1949. *The Mathematical Theory of Communication*. Urbana: University of Illinois Press.

Shaw, Scott. 1999. "The Secret Origin of (the San Diego Golden State) Comic-Con International (more or less)." In *Comic-Con International: San Diego Souvenir Book*, 94–5. San Diego: Comic-Con International.

Shelton, Gilbert, publisher. 1964. *The Austin Iconoclastic Newsletter* 1, no. 5: n.p.

Sheridan, Martin. 1942. *Comics and Their Creators*. Boston: Hale, Cushman & Flint.

Sherif, Carolyn, Muzafer Sherif, and Roger Nebergall. 1965. *Attitude and Attitude Change*. Philadelphia: W.B. Saunders Company.

Shooter, Jim. 1994. "Foreword." In *The Comic Book*, by Paul Sassiene, 6. Edison: Chartwell Books.

Simon, Joe, and Jim Simon. 2003. *The Comic Book Makers*. Lebanon: Vanguard Productions.

Simpson, Will. 2018. "Feelings in the Gutter: Opportunities for Emotional Engagement in Comics." *ImageText* 10, no. 1. https://imagetextjournal.com/feelings-in-the-gutter-opportunities-for-emotional-engagement-in-comics/.

Singer, Marc. 1999. "Invisible Order: Comics, Time and Narrative." Paper presented at the 29th Annual Popular Culture Association Conference, San Diego, California, March 31–April 3, 1999.

Singer, Marc. 2015. "Views from Nowhere: Journalistic Detachment in Palestine." In *The Comics of Joe Sacco: Journalism in a Visual World*, edited by Daniel Worden, 67–81. Jackson: University Press of Mississippi.

Slade, Michael. 1999–2000. "Michael Slade: An Unconventional Biography." Darkworlds Productions. Accessed July 1, 2000. www.specialx.net/unconbio.html.

Smart, James. 2012. "The Lovely Horrible Stuff by Eddie Campbell – Review." *The Guardian*, July 17, 2012. https://www.theguardian.com/books/2012/jul/17/lovely-horrible-stuff-eddie-campbell-review.

Smith, Colin. 2010. "The Fascist Superman, The Tyrant Aquaman, That Lil' Boy Spider-man Too: How Childish & Anti-Democratic Are Our Super-Heroes?" *Too Busy Thinking About My Comics*. Last modified July 29, 2010. http://toobusythinkingboutcomics.blogspot.com/2010/07/fasicst-superman-tyrant-aquaman-that.html.

Smith, Craig R. 1998. *Rhetoric and Human Consciousness*. Prospect Heights: Waveland.

Smith, Sidonie, and Julia Watson. 2010. *Reading Autobiography: A Guide for Interpreting Life Narratives*. Minneapolis: University of Minnesota Press.

Smith, Zack. 2007. "Jonathan Lethem on *Omega the Unknown*." *Newsarama*, July 20, 2007. http://forum.newsarama.com/showthread.php?t=121762&highlight=omega+unknown.

Snyder, Mikkel. 2020. "'Just Let Yourself Go' – Talking with Albert Monteys about 'Slaughterhouse-Five'." *Black Nerd Problems*, September 18. https://blacknerdproblems.com/just-let-yourself-go-talking-with-albert-monteys-about-slaughterhouse-five/.

Spencer, Chris, and Helen Woolley. 2000. "Children and the City: A Summary of Recent Environmental Psychology Research." *Child: Care, Health and Development* 26, no. 3: 181–97.

Spengemann, William C. 1980. *The Forms of Autobiography: Episodes in the History of a Literature Genre*. New Haven: Yale University Press.

Spiegelman, Art. 1997. "Those Dirty Little Comics." In *Tijuana Bibles: Art and Wit in America's Forbidden Funnies, 1930s–1950s*, edited by Bob Andelman, 5–10. New York: Simon & Schuster.

Spiegelman, Art. 2008. *Breakdowns*. New York: Pantheon Books.

Spiegelman, Art, and Chip Kidd. 2001. *Jack Cole and Plastic Man: Forms Stretched to Their Limits!* New York: DC Comics/Chronicle Books.

Spurgeon, Tom. 2005. "Mini-Comics: Comics' Secret Lifeblood." In *The Education of a Comics Artist: Visual Narrative in Cartoons, Graphic Novels, and Beyond*, edited by Michael Dooley and Steven Heller, 133–7. New York: Allworth Press.

Stack, Frank. 2002. "Gilbert Shelton Interviewed by Frank Stack." *The Comics Journal*. www.tcj.com/2_archives/i_shelton.html.

Stan Lee: ComiX-Man. 1995. A&E Biography. Videocassette, 42 minutes.

Steele, Edward D., and W.Charles Redding. 1962. "The American Value System: Premises for Persuasion." *Western Speech* 26: 83–91.

Steranko, James. 1970–1972. *The Steranko History of Comics*, vols. 1 and 2. Reading: Supergraphics.

Steranko, James. 1989. "Foreword." In *The Superman Archives*, vol. 1, edited by Mark Waid and Richard Bruning, 3–6. New York: DC Comics.

Stevenson, Daniel. 2008. "Year by Year Title Listing." Unpublished index.

Strömberg, Fredrik. 2003. *Black Images in the Comics: A Visual History*. Seattle: Fantagraphics Books.

Strömberg, Fredrik. 2010. *Comic Art Propaganda*. New York: St. Martin's Griffin.

Stone, Sam. 2021. "David Nakayama & Alitha E. Martinez Discuss Expanding Marvel's Avengers: War for Wakanda Into a Motion Comic." *CBR.com*, August 13, 2021. https://www.cbr.com/david-nakayama-alitha-e-martinez-marvels-avengers-war-for-wakanda-interview/.

"Superman's Dilemma." 1942. *Time*. April 13, 1942, 78. http://content.time.com/time/subscriber/article/0,33009,766523,00.html.

Swain, Emma Halstead. 1978. "Using Comic Books to Teach Reading and Language Arts." *Journal of Reading* 22: 253–8.

Sweeney, Bruce. 1984. "Jaxon." *Comics Interview*, March, 9–49.

Szasz, Ferenc Morton. 2000. "The Comic Book that Changed the Nation!" *Comic Book Marketplace*, June, 48–52.

Tabachnick, Stephen E. 2011. "Autobiography as Discovery in Epilectic." In *Graphic Subjects: Critical Essays on Autobiography and Graphic Novels*, edited by Michael A. Chaney, 101–16. Madison: University of Wisconsin Press.

Taylor, Aaron. 2007. "'He's Gotta Be Strong, and He's Gotta Be Fast, and He's Gotta Be Larger than Life': Investigating the Engendered Superhero Body." *The Journal of Popular Culture* 40, no. 2: 345–60.

Taylor, Stephanie. 2010. *Narratives of Identity and Place*. London: Routledge.

Thomas, Roy. 1998. "Stan the Man & Roy the Boy." *Comic Book Artist* 2: 6–18.

Thomas, Roy. 2005. "Introduction." In *Marvel Masterworks: Golden Age Captain America*, vol. 1, edited by Mark D. Beazley, vi–vii. New York: Marvel Comics.

Thomas, Roy, and Bill Schelly. 1997. *Alter Ego: The Best of the Legendary Comics Fanzine*. Seattle: Hamster Press.

Thompson, Don. 1970. "OK. Axis, Here We Come!" In *All in Color for a Dime*, edited by Dick Lupoff and Don Thompson, 110–29. New York: Ace Books.

Thorn, Matt. 2001. "Shôjo Manga—Something for Girls." *Japan Quarterly* 48: 43–50.

Thorndike, Robert L. 1941. "Words and the Comics." *Journal of Experimental Education* 10: 110–3.

Thrasher, Frederic M. 1949. "The Comics and Delinquency: Cause or Scapegoat." *Journal of Educational Sociology* 23: 195–205.

Tilley, Carol L. 2012. "Seducing the Innocent: Fredric Wertham and the Falsifications that Helped Condemn Comics." *Information & Culture* 47, no. 4: 383–413.

Töpffer, Rodolphe. 1965. "Essay on Physiognomy." In *Enter: Comics*, translated and edited by Ellen Wiese, 2–35. Lincoln: University of Nebraska Press.

Torres, Arturo Perez. 2007. *Super Amigos*. Open City Works. Videocassette, 82 mins.

Turner, Kathleen J. 1977. "Comic Strips: A Rhetorical Perspective." *Central State Speech Journal* 20, no. 1: 24–35.

Ujiie, Joanne, and Stephen Krashen. 1996. "Comic Book Reading, Reading Enjoyment, and Pleasure Reading among Middle Class and Chapter I Middle School Students." *Reading Improvement* 33: 51–4.

Uono, Shota, and Jari K. Hietanen. 2015. "Eye Contact Perception in the West and East: A Cross-Cultural Study." *Plos One* 10, no. 2. https://doi.org/10.1371/journal.pone.0118094.

Uricchio, William, and Roberta E. Pearson. 1991. "'I'm Not Fooled by that Cheap Disguise.'" In *The Many Lives of the Batman: Critical Approaches to a Superhero and His Media*, edited by Roberta E. Pearson and William Uricchio, 182–213. New York: Routledge.

U.S. Congress. Senate. 1954. *Juvenile Delinquency (Comic Books): Hearings before the Senate Subcommittee on Juvenile Delinquency*, 83rd Cong., 2nd sess., April 21–22, 1954.

U.S. House of Representatives. 1952. *Report of the Select Committee on Current Pornographic Materials, House of Representatives, Eighty-second Congress, pursuant to H. Res. 596: A Resolution Creating a Select Committee to Conduct a Study and Investigation of Current Pornographic Materials, 1952*. Washington, D.C.: USGPO, 1952.

Vallacher, Robin R. 1980. "An Introduction to Self-Theory." In *The Self in Social Psychology*, edited by Daniel M. Wegner and Robin R. Vallacher, 3–20. New York: Oxford University Press.

Van Hise, James. 1989. *How to Draw Art for Comic Books: Lessons from the Masters*. Las Vegas: Pioneer Books.

Vernon, Zackary. 2017. *The Comic Book Agenda: Altering Perceptions and Attitudes Towards LGBTQIA+ People through Graphic Narratives*. MFA thesis, Texas State University.

Versaci, Rocco. 2007. *This Book Contains Graphic Language: Comics as Literature*. New York: Continuum.

Viau, Michael. 2007. "Quebecois Comics." *Library and Archives Canada*. Accessed September 2007. www.collectionscanada.gc.ca/comics/027002-7000-e.html.

Victims of International Communist Emissaries. 1984. *Grenada: Rescued from Rape and Slavery*. Accessed February 13, 2008. www.ep.tc/grenada/index.html.

Vidal, Gore. 1995. *Palimpsest: A Memoir*. New York: Random House.

Viola, Ken, dir. 1987. *Masters of Comic Book Art*. Ken Viola Productions. Videocassette, 61 min.

Wallace, Harry M., and Dianne M. Tice. 2012. "Reflected Appraisal through a 21st-Century Looking Glass." In *Handbook of Self and Identity*, 2nd ed., edited by Mark R. Leary and June Price Tangney, 124–40. New York: Guilford Press.

Wareham, Edmund. 2016. "Passional Christi vnnd Antichristi." *Reformation at the Taylor Institution Library: A Bodleian Libraries Blog*. Accessed September 2, 2018. https://blogs.bodleian.ox.ac.uk/taylor-reformation/2016/01/21/passional-christi-vnnd-antichristi/.

Watson, Julia. 2011. "Autographic Disclosures and Genealogies of Desire in Alison Bechdel's Fun Home." In *Graphic Subjects: Critical Essays on Autobiography and Graphic Novels*, edited by Michael A. Chaney, 123–56. Madison: University of Wisconsin Press.

Waugh, Coulton. 1947. *The Comics*. New York: Macmillan.

Weber, Wibke, and Hans-Martin Rall. 2017. "Authenticity in Comics Journalism. Visual Strategies for Reporting Facts." *Journal of Graphic Novels and Comics* 8, no. 4: 376–97.

Wecter, Dixon. 1941. *The Hero in America: A Chronicle of Hero-Worship*. New York: Charles Scribner's Sons.

Weiner, Stephen. 2003. *Faster than a Speeding Bullet: The Rise of the Graphic Novel*. New York: Nantier, Beall, Minoustchine Publishing Inc.

Weisberg, Jessica. 2012. "Hello to Symbolia." *Columbia Journalism Review*, December 12, 2012. https://archives.cjr.org/the_news_frontier/symbolia.php.

Wertham, Fredric. 1948. "The Comics . . . Very Funny!" *Reader's Digest*, August, 15–18.

Wertham, Fredric. 1953. "What Parents Don't Know about Comic Books." *Ladies' Home Journal*, November, 50–3.

Wertham, Fredric. 1954. *Seduction of the Innocent*. New York: Rinehart.

Wertham, Fredric. 1955. "It's Still Murder: What Parents Don't Know about Comic Books." *Saturday Review of Literature*, April 9, 11–12.

Wheat, John. 2006. "Jack Jackson: A Tribute." *Southwestern Historical Quarterly* 110, no. 2: 272–5.

Whyte, Kenneth. 2009. *The Uncrowned King: The Sensational Rise of William Randolph Hearst*. Berkeley: Counterpoint.

Wickline, Dan. 2013. "Senator Patrick Leahy Praises Graphic Novel by Congressman John Lewis" *Bleeding Cool*, July 18, 2013. http://www.bleedingcool.com/2013/07/18/senator-patrick-leahy-praises-graphic-novel-by-congressman-john-lewis/.

Wiese, Ellen. 1965. "Introduction: Rodolphe Töpffer and the Language of Physiognomy." In *Enter: Comics*, translated and edited by Ellen Wiese, ix–xxxii. Lincoln: University of Nebraska Press.

Wilbers, Lina, et al. 2012. "Are Autobiographical Memories Inherently Social? Evidence from an fMRI Study." *Plos One* 7, no. 9. www.plosone.org/article/info:doi/10.1371/journal.pone.0045089.

Williams, Ian. 2011. "Autobiography as Auto-Therapy: Psychic Pain and the Graphic Memoir." *Journal of Medical Humanities* 32: 353–66.

Williams, Kristian. 2005. "The Case for Comics Journalism: Artist-Reporters Leap Tall Conventions in a Single Bound." *Columbia Journalism Review*, March/April, 51–5.

Williams, Neil. 1995. "The Comic Book as Course Book: Why and How." Paper presented at the Annual Meeting of the Teachers of English to Speakers of Other Languages, Long Beach, California, 1995.

Wilson, Anne, and Michael Ross. 2003. "The Identity Function of Autobiographical Memory: Time is On Our Side." *Memory* 11: 137–49.

Winick, Judd. 2000. *Pedro and Me: Friendship, Loss and What I Learned*. New York: Henry Holt and Company.

Wink, Walter. 1998. *The Powers that Be*. New York: Galilee, Doubleday.

Winkielman, Piotr, Norbert Schwarz, Rolf Reber, and Tedra A. Fazendeiro. 2003. "Cognitive and Affective Consequences of Visual Fluency: When Seeing Is Easy on the Mind." In *Persuasive Imagery: A Consumer Response Perspective*, edited by Linda M. Scott and Rajeev Batra, 75–90. Mahwah: Lawrence Erlbaum Associates.

Witek, Joseph. 1989. *Comic Books as History: The Narrative Art of Jack Jackson, Art Spiegelman, and Harvey Pekar*. Jackson: University Press of Mississippi.

Witek, Joseph. 1999. "Comics Criticism in the United States: A Brief Historical Survey." *International Journal of Comic Art* 1: 4–16.

Witek, Joseph. 2011. "Justin Green: Autobiography Meets the Comics." In *Graphic Subjects: Critical Essays on Autobiography and Graphic Novels*, edited by Michael A. Chaney, 227–30. Madison: University of Wisconsin Press.

Witek, Joseph. 2012. "Comics Modes: Caricature and Illustration in the Crumb Family's 'Dirty Laundry'." In *Critical Approaches to Comics: Theories and Methods*, edited by Matthew J. Smith and Randy Duncan, 1–14. New York: Routledge.

Witty, Paul. 1941. "Reading the Comics: A Comparative Study." *Journal of Experimental Education* 10: 105–6.

Wolf, Thomas. 1977. "Reading Reconsidered." *Harvard Educational Review* 47: 427.

Wolfe, Katherine M., and Marjorie Fiske. 1949. "The Children Talk about Comics." In *Communications Research 1948–1949*, edited by Paul F. Lazarsfeld and Frank N. Stanton, 3–50. New York: Harper.

Wolfe, Tom. 1968. *The Electric Kool-Aid Acid Test*. New York: Farrar, Straus, and Giroux.

Wolk, Douglas. 2007. *Reading Comics: How Graphic Novels Work and What They Mean*. Cambridge: Da Capo Press.

Woo, Benjamin. 2010. "Reconsidering Comics Journalism: Information and Experience in Joe Sacco's Palestine." In *The Rise and Reason of Comics and Graphic Literature: Critical Essays on the Form*, edited by Joyce Goggin and Dan Hassler-Forest, 166–77. Jefferson: McFarland & Company.

Wright, Bradford W. 2001. *Comic Book Nation: The Transformation of Youth Culture in America*. Baltimore: John Hopkins University Press.

Wright, Gary. 1979. "The Comic Book: A Forgotten Medium in the Classroom." *Reading Teacher* 33: 158–61.

Wright, Nicky. 2000. *The Classic Era of American Comics*. Lincolnwood: Contemporary Books.

Wylie, Philip. 1930/1976. *The Gladiator*. New York: Manor Books.

Yeung, King-To, and John Levi Martin. 2003. "The Looking Glass Self: An Empirical Test and Elaboration." *Social Forces* 81, no. 3: 843–79.

Yockey, Matt. 2012. "Retopia: The Dialectics of the Superhero Comic Book." *Studies in Comics* 3, no. 2: 349–70.

Young, Michael C., and Richard Foltin. 1974. "Comics' New Wave." *Harvard Journal of Pictorial Fiction*, 4–11.

Zajonc, Robert B. 1968. "Attitudinal Effects of Mere Exposure." *Journal of Personality and Social Psychology* 9, no. 2: 1–27.

Zehr, E. Paul. 2008. *Becoming Batman: The Possibility of a Superhero*. Baltimore: Johns Hopkins University Press.

Index

24 Hour Comics Day 35
300 41, 301–2, 281

Abel, Jessica 94, 114
Academy of Comic Art Fans and Collectors 46, 49
Acclaim Books 297
Aces High 66
Aces Weekly 285
Ackerman, Forrest J. 50
Acme Novelty Library 30, 42, 281
acting 78–9, 86
Action Comics 26, 44, 60, 66, 86, 95, 179, 182–3, 254–6
Action Philosophers! 288, 297
A.D.: New Orleans After the Deluge 209–12
Adams, Jeff 239
Adams, Neal 85, 104, 201, 265
Addicted to War 225
additive combination 95
ad hominem **235**
Adkins, Lieuen 267
Adventure 253
Adventure Comics 183, 254
Adventures into the Unknown 146
Adventures of Jesus, The 267
Adventures of Obadiah Oldbuck, The 246–7
Adventures of Superman, The (television series) 202
Adventures of Tintin, The 15, 277
Aesop 144
aesthetic layout **110–**17, 123
Aesthetics of Comics 308
affective response **58**, 71, 80, 95, 108, 118, 120, 161–2
Afshana, Syeda 213, 220
Age of Bronze 30, 281
Aguirre-Sacasa, Roberto 322–5
Ahmed, Saladin 30
Air Pirates Funnies 53
Aja, David 104
Akira 32, 282
albums 15, 277
Alcala, Alfredo 78
Aldama, Frederick Luis 25
Aldrich Family, The 141
Alexander-Bidon, Daniele 244
Alf, Richard 50
All about Me 20
All-American Comics 26, 257
All-Atomic Comics *224*, 297
Alley Awards 47, 49
All for Love 142
All in Color for a Dime 291
Alls, Rob 282
All-Star Comics 45, 258, 262
All-Star Western 258
Alter-Ego *46*
alternative comics 228, 272–4
Amazing Fantasy 47, 263
Amazing Spider-Man 47, 224, 270, 275
Amazon 286
American Born Chinese 34
American Comics Group 146, 264
American Elf 171
American monomyth 193
American Splendor 7, 156–7, 163, 170
American studies 18–19
American Visuals Corporation 252–3
Ames, Winslow 257
analyses 311–12, 318–25
Anderson, Brent 97, 205
Anderson, Dana 203
Andrae, Thomas 291
Andreas, Joel 225
Andru, Ross 115
Andy Hardy 141, 257
Andy Panda 144
Angelfood McSpade 267
Angle 81–2
Angoulême, France 252
Animal Comics 145

anime 14
anthropomorphism 144–5
anti-hero 184, 246, 277
Aquaman 262
Arab in America 167
Aragones, Sergio 54
Arcade: *The Comics Review* 272
Archer, Dan 207, 210–11, 215
Archie 293
Archie Andrews 140–2, 150–2, 257, 270, 300, 306, 317
Archie Comics 224, 260, 264, 295, 305
Argosy 253
argument 161, 215, 220, 226, 229, 231–5, 237, 298, 301, 308, 314, 319
Aristotle 221, 227, 237
Arlin, Marshall 294
Army of Principles, *An* 230–1
Arthur 257
artisan process **40**, 229
Artist, Writers & Artisans (AWA) 31
Art of News: Comics Journalism, The 211
Association of Comics Magazine Publishers (ACMP) 258
Asterix and Obelix 15–16
Astro City 205
asynchronous 71
Ater, Malcom 223
Atlas Comics 261, *see also* Marvel Comics, Timely Comics
Attack on Titan 29
audience 136
Augustine 171
Ault, Donald 291
auteur theory 41–2
authenticity 162–4, 212
authoring I **160–**1, 171, 175
Authority, *The* 277
autobiographical avatar **159–**60, 176
autobiographical pact 159
Autobiographix 169
Autry, Gene 138, 258
Avengers 196–8, 263
Avengers: *Endgame* 202
Axe, David 210, 225
Aydin, Andrew 19
Ayer, Vijaya 29
Azzerello, Brian 85

Babb, Tiffany 20
back issues 36–9, 273–4
Baetens, Jan 209
Baffled Bunny in OK with That 234
Bagge, Peter 30, 281
Bails, Jerry 42, 45–6, 49
Baker, Matt 287
Bald Knoppers 179
Bale, Christian 23
bande dessinée **15–**16, 157
Barajas, Victor 317–18
Barefoot Gen 15, 24, 155, 224
Barks, Carl 16, 145, 257
Baron Weirwulf 148
Barrier, Michael 252
Barry, Lynda 215, 286, 310, 327
Bat, The 182–3
Batcave 196–7
Batgirl 303
Batiste, Stephanie L. 85
Batman 23, 33, 60, 63, 80, 180, 182–5, 187–8, 194–5, 202–4, 249, 256–7, 262, 277, 279, 303, 307, 317, *see also* Bruce Wayne
Batman (1989 film) 276, 279
Batman (television series) 83, 263
Batman: *The Black Mirror* 5
Batman: *The Dark Knight Returns* 276–7
Batman: *The Killing Joke* 303
Batman: *The Long Halloween* 41
Baudoin, Edmund 157
Baumeister, Roy 191
Bayeux Tapestry 3, 244
Beagle Boys 300
Beaty, Bart 174
Beauchard, Pierre-Francois 158, *see also* David B.
Bechdel, Alison 7, 19, 22, 86, 89, 91, 158, 163–4, 283, 286, 306, 324
Bechdel Test **19**, 306, 324
Beck, C. C. 256
Beerbohm, Robert Lee 246, 248
Behm-Morawitz, Elizabeth 203
Belk, Russell W. 300
Bell, Blake 249
Bell, Gabrielle 283
Bell, Tony 266
Bendis, Brian Michael 30, 85, 281, 310
Ben Grimm 184, *see also* Thing, The
Benton, Mike 6, 141, 204, 248, 257–9, 261
Berger, Arthur Asa 308
Berger, Karen 31, 277, 306
Beringer, Alex 247
Berkeley Comic Art Convention 291
Berkeley Comix Convention 268
Bernofsky, Susan 11
Bertamini, Marco 85

Bessie, Adam 215
Bester, Alfred 26
Betty Cooper 141, 306
Big Bang Theory, The 52
Big Brother and the Holding Company 268
Bignell, Jonathan 63
Billy the Kid 138
Binder, Otto 26, 50
Binky Brown Meets the Holy Virgin Mary 155, 164–5
Bird, Robert M. 179
Bissette, Stephen R. 35, 60, 187, 195
Bitchy's College Daze 167
Bitz, Michael 295
Bjordahl, Hans 284
Black, White & Read All Over 311
black and white 80–1
Black Marvel 193
Blackmore, Tim 301–2
Black Panther 198
Black Panther: World of Wakanda 103
Black Summer 191
Blade, the Vampire Hunter 147
Blair, J. Anthony 237
Blanc, Mel 145
Blanch, Christina 285
Blankets 30, 90–1, 93–4, 158, 170, 281
Bleeding Cool 326
blending words and pictures 6, 70–1, 77, 85, 94–5, 120, 308, 313
blocking **78**, 316
Blonde Phantom 257
Bloom, Vic 140, 142
Blue Beetle 256
Blue Bolt 192, 196
Blum, Geoffrey 291
Boatner, E. B. 259
Boelcskevy, Marry Anne 85
Bolland, Brian 277
Boltinoff, Murray 50
Bone 28, 52, 145, 152, 283
Bongco, Mila 193, 195
Book of Sarah, The 166–7
Boondocks 222
Boone, Daniel 179
Bors, Matt 210, 226
bound reprint editions 36
Bourgeron, Frank 210
Boxers and Saints 7, 284
Boys, The 204, 276
Bradbury, Ray 50, 146, 249
braided narrativity 59
braiding **120**
Brainiac 188
branding **175**
Brat Pack 187, 191
Brave and the Bold, The 45, 262
Breakdowns: Portrait of the Artist as a Young %@!* 176
Breitweizer, Elizabeth 98
Briggs, Clare 248–9
Brinkley Girls, The: The Best of Nell Brinkley's Cartoons from 1913–1940 307
broadsheet 207, 244
Brockmeier, Jens 162
Brosch, Bob 49
Brought to Light 271
Brown, Chester 157, 159
Brown, Jeffrey 42, 54
Brown, Matthew J. 327
Browne, Ray B. 291
Brownies, The 23
Brubaker, Ed 98, 148
Bruce Wayne 63–4, 184, 197, *see also* Batman
Bruss, Elizabeth 169
Bruzenak, Ken 83, 89
BRZKR 29
Bubnis, Bernie 49, 50
Buck Rogers in the 25th Century A.D. 135
Bucky 123
Bugs Bunny 144
Bukatman, Scott 197, 202
Bullpen Bulletins 48
Bureau of Cartoons, The 222
Burford, Brendan 209, 215
Burke, Kenneth 221, 228, 231
Burns, Charles 272
Burroughs, Edgar Rice 149, 181
Burton, Tim 23, 276, 279
Busch, Wilhelm 13
Bush Junta, The 225
Busiek, Kurt 205
Buster Brown 248
Byrne, John 205, 270

C.C. Beck and Pete Costanza Studio 251
Cacioppo, John 226
Cagle, Susie 209–10
Cain and Abel 148
Callendar, Brian 233
Camelot 3000 274, 277
Camp, Brian 185, 193, 204
Campbell, Eddie 159, 168, 218–19
Campbell, Joseph 192
Campbell, Richard 137

canon **42**
Captain America 77, 121, 123, 142, 185, 189, 192, 204, 222, 229, 257–8, 261, 263
Captain America Comics *104*, 198, 200
Captain America Complex 191
Captain Atom 264
Captain Carrot and His Zoo Crew 150, 227
Captain Marvel 192, 203–4, 251, 256, 296
Captain Marvel Adventures 257
caricature 66, 84, 207, 221, 235
Caricature, La 221
Carlson, Peter E. 310
Carnet de Voyage 170
Carrier, David 308
Carter, James Bucky 295
cartoon **247**
Cartoon Books 283
cartoonist **58**
cartoon mode **84**, 85
Cartoon Movement 210, 213
Cartoon Picayune 210
Cary, Stephen 296
Caswell, Lucy Shelton 292
catharsis 146
Catron, Mike 291
Catwoman 188, 304
cave paintings 206, 221
Center for Cartoon Studies, The 219
Central Intelligence Agency 224–5
central processing **226**
Century of Women Cartoonists, A 307
Cerebus 59, 145
Chadwick, Paul 192
Cham, Jorge 327
Chandler, Raymond 203, 249
Chaos! Comics 147
character types 138, 151, 313
Charivari, Le 207, 221
Charlton Comics 148, 270
Chavanne, Renaud 104
Chaykin, Howard 83, 89
Cheap Thrills 268
Chee 285
cheesecake 305
Cheng, Kevin 220
Cheryl Blossom 141
chiaroscuro **81**, 323
Chicagoland Detective Agency 307
Chicago Style 321
Chick, Jack 224
Chick tracts **224**
Childs, Elizabeth C. 222
Chilling Adventures of Sabrina 322–5
Churchill, Winston 296–7
Chute, Hilary 177
Cioffi, Frank L. 95
City of Heroes 195
Civil War 192, 277
Civil War: Front Line
claim **314**
Claremont, Chris 270, 277
Clark Kent 181, 184, 186, 189, *see also* Superman
Classics Comics, see Classics Illustrated
Classics Illustrated 149, 297–9, 310
clear line style 85, 93, 96, 234, *see also ligne Claire*
Clock, The 180
close reading **319**
closure **118**, 120, 236–7, 308
Clowes, Daniel 30, 281
Coburn, Tom 6
Cochran, Russ 152
Cockrum, Dave 270
cognitive response **58**, 71, 95, 108
Cohen, Jonathan 228
Cohn, Neil 58, 69, 117, 120–1, 123, 308
CoJo List, The 210
Colan, Gene 147
Cold War comics 223–5
collectors 37–9
Color 80–1
Comic Art 46
Comic book **3**
Comic Book Guy 35, 43
Comicbookrealm.com 37
Comic Book Resources 326
Comic Books as History 292
Comic-Con International 27, 50, 292, 326, *see also* comic conventions
comic conventions 49–51, *see also* Comic-Con International
Comic Magazine Association of America (CMAA) 282
Comic Monthly 247
Comico 271
Comicollector, The 46
Comics **2**
Comics, The 291
Comics: Anatomy of a Mass Medium 7
Comics and Narration 308
Comics and Popular Arts Conference 326
Comics and Sequential Art 252, 292, 308
Comics and Their Creators 308
Comics Arts Conference 292, 326

Comics as Culture 292
Comics Buyer's Guide, The 37–8
Comics Code 21, 143, 146–7, 200, 227, 259–61, 266, 269, 274, 282
Comics Grid 326
Comics Guaranty, LLC (CGC) 37, 39
Comics Journal, The 291, 312
comic specialty stores 34–9, 50, 52, 271, 273–4, 279–80, 282–3, 286, 311
Comics studies 12, 20, 290–2, 312, 314, 320, 325–6
Comics Studies Society 292, 326
comic strip **4**, 12–13, 16, 104, 135, 137, 141, 144, 149, 222, 226, 227
Comic-Stripped American, The 308
Comic Town 311
Comix: A History of Comic Books in America 291
Comixology 29, 286
Common Core State Standards 296
complex narrative **59**
composition 76–97, 234–5
CompuServe 284
Conan the Barbarian 137, 269, 277
Confessions 171
Conner, Amanda 106, 115
content analysis 298, 300, 308–9
continuity 193
Contract with God, A 1, 158, 252–3, 275
conventional fragmented layout 106–7
conventional layout 74, 104–8, 117
conventional regular layout 106
conventional semi-regular layout 106, 115
Conway, Gerry 277
Coogan, Peter 180, 182–3, 185, 190, 192, 204, 292
Cooke, Jon B. 54
copyright 40, 52–3
Corben, Richard 80
Corporate Crime Comics 224
Costanza, Pete 321
Costello, Matthew J. 189
Cousin Eerie 148
Cowgirl Romances 80
Cox, Palmer 23
Craft, Jerry 13–14
Creel, George 222
Creepy 147
crime comics genre 148, 257–8, 261, 266
Crime Does Not Pay 148, 258
Crime SuspenStories 153, 259, 265
Criminal 148
critical methods 290, 302–6, 308
Crumb, Robert 88, 156, 266–8, 312
Cruse, Howard 7, 22, 275
Crypt-Keeper 148
cultural imperialism 16–18
Cuno, James 222
Curse of Spawn 293, *see also* Spawn

Dalton, Russell W. 186–7
Damnation of Charlie Wormwood 285
Dandridge, Victor, Jr. 311, 326
Daniels, Les 48, 145, 291
Daredevil 185, 190, 263, 276
Daredevil 111
Daredevil: Born Again 5
Daredevil: Yellow 41
Dark Horse Comics 28, 31, 281
Dark Knight, The 23
Dark Mansion of Forbidden, The 150
Darkroom: A Memoir in Black and White 168
Darowski, Joseph J. 189
Dauber, Jeremy 288
David B. 158, 165
Davidson, Sol 206, 221, 291
Dazzler 274
DC Comics 22, 26–8, 31, 36, 39, 50, 57, 59, 115, 136–8, 141, 143–4, 146–8, 185–7, 189, 192, 198, 200, 224, 228, 253–6, 260–5, 268–71, 274, 276–7, 279, 282, 286, 305–7
DC Comics Guide to Creating Comics, The 70
Deadman 265
Deadpool 86
Dean, James 266
Dean, Michael 273–4
Death of the New Gods 41
decompressed storytelling 69
Deitch, Kim 164
Delacorte, George 250–1, 253
Dell Publishing 144–5, 250, 257–8, 260, 264
DeMarco, Em 210
Democratic National Committee (DNC) 289
descriptive methods 290, 292, **293–**6, 308
Detective Comics 87, 183, 254–6, 261
Detective Comics, Inc. 254
Detroit Triple Fan Fair 49
Dewey, Thomas E. 289
Dexter's Laboratory 293
Diamond Comic Distributors 33–4, 280, 296
diary comics 20, 171
Diary of a Wimpy Kid 285
Dickens, Charles 297
Dick Tracy Comics 258

diegesis **3**, 87–90, **159**, 323
differentiation **137**, 151
digital comics 34, 111, 210, **284**, *see also* webcomics
Dik, Bryan J. 184
Dillon, Steve 31, 278
Din, Heeba 213, 220
direct market 35, 147, 271, **274**, 283–4
Dirks, Rudolph 13–14, 149
Disaster Capitalism Curriculum, The 65, 215–16
disjunctive combination 95
Disney, Walt 144, *see also* Walt Disney Company
distance 81
distribution 18–19, 21, 33–5, 246, 271, 273
Ditko, Steve 46–7, 50, 263–4
Dixon, Thomas R., Jr. 179
Doc Savage 115–17, 180–1, 184, 249
Doctor Aphra 149
Doctor Doom 188
Doctor Strange 203, 265
documentary **213**–19, *see also* expository mode; observational mode; participatory mode; performative mode; poetic mode; reflexive mode
Dog Man 29, 33
Donahue, Don 267–8
Donald Duck 11, 18, 144–5, 257
Donenfeld, Harry 254–6
Dony, Christophe 163
Doomsday 279
Doonesbury 222, 226
Doran, Colleen 31, 104
Doré, Gustave 246
Dorf, Shel 49, 50
Dozier, William 23
Dr. Graves 148
Dr. Manhattan 110
Dr. Occult 180, 254
DragonCon 326
Drake, Stan 86
Drawing the Times 213, 225
Drawing Words & Writing Pictures 94
Drawn & Quarterly 30
Drawn Journal, *The* 210
Dreadstar 41
Dreamer, *The* *168*, 251
Dream of a Rarebit Fiend 21
Drooker, Eric 7
Duckburg 11–12
Duncan, Randy 20, 211, 228, 239, 292, 327
Dunlavey, Ryan 288, 297
duo-specific combination 94
Durwood, Thomas 85
Dykes to Watch out For 19, 306

Early, Gerald 179, 186
early adopters **284**
Early Comic Strip, *The* 291
Eastern Color Printing Company 250–1
East Village Other 267
EC Comics 44, 146–9, 152, 258–9, 261, 265, 306, *see also* Educational Comics
EC fan-addicts 44–5, 259, *see also* fans
Eclipse Enterprises 271
Eco, Umberto 186, 191, 195, 204, 291
Educational Comics 297, *see also* EC Comics
educational comics genre 149, 296–9
Educomics 155, 224, 297
Eerie 146–7
Eggs Ackley 267
Ego comme X 157
Eightball 30, 281
eight-pagers, *see* Tijuana Bibles
Eisenhower, Dwight D. 297
Eisner, Will 5, 41, 61, 65–6, 71, 75, 81, 84–5, 88, 104, 110–11, 149, 158, 168, 197, 251–3, 275, 288, 292, 308
Eisner Awards 50, 252, 285, 319
Eisner-Iger Shop 39, 251–2, 256
Elfquest 306
Ellis, Warren 277
Ellsworth, Whitney 254
El Rassi, Toufic 167
El Refaie, Elisabeth 161–2, 169
emanata 90, 213
Emerson, Ralph Waldo 189
emotional truth 165
Emracer 28
encapsulation **61–**74, 76, 97, 118, 229–31, 308, 324
Encounter With Richard Peterson, *An* 214–15
Engle, Gary 189
Ennis, Garth 31, 276–7
Entertaining Comics, *see* EC Comics
Enthymematic 235–7
Epic Illustrated 31
Epilectic 1, 158, 165
Essai de physiognomonie (*Essay on Physiognomy*) 246
Estren, Mark 266
Ethos **227**
eugenics movement 181
Eury, Michael 188
Evanier, Mark 54

Everett, Bill 263
evidence **314**, 320–2
Evil Ernie 147, 293
exhibition 35
experiencing I **159**, 161, 169–71, 175
expository mode 215–16
Expressionism 173

Fabos, Bettina 137
Fabulous Furry Freak Brothers 266
Fago, Al 144
Fairbanks, Douglas 180
Falk, Lee 16
Famous Funnies 250–1
fanboy **43**, 44
fandom 42–53
fan fiction 53
fans **42**, 43–53, 228, 267, *see also* EC fan-addicts
Fantagraphics 30–1, 281–2, 307
Fantastic Four 46–7, 86, 184, 186, 188, 196–9, 262–3, 306
fanzines **26**, 46, 284
Faulkner, William 277
Fawcett Comics 251, 256, 258
Federal Men 254
Feiffer, Jules 291
Feldstein, Al 146, 148, 259
Fell 85
Ferguson Firsthand 211
Ferris, Emil 7, 306
Festinger, Leon 168
Feuerlicht, Roberta Strauss 297
Few Perfect Hours, A 170
Fiction House 252
Fight Night 61, 78, 106
film 22, 135–6, 146, 178, 192, 195
Fin Fang Foom 262
Finger, Bill 23, 50, 182, 256
Fingeroth, Danny 186, 190, 202
First Comics 271
Fischer, Craig 312
Fisher, Bud 23, 249
Fitzpatrick, James A. 153
Flash 45, 80, 118, 185, 187, 189, 192, 202, 262
Flash, The 118–19
Flash Gordon 135
flayed look 197
Fleener, Mary 175
Fleischer, Dave 169
Fleischer Studios 198
Flood! 7
Food Comics 297
Footnotes in Gaza 209, 211
Forest, Jean-Claude 273
Forever People 200, 269
Foss, Ronn 49
Foster, Hal 86–7, 197
Four Immigrants Manga, The 155
Fourth World, The 198, 200, 269
Fox, Gardner 45, 50
Fox, Victor 256
Fox and the Crow 144, 300
Fox Features Syndicate 76, 256
Foxy Grandpa 248
fractionalization **18**, 32
Fradkin, Ron 49
Fradon, Ramona 306
Frank 145
Frankenstein 146, 180
Frank Leslie's Illustrated Newspaper 207
Free Comic Book Day 35
freelancers **39**
Freeman, Mark 154, 162
Fresnault-Derulle, Pierre 114
Friedrich, Mike
Friends of Lulu 307
Fuchs, Erica 11–12
Fuchs, Wolfgang 7, 71, 266, 268
Funbrain 285
Fun Home 7, 22, 88, 91, 158, 163–4, 283, 306
Funnies, The 250, 253
Funnies on Parade 250–1
Funny Aminals 156, 272, 275
Funny Animals 144
funny animals genre 136–7, 144–5, 148, 151–2, 257

Gabilliet, Jean-Paul 222
Gaiman, Neil 31, 57–8, 60, 113, 147, 195, 277
Gaines, Maxwell Charles 250–1, 257–8, 297
Gaines, William 146, 148, 258–9, 265
Galactus 188, 198
Garcia, Antero 310
Gardner, Jared 156, 159, 163
Garney, Ron 29
Garriock, P. R. 85
Gasoline Alley 21, 23
Gavaler, Chris 179, 186
Gay Comics 22
Gebbie, Melinda 30, 281
Geipel, John 246
gender roles 21, 143

Gen of Hiroshima 155
genre 8, 135–52
Gerber, Steve 145
Gertler, Nat 35, 204
Ghost Rider 150
GhouLunatics 148
Gibbons, Dave 7, 110, 276–7
Giddens, Thomas 310
Giffen, Keith 85
Gill, Tom 50
Gillen, Kieron 281
Gillray, James 221
Giraud, Jean 273
Girl Town 65, 71, 106
Gladiator 181
Glascow/Northern Looking Glass 207
Gleason, Lev 287
Glidden, Sarah 209, 213
Gloekner, Phoebe 164–5
God Nose Adult Comix 267
Goethe, Johann Wolfgang von 246
GoGirl! 307
Golden Age 42, 44, 261, 288
Gold Key 31, 50, 270, 282
Goldstein, Jay 222
Goldwater, John 140, 142
good girl art 304
Good Girls 30
Goodman, Martin 46, 261–3
Gorman, Michele 296
Goscinny, René 15
Gotham City 197
Goulart, Ron 6, 183, 192, 255, 259
grading 37–9
Grand Comics Database 34
Graphic Details: *Confessional Comics by Jewish Women* 166–7
graphic medicine **233**
Graphic Medicine International Collective 326
graphic novel **4**, 5, 12, 30, 33–4, **36**, 40, 52, 155, 226–7
Gravett, Paul 98, 118, 274
Great Comic Book Heroes, *The* 291
Great Depression 202
Great Train Robbery, *The* 137
Green, Justin 155, 159, 164–5, 168, 176
Green, Karen 67, 86, 120, 125–32, 317–18
Green, Katie 176
Green Hornet 180
Green Lantern 45, 121–85, 196, 262, 277, 303
Green Lantern/Green Arrow 224
Gregory, Roberta 30, 91–2, 167, 173
Grennan, Simon 308
grid (waffle-iron) layout 104, 106, 108, 110–11
Griffin, Bill 43, 272
Groensteen, Thierry 71, 104, 108, 110–11, 120, 244, 246, 308
Gross, Theodore L. 189
Groth, Gary 272, 291
Gruenwald, Mark 276
Gryph 149
Gubiitosa, Carlo 211
Guerra, Pia 31, 278
Guibert, Emmanuel 177
Gulacy, Paul 271
Gulf Comic Weekly 250
Gunsmoke 137
Guruzhalov, Victor 220
Gusdorf, Georges 165
gutter 61–2, 74, **104**, 119
Gwen Stacy 270

Hachette 34
Hack, Robert 322–5
hardcover editions **36**
Harlequin Romance paperbacks 143, 151
Harlot's Progress, A 244–5
Harper, David 78
Harper's Magazine 207
Harry "A" Chesler Shop 251
Harvey, Robert C. 48, 62, 71, 85, 183, 291, 308
Harvey Kurtzman's Jungle Book 275
Harvey Publishing 149, 198, 200, 264, 270
Haspiel, Dean 96
Hate 30, 281
Hatfield, Charles 87, 121, 157, 191, 198–201, 205, 275, 288
Hattenstone, Simon 158
Haugaard, Kay 294
Haunted Love 150
Haunt of Fear, *The* 44, 146, 152, 259
Hawkeye Initiative 305
Hawkman 187
head shops 265, 268
Heap, The 184
Hearst, William Randolph 14, 21
Heavy Metal 273
Heck, Don 263
Heer, Jeet 205
Heisler, Florence 294
Hellboy 147, 281
Help! 266
Helvie, Forrest C. 327
Hergé 15, 277

Herman, David 159
hermeneutic images **87**, 90–4, 110, 121, 174–5, 218
Herodotus 301
Heroes World 280
Herriman, George 14, 21–4, 144
Hershey, John 15
Hibbs, Brian 34
hieroglyphics 20
Hietanen, Jari K. 15
Higgins, Dusty 7
Hiroshima 15
Hirsch, Paul 235, 239
Histoire de M. Jabot 246
Hix, Lisa 179
Hogan's Alley 248, *see also Yellow Kid, The*
Hogarth, Burne 197, 201, 253
Hogarth, William 244–5
Hogg, Trevor 85
Holkins, Jerry 285
Hollywood, *see* film
Holocaust 270, 275–6
homage 86
Homer 297
Hopalong Cassidy 258
Horkheimer, Max 11
Horn, Maurice 138, 143, 244
horror comics genre 136–7, 146–8, 150, 257–8, 261, 265, 269, 315, 322
Hosler, Jay 296, 310
House of Secrets 147, 269
Howard, Robert E. 269
Howard the Duck 145
Huey, Dewey, and Louie 11
Hugo, Victor 297
Hugo Danner 181
Hulk 42, 184, 189, 195, 263, 265
Human Top 192
Human Torch (Jim Hammond) 257, 261
Human Torch 186–7, *see also* Johnny Storm
Hybels, Saundra 167
hybrid genre forms 136–7, 149–52

Ice Haven 1
iconostasis **114**, 117, 123
ICv2 33, 287
identification 84, 165, **228–**9, **263**
Identity Crisis 192
ideology 302–4
IDW 31, 282
Iger, Samuel "Jerry" 149, 251–2
Illustrated London News 207
Image Comics 30, 278–9, 281, 305
image functions 87, 97, 174–5, *see also* sensory diegetic images; non-sensory diegetic images; hermeneutic images
ImageTexT: Interdisciplinary Comics Studies 292, 326
Imposter's Daughter, The 165
Independent News Company (IND) 254
independent publishers 40, 270–1, 273–5, 278, 281–2
individualism 139
industrial process **39**, 40, 229
Infantino, Carmine 104
inferences 87, 96–7, 118, 236
infinite canvas **113**
Inge, M. Thomas 292
Ingels, Graham 135
Injustice: Gods Among Us 286
INKS: Cartoon and Comic Art Studies 292, 326
intellectual property **52**
interanimation of meaning **94–**5
interdependent combination 95
International Comic Arts Forum 292
International Journal of Comic Art 292, 301, 326
international perspective 14–18
internet 284–5
interpretive methods 290, 298, 300–2, 308
intertextuality 92–3
In the Shadow of No Towers 163
Invisible Woman 306
Iron Man 178, 185, 189, 192, 203, 263, *see also* Tony Stark
Iron Man 3 103, 178
I Saw It 155
Is This Tomorrow? 223
It Ain't Me, Babe 306–7
It's a Good Life if You Don't Weaken 1, 157
Ivie, Larry 45

Jackie 305
Jack Lake Productions 297
Jackson, Jack "Jaxon" 266–7
Jacobs, Will 45, 280
Jaeger 113
James, Muriel 167
Jane Foster 143
Janson, Klaus 276
Japanese comics, *see* manga
Jar of Fools 7, 90
Jenkins, Henry 52, 164, 193
Jennings, John 85
Jensen, Joli 42

Jewett, Robert 191, 193
Jimmy Corrigan: The Smartest Kid on Earth 85
John Carter 180–1
Johnny Storm 186, *see also* Human Torch
Johnson, Jeffery K. 189
Joker 188, 276, 303
Jonah Hex 138
Jones, Gerard 45, 280
Jones, William B., Jr. 296–9
Joneward, Dorothy 167
Joplin, Janis 268
Josie and the Pussycats 141
Journalism 207–13
Journal of Consumer Research 300
Journal of Graphic Novels and Comics, The 292, 312, 326
Journal of Popular Culture 291
Journey into Mystery 263
Jughead Jones 141
Jumbo Comics 149
jungle comics genre 149
Justice League of America 45, 197, 262, 277
Justice Society of America 45–6, 262
juvenile delinquency
juxtaposition **2**, 66, 220, 231

Kachelmann-Prozess, Der 210
Kahn, Jeanette 306
Kaler, Dave 50
Kaluta, Mike 104
Kamandi, the Last Boy on Earth 198, 200
Kane, Bob 23, 87, 182, 256
Kane, Gil 86, 104
Kanigher, Robert 149
Kannenberg, Jr., Gene 88
Kanter, Albert L. 297
Katy Keene 141, 305
Katzenjammer Kids, The 13–14, 149, 248
Ka-Zar, Lord of the Savage Land 17
Kearns, Ciléin 233
Kearns, Nethmi 233
Keaton, Michael 23
Keep on Truckin' 267
Kefauver, Estes 153, 259–60
Kelly, Walt 42, 145, 152
Kelp-Stebbins, Sarah 211
Kelso, Megan 61
Kershl, Karl 104
Kesey, Ken
Keyhole 96
key issues **44**
Key Terms in Comics Studies 308
Kickstarter 29, 40, 284
Kid Flash 187
kids comics genre 149
Kidson, Mike 245
Kindt, Matt 29
King, Frank 21, 23
King, Martin Luther, Jr. 18–19
King, Stephen 146
King Bongo 14
King Feature Syndicate 18
Kinney, Jeff 285
Kirby, Jack 21–2, 41–3, 45–8, 50, 76–7, 85–6, 95, 104, 111, 197–201, 251, 257, 262–4, 269
Kirby, Roz 50
Kirkman, Robert 30, 281
Kirsh, Stephen 293
Kirste, Kenneth K. 81
Kirtley, Susan E. 310
Kitchen Sink Enterprises 224
Kiyama, "Henry" Yoshitaka 155
Klein, Todd 88–9
Knights of the Living Dead 7
Knowles, Christopher 202
Kobler, John 182
Kochalka, James 171
Kodansha 29
Kominsky-Crumb, Aline 156, 159, 163, 169
Krahulik, Mike 285
Kramer, Josh 210–11
Krashen, Stephen 294
Krassousky, Vincent (Vica) 222
Krazy Kat 14, 21–4, 144
Kress, Gunther 232
Krigstein, Bernie 61
Krueger, Ken 50
Krypton 192
Kryptonite 23, 185
Krys, Kuba 15
Kubert, Joe 76, 85, 149
Kuleshov Effect 113, **231**
kung fu comics genre 136, 151, 269
Kunka, Andrew J. 177
Kunzle, David 244, 246, 257, 291
Kuper, Peter 160, 163, 224
Kurtz, Scott 285
Kurtzman, Harvey 77, 149, 266, 312
Kyle, Richard 275

L'Association 158
Labarre, Nicolas 152
Labours of Hercules, The 246
La Cour, Erin 308

Lady Death 147, 305
La Guardia, Fiorello 227
Lance Lewis 135–6
Land, Greg 86
Lantz, Walter 144
Lapham, David 72
Larraz, Pepe 114
Larsen, Erik 41, 278
Last Gasp 155
Lawrence, John Shelton 191, 193
Lay, Carol 30
layout **104–**23, 231–3, 313–14, *see also* conventional layout; rhetorical layout; aesthetic layout
Leahy, Patrick 153
Lee, Harper 277
Lee, Jae 104
Lee, Joan 227, 263
Lee, Stan 15, 21–2, 46–8, 76, 85, 90, 141, 143, 187, 198–200, 224, 227, 262–3
LeFèvre, Pascal 214, 216
Legend of Wonder Woman 307
Legion of Super-Heroes 85
Lejeune, Philippe 154, 159
Lemire, Jeff 30
Lent, John 292
Leonidas of Sparta 301–2
Les Amours de M. Vieux-Bois 246–7
letter columns 45–7
lettering 78, 83, 88–9
Lev Gleason Publications 258
Lewis, John 19, 153, 224
Lewis, Shireen K. 85
Lex Luthor 187, 255
Lieber, Larry 263
Lieber, Stanley, *see* Lee, Stan
Lieber, Steve 7, 86
Liebowitz, Jack 254, 262
Liefeld, Rob 278
Liew, Sonny 98, 234
Life in Comics, A 65, 67, 86, 89, 120, 125–31, 231–2
Lighter than My Shadow 176
lighting effects 81
Lightman, Sarah 166–7
ligne Claire, *see* clear line style
Linear, the 114, 118, 121–3
Ling, Paul 186
Linthout, Caroline 163
Lippman, Walter 234–5
Lischer, Brian 233
literacy 294–6
literary perspective 12–14
Little Lulu 149
Little Nemo in Slumberland 23, 86, 248
Liu, Majorie 281
Lloyd, David 285
Location, Location, Location 219–20
Loeb, Jeph 41, 203
Lois Lane 181, 305
Lone Ranger, The 137, 180
Longstreth, Alec 66, 219–20
Looney Tunes and Merrie Melodies 144
Los Bros Hernandez 30, 281
Lost Girls 30, 281
Love, Gordon B. 46
Love and Rockets 30, 281
Loveless 138
Love Life of Harold Teen, The 141
Lovely Horrible Stuff, The 216
Lovibond, S. H. 293
Lupoff, Dick 6, 45, 49, 291
Lupoff, Pat 45, 49
Lustig, John 143
Lutes, Jason 7, 90

MacArthur Fellows Program 286
McCarthy, Joseph 145
McCay, Winsor 21, 23
McCloud, Scott 2, 19–20, 35, 65, 67, 80–1, 85, 94, 98, 114, 117–20, 173, 236, 275, 285, 292, 308
MacDonald, Heidi 78
McFadden, Benarr 182
McFarlane, Todd 278
McGregor, Don 271
Mack, David 61, 104, 111
McKelvie, Jamie 281
McLuhan, Marshall 58
McMillan, Graeme 103
McRobbie, Angela 305
Mad 265–6, 275
Madam Satan 323–5
Madden, Matt 94, 114
Mademoiselle magazine 266
Maggin, Elliot S! 203
Magneto 270
mainstream comics 265, 272–4, 281–2
Making Comics 65
Malibu Comics 31, 282
Mallia, Ġorġ 294–5
Man and Superman: A Comedy and a Philosophy 181
Manara, Milo 273
manga 14–17, 19, **29**, 32, 52, 143–4, **155**, 271, 275, 280, 282–3

manhwa **29**
Man of Steel, The
Man-Thing 147
March 19, 153, 224, 227, 286
Marge 149
Marketing 5, 46, 50
Marnell, Blair 114
Marshall, Monica 211
Marston, William Moulton 257, 306
Martian Manhunter 185, 261–2
Martin, Christophe 137
Martin, George R. R. 50, 297
Martinez, Alitha E. 103, 105
Martin Luther King and the Montgomery Story 224
Marvel Bullpen 47–8
Marvel Cinematic Universe 204
Marvel Comics 251
Marvel Comics 22, 27–8, 31, 36, 39, 46–9, 59, 103, 136–8, 141, 143, 149, 183, 185–7, 192, 197–200, 224, 228, 253, 257, 263–5, 268–71, 274, 276, 278–80, 282, 286–7, 305, 307, *see also* Atlas Comics; Timely Comics
Marvelman 276, *see also Miracleman*
Marvel Mania 46–8
Marvel Method 76
Marvel Voices: Legacy 237
Marvel Zombies 150
Mary Jane Watson 144
Maryland Comic Book Initiative 296
Massey, Pat 267
mass media 11–12, 14, 17–19, 21–2, 244, 248, 303–4, 306
Master of Kung Fu 136, 269
Matt, Joe 157, 164, 167, 169
Maus 1–2, 7, 31, 92, 156, 158, 161, 176, 272, 275–7, 287
Max and Mortiz: A Story of Seven Boyish Pranks 13
media studies perspective 19–20
medium **1**
Meet Misty 307
Megaton Man 201
Melby, Julie 222
Melville, Herman 297
memoir genre 20, 136–7, **154**, 283–4, 314
- character types 159–61
- history of the genre 154–8
- narrative patterns 170–2
- themes 162–70
- visual conventions 172–5

Menu, Jean-Christophe 158
mere exposure effect **226**
Merry Marvel Marching Society (M.M.M.S.) 48
Messaris, Paul 237
Métal Hurlant 273
Metamorpho 306
meta-panel 67
metaverse 195
metonymy **65**
Metropolis 197
Mickey Dugan 248, *see also* Yellow Kid, The
Mickey Mouse 53, 144
Micky Maus 11
Mighty Mouse 144
Mignola, Mike 147, 281
Mikkonen, Kai 75
Miles Morales 231, 237–8
Millar, Mark 277
Miller, Ann 80
Miller, Frank 41, 159, 276, 281, 301–2
Miller, Jeffery 119
Millie the Model 305
Mills, Tarpé 287, 306
mini-comics (also mini-comix) **34**, 35, 57
mint condition **37**, 38
Miracleman 191, *see also* Marvelman
Miracles of Mary, The 206
mise-en-scene 77–85
Mishler, James 147
Misiroglu, Gina 188
Miss Fury 306
Mister Miracle 200, 269
MLJ Publishing, *see* Archie Comics
Modern World, This 222
Molotiu, Andrei 4, 114–15
Moments of prime action 61–5, 103, 213, 230
Monaco, James 63
monomyth 139, 192
Monstress 1, 281
montage combination 95
Montana, Bob 140, 142
Monteys, Albert 78
Moon, Fåbio 285
Moon Knight 185–6
Moorcock, Michael 195
Moore, Alan 7, 30, 42, 110, 124, 147, 269, 276–7, 281, 303
More Fun Comics 254
Morris, Tom 203, 277
Morrison, Grant 30, 192, 277
Morrow, John 54
motion lines, *see* speed lines
Mouly, Françoise 226, 272–3
Moustafa, Ibrhim 124

movement 67, 82
movie comics genre 149, *see also* television comics genre
Mr. Fantastic 184, 188
Mr. Natural 267
Ms. Marvel 185
Mud Man 197
Mullaney, Dean 271
Mullaney, Jan 271
multimodality 295
multiplicity 193
multiverse 195
Muñoz, José 85
Murray, Chris 226
music 84
Mutt and Jeff 23, 248–9
My Favorite Thing is Monsters 7, 306
My Hero Academia 33
Mystery in Space 44
mythic criticism 300–2
myth of redemptive violence 186
myths **301**

Nagashima, Shin'ichi 155
Nakazawa, Keiji 15, 24, 155, 224
Namor, the Sub-Mariner 184, 186, 190, 257, 261
narrating I **159**, 160, 171
narrative **59**
narrative flow **117–**18, 123
narrative patterns 139, 151, 170–2
narrative problematic 142
narrative verve 60–1
Nast, Thomas 221–2, 247–8
National Allied Publications 253–4, *see also* DC Comics
National Book Award 153, 284, 286
National Periodical Publications 253, *see also* DC Comics
Natty Bumppo 179
naturalistic mode **84**, 219
Naughty Bits 30
Ndalianis, Angela 203
Neaud, Fabrice 157
Nebergall, Roger 170
negotiated reading 303
Neufeld, Josh 170, 209, 211–12
Nevins, Mark David 179, 183, 276
newave 34
Newbery Medal 14, 286
New Comics 254
New Fun Comics 254
New Funnies 144
New Gods 198–200, 269
New Journalism 211, 213–14
New Kid 13–14
newsstands 35, 50, 147
New York Comic Art Convention 273
New York Comicon 49, 50
New Yorker, The 12, 317
New York Journal 14
Nib, The 210, 213, 225
Nichols, Bill 213–15, 218
Nick of the Woods 179–80
Nietzsche, Friedrich 181, 189
1986 275–9
ninth art 15
Nobel, Carmen 211
Nolan, Christopher 23
Nolan, Michele 152
non-sensory diegetic images **87**, 90, 93, 175
North, Sterling 292–3
Norton, Bonny 294–5
Nowak, Carolyn 71–4, *see also* Nowak, Casey
Nowak, Casey 71–4, *see also* Nowak, Carolyn
Nubia and the Amazons 103, 106
Nyberg, Amy 6, 209, 213

Obadiah Oldbuck, *see Adventures of Obadiah Oldbuck, The*
observational mode 216–17
Oeming, Michael Avon 30, 281
Official Overstreet Comic Book Price Guide 34, 37, 43
Olczak, Paul 293
Old Witch 148
Oliver, Glynis 80
Olson, Richard D. 248
Omaha the Cat Dancer 145
O'Nale, Robert 120
100 Bullets 85
One Hundred Demons 158
online comics 213
onomatopoeia 244
On the Drawing Board 46
oppositional reading 303
Ormes, Jackie 19, 23
Orwell, George 164
Other **85**, 237, 304
Otsmane-Elhaou, Hassan 113
Ottaviani, Jim 297
Outcault, Richard Felton 18, 248
Ozymandias 110, 191, 276

Pacific Comics 198, 200, 271, 274
pacing 69

page as a unit of meaning 62, 96, 113–15
Paim, Augusto 210
Palestine 207, 212, 215, 284
Palmiotti, Jimmy 115
Palooka-Ville 95, 157
panel **2**, **61–**2, 74, 119, 246, 318
Panter, Gary 272
paradigmatic choice **63**, 74
paralanguage 83
parallel combination 95
parasocial relationships 143, 203, 228
Parents Magazine 258
Parker, Bill 256
participatory mode 214–15
pastiche 86
Patreon 29, 41
Patsy Walker 141
Paying for It 157, 211
Peanuts 19, 282
Peepshow 157
Peeters, Benoit 104, 108, 114, 124
Pekar, Harvey 7, 156–7, 163, 170
Penguin Random House 29, 34
Pennell, Hillary 203
Penny Arcade 285
People's Comics, The
Pep Comics 140, 222
performative mode 218–19
performing identity 169
periodicals **36**
peripheral processing 226
Perkins, Linda 96
Persepolis 158, 306
persuasion 221–38
Peter, Henry G. 257
Peter Parker 224, 228, 263–4, *see also* Spider-Man
Petty, Richard 226
Phantom, The 16–18, 179–80, 184
Philipon, Charles 221–2
Phillip Marlowe 203
Phillips, Sean 78, 85, 98, 148
physical culture movement 181–2, 255
pictorial embodiment 161–2
picture-specific combination 94
Picture Stories from American History 297
Picture Stories from the Bible 297
Pilkey, Dav 29
Pini, Richard 45
Pini, Wendy 45, 306
pirated comics 33, 286
Pizarro, David A. 191
Plastic Man 204
Plot, The 252
Plymell, Charles 267
poetic mode 219
Pogo 222
Pogo Possum 145, 152
Pollman, Joost 88
Popeye 180, 265
Porky Pig 144
Portacio, Whilce 278
PositiveNegatives 225
Potts, Carl 70, 113
Powell, Nate 19
power 302
power fantasy 256
Power Rangers
Powers 30, 281
Preacher 278
preferred reading 303
Preiss, Byron 5
prestige format 276
Pretty in Ink: American Women Cartoonists 1896–2013 307
primary movement 82
Princess of Mars, A 181
Prisoner on a Hell Planet 165
Prize 198, 200
Prize Comics 146
production 21, 246
Professor Xavier 187
proliferating narrativity **60**, 69
Promethea 110
propaganda 221, 223–6
pro-social mission 184
psychological image **91**
Puck 247
Pudovkin, Vsevolod 65
Pulitzer Prize 1, 31, 158, 176, 276
pulp magazines 26, 249, 254
Punch 207, 247
Punisher 184, 277
Pustz, Matthew 43, 263
PvP 285

qualitative research **300–1**
Qualter, Terence 221
quantitative research **298**
Quart, Alissa 212
Quesada, Joe 61, 111, 253, 282
Quicksilver 185
Quinones, Joe 121

R. Crumb Head Comix 268
Radical America Komiks 265

Raeburn, Daniel 268
Rall, Hans-Martin 207, 211–12
Rall, Ted 209, 213
Rank, Hugh 230
Rank, Otto 192
Raw 272, 276
Rawhide Kid 138
Raymond, Alex 86
readership 6, 44, 46, 50–1
reading path 70, 113, 117–18, 123
realism 66, 84, 164, 174–5, 213, *see also* naturalistic mode
Real Screen Comics 144
Real War Stories 271
reboots **59**
Redding, W. Charles 203
redemptive arc **171–**2
Reeves, Keanu 29
reflected appraisals 167–8
reflexive mode 219–20
Regalado, Aldo 202
Reggie Mantle 141
Reinventing Comics 285
Reitberger, Reinhold 7, 71, 94, 266, 268
representation 304
RESIST! 225
reviews 311–18, **312**
Revue dessinee, Le 210
Reynolds, Richard 188
rhetoric **108**, 162
rhetorical content layout **108–**10
rhetorical criticism 301
rhetorical layout **108–**11, 117
rhetorical subtext layout **110**
Ricca, Brad 182, 255
Rice, Anne 297
Richard Dragon, Kung Fu Fighter 136
Richie Rich 149, 300
Riddler 188
Rifas, Leonard 222–4, 293, 297
Riverdale 22, 141
Road to Wakanda: Fathers and Sons 103
Robbins, Daniel 221
Robbins, Trina 140–1, 292, 306–8
Roberson, Chris 203
Robertson, Darick 276
Robin 187, 202
Robin Hood 261
Rocket's Blast Comicollector 46
Rogers, Mark C. 39, 40
Rogers, Roy 138
Rogofsky, Howard 49
Rolling Stones 268
romance comics genre 135, 142–4, 148, 150–2, 200, 257–8, 261
Ronin 276
Rorschach 111, 191, 276
Rosati, Melissa 32
Rosenkranz, Patrick 164–5, 167, 267–8, 272
Roth, Gary 294
Rowson, Martin 7
Royer, Mike 50
Rozanski, Chuck 273–4, 279–80
Rubin, Rebecca 202
Rubinstein-Avila, Elaine 295
Rucka, Greg 7
Russell, P. Craig 75
Ryan, Marie-Laure 59, 60

Sabin, Roger 43, 266, 272–4
Sabre: Slow Fade of an Endangered Species 271
Sabrina the Teen-Age Witch 141
Sacco, Joe 168, 173, 208–13, 215–16, 218, 236, 275, 284
Safe Area Goražde 209
Saga 1, 59, 76, 281
Sailor Moon 29
Sale, Tim 41
sales 5, 33–8
Salkowitz, Rob 54
Saltus, Elinor 297
Sandell, Laurie 165
Sandman 5–8, 31, 113, 147, 277
Sandow, Eugen 181–2
Santa Claus 247, 259
Saraceni, Mario 81, 119
Satrapi, Marjane 158, 306
Saunders, Ben 205
Savage Dragon 41
scarcity **37**
Scarlet Pimpernel, The 180–1
Scarlet Witch 143
scene **62**, 96
Schelly, Bill 49, 50, 263, 275
Schiller, Friedrich 11
Schlenker, Barry R. 169, 171
Schodt, Frederik 155
scholarship 290, 308
Scholastic Books 28–9, 283
School of Visual Arts 252–3
Schulz, Charles 19, 282
Schulz, Juergen 221
Schwartz, Adam 295
Schwartz, Delmore 297
Schwartz, Julius "Julie" 26, 44–6, 49, 50, 262

Science Fiction 255
science fiction comics genre 135–6, 152, 200, 265, 319
Scott, Naomi 143
Sea Gate Distribution 274
secondary movement 82
Second World War 14, 142, 149, 198, 261, 276, 288–9
secret/dual identity 180, 185–6, 249
Seduction of the Innocent 259, 291
self-concept 67, 176, *see also* reflected appraisals; social comparisons; self-perception
self-perception 168–9
Senate Subcommittee to Investigate Juvenile Delinquency 259, 261
sensory diegetic images **87–**9, 93, 174–5
sequence **62**
sequence metaphor 66
sequential art 1–2, 244, 247
sequential dynamism **115**, 117, 123
Sequential Tart 306
Sergeant Frank Rock 149
Serrano, Nhora Lucía 24–5
Seth 95, 157
setting 138–9
Seuling, Phil 49, 50, 273
Severin, Marie 306
Seymore, Ryan 311, 326
Shachtman, Noah 226
Shadow, The 180, 182, 249, 256
Shakespeare, William 297, 299
Shanower, Eric 30, 281
Sharen, Bob 80
Shaw, George Bernard 181
Shaw!, Scott 50
Sheena 16, 149
Shelley, Mary 146
Shelton, Gilbert 266–7
Sheridan, Martin 308
Sherif, Carolyn 170
Sherif, Muzafer 170
Shield, The 140, 222, 264
shôjo manga 143
Shooter, Jim 5
shop system 251–2, 257
Short Order Comix 156
Showcase 45, 262
Shuster, Joe 23, 180, 182, 205, 254–5
sidekicks 187
Siegel, Jerry 23, 180–2, 205, 254
Silver Age 45
Silver Surfer 198
Silvestri, Marc 278
Sim, Dave 86, 88, 145
Simek, Artie 48
Simon, Joe 77, 142, 198–200, 251, 257
Simone, Gail 303, 306
Simonson, Walter 83, 114
Simple J. Malarkey 145
simple narrative **59**
Simpson, Don 201
Simpson, Will 118
Simpsons, The 43, 52
Sin City 41, 281
Singer, Marc 195, 204
Sinnott, Joe 48
Skywald Publishing 269
slabbed **37**
Slade, Michael 259
Slam Bradley 254
slapstick 141, 144, 246
slash fiction 53
slice of life story 170–1
Small, David 165, 171
Smile 29, 176
Smith, Barry 104
Smith, Colin 191
Smith, Jeff 28, 31, 145, 152, 283
Smith, Matthew J. 20, 327
Smith, Sidonie 162, 164
Snatch Comics 265
Snow Crash 195
Snyder, Mikkel 78
Snyder, Scott 30
Soba 216
social comparison 168
social judgement theory 170
social scientific research, *see* descriptive methods
So Close, Faraway 210
Sōjō, Toba 144
Something is Killing the Children 33
Soremsky, Bo 210
sound 88
Sound and the Fury, The 277
sound effects 83
Sousanis, Nick 86, 125–31, 231, 317–18
Spanjers, Rik 308
Spawn 278, *see also Curse of Spawn*
Spectre 150
speculators **43**, 44, 279
speed lines **67–**8
Speedy 224
Spencer, Nick 30
Spengemann, William C. 154

Spider, The 182, 249
Spider-Man 15, 40, 47, 60, 187, 189, 191, 202–4, 224, 237, 263, 265, 277–8, 286, 307, 317, *see also* Peter Parker
Spider-Man Loves Mary Jane 144
Spiegelman, Art 1, 31, 61, 92, 94, 97, 156, 158, 161, 163, 165, 176, 225, 238, 265, 272–3, 275–6
Spire Christian Comics 224
Spirit, *The* 111, 252–3, 288
Spirit Section, *The* 41, 252
splash page 41, 68, 110–11
spoiler **316**, 320, 322
Squadron Supreme 191, 276
Stack, Frank 266–7
staffer **39**
standardization **137**, 151
Stan Lee's Superheroes 202
Stan's Soapbox 48
Staples, Fiona 76, 281
Starlin, Jim 41
Star Ranger 137
Startling Comics 135
Star Trek 282
Star Wars 23, 149
state of grace 60–1, 195
Steele, Edward 203
Steinberg, Flo 50
Stephenson, Neil 195
Steranko, Jim 104, 121, 123, 201, 287, 291
Steranko History of Comics, *The* 291
stereotypes 43, 51, **66–**7, 279, 304
Stevenson, Daniel 257–8, 261
Steve Rogers, *see* Captain America
Stitches 165, 171–2
Stoddard, David 211, 239
Stone, Sam 103
Story of Harry S. Truman, *The* 223, 289–90
Strange Adventures 44, 265
Strangers in Paradise 59
strawman 230–1
Strömberg, Fredrik 223–4
Stuck Rubber Baby 7, 22, 275
Studies in Comics 292
Style 66, 77, 96, 161, 208
Sub-Mariner, *see* Namor
subscription sales 273
Substack 29–30
subtext 91, 111
Sugarshock! 285
Sullivan, Vincent 182, 254–6
Sumner, Eloise 322–5
Sundered Worlds, *The* 195
Supergirl 106–7, 110, 115
Superhero City 195
superhero comics genre 30, 33, 46, 110, 136–7, 140, 145, 150, 178–205, 243, 249, 252, 256–7, 261, 264, 268–9, 275–6, 281, 287, 303
  character types 183–8
  narrative patterns 192–5
  setting 195–7
  themes 188–92
  visual conventions 197, 201–2
Superman 18, 23, 26, 40, 42, 59, 60, 65, 95, 140, 179–81, 183, 185–6, 189, 191, 195, 202–5, 249, 255–7, 262, 268, 276–7, 279–80, 296, *see also* Clark Kent
Superman 37, 181, 256
Superman: *Birthright* 60
Superman: *Peace on Earth* 191
Superman: *Secret Origin* 60
Superman: *The Movie* 28
Superman's Girlfriend Lois Lane, *see* Lois Lane
Superman's Pal Jimmy Olsen 199–200, 269
supervillain 187–8, 190–1, 197, 204
Swain, Emma Halstead 294
Swamp Thing 31, 147, 184, 269, 277
Swan, Curt 205
swiping 86
sword and sorcery comics genre 137, 151, 269
SYFY 150
Symbolia 210
symbols **66**
Synchopated 209
synchronous **71**
synecdoche **65**, **89**, 93
syntagmatic choice 62–3, 74
System, *The* 232
System of Comics 308
Szurek, Dave 49

T.H.U.N.D.E.R. Agents 264
tabular, the 114, 117–18, 121–3
Takeda, Sana 281
Talbot, Bryan 173, 238
Talbot, Mary 173
Tale of One Bad Rat, *The* 1
Tale of Two Pandemics 212
Tales from the Crypt 44, 146, 148, 152, 259
Taniguchi, Jiro 219
Tapas 29, 40
Tarzan 16, 149, 180, 184, 197, 249
Taylor, Aaron 195, 201

Taylor, Michael Ray 211, 238
Teenage Mutant Ninja Turtles 272
Teen-Age Temptations 316
teen humor comics genre 136–7, 140–2, 148, 151, 257
Teen Titans 187
television 22, 135–6, 143, 146, 195, 200, 202, 204, 260–1, 293
television comics genre 261, *see also* movie comics genre
Telgemeier, Raina 29, 176, 306
Templesmith, Ben 85
tenor **66**
terministic/imagistic screen **231**, 237
Terry-Toons 144
Texas Ranger 266–7
THE Austin Iconoclastic Newsletter 266–7
themes 139, 151
thesis **314**, 319–20, 322
Thing, The 263, *see also* Ben Grimm
Third World Distribution 267
Thomas, Roy 45–6, 49, 269
Thompson, Craig 30, 91, 93–4, 158, 170, 281
Thompson, Don 6, 46, 49, 263, 291
Thompson, Kelly 30
Thompson, Maggie Curtis 46, 49
Thor 143, 185, 198, 202, 263
Thorn, Matt 143
Thorndike, Robert 294
thought balloon 90
Thrillbent 285
thumbnail breakdowns **62**, 71, 113–14
Tice, Dianne M. 167
tier **104**
Tijuana Bibles 265
Tilley, Carol 259
time 68–9
Time 276
Time^2*: The Epiphany*
Timely Comics 196, 198–9, 257, *see also* Atlas Comics; Marvel Comics
Time Warner, Inc. 27, *see also* Warner Brothers
Timmons, Anne 307
To Afghanistan and Back 209
Tobocman, Seth 224
To Kill a Mockingbird 277
Tolkien, J. R. R. 13, 152
Tomb of Dracula, The 66, 147, 269
Tomb Raider 282
Tony Stark, *see* Iron Man
Top Cow 31, 282
Töpffer, Rodolphe 245–7
Top Shelf 30
Torchy Brown in Dixie to Harlem 19, 23
To the Heart of the Storm 158
Toulmin, Stephen 232
Tower Comics 141, 264
trade paperbacks (TPB) 5, 36
Tran, GB 158, 176
Treasure Chest of Fun and Fact 224
Triggs, Teal 272
True Comics 296
Truman, Harry S. 289
Tsuge, Yoshiharu 155
Turner, Kathleen 226, 237
Two-Fisted Science 297
Two-Fisted Tales 149, 152, 259
Two-Gun Kid, The 138
Tynion, IV, James 30
Tokyopop 32

Uderzo, Albert 15
ugly (brut) art style 85, 93, 96, 234, 324
Ujiie, Joanne 294
Umbrella Academy, The 22
Uncle Creepy 148
Uncle Sam 247
Uncle Scrooge McDuck 11, 16, 145, 257, 300
underground comix 19, 21–2, 149, **155–**7, 243, 253, 264–9, 271–3, 275–6
Underground Press Syndicate 267
Understanding Comics 19, 94, 292
University of Florida 292
University Press of Mississippi 42, 292
Unstoppable Wasp, The 107–8
Uono, Shota 15
Updike, John 274
Uslan, Michael 50

valence **315**
Valentino, Jim 278
Vampirella 147
Vanderheyden, Karen 295
Van Hise, James 80, 86, 97
van Leeuwen, Theo 232
Van Lente, Fred 288, 297
Varley, Lynn 276
Vassallo, Michael J. 249
Vaughan, Brain K. 31, 76, 278, 281
Vault-Keeper 148
Vault of Horror 44, 146, 152, 259, 265
vehicle 66
Veitch, Tom 60, 195
Vernon, Zackary 225
Veronica Lodge 141, 300, 306

Versaci, Rocco 156
Vertigo 31, 138, 147, 277
V for Vendetta 285
Vidal, Gore 154
Vietnamerica 158
Vigilante, The 184
vigilantes 179, 183, 186, 191, 276–7
violence 183, 186–7
virtual community 44
Vision 143
visual conventions 140
visualized sound 77, 82–3
Visual Language of Comics, The 308
visual metaphor 67, **91**, 94, 155, 165, 231
Viz Communications 29, 32, 271, 282–3
Vulture Demoness 267

Walking Dead 22, 281
Walking Man, The 219
Wallace, Henry M. 167
Waller, Reed 145
Walt Disney Company 11, 16, 27–8, 53, 145, 202, 257, 287, *see also* Disney, Walt
Walt Disney's Comics and Stories 144, 257
war comics genre 149
Ware, Chris 30, 42, 85, 281
Ware, Hames 42
War is Boring 210, 226
Warlock 41
Warlord 137
Warner, Andy 210
Warner Brothers 28, 144, 202, 257, *see also* Time Warner, Inc.
Warren Publishing 147–8, 269–70
Warrior 276
Wasteland 7
Watchmen 7, 22, 110–11, 191, 204, 276
Watson, Julia 162, 164
Waugh, Frederick Coulton 6, 291
Weaver, Lila Quintero 168
Weaver, Richard L. 167
webcomics 12, 20, 29, 34, 40, 113, 210, 226, 229, **284–**6
Weber, Wibke 207, 211–12
Webtoons 29, 40
Wecter, Dixon 189
Wednesday Comics 115, 121–2
Wein, Len 50, 147, 269–70
Weird Science 44, 152, 259
Weisberg, Jessica 213
Weisinger, Mort 26, 50
Wells, H. G. 299
Werewolf by Night 269
Wertham, Fredric 258–60, 291, 297
West, Adam 23
western genre 136–40, 150–1, 257–8, 261
Western Picture Stories 137
Wheat, John 267
Whedon, Joss 285
Wheeler-Nicholson, Major Malcolm 253–4
Where the Buffalo Roam 284
Whiteman 267
Whiteout 7
Who's Who of American Comic Books, The 42
Who Understands Comics? 58
Who Wants to Be a Superhero? 202
Whyte, Kenneth 14
Wicked + Divine, The 281
Wiese, Ellen 246
Wildenberg, Harry I. 250–1
Williams, Ian 176
Williams, Kristian 211
Williams, Neil 295
Williams III, J. H. 104, 110, 124
William Tell 11
Will Kane 203
Wilson, S. Clay 272
Wimmen's Comix 149, 156, 307
Windsor-Smith, Barry 269, 277
Wink, Walter 186
Winkielman, Piotr 220
Witek, Joseph 7, 156, 175, 292, 308
Witty, Paul 294, 306
Wizard 43
Woggon, Bill 141
Wolfe, Ron 7
Wolfman, Marv 147
Wolk, Douglas 169
Wolverine 184, 277, 279
Women and the Comics 292, 307
Women in Refrigerators 303
Women Write about Comics 306, 326
Wonder Man 256
Wonder Wart-Hog 266
Wonder Woman 204, 257, 262, 306
Woo, Benjamin 161–4
Wood, Wally 85
Woodring, Jim 145
Woody Woodpecker 144
Worcester, Kent 205
word balloons 88
word-specific combination 94
work-for-hire **39**, 200, 279
Worku-Dix, Benjamin 225
World Superhero Registry 202